Multicultural Issues in Social Work

Edited by

Patricia L. Ewalt
Edith M. Freeman
Stuart A. Kirk
Dennis L. Poole

with a foreword by

Senator Daniel K. Inouye

NASW PRESS
National Association of Social Workers
Washington, DC

Jay J. Cayner, ACSW, LSW, *President*
Robert H. Cohen, JD, ACSW, *Executive Director*

Linda Beebe, *Executive Editor*
Nancy Winchester, *Editorial Services Director*
K. Hyde Loomis, *Senior Editor*
Christina A. Davis, *Staff Editor*
Stephen D. Pazdan, *Staff Editor*
Marcia D. Roman, *Staff Editor*
Bill Cathey, *Typesetter*
Sarah Lowman, *Editorial Secretary*
Bernice Eisen, *Indexer*

First impression, February 1996
Second impression, March 1997

Library of Congress Cataloging-in-Publication Data
Multicultural issues in social work / edited by Patricia L. Ewalt . . .
   [et al.] ; with a foreword by Senator Daniel K. Inouye.
      p.   cm.
   Includes bibliographical references and index.
   ISBN 0-87101-266-9
   1. Social service--United States. 2. Multiculturalism--United
States.   I. Ewalt, Patricia L.
HV41.M84   1996
362.84'00973--dc20   96-3663
                                                            CIP

Printed in the United States of America

Contents

Foreword

Multicultural Issues in Social Work was designed to help professionals in the human services understand and appreciate cultural diversity. Greater understanding must be supported by sound research to rebut some of the rhetoric and distortions in the public arena. This unique collection of chapters reflects solid, heavy-duty research. However, this book also contains thoughtful essays and practice pieces that will attract individuals who don't normally look at research, enabling them to understand the underpinnings of research. Chapters from outstanding writers in the field address policy, law, education, health care, and the delivery of services; they look at many different racial and ethnic groups as well as age groups from children to elders. Knowledge in these areas is essential for human services workers who must possess cross-cultural competency if they are to succeed in alleviating human problems and helping individuals remain productive and healthy citizens.

Issues surrounding cultural diversity permeate modern society and thus must be addressed in all settings; however, the workplace is often the focus for concerns and conflicts that may arise. In my own state of Hawaii, cultural diversity is the rule, not the exception. This diversity is not only accepted but sought after by organizations seeking to compete in the international market. Our society is changing so rapidly that a diverse workforce is becoming commonplace. For example, it is estimated that in the very near future, 85 percent of the new jobs in the labor force will be filled by women, minorities, and immigrants. Projections show that as the labor pool becomes more diverse, the number of people with technical skills will shrink. It would therefore seem logical that the contributions of every employee should be maximized. Organizations that are looking to the future will have to evaluate the impact that diversity in our society will have on the marketing of their products and services. What better way for an organization to ensure innovation than through the cultivation of a diverse workforce. Certainly one must have an understanding of multicultural differences to achieve this goal.

As society evolves, we encounter more diversity in our work-places, in our neighborhoods, and in every other facet of our lives. Our entire country depends on individuals obtaining a greater understanding of the similarities and differences among ethnic, racial, and cultural groups. Certain professions will have to play a key role if we are to obtain this fuller understanding, and social work is clearly among the most important. I applaud the NASW Press for producing this scholarly, valuable book, which definitely provides knowledge needed by human services workers to pro-mote and foster cross-cultural understanding.

Daniel K. Inouye
January 1996   United States Senator, Hawaii

Introduction

Multicultural Issues in Social Work presents a collective vision of multiculturalism in social work practice. The book reflects the multicultural reality of this country and its increasingly multicultural families and individuals. It paves the way for practice and research based on the knowledge that individuals cannot readily be identified in single cultural categories.

In this book *multiculturalism* refers to the professional disposition to acknowledge, appreciate, and understand cultural diversity. The concept contrasts sharply with ethnocentrism—the tendency to view reality only from the perspective of one's own culture and to disfavor other cultures or view them as inferior. Ethnocentrism breeds cultural intolerance, ignorance, and prejudice. Social work demands flexibility in the helping role, a willingness to appreciate and learn from other cultures, and skills to intervene in divergent cultural settings. Multicultural perspectives, therefore, should permeate the entire curriculum of social work education and all methods of professional practice.

The book contains knowledge about various age groups—children, youths, young adults, and older people—and about various racial and ethnic groups—American Indian, African American, Asian, Pacific Islander, Caucasian, Latino. These groups vary not only among but also within themselves. The book also recognizes cultures that exist for reasons in addition to race and ethnicity—for example, a place of residence or physical condition shared in common.

The book contains sections focused on multicultural practice, law and policy, populations, education, health care, and service delivery. It contains specific knowledge for all parts of the social work curriculum, including social policy, research, human behavior, and practice. Students and educators in concentrations will find resources for practice in organizations and communities, health, school social work, aging, children and families, and other sectors.

The chapters clarify how multiculturalism encourages a positive focus on human diversity within the context of clients', practitioners', and other key actors' complex environments. Social workers' approach to practice has too often ignored the rich and positive diversity among people, assuming that a focus on multiculturalism emphasizes cultural differences in a negative way. This approach brings to mind the Chinese proverb, "The only way around a situation is through it." Social work's way of attempting to go around instead of addressing the issue of multiculturalism may have hampered professionals' efforts to develop a more positive and direct understanding of cultural variation. A positive approach is more likely to unite social workers and to help them manage together the adverse economic, political, and social conditions presently confronting U.S. society.

Social work literature has just begun to identify more positive and strengths-oriented approaches to diversity and a multicultural perspective. With its emphasis on social welfare and social justice, it is appropriate for this profession to take a leadership role in theory building and advocacy for the development of multicultural perspectives. Implicit in these perspectives is the requirement to address social structures that create and maintain oppressive conditions that dehumanize both the oppressed and those who witness oppression and to promote people's resiliency in coping with such conditions. Many of these perspectives also acknowledge and value similarities *and* differences among people from various racial, ethnic, cultural, and religious groups. Multicultural perspectives are inclusive rather than exclusive by viewing the strengths, traditions, and contributions of all groups as essential to the development and well-being of a society.

Multicultural Issues in Social Work addresses multiculturalism from this broad and most inclusive framework and also provides in-depth discussions about specific areas of human diversity from an ecological perspective. It is designed for social work students, practitioners, educators, researchers, and policy analysts in a variety of settings, fields of practice, and practice modalities. It should also be useful to policymakers and researchers and to practitioners in other disciplines.

This book has been made possible through the contributions of the many authors, who recognized the necessity of multicultural knowledge for practice. We acknowledge with appreciation the importance of their work.

Patricia L. Ewalt
Edith M. Freeman
Stuart A. Kirk
Dennis L. Poole

Part I

MULTICULTURAL PRACTICE

The Multicultural Mosaic

Michael Yellow Bird, Rowena Fong, Petra
Galindo, Jack Nowicki, Edith M. Freeman

We five authors represent five different ethnic groups: First
Nations, Asian Americans, Latinos, European Americans,
and African Americans. We have written about multiculturalism from our professional perspectives and from our unique
personal experiences as members of these particular groups. Because the members of each ethnic group have diverse perspectives, we speak for ourselves rather than for our ethnic groups.
Obviously, not all ethnic, religious, and cultural groups are represented, given the limited number of authors who could be invited
to share their points of view. It is hoped that, as is true in other
situations, the essence of multiculturalism has been captured in
this chapter by combining diverse voices and experiences.

MULTICULTURALISM AND FIRST NATIONS: MICHAEL YELLOW BIRD

Numerous cultures have existed among the First Nations of the
Americas since time immemorial. Before the European invasion
of Turtle Island (Wright, 1993), almost all of the lands in the
Americas had been occupied or discovered by the indigenous
populations and, thus, resonated with an enormous amount of
life and human diversity. It is estimated that before 1492, hundreds of mutually unintelligible aboriginal languages and dialects existed (Owen, Deter, & Fisher, 1967) and that the population
north of Mexico numbered as many as 18 million (Dobyns, 1983).

Although First Nations cultures share many similar social, political, and economic characteristics, many are as different from
one another as the lands, waters, and forests that they occupy.
Indeed, diversity among indigenous peoples may be best expressed in the relationship that each nation has with its natural
environment. For example, the salmon, and the rivers where they
migrate and spawn, are as sacred and important to the Coast

Salish, Tsimshian, and Kwakiutl of the Northwest coast as the Missouri River and corn are to the Sahnish, Hidatsa, and Mandan of the Northern Plains. Likewise, the buffalo and the Black Hills are as important to the Dakota, Lakota, and Nakota as the walleye, forests, and wild rice lakes are to the Anishinabe people of the Great Lakes region.

Along with this diversity, it is important for school social workers to remember that Euro-American education systems, especially the government and missionary "Indian" boarding schools (forced acculturation camps), were very oppressive and specifically constructed to eliminate the cultural traditions and practices of First Nations peoples. Indigenous languages were systematically suppressed, and the race and national identities of the students were systematically ignored by school officials. For example, on February 2, 1887, J.D.C. Atkins, commissioner of Indian affairs, wrote to all government and missionary school officials that educating "Indian" students in their indigenous languages "is not only of no use to them, but is detrimental to the cause of their education and civilization, and no school will be permitted on the reservation in which the English language is not exclusively taught" (Prucha, 1975, p. 175). The education of First Nations peoples has been, more often than not, synonymous with the loss of culture (Yellow Bird & Snipp, 1994).

Despite these efforts, many First Nations have been able to maintain and recover important aspects of their indigenous beliefs, practices, and languages that were suppressed or lost through cultural genocide. Today in the United States, more than 500 federally recognized First Nations groups and many unrecognized groups petitioning for federal recognition attest to the strengths and resiliency of these groups. Equally important are the many First Nations elementary and secondary schools and community colleges that have established language programs that are helping to restore their cultures.

There is a lot that school social workers can do to promote multiculturalism for First Nations peoples. They can carefully examine the history of the oppressive education of First Nations peoples, educate others, and speak out against the oppressive education that First Nations students encounter today. They can actively recognize the strengths and resiliency of First Nations peoples and the importance that these groups place on their cultures by helping to promote more awareness of First Nations cultures. To me, this means going beyond the traditional "Native American" day/week or Indians and pilgrims "Thanksgiving" themes.

Social workers in school settings can also play key roles in helping schools and community agencies to collaborate with First Nations organizations. There is much to be done to increase understanding between First Nations peoples and the Euro-American education system. Social workers can help First Nations communities to identify existing needs related to their education, and they can help to sensitize school personnel about the differences in First Nations cultures.

NOT SIMPLY "ASIAN AMERICANS": ROWENA FONG

"Not Simply 'Asian Americans'" is part of the title of an article that I cowrote for *Social Work* (Fong & Mokuau, 1994). The title, while relevant to multiculturalism, implies that there is ethnic diversity among Asians. When one ignores the heterogeneity of a population and offers prescriptions for social work practice predicated on a generic perspective, not only are specific subgroups neglected, but there is also a tendency to perpetuate stereotypes and racism.

School social workers need to recognize the diversity that exists among Asians, a category that encompasses Chinese, Japanese, Koreans, Vietnamese, Filipinos, Laotians, Thais, Cambodians, Asian Indians, and others. There are refugees, immigrants, native-born children of immigrants, and people who have lived in America for several generations. Even among Chinese people there is considerable diversity. For example, a Chinese child who recently arrived from the People's Republic of China is likely to come with an educational experience emphasizing the importance of the collective over the individual. A child from Taiwan may bring high parental pressures for individual achievement. A child from Chinatown may be the first person in her family to go beyond grade school. A Chinese youngster from the suburbs may have two parents with doctorates. These frameworks are very different even if the Chinese have the same last names or speak the same dialects. Similar diversity occurs in other Asian groups such as Filipinos and Asian Indians, both of which have large immigrant populations.

Multiculturalism forces the social worker to examine (for example) Chinese clients not just from the viewpoint that they are different from Japanese or Tongan students, but also that the Chinese student who comes from China in the era of the single-child policy will not be like the Chinese student from Boston in the era of child welfare reform policy. Multiculturalism demands that social workers give up mere cultural sensitivity as the end-point and instead use it as a means to achieve cultural competency at various interactive cultural and environmental levels.

Born and raised in the 1950s and 1960s as a second-generation bilingual Chinese American, I grew up in a small, working-class city near Boston and attended the local public schools. There were four Chinese families including my own immigrant family residing in this city. Although I lived in a bicultural world, I was not aware of multiculturalism. I knew only Chinese culture and a conglomerate white culture, mostly Jewish, Irish, and Italian.

In the 1970s and 1980s, after being educated on both coasts at Berkeley, Wellesley, and Harvard, I began to be more aware of multiple cultures. I experienced ethnic culture and race interacting with preferential social class. I came to understand social worlds that were not just Chinese or white, but poor American-born Chinese, rich national Japanese, and rich white, among many other varieties. In the mid-1980s, an undergraduate teaching job in the Midwest forced me to deal with multiculturalism in terms of urban and rural differences and in terms of Midwest norms and their negative valuation of my ethnic identity. The book *It's Crazy to Stay Chinese in Minnesota* (Telemaque, 1978) summarized it all.

When I taught in the People's Republic of China during the student demonstrations in the spring of 1989, multiculturalism took on another dimension. That is, I experienced my own familiar Chinese culture with a new twist of awareness that communism and democracy had very different effects on it. Here I came to understand that ethnic culture is decidedly affected by ideology.

Personal experiences have led me to understand multiculturalism as my individual identity being affected by environments at several levels simultaneously. My own immigrant background was challenged when I attended elite educational institutions with preferential social class differences, when I interacted with conservative norms in white-dominated geographic locations, and when I encountered differing ideologies in Chinese-dominated cultures. This interaction forced me to be more clear about what my roots were, how important they were to me, and how much I was not willing to give them up despite my new environments. Multiculturalism is not one culture imposing itself on another culture. Multiculturalism is several components of culture—ethnic identity, geographic location, and philosophical ideologies—challenging the individual to decide what stays and what does not.

ALGO PERSONAL/A PERSONAL STORY: PETRA GALINDO

For me, the term "multiculturalism" has to do not only with an awareness but also with an acknowledgment of the effect of culture on individual behavior. My use of the term "culture" is taken from two of many definitions: (1) patterns of thinking, feeling, and behaving characteristic of a people that stem from the value orientations transmitted from generation to generation, the purpose of which is to guide individual behavior to ensure the survival of the society and (2) ideas, beliefs, viewpoints, values, and feelings that are shared by any designated group of people in a given society (Arce, 1993). Encompassed within these two definitions is the broadening of the term to include not only ethnicity and race but also any shared experience with a system of values that a particular group, such as a nation or a profession, may reflect.

Nineteen years of working with an extremely diverse cross-section of children and families as a paraprofessional and professional in a variety of settings (often in Spanish or in collaboration with an interpreter) gives me an appreciation for many unique ways of seeing the world. Currently, through direct contact with students, their families, and the individual staff members of the Los Angeles Unified School District, I have been able to learn about many worldviews from working together—that is, both listening and talking—with students to help them solve the problems they bring to my attention.

In terms of my ethnic and cultural background, as the oldest of seven children of a Mexican American mother with a large extended family and a Mexican immigrant father, and having grown up in an ethnically diverse working-class suburban community of Los Angeles, I have come to value my own unique experience. My father had a sixth-grade education in Mexico and attended adult education classes to learn English, obtain his general equivalency diploma, and ultimately become a naturalized citizen while working as a truck driver in Los Angeles (I was in high school at the time). My mother took total responsibility for raising us. She was the listener and my father was the talker, in heavily accented English laden with Spanish *dichos* (proverbs). They continue to teach me today, my father now the listener (to my much-improved Spanish) and my mother the talker, telling stories of her early years.

My father's late-night stories about his personal experiences with coworkers and supervisors always taught me tolerance, even when I could not understand his tolerance of discriminatory behavior toward him. In school social work practice I am constantly challenged to understand the world through each student's eyes and his or her family's experience. It never ceases to amaze me that stories that are surprising and different communicate a universal need to be understood. Ultimately, multiculturalism is about person-to-person contact, which comes through communication and takes time. This contact can make a difference in the successful living of individuals from many cultures.

AFFIRMING CULTURAL DIVERSITY: JACK NOWICKI

We seem to be moving from the idea of our culture as a "melting pot" to the idea of it being a "salad bowl," thinking of our many different cultural groups as the ingredients of a delicious salad. In the salad analogy, our culture, or society, is the salad dressing that enhances and ties together the diverse flavors of the individual ingredients. I use the analogy here to honor whoever first used it to describe a shift toward the idea of multiculturalism that is evolving in our understanding about how to acknowledge, respect, and appreciate cultural diversity. Affirming cultural diversity, according to Nieto (1995), "implies that cultural, linguistic, and other differences can and should be used as a basis for learning and teaching, . . . are an important and necessary starting point for all interactions, and can enrich the experiences of each individual" (p. 1). When staffing public schools and social services agencies, organizations need to go beyond recruiting a culturally diverse staff and focus on retention, that is, finding ways to keep such a diverse staff by identifying their unique contributions and incorporating that uniqueness in all programs and services. When these staff reflect a multicultural population, the richness of cultural differences is modeled for the various populations of students and families in the community.

In terms of social work practice between schools and social services agencies, workers need to plan and implement programs and services that recognize the strength in youths' individual differences and use that strength to empower them. Such programs include developing collaborations with neighborhood organizations, churches, and agencies to respond to neighborhoods' specific needs and implementing services to meet those needs in the neighborhoods. In school social work practice, affirming cultural diversity means working with youths to acknowledge their cultural heritage and drawing on youths' varied cultural experiences to increase their creativity in finding solutions that work for them. When youths are sensitive to and draw on the strengths of their individual cultural backgrounds, they increase the variety of their options and empower both individual members and the group. The challenges for social workers in schools and community agencies are staying committed to honoring cultural diversity, focusing on youths' competencies rather than their deficits, and increasing flexibility in responding to youths.

As a second-generation Polish American man who was raised in a military family by a father whose behavior reflected melting pot ideology, my experience was one of disconnection with my cultural heritage (speaking a different language than my grandparents) and feeling like an outsider (as an Army "brat") in the bicultural community of El Paso, Texas, where I spent the majority of my youth. Fortunately, my father taught me to disdain cultural discrimination by sharing stories about his youth in the Polish ghetto where he was raised and from which he "escaped." My upbringing and my self-imposed immersion in the counterculture and the community action movement of the 1960s contributed heavily to my views on cultural diversity. These life experiences left me with a fierce defense of individual freedom, a natural distrust of bureaucratic intention, and a strong belief in the value of accepting and honoring people for who they are and how they can contribute.

I AM A HUMAN BEING: EDITH M. FREEMAN

At some point during his life as a celebrated Roman playwright, Publius Terentius Afer (c. 195–158 B.C.), called "Terence," wrote the following: "I am a human being, therefore, anything human cannot be alien to me." This quote reflects the meaning Terence must have derived from his life and experiences as an African living in Carthage who was captured and sent as a slave to Rome and who finally regained his freedom after many years (Barrett, 1995). In this quote, Terence alludes to his positive self-image and to the common human condition that unites people of all ethnic groups.

Recognizing the universality of the human condition is one side of the coin of multiculturalism, and acknowledging and appreciating the unique culture and contributions of each ethnic group in this pluralistic society is the other side.

From my professional perspective, this duality is what multiculturalism means in school social work practice, although it may not always be understood or accepted by school administrators, other staff, students, or parents. The school social worker can emphasize that as a universal setting in the lives of children and youths, the school presents many opportunities to influence childrens' attitudes about differences among ethnic groups and about themselves in relation to their own ethnic group. During early childhood individuals become aware of ethnic differences in general, and during the ages of five to eight years they are socialized to make value judgments about the relative worth of each group in terms of how it is different (McRoy & Freeman, 1986).

This age range represents an optimal period to counteract any negative socialization by helping children understand the different cultural contributions of all groups to this society. Children should know about the role of oppression and its effects in diminishing the lives and opportunities of some ethnic groups. They need to learn how the sense of entitlement and privilege experienced by some majority group members (McIntosh, 1991) can erode these group members' common human bond with the members of other ethnic groups, as Terence so eloquently reminds us. Therefore, in addition to a focus on differences, for multiculturalism to be effective, school social workers should help schools include members of different ethnic groups in curricula and books and as speakers and staff. Emphasizing the commonalities across all groups can provide other opportunities to strengthen multicultural learning in peer counseling groups, particularly when the facilitators are from different ethnic backgrounds.

This professional perspective bears a close relationship to my personal ideas about multiculturalism as an African American who was raised in the Midwest. In my family, we were reminded often that all people should be treated with dignity and respect even if their customs are different and we do not agree with their ideas. We also learned that as African Americans, we could not allow ourselves to be defined by others who might not see our self-worth and value; instead, we must define who we are. This has meant maintaining the customs and values that define me as an African American and those that make me a part of humanity. At yet another level, it has been meaningful to identify simultaneously with my African origins before the diaspora (creating a sense of unity with black people in the United States, Canada, the Caribbean, South America, Europe, and Africa) and with the unique experiences of black people in America that have both transformed and maintained our formerly subjugated African values. This knowledge highlights the common bond and the diversity among black people as an ethnic group as well as the diversity among African Americans in this country.

As a young woman I participated in church-sponsored joint youth group activities with members of other ethnic groups, but I was aware that the "separate but equal" doctrine continued to include Sunday worship services. Although I was more comfortable in my ethnic church at age 15, these youth group activities made it possible for me to explore previously unknown similarities among various groups and demystify some of the differences. Other influences on my ideas about multiculturalism included the Pan African and civil rights movements, which reframed political action positively by emphasizing that you've got to know who you are to make a united political stand. These movements also made it clear that taking pride in your own group does not mean devaluing others. Alex Haley's (1976) landmark book *Roots* as well as other meaningful black literature helped me understand also that to know who you are, you've got to know where you've been. All of these experiences have contributed to what I hope is an openness to multiculturalism, a celebration of our similarities, and an appreciation of the differences.

AS FOR TOMORROW. . .

As the different voices have spoken here, it is clear that these perspectives and experiences represent the rich multicultural mosaic that exists in school and community social work practice. As mosaics are designed to do, this one blends the common themes while highlighting and contrasting differences in a way that enriches the clarity and beauty of the artwork separately and as a whole. Some of the social, cultural, economic, and political arguments of today may attempt to distort the mosaic's inherent truth. Such arguments emphasize, for example, that a focus on multiculturalism is divisive rather than inclusive, that it involves a valuing of some groups over others instead of a valuing of all groups. It is through the valuing of all groups that we can become more hopeful about the future of this society and about the outcomes of school social work practice. In her presidential inaugural poem, *On the Pulse of Morning*, Maya Angelou speaks of multiculturalism and hope for positive change:

> Here on the pulse of this new day
> You may have the grace to look up and out
> And into your sister's eyes,
> And into your brother's face,
> Your country,
> And say simply
> Very simply
> With hope —
> Good Morning.*

REFERENCES

Angelou, M. (1993). *On the pulse of morning: The inaugural poem.* New York: Random House.

Arce, A. A. (1993, May 27). *Transference issues in cross cultural therapy* (Simon Bolivar Award Lecture). Presented at the annual meeting of the American Psychiatric Association, San Francisco.

Barrett, A. A. (1995). Terence. In *World book encyclopedia* (Vol. 19, p. 173). Chicago: Scott Fetter.

Dobyns, H. (1983). *Their number become thinned*. Knoxville: University of Tennessee Press.

Fong, R., & Mokuau, N. (1994). Not simply "Asian Americans": Periodical literature review on Asians and Pacific Islanders. *Social Work, 39*, 298–305.

Haley, A. (1976). *Roots: The saga of an American family*. New York: Dell.

McIntosh, P. (1991). *Understanding privilege*. Paper presented at a Wellesley College Center for Research on Women seminar on curriculum development and cultural diversity, Wellesley, MA.

McRoy, R. G., & Freeman, E. M. (1986). Racial-identity issues among mixed-race children. *Social Work in Education, 8*, 164–174.

Nieto, S. (1995, March 28). *Cultural competency*. Paper presented at the Regional Network for Children Conference, Upton, TX.

Owen, R. C., Deter, J., & Fisher, A. D. (1967). *The North American Indians: A sourcebook*. New York: Macmillan.

Prucha, F. P. (1975). *Documents of United States Indian policy*. Lincoln: University of Nebraska Press.

Telemaque, E. W. (1978). *It's crazy to stay Chinese in Minnesota*. New York: Nelson Thomas.

Wright, R. (1993). *Stolen continents: The "new world" through Indian eyes*. Toronto: Penguin Books.

Yellow Bird, M. J., & Snipp, M. C. (1994). American Indian families. In R. C. Taylor (Ed.), *Minority families in the United States: A multicultural perspective* (pp. 177–201). Englewood Cliffs, NJ: Prentice Hall.

This chapter was originally published in the July 1995 issue of Social Work in Education, *vol. 17, pp. 131–138.*

2

Undermining the Very Basis of Racism—Its Categories

Paul R. Spickard, Rowena Fong, and
Patricia L. Ewalt

The fastest-growing racial category in the past two U.S. censuses was "other" (Spickard & Fong, 1995), which suggests
significant changes in the U.S. racial scene. How social
workers and policymakers understand race and deal with racial
issues is changing rapidly and will continue to change, because
U.S. society's understanding of race is changing in fundamental
ways.

RACIAL CATEGORIES

Expanding Numbers

The number of racial categories is growing rapidly as Americans
become aware of the multiplicity of peoples who live in the United
States. At the same time, the boundaries between those categories are becoming blurred.

Not so long ago, the racial consensus in the United States was
the "one-drop" rule or "the rule of hypodescent" (Daniel, 1992a).
U.S. society was widely spoken of as consisting of two races, one
white and one black. The white–Caucasian–European race was
deemed biologically pure. People with any known African ancestry ("one drop of black blood") were put in the black–Negro–
African American category. Other people—those who were neither white nor black—were seldom noted or were placed on the
margins (Daniel, 1992b; Spickard, 1992). The roots of this unusual
system reach deep into the history of racial domination in the
United States (Jordan, 1969; Williamson, 1980). Other countries—
for example, Brazil, Mexico, and most Caribbean countries—
have more complex and subtle racial systems (Degler, 1971;
Vasconcellos, 1925/1979).

The racial categories in the 1940 census were white and non-white (by the latter, the census takers meant mainly African Americans). During the next three censuses, the number of categories slowly increased, exploding in the 1980 and 1990 censuses. There were 43 racial categories and subcategories on the 1990 census forms, including white; black; American Indian, Eskimo, or Aleut; Asian or Pacific Islander, with 11 Asian subcategories and four Pacific Islander subcategories; other race; and a Hispanic origin grid with 15 subcategories that included Mexican, Puerto Rican, Cuban, and other Hispanic (U.S. Bureau of the Census, 1992). This multiplication of racial categories stems in part from the growing numbers of immigrants, particularly from Asia and Latin America, and their descendants. In 1990 the U.S. population was 76 percent white, 12 percent African American, 9 percent Hispanic, and 3 percent Asian. Conservative projections for 2050 are 52 percent white, 16 percent African American, 22 percent Hispanic, and 10 percent Asian ("The New Face of America," 1993).

Deconstructing Race

The multiplication of racial categories suggests a deconstruction of the very notion of race. For a long time, most Americans and others who had imbibed European ideas thought of race as a biological fact. Starting with the Linnaean pyramid of biological taxonomy, from kingdom to phylum to class to order to family to genus to species, 19th-century pseudoscientific racists such as Johann Friedrich Blumenbach and Joseph Arthur comte de Gobineau tried to extend the system down one more level and so created the idea of discrete human races. Based on geographic origin and observed physical features, these races were supposed to have distinct characterological qualities as well.

However, it is widely recognized today that these racial ideas did not in fact spring from biological differences. Instead, they were mainly props used to justify European colonialism and white hegemony in multiracial societies (Spickard, 1992). Occasionally, there is a throwback to the era of pseudoscientific racist thinking, such as last year's best-selling book *The Bell Curve* (Herrnstein & Murray, 1994). However, in recent years social scientists have come to understand what biologists have long recognized—that race is a social and not a biological construct (Fraser, 1995; Marks, 1995). As geneticist James C. King (1981) put it,

> Both what constitutes a race and how one recognizes a racial difference are culturally determined. Whether two individuals regard themselves as of the same or of different races depends not on the degree of similarity of their genetic material but on whether history, tradition, and personal training and experiences have brought them to regard themselves as belonging to the same group or to different groups.... There are no objective boundaries to set off one subspecies from another. (pp. 156–157)

MULTIRACIAL CONSCIOUSNESS

One of the spurs to the change in racial thinking is the rapid rise of multiracial consciousness. Since the 1960s the rate of intermarriage has skyrocketed; the percentage of Asian and Hispanic people who marry outside their ancestral group has increased from less than 10 percent in the post–World War II generation to more than 40 percent in the closing years of this century. American Indians have sustained a 50 percent outmarriage rate throughout the past half-century. Even outmarriage rates for African Americans, which have been much lower, have sharply increased.

Along with intermarriage, the number of people who have multiple racial ancestries has increased. For some groups, such as Japanese Americans, the majority of children born in the 1990s are of mixed-race parentage (Kalmijn, 1991; Spickard, 1989).

As the mixed-ancestry population has increased, their identity options have also changed. Previously, people with multiple ancestries were typically allowed only one identity, usually specified by society at large. "One drop of black blood" made one an African American in the eyes of white America. A single non-Chinese parent made one not Chinese in the eyes of Chinese America (Spickard, 1989). In the 1950s and 1960s, author Greg Williams, although he looked white to most people, grew up under the black racial category because people knew his father as black (Williams, 1995). Others, like some of author Shirlee Taylor Haizlip's (1994) relatives, were accepted as white, but to do so they had to hide the African part of their ancestry.

These days the options for people like Williams and Haizlip are different. Some choose among their ancestral heritages; others refuse to choose and embrace them all. Teenage golf phenomenon Tiger Woods is frequently referred to by sportswriters as "the great black hope of the golf world," yet he says, "My mother is from Thailand. My father is part black, Chinese, and American Indian. So I'm all of those. It's an injustice to all my heritages to single me out as [only] black" (Goodman, 1995, p. A6). Not long ago, most observers would have said he was deluded—he was in their estimation really black. Now, his multiracial consciousness is taken seriously.

A recent *Newsweek* cover asked, "What Color Is Black?" (Morganthau, 1995). Scholarly books bear titles like *Ethnic Options* (Waters, 1990) and *Making Ethnic Choices* (Leonard, 1993). Psychologist Maria Root (in press) has set forth a "Bill of Rights for Racially Mixed People," claiming, for example, the rights "not to keep the races separate within me . . . not to justify my ethnic legitimacy . . . to identify myself differently than strangers expect me to identify . . . to identify myself differently in different situations . . . to change my identity over my lifetime . . . to have allegiances and identify with more than one group." Also, there is currently a campaign by such groups as the Association of Multi-Ethnic Americans and Project Race to change the category systems of the U.S. census, the Office of Management and Budget, and various state governments (which would affect school forms and other bureaucratic papers) to either include a multiracial category or to allow a person to check more than one box (Fernandez, in press; Wood, 1994).

All this is not to suggest that race is unimportant in America. On the contrary, it remains a highly salient factor in social and political relationships. However, race as an idea, in an era of multiplicity and mixing, is becoming an increasingly fluid construct. One of the hopeful possibilities in such a situation is that as the idea of race becomes less fixed, it may be more difficult for racism to find clear targets. As Glass and Wallace (in press) insisted,

> Race cannot be ignored as a conceptual framework because of its theoretical inadequacy for capturing the phenomenon of race, nor because of its simplistic use of reified notions for historically dynamic meanings and practices. Nor can the politics of race be transcended by a mental act of some sort (like a change in belief, or an act of will) nor wished away in a fantasy of color blindness. . . . But an even stronger challenge to race can come from people at the margins to all racial centers; that is, from people expressive of multiracial

existence and evident human variation, who resist efforts to
be subdued and brought within racial orders.

RACIAL UNDERSTANDING AND SOCIAL WORK

Because the United States is home to many different peoples,
social workers' training and practice need to embrace understanding of all kinds of people. There is a growing literature designed
to help social workers achieve competence in dealing with various racial and cultural groups (Browne, Fong, & Mokuau, 1994;
Fong & Mokuau, 1994; Furuto, Biswas, Chung, Murase, & Ross-
Sheriff, 1992; Gibbs & Huang, 1989; Gray & Nybell, 1990; Lum,
1992; Matsuoka, 1990; McAdoo, 1993; Sandau-Beckler, Salcido,
& Ronnau, 1993).

As the variety of peoples in the nation continues to expand, as
an increasing number of people maintain multiple racial and cultural identities, and as ideas about race change rapidly, the simple
understanding of race and the easy targets of racism grow more
complex. It is important that we examine the implications for
social workers and policymakers of these changes in racial ideas.

REFERENCES

Browne, C., Fong, R., & Mokuau, N. (1994). The mental health of Asian and
    Pacific Island elders. *Journal of Mental Health Administration, 21,* 52–59.
Daniel, G. R. (1992a). Beyond black and white: The new multiracial con-
    sciousness. In M.P.P. Root (Ed.), *Racially mixed people in America* (pp. 333–
    341). Newbury Park, CA: Sage Publications.
Daniel, G. R. (1992b). Passers and pluralists: Subverting the racial divide. In
    M.P.P. Root (Ed.), *Racially mixed people in America* (pp. 91–107). Newbury
    Park, CA: Sage Publications.
Degler, C. N. (1971). *Neither black nor white: Slavery and race relations in Brazil
    and the United States.* New York: Macmillan.
Fernandez, C. A. (in press). Government classification of multiracial/
    multiethnic people. In M.P.P. Root (Ed.), *Racially mixed people in the new
    millennium.* Newbury Park, CA: Sage Publications.
Fong, R., & Mokuau, N. (1994). Not simply "Asian Americans": Periodical
    literature review on Asians and Pacific Islanders. *Social Work, 39,* 298–312.
Fraser, S. (Ed.). (1995). *The Bell Curve wars: Race, intelligence, and the future of
    America.* New York: Basic Books.
Furuto, S. M., Biswas, R., Chung, D. K., Murase, K., & Ross-Sheriff, F. (Eds.).
    (1992). *Social work practice with Asian Americans.* Newbury Park, CA: Sage
    Publications.
Gibbs, J. T., & Huang, L. N. (1989). *Children of color: Psychological interventions
    with minority youth.* San Francisco: Jossey-Bass.

Glass, R. D., & Wallace, K. R. (in press). Challenging race and racism: A framework for educators. In M.P.P. Root (Ed.), *Racially mixed people in the new millennium.* Newbury Park, CA: Sage Publications.

Goodman, E. (1995, April 15). Obsessed with racial classes. *Honolulu Advertiser,* p. A6.

Gray, S. S., & Nybell, L. (1990). Issues in African American family preservation. *Child Welfare, 69,* 513–524.

Haizlip, S. T. (1994). *The sweeter the juice: A family memoir in black and white.* New York: Simon & Schuster.

Herrnstein, R. J., & Murray, C. (1994). *The bell curve: Intelligence and class structure in American life.* New York: Free Press.

Jordan, W. D. (1969). *White over black.* Chapel Hill: University of North Carolina Press.

Kalmijn, M. (1991). Trends in black/white intermarriage. *Social Forces, 72,* 119–146.

King, J. C. (1981). *The biology of race.* Berkeley: University of California Press.

Leonard, K. I. (1993). *Making ethnic choices: California's Punjabi-Mexican Americans.* Philadelphia: Temple University Press.

Lum, D. (1992). *Social work practice and people of color: A process-stage approach* (2nd ed.). Pacific Grove, CA: Brooks/Cole.

Marks, J. (1995). *Human biodiversity: Genes, race, and history.* New York: Aldine de Gruyter.

Matsuoka, J. (1990). Differential acculturation among Vietnamese refugees. *Social Work, 35,* 341–345.

McAdoo, H. P. (Ed.). (1993). *Family ethnicity: Strength in diversity.* Newbury Park, CA: Sage Publications.

Morganthau, T. (1995, February 13). What color is black? *Newsweek,* pp. 62–72.

The new face of America: How immigrants are shaping the world's first multicultural society. (1993, Fall). *Time* [Special issue].

Root, M.P.P. (in press). A bill of rights for racially mixed people. In M.P.P. Root (Ed.), *Racially mixed people in the new millennium.* Newbury Park, CA: Sage Publications.

Sandau-Beckler, P., Salcido, R., & Ronnau, J. (1993). Cultural-competent family preservation services: An approach for first-generation Hispanic families in an international border community. *Counseling and Therapy for Couples and Families, 1,* 313–323.

Spickard, P. R. (1989). *Mixed blood: Intermarriage and ethnic identity in twentieth-century America.* Madison: University of Wisconsin Press.

Spickard, P. R. (1992). The illogic of American racial categories. In M.P.P. Root (Ed.), *Racially mixed people in America* (pp. 12–23). Newbury Park, CA: Sage Publications.

Spickard, P. R., & Fong, R. (1995). Pacific Islander Americans and multiethnicity: A vision of America's future? *Social Forces, 73,* 1365–1384.

U. S. Bureau of the Census. (1992). *1990 census of population: General population characteristics (CP-1-1).* Washington, DC: U.S. Government Printing Office.

Vasconcellos, J. (1979). *La Raza cósmica* (D. T. Jaen, Trans.). Los Angeles: California State University, Centro de Publicaciones. (Original Spanish work published 1925)

Waters, M. C. (1990). *Ethnic options: Choosing identities in America*. Berkeley: University of California Press.

Williams, G. H. (1995). *Life on the color line*. New York: Dutton.

Williamson, J. (1980). *New people: Mulattoes and miscegenation in the United States*. New York: Free Press.

Wood, J. (1994, December). Fade to black: Once upon a time in multiracial America. *Village Voice*, pp. 25–34.

Wright, L. (1994, July 25). One drop of blood. *New Yorker*, pp. 46–55.

This chapter was originally published in the September 1995 issue of Social Work, *vol. 40, pp. 581–584.*

A Multiracial Reality: Issues for Social Work

Rowena Fong, Paul R. Spickard, and Patricia L. Ewalt

In an age when countless people migrate around the globe, the ethnic categories Americans encounter and recognize have multiplied dramatically. Intermarriage has created people who do not fall neatly into one or another of an ever-longer list of categories. This makes for what novelist Dorothy West (1995) called "the overlapping worlds and juxtaposed mores" (p. 63) of racially postmodern America. Simple binary thinking about race in the United States as black and white, which characterized earlier eras, no longer applies (Camper, 1994; Root, 1992, 1995; Zack, 1995).

What issues does this new complexity raise for social work practitioners and researchers? In direct practice, social policy, competing individual and community values, research methods, and theory building, the multiracial reality has implications for social workers.

DIRECT PRACTICE

In direct practice it is important to rethink assessment to take clients' multiraciality fully into account. If a client appears African American, he or she is likely to be identified by others as black regardless of his or her other ethnicities. Social workers must recognize that the person may well have a white or Latino or Asian or American Indian parent or earlier forebear. Social workers have a responsibility to consciously reverse the historic binary system, enforced more strongly against African Americans than people of any other race or ethnicity, by seeking to understand the full background of clients and clients' perceptions of their identities, rather than allocating them into preconceived categories. Assessment should explore the multicultural environmental components that have shaped the client's upbringing, current functioning, and hopes for the future.

Zastrow and Kirst-Ashman (1990) advocated a Behavior Dynamics Assessment Model (BDAM), which weighs the effects of diversity, including race or ethnicity, in assessing the life events of the individual. Fong (in press) adapted the BDAM model to a more subtle characterization of Asian clients. Similar assessment procedures and tools need to be developed to reflect the complex identities of multiracial clients. Researchers at the University of Hawaii are doing promising work on a protocol to measure multiethnic identities but have not yet completed their work (Horvath, Marsella, & Yamada, 1995).

SOCIAL POLICY

The existence of a substantial racially mixed population, along with the increasing social option of identifying oneself multiply, suggests that social workers may have to recast the dialogue about what have been regarded as "transracial" adoptions. It has for many years been more or less settled policy to place children for adoption with parents of like ancestry—for example, to place Cuban American children, if at all possible, with Cuban American couples.

The lead position in this regard has been taken by the National Association of Black Social Workers, which said in 1974, "Only a black family can transmit the emotional and sensitive subtleties of perception and reaction essential for a black child's survival in a racist society" (cited in Smith, 1995, p. 3). There is much to recommend this sentiment, for it is far more likely that an average black family can prepare a child for the distinctive pressures and disabilities that American society places on African Americans than almost any white family (Ladner, 1977). Similar arguments can be made for placement of American Indian, Mexican American, and Asian American children.

Yet this policy, formulated in the 1970s, assumed that all children are members of only one race. In fact, many children available for adoption today are of mixed parentage. With what sort of family, then, should they be placed? Should social workers hold children for parents of the same ethnic mix? Should they be placed systematically with parents from one group or the other? These questions are a subset of larger debate on the advisability of adoption of children of color by white families and of children from Third World countries by U.S. families (Bagley, 1993; Bartholet, 1993; Reddy, 1994; Register, 1991; Simon & Altstein, 1987, 1992; Smith, 1995).

The Multiethnic Placement Act of 1994 (P.L. 103-382) challenges the traditional practice of using race and ethnicity as the deciding factor in adoption. The act

> bans discrimination in placement decisions based solely on race, color, or national origin. . . . It allows agencies to consider the cultural, ethnic, or racial background of children and the capacity of the prospective foster or adoptive parents to meet the needs of the children based upon their background; and stipulates that agencies engage in active recruitment of potential foster or adoptive parents who reflect the racial and ethnic diversity of the children needing placement. (cited in Smith, 1995, p. 3)

Our point here is not to take a side in the debate about the advisability of placing a child who is clearly of one racial and cultural group with a family that is clearly of another—for example, placing a Mexican American child with a Chinese American family. Rather, we wish to observe that a child who is mixed Mexican and Chinese probably belongs as much with a Chinese family as with a Mexican family. So, too, a child of mixed African American and European American biological parentage may be as appropriately placed with a white family as with a black family. In either case, the adoptive parents will have some cultural stretching to do.

Some may object, arguing that children of African American heritage, for example, should be reared by black families because only those families can sufficiently nurture children's positive black identities. African American psychologist Prentice Baptiste (1983) argued the contrary:

> Biologically, these [biracial] children are neither Black nor White, but equally a part of both races. But the Jim Crow traditions and laws will attempt to define all of them as Black regardless of their phenotypic appearance. Parents of interracial children must counter this attempt by teaching them that they are and culturally can be members of both races. Positive models of both races must be very apparent to these children during early years of development. (p. 1)

Obviously, this is an issue that policymakers and practitioners in adoptions and foster care will continue to ponder and debate.

However, what seems lacking in the debate is consideration of the impact on foster care placement versus considerations of the child's multiracial ethnic identity.

The Casey Family Program is a national long-term foster care agency whose commitment to cultural competency is pervasive throughout program and policy. To ensure understanding of the multiracial families the program serves, its five-year strategic plan (Casey Family Program, 1995) includes as a goal to "strengthen diversity and cross-cultural understanding," including understanding of multiraciality. The program is currently providing training to its employees on ethnic socialization and ethnic identity development of children and youths (Helms, 1990; Phinney, 1990, 1993; Sue & Sue, 1990).

COMPETING INDIVIDUAL AND COMMUNITY VALUES

The upcoming census has provoked a great debate about how to characterize people of mixed heritage (Fernandez, 1995; Graham, 1995; Jones, 1994; Office of Management and Budget, 1995; Wood, 1994). Is it desirable to allow people to identify themselves as multiracial rather than forcing them to choose among ethnic and racial categories?

At the individual level, psychological benefits may accrue to a multiracial individual from opportunities to adopt a multiracial consciousness. For individuals of mixed parentage, it is generally healthful and empowering to embrace both, or all, parts of themselves (Daniel, 1992; Gibbs & Hines, 1992; Hall, 1992; Spickard, 1989).

However, there may be costs for social groups of recognizing multiracial identities. Some African American civic leaders, for example, worry that if "biracial" and "mixed" become accepted ethnic identities, individuals with dual heritages will cease to identify as African Americans and that their numbers and talents will become unavailable to the African American community (Daniel, 1992; Office of Management and Budget, 1995; Wood, 1994). Mass (1992) echoed this concern, reporting that there is fear in the Japanese American community that it may "disappear" because mixed people may "hasten assimilation into mainstream culture" (p. 277).

There are potential costs to Japanese and African Americans, as well as to other groups, in terms of counting their populations.

According to Wright (1994), 75 percent to 90 percent of people who identify themselves in the census as black could alternatively classify themselves as multiracial. If even a small proportion did so, civil rights programs, including those related to housing, employment, and education, would be severely affected. Yet recognition of multiraciality need not necessarily decrease the community of color. Among Native Americans, a high rate of interracial marriage over the past half-century has resulted in increasing numbers. There is continued need for policy discussion on these issues with concern for both individual and group well-being.

RESEARCH METHODS

There are practical problems related to research and the knowledge base on which many policy decisions are made. On the one hand, the new multiracial consciousness makes demographic data more complicated and less clear. Are the caseworker and the researcher to record a half-black, half-Chicano client as Mexican American, African American, both, neither, other, mixed, or something else? The complexity and indefiniteness of this situation may result in a cumulative loss of clarity in keeping statistics and thus in our understanding of the populations we serve.

On the other hand, if we continue to do research and demographic analysis with the assumption that each person is only black or only white or only Vietnamese, then we have failed to describe and understand the realities of many people's human experience. Recent research has shown that the commonly used monoracial category systems do not accurately reflect the ethnic identities of many people. Nautu and Lang (1995) found that Pacific Islander Americans—most of them racially mixed people—displayed no measurable consistency when identifying themselves on census, school, and employment affirmative action forms. When studying populations that include people of mixed race and ethnicity, an increasingly likely circumstance, researchers will have to question to what extent race or ethnicity in fact has meaningful explanatory capability.

THEORY BUILDING

The final question raised by the current state of racial category deconstruction is a theoretical one with implications for social work that are not yet fully clear. Social workers are in the habit of locating their clients along analytical axes, of which race and class are two (Zastrow & Kirst-Ashman, 1990). Traditionally, race has been seen as a biological attribute (with obvious social ramifications), whereas class has always been understood to be socially constructed. Most of the recent work on race concludes, however, that it is not a biological fact at all, but rather a social and political construct that uses physical markers (King, 1981; Marks, 1995; Spickard, 1992). Race, therefore, must be considered a social consequence and not a cause of human behavior. What implications will this understanding have for theory building in years to come? This question and the other issues posed in this editorial are challenges for social workers in a 21st century when increasing numbers of clients will be multiracial.

REFERENCES

Bagley, C. (1993). *International and transracial adoptions.* Aldershot, UK: Avebury.

Baptiste, H. P. (1983). Rearing the interracial child. *Communique, 1*(3), 1, 4.

Bartholet, E. (1993). Adoption and race. In E. Bartholet (Ed.), *Family bonds: Adoption and the politics of parenting* (pp. 86–117). Boston: Houghton-Mifflin.

Camper, C. (Ed.). (1994). *Miscegenation blues: Voices of mixed race women.* Toronto: Sister Vision Press.

Casey Family Program. (1995). *Building toward a new century: Strategic plan 1995–2000.* Seattle: Author.

Daniel, G. R. (1992). Beyond black and white: The new multiracial consciousness. In M.P.P. Root (Ed.), *Racially mixed people in America* (pp. 333–341). Newbury Park, CA: Sage Publications.

Fernandez, C. A. (in press). Government classification of multiracial/ multiethnic people. In M.P.P. Root (Ed.), *The multiracial experience: Racial borders as the new frontier.* Newbury Park, CA: Sage Publications.

Fong, R. (in press). Child welfare practice with Chinese families: Assessment issues for immigrants from the People's Republic of China. *Journal of Family Social Work.*

Gibbs, J. T., & Hines, A. M. (1992). Negotiating ethnic identity: Issues for black–white biracial adolescents. In M.P.P. Root (Ed.), *Racially mixed people in America* (pp. 223–238). Newbury Park, CA: Sage Publications.

Graham, S. (1995). Grassroots advocacy. In N. Zack (Ed.), *American mixed race: The culture of microdiversity* (pp. 185–190). Lanham, MD: Rowman & Littlefield.

Hall, C.C.I. (1992). Please choose one: Ethnic identity choices for biracial individuals. In M.P.P. Root (Ed.), *Racially mixed people in America* (pp. 250–264). Newbury Park, CA: Sage Publications.

Helms, J. (1990). An overview of black racial identity theory. In J. Helms (Ed.), *Black and white racial identity: Theory, research, and practice* (pp. 8–66). New York: Greenwood Press.

Horvath, A.-M., Marsella, A. J., & Yamada, S. Y. (1995, May 11). *A behavioral measure of ethnocultural identification: Implications for the measurement of multi-identified students.* Paper presented to the Ethnicity and Multiethnicity Conference, Brigham Young University–Hawaii.

Jones, L. (1994). Is biracial enough? (Or, What's this about a multiracial category on the census?: A conversation). In L. Jones (Ed.), *Bulletproof diva: Tales of race, sex, and hair* (pp. 53–66). New York: Doubleday.

King, J. C. (1981). *The biology of race.* Berkeley: University of California Press.

Ladner, J. (1977). *Mixed families: Adopting across racial boundaries.* Garden City, NY: Doubleday.

Marks, J. (1995). *Human biodiversity: Genes, race, and history.* New York: Aldine de Gruyter.

Mass, A. J. (1992). Interracial Japanese Americans: The best of both worlds or the end of the Japanese American community? In M.P.P. Root (Ed.), *Racially mixed people in America* (pp. 265–279). Newbury Park, CA: Sage Publications.

Multiethnic Placement Act of 1994, P.L. 103-382, 103 Stat. 4868 (October 28, 1994).

Nautu, D., & Lang, R. (1995, June). *What do you call a Pacific Islander American?* Paper presented to the Association for Asian American Studies, Oakland, CA.

Office of Management and Budget. (1995, August 28). Standards for the classification of federal data on race and ethnicity. *Federal Register, 60*(166), 44674–44693.

Phinney, J. (1990). Ethnic identity in adolescents and adults: Review of research. *Psychological Bulletin, 108,* 499–514.

Phinney, J. (1993). A three-stage model of ethnic identity development in adolescence. In M. E. Bernal & G. P. Knights (Eds.), *Ethnic identity: Formation and transmission among Hispanics and other minorities* (pp. 61–79). Albany: State University of New York Press.

Reddy, M. T. (1994). *Crossing the color line: Race, parenting, and culture.* New Brunswick, NJ: Rutgers University Press.

Register, C. (1991). *"Are those kids yours?" American families with children adopted from other countries.* New York: Free Press.

Root, M.P.P. (Ed.). (1992). *Racially mixed people in America.* Newbury Park, CA: Sage Publications.

Root, M.P.P. (Ed.). (1995). *The multiracial experience: Racial borders as the new frontier.* Newbury Park, CA: Sage Publications.

Simon, R. J., & Altstein, H. (1987). *Transracial adoptees and their families: A study of identity and commitment.* New York: Praeger.

Simon, R. J., & Altstein, H. (1992). *Adoption, race, and identity: From infancy through adolescence.* New York: Praeger.

Smith, R. (1995, July). The adoption equation, minus race: Can agencies' decisions be colorblind? *NASW News,* pp. 3–4.

Spickard, P. R. (1989). *Mixed blood: Intermarriage and ethnic identity in twentieth-century America*. Madison: University of Wisconsin Press.

Spickard, P. R. (1992). The illogic of American racial categories. In M.P.P. Root (Ed.), *Racially mixed people in America* (pp. 12–23). Newbury Park, CA: Sage Publications.

Sue, D., & Sue, D. (1990). Racial/cultural identity development. In D. Sue & D. Sue (Eds.), *Counseling the culturally different: Theory and practice* (pp. 93–117). New York: Wiley–Interscience.

West, D. (1995). *The wedding*. New York: Doubleday.

Wood, J. (1994, December). Fade to black: Once upon a time in multiracial America. *Village Voice*, pp. 25–34.

Wright, L. (1994, July 25). One drop of blood. *New Yorker*, pp. 46–55.

Zack, N. (Ed.). (1995). *American mixed race: The culture of microdiversity*. Lanham, MD: Rowman & Littlefield.

Zastrow, C., & Kirst-Ashman, K. (1990). *Understanding human behavior and the social environment* (2nd ed.). Chicago: Nelson-Hall.

This chapter was originally published in the November 1995 issue of Social Work, *vol. 40, pp. 725–728.*

The Misconstruing of Multiculturalism: The Stanford Debate and Social Work

Ketayun H. Gould

The 1990 census shows that the racial and ethnic composition of the American population changed more dramatically in the past decade than at any time in the 20th century, with nearly one in every four Americans identifying themselves as black, Hispanic, Asian and Pacific Islander, or American Indian (Barringer, 1991). In 1980 one in every five Americans had a nonwhite background. White people (excluding people who classified themselves as having Hispanic ancestry) now make up slightly less than 76 percent of the resident population. These statistics also reflect the fact that in recent years, more than four in five legal immigrants to the United States have been of non-European ancestry (Barringer, 1991). The 1990 census shows that the number of foreign-born residents reached an all-time high of 20 million. The previous peak, in 1980, was about 14 million (Vobejda, 1992).

Moreover, these trends certainly underscore the need for the social work profession to speak out publicly to urge a societal commitment to the values of racial, ethnic, and cultural diversity—values that have been recognized as being part of the profession's "system of ethics" (Council on Social Work Education [CSWE], 1988). However, at this point, there is an equally compelling reason for the profession to present its perspective on cultural diversity, a challenge that has been generally unheeded. I am referring to the current social discourse on multiculturalism, or rather the misconstruing of the concept of multiculturalism, which has polarized the debate in society, the educational community, and even the social work field (Lawrence,

1992). Although this controversy initially started on college campuses, there are so many hidden levels to this discourse that it has catapulted an academic debate into a public exchange involving the popular print and broadcast media (see, for example, D'Souza, 1991b).

This article undertakes an analysis of the concept of multiculturalism to demonstrate the complexity of this perspective, which has been lost in the acrimonious exchange surrounding the term—a debate that also covers other issues and that has given rise to the term "political correctness" (Hartman, 1991). Specifically, some of the main ideas and value imperatives involving the dispute over the definition of multiculturalism are outlined. This background information provides a framework to investigate how the social work literature has dealt with the concept of multiculturalism and whether the profession's long-term experience in dealing with cultural diversity has left it with any better ability than the current campus advocates to implement a multicultural curriculum. The discussion then considers an alternative model—one that uses the original definition of multiculturalism developed in the literature on intercultural communication. The author argues for a paradigmatic shift to a framework that informs thinking at a transcultural level rather than a model that merely provides specific strategies for ethnic-sensitive practice. The shift might extricate the profession from the forced dichotomies of white people versus people of color, established immigrants versus new immigrants, and American minorities versus Third World cultures. As Hartman (1990) said, "a new world demands new responses and major changes on the international, national, professional, and personal levels" (p. 291).

ASSUMPTIONS, VALUES, AND INTERPRETATIONS

All sides of the debate on multiculturalism seem to agree that the fact of demographic change has altered the complexion of U.S. society. Hence, there is no dispute when the definition of multiculturalism simply implies the existence of a culturally pluralistic society. However, as soon as the model moves beyond this basic descriptive level and suggests a prescriptive dimension, especially one that implies a transformation of professional and societal roles, the lines become sharply drawn on prospective strategies.

The pivotal point in understanding why the discourse on multiculturalism is so acrimonious is the following: The complex and subtle dimensions of the theoretical concept of multiculturalism have been politicized by ideologically driven interpretations of the term that have structured the dialogue. Given the fact that the original controversy was centered in academic settings before it escalated into a public debate, it might be instructive to use the example of the multicultural curriculum dispute at Stanford University (the most publicized account of this controversy) to illustrate its wider significance. It is important to remember, however, that the debate at Stanford was only a small piece of the struggle that has plagued many college campuses and public schools (see, for example, Berger, 1989; Bernstein, 1990; D'Souza, 1991a, 1991b; Goodstein, 1991; Woodward, 1991).

Although the debate over what came to be known as the "Stanford-style multicultural curriculum" was quite involved, it is clear that the focal point of the controversy was the content of a core curriculum on Western civilization that was required of all undergraduate students. Established in 1980, Stanford had decreed a canon—a set of 15 required "great books" by writers such as Plato, Aristotle, Homer, Aquinas, Marx, and Freud—that would familiarize the students with great traditions, philosophy, literature, and history of the West.

By 1987 a newly formed Rainbow Coalition demanded substantial revision of the three-course Western culture requirement that included the abandonment of the idea of studying 15 required books all by white males. To many in the university community, the canon conveyed a white, male, Eurocentric bias that denied the history and intellectual contributions to society of people of color, women, and other oppressed groups. In 1988 the Stanford Faculty Senate voted 39 to 4 to change the Western culture curriculum to a new three-course sequence called "Cultures, Ideas, and Values" (CIV). The term "Western," along with the 15-book requirement, was eliminated. The concept of cultures was introduced to emphasize a pluralistic perspective. All three courses had to study at least one non-European culture, and the professors had to give substantial attention to issues of race and gender.

The proposed changes brought on a predictable avalanche of responses from both the academic world and the wider community. In the turn of events at Stanford and the conservative mood of the country, the idea of multiculturalism became synonymous with a so-called "minority perspective"—a "politically correct" movement that opponents claimed imposed "intellectual conformity in the name of a putative commitment to diversity" (D'Souza, 1991b, pp. xii–xiv). This entanglement with the issues of free speech and academic freedom made enemies such as traditional conservatives and traditional liberals join together in their opposition to the demands for societal changes that were advocated by the supporters of multiculturalism (Woodward, 1991).

Furthermore, the polarization was accentuated by the question the Stanford Rainbow Coalition raised about the value of learning about American nonwhite groups as opposed to Third World cultures: A member of the coalition stated, "We're not saying we need to study Tibetan philosophy. . . . We're arguing that we need to understand what made our society what it is" (Mooney, 1988, p. A-11). In fact, it seems that the value of studying non-Western societies was a political football for all sides. Opponents of the "new multiculturalism" supported it to demonstrate the provincialism of the Rainbow Coalition, and the Stanford administration opposed it because it did not want to hire new faculty with expertise in cultures of developing countries (D'Souza, 1991a).

The debate reflects the very real tensions and challenges that confront today's college administrators and students. However, many academic programs have resolved issues surrounding the establishment of a multicultural curriculum without this kind of publicity (Dye, 1991). Nevertheless, it is clear that the dictum that Americans are a single people of diverse backgrounds is no longer sufficient to provide a basis for consensus on how to create a core intellectual experience that truly reflects a pluralistic society.

SOCIAL WORK PERSPECTIVE

Multiculturalism is, of course, a crucial issue for the social work profession. From both the education and practice points of view, the profession has recognized and implemented the principle that students must be prepared to understand and appreciate racial, cultural, and social diversity. Thus, there is no question that the social work field has long passed the point where it needs to have a Stanford-style debate on the value of implementing a multicultural curriculum. But the question that remains to be explored is whether social work's long-term experience in developing a culturally pluralistic perspective has left the profession with any better grasp of the complex and subtle dimensions of the concept of multiculturalism than the recent participants in the Stanford-style curriculum debate.

An initial step that might provide a basis to evaluate this question is a historical perspective on the profession's involvement with the concept of multiculturalism. Influenced by the activities of the civil rights movement of the 1960s and the subsequent demands for action on behalf of minority rights within the profession, social work began a halting move in 1973 to acknowledge that "ours is a pluralistic society"—a fact that has "implications . . . for sensitive and effective social work intervention." These words are part of the CSWE's (1973) *Guidelines for Implementation of Accreditation Standard 1234A*, which requires that "a school must make special, continual efforts to enrich its program by providing racial, ethnic, and cultural diversity" (p. 1). In practice, however (not unlike the Stanford scenario), educating for pluralism became equated with teaching about people of color. Furthermore, the content was tailored primarily to fit the needs of the dominant group of white social work students by including sufficient information about specific cultures to enable students to engage in what was believed to be ethnic-sensitive practice.

In reality, social work established a one-directional model of learning pluralism (a contradiction in itself) that at best taught students to look at, rather than into, the lives of people of color (Leigh, 1983). As a result, students and faculty never interpreted the CSWE standard as prescribing an intercultural learning experience—an integral part of a multicultural worldview. In a less blatant fashion than the Stanford incident, many in social work education compartmentalized and otherwise ignored this part of the curriculum because they felt that it pertained only to students of color and that it contained "a lot of propaganda" (Lawrence, 1992, p. 384). Furthermore, the situation did not alter substantially when the ethnically sensitive content was supposedly integrated into the total curriculum.

In addition, it is also worth noting that the term "multiculturalism" was never used in the CSWE standard. Perhaps the professional failure in spelling out the concept clearly might be better understood if the problem is viewed in terms of the broader societal context. In an ethnically stratified country like the United States, multiculturalism is not part of the societal norm. Despite the ease with which the profession speaks about cultural plurality, social stratification provides an implicit endorsement of the value of "Angloconformity" (Gordon, 1964). Consequently, not only is there an underlying denial of the equivalent value of the cultures of people of color (making multiculturalism a devalued norm), but it is only for the people of color that "multicultural competency" (Seelye & Wasilewski, 1979) is a necessity for survival. Conversely, the lack of pressure for white people to master the same skills leads to a mechanical process of learning about "different" groups—a social reality that is hard to overcome through professional mandates to teach cultural pluralism.

By the mid-1970s, social work publications included an occasional piece that used the concept of multiculturalism. Often, the definition did not go any further than the descriptive level as the authors tried to exhort the profession to be effective change agents in a "multicultural, pluralistic society" (see, for example, Sanders, 1975). The concept was also used to define a multicultural and pluralistic perspective as "the effort towards a positive view of ethnicity and a 'new pluralism' . . . that accepts uniqueness and balances identification with a small group against commitment to society as a whole" (Sanders, 1975, p. 98). Not unlike the Stanford proponents of "new multiculturalism," Sanders also worried that these partisan efforts carried "risks and difficulties . . . [and] the possibility of conflict between diverse ethnic and cultural groups leading to further tensions and social polarization" (p. 98).

Interestingly, the complex and subtle dimensions of the concept of multiculturalism did not emerge in the social work literature in the area of cross-cultural practice with the varied ethnic groups in this country. Rather, it was scholars interested in the international and cross-cultural area of social work practice who addressed the issues involved in delineating the theoretical concept of multiculturalism. This development can be explained easily by the fact that these authors became aware early on of the literature on intercultural communication, which focused heavily, if not exclusively, on the international arena. By the mid-1970s, the writings of people like Adler (1986) on "multicultural man" were seminal in influencing social work educators like Sanders (1977, 1980), who was a pioneer in establishing a social work curriculum with an international–cross-cultural perspective. In fact, Sanders's (1980) article "Multiculturalism: Implications for Social Work" stood by itself in concentrating on "the implications of the multicultural perspective with all its ramifications for social work" (p. 9).

Although Sanders made a consistent effort to relate the cross-cultural aspects of multiculturalism to both the national and international arenas, the lack of emphasis on international concerns in the profession prevented the literature on intercultural communication from influencing social work practice with various ethnic groups and people of color in this country in any significant way. Sikkema (1984) explained the barrier in moving from an Amerocentric to an international perspective in the area of cross-cultural practice: "Social work education is more likely to include the limited objective of learning specifically to work with a given minority group . . . rather than the broad objective of having students develop a multicultural perspective and competence" (pp. 96–97). Indeed, this is the crux of the problem in the present debate on multiculturalism. Learning about other cultural groups, or even having the perspective of another culture, is a necessary but not a sufficient step in achieving a multicultural worldview—a more encompassing concept both in theory and practice.

The changing demographics of the 1990s have made it impossible for the profession to continue its "add and stir" strategy to teach about a wide variety of ethnic groups. In fact, the social work literature of the 1980s and 1990s reflects a growing dissatisfaction with the old methods of dealing with an increasingly ethnically complex environment (Nakanishi & Rittner, 1992). The influx of new immigrants from Third World countries certainly revolutionized the size and complexity of the problem of dealing with nonwhite communities, and at the same time it succeeded in introducing an added dimension of internationalizing domestic practice (Healy, 1987; Rosenthal, 1991).

A review of the literature reveals that the profession reacted to this trend in several positive ways. An editorial in social work's professional journal gave a strong signal of commitment when it called on social workers to "work with the increasingly diverse population in this country and to understand the culture, the needs, and the experiences of the new immigrants and refugees" (Hartman, 1990, p. 292). Healy (1987) drew attention to the problem when she stressed the fact that "making a sharp dichotomy between the domestic and the international is no longer functional or responsible" (p. 409). Several authors responded to the challenge by developing models of social work practice with racial and ethnic groups (Devore & Schlesinger, 1987; Green, 1982; D. Lum, 1986) or more recently by developing cross-cultural models of practice that tried to capture the reality and meaning of the cultural experience for both immigrants and indigenous nonwhite communities (see, for example, Chau, 1990; Nakanishi & Rittner, 1992; Rodwell & Blankebaker, 1992).

Others concentrated on broadening the concept of the "dual perspective" that had been used to characterize the personal and social self-images developed by members of different ethnic backgrounds (Norton, 1978) to include the "dual socialization" of the "bicultural" immigrant (deAnda, 1984; De Hoyos, De Hoyos, & Anderson, 1986). And, more importantly for the purposes of this article, recent literature has demonstrated an interest in re-examining the contributions of multicultural service models (developed in related fields of practice) that had been ignored as more applicable in the international rather than the domestic arena of practice (Canda & Phaobtong, 1992; Garland & Escobar, 1988).

None of these strategies, however, has addressed the question of whether social work's quest to provide racial, ethnic, and cultural diversity in its education and practice efforts might be flawed because the basic premise underlying the main concept is ill-defined. In other words, like the Stanford scenario, a fundamental paradigmatic shift might be the first step in developing an alternative model: a change from viewing multiculturalism as merely a "practice" extension of the minority perspective to a framework that can help all groups in society orient their thinking at a transcultural level.

ALTERNATIVE MODEL

Inevitably, a profession concerned with societal inequities might be inclined to translate teaching and practice about "cultural diversity" as educating its students for competent practice with racially diverse groups. In reality, this approach has not been conducive to fostering intercultural learning (Nakanishi & Rittner, 1992), because students have come to view multiculturalism in purely objective terms—as information about other cultures that has to be mastered to work effectively with clients from "different" groups in the broader society (CSWE, 1973). Several authors have recognized this distancing and have stressed the incorporation of an experiential and affective component along with the cognitive content as an antidote in developing a successful curriculum on multicultural issues (see, for example, Montalvo, 1983; Nakanishi & Rittner, 1992). However, perhaps the problem begins at a more basic level—with the theoretical model itself and its definition of multiculturalism. If the ideological assumptions about broadening the horizons of the dominant groups about cultural diversity in society are to be realized, both social work and the Stanford advocates might re-examine the original definition of multiculturalism that was developed in the literature on intercultural communication. This particular orientation is valuable, because the intercultural communication literature does not buy the basic assumption in American thought that similarities rather than communicative contrasts are the basis for establishing cultural contact.

Fundamentally, multiculturalism presents a paradigm that goes beyond intercultural learning and multicultural competency. Its vision of an ethnically complex society provides a prescriptive rather than a descriptive model that answers Hartman's (1990) call for an orientation that can "deal with the diversity of the world within ourselves" (p. 291) and that incorporates the existence of a multitude of equivalent cultural realities within society. At bottom, then, a multicultural framework eschews the basic assumption that cultural identity has to be undimensional—that becoming more of something else automatically means becoming less of the original (McLeod, 1981; Saltzman, 1986). More specifically, field studies by anthropologists like McFee (1968) among the Blackfeet tribe have revealed that concepts like "levels of acculturation" that assume a continuum model fail to measure the situational factors that determine whether characteristics of the original culture will be retained or replaced. McFee suggested that straight line measurements lead us into making the "container" error (for example, if an individual scores 75 percent on an "Indian" scale, he or she should be limited to a score of 25 percent on a "white" scale). McFee presented a matrix model as being more meaningful than the continuum model for the assessment of experiences of multicultural individuals, whom he called "150 percent men." Similar themes have been echoed by authors like Adler (1986), Bennett (1986), Bochner (1981), Heath (1977), and Saltzman (1986) using such concepts as "multicultural man," "mediating person," "maturity," and "intercultural competence."

Defined in this manner, multiculturalism strives to describe the subjective experiences of people who are struggling with what Bennett (1986) called the total integration of ethnorelativism. It is a framework that goes beyond encouraging intercultural learning and multicultural competency to building a multicultural identity for all groups. In this respect, there is a difference in degree, if not in kind, between multiculturalism and any one ethnic or cultural perspective. Multiculturalism is built on an organizing principle that puts the onus on both the dominant community and community members of color to consider the fact of their "ethnic psychological captivity" (Hoopes, 1979). At the same time, the framework does not over-emphasize the subjective experiences of people at the expense of examining institutional and societal forces that might affect majority–minority relations. In fact, the model recognizes the fact that conflict might be the inevitable result when the values of the dominant group confront those of the nondominant group: "The relationship of power to cultural imperialism is very important" (Prosser, 1978, p. 39). However, part of what multiculturalism is seeking to accomplish, in the words of Geertz (1973), is an understanding of social discourse in the cultural context—that is, a cultural dialogue.

In addition, multiculturalism espouses a line of thinking that has profound implications for people of color. The model seeks to redefine the traditional conceptions of marginality as involving people in the out-groups who change their behavior to be more like the people of the in-groups. The multicultural perspective tries to interpret the actions of people who do not reflect only one culture in contextual terms: "Marginal people who fall may be rootless or alienated. Those who rise may be synthesizers; can transcend boundaries" (J. Lum, 1986, p. 386). This conceptualization has definite societal implications, because it subscribes to the idea that although movement of people across cultural boundaries might cause conflict, "marginality is an essential component in a healthy social system. Effective social systems endure the tensions brought about by the need for unity and the need for marginality and social change" (J. Lum, p. 386). "Our global village" (Hartman, 1990, p. 291) certainly needs leaders who "find their identities in the synthesis of groups. They [can] synthesize majority–minority relations into new social orders" (J. Lum, 1986, p. 387) and "create a new concept out of the various elements that were previously part of different worlds" (Bochner, 1981, p. 19).

IMPLICATIONS FOR SOCIAL WORK

The controversy surrounding the debate on the "new multiculturalism" is not over. Early (1992) branded what he called the "current hysteria over multiculturalism" as "that peculiarly American temperamental confluence of enthusiasm and moralism" (p. 48). Certainly, the mingling of issues surrounding "political correctness" with multiculturalism has forced both sides of the debate into a dichotomous position: advocates of liberal education versus advocates of the oppressed. Although the profession might be reluctant to acknowledge that the current controversy surrounding multiculturalism might reflect social work's dilemmas about promoting multicultural education and practice, there is an underlying similarity. Despite the fact that the profession, in principle, has endorsed the value of implementing a multicultural curriculum, there has always been an unease involving the "mission of social work"—whether social work education was trying to "achieve a kind of rainbow collectivist society" by teaching required courses that "contain a lot of propaganda designed to make approved minority students feel good and everyone else feel guilty" (Lawrence, 1992, p. 384).

Perhaps, for professionals who agree with Lawrence (1992), a careful re-examination of the concept of multiculturalism might open up new dimensions of meaning that would lead to a less pessimistic view about the future of social work. By offering a paradigm that informs thinking at a transcultural level and not just a model that provides specific strategies for ethnic-sensitive practice, the multicultural perspective might serve to replace rather than preserve the color lines that have divided social work faculty and students. At the same time, the model has the potential of involving white faculty and students in curriculum building that could affect nonwhite people rather than feel, as Lawrence (1992) said, that "Students and faculty that disagree had better keep their mouths shut" (p. 384). Thus, a true multicultural perspective might heal culturally assigned rifts such as white people versus people of color, established immigrants versus new immigrants, and established American ethnic communities versus Third World cultures.

Lawrence's (1992) other concern about the mission of social work might be addressed along the same lines, as long as he is really contesting the means rather than the ends in achieving cultural diversity. The second term he uses in the phrase "rainbow collectivist society" is the key in allaying Lawrence's fear that the profession is pushing a partisan ideology that favors nonwhite people. A collectivist perspective in a multicultural worldview does not exclude white people. It just gives them an equivalent rather than a dominant voice to settle societal differences in an ethnically complex environment. Perhaps Bennett (1986) said it best: "Today, the failure to exercise intercultural sensitivity is not simply bad business or bad morality, it is self-destructive. So we face a choice: overcome the legacy of our history, or lose history itself for all time" (p. 27).

REFERENCES

Adler, P. S. (1986). Beyond cultural identity: Reflections on cultural and multicultural man. In L. A. Samovar & R. Porter (Eds.), *Intercultural communication: A reader* (3rd ed., pp. 389–408). Belmont, CA: Wadsworth.

Barringer, F. (1991, March 11). Census shows profound change in racial makeup of the nation. *New York Times,* pp. A1, A12.

Bennett, M. J. (1986). Towards ethnorelativism: A developmental model of intercultural sensitivity. In R. M. Paige (Ed.), *Cross-cultural orientation: New conceptualizations and applications* (pp. 27–69). Lanham, MD: University Press of America.

Berger, J. (1989, April 12). Ibn Batuta and sitar challenging Columbus and piano in schools. *New York Times,* pp. A1, B6.

Bernstein, R. (1990, November 4). The language of the U.S. *Champaign–Urbana News–Gazette,* pp. B1–B5.

Bochner, S. (1981). The social psychology of cultural mediation. In S. Bochner (Ed.), *The mediating person* (pp. 6–36). Cambridge, MA: Schenkman.

Canda, E. R., & Phaobtong, T. (1992). Buddhism as a support system for Southeast Asian refugees. *Social Work, 37,* 61–67.

Chau, K. L. (1990). A model for teaching cross-cultural practice in social work. *Journal of Social Work Education, 26,* 124–133.

Council on Social Work Education. (1973, February 12). *Guidelines for implementation of accreditation standard 1234A.* New York: Author.

Council on Social Work Education. (1988). *Handbook of accreditation standards and procedures.* Washington, DC: Author.

deAnda, D. (1984). Bicultural socialization: Factors affecting the minority experience. *Social Work, 29,* 101–107.

De Hoyos, G., De Hoyos, A., & Anderson, C. B. (1986). Sociocultural dislocation: Beyond the dual perspective. *Social Work, 31,* 61–67.

Devore, W., & Schlesinger, E. S. (1987). *Ethnic-sensitive social work practice* (2nd ed.). Columbus, OH: Merrill.

D'Souza, D. (1991a). Multiculturalism 101: Great books of the non-Western world. *Policy Review, 56,* 22–30.

D'Souza, D. (1991b). *Illiberal education: The politics of race and sex on campus.* New York: Vintage Books.

Dye, N. S. (1991, March 31). What color is your reading list? [Book Review]. *New York Times,* p. 12.

Early, G. (1992). Multiculturalism and American education. *Washington University Magazine and Alumni News, 62*(1), 48–49.

Garland, D. R., & Escobar, D. (1988). Education for cross-cultural social work practice. *Journal of Social Work Education, 24,* 229–241.

Geertz, C. (1973). *The interpretation of culture.* New York: Basic Books.

Goodstein, L. (1991, November 9). Changing face of CCNY affects about face in campus sympathies. *Washington Post,* p. A17.

Gordon, M. M. (1964). *Assimilation in American life: The role of race, religion, and national origins.* New York: Oxford University Press.

Green, J. W. (1982). *Cultural awareness in the human services.* Englewood Cliffs, NJ: Prentice Hall.

Hartman, A. (1990). Our global village [Editorial]. *Social Work, 35,* 291–292.

Hartman, A. (1991). Words create worlds [Editorial]. *Social Work, 36,* 275–276.

Healy, L. M. (1987). International agencies as social work settings: Opportunity, capability, and commitment. *Social Work, 32,* 405–409.

Heath, D. J. (1977). *Maturity and competence: A transcultural view.* New York: Gardner Press.

Hoopes, D. S. (1979). Intercultural communications: Concepts and the psychology of intercultural experience. In M. D. Pusch (Ed.), *Multicultural education: A cross-cultural training approach* (pp. 10–38). New York: Intercultural Press.

Lawrence, H. (1992). Do "words create worlds?" Readers respond [Letters]. *Social Work, 37,* 384.

Leigh, J. (1983). The black experience with health care delivery systems: A focus on the practitioners. In A. E. Johnson (Ed.), *The black experience: Considerations for health and human services* (pp. 115–129). Davis, CA: International Dialogue Press.

Lum, D. (1986). *Social work practice and people of color: A process-stage approach.* Monterey, CA: Brooks/ Cole.

Lum, J. (1986). Marginality and multiculturalism: Another look at bilingual/ bicultural education. In L. A. Samovar & R. Porter (Eds.), *Intercultural communication: A reader* (3rd ed., pp. 384–388). Belmont, CA: Wadsworth.

McFee, M. (1968). The 150% man, a product of Blackfeet acculturation. *American Anthropologist, 70,* 1096–1103.

McLeod, B. (1981). The mediating person and cultural identity. In S. Bochner (Ed.), *The mediating person* (pp. 37–52). Cambridge, MA: Schenkman.

Montalvo, F. F. (1983). The affective domain in cross-cultural social work education. *Journal of Education for Social Work, 19*(2), 48–53.

Mooney, C. (1988, December 14). Sweeping curricular change is underway at Stanford. *Chronicle of Higher Education,* p. A11.

Nakanishi, M., & Rittner, B. (1992). The inclusionary cultural model. *Journal of Social Work Education, 28,* 27–35.

Norton, D. G. (1978). *The dual perspective: Inclusion of ethnic minority content in social work curriculum.* New York: Council on Social Work Education.

Prosser, M. H. (1978). *The cultural dialogue: An introduction to intercultural communication.* Boston: Houghton Mifflin.

Rodwell, M. K., & Blankebaker, A. (1992). Strategies for developing cross-cultural sensitivity: Wounding as metaphor. *Journal of Social Work Education, 28,* 153–165.

Rosenthal, B. S. (1991). Social workers' interest in international practice in the developing world: A multivariate analysis. *Social Work, 36,* 248–252.

Saltzman, C. E. (1986). One hundred and fifty percent person: Models for orientating international students. In R. M. Paige (Ed.), *Cross-cultural orientation: New conceptualizations and applications* (pp. 247–268). Lanham, MD: University Press of America.

Sanders, D. S. (1975). Dynamics of ethnic and cultural pluralism: Implications for social work education and curriculum innovation. *Journal of Education for Social Work, 11*(3), 95–100.

Sanders, D. S. (1977). Developing a graduate social work curriculum with an international–cross-cultural perspective. *Journal of Education for Social Work, 13*(3), 76–83.

Sanders, D. S. (1980). Multiculturalism: Implications for social work. *International Social Work, 23*(2), 9–16.

Seelye, N., & Wasilewski, H. (1979). Historical development of multicultural education. In M. D. Pusch (Ed.), *Multicultural education: A cross-cultural training approach* (pp. 47–61). New York: Intercultural Press.

Sikkema, M. (1984). Cross-cultural learning in social work education. In D. S. Sanders & P. Pedersen (Eds.), *Education for international social welfare* (pp. 93–105). Honolulu: University of Hawaii, School of Social Work.

Vobejda, B. (1992, April 16). America's many tongues: Immigration changing how the nation speaks. *Washington Post,* pp. A1, A14.

Woodward, C. V. (1991, July 18). Freedom and the universities. *New York Review of Books, 41*(13), 32–37.

This chapter was originally published in the March 1995 issue of Social Work, *vol. 40, pp. 198–205.*

5

Understanding the Empowerment Process: Does Consciousness Make a Difference?

Lorraine M. Gutiérrez

Empowerment is the process of increasing personal, interpersonal, or political power so that individuals, families, and communities can take action to improve their situations. The social work, community psychology, and health care fields present empowerment as a means to address the problems of powerless populations and to mediate the role powerlessness plays in creating and perpetuating social problems (Fagan, 1979; Gutiérrez, 1990; Rappaport, 1987; Solomon, 1976; Swift & Levin, 1987). Within each field, empowerment has been described as a new way of thinking about developing programs, policies, and services.

Although the social work literature describes empowerment as a method that can incorporate multiple levels of intervention, most of the current work has focused on individual or interpersonal empowerment (Parsons, 1991; Pinderhughes, 1990; Simon, 1990; Solomon, 1976; Staples, 1990). The literature has discussed processes and methods for moving individuals to gain personal power or to develop the ability to influence others. Very little systematic or empirical research has focused on the political dimensions of empowerment and ways in which it can contribute to collective action or social change. This study investigates how a psychological process can contribute to political empowerment.

PSYCHOLOGICAL PROCESS OF EMPOWERMENT

Theories of empowerment focus on how beliefs about the self can contribute to individual, community, and social change. For individuals to engage in social action, they must first develop a

43

sense of critical consciousness (Freire, 1973; Gutiérrez, 1989; Kieffer, 1984; Pecukonis & Wenocur, 1994; Swift & Levin, 1987; Zimmerman & Rappaport, 1988). The development of a critical consciousness has been described as involving three psychological processes (Gutiérrez, 1990; Kieffer, 1984; Pecukonis & Wenocur, 1994; Swift & Levin, 1987):

1. *Group identification* includes identifying areas of common experience and concern, a preference for one's own group culture and norms, and the development of feelings of shared fate; group membership becomes a central aspect of one's self-concept (Gurin, Miller, & Gurin, 1980).
2. *Group consciousness* involves understanding the differential status and power of groups in society. For members of oppressed groups, this leads to feelings of relative deprivation, power discontent, and a tendency to blame the system for problems related to group membership. This understanding can draw connections between personal problems and social structure (Gurin et al., 1980; Klein, 1984).
3. *Self and collective efficacy* refers to beliefs that one is capable of effecting desired changes in one's life (Bandura, 1982; Pecukonis & Wenocur, 1994). In the literature on critical consciousness, self and collective efficacy is described as perceiving one's self as a subject (rather than object) of social processes and as capable of working to change the social order (Fay, 1987; Freire, 1973; Gutiérrez, 1989).

Empowerment theory suggests that these components often develop sequentially and can be mutually reinforcing. The components can develop independently or in conjunction with one another. Feedback loops allow the experience of group consciousness to heighten a sense of group identification or the exercise of collective efficacy to deepen a sense of group consciousness. In these ways critical consciousness is at once a process and a cognitive state.

How can critical consciousness contribute to empowerment? Individuals and groups that believe in their ability to effect change are more likely than others to make efforts to increase their power (Bandura, 1982). For individuals and communities to understand that their problems stem from a lack of power, they must first comprehend the structure of power in society. An understanding of how group membership can affect life circumstances is crucial for identifying powerlessness as a source of problems.

EMPOWERMENT AND THE LATINO COMMUNITY

Latinos are one of the fastest growing and most economically deprived ethnic groups in the United States. (This article uses the term "Latino" instead of "Hispanic" to describe people living in the United States whose ancestry is Latin American.) As a group, Latinos have fewer median years of education and less participation in higher education than the rest of the population. Latinos' median income is only slightly higher than that of African Americans, they are concentrated in the secondary labor market, and their rate of poverty is double the national average. For the two largest Latino subgroups—Mexican Americans and Puerto Ricans—these status and income trends do not improve substantially for succeeding generations (Castex, 1994; Chapa & Valencia, 1993).

Despite these commonalities, the Latino group is quite heterogeneous: It includes new immigrants and descendants of some of the original inhabitants of the North American continent, undocumented aliens and American citizens, English- and Spanish-speaking people, people of different national origins, and people who identify closely with their ethnic heritage and those who do not. It is important that social work research and practice with Latinos recognize this heterogeneity and how it can affect outcomes (Castex, 1994; Chapa & Valencia, 1993; Hayes-Bautista & Chapa, 1987; Portes & Truelove, 1987).

The social work literature on Latinos typically has focused on the role of cultural factors in the development and provision of services (Ghali, 1982; Gomez, 1983; Queralt, 1984; Rogler, Malgady, Constantino, & Blumental, 1987; Vega & Miranda, 1985; Watkins & Gonzales, 1982). The focus of this approach has been on understanding one's own personal attributes and values, gaining knowledge about the culture of different groups, and developing skills for cross-cultural work (Chau, 1990; Gallegos, 1982). The model is based on the notions that society is multicultural and that positive gains can result from learning about different groups and incorporating culture into agency procedures, structures, and services (Devore & Schlesinger, 1987; Gallegos, 1982).

The empowerment perspective expands the cultural competence model by focusing on how Latinos have experienced racism and discrimination (Longres, 1982; Portes, Parker, & Cobas, 1980). The model is based on the assumption that the condition of Latinos in society will change only if they gain greater power in political and social arenas. The role of community organizations would go beyond service provision to developing the means for Latinos to work together to overcome conditions of powerlessness (Padilla, 1985).

Empowerment theory suggests that if Latinos as a group are to become politically empowered, they must develop a group identification and consciousness that transcends specific national origin identity. This "pan-Latino" identity would not replace subgroup identification but would supplement it (Padilla, 1985). Given the diversity of the U.S. Latino population, difficulties in developing solidarity could be a barrier to empowerment practice. Research on the empowerment process with Latinos must study how specific and broader group identifications and consciousness can produce empowerment for this diverse population, potentially illuminating the empowerment process for other populations as well.

A combination of contact within and outside of subgroups is necessary for the development of ethnic consciousness. Contact outside of the group contributes to the development of feelings of relative deprivation and provides information about the status and power of other groups (Crosby & Clayton, 1987; Hurtado, 1982; Tajfel, 1981) and also provides the opportunity for critical incidents that will make group membership and status salient (Brewer & Kramer, 1985; Gurin & Brim, 1984; Rosenberg, 1981). Furthermore, close contact with group members, either in discussions about status or in the context of intergroup conflict, is also necessary for developing a perception of a sense of common fate and of blaming the system (Espinoza & Garza, 1985; Gutiérrez, 1989; Tajfel & Turner, 1985; Zander, 1979).

Cognitive styles, self-structures, and perceptions of other groups are crucial to the development of a Latino ethnic consciousness. A complex attributional style and high need for cognition that involve an interest in understanding the causes and effects of social situations will lead individuals to think more about their own social situation (Cacioppo & Petty, 1982; Fletcher, Danilovics, Fernandez, Peterson, & Reeder, 1986), which can lead to a deeper understanding of group status and power and encourage cognitive centrality. Individuals whose self-structures include group identification and an interest in political issues will selectively attend to social stimuli involving group status, which will encourage perceptions leading to the development of group consciousness (Crosby & Clayton, 1987; Gurin & Markus, 1987). Individuals who perceive intergroup relationships as illegitimate and unstable and group boundaries as impermeable are more apt to develop a collective orientation to change (Tajfel 1981).

To what degree do the existing studies on Latino ethnic consciousness support this model? Contact within the group (Gutiérrez, 1989; Padilla, 1985; Rodriguez, 1986) and negative contact outside of the group (Portes, 1984; Portes et al., 1980) can have a strong positive effect on the development of ethnic consciousness among Latinos, particularly for Mexican Americans born in the United States (Gutiérrez, 1989). No research has been done testing the effects of individual factors on Latino ethnic consciousness, so knowledge about that aspect of the model is incomplete.

METHOD

Hypotheses

Four hypotheses were tested in this study:

1. When engaged in discussions focused on common problems and experiences, a diverse group of Latinos can develop a sense of Latino ethnic consciousness.
2. The belief that individual, interpersonal, or community problems are related to group status and power will be associated with the development of a Latino ethnic consciousness.
3. More active strategies for solving individual, interpersonal, or community problems will be associated with the development of a Latino ethnic consciousness.
4. Political participation and social change will be associated with the development of a Latino ethnic consciousness.

Study Design

Descriptive and qualitative literature on empowerment has discussed surveys of individuals already involved in community action (Checkoway & Norseman, 1986; Freire, 1973; Kieffer, 1984; Maton & Rappaport, 1984; Zimmerman & Rappaport, 1988).

Methods for developing critical consciousness and assessment of its effects on the process of empowerment have not been studied empirically. The study reported in this article used a completely randomized one-factor, parallel-groups experimental design to test the cause-and-effect relationships among participation in groups, the development of an ethnic consciousness, and the effects of ethnic consciousness on empowerment.

Sample

Participants were a random sample of Latino undergraduate students attending a large, predominantly white midwestern university. A listing of all Latino undergraduates ($N = 677$) was provided by the university. Using a table of random numbers, a sample, stratified by gender, was selected from this list. Latinos in this sample were contacted individually by phone and invited to participate in a study of the experiences of Latino students at the university. Seventy-three students (77 percent of those contacted) agreed to participate and were randomly assigned to one of three groups, two experimental (consciousness raising and ethnic identity) and one control. Efforts were made to balance all groups by gender. All participants received reimbursement for their time.

The sample was composed of almost equal numbers of men and women (Table 5-1). Most of the 73 participants were born in the United States (78 percent) and grew up here (75 percent). The average age was 19, and most (70 percent) were in their freshman or sophomore years. All major Latin American groups were represented, with 31 percent not specifying a national origin. More than half described themselves as having more than one ethnic background; however, the majority (72 percent) identified primarily with their Latino heritage. Sixty percent said that their first language was English and described English as the primary language they used, which is not atypical for Latinos born in the United States (Castex, 1994; Chapa & Valencia, 1993).

Cross-tabulations and chi-square tests of association found no significant differences between participants in the experimental groups. This suggests that any differences found after the experiment were not caused by some preexisting sociodemographic factor that could influence the development of an ethnic consciousness such as social status, gender, or nativity.

TABLE 5·1
Sample Characteristics

Characteristic	Percentage of			
	Control Group (*n* = 23)	Ethnic-Identity Group (*n* = 24)	Consciousness-Raising Group (*n* = 26)	Total (*N* = 73)
Gender				
Male	44	46	54	48
Female	56	54	46	52
Nativity				
Latin America	26	25	12	20
United States	74	71	88	78
Other	0	4	0	2
Language use				
Spanish	35	38	39	37
English	61	58	61	60
Other	4	4	0	3
Social status/class				
Poor	0	4	0	1
Working	30	42	48	40
Middle	17	4	28	17
Upper	44	33	12	30
Wealthy	9	17	12	12

Study Groups

Twenty-three Latinos participated in a control group. These participants came to an office and were administered the dependent measures individually by the investigator or a research assistant, both of whom were Latino. After completion of the questionnaire, participants had an opportunity to ask questions about the study. All participants received a list of university-based Latino resources and social activities.

Fifty participants were assigned to one of two experimental groups: One group was developed to arouse participant's feelings of ethnic identification (*n* = 24) and the other to arouse Latino ethnic consciousness (*n* = 26). The groups were conducted using a focus group method (Kreuger, 1988). Each focus group was attended by an average of 12 participants, was two hours in length, and was co-led by two Latino graduate student facilitators, a Mexican American man and a Puerto Rican woman.

Leaders of the ethnic-identity group focused on the meaning of being Latino and identified shared values and feelings. The discussion of Latino identity was primarily positive and dealt with commonalities between Latino students on campus and in society. If the discussion turned to negative experiences on campus, these problems were dealt with through a discussion of the resources and services available to Latino students.

Leaders of the consciousness-raising group focused on how being Latino had affected experiences at the university and on how group efforts for change could be developed and used. Each group session began with a discussion of commonalities among Latinos but moved quickly to problems faced by Latinos at the university and how societal values and conditions contributed to these problems. The problems most commonly mentioned were negative stereotyping and the lack of contact among Latino students. The end of each session was devoted to group problem solving that examined how individual Latino students could be involved in ameliorating their situations.

Measures

Measures were adapted from existing measures on group consciousness or developed from consultation with the university's Office of Minority Affairs, Minority Student Services, and Latino Studies. The full questionnaire was pretested with a small group of Latino graduate students and faculty at the university and participants in a Latino research methods course to assess the face validity of the measures and the ease of administration.

The measure of Latino ethnic consciousness was adapted from those used in the National Survey of Mexican Americans (Hurtado, 1982). This measure has been used extensively in research on Mexican Americans to investigate the structure, development, and significance of ethnic consciousness. Research on Chicano ethnic consciousness has found these scales to be valid and reliable measures of the concepts in question (Gutiérrez, 1989; Hurtado, 1982; Rodriguez, 1986). The survey was adapted to a mixed Latino group by changing all references to Mexican Americans to Latinos. The alpha coefficient was .77.

Three measures were developed. Cognitive orientations to empowerment, problem construal, and change strategy were measured through responses to vignettes that presented Latino students with specific problems. A political level of empower-ment, ethnic activism, was measured by levels of interest in par-ticipating in activities to improve the status of Latinos at the uni-versity. Although the sample size was small, factor analysis was used to construct scales. The reliability of these scales was then tested through the calculation of alpha coefficients.

Vignettes

Participants were presented with six vignettes that were written for this study based on actual experiences of university students. These vignettes had different levels of ambiguity about individual or structural causes of the problems presented. The following is an example of a high-ambiguity vignette:

> Roberto is just starting his sophomore year at the university. When he was in high school Roberto did very well: He had a 3.8 grade point average, was in the top 10 percent of his class, and scored more than 1,200 on the SATs [Scholastic Aptitude Tests]. However, since Roberto has entered college, he has not done as well. His grade point average is only 2.7 and he has received many grades of incomplete. Roberto is starting to wonder if he is really good enough to make it at the university.

The following is an example of a low-ambiguity vignette:

> Belinda and her friends have been active in organizing a se-ries of speakers on Latino issues for the campus community. One evening the group worked hard putting up posters on all of the major campus buildings. Belinda went to bed that evening satisfied that their job was well done. However, the next morning as Belinda walked to class, she noticed that most of the posters had been pulled down and those that remained were covered with ethnic slurs.

Scales and Model

Using responses to the vignettes, a measure for problem construal was developed. Participants indicated on a five-point scale (1 = not at all to 5 = totally) the degree to which the following caused the problems described in the vignette: the actor's personality or behavior, other actors, the university, or society. A factor analysis of responses to the possible causes resulted in a two-factor solu-tion: one representing larger system construal (the university or society) and the other representing individual and interpersonal construal (the actor's behavior or personality or other actors). The scale was developed based on the summary score of the variables that constituted larger system construal. The alpha coefficient for this scale was .91.

A change strategy scale was also developed from responses to the problems presented in the vignettes. Participants responded to open-ended questions about actions the actor in the vignette could take (for example, What can he or she do? What is the best thing to do?). Responses to the question about the best thing to do were then coded according to the type of action being advocated, resulting in an ordinal scale with a value of 1 = no action should be taken to 4 = social mobilization is appropriate. Responses to all vignettes were summarized into a score measuring change strategy. The alpha coefficient for this scale was .49, indicating that the measure is not as reliable as that for construal. The lower internal reliability of this scale may be a result of the range of situations that were represented by the vignettes as well as the difficulty in categorizing some responses.

A measure of political empowerment was developed from responses to a series of questions about interest in participating in Latino-oriented activities such as attending salsa music concerts, tutoring Latino high school students, or picketing for the United Farm Workers. Results from a factor analysis on these items generated a two-factor solution: a cluster of cultural activities and a cluster of community involvement and political action activities. The six activities that were more activist in nature (tutoring, picketing, recruiting, meeting, demonstrating, and orienting) were summarized into an ethnic activism scale. The alpha coefficient for this scale was .87.

The proposed model suggests that Latino ethnic consciousness can result from participation in discussion groups oriented toward developing a heightened sense of ethnic identity, understanding the connection between personal and group problems, and analyzing how individuals can play a role in social change. The model assumes that discussion of cultural similarity between Latinos will produce less Latino ethnic consciousness than a discussion that involves both cultural similarity and an analysis of group-based problems and solutions. The direct effects of group condition on the consciousness-raising and empowerment measures were analyzed using analyses of variance (ANOVAs) and planned comparisons.

The model suggests also that developing an ethnic consciousness regardless of its origin will contribute to the empowerment process. A full test of this model would require a longitudinal design. However, multivariate techniques can show the magnitude of the relationships between these variables. The relationship between ethnic consciousness and empowerment was tested through path analysis.

RESULTS

Analyses to assess the relationship between participation in the three study groups and Latino ethnic consciousness and empowerment used a one-way ANOVA with one set of a priori orthogonal planned comparisons and a polynomial test of linearity. The comparisons assessed the statistical significance of observed differences between the control group and the two experimental groups and between the ethnic-identity and the consciousness-raising groups. The model predicted that the two experimental groups together would have higher scores than the control group and that a significant linear trend would be found (control group < ethnic-identity group < consciousness-raising group).

The first analysis looked at the group effects on the measure of ethnic consciousness (Table 5-2). As predicted, the highest levels of ethnic consciousness were associated with the consciousness-raising group and the lowest levels with the control group [$F(2, 72) = 9.96, p < .001$]. A statistically significant difference was also observed between the ethnic-identity and consciousness-raising groups together in contrast to the control group [$t(70) = 2.16, p < .05$].

The next analyses considered group effects on problem construal and change strategy. As predicted, participants in the consciousness-raising group used structural explanations more than those in the ethnic-identity or control groups [$F(2, 70) = 4.86, p < .05$]. The contrast between the ethnic-identity and the consciousness-raising groups was also statistically significant [$t(70) = 2.29, p < .03$]. The greatest difference was between the consciousness-raising and the other two groups.

As expected for change strategy, participants in the consciousness-raising group had higher scores on ethnic activism ($M = 3.28$)

TABLE 5-2

Mean Scores on Outcome Measures

Item	Control Group ($n = 23$)	Ethnic-Identity Group ($n = 24$)	Consciousness-Raising Group ($n = 26$)
Ethnic consciousness			
M	2.63	2.97	3.24
SD	.80	.58	.61
Problem construal			
M	2.85	2.88	3.39
SD	.93	.85	.77
Change strategy			
M	2.70	2.62	3.13
SD	.47	.50	.40
Ethnic activism			
M	2.75	3.24	3.28
SD	1.22	.96	.83

NOTE: Differences are significant at the .10 level.

than those in the control group ($M = 2.75$) or ethnic-identity group ($M = 3.24$) [$F(2, 72) = 3.33$, $p < .10$] (Table 5-2). The main difference was between participants in the experimental groups ($M = 3.26$) and those in the control group ($M = 2.75$) [$t(70) = 1.78$, $p < .10$].

Regression analyses were run that looked at the joint effects of ethnic consciousness, change strategy, and problem construal on ethnic activism and that looked at the effects of ethnic consciousness on change strategy and ethnic activism. Partial betas were then entered into the model. Ethnic consciousness had statistically significant effects on both problem construal and change strategy, but the direct and indirect influences on each dependent variable differed (Figure 5-1). Most of the change in ethnic activism is due to the direct effect of ethnic consciousness (95 percent), suggesting that the effects of problem construal and change strategy are minimal when predicting behavioral intention. In contrast, the ratio of direct to indirect effects in predicting change strategy (62 percent) suggests that problem construal and change strategy are more significant in mediating the relationship between ethnic consciousness and advocating action-oriented collective responses to individual problems.

Figure 5-1

Path Model: Connection between Consciousness and Ethnic Activism

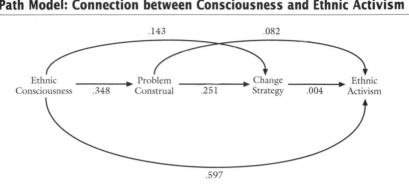

DISCUSSION

What do these results tell us about the empowerment process? Data from the ANOVAs suggest that group discussion and problem-solving processes can contribute to the development of a Latino ethnic consciousness. Participants in the consciousness-raising group had a higher overall mean score on ethnic consciousness than those in the other two groups, with participants in the control group having the lowest levels of ethnic consciousness and participants in the consciousness-raising group having the highest. Therefore, for Latinos to develop a sense of ethnic consciousness, simple group contact or discussion concerning ethnic identity will not be as influential as discussion that involves a critical appraisal of the social situation and the generation of solutions to problems related to Latino status.

Data from the path analysis suggest that an ethnic consciousness can affect one's thinking about specific problems and strategies for change. These findings demonstrated a strong direct effect of consciousness on problem construal or specific problems and on intention to engage in activism. The relationship between ethnic consciousness and change strategies was weaker but still positive. These results reflected the participants as a whole, regardless of experimental group membership, suggesting a particularly strong relationship between these variables.

Therefore, results from this experiment supported the theoretical propositions about the process of consciousness raising and the importance of ethnic consciousness to empowerment. Participants high in ethnic consciousness were more likely to attribute problems of Latinos to social and structural factors and to suggest collective solutions to individual problems. Path analysis indicated a strong direct effect of ethnic consciousness on ethnic activism and therefore on political empowerment.

CONCLUSION

This study is a first step in identifying how the empowerment process takes place. It is especially significant for organizers interested in working with diverse communities. Additional research is needed that further investigates the influence of ideology, analysis, and consciousness in interaction with efficacy on the process of political empowerment.

Although this study lends some support to empowerment theory, the design precluded any identification of long-lasting effects. The experiment demonstrated that consciousness raising has immediate effects on ethnic consciousness, but the study could not provide evidence that the observed changes would persist. A second limitation is the focus on attitudes rather than actual behavior. There was no indication whether participants high in ethnic activism actually participated more than others. To determine if the group discussion had any lasting or behavioral result, a follow-up study is needed.

The empowerment perspective is one way the social work profession can reconcile the often competing goals of individual casework and social change. This reconciliation can result in a vital practice integration of the personal and the political. Participants in the consciousness-raising group were able to move quickly from a consideration of common cultural traits and values to an awareness of the political nature of their status as Latinos. This was accomplished with a group process that focused simultaneously on group commonality, status, and problem solving, suggesting that political empowerment need not only be a goal for the social work profession, but can also become a method of practice.

REFERENCES

Bandura, A. (1982). Self-efficacy mechanism in human agency. *American Psychologist, 37*, 122–147.

Brewer, M., & Kramer, R. (1985). Psychology of intergroup attitudes and behavior. *Annual Review of Psychology, 36,* 219–243.

Cacioppo, J., & Petty, R. (1982). The need for cognition. *Journal of Personality and Social Psychology, 42,* 116–131.

Castex, G. (1994). Providing services to Hispanic/Latino populations: Profiles in diversity. *Social Work, 39,* 288–296.

Chapa, J., & Valencia, R. (1993). Latino population growth, demographic characteristics, and educational stagnation: An examination of recent trends. *Hispanic Journal of the Behavioral Sciences, 15,* 167–187.

Chau, K. (1990). A model for teaching cross-cultural practice in social work. *Journal of Social Work Education, 26,* 124–133.

Checkoway, B., & Norseman, A. (1986). Empowering citizens with disabilities. *Community Development Journal, 21,* 270–277.

Crosby, F., & Clayton, S. (1987). Male sympathy and the situation of women: Does personal experience make a difference? *Journal of Social Issues, 42,* 55–66.

Devore, W., & Schlesinger, E. (1987). *Ethnic-sensitive social work practice* (2nd ed.). St. Louis: C. V. Mosby.

Espinoza, J., & Garza, R. (1985). Social group salience and interethnic cooperation. *Journal of Experimental Social Psychology, 21,* 380–392.

Fagan, H. (1979). *Empowerment: Skills for parish social action.* New York: Paulist Press.

Fay, B. (1987). *Critical social science.* Ithaca, NY: Cornell University Press.

Fletcher, G., Danilovics, P., Fernandez, G., Peterson, D., & Reeder, G. (1986). Attributional complexity: An individual differences measure. *Journal of Personality and Social Psychology, 51,* 875–884.

Freire, P. (1973). *Education for critical consciousness.* New York: Seabury Press.

Gallegos, J. (1982). The ethnic competence model for social work education. In B. White (Ed.), *Color in a white society* (pp. 1–9). Silver Spring, MD: National Association of Social Workers.

Ghali, S. (1982). Understanding Puerto Rican traditions. *Social Work, 27,* 98–102.

Gomez, E. (1983). The San Antonio model: A culture-oriented approach. In G. Gibson (Ed.), *Our kingdom stands on brittle glass* (pp. 96–111). Silver Spring, MD: National Association of Social Workers.

Gurin, P., & Brim, O. (1984). Change in self in adulthood: The example of sense of control. In P. Baltes & O. Brim (Eds.), *Life span development and behavior* (pp. 281–334). New York: Academic Press.

Gurin, P., & Markus, H. (1987). *Group identity: The psychological mechanisms of durable salience.* Unpublished manuscript.

Gurin, P., Miller, A., & Gurin, G. (1980). Stratum identification and consciousness. *Social Psychology Quarterly, 43,* 30–47.

Gutiérrez, L. (1989). Critical consciousness and Chicano identity: An exploratory analysis. In G. Romero (Ed.), *Estudios Chicanos and the politics of community* (pp. 35–53). Berkeley, CA: NACS (National Association for Chicano Studies) Press.

Gutiérrez, L. (1990). Working with women of color: An empowerment perspective. *Social Work, 35,* 149–154.

Hayes-Bautista, D., & Chapa, J. (1987). Latino terminology: Conceptual bases for standardized terminology. *American Journal of Public Health, 77*, 61–68.

Hurtado, A. (1982). *Domination and intergroup relations: The impact on Chicano linguistic attitudes.* Unpublished doctoral dissertation, University of Michigan, Ann Arbor.

Kieffer, C. (1984). Citizen empowerment: A developmental perspective. In J. Rappaport, C. Swift, & R. Hess (Eds.), *Studies in empowerment: Toward understanding and action* (pp. 9–36). New York: Haworth Press.

Klein, E. (1984). *Gender politics: From consciousness to mass politics.* Cambridge, MA: Harvard University Press.

Kreuger, R. (1988). *Focus groups: A practical guide for applied research.* Newbury Park, CA: Sage Publications.

Longres, J. (1982). Minority groups: An interest-group perspective. *Social Work, 27*, 7–14.

Maton, K., & Rappaport, J. (1984). Empowerment in a religious setting: A multivariate investigation. In J. Rappaport, C. Swift, & R. Hess (Eds.), *Studies in empowerment: Toward understanding and action* (pp. 37–70). New York: Haworth Press.

Padilla, F. (1985). *Latino ethnic consciousness: The case of Mexican Americans and Puerto Ricans in Chicago.* Notre Dame, IN: University of Notre Dame Press.

Parsons, R. (1991). Empowerment: Purpose and practice in social work. *Social Work with Groups, 14*(2), 7–22.

Pecukonis, E., & Wenocur, S. (1994). Perceptions of self and collective efficacy in community organization theory and practice. *Journal of Community Practice, 1*(2), 5–22.

Pinderhughes, E. (1990). *Understanding race, ethnicity and power: The key to efficacy in clinical practice.* New York: Free Press.

Portes, A. (1984). The rise of ethnicity: Determinants of ethnic perceptions among Cuban exiles in Miami. *American Sociological Review, 49*, 383–397.

Portes, A., Parker, R., & Cobas, J. (1980). Assimilation or consciousness: Perceptions of U.S. society among recent Latin American immigrants to the United States. *Social Forces, 59*, 200–224.

Portes, A., & Truelove, C. (1987). Making sense of diversity: Recent research on Hispanic minorities in the United States. *Annual Review of Sociology, 13*, 359–385.

Queralt, M. (1984). Understanding Cuban immigrants: A cultural perspective. *Social Work, 29*, 115–121.

Rappaport, J. (1987). Terms of empowerment/Exemplars of prevention: Toward a theory for community psychology. *American Journal of Community Psychology, 15*, 117–148.

Rodriguez, J. (1986). *Effects of contact on the development of identity and political consciousness among people of Mexican descent.* Unpublished doctoral dissertation, University of Michigan, Ann Arbor.

Rogler, L., Malgady, R., Constantino, G., & Blumental, R. (1987). What do culturally sensitive services mean? The case of Hispanics. *American Psychologist, 42*, 565–570.

Rosenberg, M. (1981). The self concept: Social product and social force. In M. Rosenberg & R. Turner (Eds.), *Social psychology* (pp. 593–624). New York: Basic Books.

Simon, B. (1990). Rethinking empowerment. *Journal of Progressive Human Services, 1,* 27–40.

Solomon, B. (1976). *Black empowerment.* New York: Columbia University Press.

Staples, L. (1990). Powerful ideas about empowerment. *Administration in Social Work, 14,* 29–42.

Swift C., & Levin, G. (1987). Empowerment: An emerging mental health technology. *Journal of Primary Prevention, 8*(1–2), 71–94.

Tajfel, H. (1981). *Human groups and social categories.* Cambridge, MA: Cambridge University Press.

Tajfel, H., & Turner, J. (1985). The social psychology of intergroup behavior. In S. Worchel & W. Austin (Eds.), *Psychology of intergroup relations* (pp. 7–24). Chicago: Nelson Hall.

Vega, W., & Miranda, M. (1985). *Stress and Hispanic mental health: Relating research to service delivery.* Rockville, MD: U.S. Department of Health and Human Services.

Watkins, T., & Gonzales, R. (1982). Outreach to Mexican Americans. *Social Work, 27,* 68–73.

Zander, A. (1979). Psychology of group process. *Annual Review of Psychology, 30,* 417–451.

Zimmerman, M., & Rappaport, J. (1988). Citizen participation, perceived control, and psychological empowerment. *American Journal of Community Psychology, 16,* 725–750.

This chapter was originally published in the December 1995 issue of Social Work Research, *vol. 19, pp. 229–237.*

6

The Organizational Context of Empowerment Practice: Implications for Social Work Administration

Lorraine Gutiérrez, Linnea GlenMaye, and Kate DeLois

During the past two decades, empowerment practice in the human services has emerged from efforts to develop more effective and responsive services for women, people of color, and other oppressed groups. The goal of this method of practice is to address the role powerlessness plays in creating and perpetuating personal and social problems. It can be distinguished by its focus on developing critical awareness, increasing feelings of collective and self-efficacy, and developing skills for personal, interpersonal, or social change (Bricker-Jenkins & Hooyman, 1991; Freire, 1973; Gutiérrez, 1990; Pinderhughes, 1989; Rappaport, 1981; Solomon, 1976; Staples, 1991). Within our increasingly diverse society, empowerment has emerged as one perspective on practice that can be inclusive and supportive of diversity.

The literature describing empowerment practice is based primarily on empowerment theory and case examples of empowerment practice. The focus of this literature has been on definitions of empowerment practice (Parsons, 1991; Rappaport, 1981; Simon, 1990; Staples, 1991; Swift & Levin, 1987) and the description of specific methods (Freire, 1973; Solomon, 1976) and outcomes (Gutiérrez & Ortega, 1991; Maton & Rappaport, 1984; Zimmerman & Rappaport, 1988). Less attention has been paid to how the structure, culture, and management of human services organizations can support the empowerment of workers and consumers. Yet some have argued that if clients and consumers of services are to gain power, some modifications may be required in the administration of organizations that serve them (Gerschick, Israel, & Checkoway, 1989; Mathis & Richan, 1986; Pinderhughes, 1989; Sherman & Wenocur, 1983; Zimmerman, in press). This article begins to address this gap by identifying issues experienced by workers and administrators in organizations that focus on the empowerment of consumers.

EMPOWERMENT PRACTICE IN SOCIAL WORK

The term "empowerment" is ubiquitous, used by presidents and poets alike, yet its meaning often seems hazy and undeveloped. In the field of social work, a similar lack of clarity prevails. The concept of empowerment has been unevenly developed and has been used in different ways. Some describe empowerment primarily as a goal, others as a process, others as a form of intervention. This lack of clarity has contributed to considerable confusion in the field regarding the use of the term "empowerment" and the degree to which empowerment represents a particular type of practice (Simon, 1990; Staples, 1991). Yet a review of the literature suggests that a working definition of empowering social work practice can be developed (Bricker-Jenkins & Hooyman, 1987; Gutiérrez, 1990; Solomon, 1976). The goal of effective practice is not coping or adaptation but an increase in the actual power of the client or community so that action can be taken to change and prevent the problems clients are facing. Because the effects of powerlessness can occur on many levels, efforts toward change can be directed at any level of intervention or can include multiple levels of intervention. Most scholars would agree that the empowerment of a group or community is the ultimate goal and that this requires change on multiple levels.

Research with practitioners concerning their definition of empowerment suggests ways in which this method is being integrated into practice. When asked to define empowerment, practitioners describe a psychological process of change. One critical element of this change is gaining awareness of the power that exists within any individual, family, group, or community. This focus on empowerment as a process is emphasized by practitioners involved in different levels of practice (for example, individual, group, or community work) and with different populations. The applicability of empowerment to varying foci of practice suggests an underlying unity to the concept: Although practitioners may work with individuals, groups, or communities that have different goals, empowerment is described as a method for developing personal and interpersonal power through a process of self-awareness. Therefore, changes within the self are considered to be an important element of change on different levels (Gutiérrez, GlenMaye, & DeLois, 1992).

Practitioners also identify common practice perspectives that cut across different levels of empowerment intervention. These themes emphasize the education of consumers to enable them to comprehend the social environment, the need to involve consumers in developing concrete skills for surviving and developing social power, the importance of recognizing and building on strengths, and the use of democratic processes in working with clients. These practitioners placed equal emphasis on these methods and did not believe that any one was more important than the other. Their descriptions of empowerment-based work presented a challenging blend of the practical and concrete, such as helping people to develop word-processing skills while concurrently developing a critical awareness regarding their position and potential in the world (Gutiérrez et al., 1992).

This brief description of empowerment practice suggests that implementation of empowerment-based programs may require particular administrative practices. For example, the literature and interviews with workers indicate that empowerment practice is consciously consumer oriented and driven. Often this practice involves clients or consumers in the planning, governance, or implementation of programs and suggests that the successful implementation of empowerment-based programs may require the use of participatory management techniques and the creation of an organizational culture that is based on working in partnership with others.

To learn more about the ways in which social services organizations can most effectively support the development of empowerment-based services, an exploratory qualitative study was conducted with a small group of agencies engaged in empowerment practice. Open-ended interviews were conducted to identify the influences on practitioners' ability to implement empowerment methods in existing social services agencies. Although findings from this small, qualitative study should not be viewed as representative of the conditions in all social work agencies, themes identified from this study can provide the basis for further research in this area.

METHOD

A multiple case study method was used to identify those organizational factors that could support or enhance empowerment practice. This qualitative method has been used successfully in efforts to ground theoretical principles in practice in relation to feminist social work (Bricker-Jenkins & Hooyman, 1986), educational administration (Greene & David, 1984), management of alternative services (Gutiérrez, 1986), and business administration (Peters & Waterman, 1982).

Sample Selection

The sample consisted of a reputational sample of human services organizations engaged in empowerment practice in a large ethnically diverse city. After consulting with key informants from the University of Washington School of Social Work and the community, the research team generated a list of 27 agencies representing five specific population groups and five fields of practice (Table 6-1). Each organization was then contacted, told about the study, and asked if they would describe themselves as engaged in empowerment practice. From this list, six nonprofit organiza-

Table 6-1

Specific Fields of Practice and Population Groups Represented in the Study

Agency Characteristic	No. of Programs
Field of practice	
Mental health	4
Family and children's services	7
Education	2
Employment	4
Advocacy	5
Specific populations	
Women	12
Gay men and lesbians	3
People of color	5
Older people	2
Youths	4

NOTE: Some programs are listed under both field of practice and specific populations.

tions were selected for study: two serving women, two developed by and for people of color, one serving youths, and one primarily focused on issues of older people. These organizations were selected because of their involvement with populations that have been associated with empowerment-based services. The directors of these agencies were contacted by phone and invited to participate in the study. As an incentive, each agency received a small donation.

Data Collection

Data were gathered through structured, taped, individual interviews with a staff person and administrator directly engaged in empowerment practice at each agency. The interviews were conducted on site by a doctoral research assistant and averaged 90 minutes. The interviewer followed a standard interview protocol oriented toward getting a picture of how the agency and the practitioner defined, carried out, and evaluated empowerment practice. Specific questions were asked to identify ways in which the agency's structure, policies, and personnel practices supported or worked against empowerment practice. The standard protocol was also supplemented by questions that probed for the clarification and expansion of initial responses. All interviews were taped and transcribed for analysis.

Data Analysis

The objectives of this research guided the process of data analysis. A modified grounded theory method was used to answer the primary research questions. These data were independently analyzed by three readers to address each research question. The three readers then met to discuss their findings and to work toward a common understanding. Areas of agreement and disagreement concerning core themes were noted during each meeting and became the focus for discussion. Examples from the transcripts were used to deal with disagreements or differences in perspective. When the readers were satisfied that all themes had been identified from an interview, they moved on to the next transcript. When all transcripts had been completed, notes from the analytic meetings were used to identify common themes across interviews. These themes then became the central findings of the study.

RESULTS

Participant responses to questions concerning barriers and supports to empowerment practice can be grouped into several major thematic areas. One initial finding was that the barriers and supports, as identified by participants, did not stand in isolated and total opposition to each other; rather, the responses of participating agencies revealed that the barriers were often ameliorated by the presence of factors that supported an empowering atmosphere within the agency or organization. This connection between barriers to empowerment and supports for empowerment was not explicitly stated by the participants but can be inferred from the comparison of responses to questions about each.

Barriers

The barriers to maintaining and implementing an empowerment-based approach in the organizational context can be grouped into four major areas: funding sources, social environment, intrapersonal issues, and interpersonal issues. Although these areas have considerable overlap and connections, they are described here as discrete conceptual themes for the purpose of clarity.

Expectations of Funding Sources. Most participants said that using an empowerment approach was more time-consuming than using traditional approaches. This longer time frame for organizational and interventive efforts emerged from the commitment to work collaboratively with consumers—that is, at their pace and within their chosen parameters—and with each other.

The slower pace of practice can in turn affect funding because of the requirements and expectations of funding sources. One participant described funders as not adequately taking the situation and needs of clients into account when making policy directives and regulations; therefore, agencies using an empowerment perspective must somehow work around the rules of funders to maintain their commitment to empowerment approaches. Managers must also evaluate whether a form of funding will compromise the empowerment perspective. This type of conflict was described by the director of an Afrocentric mental health agency:

> There's a decision that's been made by [a government funder] . . . that all consumers will be enrolled on the 24-hour protocol with all agencies so that they can receive services. . . . And so that type of decision has impact on clients, but it's a

> funding problem, because in order to get our money,
> everybody's got to be able to be enrolled. We have to inform
> clients in writing, face to face, and make sure that they have
> full understanding of what that means.

Another barrier to funding access is the difficulty of measuring positive outcomes and incremental changes over time. As one participant observed, "People get funding [for] things they can see. . . . People want . . . things that are measurable. . . . [T]he piece that looks at empowerment . . . is really hard to measure and it is really hard to get funding for." Access to funding can also be compromised or jeopardized by the empowerment commitment and the philosophy of agencies and organizations. As one participant stated, giving people power may not be a high priority for many funders, "and I don't know that . . . funding sources and the government are all that interested in people having that kind of power."

Social Environment. Several participants stated that some barriers they encountered in their empowerment-based services involved interactions with other human services agencies. In some situations, differing philosophies or politics of more traditional service providers negatively affected the willingness or ability of empowerment-based agencies to refer clients to other services. One participant described this situation as follows: "When I begin to use outside resources . . . everybody's got their own agenda. . . . A lot of people are very set in their ways, and . . . so the field itself . . . often represents the most barriers for a [client] because [of] the inconsistency in approaches."

Competition between agencies and organizations can also have a negative impact on interagency cooperation. As one participant explained, "I think that the fact that [competition] does happen does affect the ability of programs like this to work, because you really do need interagency cooperation between the [services] because we serve the same clients." Difficulties with securing cooperation from other service providers can directly influence the ability to serve clients and can also affect access to funds, because increasing numbers of funders expect evidence that service providers will work together and demand evidence of cooperative effort.

Competition within a community can also impede an organization's ability to gain access to other types of resources.

For one advocacy organization, competition for the energy and commitment of staff and volunteers may be a barrier to survival and growth. As one participant stated, "We did a survey one time and found that members of [our organization] on average belong to about five other organizations which also took their energy.... I think that happens to a lot of groups, a lot of people.... They just aren't empowering us, if you see what I mean.... People are kind of exhausted with everything else ... and don't turn out [for meetings] like I feel I would like to see them."

Intrapersonal Issues. Intrapersonal barriers involved characteristics of the clients or workers that seemed to interfere with empowerment practice. One such barrier is the challenge of the client's mental or physical condition, especially when working with chronic problems. Participants working in community mental health or with violent families described the difficulty in using a consumer-driven approach when progress was incremental or discontinuous.

The longer time frame for interventions often means that staff must wait longer to see positive results. As one participant stated, when things are moving along at an agency-defined pace, "it makes you feel like you're doing more." For those workers who are likely to become overinvolved with the outcome of clients, frustration and impatience with the process can result. One participant described this "ego involvement" on the part of staff as a problem, "because intellectually, . . . you'd like this grander scheme. . . . What can . . . I do to make this different so that it's [going] to impact this [client]? . . . So it's more internal stuff. . . . It's that sort of internal struggle."

Interpersonal Issues. The interpersonal barriers that emerged from the data revolved around the relationship between staff and clients. A dilemma regarding consumer choice can go beyond the problem of ego involvement when encouraging choice may require letting go of outcomes or when the most essential well-being of clients is at stake. Some participants described the process of letting go as involving some agonizing of conscience and will that, according to one participant who works with violent families, may lead to a decision by the worker to abandon the empowerment approach: "I have to respect people's choices. Once in a while ... if we get someone where the abuse is in the real late stage where it's getting real close to lethal, we drop the empow-

erment model and we . . . confront people with . . . the seriousness of the situation. . . . But that's fairly rare."

More often, participants describe the letting go process in terms
of reaching an understanding with clients about responsibility
and ownership of the problem: "It's [the client's] decision. . . . I
can only suggest . . . if you don't want to go along with it, that's
fine. . . . I take credit for my behavior. But at the same time . . . the
credit belongs to those who have made it. It doesn't belong to
me." This process of encouraging independence and autonomy
within the empowerment relationship was not always an easy
one for workers. Disappointment was identified by some as a
possible negative consequence of not letting go and one of the
barriers encountered in using an empowerment approach. The
theme of disappointment, as related to autonomy and choice, and
the resulting dilemmas of these participants were echoed in the
responses from an advocacy organization. The disappointment
in this case stems from not being able to let go of the desire for
organizational success. As one participant stated, "I've come to
question that as to whether we don't need to . . . remove ourselves [as primary organizers] from it and let it sink or swim. At
least to some partial degree."

Supports for Empowerment

The supports identified by participants for maintaining and facilitating an empowerment-based approach in an agency or organizational setting were grouped into three major areas: staff
development, enhanced collaborative approach, and administrative leadership and support. As with barriers, in actual administrative practice these factors are interrelated, but for the purposes
of the article they are discussed separately.

Staff Development. Administrators and staff alike identify staff
development as one of the most important aspects of maintaining an empowerment approach in an agency or organization. Staff
development, as described by participants, involves four different aspects:

1. provision by agencies of advanced training and in-service
   training. Access to conferences, training, and educational
   opportunities is identified as being integral to the empowerment atmosphere of the organization. In this regard one

participant said, "I think the other part of empowerment, as far as inside, is . . . the amount of training that we . . . are entitled to. . . . When we first got on board, [the administrator] sent us all down to San Francisco . . . and I think that this is really empowering to get . . . training that comes through town. . . . We are encouraged to go . . . and that in itself is really empowering."

2. entrepreneurial support. Being given the encouragement and opportunities to develop programs and professional skills that match their own personal interests is an important part of the empowerment of staff in an agency: "They're encouraged that if they see a trend in their case load . . . to . . . go ahead and develop [a program]. . . . It keeps staff kind of willing to extend themselves and to . . . branch out so that they have areas of interest."

3. being rewarded through promotions and salary increases for pursuing self-defined learning goals: "The more I took on and the more areas I wanted to go . . . the more I was rewarded, both with money and a change in responsibility. . . . I do see that as empowerment. Because you're not coming into a structure, and you're not getting your raise at 4 percent because you've been there a year."

4. the provision of flexible hours and encouragement toward self-care: "This office is really flexible. . . . If I need space . . . time. . . . Whatever I need to take care of . . . myself as a person, it's given to me. . . . Taking care of your well-being is important in this agency."

Enhanced Collaborative Approach. Several participants mentioned the importance of having a teamlike approach in maintaining the atmosphere of empowerment in an agency or organization. This collaborative approach includes a sharing of power and information among all levels of staff. One participant described, for example, how the board "really values the staff input. . . . They listen so carefully to what the staff wants and . . . needs. . . . [The former director] did a lot of work to . . . open up the communication, and to make sure there wasn't so much mystery about what both groups were doing." The use of a collaborative approach—or teamwork—is also seen as an antidote to burnout and as a way to combine energies and talents: "I think when the team concept begins to really get into place, you start getting empowerment, because you begin to have other people and yourself, police yourself. . . . You just can't . . . hot dog anymore." Another participant said, "There are going to be times in which we need to come together, and [we] are much more powerful because of that and that is empowering in itself."

Another aspect of incorporating an enhanced collaborative approach is the use of peer supervision and review, which serve to build relationships and support systems among staff and strengthen the horizontal structure of the organization. In addition, the collaborative approach can be enhanced by two factors that were often named as being important to the continued sense of empowerment among staff: a sense of safety and a shared philosophy.

Staff must feel free to take risks in confronting each other (for example, on issues of sexism, racism, homophobia, and abuse of power), venting their frustrations, and developing new programs and ideas. According to one participant, "It is important for us to have a safe place in which we can talk about the issues of our people." Another stated, "The staff call each other on instances where they feel someone might be being too direct and . . . telling a [client] what to do. And so we try to keep aware of that and bring it up in staff meetings."

Sharing the basic philosophy of the agency with its empowerment perspective was mentioned directly by one participant and can be inferred from the responses of others. In response to a question regarding supports, one participant emphasized the need to keep the empowerment philosophy intact. Another identified the importance of building a staff with a similar outlook, commitment, and shared attitude of questioning the system.

Administrative Leadership and Support. Advocacy and encouragement of the empowerment orientation by the leadership of the agency or organization is frequently mentioned by participants as being of fundamental importance. Frequently the administrative leader is also responsible for the vision and development of the program.

Having an administrator on your side as an advocate for consumers and staff is seen by many participants as a critical support for maintaining an atmosphere of empowerment. For instance, one participant stated, "To know that someone's at your back. Somebody is going to look out for you, [the executive director] you know. She may yell at me later, but she is not going to let nobody else dog me out, you know."

Administrative staff who are able to advocate for the organization with external systems can support empowerment-based programs in the agency. For example, the coordinator of a program for low-income women described how the efforts of an influential grant writer were critically important in influencing funding sources. These supports can play a crucial role in developing an organizational culture that is supportive of the empowerment of board, staff, volunteers, and consumers.

DISCUSSION

Administrators and workers were asked a series of questions to identify supports and barriers to empowerment practice in their organization. From this inquiry factors that affected different levels of administrative practice were identified. These themes generated new demands on administrators and supervisors in human services organizations. In their descriptions of how empowerment practice can be developed and sustained, these administrators and workers highlighted how a balance of internal and external barriers and supports can affect the ability to work effectively. Many of the external conditions identified as potential barriers to empowerment practice, such as lack of funding or community environment, could be directly challenged by careful, motivated, and effective leadership within the organization. Similarly, those difficulties experienced by workers with their own feelings or the reactions of clients could be counteracted by staff development, peer supervision and review, and team-building activities. Many of the respondents felt that an effective system of leadership in the organization that advocated and practiced empowerment methods was the one factor that made their work possible.

The results of this research are important to social work administrators in a number of ways. If an empowerment-based paradigm is gaining ascendency in the social work field, we need to develop ways in which organizational practice can support these programs. Moreover, we need to develop methods that are more than just ideas that exist only in our professional discourse, but that are, as Hartman (1993) urged, ideals that can be implemented in real settings in full recognition of the barriers and obstacles to empowerment. As Hartman suggested, we need to have the courage to examine the client–worker relationship as a system of power, and we must begin to question treatment approaches that increase the power of workers rather than the power of clients. Radical sharing of power in the client–worker relationship consists of more than techniques for increasing client skills or even client self-determination. It involves power sharing and power shedding (Hartman, 1993), a professional stance that implies transformative changes in how the work of professionals is evaluated and rewarded. Moving toward empowerment-based approaches, then, requires the full commitment of agency administration and staff.

Our data suggest that the motivation and influence of social services administrators are key factors in creating and sustaining an empowerment-based approach. Administrators must understand and address the challenges and implications of shared decision making, delayed or ambiguous outcomes, and the blurring of professional and personal boundaries. Some traditional social work clinical models and management practices have addressed this aspect of the empowerment paradigm. For instance, the concept of parallel process (Eckstein & Wallerstein, 1958), a term familiar to therapists, may be invoked to suggest the importance of the supervisor–worker relationship to the overall effectiveness of the therapeutic relationship. Parallel process models propose that the interaction of the supervisor and supervisee has a profound impact on the progress of clients in therapy (Carkhuff, Kratochvil, & Friel, 1968; Davenport, 1984; Friedlander, Siegel, & Brenock, 1989; Hartman & Brieger, 1992; Rubin, 1989; Rubinstein, 1992; Schneider, 1992). In this model, supervision and counseling are seen as reciprocal and interlocking processes (Friedlander et al., 1989). Parallel process models suggest that difficulties in supervision will be reflected in the client–worker relationship and that supervisors' attitudes and ways of addressing conflict and problems will find their way, for better or worse, into the therapeutic process (Rubinstein, 1992). Practitioners who adhere to parallel process approaches point out how the neglect of difficulties between the supervisor and therapist provides a model for the therapist of how not to communicate with clients (Rubin, 1989).

The parallel process model provides points of connection to empowerment-based approaches and illustrates the findings of our study that the ability of individual workers to share their power with clients and to engage in the range of interventions required for empowerment-based practice can be dependent on the support they receive for this type of work and on their own feelings of personal power. However useful the concept of parallel process may be in describing the similar power dynamics of the supervisory and therapeutic relationship, it does not fully explain and model how actual power may be transferred from the worker to the client. Power differentials among supervisors, workers, and clients, however, present a continuing source of questions, dilemmas, and conflicts. In an empowerment-based approach, awareness of the power imbalance must be followed by movement toward partnership.

Our study highlighted the conflicts and contradictions inherent in attempts to share power in situations in which the stated goal of self-determination and the sometimes necessary function of social control are thrown into tension in the client–worker relationship. Many participants noted this tension and struggled to articulate ways to integrate client self-determination with their commitment to provide interventions that promoted personal safety and health. On occasion, participants discovered dilemmas regarding the responsible use of their power, such as cases in which they could not in good conscience support decisions of clients to return to abusive situations. In this regard, Hartman (1993) suggested that there may be times when social workers must limit client self-determination to prevent behavior that is antisocial, in the recognition that social workers have legitimate power that can be used protectively. These dilemmas and others call for heightened sensitivity and wisdom on the part of administrators and highlight the need for more clarity regarding the tension between individual freedom and social responsibility, along with the need for strategies to increase both.

Our data suggest, in line with earlier studies (Holland, Konick, Buffum, Smith, & Petchers, 1981), that those organizations that empower workers by creating an employment setting that provides participatory management, the ability to make independent decisions about their work, communication and support from administrators, and opportunities for skill development will be more capable of empowering clients and communities. Researchers who promote the expansion of participatory management also point out, however, that political conditions that limit control over resources and policies severely limit its use in public welfare settings (Weatherley, 1985). Clearly, there is still much work to be done in clarifying and strategizing an administrative and practice method that can overcome the barriers and limitations of empowerment-based practice.

The results of this study, however, demonstrate that some organizations are implementing and struggling with the barriers and supports to empowerment-based practice. In the process, these workers and, by extension, their clients are describing themselves as empowered. The supports to empowerment-based practice identified in this study—staff development, collaborative approaches, a safe environment, a shared philosophy, and administrative leadership and support—can provide a starting place for staff and administrators to discuss and, it is hoped, to ultimately commit to empowerment-based paradigms in the human service.

REFERENCES

Bricker-Jenkins, M., & Hooyman, N. (1986). *Not for women only: Social work practice for a feminist future.* Silver Spring, MD: National Association of Social Workers.

Bricker-Jenkins, M., & Hooyman, N. (1991). *Feminist social work practice in clinical settings.* Beverly Hills, CA: Sage Publications.

Carkhuff, R. R., Kratochvil, D., & Friel, T. (1968). Effects of professional training: Communication and discrimination of facilitative conditions. *Journal of Counseling Psychology, 15,* 68–74.

Davenport, J. J. (1984). The Saturday center: A training institution in process. *Clinical Social Work Journal, 12,* 347–355.

Eckstein, R., & Wallerstein, R. S. (1958). *The teaching and learning of psychotherapy.* New York: Basic Books.

Freire, P. (1973). *Education for critical consciousness.* New York: Seabury Press.

Friedlander, M. L., Siegel, S. M., & Brenock, K. (1989). Parallel processes in counseling and supervision: A case study. *Journal of Counseling Psychology, 36,* 149–157.

Gerschick, T., Israel, B., & Checkoway, B. (1989). *Means of empowerment in individuals, organizations, and communities: Report from a retrieval conference.* Ann Arbor: Center for Research on Social Organizations, University of Michigan.

Greene, D., & David, J. (1984). A research design for generalizing from multiple case studies. *Evaluation and Program Planning, 7,* 75–85.

Gutiérrez, L. (1986, March). *Alternative services and community organization: Opportunities and dilemmas.* Paper presented at the Symposium on Community Organization and Social Administration, Council on Social Work Education, Miami.

Gutiérrez, L. (1990). Working with women of color: An empowerment perspective. *Social Work, 35*, 149–154.

Gutiérrez, L., GlenMaye, L., & DeLois, K. (1992, July). *Improving the human condition through empowerment practice.* Paper presented at World Assembly: NASW's Annual Meeting of the Profession, Washington, DC.

Guitérrez, L., & Ortega, R. (1991). Developing methods to empower Latinos: The importance of groups. *Social Work with Groups, 14*(2), 23–44.

Hartman, A. (1993). The professional is political. *Social Work, 38*, 365–366, 504.

Hartman, C., & Brieger, K. (1992). Cross-gender supervision and sexuality. *Clinical Supervisor, 10*(1), 71–81.

Holland, T. P., Konick, A., Buffum, W., Smith, M. K., & Petchers, M. (1981). Institutional structure and resident outcomes. *Journal of Health and Social Behavior, 22*, 433–444.

Mathis, T., & Richan, D. (1986, March). *Empowerment: Practice in search of a theory.* Paper presented at the Annual Program Meeting of the Council on Social Work Education, Miami.

Maton, K., & Rappaport, J. (1984). Empowerment in a religious setting: A multivariate investigation. In J. Rappaport, C. Swift, & R. Hess (Eds.), *Studies in empowerment: Toward understanding and action* (pp. 37–70). New York: Haworth Press.

Parsons, R. (1991). Empowerment: Purpose and practice in social work. *Social Work with Groups, 14*(2), 7–22.

Peters, T., & Waterman, R. (1982). *In search of excellence: Lessons from America's best run companies.* New York: Harper & Row.

Pinderhughes, E. (1989). *Understanding race, ethnicity, & power: The key to efficacy in clinical practice.* New York: Free Press.

Rappaport, J. (1981). In praise of paradox: A social policy of empowerment over prevention. *American Journal of Community Psychology, 9*(1), 1–25.

Rubin, S. S. (1989). Choice points in psychotherapy, supervision: On the experiences of supervisors in supervision. *Clinical Supervisor, 7*(2–3), 27–41.

Rubinstein, G. (1992). Supervision and psychotherapy: Toward redefining the differences. *Clinical Supervisor, 10*(2), 97–116.

Schneider, S. (1992). Transference, counter-transference, projective identification and role responsiveness in the supervisory process. *Clinical Supervisor, 10*(2), 71–84.

Sherman, W., & Wenocur, S. (1983). Empowering public welfare workers through mutual support. *Social Work, 28*, 275–279.

Simon, B. (1990). Rethinking empowerment. *Journal of Progressive Human Services, 1*, 27–40.

Solomon, B. (1976). *Black empowerment.* New York: Columbia University Press.

Staples, L. (1991). Powerful ideas about empowerment. *Administration in Social Work, 14*(2), 29–42.

Swift, C., & Levin, G. (1987). Empowerment: An emerging mental health technology. *Journal of Primary Prevention, 8*(1–2), 71–92.

Weatherly, R. A. (1985). Participatory management in public welfare: What are the prospects? In S. Slavin (Ed.), *An introduction to human services management: Vol. 1, Social administration: The management of the social services* (pp. 270–281). New York: Haworth Press.

Zimmerman, M. A. (in press). Empowerment: Forging new perspectives in mental health. In J. Rappaport & E. Seidman (Eds.), *Handbook of community psychology.* New York: Plenum Press.

Zimmerman, M., & Rappaport, J. (1988). Citizen participation, perceived control, and psychological empowerment. *American Journal of Community Psychology, 16,* 725–750.

This chapter was originally published in the March 1995 issue of Social Work, *vol. 40, pp. 249–258.*

7 RAP: A Framework for Leadership of Multiracial Groups

Larry E. Davis, Maeda J. Galinsky, and
Janice H. Schopler

Despite social work's long tradition of serving multiracial groups and the growing opportunities to learn about racial dynamics, practitioners are often ill prepared to address racial issues in the groups they lead. The availability of information about the impact of race on group work practice does not necessarily ensure effective leadership of multiracial groups. Race is such an emotionally charged area of practice that leaders may fail to identify and deal with racial issues because they wish to avoid racial confrontations, are anxious, or perhaps are unsure about how to proceed. This article proposes a framework for practice with racially mixed groups that explicitly recognizes the interplay among the leader's ability to act, the racial dynamics of the group, and the imperatives for intervention.

INFLUENCE OF RACE IN GROUP WORK PRACTICE

Social Forces

Whenever people of different races come together in groups, leaders can assume that race is an issue, but not necessarily a problem. Race is an issue in multiracial groups because it is a very apparent difference among participants and one that is laden with highly sensitive social meaning. The racism and institutional discrimination found in society at large become a salient part of a group's social reality when group composition includes people of more than one race. Typically, observations of racial differences are accompanied by inferior–superior ascriptions of social class and status (Davis & Proctor, 1989). Although some practitioners continue to believe that the model of intervention transcends the importance of demographics when people of different races come together for a common purpose, this "color blind" approach denies the significance of race (Davis & Proctor, 1989; Griffith, 1977; Lum, 1986).

The issue of race and its influence on group work practice is of increasing importance for several reasons. Our population is rapidly becoming more racially diverse (for example, Chau, 1990b; Henry, 1990). The population groups with the fastest rate of growth—black people, Hispanics, Asians, and other people of color (for example, American Indians)—are most likely to require social work services because they are disproportionately at risk for social perils such as poverty, drug abuse, family violence, teenage pregnancy, and homelessness. These societal changes have increased the likelihood that social workers will be leading groups where racial differences exist among members and between leaders and members. Relationships among members and workers and between groups and their environments may be strained by the racism and institutional discrimination so prevalent in society.

In response to these developments, group work frequently is the method of choice. Group methods that emphasize both individual change and institutional change are often the most appropriate approach for empowering clients, for advocating for more accessible and culturally responsive services, for affirming ethnic identity and heritage, and for promoting intercultural acceptance and interdependence (Chau, 1990b; Gutierrez, 1990; Northen, 1990).

Practice Literature

Coyle (1930) first alerted group workers to the impact of race, ethnicity, and culture in 1930, and attention to these factors has increased over the years, with a surge of publications in the past decade (Chau, 1990c; Davis, 1984a, 1984b; Davis & Proctor, 1989). Recent authors have described the impact of racial and cultural factors on groups formed for specific purposes ranging from counseling and stress reduction (Bilides, 1990; Child & Getzel, 1989; Malekoff, Levine, & Quaglia, 1987) to dealing with racial and cultural concerns (Ciullo & Toriani, 1988; Mullender, 1990; Rhule, 1988; Van Den Bergh, 1990). They have also reported on experiences in groups serving members with specific ethnic, racial, or cultural identities, including black people and Vietnamese and other Asians (Boyd-Franklin, 1987; Chan, 1990; Gutierrez, 1990; Lewis & Ford, 1990; Lewis & Kissman, 1989; Tsui & Schultz, 1988). Several authors have also begun to conceptualize the special requirements of racially and ethnically sensitive practice with multiracial groups (Chau, 1990a; Glassman & Kates, 1989; Hurdle, 1990).

The literature on race and group work provides rich practice content, identifies many problems and issues, and offers some general constructs to guide multiracial practice. Much of this literature, however, is based on accounts of single-group experiences. Furthermore, information and principles are often specific to a particular race and may not generalize to a multiracial situation. What is lacking in this literature is specific guidance for practice that is based on a conceptualization of the group dynamics, interpersonal reactions, and special demands for leadership that are likely to occur when people of different races, ethnic backgrounds, and cultures come together in groups. To address this need, we propose a framework to validate leaders' concerns, alert practitioners to potential areas of difficulty, help them understand the underlying racial dynamics, and guide selection of interventions appropriate to the specific multiracial situation.

Practice Experience

In developing a conceptual framework for leadership of multiracial groups, we have been influenced by the experience of practitioners who have led such groups. Over a two-year period, we tested ideas and assumptions based on our review of the literature and our own experience by collecting information from professional leaders of multiracial groups at national and international workshops and from students in our group work classes. Our multiracial sample of 51 workshop participants and 66 students completed 117 anonymous, structured questionnaires indicating their concerns, experiences, and suggestions for working with multiracial groups.

When asked about the types of multiracial situations they had encountered as members or leaders of groups, all of the 117 respondents checked one or more of the following categories: imbalance in racial composition (87 respondents), racial tensions or conflicts between worker and members (56), outside racial tensions or conflicts brought into the group (56), racial tensions or conflicts among members (53), and difficulty in introducing the topic of race (47). In addition, when respondents were asked to consider 11 situations that could be of potential concern in leading multiracial groups, all of the respondents indicated some concerns. The most frequently checked concern (75 of the 117 respondents) was that members would perceive the leader as having insufficient understanding of issues. Slightly more than half of the respondents (65) indicated concern that members would not participate in activities and discussions because of racial tension; half (58) expressed concern with racist behavior such as members being condescending and rude or using racial slurs.

In order of decreasing frequency, other concerns checked by a substantial number of participants were as follows: members would stop coming because of racial tensions (46), members would verbally attack each other (42), leader would be perceived as having insufficient skills (31), leader would be rejected because of race (30), leader would be perceived as racist (30), and leader would be verbally attacked (18). A few respondents also checked the remaining categories: members would physically attack each other (13) and the leader would be physically attacked (3).

To gain additional practitioner perceptions about leadership of multiracial groups, we asked respondents at two workshops for other comments and suggestions. We also conducted telephone interviews with 18 practitioners who volunteered at the workshops to give us additional information about their experiences. These interviews and open-ended questionnaire responses enriched our understanding of the demands of current practice and further sharpened our thinking about the factors that should be considered in the conceptual framework.

RAP FRAMEWORK

The RAP framework addresses the leader's ability to act, the racial dynamics of the group, and the imperatives for leader action (Figure 7-1). Each of these components acts on and is acted on by the others. Each part of the framework can be examined as a separate unit, but it is the interplay among components that determines the group's reaction to the multiracial experience.

Leader's Ability to Act

The ability to respond to racial issues is jointly determined by the interaction of leader comfort and competence. To be comfort-

Figure 7-1

RAP Framework

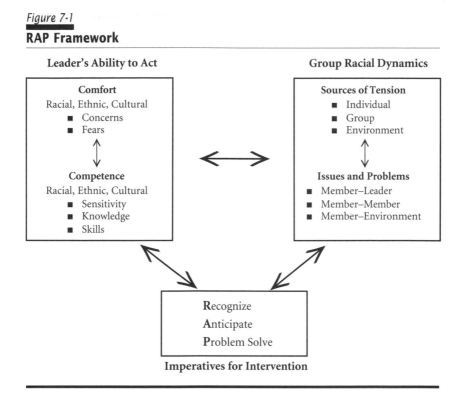

Leader's Ability to Act

Comfort
Racial, Ethnic, Cultural
- Concerns
- Fears

Competence
Racial, Ethnic, Cultural
- Sensitivity
- Knowledge
- Skills

Group Racial Dynamics

Sources of Tension
- Individual
- Group
- Environment

Issues and Problems
- Member–Leader
- Member–Member
- Member–Environment

Recognize
Anticipate
Problem Solve

Imperatives for Intervention

able enough to use their knowledge, skills, and sensitivity when confronted with a racially tense situation, leaders need to have a realistic sense of their concerns and fears and be able to cope with them. Unrealistic fears or too much anxiety and concern can be incapacitating. Furthermore, to be able to intervene competently, leaders not only need to know what to do and how to do it, but also need to be able to recognize racial issues.

The need for leader competence in responding to racial differences is assumed in all of the publications related to group work and race that we reviewed and is often explicitly stated (Chau, 1990a; Ciullo & Toriani, 1988; Davis, 1981, 1984a; Davis & Proctor, 1989). Structured experiences useful in developing group leader awareness of racial, ethnic, and cultural dynamics are also becoming more available (Abels & Abels, 1991; Glassman, 1990; Muston & Weinstein, 1988; Roundtree, 1991).

Generally, however, the anxieties and fears that affect leader responsiveness to racial, ethnic, and cultural differences receive less attention. Davis (1984a) proposed that leader fears related to unmanageable resistance, losing control, excessive hostility, acting out, overwhelming dependency, and group disintegration are often realistic, but not expressed, and he noted that fears about creating or increasing racial tensions in the group may make leaders hesitant about intervening. Some authors (Boyd-Franklin, 1987; Child & Getzel, 1989; Davis, Sharfstein, & Owens, 1974; Hurdle, 1990) indicated that discomfort about discussing race can create group tensions. More often than not, however, there seems to be an implicit assumption that leaders who are knowledgeable and sensitive will be comfortable in dealing with these racial issues. The reality of leader concerns and fears about practice with multiracial groups has been affirmed by the accounts of practitioners and students in our pilot data. The detail leaders used in describing their worries and the intensity of their discussions about racial issues in the workshops and classes speak to their significance.

The importance of recognizing the effect of leader anxieties is supported by the discussions of Williams (1966), Yalom (1966), and more recently Reid (1988), who examined the fears of neophyte group leaders. These authors noted that some anxiety is useful but emphasized that anticipating and predicting anxiety help keep it within manageable bounds and promote greater competence. Thus, the degree of leader comfort in dealing with racial issues can have implications for how leaders view problems and issues and how they intervene. Leaders who profess no concerns about race and those who are immobilized by their fears may deny the significance of race, avoid the subject, and overlook racial incidents in their group. Leaders who have a more realistic level of concern and who are in touch with their feelings are likely to become better informed, will be more sensitive to issues, and should be more responsive and effective when problems arise.

Group Racial Dynamics

The racial dynamics of multiracial groups evolve from the interplay among the sources of racial tensions and the way racial issues and problems are manifested in the group. By recognizing the sources of tensions, leaders can often prevent problems from occurring. When problems do arise, an understanding of underlying causes can facilitate resolution of problems.

Sources of Racial Tension. Tensions may lie within the individuals who are in the group, derive from the nature of the group itself, and flow from the immediate and more remote environments. In any case, these tensions influence member beliefs and actions both within and outside the group. Leaders thus need "trifocal vision" to recognize and cope with the issues that arise in their groups.

Foremost among the individual characteristics that should be considered are the races of the participants; their racial, ethnic, and cultural experiences; and their racial self-concepts (Robinson, 1989). Each leader and member in any multiracial group has a unique racial self-concept that has been shaped by family of origin, personality, individual talents and skills, and life experiences. Furthermore, individuals come with personal prejudices and stereotypes. Tensions stem from the way specific individual participants differ in their racial, ethnic, and cultural beliefs, perceptions, and responses. General knowledge about how different population groups tend to view power, authority, status, and interpersonal boundaries as well as typical cultural and family expectations and behavior can alert leaders to general areas of difference (for example, Chau, 1990a; Davis & Proctor, 1989; Hurdle, 1990). Leaders must, however, be cautious about generalizing knowledge about population characteristics to individuals in their groups.

The group dimensions that can become sources of racial tension may temper all group interactions or they may remain dormant for much of the group's life, only to be activated by some critical incident that divides the group along racial, ethnic, or cultural lines. Leaders need to be particularly sensitive to the specific races represented in the group and the number of persons of each race. Solo membership and marked imbalance in numbers can create problems. Unequal numbers of members of each race can lead to subgrouping and domination by members of a particular race. In addition, a group that has a relatively equal number of each race represented may appear racially balanced, but members may perceive themselves to be in a "psychological minority" if their proportion in the group is less than their usual expectations (Davis, 1979; Davis & Proctor, 1989).

The purpose and goals of the group as well as its culture and norms can be a significant source of tension, particularly if participants of different races have different expectations about what the group's focus should be (Chau, 1990a). Group purposes related to individual change, support, and advocacy are often in conflict. If norms do not promote recognition and respect of differences, member equality, and open discussion of issues related to race, ethnicity, and culture, the group atmosphere can be cautious, mistrustful, and guarded. Tensions may also evolve from forces related to group development because participants will all have their own ideas about when and how it is appropriate to share intimacies, confront others, and deal with power differentials (Glassman & Kates, 1989). Furthermore, members of different races may be unwilling to engage in honest expressions of opinions and feelings in racially mixed groups.

The environmental factors that need to be considered as sources of tension include the climate of society, events in the members' neighborhoods, the sponsoring organization's reputation for responsiveness to racial concerns, and the way that people who are significant in the immediate lives of group members view the group. Such external forces as lack of accessible services, culturally inappropriate services, institutional discrimination, inflammatory social incidents, and hostile social interactions are often replayed within the group. Epidemiological data support the negative impact of a racially dissonant environment on feelings and behavior in multiracial relationships (Tweed et al., 1990).

Neighborhoods may create ethnic and socioeconomic boundaries that are difficult for members to cross, even when they share the same concerns (Malekoff, Levine, & Quaglia, 1987). Members will be affected by what is happening in their home communities and in their own homes, and these events will create tensions whether or not the events are spoken of in the group. Furthermore, the way the sponsoring organization is viewed by people who are important in the members' lives will affect their confidence in the efficacy of services and their commitment to participation in the group.

Racial Issues and Problems. Issues related to race, ethnicity, and culture are always present in multiracial groups. Racial issues and problems need to be addressed from two vantage points: the nature or content of the issue or problem itself and the parties involved, whether leaders, members, or the environment. Although the specific nature of the issues or problems will vary with each group, racial issues or problems can occur at three levels: between the leaders and members, among members, and between members and the environment.

Issues and problems are likely to arise in member–leader relationships whenever racial differences exist. Some common manifestations include a leader who is the only representative of a particular race and who feels isolated; leaders who are insensitive to the particular racial, ethnic, and cultural expectations of the members and unknowingly alienate members by poorly timed or inappropriate comments; members who doubt the ability of leaders to be helpful because of their race and are reluctant to self-disclose, are resistant, withdraw from activities and discussion, or leave the group; and people of color whose leadership status is incongruent with members' expectations and who find their competence challenged by members of the same or other races.

Typically, member–member issues and problems involve differences in perceptions and behaviors that stem from past experience and socialization as well as the current group experience. Some indications of issues and problems related to member relationships include members who have concerns about how they will be perceived and fears about being rejected, members who engage in racist behaviors that lead to verbal and physical attacks, members of different races who form subgroups and struggle to dominate the group, members who avoid discussion of sensitive topics, and members who withdraw from participation or do not return to groups where they feel isolated or under attack because of their race.

Issues and problems in member–environment relationships may be apparent in the way members perceive the group, interact with each other, and deal with others in the environment. Problematic relationships with the environment may relate to a range of situations including the following: the institutional racism in both the local community and throughout society that affects members' racial attitudes and their behavior and influences the extent of support for group activities, members' reluctance to attend meetings that are held in unfamiliar territory or that are sponsored by organizations perceived as unresponsive to the needs of particular racial groups, current neighborhood or societal conflicts reflected in member interactions, and pressure on members from family and friends to perpetuate traditional styles of interaction based on animosity and fear.

Imperatives for Intervention

The RAP framework assumes that effective outcomes in any multiracial group require that leaders carry out three essential tasks. First, they must recognize (**R**) the critical importance of the racial dynamics of the group and their own ability to act. Second, they must anticipate (**A**) the sources of racial tension and help members deal with these tensions. Third, they must be prepared to problem solve (**P**) if issues become problems. The application of these imperatives for action is illustrated by a group session in which leader action is essential to deal with multiracial issues and problems. This case study is analyzed from the perspective of the three imperatives for action to explain what the leader did and what the leader might have done.

CASE STUDY

A support group of persons with cancer meets weekly at a local hospital in a medium-sized community. Although the group is open-ended, a stable group of seven women, four white and three black, have met for the past three weeks. The group members are beginning to trust each other, share personal experiences with friends and family, and discuss ways of coping. Four days before the meeting under discussion, an incident occurred in the community in which a white police officer shot a black youth. Racial tensions in the community have been high since then.

All seven members are in attendance at the fourth meeting. The meeting begins with the social worker, a black woman, greeting members and asking them how they have been doing this week. The members talk about how they are feeling physically and emotionally. Conversation is much more guarded, however, than at the previous meetings. Black people and white people avoid looking at each other, and there is little cross-racial communication.

Members start talking about experiences they have recently had with the medical care system, and a couple of interchanges suggest that racial tensions are running high. One of the white members mentions by name a secretary and a nurse. She says they were very rude to her the last two times she was at the clinic and that she is going to report them to someone. Race is not mentioned but all members are aware that the people involved are black. Shortly thereafter, one of the black members describes an emotional healing session she participated in at her church. A white member remarks, "If you people were less emotional and paid more attention to facts, you'd do better in this world." A black member retorts with obvious anger, "You don't seem to be doing too well yourself."

The leader intervenes in the session and asks the members what is going on in the group, stating she feels the atmosphere has changed. Members do not reply, and the group worker notes that they have seemed caring and supportive of each other until today. She asks what makes this meeting different, but no one responds, and members appear tense and uncomfortable. The worker reminds the women that they agreed to discuss group problems with each other in the group. She inquires whether the recent shooting of a young black man in the community by the police has anything to do with what is going on with members right now. The more outspoken members, one black and one white, say yes, and others chime in to express their agreement. One of the white women says she does not feel safe discussing personal matters in the group anymore. A black member then states that the white member would not know anything about not feeling safe until she puts herself in the shoes of a black person facing a white police officer.

At this point the leader initiates a discussion of the community racial incident. She starts by establishing rules that there are to be no racial slurs, no name calling, and no threats. Members, however, should be free to express feelings without being put down. With a few gentle proddings from the leader and these baseline instructions, members begin to express their feelings.

The leader notes how hard it must be for the women to talk about issues related to having cancer, given the racial tensions in the community right now. She reminds members of the ways they have been supportive of each other in previous meetings and asks if they would like to continue as a group. All of the members nod in agreement. One of the black members then states that so far this group has been very helpful. A white member replies that she feels the same way, but after the shooting of the black youth she does not know if the group would ever be able to deal with personal concerns as freely as they had in previous weeks. The worker states that by facing racial issues openly as they have today, they are finding ways to discuss difficult matters. She praises the group for being honest with each other and for their willingness to tackle problems.

The group members agree that they need the support the group has been providing. After a few more minutes of discussion about the racial incident, the women proceed to talk about some of the challenges they face because they have cancer. One of the members describes how upset she was when a neighbor was afraid to let her child play in the member's home for fear that he might catch cancer. The members get into an intense discussion of people's fears of those who have cancer and the stigma attached to the disease.

Recognize

Recognizing critical racial, ethnic, and cultural differences in any group requires leaders to be self-aware as well as aware of the group's racial dynamics. To carry out this task, leaders must engage in ongoing self-assessment and assessment of the group, its members, and their environment. To become effective in recognizing differences that are salient in the group, leaders of multiracial groups need to

- be prepared to be responsive to racial, ethnic, and cultural differences between leaders and members and among members
- know and respect the history, norms, and culture of the populations represented in the group
- examine their own racial, ethnic, and cultural attitudes and values
- obtain supervision or consultation from practitioners who are of the same race as members or other effective leaders of multiracial groups when members are of different races
- become familiar with resources (agencies, professionals, community leaders) in the community that are responsive to the needs of the racial groups represented in the group and be willing to refer when racial issues preclude effective helping relationships in the group

- become aware of various forms of institutional discrimination and their impact on different population groups in the community
- become aware of racial tensions that exist due to events, beliefs, and issues in the society at large or the members' neighborhoods
- become aware of the concerns and issues that individual members may have about racial, ethnic, and cultural differences.

The leader of the cancer support group was aware of the impact of racial differences on the group dynamics and knew she needed to be responsive to racial issues and problems. She had firsthand experience with the institutional discrimination faced by minorities in her community. She was familiar with local resources geared to specific racial groups and continuously tried to increase her understanding of the history, norms, and cultures of the many racial groups present in the city. Despite her preparation for dealing with racial issues, the social worker thought that some white members might not want her as their leader. Up to this point, she had been hesitant to introduce a discussion of racial differences because she was afraid her responses to members might not appear neutral.

Following the shooting of the black youth, the social worker considered the potential impact of this community racial incident on the group members. She expected that racial feelings might be intense when the group met, but she did not know exactly how the women might be responding to the news of the shooting. Because of her own personal concerns, the worker realized she had not learned much about the specific racial attitudes of the current members. Even though she expected some conflict among members at this stage of group development, she anticipated that conflict might be more pronounced in the current group because of the members' responses to the community racial turmoil.

Before the group meeting, the social worker consulted with her white supervisor for the first time about her racial concerns and fears. They had a productive discussion of their own racial differences and perceptions. Following the supervisory session, the social worker felt more confident about her ability to be helpful to the group in discussing racial issues. She knew that giving group members an opportunity to discuss how community racial tensions were affecting their work together would probably relieve potential group tensions. At this point, however, she was not comfortable enough to raise the issue in the group and decided to wait until she got a sense of how members were feeling.

Anticipate

Anticipating how individual members and the group as a whole will be affected by racial issues and problems requires a preventive as well as an interventive stance. As the group begins to meet, the leader will need to anticipate potential sources of tension in composing the group, formulating the purpose, and structuring the group's work together. Because relationships among participants and with the environment change over time, anticipating tensions is an ongoing leadership responsibility, and the leader may need to alter his or her approach as new issues emerge. To anticipate tensions and help members deal with them effectively, leaders must

- develop a repertoire of helping responses and select a leadership style that is culturally appropriate to the specific racial configuration, even if this is less comfortable than their typical approach
- when coleaders are of different races, discuss potential problems ahead of time and be sure to portray equal status in the group (ensuring that neither leader is seen as the helper)
- avoid having only one member of any race, but if the group has a solo member, acknowledge how difficult this situation may be for that person, and do not expect members to serve as representatives of their race or ethnic group
- strive for "psychological balance" when composing groups; if composition is imbalanced, discuss possible sources of discomfort and consider adding members to create a more favorable balance of races
- help the group formulate a purpose that is responsive to concerns and needs expressed by the members; when environmental conditions are barriers to the achievement of individual goals, take action and empower members to obtain their rights and acknowledge the importance of environmental as well as individual change

- acknowledge in the initial contacts and sessions the racial and ethnic differences that exist in the group and discuss their potential salience; state that race is a difficult issue to discuss and that individuals often feel awkward with persons of different races and backgrounds
- encourage the development of norms of tolerance and mutual respect; state that tolerance is important because of differences in the social reality of each member
- announce in initial sessions that sometimes people do and say things that are racially inappropriate; state that in this group any comments that may be considered insulting will be thoroughly discussed.

The social worker did not have a voice in selecting members for the cancer support group, but she was aware of the psychological imbalance that may have been created by the group's composition. The white members were not accustomed to meeting in a group with such a high proportion of black members. In addition, the leader was also black, an unusual situation for most white people. Because she did not have a coleader, the social worker was not able to model a relationship of equality. Whenever the need arose, however, she was prepared to discuss race openly with the group, to use a leadership style that was more active than her typical nondirective facilitative approach, and to stand by any solo members of a particular race who might come to the group.

The leader was developing a repertoire of culturally specific responses appropriate to different racial and ethnic groups. On the one hand, she felt particularly confident about her knowledge of the customs and beliefs of local black and white populations. On the other hand, she felt awkward about introducing race as a topic for consideration before it became an obvious issue for the group. In this case, if she had initially noted the importance of race to members, some of the group tensions associated with the community racial incident might have been tempered.

From the beginning of the group, the leader encouraged members to tolerate their differences and show respect for each other whether or not they agreed with each other. Even though the general norms of the group did not specifically address race and ethnicity, they served the group well. Without these norms as a backdrop, discussing the community racial incident would have been more difficult. In addition, the goals of the group were relevant to all of the members, and sharing a common diagnosis of cancer had enhanced the development of group bonds.

Problem Solve

Whenever there are incidents related to racial, ethnic, or cultural issues, the leader must intervene at the individual, group, or environmental level to resolve the situation. Although leaders have primary responsibility for ensuring that problematic situations are dealt with, they must also involve members in confronting and resolving problems within and outside the group. To be effective in addressing problems, leaders should

- use interventions and goals that are culturally acceptable and appropriate for members; if misinterpretations of leaders occur, discuss how persons have different perspectives based on race or ethnicity
- convey respect and genuineness through behavior (no phony language or slang) and gear attending skills and nonverbal behaviors to the culture of members (for example, observe cultural norms related to factors such as eye contact and personal space)
- encourage members to discuss racial, ethnic, and cultural issues and to resolve conflicts; focus on the positive contributions of diversity; and promote understanding of issues and resolution of problems
- stop the action and confront directly when there is a problem between persons of different races; have members confront and problem solve; and when antagonists need time to cool off, do not involve them for a time
- provide some rules when involving members in problem solving (for example, no name calling) and provide a framework for discussion so the situation will not escalate
- use structured problem-solving processes; design exercises that involve members in facilitative interactions (for example, role-play problematic situations, verbally reward cooperative behavior)
- help members gain skills in confronting and dealing with problems related to race and ethnicity outside the group

- be prepared, if necessary, to intervene in the environment to confront racial, ethnic, and cultural issues, resolve conflicts, and promote system responsiveness; be prepared to advocate on members' behalf and, when appropriate, to involve members in actions that will bring about a more just and responsive environment.

The social worker was very careful to guide members of the cancer support group toward discussion of what was occurring in the group and an explicit statement of what was causing the tensions among them. The group members, both black and white, seemed to want to discuss the racial tensions. By providing a structure for members' expression, the worker was trying to create a safe and secure place where these women would be free to share their feelings. The leader gave each person a chance to talk without interruption, established rules about what could be stated, and spoke openly about race herself. She ensured that members of different races alternated in giving their initial perceptions so that no one racial group felt overwhelmed. She conveyed respect for members by her demeanor and insisted that members also show respect for one another. The leader acknowledged that negative community events could be carried into the group and create problems, and she modeled ways in which racial tensions could be confronted. The social worker also resolved to explore the members' perceptions of rude behavior by clinic staff, perhaps by talking directly to staff or suggesting some in-service training if racial issues existed.

Discussion

This situation illustrates the interdependence of the leader's ability to act, the racial dynamics of the group, and the imperatives for action. Although the social worker had developed the competence to deal effectively with racial problems, she found it difficult to initiate discussions about race. Before the group meeting, she recognized the critical racial dynamics of the group. She was well aware of her own discomfort and was working to overcome her hesitancy about intervening more directly around racial matters. She also anticipated correctly that the community racial incident would have repercussions for the group. Thus, she was able to act promptly and effectively to help the group deal with the racial tensions that interfered with goal achievement, threatened group survival, and negatively affected individuals in the group. Further, the caring, respectful relationships she had modeled and nurtured in earlier sessions provided a foundation for structuring productive problem solving. Members were able to discuss racial tensions and to move on to renew their commitment to each other and to the group.

CONCLUSION

The RAP framework provides conceptual guidance for leaders of multiracial groups. Identifying the critical factors that influence the leader's ability to act, the forces that characterize the racial dynamics of multiracial groups, and the imperatives for intervention constitute a comprehensive framework for intervention. Furthermore, the attention to the emotional components in both the leader's ability to act and the group's racial dynamics should directly address leader concerns and member discomfort about confronting racial issues and problems. Because measures can be developed for all of the constructs, the model provides a framework that can be applied in practice, that can be tested through research, and that can promote more effective outcomes when people with varied racial, ethnic, and cultural backgrounds come together in groups.

REFERENCES

Abels, P., & Abels, S. L. (1991). The basic game. *Social Work with Groups, 14*(3), 123–126.

Bilides, D. G. (1990). Race, color, ethnicity, and class: Issues of biculturalism in school-based adolescent counseling groups. *Social Work with Groups, 13*(4), 43–58.

Boyd-Franklin, N. (1987). Group therapy for black women: A therapeutic support model. *American Journal of Orthopsychiatry, 57,* 394–401.

Chan, L. (1990). Application of single-session groups in working with Vietnamese refugees in Hong Kong. *Social Work with Groups, 14*(3), 103–120.

Chau, K. L. (1990a). Social work with groups in multicultural contexts. *Groupwork, 3*(1), 8–21.

Chau, K. L. (1990b). Introduction: Facilitating bicultural development and intercultural skills in ethnically heterogeneous groups. *Social Work with Groups, 13*(4), 1–5.

Chau, K. L. (Ed.). (1990c). Ethnicity and biculturalism: Emerging perspectives of social group work [Special issue]. *Social Work with Groups, 13*(4).

Child, R., & Getzel, G. S. (1989). Group work with inner city persons with AIDS. *Social Work with Groups, 12*(4), 65–80.

Ciullo, R., & Toriani, M. V. (1988). Resolution of prejudice: Small group interaction and behavior in latency-age children. *Small Group Behavior, 19,* 386–394.

Coyle, G. (1930). *Social process in organized groups.* New York: Richard R. Smith.

Davis, L. (1979). Racial composition of groups. *Social Work, 24,* 208–213.

Davis, L. (1981). Racial issues in the training of group workers. *Specialists in Group Work, 6*(3), 155–160.

Davis, L. (1984a). The essential components of group work with black Americans. *Social Work with Groups, 7*(3), 95–109.

Davis, L. (Ed.). (1984b). Ethnicity in social group work practice [Special issue]. *Social Work with Groups, 7*(3).

Davis, L. E., & Proctor, E. K. (1989). *Race, gender, and class: Guidelines for practice with individuals, families, and groups.* Englewood Cliffs, NJ: Prentice Hall.

Davis, M. I., Sharfstein, S., & Owens, M. (1974). Separate and together: All black therapy group in the white hospital. *American Journal of Orthopsychiatry, 44,* 19–25.

Glassman, U. (1990). Teaching ethno-racial sensitivity through groups. *Social Work with Groups, 14*(3), 127–130.

Glassman, U., & Kates, L. (1989, October). *Group work method and ethnic-sensitive practice.* Paper presented at the 11th Annual Symposium, Association for the Advancement of Social Work with Groups, Montreal.

Griffith, M. S. (1977). The influence of race on the psychotherapeutic relationship. *Psychiatry, 40,* 27–40.

Gutierrez, L. M. (1990, March). Working with women of color: An empowerment perspective. *Social Work, 35,* 149–153.

Henry, W. A. (1990, April 9). Beyond the melting pot. *Time,* pp. 28–31.

Hurdle, D. E. (1990). The ethnic group experience. *Social Work with Groups, 13*(4), 59–69.

Lewis, E. A., & Ford, B. (1990). The network utilization project: Incorporating traditional strengths of African-American families into groupwork practice. *Social Work with Groups, 13*(4), 7–22.

Lewis, E. A., & Kissman, K. (1989). Factors linking ethnic-sensitive and feminist social work practice with African-American women. *Arete, 14*(2), 23–31.

Lum, D. (1986). *Social work practice and people of color: A process–stage approach.* Monterey, CA: Brooks/Cole.

Malekoff, A., Levine, M., & Quaglia, S. (1987). An attempt to create a new "neighborhood": From suburban isolation to mutual caring. *Social Work with Groups, 10*(3), 55–68.

Mullender, A. (1990). The ebony project—Bicultural groupwork with transracial foster parents. *Social Work with Groups, 13*(4), 23–41.

Muston, R., & Weinstein, J. (1988). Race and groupwork: Some experiences in practice and training. *Groupwork, 1,* 30–40.

Northen, H. (1990). Foreword: Ethnicity and biculturalism: Emerging
    perspectives of social group work. *Social Work with Groups, 13*(4), xix–xx.
Reid, K. (1988). "But I don't want to lead a group!" Some common problems
    of social workers leading groups. *Groupwork, 2*, 124–134.
Rhule, C. (1988). A group for white women with black children. *Groupwork, 1*,
    41–47.
Robinson, J. B. (1989). Clinical treatment of black families: Issues and strate-
    gies. *Social Work, 34*, 323–329.
Roundtree, R. L. (1991). What's new? *Social Work with Groups, 14*(3), 131–133.
Tsui, P., & Schultz, G. (1988). Ethnic factors in group process: Cultural
    dynamics in multi-ethnic therapy groups. *American Journal of
    Orthopsychiatry, 58*, 136–142.
Tweed, D. L., Goldsmith, H. F., Jackson, D. J., Stiles, D., Rae, D. S., & Kramer,
    M. (1990). Racial congruity as a contextual correlate of mental disorder.
    American Journal of Orthopsychiatry, 60, 392–403.
Van Den Bergh, N. (1990). Managing biculturalism at the workplace: A group
    approach. *Social Work with Groups, 13*(4), 71–84.
Williams, M. (1966). Limitations, fantasies, and security operations of
    beginning group psychotherapists. *International Journal of Group Psycho-
    therapy, 16*, 150–162.
Yalom, I. D. (1966). Problems of neophyte group therapists. *International
    Journal of Social Psychiatry, 12*(1), 52–59.

This chapter was originally published in the March 1995 issue of Social
Work, *vol. 40, pp. 155–167.*

8

The Challenge of Racial Difference: Skills for Clinical Practice

Enola K. Proctor and Larry E. Davis

R ace continues to have significant—sometimes volatile—effects on personal relationships, both in society at large and in professional practice. This reality often surprises and disappoints well-intentioned social workers, many of whom have worked actively for civil rights. Although much progress has been made over the past three decades, serious problems and inequities remain. And just as racial injustice continues to negatively affect the plight of minorities in society, racial tensions continue to impede professional helping endeavors.

This article explores societal factors that contribute to the intrusion of race on personal relationships and identifies three concerns that clients experience about working with racially dissimilar practitioners. Case examples illustrate how these concerns are typically mishandled by practitioners and demonstrate how workers can effectively handle those concerns in ways constructive to the helping endeavor.

SOCIAL CONTEXT OF RACE

A number of factors contribute to the sustainment of race as a salient issue for practice. First, minority groups of color are growing faster than the white American population. During the 1980s the African American population grew by 13 percent, the Native American population by 38 percent, the Hispanic population by 53 percent, and the Asian population by 107 percent (Barringer, 1991). In 1980 one in five Americans was nonwhite; by the end of the century, one of three Americans is expected to be nonwhite (Davis, Haub, & Willette, 1983). As America becomes more diverse, the likelihood that practitioner and client will be of different racial backgrounds increases each year.

Second, despite the growth in their numbers, nonwhites continue to be largely segregated from whites and from mainstream America (Farley, 1991). Although illegal, racial segregation in employment, housing, and education is still more the rule than the exception (Dewart, 1991; Wilson, 1987). By and large whites and nonwhites continue to go to different schools, live in different neighborhoods, attend different churches, and socialize in different parts of the city. Because they live in different worlds, some argue that racial groups have different worldviews (Sue, 1981).

When minority and majority populations do interact, the toll of segregation is apparent in their personal relationships. Those who live separately neither know nor understand each other; in turn, they do not trust one another. White people, in particular, know very little about the social realities of nonwhite cultures. Many white practitioners have virtually no meaningful contact with minorities before seeing them as clients. Although schools of social work provide students with content on minority groups, that exposure is too often superficial and abstract (Proctor & Davis, 1983). Knowledge of the cultural nuances of a people depends on meaningful personal interactions. Thus, cross-racial professional interactions are hampered by the pervasiveness of segregation and separation in society.

Third, historically and at present, majority–minority relationships in the United States are negatively charged. Throughout U.S. history, contact between white and nonwhite groups has been fraught with injustice and exploitation, typically on the part of whites toward nonwhites (Cunningham, 1930a, 1930b; Daniels, 1971; Daniels & Kitano, 1970; Ginsburg, 1962). Awareness of this social–political legacy leaves both groups uncomfortable discussing race. Each fears that acknowledging race and its effects will arouse anger or ill will in the other. In particular, nonwhite people often fear renewed rejection from white people, and white people fear some form of racial retaliation or "reverse discrimination" from nonwhites. Of course, as the economic status of most minority groups and African Americans in particular continues to deteriorate, racial hostility and degradation are perpetuated (Dewart, 1991; Wilson, 1987).

The combination of these social forces may be quite ominous for personal and professional cross-racial interactions. Although economic problems are likely to increase the numbers of minority group members who need social work services, the white professionals who will be asked to help them may have little prior contact with these groups and hence little substantive knowledge of them. At the same time, minorities are apt to be increasingly distrustful of representatives from "the system." As a worst-case scenario, society may confront increasing numbers of minority clients who must be helped by white practitioners who understand too little about them and for whom their clients have too little trust.

RACE IN HELPING RELATIONSHIPS

The interpersonal relationship is widely viewed as a key ingredient in professional helping (Derlega, Hendrick, Winstead, & Berg, 1991; Proctor, 1982). The helping literature takes "as a given that therapeutic gain, broadly construed . . . is based on a significant relationship with another person, characterized by feelings of mutual respect, acceptance, and liking or positive regard" (Wills, 1982, p. 2). Studies of client perceptions of therapy support the view that the relationship contributes to treatment gain (Ford, 1978; Saltzman, Luetgert, Roth, Creaser, & Howard, 1976; Strupp, 1977).

Yet in cross-racial helping, the professional faces a formidable challenge—the development of a relationship qualitatively different than either party may have previously experienced with a racially dissimilar other.

Until the late 1960s race was largely ignored in the professional literature. Indeed, "color-blind practice" was encouraged as an attempt to avoid racial bias. Commonly, professionals denied awareness of, or feigned blindness to, client race in an attempt to treat minority clients "just like any other" client (Cooper, 1973; Davis & Proctor, 1989; Thomas & Sillen, 1976). Color-blind practice was assumed to control for client–worker racial differences, to foster the conveyance of "true regard" for minority clients, and to ensure that all clients were treated equally. The acknowledgment of racial difference was seen as akin to racism.

However well intentioned, color-blind practice is associated with a number of negative consequences. First, such practice is unrealistic. Race, reflected in skin color, is readily apparent and cannot be easily ignored. Studies show that children become aware of racial difference by the age of four or five years (Goodman, 1952). Thus, color-blind practice is based on the pretense of the nonexistence of the obvious.

Second, ignoring race is potentially destructive because that which is ignored is, in fact, a major element in the client's self-definition and social reality. As Griffith (1977) noted, the "any other client" ideal in color-blind practice is really any other white client. "Color-blind" workers are left with an unrealistic, abstract view of their clients and their problems. The pretense of color blindness curtails the practitioner's ability to question and the client's ability to disclose, thereby constraining the helping relationship. Finally, color-blind practice is escapist, enabling professionals to avoid both the cognitive and affective components of America's racial turmoil. The color-blind professional is excused from confronting racial injustice and its impact on the client's social reality.

Clients want therapeutic relationships in which they feel understood, in which they trust their workers, and in which they have confidence in the worker's ability (Frank, 1961). The professional must establish credibility and trust (Brody, 1987) and, through words and actions, address and move beyond the client's race-related concerns.

How are such qualities achieved, given the social context of cross-race relationships? With what baggage do clients approach cross-racial professional relationships? How do workers' prior experiences hinder their efforts? What professional skills are necessary?

CLIENT CONCERNS AND WORKER SKILLS

Is the Helper a Person of Goodwill?

The most widespread concern of minority clients working with majority workers is fear that the worker harbors ill will toward members of their race. Such concerns are rooted, in part, in the racism and disrespect that minority group members experience every day.

Clients manifest this concern in many ways. The wary client will closely observe the worker's actions and listen carefully to the words. Clients will easily discern negative feelings or attitudes. Although workers' negative perceptions of clients (Wills, 1978) are not limited to cross-racial situations, these all-too-common behaviors carry special significance to the minority client, who often experiences a lack of goodwill and respect in everyday life and for whom the helping relationship should be qualitatively different.

Not infrequently, practitioners convey—albeit inadvertently—a lack of goodwill toward their clients, as in the following exchange:

> Worker: Come in, Mary, and have a seat. I'll be with you in just a minute.

After shuffling a few papers out of the way and answering a phone call, the worker turns to the client and says,

> Worker: Now, let's see. How can I help you? What brings you here today?

> Client: Well, as I already told the receptionist when I called, I've been having some problems. Were you expecting me, or are you busy? I thought this was the time I was supposed to come.

> Worker: Oh, it is. It's just been one of those days. I hope we don't have any more interruptions. Go ahead, what were you saying? What brings you here?

In the haste and interruptions of a busy day, the worker has failed to focus on the client and the client's problems. Several behaviors have conveyed a lack of attention to and respect for the client; those behaviors include calling the client by her first name, not being ready to immediately attend to the client, allowing the session to be disrupted by a phone call, appearing distracted after the client enters the office, and ignoring the client's attention to her distraction.

Each of these actions is undesirable regardless of client race. Research has confirmed the importance of goodwill and respect for work with all clients. Studies show that such perception enhances the client's desire to work with the helper (Hollander-Goldfein, Fosshage, & Bahr, 1989), increases the client's liking for the worker (Hollander-Goldfein et al., 1989), and contributes to client trust (LaFromboise & Dixon, 1981; Roll, Schmidt, & Kaul,

1972). Of course, trust has long been recognized for its important role in the helping relationship; empirical findings demonstrate that clients who trust their worker are more likely to continue in treatment (Terrell & Terrell, 1984), to self-explore and self-disclose, to be susceptible to the helper's influence (Roll et al., 1972), and to make greater treatment progress (Okun, 1976; Patterson, 1985).

Respect and professional courtesy are particularly important with minority clients, to whom society frequently gives less. That minority clients have difficulty trusting white social workers and that lack of trust impedes effective helping are widely acknowledged in the practice literature. Minority clients who are mistrustful of their white practitioners are apt to hold negative expectations of counseling, are more likely to view their white counselors as less helpful (Watkins, Terrell, Miller, & Terrell, 1989), and are at greater risk of dropping out of treatment (Terrell & Terrell, 1984). With minority clients, the professional needs to send clear signals of respect and positive regard.

Signals of respect and goodwill may be conveyed in several ways. Social workers are advised to extend a warm greeting to the client, to move physical barriers that inhibit communication out of the client's way, and to address the client by his or her last name. The client should be given an opportunity to get settled before the worker begins to talk. Privacy should be maximized, and the worker should appear unhurried with the client and refer to the shortage of time only in the final minutes of the session (Johnson & Fawcett, 1987; LaFromboise & Dixon, 1981). These principles are reflected in the following example:

> Worker: Good morning, Mrs. Williams. Please come in and have a seat where you'll be comfortable. May I take your coat? I've been looking forward to seeing you today. I know from the receptionist's notes that you called last week for an appointment. I hope that waiting until today to see me hasn't been a problem.

Such remarks convey that the worker is prepared for the client, has reviewed available information, and is concerned for the client's convenience. Respect can be further conveyed by briefly describing the helping process to the client and providing a rationale for asking questions. For example, the worker might explain,

> Worker: Today I'll want to understand what brings you to
> our agency. I want you to have plenty of opportunity to tell
> me about your situation and concerns, but I will probably
> ask you some questions to be sure that I understand your
> needs as clearly as possible. Does that sound OK to you?

Providing a rationale for questioning is particularly important in cross-racial situations, as historically minorities have had to protect themselves from potential white abuses by engaging in what is referred to as "healthy paranoia" (Grier & Cobbs, 1968).

Both what the worker says and how it is said contribute to the client's perception of goodwill. Selective and appropriate worker self-disclosure can produce a mutual, rather than imbalanced, expectation of information sharing and contribute to a sense of goodwill toward the client. Maintaining topic consistency, paraphrasing accurately, assuring confidentiality, and providing follow-up to the client's comments affirm the worker's sincere interest in the client (LaFromboise & Dixon, 1981). Minority clients are likely to be particularly sensitive to the degree of congruence between a worker's verbal and nonverbal messages.

Physical cues are particularly important. The worker can convey genuine interest and trustworthiness by moving toward the client; by maintaining an upright, relaxed posture; and through affirmative head nods and eye contact (Johnson & Fawcett, 1987; LaFromboise & Dixon, 1981). On the other hand, maintaining an excessively casual posture, leaning away from the client, occupying oneself with other work, or tapping a pencil contribute to the perception of lack of interest.

Roll, Schmidt, and Kaul (1972) offered the following definition of trustworthiness: "A trustworthy person respects your needs and feelings. You believe that the information and opinions he offers are true and for your own good, rather than for some selfish purposes. . . . You feel sure he would never use the information against you. He has no hidden purpose in what he says and does, but instead is open and honest" (p. 538). LaFromboise and Dixon (1981) suggested that racial similarity between helper and client may be less important than the worker's level of skill in using culturally appropriate communicative and trustworthy behaviors in the interview. Social workers should be encouraged that the behaviors associated with perceived counselor trustworthiness can be learned, and workers can be trained to work with dissimilar clients.

Is the Help Offered Valid and Meaningful to Me?

A second concern often experienced by clients in cross-racial help-ing is whether their social reality is understood and appreciated by the helper. The client may wonder, "Does the practitioner have sufficient knowledge of my world to be of real assistance to me?"

The most likely target of this question is the white professional working with the minority client. Although failure to understand clients is a problem for both white and nonwhite practitioners, those at greatest risk are white practitioners, most of whom do, in fact, have limited experience with minority communities, cul-tures, and concerns. In contrast, minority practitioners have been required to learn, through their life experiences as minority group members, a great deal about white Americans. Thus, indepen-dent of other concerns about the helper's goodwill or skill level, the skeptical minority client may say, "Yes, my practitioner is a person of goodwill—well meaning and genuinely trying to help me—and yes, my practitioner is professionally trained, but what does this white person know about being a minority in America?" In this instance, the client worries less about the practitioner's doing any harm than about whether the worker will be able to do any good because he or she lacks knowledge of the client's culture. Such skepticism is healthy in that it has contributed to the survival of minorities in America.

Social workers display their lack of understanding of clients' social realities in many ways. A basic part of the failure to under-stand the client's social reality is the failure to understand the client's language and what various expressions and terms mean to him or her. Not surprisingly, most practitioners may attempt to hide the fact that they are often ignorant about the culture, values, and norms that are expressed through the client's ver-nacular. Although the practitioner may mean well, fear of losing professional credibility leads to a reluctance to acknowledge lack of understanding of what the client says, means, or experiences in day-to-day life. Yet such attempts are likely to backfire as the client recognizes the worker's pretense, and the lack of credibil-ity becomes compounded by the worker's pretense and failure to confront his or her own ignorance of the client's world.

The following scenario illustrates a white worker's lack of com-prehension of a black client's language and subsequent attempts to gloss over this basic misunderstanding:

> Client: Like I was saying, Fred, I miss my main squeeze very much even though I've got so many hammers after me.

> Worker: Well, Joe, it sounds like you're in good spirits. I am surprised in light of the fact that last week you were unhappy over your wife leaving you. Are you feeling better because of the woodworking you're doing?

This worker did not understand what the client said—that the client misses his wife, despite the fact that a number of other females ("hammers") are pursuing him.

Given the continuing legacy of segregation in society, failure to understand language and cultural nuances across racial boundaries should not be surprising. Yet understanding the client and the client's social reality may be one of the most critical issues in cross-racial practice (Sue, 1981). As the above example makes apparent, misunderstanding words and symbols, as well as the meaning of certain behaviors, of racially dissimilar clients is a serious liability. Failure to understand can damage the likelihood of continued participation by the client. The client may conclude that the practitioner is not listening, is not very smart after all, or does not care enough to try to understand. Consequently, the helping effort may be dismissed as futile or irrelevant.

The worker's efforts to understand the client can be communicated in several ways. First, the worker should acknowledge immediately any difficulty in hearing or comprehending the client. The conversation can be interrupted politely, so that clarification can be sought. The worker can indicate to the client his or her failure to understand what the client said or meant. For example, the worker might have said:

> Worker: Just a minute, Joe. I think that I might have missed something here. Perhaps you'll be good enough to explain to me one more time what you meant. In particular, what did you say about hammers—are you making something?

Such a question does reflect some ignorance on the practitioner's part. But more importantly, it also signals to the client that the practitioner is listening and is trying to better understand. The worker might also have acknowledged that it seemed to him that the comment about hammers did not seem to follow their earlier discussions. This addition emphasizes that the client's earlier comments were heard and remembered.

Although it may be somewhat humbling, or even embarrassing, to the practitioner, willingness to admit ignorance about something the client has said or done is extremely important. The interruption may momentarily disrupt the flow of communication, but it will benefit the helping process in the long run. This may be a very difficult piece of advice to accept. In response to such advice, most white people counter, "Why acknowledge ignorance? Why raise the racial issue if the client has not?" Workers often believe that it is important to act professional or all-knowing.

Acknowledging unfamiliarity with the client's language or culture may threaten professional identity. Yet by acknowledging misunderstanding or failure to comprehend, the worker is likely to enhance the level of rapport with the client. The worker's honesty and genuine interest in the client are conveyed. The worker shows no need to be a know-it-all and demonstrates a willingness to receive help from the client as well as to offer it.

According to studies, rapport with a different-race client is likely to increase as workers gain interracial experience (Heffernon & Bruehl, 1971; Phillips, 1960). Workers should assume, therefore, as they increase their exposure to racially dissimilar clients, that scenarios such as the one above will occur less frequently.

Is the Helper Trained and Skilled?

A third concern common to clients in cross-racial helping situations pertains to the worker's training and skill. This concern leads the client to wonder, "Does the worker have professional expertise or mastery of skills that can resolve my problems? Is this worker adequately skilled or trained as a practitioner?"

Like the two other concerns, this issue also comes with considerable sociopolitical history: It is rooted in the context of segregation and mistrust. This concern is somewhat different, however, in that minority professionals working with majority clients are most likely to experience it. The historic underrepresentation of minorities among professionals results in the general expectation—among both black and white clients—that professionals will be white (Proctor & Rosen, 1981). Such expectations are based in part on reality, as minorities continue to be underrepresented in the social work and counseling professions.

Yet another source of such expectations is racial bias. In U.S. society, race has been consistently associated with status. Over time and over situations, minorities of color have tended to occupy roles of lower status. Unfortunately, such repeated observations contribute to an expectation that race and status are associated for individuals.

In a comparable analysis of the role of gender bias in society, Kiesler (1975) labeled cognitive bias based on past information about a group "actuarial prejudice." Although based on past observations, actuarial prejudice leads to expectations of present or future inferior performance. Gender and race become cues for status. Observation of an individual's race leads to assumptions and conclusions about that individual's status. So consistent has been the pattern between race and status in U.S. society that we often depend on race as a cue for status. The minority professional, then, presents a status incongruence: The high status accorded on the basis of professional training is incongruent with the low status as a function of race.

White clients—and some minority clients, too—may respond to minority professionals with surprise and skepticism; they may even challenge the minority professional's competence. Such reactions may be thinly veiled in questions about the worker's training, education, and experience. And without preparation for the situation, the minority professional may become defensive and respond with discomfort, anxiety, and negative feelings toward client:

> Worker: Good morning, Mrs. Simmons. Please come in and have a seat. I've been looking forward to meeting you. As you may remember, I was the intake worker you spoke with Monday on the phone. I know that you were feeling quite upset that day about your conflict with your daughter; you seemed to feel you didn't know where to turn for help. I'm glad to meet you so that we could have a chance to talk in person about your situation.
>
> Client: Oh, so that was you on the phone? I remember you said you would see me today, but when I saw you, I didn't realize that you were the same Mrs. Randolph.
>
> Worker: Yes, I'm the same one. I'm the only Mrs. Randolph who works here. Didn't I say that I would be meeting with you today?

Client: Yes, but, well, I guess I'm surprised. I thought maybe you were the receptionist but didn't expect you to be the real worker, you know?

Worker: Well, there's no need to be surprised, since I told you that I'd see you. Now, let's see, what were you telling me about your problem with your daughter?

In her frustration at the client's reaction to meeting her in person and discovering her race, the worker has failed to focus on the underlying issue—the client's challenge to her competence.

The client's perception that the worker is competent has consequences far beyond the worker's own comfort level. Research findings suggest that clients who view their helpers as competent are more likely to trust the worker (Hollander-Goldfein et al., 1989; Kaul & Schmidt, 1971; Roll et al., 1972; Strong & Schmidt, 1970a, 1970b), are more likely to be influenced by the worker (Stoltenberg, Pace, & Maddux, 1986), are more likely to continue in treatment (Stoltenberg et al., 1986), and are more likely to expect treatment to have a positive effect on the presenting problem (Strong & Dixon, 1971). In short, a perception of worker competence appears to be critical to the success of the helping endeavor.

Social workers may wish that clients came to helping situations already accepting their competence. Yet workers may have to deliberately work toward a perception of their competence, particularly when perceptions are affected by societally based racial biases.

Signals of competence may be conveyed in several ways. Studies show that a worker's competence can be conveyed through the position of a desk and chairs, the attractiveness of the meeting space, the display of diplomas and professional certificates, and journals and books on the shelves (Bloom, Weigel, & Trautt, 1977; Heppner & Pew, 1977; Siegel & Sell, 1978). Professional dress and deportment also may be helpful (Kerr & Dell, 1976). Studies also point to the importance of "reputational cues," or the cues given by others about a worker's competence (Atkinson & Carskaddon, 1975; Strong & Schmidt, 1970a, 1970b), highlighting the importance of mutual respect among agency staff, particularly with respect to minority colleagues.

The social worker's own confidence is also important. Helpers should be both attentive to their clients and confident—

unhalting—in their responses (Sprafkin, 1970). The worker who can direct and structure the session, who is willing to answer appropriate questions about her background and training, and who can address even sensitive issues of racism or prejudice is likely to enhance the client's perception of his or her competence. These approaches to enhancing the client's perception of credibility are illustrated in the following scenario:

> Client: So you're the therapist, and not just a receptionist who screens calls and all that? How long have you been working here?

> Worker: Yes, I'm a therapist. I've been a social worker here for five years.

> Client [Looking around, noticing the worker's framed degrees, neat and tidy office, and shelved journals]: I see. Did you go to school and all? I mean, do you have much training? Are those your degrees?

> Worker: Yes, Mrs. Simmons, I'm professionally trained and licensed as a social worker. In addition to my college degree, I have a master's degree from the graduate school of social work. I'm wondering if you are concerned about my training and my ability to help you with your situation?

> Client: Well, I was just sort of surprised . . . you know, you seem different than I expected. I guess that from talking to you over the phone, I didn't expect you to be so, well, you know, so . . . so . . . young?

> Worker: Thank you for the compliment. Some days I don't feel so young. Actually, I've been working in this field for 15 years, five at this agency. I supervise, as well as help people like yourself who are experiencing conflicts with their children. Also, I teach courses in child development part-time at the university. In fact, parent–child relationships are my area of specialty. But of course, the really important issue is whether I can be helpful to you, Mrs. Simmons. I sense some concern on your part. You said you were surprised at meeting me. I wonder if you're surprised also that I'm African American?

> Client: Oh, no. Well, maybe. You didn't sound black. I mean, I guess I just assumed that you would be white. I mean, you were so well spoken and all. Oh, I didn't mean that you

wouldn't be educated and trained and all. Oh, I don't know what I mean. . . . Did you say you have kids of your own?

Worker: Yes, I do have children. And I enjoy working with parents and their children. I find that usually we can be help-ful in working toward better ways of communicating. I hope you'll find that we're able to work together well. If at any point, you feel that someone else would be better able to help you, I hope you'll let me know. I could arrange to transfer you to another worker. I'll tell you what. If at the end of our time together today you think you'd prefer another worker, I'll be happy to arrange that. But we seemed to understand each other so well over the phone, and I think we can work well together. If it's agreeable to you, I suggest that we give ourselves a chance today to work together in person. I'm ea-ger to work with you and see if I can't help you. Are you willing to give us a chance today?

Client: Yes, let's do. You know, I've been thinking about some of the questions you asked me Monday, and I realized some things about the problem with my daughter. . . .

This worker has conveyed her competence through professional deportment, through her self-confidence, and through her will-ingness to directly address the client's concerns about her race. Studies suggest that initial encounters have the greatest effect on the development of rapport and continued interaction (Mizio, 1972; Newcomb, 1947; Weissman, Geanakoplos, & Prusott, 1973). Fortunately, repeated contact itself appears to foster in-creased positive feelings (Zajonc, 1968). Hence, workers who are able to foster initial positive encounters also improve their prob-abilities of sustaining their cross-racial encounters. The above vignette illustrates how a worker and client might move beyond the initial issue of their racial difference to focus on the client's problem.

CONCLUSION

Racial difference poses formidable challenges to the helping rela-tionship. Often, the racially dissimilar social worker and client approach each other with little understanding of each other's social realities and with unfounded assumptions and unrealistic expec-tations. Unfortunately, they are rarely willing to acknowledge such differences or their potential effect on their relationship.

Yet the quality of their interaction and the fruitfulness of their work depends on their ability to develop and invest in a trusting, open relationship. Although it is clear that race affects the process of helping, there is no conclusive evidence that racial dissimilarity necessarily impairs treatment outcome (Davis & Proctor, 1989). In fact, there is evidence that experienced, sensitive, and skilled practitioners can work effectively with racially dissimilar clients.

Practitioners should appreciate that the stresses associated with racial dissimilarity are rooted in society. They should critically examine the breadth of their own exposure to minority communities and cultures. When that exposure is limited, they should seek and obtain interethnic experiences. Their own clients should not bear the burden of educating their workers about the realities of racial injustice. Social workers should be informed, should be exposed to other ethnic cultures and histories, and should be comfortable with difference.

Yet the social worker's responsibility extends beyond personal comfort with racially dissimilar clients. The professional also should aim to make the client sufficiently comfortable that racial difference can be acknowledged and that concerns about goodwill, understanding, and competence can be expressed. The professional is responsible for acquiring skills to enhance client comfort, to foster trust, to convey understanding, to communicate professional competence, and to express caring and goodwill. Such skills are essential for effectiveness in clinical practice.

REFERENCES

Atkinson, D. R., & Carskaddon, G. (1975). A prestigious introduction, psychological jargon, and perceived counselor credibility. *Journal of Counseling Psychology, 22,* 180–186.

Barringer, F. (1991, March). Census shows profound change in racial makeup of the nation: Shift toward minorities since 1980 is sharpest. *New York Times,* pp. A-1, A-8.

Bloom, L. J., Weigel, R. G., & Trautt, G. M. (1977). Therapeugenic factors in psychotherapy: Effects of office decor and subject–therapist sex pairing on the perception of credibility. *Journal of Consulting and Clinical Psychology, 45,* 867–873.

Brody, C. M. (1987). White therapist and female minority clients: Gender and culture issues. *Psychotherapy, 24,* 108–113.

Cooper, S. (1973). A look at the effect of racism on clinical work. *Social Casework, 54,* 76–84.

Cunningham, H. (1930a). A history of the Cherokee Indians. *Chronicles of Oklahoma, 8*(3), 291–314.

Cunningham, H. (1930b). A history of the Cherokee Indians. *Chronicles of Oklahoma, 8*(4), 409–440.

Daniels, R. (1971). *Concentration camps U.S.A.: Japanese Americans and World War II.* New York: Holt, Rinehart & Winston.

Daniels, R., & Kitano, H. (1970). *American racism.* Englewood Cliffs, NJ: Prentice Hall.

Davis, C., Haub, C., & Willette, J. (1983). U.S. Hispanics–Changing the race of America. *Population Bulletin, 38,* 38–41.

Davis, L. E., & Proctor, E. K. (1989). *Race, gender, and class: Guidelines for practice with individuals, families, and groups.* Englewood Cliffs, NJ: Prentice Hall.

Derlega, V., Hendrick, S., Winstead, B., & Berg, J. (1991). *Psychotherapy as a personal relationship.* New York: Guilford Press.

Dewart, J. (Ed.). (1991). *The state of black America.* New York: National Urban League.

Farley, R. (1991). *Racial conflict and ethnic issues in the United States: The melting pot and the color line.* Unpublished manuscript, University of Michigan, Populations Studies Center, Ann Arbor.

Ford, J. D. (1978). Therapeutic relationship in behavior therapy: An empirical analysis. *Journal of Consulting and Clinical Psychology, 46,* 1302–1314.

Frank, J. D. (1961). *Persuasion and healing.* Baltimore: Johns Hopkins University Press.

Ginsburg, R. (1962). *One hundred years of lynchings.* New York: Lancer Books.

Goodman, M. (1952). *Race consciousness in young children.* Cambridge, MA: Addison-Wesley Press.

Grier, W., & Cobbs, P. (1968). *Black rage.* New York: Bantam Books.

Griffith, M. S. (1977). The influences of race on the psychotherapeutic relationship. *Psychiatry, 40*(1), 27–40.

Heffernon, A., & Bruehl, D. (1971). Some effects of race of inexperienced lay counselors on black junior high school students. *Journal of School Psychology, 9,* 35–37.

Heppner, P. P., & Pew, S. (1977). Effects of diplomas, awards, and counselor sex on perceived expertness. *Journal of Counseling Psychology, 24,* 184–190.

Hollander-Goldfein, B., Fosshage, J. L., & Bahr, J. M. (1989). Determinants of patients' choice of therapist. *Psychotherapy, 26,* 448–461.

Johnson, M. D., & Fawcett, S. B. (1987). Consumer-defined standards for courteous treatment by service agencies. *Journal of Rehabilitation, 53,* 23–26.

Kaul, T. J., & Schmidt, L. D. (1971). Dimensions of interviewer trustworthiness. *Journal of Counseling Psychology, 18,* 542–548.

Kerr, B. A., & Dell, D. M. (1976). Perceived interviewer expertness and attractiveness: Effects of interviewer behavior and attire and interview setting. *Journal of Counseling Psychology, 23,* 553–556.

Kiesler, S. (1975). Actuarial prejudice toward women and its implications. *Journal of Applied Social Psychology, 5*(3), 201–216.

LaFromboise, T. D., & Dixon, D. N. (1981). American Indian perception of trustworthiness in a counseling interview. *Journal of Counseling Psychology, 28*, 135–139.

Mizio, E. (1972). White worker–minority client. *Social Work, 17*, 82–86.

Newcomb, T. (1947). Autistic hostility and social reality. *Human Relations, 1*, 69–87.

Okun, B. F. (1976). *Effective helping: Interviewing and counseling techniques.* North Scituate, MA: Duxbury.

Patterson, C. H. (1985). *The therapeutic relationship: Foundations for an eclectic psychotherapy.* Monterey, CA: Brooks/Cole.

Phillips, W. (1960). Counseling Negro pupils: An educational dilemma. *Journal of Negro Education, 29*, 504–507.

Proctor, E. K. (1982). Defining the worker–client relationship. *Social Work, 27*, 430–435.

Proctor, E. K., & Davis, L. E. (1983). Minority content in social work education: A question of objectives. *Journal of Education for Social Work, 19*(2), 85–93.

Proctor, E. K., & Rosen, A. (1981). Expectations and preferences for counselor race and their relation to intermediate treatment outcomes. *Journal of Counseling Psychology, 28*, 40–46.

Roll, W. V., Schmidt, L. D., & Kaul, T. J. (1972). Perceived interviewer trustworthiness among black and white convicts. *Journal of Counseling Psychology, 19*, 537–541.

Saltzman, C., Luetgert, M. J., Roth, C. H., Creaser, J., & Howard, L. (1976). Formation of a theraputic relationship: Experienced during the initial phase of psychotherapy as predictors of treatment duration and outcome. *Journal of Consulting and Clinical Psychology, 44*, 546–555.

Siegel, J. C., & Sell, J. M. (1978). Effects of objective evidence of expertness and nonverbal behavior on client perceived expertness. *Journal of Counseling Psychology, 25*, 188–192.

Sprafkin, R. P. (1970). Communicator expertness and changes in word meaning in psychological treatment. *Journal of Counseling Psychology, 17*, 191–196.

Stoltenberg, C. D., Pace, T., & Maddux, J. E. (1986). Cognitive style and counselor credibility: Effects on client endorsement of rational emotive therapy. *Cognitive Therapy and Research, 10*(2), 237–243.

Strong, S. R., & Dixon, D. N. (1971). Expertness, attractiveness, and influence in counseling. *Journal of Counseling Psychology, 18*, 562–570.

Strong, S. R., & Schmidt, L. D. (1970a). Expertness and influence in counseling. *Journal of Counseling Psychology, 17*, 81–87.

Strong, S. R., & Schmidt, L. D. (1970b). Trustworthiness and influence in counseling. *Journal of Counseling Psychology, 17*, 197–204.

Strupp, H. H. (1977). *A reformulation of the dynamics of the therapist's contribution.* In A. S. Gurman & A. M. Razin (Eds.), Effective psychotherapy: A handbook of research. (pp. 1–22). New York: Pergamon Press.

Sue, D. W. (1981). *Counseling the culturally different: Theory and practice.* New York: John Wiley & Sons.

Terrell, F., & Terrell, S. L. (1984). Race of counselor, client sex, cultural mistrust, and premature termination from counseling among black clients. *Journal of Counseling Psychology, 31*, 371–375.

Thomas, A., & Sillen, S. (1976). *Racism and psychiatry*. Secaucus, NJ: Citadel Press.

Watkins, C. E., Jr., Terrell, F., Miller, F. S., & Terrell, S. L. (1989). Cultural mistrust and its effects on expectational variables in black client–white counselor relationships. *Journal of Counseling Psychology, 36*, 447–450.

Weissman, M., Geanakoplos, E., & Prusott, B. (1973). Social class and attrition in depressed outpatients. *Social Casework, 54*, 162–170.

Wills, T. A. (1978). Perceptions of clients by professional helpers. *Psychological Bulletin, 85*, 968–1000.

Wills, T. A. (1982). *A study of helping relationships*. In T. A. Wills (Ed.), Basic processes in helping relationships (pp. 1–12). New York: Academic Press.

Wilson, J. (1987). *The truly disadvantaged*. Chicago: University of Chicago Press.

Zajonc, R. (1968). Attitudinal effects of mere exposure. *Journal of Personality and Social Psychology, 9*, 1–27.

This chapter was originally published in the May 1994 issue of Social Work, *vol. 39, pp. 314–323.*

Part II

LAW AND POLICY

9 Immigration Statuses and Their Influence on Service Provision, Access, and Use

Diane Drachman

Although the U.S. Bureau of the Census does not obtain information on immigration, it does provide statistics on the foreign-born population in the United States. According to the 1970 U.S. census, 9,619,302 foreign-born individuals were residing in the United States (U.S. Bureau of the Census, 1970). By 1980, 14,079,906 foreign-born individuals were living in the United States (U.S. Bureau of the Census, 1980), and by 1990, the number of foreign-born people residing in the United States was 19,767,316 (U.S. Bureau of the Census, 1990). Therefore, the newcomer population increased 46 percent between 1970 and 1980 and 40.4 percent between 1980 and 1990. One demographer stated, "Immigration to the United States has reached levels not attained since early in this century" (Bouvier, 1981, p. 1), and it is estimated that 33 percent to 40 percent of the nation's population growth is attributable to immigration (Suro, 1991).

Unlike the mass migration that occurred early in the century, when most people came from Europe, recent newcomers have been arriving mainly from Asia, the West Indies, Central America, the Middle East, Eastern Europe, and Africa. There has been considerable growth of the Asian and Latino populations in the United States. In the past decade, the Asian population has more than doubled, and the Latino population grew by more than 50 percent (Butterfield, 1991; Gonzalez, 1991).

The residence patterns of many newcomers have also shifted. For example, before 1980, Asian Americans primarily settled in a few states such as California and Hawaii and in urban centers such as New York City, San Francisco, and Los Angeles (Butterfield, 1991). By the end of the 1980s, the Asian population had settled throughout the nation, and in some states the growth of this population was stunning. The Asian American population in New Jersey increased 162 percent to 272,521, in Texas it increased 165 percent to 319,459, in Rhode Island it increased 245 percent to 18,325, in Alabama it increased 124 percent to 22,000, in Mississippi it increased 76 percent to 13,000, and in Louisiana it increased 73 percent to 41,000 (Butterfield, 1991).

The Asian American population is also diverse in national origin, culture, ethnicity, and social and economic backgrounds. Groups now residing in the United States include Filipinos, Chinese, Vietnamese, Koreans, Japanese, Asian Indians, Cambodians, Laotians, and Pacific Islanders (Butterfield, 1991). The Latino population is also diverse and includes people from Cuba, Mexico, the Dominican Republic, Chile, Columbia, Guatemala, Ecuador, Nicaragua, and El Salvador. Like the Asian American groups, Latino newcomers are spread throughout the nation.

The cultural and ethnic diversity of the new wave of migration is reflected in a section of Los Angeles where Salvadorans, Armenians, Filipinos, Thais, Greeks, Italians, Vietnamese, Tamils from Sri Lanka, and Mixtec Indians from Mexico's Oaxaca Province all live within a few blocks (Mydans, 1991). Thus, the new wave of migration is characterized by people who are diverse in culture, ethnicity, and race, people who have come from all corners of the world and who have settled throughout the nation.

The rise of newcomer populations is evident in the educational, political, and workplace arenas. In the educational arena the increase in school enrollment is attributable in some regions to the influx of foreign-born students (Barron, 1991). In the political arena politicians compete for the support of newcomer constituencies (Crossette, 1988). In the workplace, the U.S. Department of Labor estimates that immigrants will represent 22 percent of the new workers in the labor force by the beginning of the 21st century (Johnston & Packer, 1987). Many will be the adult children of immigrants who arrived in the United States during the 1970s and 1980s.

LEGISLATIVE BACKGROUND

From 1924 to 1965 immigration to the United States was primarily based on the national origins quota system, which, in accordance with the Immigration Act of 1924, limited the yearly quota for each country to 3 percent of the individuals born in that country who were residing in the United States as enumerated in the 1890 census (Briggs, 1984). Because most of the white population in 1890 was of northern or western European ancestry, countries in northern and western Europe received the largest quotas. The system restricted the immigration of people from Asian and Pacific countries and from Eastern and Southern Europe and totally excluded immigrants from Africa (Abrams, 1984; Seller, 1984).

The national origins quota system was a product of racial and ethnic tensions and economic concerns that arose at the turn of the 20th century, when there was unprecedented growth in both the number of immigrants and the mix of nationalities (Levine, Hill, & Warren, 1985). Anti-Asian sentiments in the western United States were strong, and interethnic tensions between newly arrived groups from eastern and southern Europe and the earlier immigrants from northern and western Europe were prominent in the East (Levine et al., 1985). Economic concerns that the new arrivals would take jobs needed by U.S. workers prevailed (Briggs, 1984; Seller, 1984). The hotly debated issue of immigration led Congress to mandate a commission to study immigrants, and the 1911 commission report ultimately supported the popular belief that immigrants from southern and eastern Europe were less adaptable to U.S. society and less desirable than their counterparts from northern and western Europe (Morris, 1985). Although the quota system was modified in 1929 by using the 1920 census as the basis for allocating the flow of immigrants, the system nonetheless continued for approximately 40 years (Briggs, 1984). It exerted both quantitative and qualitative control over immigration by restricting the number of people allowed to enter the country and determining who was permitted entry.

The Immigration and Nationality Act of 1965 (P.L. 89-236) created a major policy shift by abolishing the national origins quota system. This act and the amendments to it in the decades following its passage have been the basis of present immigration policy (Abrams, 1984). Three policy emphases predominated in the 1965 act: (1) restriction on the number of people permitted to enter the country; (2) family reunification (a humanitarian force) that favored the immigration of relatives of U.S. citizens or relatives of individuals who had previously entered as immigrants (family-based immigration); and (3) an economic emphasis, aimed at the labor market, which encouraged individuals with occupational skills deemed needed by the United States and discouraged individuals outside the family reunification preference by requiring them to obtain documentation from the U.S. Department of Labor certifying they were not taking a job from an American (Abrams, 1984). A system of preferences for the admission of newcomers was established, and these preferences reflected both the family reunification and labor market emphases. Percentages were also established for each preference category. In amendments to the Immigration and Nationality Act of 1965, an annual worldwide admission quota was set, all countries were allotted a yearly admission ceiling of 20,000, and a separate admission policy was established for refugees (Briggs, 1984).

Economic and humanitarian issues and immigration control were prominent forces in the Immigration Reform and Control Act of 1986 (IRCA) (P.L. 99-603), commonly referred to as the "amnesty program" (Greenhouse, 1991). The humanitarian force was contained in four legalization programs: (1) amnesty for undocumented people who were living continuously in the United States before 1982; (2) access to permanent legal resident status for Cuban and Haitian entrants provided they were living in the United States before January 1, 1982; (3) access to temporary and later permanent legal resident status for special agricultural workers; and (4) a registry update for documented and undocumented people provided they were living in the United States before January 1, 1972 (Bogen, 1988; Finch, 1990).

Although the legalization programs were important aspects of the law, the legislation was primarily aimed at controlling illegal immigration. The concern about illegal immigration primarily revolved around the view that undocumented people absorb jobs needed by U.S. workers and depress wages. The legislation established a two-pronged strategy to deal with the economic issues: sanctions against employers who knowingly hired undocumented workers and increased border control.

Under the Immigration Act of 1990 (P.L. 101-649), the total number of legal immigrants permitted to enter the United States annually was increased to 700,000. The annual minimum for family-sponsored immigration was raised to 226,000 (Ross, 1991), and annual employment-based immigration was increased to 140,000 (Clark, 1991). Countries that sent relatively few immigrants in recent years obtained 40,000 visas, and 55,000 visas were allocated between 1992 and 1994 for spouses and children of individuals who legalized their status under IRCA (Pear, 1990).

Although this legislation reflected the continued emphasis in immigration policy on family reunification, the impetus for the legislation was primarily economic. Because of projections of a short supply of skilled labor in the 1990s, particularly in the fields of engineering, medicine, and basic science, Congress, the U.S. Department of Labor, and many economists saw legal immigration as a way to correct the imbalance in labor supply and demand (Pear, 1990). Therefore, the 1990 act gave priority to alien workers with extraordinary ability, such as outstanding professors and researchers and multinational executives or managers (Clark, 1991). The act also created an immigrant investor visa under the category of "employment creation" (Chin, 1991, p. 65). The Senate viewed this category as creating employment for U.S. workers and thus bringing new capital into the country (Chin, 1991). The preference system for the allotment of immigrant visas was also changed under this act. Two broad categories of preferences—family sponsored and employment—were developed, and preferences within each of these categories were outlined (Clark & McLaughlin, 1994; Silverman, 1994).

Recurring historic themes in immigration policy surfaced in the debate over the Immigration Act of 1990. The Departments of Labor and Justice as well as the president were concerned that the bill was too "heavily weighted in favor of family-sponsored immigration at the expense of business-sponsored immigration" (Nash, 1990, p. A23). Others questioned how immigration policy would improve the economy because they viewed immigrants as "filling the ranks of those on welfare" (Nash, 1990, p. A23). Embracing educated workers from abroad raised concern that the country was "abandoning inner-city blacks" (Nash, 1990, p. A23). Others suggested that high numbers of immigrants would take jobs from Americans (Nash, 1990).

IMMIGRATION STATUSES

The economic and humanitarian forces and racial issues that emerged in the debate over legislation and that historically have shaped immigration legislation and policy (Seller, 1984) are reflected in the immigration statuses assigned to newcomers. All newcomers to the United States require U.S. government permission to enter the country. The Immigration and Naturalization Service (INS), which implements and enforces immigration policy, assigns the newcomer an immigration status. The varied immigration statuses carry different service entitlements.

Refugee

A *refugee,* as defined by the Refugee Act of 1980 (P.L. 96-212), is a person who is outside of and unable or unwilling to avail himself or herself of the protection of the home country because of persecution or fear of persecution on account of race, religion, nationality, membership in a particular social group, or political opinion. The individual who requests refugee status makes an application from abroad, often from a country of asylum, that the INS accepts or rejects.

Unlike an immigrant, who generally has the opportunity to plan and prepare to leave the native country, the refugee often flees or is forced to leave suddenly and therefore leaves with few possessions. In recognition of this common refugee experience, the Refugee Act of 1980 entitles refugees to special assistance aimed at economic self-sufficiency. Refugees, therefore, receive resettlement services that consist of relocation assistance, financial aid, medical care, English language training, employment and vocational counseling, and job placement for 18 months. Refugees are also entitled to the same services as U.S. citizens, including Supplemental Security Income (SSI), Aid to Families with Dependent Children (AFDC), Medicaid, and food stamps. After one year of residence in the United States, the refugee may adjust the status to immigrant (legal permanent resident). Because the services and entitlements available to refugees are the most generous among the categories of newcomers, the issue of who is accepted as a refugee is central to immigration policy. In addition to humanitarian considerations, the assignment or denial of refugee status often revolves around foreign policy goals and ideological preconceptions, which influence immigration procedures and ultimately access to services. An examination of those individuals accepted and rejected as refugees illustrates the controversy surrounding this status.

Following World War II and during the Cold War era, large groups of people from communist countries were admitted into the United States. The United States responded to uprisings in communist Hungary and Cuba by admitting thousands of people. The Refugee Escapee Act of 1957 narrowly defined a *refugee* as a persecuted person who escaped from a communist country or communist-dominated area or a person who fled the persistent turmoil of the Middle East (Briggs, 1984). A similar definition was used in the Immigration and Nationality Act of 1965 (Briggs, 1984). The United States had a special obligation to countries in Indochina because of the Vietnam War, and the anti-communist theme also played a role in the admission of many refugees from Southeast Asia (Morris, 1985). This trend has continued; one study reported that 94 percent of the 94,505 refugees approved for admission in 1989 came from communist countries (Howe, 1990).

In addition, INS procedures have been different for individuals from communist countries. In accordance with the Refugee Act of 1980, all individuals seeking asylum have been required to demonstrate a well-founded fear of persecution should they return to their native country. However, approval for refugee applications from Soviet Armenians who arrived in the late 1980s was "virtually automatic even though they did not claim persecution when interviewed by the INS" (Taubman, 1988, p. A1). Thus, this group was permitted to bypass the eligibility requirement for refugee status established by law.

Unlike people fleeing persecution from communist countries, Haitians faced detention and deportation and interdiction at sea. Although oppression and persecution of Haitians under the Duvalier regimes were amply documented, the "enormity of human rights violations committed by these regimes and the extent to which they . . . motivated many Haitians to emigrate [was] persistently overlooked by the United States Government" (DeWind, 1990, p. 10). The INS assertion that Haitians were economic migrants rather than refugees has been considered by many as motivated both by a political interest in maintaining Haiti as an ally in its anti-communist foreign policy and by racism (DeWind, 1990). From 1981 to 1989, of the 21,369 Haitians interdicted at sea, only six were permitted entry (Refugee Reports, 1989). Of the Haitians who reached U.S. territory, many were apprehended and placed in detention centers, where they awaited

a decision on deportation or entry. Detention center stays ranged
from months to years. Those who escaped the attention of the
INS were undocumented. Workers in contact with the undocumented Haitian population not only had difficulty obtaining
needed services for their clients but also encountered clients' distrust and wariness of service personnel and institutions, attributable in part to the harsh U.S. reception.

Asylee — Services Limited

An *asylee* is essentially a refugee. The asylee, however, applies
for asylee status from U.S. territory, whereas the refugee applies
for asylum in the United States from another country. The service benefits for an asylee are uncertain, despite the fact that the
definition of refugee and asylee statuses is the same. Moreover,
an individual who applies for asylee status waits a long time for
status determination, and during the wait the individual remains
ineligible for many services.

Parolee

A *parolee* is an individual who is admitted into the United States
under emergency conditions or is admitted if the person's entry
is considered in the public interest. This immigration category
has no relationship to the parole status connected to the correctional system. A parolee enters the country under the U.S. attorney general's parole authority, and thousands have entered the
country under this immigration status. A parolee is not entitled
to federal benefits. Several reasons for the admission under parolee status of emigres from the former Soviet Union in the late
1980s illustrate the political, economic, and humanitarian issues
involved in the assignment of this status.

During the Gorbachev era, a political debate in Congress
emerged, with some members suggesting that recent newcomers
from the Soviet Union could no longer be considered refugees
under the new Soviet policy of openness (Pear, 1989). In line with
this thinking it was increasingly difficult for the U.S. government
to portray citizens of a newly allied country as experiencing persecution. The influx of so many Soviet Jews also raised economic
concerns regarding expenditures for resettlement benefits to which
Soviet emigres would be entitled if they were permitted entry as
refugees. A plan was therefore devised to curb the admission of

Soviet Jews (Pear, 1989). This plan created a controversy in Moscow because all citizens who had received permission to leave the Soviet Union had previously been assured admission into the United States (Cullen, 1988). Moreover, some individuals who had received their exit visas from the Soviet government and followed common procedures associated with departure permission by relinquishing apartments, terminating employment, renouncing Soviet citizenship, and giving up entitlements to housing and medical care found themselves stranded in Moscow as the United States either refused them refugee status or terminated the process of visa applications (Barringer, 1988). To deal with the crisis, the INS permitted some to enter as parolees.

After arrival in the United States, emigres encountered the high costs of housing, utilities, and other services as well as difficulty obtaining work. These circumstances forced some to request services that had been entitlements in the Soviet Union, and it seemed logical to expect similar entitlements in the United States. When workers explained the limitations on U.S. services, the emigres assumed workers were withholding them; this was a common experience with service personnel in the Soviet Union. The parolee–emigres knew compatriots who had received more services than they were able to secure because they had been designated as refugees, and workers were often unable to explain why some emigres had different immigration statuses than others. Reactions among parolee–emigres to this situation included rage, depression, confusion, unrelenting pursuit of workers, persistent demand for services, and a sense of impotence (Drachman & Halberstadt, 1992).

Immigrant

An *immigrant* is an individual lawfully granted permission to permanently reside in the United States. An individual obtains permanent residence in different ways, and service access and entitlements vary in accordance with the way this status is achieved. For example, many individuals seeking permanent residence require sponsorship. A *sponsor* is a person or an organization guaranteeing economic support of the immigrant for the first three years of the immigrant's residence in the United States. Although an immigrant who is sponsored is entitled to many of the services available to citizens (AFDC, food stamps, SSI), eligibility requirements for these entitlements are more restrictive than those applied to citizens. For example, a sponsored immigrant who requests AFDC within the first three years of residency in the United States must qualify based on his or her own income plus the income and resources of the sponsor. In contrast, a citizen qualifies on the basis of his or her own income and resources only.

An individual who becomes an immigrant through adjustment of status from refugee to immigrant has no additional restrictions and is subject to the same service eligibility requirements as those applied to citizens. Other disincentives for service use exist, however; for example, an immigrant who has received welfare funds and who wishes to sponsor the immigration of a family member is likely to be denied sponsorship and immigration of the relative.

Temporary Resident

Temporary residents have legal permission to live and work temporarily in the United States. They are eligible to become permanent residents after a set period and must do so or lose their legal status. Many individuals in this group are undocumented people who legalize their status through the amnesty program established under IRCA. Individuals who become temporary residents through the amnesty program are ineligible for many major federal entitlements for five years following assignment to this status. Thus, a temporary resident who is an unemployed single parent of three children is ineligible for AFDC and food stamps until five years after assignment to this status have lapsed.

Undocumented Person

Undocumented people are individuals who have no current authorization to be in the United States. This group consists of people who enter illegally and people who enter legally under a nonimmigrant status for a temporary period (for example, students or tourists) and who remain in the United States after their visas expire. Undocumented people are subject to deportation. They are ineligible for federally funded cash assistance programs and many other social services.

There is a sizeable undocumented population in the United States. Statistics on the size of this group vary widely, and estimates have ranged from 2 million to 6 million (Brinkley, 1994;

Thornton, 1986). Recently the population has been estimated at 3.85 million (Sontag, 1994). Problems in the counts are numerous. First, there is difficulty in obtaining accurate statistics because undocumented people tend to lead invisible lives for fear of deportation. Second, many of these individuals leave the United States and then return. Third, different political views on the population contribute to exaggeration and underestimation of the count. Fourth, statistical methods used in the counts have been criticized (Hill, 1985). Although more than 3 million undocumented people attempted to legalize their status under IRCA, many did not qualify because they arrived after the January 1, 1982, cutoff date for establishing residency (Greenhouse, 1991). Those who qualified are now either temporary or permanent legal residents and entitled to benefits associated with these immigration statuses. However, the many who did not qualify remain undocumented.

To control illegal immigration the law requires employers to verify citizenship or work authorization papers of all new employees and sanctions individuals or businesses who knowingly hire undocumented people. Thus, undocumented people have major difficulties obtaining work. The wages of undocumented people who are able to secure jobs are often so low that their subsistence is in jeopardy. Some who work in factories earn $2.00 an hour (Gonzalez, 1989), and others make deliveries solely for tips. Moreover, some employers who have chosen to violate the ordinance have decided they can minimize their losses in the event of fines by hiring individuals at the cheapest wage possible (Gonzalez, 1989).

In addition to low wages, the fear of deportation fosters a tendency among undocumented people to avoid needed services such as health care (Gelfand & Bialik-Gilad, 1989). Fear of deportation leads some to avoid the police after having been assaulted (Gonzalez, 1989). Some refuse to report landlords for housing violations, and some keep their children out of school (Gonzalez, 1989).

Undocumented people who seek to obtain legal authorization to live and work in the United States must return to their country of citizenship or legal residence and apply from that country for legal entry into the United States. This procedure separates many families. Furthermore, the wait for legal entry may take years because the annual demand for entry by unskilled workers is greater than the yearly visa allotment for this group.

The following vignette illustrates the influence of policy on the life of an undocumented person and on service provision. Although the example reflects the experience of a single individual, many of the circumstances surrounding the person's life are commonly associated with the undocumented immigration status. A 19-year-old mother lives with her two small children in a shelter for homeless women. The mother arrived in this country when she was 14 with an aunt who was raising her after her mother died. The aunt died in the United States, and her partner did not want to raise the child. The teenager eventually became homeless and later had the two children. Although she is an undocumented person, her children are U.S. citizens because they were born in this country. However, she is ineligible for AFDC, and as a result the shelter receives no reimbursement from AFDC for the care of the family. She cannot obtain work because of her undocumented status, and she is ineligible for public housing. Even if she obtained work, her undocumented status would probably keep her wages down, and there would be no funds for child care.

Undocumented people and service providers alike are often unfamiliar with the rights associated with this status. Undocumented children have the right to public education (Schuck, 1987). Moreover, children who are born on U.S. soil are considered U.S. citizens even if their parents are undocumented (Schuck, 1987). These children are therefore entitled to the rights of all citizens, which implies that in some cases undocumented parents may apply for benefits on behalf of their children (Schuck, 1987). Regional ordinances also influence undocumented peoples' service access, use, and provision. For example, city agencies in New York City are prohibited from submitting information on an individual to federal authorities unless the person committed a crime (Gonzalez, 1989).

Current anti-immigration sentiments, however, are threatening the rights of undocumented people (Hernandez, 1994; Tien, 1994). The passage of California's Proposition 187, which denies most social services to undocumented people including schooling for children and basic health care, reflects that threat. Constitutional issues surrounding Proposition 187 (Ayres, 1994) are likely to be raised in the courts for many years, during which time the rights of this group in California will be uncertain.

IMPLICATIONS FOR SERVICES

Although many of the new arrivals have adapted well to living in the United States, many are in need of services. These service needs have been identified by individuals and organizations in contact with the newcomers and by practitioners in diverse settings such as hospitals and mental health organizations, schools, and workplaces (Drachman & Ryan, 1987). Commonly reported problems include economic hardship, marital discord, depression, wife and child abuse, drug and alcohol abuse, school problems, and parent–child conflict (Drachman & Ryan, 1987). For the undocumented population, problems of extreme poverty, substandard housing, and health care have been cited (Gelfand & Bialik-Gilad, 1989).

Regardless of immigration status, newcomers commonly experience stress (Shuval, 1982). For many the stress involves leaving family, friends, community, and homeland, followed by arriving in a new country, finding housing, learning a new language, adjusting to a new environment, and securing employment. For some, the migration process itself is traumatic, involving abrupt departure from the native country, loss of lives of family members or friends, and experiences of violence followed by living in limbo until reaching the country of final destination (Kinzie, 1985; Westermeyer, 1985). Adjustment is more difficult when the cultures of the countries of origin and destination are very different. The immigration policy of the receiving country may be harsh on the newcomer, thus complicating adjustment (Stepick, 1984).

Knowledge of the regulations and procedures of the INS is necessary to assist and advocate for clients and influence policy. For example, knowledge that there is a long wait for asylees to be granted an INS asylum hearing during which time asylees have limited or no access to services implies a need for advocacy to shorten the wait. Families who are separated due to migration implies the need for knowledge of the preference system used for sponsorship to reunify families. There is a need to influence policy to broaden the U.S. definition of refugee. Critical concepts embedded in the definition are a well-founded fear of persecution and being outside one's country of citizenship. This definition, however, does not include people fleeing poverty, even though it may be as dangerous for these migrants to return to poverty as it would be for others to return to persecution.

Familiarity with the issues surrounding the different immigration statuses and an understanding that entitlements vary from status to status are necessary for effective service delivery. The limited information about newly arrived individuals and groups, the problems associated with the migration process, the entitlements and problems connected to each immigration status, and the paucity of information service providers have about the INS imply a need for the development of programs aimed at gathering information to assist and connect individuals to appropriate resources and services. Such information can be obtained from service organizations familiar with specific groups such as immigrants from the republics of the former Soviet Union; refugees from Southeast Asia; undocumented populations from Nicaragua, El Salvador, Guatemala, Mexico, and countries from Africa and Asia; and children who have been terrorized by war in their native country and who have arrived in the United States as either refugees or undocumented children.

The fear of deportation is a central concern for the undocumented population and fosters avoidance of service systems. This population is therefore at gravest risk because health, economic, housing, and family needs may not be met. However, undocumented people have certain rights and entitlements, and effective service delivery is dependent on familiarity with these rights and entitlements. Advocacy work and contact with lawyers familiar with immigration law may also be necessary to assist individuals in securing a right. Because undocumented people are ineligible for cash assistance programs and many other services, service providers need knowledge of services that exist outside the "mainstream of public social welfare agencies" (Gelfand & Bialik-Gilad, 1989, p. 23). Contact with human rights organizations may be needed to obtain information on further avenues for assistance to this group.

CONCLUSION

World conditions and events such as civil war, famine, war between countries, poverty, oppression, and ethnic conflict create migration and populations of displaced people. The foreign, economic, and domestic policies of each nation-state determine whether displaced populations remain displaced or are permitted entry. International social work in the field of immigration therefore requires an understanding of the interrelationship of the policies and conditions in both sending and receiving countries.

REFERENCES

Abrams, F. S. (1984). American immigration policy: How strait the gate? In R. R. Hofstetter (Ed.), *U.S. immigration policy* (pp. 107–136). Durham, NC: Duke University Press.

Ayres, D. (1994, October 22). Feinstein faults aliens proposal. *New York Times*, p. A1.

Barringer, F. (1988, July 14). Ire in Moscow at Americans on visa delay. *New York Times*, p. A9.

Barron, J. (1991, March 28). Sudden jump in school rolls may be trend. *New York Times*, p. B1.

Bogen, E. (1988). *The Immigration Reform and Control Act of 1986: Its effects on New York City and on city government.* New York: Department of City Planning, City of New York, Office of Immigrant Affairs.

Bouvier, L. (1981). *Immigration and its impact on U.S. society.* Washington, DC: Population Reference Bureau.

Briggs, V. M. (1984). *Immigration policy and the American labor force.* Baltimore: Johns Hopkins University Press.

Brinkley, J. (1994, October 15). California's woes on aliens appear self-inflicted. *New York Times*, p. A1.

Butterfield, F. (1991, February 24). Asians spread across a land and help change it. *New York Times*, p. A22.

Chin, F. E. (1991). Immigrant investor visas. In *Immigration Act of 1990* (91-14.01, pp. 65–98). Boston: Massachusetts Continuing Legal Education.

Clark, S. (1991). Summary of employment-based immigrant provisions: Immigration Act of 1990. In *Immigration Act of 1990* (91-14.01, pp. 23–48). Boston: Massachusetts Continuing Legal Education.

Clark, S., & McLaughlin, M. (1994). Employment-based immigrant visas. In *Immigration law basics* (95-14.02, pp. 161–209). Boston: Massachusetts Continuing Legal Education.

Crossette, B. (1988, June 11). U.S. legislators and aid group going to Hanoi. *New York Times*, p. A11.

Cullen, R. (1988, November 30). For a quiet deal on Soviet emigrants. *New York Times*, p. A31.

DeWind, J. (1990). Haitian boat people in the United States: Background for social service providers. In D. Drachman (Ed.), *Social services to refugee populations* (pp. 7–56). Washington, DC: National Institute of Mental Health.

Drachman, D., & Halberstadt, A. (1992). A stage of migration framework as applied to recent Soviet emigres. *Journal of Multicultural Social Work, 2,* 63–78.

Drachman, D., & Ryan, A. S. (1987). Social work practice with refugee populations: Curriculum development in social work education. In D. Drachman & A. Ryan (Eds.), *Final report to National Institute of Mental Health* (pp. 43–61). Washington, DC: U.S. Department of Health and Human Services.

Finch, W. (1990). The Immigration Reform and Control Act of 1986: A preliminary assessment. *Social Service Review, 64,* 245–260.

Gelfand, D., & Bialik-Gilad, R. (1989). Immigration reform and social work. *Social Work, 34,* 23–27.

Gonzalez, D. (1989, May 19). Poor and illegal Mexicans lose hope in New York. *New York Times,* p. B1.

Gonzalez, D. (1991, May 26). Hispanic voters struggle to find strength in their numbers. *New York Times,* p. B3.

Greenhouse, L. (1991, February 20). High court rules aliens can sue over procedures in amnesty law. *New York Times,* p. A4.

Hernandez, R. (1994, June 11). Illegal immigrants don't get benefits. *Hartford Courant,* p. E8.

Hill, K. (1985). Illegal aliens: An assessment. In D. Levine, K. Hill, & R. Warren (Eds.), *Immigration statistics: A story of neglect* (pp. 225–250). Washington, DC: National Academy Press.

Howe, M. (1990, March 16). Study asks new safeguards for refugees seeking asylum. *New York Times,* p. A11.

Immigration Act of 1924, 43 Stat. 153.

Immigration Act of 1990, P.L. 101-649, 104 Stat. 4978.

Immigration and Nationality Act of 1965, P.L. 89-236, 79 Stat. 911–920, 922.

Immigration Reform and Control Act of 1986, P.L. 99-603, 100 Stat. 3359.

Johnston, W., & Packer, A. (1987). *Workplace 2000: Work and workers for the 21st century.* Indianapolis: Hudson Institute.

Kinzie, J. D. (1985). Overview of clinical issues in the treatment of Southeast Asian refugees. In T. C. Owan (Ed.), *Southeast Asian mental health: Treatment, prevention, services, training, and research* (pp. 113–135). Washington, DC: U.S. Department of Health and Human Services.

Levine, D. B., Hill, K., & Warren, R. (1985). Immigration policy: Past to present. In D. Levine, K. Hill, & R. Warren (Eds.), *Immigration statistics: A story of neglect* (pp. 13–25). Washington, DC: National Academy Press.

Morris, M. (1985). *The beleaguered bureaucracy.* Washington, DC: Brookings Institution.

Mydans, S. (1991, June 2). Vote in a melting pot of Los Angeles may mirror the future of California. *New York Times,* p. A34.

Nash, N. (1990, October 4). Immigration bill approved in House. *New York Times,* p. A23.

Pear, R. (1989, September 3). U.S. drafts plan to curb admission of Soviet Jews. *New York Times,* p. A1.

Pear, R. (1990, October 20). Congress sets tentative pact on immigration rise. *New York Times,* p. A9.

Refugee Act of 1980, P.L. 96-212, 94 Stat. 102.

Refugee Escapee Act of 1957, 71 Stat. 639.

Refugee Reports. (1989, October 20). *Update*. Washington, DC: U.S. Committee for Refugees.

Ross, S. (1991). Family-sponsored immigration. In *Immigration Act of 1990* (91-14.01, pp. 1–22). Boston: Massachusetts Continuing Legal Education.

Schuck, P. H. (1987). The status and rights of undocumented aliens in the U.S. *International Migration, 25*, 125–140.

Seller, M. (1984). Historical perspectives on American immigration policy: Case studies and current implications. In R. R. Hofstetter (Ed.), *U.S. immigration policy* (pp. 137–162). Durham, NC: Duke University Press.

Shuval, J. T. (1982). Migration and stress. In L. Goldberger & S. Breznitz (Eds.), *Handbook of stress: Theoretical and clinical aspects* (pp. 677–691). New York: Free Press.

Silverman, H. (1994). Family-sponsored immigration. In *Immigration law basics* (95-14.02, pp. 119–147). Boston: Massachusetts Continuing Legal Education.

Sontag, D. (1994, June 10). New York officials welcome immigrants, legal or illegal. *New York Times*, p. A1.

Stepick, A. (1984). Haitian boat people: A study in the complicating forces shaping U.S. immigration policy. In R. R. Hofstetter (Ed.), *U.S. immigration policy* (pp. 163–196). Durham, NC: Duke University Press.

Suro, R. (1991, March 30). Behind the census numbers, swirling tides of movement. *New York Times*, p. B1.

Taubman, P. (1988, July 8). U.S. holding up visas for Soviet emigres. *New York Times*, p. A1.

Thornton, M. (1986, January 12). Aliens law to change nation, experts say. *Washington Post*, p. A16.

Tien, C. L. (1994, October 31). America's scapegoats: Immigrant-bashing is hurting the native and foreign born alike. *Newsweek*, p. 19.

U.S. Bureau of the Census. (1970). *U.S. census of population 1970* [Final Report P.C. (1)-C1]. Washington, DC: U.S. Government Printing Office.

U.S. Bureau of the Census. (1980). *U.S. census of population 1980* (Final Report P.C. 80[1]-C1). Washington, DC: U.S. Government Printing Office.

U.S. Bureau of the Census. (1990). *Census of population and housing 1990* (Summary tape file 3). Washington, DC: U.S. Bureau of the Census.

Westermeyer, J. (1985). Mental health of Southeast Asian refugees: Observations over two decades from Laos and the United States. In T. C. Owan (Ed.), *Southeast Asian mental health: Treatment, prevention, services, training, and research* (pp. 65–90). Washington, DC: U.S. Department of Health and Human Services.

This chapter was originally published in the March 1995 issue of Social Work, *vol. 40, pp. 188–197.*

Social Integration of Salvadoran Refugees

André G. Jacob

For the past 15 years, tens of thousands of refugees have sought asylum in the industrialized capitalist countries of North America and Europe. In 1990 Germany opened its borders to 19,000 refugees, while 40,000 went to France (Haut conseil ê l'intégration [HCI], 1991) and 30,000 to Canada (Ministère des communautés culturelles et de l'immigration du Québec, 1990). In these countries, legal immigrants are welcome, but refugees generally are not. A large proportion of refugees are never able to obtain legal refugee status.

In the context of current social and political difficulties, a large majority of refugees display traits that may make them targets of constant discrimination. Many natives of countries in Latin America, Africa, and Asia are discriminated against because of physical features such as skin color, eye shape, and hair type, as well as language, customs, beliefs, political convictions, and working-class origin.

Refugees avail themselves of both public and private social services. The demand for services has increased greatly in recent years, and social workers with training in refugee issues are sorely needed. Only a few agencies offer special programs to assist refugees, such as the Toronto Centre for Victims of Torture and the Douglas Hospital in Montreal, which offer programs to help victims of torture and adolescent refugees who have come into Canada alone.

In general, social services organizations have developed a systematic approach to working in a multiethnic milieu; however, little thought has been given to specific practice to help refugees. It is essential to analyze in greater depth the characteristics and dynamics involved in the social integration of refugees and to better train social workers and develop programs geared to the needs of refugees, who often find themselves greatly disadvantaged in society.

This point of view has led the author to conduct research with a variety of groups, including Salvadoran, Iranian, Ethiopian, Somali, and Lebanese refugees. This article is a summary of a study I conducted with Salvadoran refugees in Canada. My aim was to discover how refugees integrate into the social environment of the host country, as considered from cultural, economic, and political points of view, and ensure their economic, social, emotional, and cultural well-being.

METHODOLOGY

Study and Sample

This qualitative study, carried out with 22 Salvadoran refugees (11 men and 11 women) who arrived in Canada between 1984 and 1989 and who came from rural backgrounds, combined an analysis of the literature and an analysis of their life stories. Little literature exists that pertains to the lives of Salvadoran refugees (Jacob & Bertot, 1991; Neuwirth, 1989; Sehl & Naidoo, 1985; Thomson, 1986); therefore, the study is principally based on the information provided by the refugees themselves in response to themes suggested by the author relating to their childhood, adolescence, and adult life; family life; education; work experiences; political experiences; the migration process; the social integration process; and future plans. Questions were asked in Spanish to allow the individual to relate his or her personal story in depth using his or her native language.

Study group members had an average age of 23 years and less than 11 years of education. All held casual, low-income jobs (averaging Can$11,000 per year) including driving taxis; working in restaurants, hotels, or as domestics; or working in small- and medium-sized factories, specifically in the textile industry.

Seven refugees had resided in the United States for at least a year before coming to Canada. Six had been in Mexico for at least six months, and the others had come to Canada directly from El Salvador. Thirteen participants were refugee claimants, and five had already obtained refugee status. None were living in Canada illegally, because according to Canadian immigration law individuals are allowed to apply for refugee status on arrival.

Definitions

Integration is defined here as participation in different sectors of social life that follows a process of conflict, negotiation, and compromise. This definition is accepted in official political spheres and by numerous researchers (Reynaud, 1989; Schnapper, 1991): "Integration is above all the product of competing and often conflicting standards issuing from different groups. Integration is a result of those conflicts, negotiations and compromises which arise within competing systems of regulations, and which often concern the very rules being challenged" (Schnapper, 1991, pp. 97–98). The meaning of participation can be found in official definitions such as those put forth by France or Quebec. The HCI described integration as a participatory process:

Integration must be conceived as a middle road between assimilation and insertion, but also as a specific process by which various different elements participate actively in the society of the nation. The subsistence of specific cultural, social and moral norms is accepted along with the belief that the whole is enriched by this plurality, this complexity. (HCI, 1991, p. 18)

The position held by the Quebec government is similar: "We wish to build a democratic society in which everyone's participation and contribution is welcomed and expected" (Ministère des communautés culturelles et de l'immigration du Québec, 1990, p. 15).

This currently accepted definition of integration, although based on profoundly humanistic values and ideas and applicable to immigrants in general, is not necessarily suitable to define the process of social integration as experienced by refugees, because they are often discriminated against and rejected by society. The best way to examine refugee social integration is to be attentive to the point of view of the refugees themselves.

DISCUSSION

Sociodemographic Factors

Four sociodemographic factors must be considered as the main determining factors in the cultural adaptation process of refugees: (1) reasons for departure, (2) age, (3) gender, and (4) marital status.

Reasons for Departure. Study participants' accounts corroborated results obtained by other researchers who carried out similar studies with various groups of refugees (Rogge, 1987; Vinar, 1989; Williams & Westermeyer, 1986). Reasons for departure significantly affect the stress level of individuals depending on the circumstances of their departure. In this study, all refugees left their country in a hurry and were obliged to go underground (first in the country of origin and then either in Mexico or the United States in some cases). Their illegal situation caused great anxiety.

Several refugees found themselves in life-or-death situations, became panic-stricken, or were traumatized by nightmarish circumstances. Some refugees saw their parents being assassinated by military patrols or death squad. One woman's husband had disappeared because he was a trade union leader. Another woman was tortured and raped in front of her children. All these individuals admitted to having difficulty adapting after having experienced such trauma. Twelve refugees said they had left their country hurriedly after being directly threatened by the arrest or assassination of a close friend or relative. The others left for indirect reasons, such as to avoid military service or to escape war or economic strife.

Age, Gender, and Marital Status. For the most part these refugees were young adults, which seemed to be advantageous to their cultural adaptation. Nevertheless, the determining factors were not so much age as gender and marital status. Single men expressed stronger and more frequent feelings of isolation and seemed to suffer greatly from being separated from their families, especially from their mothers. This phenomenon is directly related to the great importance the Salvadoran refugees place on family and the interdependence among family members. The young Salvadoran men had great difficulty coping with exile: As the uncontested family leader and economic pillar, the male participants were admired and venerated for their role of authority and of provider, yet at the same time they seemed to idolize their mothers, to whom they remained eternally devoted and on whom they were emotionally dependent.

As for the young Salvadoran women, although they too suffered from separation from the family, it seemed to affect them less. This phenomenon may be because the upbringing of Salvadoran women prepares them to adapt to various situations with an eye toward the future. The testimonies in the study reflected that these women confront hardships with courage and, in the face of new situations, assume responsibilities that are traditionally attributed to men.

Postmigration Variables

Many postmigration variables can affect the process of adaptation, including the programs and integration procedures set up by the host country (including those for learning the language) and the refugee's socioeconomic situation, length of stay, attitudes and perceptions concerning the host country, and integration into the work force. In this study, five variables were analyzed: (1) integration policies, (2) family life, (3) social networks, (4) future plans, and (5) isolation.

Integration Policies. Salvadoran refugees' perceptions of Canadian integration policies were varied. In general, they felt positive, but some criticized the brusque attitude with which immigration officers conducted their first interview.

In the refugees' view, the French language instruction programs were inadequate. Access to these courses was limited for refugees, especially for working-class individuals with a low level of education. Women with children confronted a lack of child care. Also, the poor quality of instruction did not allow refugees to become familiar with the pronunciation and vocabulary specific to an area. Furthermore, the language policy is often contradictory; in Quebec, learning French is mandatory, but many refugees needed to speak English in the workplace.

Family Life. The presence of close family can alleviate feelings of solitude among refugees (Allodi & Rojas, 1983; Brody, 1970; Chan & Andra, 1987; Chan & Lam, 1983). Nevertheless, the absence or presence of a father, mother, siblings, or children cannot totally account for the varying degrees of difficulty experienced by the Salvadoran refugees during their first few months in Canada. Feelings such as nostalgia for the homeland, loneliness, and reluctance to espouse values and norms prevalent in the host country were common.

The clash of values had an even greater effect on the process of cultural adaptation than does separation from one's family. For example, Salvadoran refugees who lived in Canada with family members expressed problems relating to the disintegration of the extended family, with its spirit of mutual help, which they felt was being replaced by an attitude of individualism. The improvement of a refugee's economic situation seemed to foster this individualism.

In general, the Salvadoran men experienced more difficulty in adapting than did women because of role changes imposed on them by their new situation. Paradoxically, the men were extremely dependent on their mothers for emotional security and family stability, because often the mother was the only stable element in their tumultuous lives. Obliged to play the role of family provider or to make a major contribution to family survival, the men left it up to the mother to assume daily household tasks and to ensure the continuity of family life. This concept of the mother's role undoubtedly differs among refugees of urban origin who are used to the lifestyle of the nuclear family. Refugee families of rural origin are probably much closer to the traditional model of the extended family (Thomson, 1986; Yedid, 1982). The traditional model of the extended family was by far the preferred family model because of its strong social and emotional ties and the control, security, and mutual help it affords. The refugees made constant reference to this model and showed behavior patterns consistent with this mode of living. For example, the men felt obligated to support their mothers financially, even if the mothers still lived in El Salvador. Some of the women mentioned that they looked after their younger and older brothers and nieces and nephews.

The presence of kin is a decisive factor in choosing the country of refuge, because established family members offer the newly arrived refugee a built-in support system. The presence of family members helps reduce the loneliness and stress during the first few months of cultural adaptation.

However, the presence of family is not a guarantee for successful cultural adaptation in a new country. Other key factors exist, such as learning the new language and integrating into the work force. In some cases the presence of relatives is not sufficient to offset loneliness among refugees (Bertot & Jacob, 1991; Chan,1984; Hitch & Rack, 1980; Myers & Neal, 1978). Also, if family members could not maintain the relationships they had before migration, the refugees experienced increased difficulty in adapting to the new environment and felt more marginal in

society unless they were able to develop satisfying social relationships in other networks.

Social Networks. Social relationships were important to satisfying the refugees' need for communication and enabling them
to avoid isolation. However, for those who did not speak French,
communication remained confined to the Spanish-speaking
milieu, and some refugees experienced mistrust and exclusion
as they found themselves caught in situations of reciprocal
incomprehension.

Also, despite the expressed need for unity and solidarity among
Salvadorans and Latin Americans in general, there was no well-
defined Salvadoran community in Canada to provide a sense of
belonging and offset the feelings of isolation. With the exception
of individuals who joined forces for political activities, social life
was centered around the family and around sports and recreational activities involving Salvadorans and Spanish-speaking
groups.

The presence of a community of compatriots in their midst
directly influences refugees' psychological well-being and ability to adapt. Martin and Martin (1985) made reference to the solidarity and tradition of interethnic mutual help. Abou (1986) confirmed the basic human need for "an organic form of solidarity
linking the individual to a group which makes one feel secure
and at home, known and recognized by others" (p. 32).

New arrivals depend on their own cultural community for a
social support system that helps to attenuate the stress of cultural immigration and integration. Many researchers have at-
tested to the importance of the community as a social support
network (Chan, 1984; Lin, Tardiff, Doretz, & Goresky, 1978; Pilisuk
& Froland, 1984; Tran, 1987; Walsh & Walsh, 1987; Wood, 1988).
Their conclusions are similar to those of Bruhn and Phillipp (1984),
who classified four main categories of social support: (1) moral,
material, and technical support; (2) negative stress modification;
(3) reinforcement of optimism and hope; and (4) help in master-
ing and using new behavior mechanisms in cultural adaptation
situations.

The workplace was the most significant nonfamily social network for these Salvadoran refugees. Although social relationships
at work were not always positive for many refugees, they nevertheless attached a great deal of importance to these contacts.

Often the opinions refugees formed about the Quebecois population were directly related to the quality and frequency of interaction in the workplace.

These Salvadoran refugees were much more concerned about the quality of interaction at work than they were about their qualifications for the job or about receiving recognition for their competence. In this they differed from other immigrant and refugee groups, for whom job qualifications and recognition are of paramount importance to cultural adaptation (Chan, 1984; Nguyen, 1982). This phenomenon can be explained by the fact that immigrants with a fairly high level of education have not been conditioned to accept employment merely to survive without feeling any shame, whereas refugees of rural origin, who have lower levels of education, have not acquired a professional status on which to base their social standing. For the refugees who were more politicized, the workplace was important for developing skills that would be useful when they returned to El Salvador.

Future Plans. Three main projects preoccupied these young Salvadoran refugees: (1) furthering their education, (2) improving their material situation, and (3) returning to their own country.

The desire to continue their education was much more prevalent among the refugees who wanted to return to El Salvador. Their motivation was to help their compatriots and to make a contribution to rebuild the country. From this vantage point, continuing their education was of social and political significance. Other refugees, however, wanted to return to school so they could consolidate their financial and social situation to establish themselves firmly in Canada.

Returning to their country was a project shared by many of these Salvadoran refugees. Returning was a clear priority for those who were politically active; those who were not remained attached to their country but had no plans to return in the near future.

The plan to return for political reasons seemed to be a determining factor in the adaptation process for some Salvadoran refugees. They pointed out that their problem was not that of adapting to Quebec society, but rather of adapting to their particular situation, which they considered temporary. These refugees were determined to make the most of their situation so that it would benefit their people. Those refugees with political and social ideals generally established more contacts with the Quebecois population than did those who were primarily concerned with their personal well-being.

Isolation. As outlined by Vasquez (1983), many of the Salvadoran refugees went through a phase of introspection generated by a state of mourning for their country, which brought them to reject all that surrounds them while considering themselves to be rejected. This phenomenon seems to be experienced by all refugees.

Furthermore, isolation is difficult to identify with any precision, because it is a highly subjective phenomenon. One person may be very happy living alone, whereas the next person is not able to tolerate such a situation. The refugees' feelings of isolation were identified by making connections between various determining factors such as the presence of family and a Salvadoran community and language proficiency.

CONCLUSION AND RECOMMENDATIONS

In general, the more difficult the premigration experiences, the more complex the cultural adaptation process. Such conclusions seem valid for other refugee groups from Third World countries where repressive regimes are in place, such as Iran, Ethiopia, Somalia, and Guatemala (Bertot & Jacob, 1991).

To help with cultural integration, more systematic and organized forms of specialized services geared to the client's individual needs are needed. Information on available services could be improved, particularly concerning public services. Furthermore, these services would be more accessible if they were provided in the clients' native language.

Much effort has been made among public and private agencies to ensure that social workers are better trained and able to obtain increased refugee participation in the agencies' programs. In 1989 the Quebec Ministry of Health and Social Services began to create and implement new policies designed specifically to improve the integration of refugees into the social system. Other organizations could create and implement similar policies.

REFERENCES

Abou, S., (1986). *L'identité culturelle: Relations interethniques et problèmes d'acculturation* [Cultural identity: Interethnic relations and acculturation problems]. Paris: Anthropos.

Allodi, F., & Rojas, A. (1983). The health and adaptation of victims of political violence in Latin America. In P. Pichot, P. Berver, R. Wolf, & K. Tau (Eds.), *Psychiatry: The state of the art.* New York: Plenum Press.

Bertot, J., & Jacob, A. (1991). *L'intégration des refugiés, deux études de cas: les Salvadoriens et les Iraniens* [Integration of refugees: Two case studies: Salvadorans and Iranians]. Montreal: Méridien.

Brody, E. (1970). *Behavior in new environments: Adaptation in migrant populations.* Beverly Hills, CA: Sage Publications.

Bruhn, J., & Phillipp, B. (1984). Measuring social support: A synthesis of current approaches. *Journal of Behavioral Medicine, 7,* 151–169.

Chan, K. B. (1984). Mental health needs of Indochinese refugees: Toward a national refugee resettlement policy and strategy in Canada. In D. Lumsden (Ed.), *Community mental health action: Primary prevention programming in Canada.* Ottawa: Canadian Public Health Association.

Chan, K. B., & Andra, D. M. (1987). *Uprooting loss and adaptation: The resettlement of Indochinese refugees in Canada.* Ottawa: Canadian Public Health Association.

Chan, K. B., & Lam, L. (1983). Resettlement of Vietnamese–Chinese refugees in Montreal, Canada: Some psycho-sociological problems and dilemmas. *Canadian Ethnic Studies, 15,* 1–17.

Haut conseil ê l'intégration. (1991). *Pour un modèle français d'intégration* [Toward a French model of integration]. Paris: La Documentation française.

Hitch, P. J., & Rack, P. H. (1980). Mental illness among Polish and Russian refugees in Bredford. *International Journal of Psychiatry, 137,* 206–211.

Jacob, A., & Bertot, J. (1991). *Intervenir avec des immigrants et des réfugiés* [Working with immigrants and refugees]. Montreal: Méridien.

Lin, T. Y., Tardiff, K., Doretz, G., & Goresky, W. (1978). Ethnicity and patterns of self-seeking. *Culture, Medicine and Psychiatry, 2*(2), 4–13.

Martin, J. M., & Martin, E. P. (1985). *The helping tradition in the black family and community.* Silver Spring, MD: National Association of Social Workers.

Ministère des communautés culturelles et de l'immigration du Québec. (1990). *Enoncé de politique en matière d'immigration et d'intégration* [Policy of immigration and integration]. Quebec: Editeur officiel du Québec.

Myers, D. H., & Neal, C. D. (1978). Suicide in psychiatric patients. *British Journal of Psychiatry, 138,* 113–118.

Neuwirth, G. (1989). *The settlement of Salvadoran refugees in Ottawa and Toronto: An exploratory study.* Ottawa: Employment and Immigration Canada.

Nguyen, S. D. (1982). The psycho-social adjustment and mental health needs of Southeast Asian refugees. *Psychiatric Journal, University of Ottawa, 7*(1), 26–35.

Pilisuk, M., & Froland, C. (1984). Kinship, social networks, social support and health. *Social Science and Medicine, 12,* 273–280.

Reynaud, J. D. (1989). *Les règles du jeu, l'action collective et la régulation sociale* [The rules of the game, collective action, and social regulation]. Paris: Armand Colin.

Rogge, J. (1987). *Refugees: A Third World dilemma.* Totowa, NJ: Roman & Littlefield.

Schnapper, D. (1991). *La France de l'intégration* [The France of integration]. Paris: Gallimard.

Sehl, M., & Naidoo, J. (1985). The adaptation of Salvadoran refugees in Canada. *Multiculturalism, 9*(1), 25–28.

Thomson, M. (1986). *Women of El Salvador—The price of freedom*. London: Zeb Books.

Tran, T. V. (1987). Ethnic community supports and psychological well-being of Vietnamese refugees. *International Migration Review, 21*(3), 577–589.

Vasquez, A. (1983). L'exil, une analyse psychosociologique [Exile, a psychosociological analysis]. *L'Information psychiatrique, 59*(1), 12–18.

Vinar, M. (1989). *Exil et torture* [Exile and torture]. Paris: Denoel.

Walsh, A., & Walsh, P. A. (1987). Social support, assimilation and biological effective blood pressure levels. *International Migration Review, 21*(3), 577–589.

Williams, C. L., & Westermeyer, J. (1986). *Refugee mental health in resettlement countries*. New York: Hemisphere.

Wood, M. (1988). *Revue de la littérature sur la santé mentale des migrants* [Review of literature on the mental health of migrants]. Montreal: Girame editeur.

Yedid, H. (1982). Quelques problèmes de réinsertion chez les réfugiés Cambodgiens de France [Some incorporation problems of Cambodians in France]. *Asemi, 13*, 1–4.

This chapter was originally published in the May 1994 issue of Social Work, *vol. 39, pp. 307–313.*

Deaf and Hard-of-Hearing Clients: Some Legal Implications

Maureen K. McEntee

Hearing impairment affects one of every 16 Americans. One of every 100 Americans is profoundly deaf, that is, unable to hear speech well enough to understand it (Schein & Delk, 1974). These people often use American Sign Language (ASL) as their primary language, and, in fact, ASL is the third most used language in the United States. Because ASL has a different grammatical structure than English, English is a second language for most ASL users, and they may find written communication difficult, if not impossible (and definitely inefficient). Speech and speechreading may also be ineffective avenues to communication for them; less than one-third of all English sounds are visible on the lips, so even the best speechreader has to guess at the rest.

With the passage of a variety of federal laws requiring accessibility to services and places for people with disabilities and with an ever-increasing number of people receiving services in community settings, social workers can expect more deaf and hard-of-hearing people on their caseloads. Therefore, social workers need at least a basic understanding of the major pieces of legislation that affect the provision of services to deaf people.

LEGISLATIVE BACKGROUND

Rehabilitation Act of 1973

The Rehabilitation Act of 1973 addressed the needs of disabled people at different ages. Title V was designed to ensure that programs receiving federal funds could be used by disabled individuals. The four major sections of Title V prohibit discrimination and require accessibility in employment; education; and health, welfare, and social services.

Section 504 of the Rehabilitation Act of 1973 is of special concern because of its accessibility requirements. If an agency receives federal funds directly or indirectly, it must make its facilities accessible to people with disabilities. Such agencies include elementary and secondary schools, colleges and universities, hospitals, nursing homes, vocational rehabilitation facilities, public welfare offices, state and local governments, police and fire departments, parks, recreational facilities, mass transit systems, airports and harbors, subsidized housing programs, legal services programs, and most parts of the judicial system. Although the Education for All Handicapped Children Act of 1975 applies only to school-age children, schools receive federal funding and are therefore required to comply with Section 504 in all their programs, including continuing adult education classes that take place in the school after school hours (DuBow et al., 1986; U.S. Department of Health, Education, and Welfare, 1977).

Although Section 504 appears to include most programs, there are some technicalities that have led to a possible weakening of a civil rights interpretation. In *Grove City College v. Bell* in 1984, the Supreme Court narrowed the application of civil rights by holding that if a college receives federal aid for only one program, that program is the only part of the institution that must comply with nondiscrimination laws. Thus, if the psychology department of a college were to receive federal funding, but the science department did not, a deaf student might be entitled to interpreter services only for the psychology course.

United States v. Baylor University Medical Center (1985) dealt with organizations in which federal monies go into the general operating budget; such organizations must comply with Section 504 in all of their programs. In this case, the hospital received reimbursement from the federal government for its inpatient and emergency room services under the Medicare program. A federal court of appeals upheld that the hospital was bound by Section 504, even though the deaf person needing the interpreter did not receive Medicare or Medicaid funding.

Americans with Disabilities Act

The Americans with Disabilities Act (ADA) of 1990 provides antidiscrimination protection for all people with physical or mental impairments that substantially limit one or more major life activities. (For a summary of the ADA's titles covering employment, public services, public accommodation, privately operated services, and the telecommunications relay services, see Jones, 1991; Parry, 1990). Social services providers will need to develop expanded skills in client advocacy, business and client consultation, and education (Benshoff & Souheaver, 1991), and they will need to address the issue of hearing impairment, an area that has been overlooked in the past.

Accessibility requires different interventions depending on the deaf individual's preference. Many deaf and hard-of-hearing people use TT (Teletext) or TDD (Telecommunications Device for the Deaf) for telephone contact. Some may prefer to use assistive listening devices (for example, auditory loops), but for most deaf people, communication requires the services of an interpreter, either sign language or oral.

A telecommunications relay service allows deaf, hearing-impaired, and speech-impaired people who use TT/TDD to call non-TT/TDD users. The ADA required the implementation of a telecommunications relay service operating in all states 24 hours a day by July 26, 1993 (Strauss, 1993). Through this service, TT and non-TT users are able to contact each other by way of a central relay station. The relay operator or communications assistant speaks the printed message from the TT user and types the spoken message on the TT for the non-TT user. As a result, TT users are able to contact social services agencies even if the agency does not have a TT system.

Additionally, the ADA may require an agency to use assistive listening devices. Such devices may include auditory loops, FM systems, or other auditory training devices. Assistive listening devices overcome the problem of distance between the speaker and listener and the added difficulty of background noise. Auditory loops (for example, infrared systems and hard wire systems) can be portable or built into a room. They require a microphone for the speaker. The listener is required to be within the loop (wire) area and to have a "T" switch on his or her hearing aid. FM and other systems require the listener to have a receiver in addition to or in place of his or her hearing aid. FM systems use a microphone and receiver and transmit auditory signals to the listener via radio frequencies.

Internal Revenue Code

The Internal Revenue Code has regulations that affect disabled people. Briefly, there are two pertinent sections. The first provides tax credits to the employer in the amount of 40 percent of the first $6,000 of the first-year wages of a new employee who has a disability. The employee must have been employed for at least 90 days or have completed at least 120 hours of work for the employer (Internal Revenue Code, Title 26, section 51).

The other relevant section, the Disabled Access Tax Credit (Title 26, section 44), is available to small businesses (less than $1 million gross receipts for preceding tax year or 30 or fewer full-time employees). The business can deduct 50 percent of "eligible access expenditures" for the taxable year that exceed $250 but do not exceed $10,250. Eligible access expenditures are expenses for construction or services that enable the small business to comply with applicable requirements under the ADA. Such expenditures include the cost of removing communication barriers, which in the case of deaf people would include providing "qualified interpreters or other effective methods of making aurally delivered materials available to individuals" and acquiring or "modify[ing] equipment, or devices for individuals" (Internal Revenue Code, Title 26, section 44).

MANDATED USE OF INTERPRETERS

Certification of Interpreters

It is necessary to understand the role and function of an interpreter in any setting (National Registry of Interpreters of the Deaf, 1979). According to DuBow et al. (1986), interpreting English into ASL and vice versa requires a great deal of skill; "relying on amateurs who may know some sign language is a frequent error" (p. 2). Therefore, using professional certification as a criteria for skill may be helpful. Deaf or hard-of-hearing people who rely chiefly on speechreading and do not use sign language may require an oral interpreter rather than a sign interpreter.

Generally, both sign and oral interpreters should be certified by the National Registry of Interpreters for the Deaf (RID), which conducts national evaluations of interpreters. Certified interpreters follow the RID *Code of Ethics* (National Registry of Interpreters for the Deaf, 1979), which mandates things such as confidentiality. RID certification gives both the hearing and deaf consumer of interpreter services some assurance of the skills and capabilities of the interpreter.

The need for qualification of interpreters is exemplified by a rape case in Virginia involving a deaf woman and a "qualified," although unskilled and uncertified, interpreter. As recounted in DuBow et al. (1986),

> When the prosecutor asked the victim what had happened, she gave the sign for "forced intercourse." The interpreter said that her reply was "made love," the sign for which is completely different. Later, when she answered "blouse" to the prosecutor's question of what she was wearing, the interpreter told the court "short blouse," creating the impression that she had dressed provocatively. (p. 124)

Mental Health Facilities

To increase access to services, federal laws (for example, Section 504) dictate the use of interpreters in mental health settings. Despite this, McEntee (1993), in a survey of all mental health centers in one state, found that 29 percent of the 28 respondents flatly stated that they were not accessible to deaf people. Additionally, 39 percent stated that they did not provide interpreters, even though 72 percent of the agencies indicated that they had served deaf individuals; of these 72 percent, only 25 percent used certified interpreters.

Federal and State Courts

Federal law dictates the use of interpreters, especially in the courts. Adopted in 1979, the Bilingual, Hearing, and Speech-Impaired Court Interpreter Act requires the appointment of a qualified interpreter in any criminal or civil action initiated in the federal courts by the federal government in which a deaf, speech-impaired, or non-English-speaking person must participate. The director of the Administrative Office of the U.S. Courts determines the qualifications required of court-appointed interpreters. Under this act, each district court must maintain on file in the office of the clerk a list of certified interpreters. The interpreter services are paid for by the federal government. It is up to the judge to apportion the interpreter fees among the parties or impose their costs on the losing party. The law, however, does not provide interpreters for actions initiated by a deaf person.

The U.S. Department of Justice's (1980) analysis of its Section 504 responsibilities requires the appointment of an interpreter in both civil and criminal proceedings in federal courts or in state courts covered by Section 504:

> Court systems receiving Federal financial assistance shall provide for the availability of qualified interpreters for civil and criminal court proceedings involving persons with hearing or speaking impairments. Where a recipient has an obligation to provide qualified interpreters under this subpart, the recipient has the corresponding responsibility to pay for the services of the interpreters. (p. 630)

Law Enforcement Agencies

Additionally, U.S. Department of Justice regulations require police departments receiving federal funds to obtain an interpreter. Specifically, the regulations state,

> Law enforcement agencies should provide for the availability of qualified interpreters (certified, where possible, by a recognized certification agency) to assist the agencies when dealing with hearing-impaired persons. Where the hearing-impaired person uses American Sign Language for communication, the term "qualified interpreter" would mean an interpreter skilled in communicating in American Sign Language.
>
> It is the responsibility of the law enforcement agency to determine whether the hearing-impaired person uses American Sign Language or Signed English to communicate.
>
> If a hearing-impaired person is arrested, the arresting officer's Miranda warning should be communicated to the arrestee on a printed form approved for such use by the law enforcement agency where there is no qualified interpreter immediately available and communication is otherwise inadequate. The form should also advise the arrestee that the law enforcement agency has an obligation under Federal law to offer an interpreter to the arrestee without cost and that the agency will defer interrogation pending the appearance of an interpreter. (U.S. Department of Justice, 1980, p. 503)

It should be noted that this regulation does not limit the right to interpreters to arrested persons. Complainants and victims are also entitled to have interpreters.

CONCLUSION

The Americans with Disabilities Act is far reaching, and its effects will undoubtedly touch the social work profession in diverse and profound ways. To be effective advocates, social workers need to be aware of the various pieces of legislation that affect the lives of our clients. The profession also needs to be aware that services must be rendered in a different manner when working with deaf and hard-of-hearing people. Social workers need to be aware of their own communication modes and how to use support personnel and equipment.

Social work agencies must develop policies that address the communication needs of deaf and hearing-impaired individuals. Agencies need to review the need for assistive listening devices and other specialized equipment in their offices to meet the new legal requirements and to best fit the needs of potential clients. They should obtain a list of interpreters with specialized skills in mental health, substance abuse, or other areas of interpreting expertise. Social services agencies should develop emergency protocols, and they should redesign intake assessments to reflect the differences of people with hearing loss.

The profession's example can set the tone for further interventions and interactions. We can ensure that the legal and civil rights of our clients are protected so that they can receive the best services and have the greatest chance of self-determination. Any less will serve neither the client nor the profession.

REFERENCES

Americans with Disabilities Act of 1990, P.L. 101-336, 104 Stat. 327.

Benshoff, J. J., & Souheaver, H. D. (1991). Private sector rehabilitation and the Americans with Disabilities Act. *Journal of Applied Rehabilitation Counseling, 22*(4), 27–31.

Bilingual, Hearing, and Speech-Impaired Court Interpreter Act, 28 U.S.C. §1827 (1979).

DuBow, S., Goldberg, L., Geer, S., Gardner, E., Penn, A., Conlon, S., & Charmatz, M. (1986). *Legal rights of hearing-impaired persons* (3rd ed.). Washington, DC: Gallaudet University Press.

Education for All Handicapped Children Act of 1975, P.L. 94-142, 89 Stat. 773.

Education of the Handicapped Act Amendments of 1986, P.L. 99-457, 100 Stat. 1145.

Grove City College v. Bell, 465 U.S. 555 (1984).

Jones, N. L. (1991). Essential requirements of the act: A short history and overview. *Milbank Quarterly, 69* (Suppl. 1–2), 25–54.

McEntee, M. K. (1993). Mental health and crisis intervention service availability for the deaf. *American Annals of the Deaf, 138*(1), 26–30.

National Registry of Interpreters for the Deaf. (1979). *Code of ethics* (rev.). Silver Spring, MD: Author.

Parry, J. W. (1990). The Americans with Disabilities Act (ADA). *Mental and Physical Disability Law Reporter, 14*(4), 292–298.

Rehabilitation Act of 1973, P.L. 93-112, 29 U.S.C. §794.

Rehabilitation Act of 1973, P.L. 96-88 Section 504. 28 CFR §42.503, Subpart G (1980).

Schein, J., & Delk, M. (1974). *The deaf population of the United States.* Silver Spring, MD: National Association for the Deaf.

Strauss, K. P. (1993). Implementing the telecommunications provisions. *Milbank Quarterly, 69*(Suppl. 1–2), 238–267.

United States v. Baylor University Medical Center, 936 F.2nd 1039 (5th Cir 1984). Cert. den. 105 S. Ct. 958 (January 21, 1985).

U.S. Department of Health, Education, and Welfare. (1977). HEW Section 504 regulations. *Federal Register, 42*(22), 676.

U.S. Department of Justice. (1980). Analysis of Section 504. *Federal Register, 45*(37), 630.

This chapter was originally published in the March 1995 issue of Social Work, *vol. 40, pp. 183–187.*

The Impact of Hate Violence on Victims: Emotional and Behavioral Responses to Attacks

Arnold Barnes and Paul H. Ephross

The importance of crime as a major social problem in the United States has been well documented (Bureau of Justice Statistics, 1988). Since the mid-1960s, American society has been increasingly concerned about the problems experienced by victims of crime (Greenberg & Ruback, 1984). This interest has led to the development of a variety of victim service programs (Elias, 1986; Schultz, 1987) and a new area of social research that focuses on victims rather than on criminals (Ochberg, 1988). However, the plight of one class of crime victims, those experiencing hate violence, has been little changed by these developments.

Hate violence crimes are those directed against persons, families, groups, or organizations because of their racial, ethnic, religious, or sexual identities or their sexual orientation or condition of disability. These crimes include arson of homes and businesses, harassment, destruction of religious property, cross burnings, personal assaults, and homicides. Hate violence has a long history in the United States (Brown, 1989). Although it is difficult to estimate the current prevalence of hate violence in the United States (U.S. Commission on Civil Rights, 1986; Weiss, 1990), many sources suggest that the level of this type of crime has increased in the past several years (Anti-Defamation League of B'nai B'rith, 1991; Community Relations Service, 1990). Also, in recent years the media have increasingly provided information on the explosion of hate violence on college campuses (Collison, 1987) and on the capacity of hate violence to spark large-scale urban disturbances ("Black Child," 1991). With the passage of the Hate Crime Statistics Act, data on the prevalence of ethnoviolence (hate violence on the basis of race or ethnicity) nationwide will be compiled by the U.S. Attorney General for the years 1990 through 1994 (National Institute Against Prejudice and Violence, 1990).

Research is beginning to identify the effects of various types of personal crime on victims (Davis & Friedman, 1985). However, despite the social importance of hate violence, there is little available information on how it affects victims (Weiss & Ephross, 1986). The present study examines the nature of hate violence and the impact of these crimes on victims.

METHOD

Research Design and Sampling

Using an exploratory research design, the National Institute Against Prejudice and Violence conducted a pilot study of the effects of hate violence on minority group members (Ephross, Barnes, Ehrlich, Sandnes, & Weiss, 1986). A purposive sample of victims was obtained by contacts between members of the institute's staff and officials of human rights agencies, social services agencies, community relations agencies, and special units of police departments in several urban areas. These areas included Alexandria, Virginia; Baltimore; Cleveland; Philadelphia; Oakland, California; Rockville, Maryland; San Jose, California; Suffolk County, New York; and Statesville, North Carolina.

Data Collection and Analysis

The technique of focus group interviewing was used in the study. A focus group is a small group convened to share feelings, thoughts, and reactions to a particular subject (Lydecker, 1986). Ten focus group meetings and some individual interviews were held at sites in the victims' communities.

Each focus group meeting was conducted by two members of the institute's research staff. The institute's staff guided the interviews by posing a prepared set of open-ended questions for each group. With the permission of the participants, each meeting was audiotaped. Participants were assured of confidentiality.

Participants also completed questionnaires. Initially, the questionnaires obtained data on the demographic characteristics of victims and the types of crime they experienced. After the third focus group, the questionnaires were revised to include seven items measuring victims' emotional responses to the hate violence incidents.

The audiotape of each interview was reviewed by pairs of institute researchers working independently. Vignettes describing each victim's experience were written by the first reviewer and then checked for reliability by a second reviewer. In addition to these procedures, the first author analyzed each audiotape using a content analysis procedure (Mostyn, 1985). Complete results from the content analysis were not available for inclusion in the pilot study report (Ephross et al., 1986).

FINDINGS

Study Sample

The current report deals with the 59 focus group participants (out of 72) for whom complete information is available. The ethnic and religious backgrounds of the study sample are presented in Table 12-1.

Table 12-1

Ethnic and Religious Characteristics of Sample (*N* = 59)

Characteristic	*n*	%
Ethnicity		
Black	20	33.9
White	14	23.7
Cambodian	11	18.6
Hmong	5	8.5
Korean	4	6.8
Vietnamese	2	3.4
Laotian	1	1.7
Chinese	1	1.7
Hispanic	1	1.7
Religion		
Protestant	19	32.2
Buddhist	14	23.7
Jewish	9	15.3
Roman Catholic	7	11.9
Islamic	1	1.7
No affiliation	2	3.4
Not ascertained	7	11.9

The diversity of the group is apparent, although the nonsystematic method of sampling resulted in a seeming oversampling of Southeast Asian victims and an undersampling of Hispanic victims. Forty-one percent of the 59 victims were foreign born. They were almost equally divided by sex (54 percent male, 46 percent female) and ranged in age from 16 to 67 years. The median age was 39 years. Sixty-three percent of the participants were married. The sample's median household income was $15,500; the range was from $5,000 or less to over $50,000.

Acts of Violence

The interviews focused primarily on the most recent personal attack that participants had experienced. The total number of recent attacks for the sample was 53, rather than 59, because the sample included six couples who mutually experienced six attacks. As indicated in Table 12-2, for slightly more than two out of five respondents (44.1 percent), the most recent attack had

Table 12-2
Attacks Reported by Victims

Frequency and Nature of Attack	n	%
Frequency of attacks (n = 59)[a]		
Experienced one discrete attack only	26	44.1
Experienced multiple attacks that were		
discrete incidents	6	10.2
Experienced multiple interconnected attacks	27	45.8
Nature of most recent attack (n = 68)[b]		
Physically assaulted	11	16.2
Verbal harassment (ethnic slurs, threats, and insults)	11	16.2
Mail or telephone threats, harassment	11	16.2
Symbols or slogans of hate on or near property		
of victim	10	14.7
Attacks on homes (shots fired, rocks or other		
missiles hurled)	6	8.8
Other acts of vandalism	5	7.4
Other acts (false fire alarms, false accusations)	2	2.9
Possible hate violence attacks (robberies,		
attempted robberies)	9	13.2
Alleged attacks by police	3	4.4

[a]Fifty-nine persons, including six couples, were interviewed. They discussed 53 attacks (the most recent).

[b]Some of the attacks were multiple in nature but occurred on the same date.

occurred in a single time period and had been their first hate violence victimization. One-tenth of the respondents (10.2 percent) reported experiencing one or more prior hate violence incidents that appeared to be unrelated to the most recent attack. For slightly more than two out of five respondents (45.8 percent), the most recent incident was actually the latest in a series of related attacks. Some of these serial attacks ranged over several months and some over three years.

Some of the most recent attacks reported by respondents included multiple crimes that occurred on the same date (Table 12-2). Because of the multiple nature of some attacks, the total number of crimes experienced by victims in recent attacks was 68 rather than 53.

Physical assault, verbal harassment, and mail or telephone threats were the most frequently reported crimes (Table 12-2). These three categories together accounted for almost 49 percent of the experiences of respondents. The next most common attacks (14.7 percent) were symbols or slogans of hate on or near the personal property of victims. Attacks on homes and other acts of vandalism, respectively, accounted for 8.8 percent and 7.4 percent of the incidents. Robberies and attempted robberies were considered possible hate violence attacks because the motives of the offenders were unclear. However, it should be noted that victims of these crimes perceived them as crimes motivated by prejudice.

Impact of Attacks on Victims and Their Families

The majority of the 59 victims (76 percent) did not receive physical injuries as a result of the most recent attack. Minor injuries were sustained by 10 percent, and 9 percent received medical treatment for injuries inflicted in the attack. The severe injuries inflicted on 5 percent of the victims required hospitalization. In 41 percent of the most recent attacks, victims incurred property damage.

Participants identified several emotional reactions to the most recent attack on them (Table 12-3). Irwin, a Jewish victim who had a swastika spray-painted on his mailbox, identified his response as "mostly a feeling of anger." The most prevalent emotion was anger at the perpetrator, which nearly 68 percent of the participants reported. Fear of injury was the next most frequently

Table 12-3

Victims' Emotional Responses to Hate Violence (N = 59)

Response	n	%
Anger at perpetrator	40	67.8
Fear that family or self would be injured	30	50.8
Sadness about the incident	21	35.6
Feeling of powerlessness to do anything about incident	12	20.3
Suspicion of other people	12	20.3
Fear that family or self would be killed	11	18.6
Feeling bad about self as a person	3	5.1

NOTE: The percentages represent victims' indications of feelings at the time of most recent attack.

cited emotion, with nearly 51 percent of the participants indicating fear that they or their families would be physically injured. A number of victims (approximately 36 percent) were saddened by the incident.

About one-third of the participants (33.9 percent) reported behavioral changes as both coping responses to the most recent attack and as attempts to avoid potential future victimization. These behavioral changes included moving out of the neighborhood, decreasing social participation, purchasing a gun or increasing readiness to use a gun, buying initial or additional home security devices, and increasing safety precautions for children in the family. Somala, a Cambodian refugee, was assaulted by a black man in a suburban park. Shortly after the attack, Somala moved to another county. She moved because of fear that the man would find her and attack again, and she subsequently avoided the county in which the attack occurred. Somala's responses represent the avoidance behavioral coping that some victims adopted.

In contrast to avoidance, the behavioral coping of some victims consisted of preparations for retaliation. One black man stated, "I am scared that I might catch one of these people. . . . The scariest thing is I got guns and can use them."

DISCUSSION AND IMPLICATIONS

In examining the most recent hate violence incidents, the study found considerable variation in both the type and intensity of attacks. This finding is consistent with those of other recent investigations of hate violence (for example, U.S. Commission on Civil Rights, 1986; Wexler & Marx, 1986). The characteristics of some attacks appeared to be consistent with conventional definitions of social terrorism (Gurr, 1989), particularly evident in the finding of the current study that more than half of the participants experienced multiple attacks.

In comparing the emotional and behavioral responses of victims of hate violence with those of victims of personal crimes such as assault and rape, several similarities were identified. Investigators have reported intense rage or anger (Bard & Sangrey, 1986); fear of injury, death, and future victimization (Davis & Friedman, 1985); sadness (Ochberg, 1988); and depression (Shapland, Willmore, & Duff, 1985) as elements of victims' potential reactions to crime. Thus, to some extent, the predominant emotional responses of hate violence victims appear similar to those of victims of other types of personal crime. The behavioral coping responses of hate violence victims are also similar to those used by other victims of crime (Davis & Friedman, 1985; Wirtz & Harrell, 1987).

Crime victims often experience feelings of powerlessness and increased suspicion of other people (Bard & Sangrey, 1986). These emotions were also reported by victims of hate violence. A major difference in the emotional response of hate violence victims appears to be the absence of lowered self-esteem. The ability of some hate violence victims to maintain their self-esteem may be associated with their attribution of responsibility for the attacks to the prejudice and racism of the perpetrators.

Some limitations of this study need to be mentioned. First, the participants interviewed in the study had all contacted the police, human rights agencies, or other organizations. Thus, study findings are most relevant to the population of victims who report hate violence. Second, the generalizability of the findings to this population may be affected by the relatively small size and nonrandom nature of the sample.

Although responsibility for responding to hate violence is primarily allocated to community relations agencies, social workers in a wide array of settings encounter clients who have experienced this type of victimization. Thus, social workers must have knowledge of characteristics of hate violence, victims' reactions to attacks, and community resources that address hate violence.

Practitioners can assist victims in managing the stress of hate violence. As with victims of other types of crime, short-term interventions appear best suited for meeting the needs of hate violence victims (Young, 1988). Group work services may also be beneficial (Weiss & Ephross, 1986). With highly traumatized victims, specialized psychotherapy may be required (Ochberg, 1988). To prevent hate violence, social workers need to assist in educating citizens about this problem (Weiss, 1990).

REFERENCES

Anti-Defamation League of B'nai B'rith. (1991). *1990 audit of anti-Semitic incidents*. New York: Author.

Bard, M., & Sangrey, D. (1986). *The crime victim's book* (2nd ed.). New York: Brunner/Mazel.

Black child and a Hasidic man die, igniting clashes in Brooklyn. (1991, August 21). *New York Times*, p. A1.

Brown, R. M. (1989). Historical patterns of violence. In T. R. Gurr (Ed.), *Violence in America: Protest, rebellion, reform* (Vol. 2, pp. 23–61). Newbury Park, CA: Sage Publications.

Bureau of Justice Statistics. (1988). *Report to the nation on crime and justice* (2nd ed.). Washington, DC: U.S. Department of Justice.

Collison, M. N.-K. (1987, March 18). Racial incidents worry campus officials, prompt U. of Massachusetts study. *Chronicle of Higher Education*, pp. 1, 41–43.

Community Relations Service. (1990). *The annual report of the Community Relations Service*. Washington, DC: U.S. Department of Justice.

Davis, R. C., & Friedman, L. N. (1985). The emotional aftermath of crime and violence. In C. R. Figley (Ed.), *Trauma and its wake* (pp. 90–112). New York: Brunner/Mazel.

Elias, R. (1986). *The politics of victimization: Victims, victimology and human rights*. New York: Oxford University Press

Ephross, P. H., Barnes, A., Ehrlich, H. J., Sandnes, K. R., & Weiss, J. C. (1986). *The ethnoviolence project: Pilot study*. Baltimore: National Institute Against Prejudice and Violence.

Greenberg, M. S., & Ruback, R. B. (1984). Criminal victimization: Introduction and overview. *Journal of Social Issues, 40*(1), 1–7.

Gurr, T. R. (1989). Political terrorism: Historical antecedents and contemporary trends. In T. R. Gurr (Ed.), *Violence in America: Protest, rebellion, reform* (Vol. 2, pp. 201–230). Newbury Park, CA: Sage Publications.

Lydecker, T. H. (1986, March). Focus group dynamics. *Association Management*, pp. 73–78.

Mostyn, B. (1985). The content analysis of qualitative research data: A dynamic approach. In M. Brenner, J. Brown, & D. Cantor (Eds.), *The research interview: Uses and approaches* (pp. 115–145). Orlando, FL: Academic Press.

National Institute Against Prejudice and Violence. (1990). Federal Hate Crime Statistics Act signed into law. *FORUM, 5*(2), 5.

Ochberg, F. M. (1988). Post-traumatic therapy and victims of violence. In F. M. Ochberg (Ed.), *Post-traumatic therapy and victims of violence* (pp. 3–19). New York: Brunner/Mazel.

Schultz, L. G. (1987). Victimization programs and victims of crime. In A. Minahan (Ed.-in-Chief), *Encyclopedia of social work* (18th ed., Vol. 2, pp. 817–822). Silver Spring, MD: National Association of Social Workers.

Shapland, J., Willmore, J., & Duff, P. (1985). *Victims in the criminal justice system.* Brookfield, VT: Gower.

U. S. Commission on Civil Rights. (1986). *Recent activities against citizens and residents of Asian descent.* Washington, DC: Author.

Weiss, J. C. (1990). Ethnoviolence: Violence motivated by bigotry. In L. Ginsberg et al. (Eds.), *Encyclopedia of social work* (18th ed., 1990 Suppl., pp. 307–319). Silver Spring, MD: NASW Press.

Weiss, J. C., & Ephross, P. H. (1986). Group work approaches to "hate violence" incidents. *Social Work, 31,* 132–136.

Wexler, C., & Marx, G. T. (1986). When law and order works: Boston's innovative approach to the problem of racial violence. *Crime & Delinquency, 32,* 205–223.

Wirtz, P. W., & Harrell, A. V. (1987). Victim and crime characteristics, coping responses, and short- and long-term recovery from victimization. *Journal of Consulting and Clinical Psychology, 55,* 866–871.

Young, M. A. (1988). Support services for victims. In F. M. Ochberg (Ed.), *Post-traumatic therapy and victims of violence* (pp. 330–351). New York: Brunner/Mazel.

This chapter was originally published in the May 1994 issue of Social Work, *vol. 39, pp. 247–251.*

13

A Society without Poverty—
The Norwegian Experience

Katherine van Wormer

Yes, there is another way.

I went to Norway to teach American methods of alcoholism treatment and to learn of life in a welfare state. My stay of almost two years informed me in the way that firsthand experience informs—rudely, indelibly. My family and I have experienced the Norwegian community—the schools, social services, the health care system. And I have come to see how each dimension is connected to every other dimension of the cultural whole. In the high quality of life in Norway is the key to the larger pattern.

To the American visitor, the lack of poverty is striking, even puzzling. The outsider is inclined to see what is in terms of what is not: the southerner noting, for instance, the complete absence of palm trees. The Norwegian, meanwhile, is aware neither of the lack of poverty nor the absence of palm trees.

To understand the lack of poverty, you have to first understand poverty. And I am speaking of poverty in a rich society, there being no need to explain poverty in the absence of resources. The sociologists of the 1960s conceived of the existence of poverty in a prosperous society as functional for the total community. What were the social functions of poverty? (For a literature review, see Blau, 1988.) Poverty or the threat of poverty provided a steady pool of compliant workers; poverty provided jobs for bureaucrats who were to ameliorate the poverty; the poverty of some provided for a natural division of classes. The existence of poverty in America is consistent with teachings of the Protestant ethic and the survival-of-the-fittest mentality.

Whereas Americans think individually, Norwegians tend to think collectively. Whereas Americans value competition,

Norwegians value cooperation. The thesis of this article is that poverty persists in the United States because our values say it will persist. It does not persist in Norway because the society chooses not to tolerate it. This article examines the general economic conditions in Norway and views them against the Norwegian cultural context—values of egalitarianism and the collective will, trust in the social system, and above all a tradition of kindness to the weaker members of society. Implications for the United States and for American social workers are drawn.

NORWEGIAN ECONOMY

Norway is a socialist country in terms of social policy but a capitalist nation in terms of the ownership of business. Because of Norwegian control of North Sea oil industries, a great deal of wealth is available to the nation. This fact helps compensate for the poor agricultural conditions—rocky, mountainous land and a short growing season.

Personal income taxes in Norway are among the highest in the world. The higher the income, the higher the percentage of taxes paid. The value-added tax is a sales tax of 20 percent on virtually all items sold. Consequently, food and services are extremely expensive in Norway.

Income differences across occupational groups are relatively slight. Virtually no group of employees earns more than twice the average earnings of all employees (Selbyg, 1987). The equalization of income is a reality in Norway.

Poverty

Official estimates put the percentage of people living in poverty at 16.0 percent in the United States and 4.8 percent in Norway (Zimbalist, 1988). In fact, these figures were based on relative income in each country. My personal impression is that the gap between poverty in the United States and Norway is much higher than the numbers indicate. Even in my work with alcoholics, I did not come across one truly impoverished person. When an individual gets into economic trouble, the state provides help. Statistics on poverty thus do not portray the reality in a cradle-to-grave, highly protective society.

Kohlert's (1989) description of the universalism philosophy in welfare is pertinent to Norway. Universalism views those in need as no different from other people. Benefits-for-all programs can effectively prevent the occurrence of poverty in the first place. Such programs as redistribution of wealth, guaranteed income, and children's allowance schemes are examples. Theoretically, benefits from the state are rights, not privileges, and schools teach children that they have earned them. No one will go homeless, hungry, or sick (Henriksen, 1988).

Norway's family policy provides a universal tax-free child allowance for all children younger than 16. Single mothers or fathers receive double the allowance for each child. Older children are eligible for educational stipends. Actually, the amount of the family allowance, about $100 per child, is far below the cost of caring for a child and needs to be increased considerably to keep up with inflation. Elderly people are guaranteed a basic pension. In short, considerable sums are filtered through the tax and social systems to those who need assistance. The result is a society in which there are few truly rich or poor individuals.

Homelessness and Housing

Homelessness is simply not a problem in Norway as it is in some other countries. The government subsidizes low-cost housing so that adequate housing is available to everyone. If a person loses a home through inability to pay the rent, for instance, the social office will assist that person in finding other suitable housing. Housing and income are provided for refugees when they arrive. Like Sweden (Zimbalist, 1988), Norway has no deteriorated housing anywhere. Buildings are well-maintained and warmly heated. In many homes, flowers, visible through well-lighted windows, give a cheerful impression in all the neighborhoods.

Health Care

A recent feature article in the leading Oslo paper carried the headline "Norway Teaches USA on Health Services for Children" (1990). The medical professor interviewed in the article described an international conference attended in Washington, DC. According to Professor Lie, "America totally lacks official health care for children. . . . In infant mortality and death of children due to violence and accidents, the USA is far ahead of Europe and Canada. Twenty-five percent of American children live in poverty" [author's translation] (p. 11).

The public health service and the hospitals are the responsibility of the government. A hospital stay is free, and medicine and primary health care cost minor sums. Mothers or fathers of newborn infants receive extended paid leaves of absence.

Present health policies give Norwegians one of the longest life expectancy rates in the world. Access to excellent health care is not available only to a certain class of citizens but to all members of society. In contrast to the United States, which has the best technology in health care in the world but lags behind other developed countries in coverage, care in Norway is readily available to all.

NORWEGIAN CULTURE

Two countries of great natural resources and highly industrious people move in different directions. Why? The persistence of poverty in the United States and the elimination of poverty in the Nordic countries reflect the cultural values of the two respective countries. In the United States there are many opportunities, but the cost of failure is high; in Norway there is great security, but the cost of security is high.

Three dominant cultural orientations of Norwegians may provide clues to the economic structure: (1) egalitarianism and the collective ideal, (2) trust in the social system, and (3) kindness toward the weak and vulnerable. These cultural orientations are consistent with those observed by Stevens (1989).

Egalitarianism and the Collective Ideal

The link between these dual concepts is in the tendency toward unity that is evidenced in all areas of Norwegian life. The stress on egalitarianism is exemplified in the organization of schools. Competition is largely absent. Children do not receive grades until they are 13, and then only rarely. Homework is minimal, and there are no special classes according to achievement level. Sports are noncompetitive as well; there are no school teams. There are no class officers. Teachers are addressed by their first names until the gymnasium, or high school. Norms favor belonging to the group and not rising above the group (Stevens, 1989).

Group conformity experiments by Milgram (1977) objectify the phenomenon of the collective ideal. A cultural comparative study of conformity to group norms in Norway and France indicated that the pull toward conformity, even to obvious judgmental fallacies, was significantly stronger among the Norwegians than among the French. In addition, although Norwegians accepted criticism impassively, the French subjects made pointed retaliatory responses.

"Do not stand out from the crowd" is the unwritten cultural norm. In my work in alcoholism treatment, the group was used to positive and compelling effect. Clients who were full of denial and minimization of their problems on day 1 seemed to all have undergone some sort of strange transformation by day 28. Never have I observed such consistent turnover of arguments and beliefs in treatment groups in the United States. Trust in the group is exceedingly strong in Norway (Ekstrom, 1988). The group in America is powerful, but in Norway it is more powerful still.

Woe to the group member in Norway who even mentioned connections with wealth or power! Indeed, the only insults uttered in the treatment groups were related either to lying or to bragging. "You are not one of us. You feel superior to the rest of the group" is a hard-hitting complaint.

This verbal enforcement of egalitarianism is reified in the tax system, which demands a heavy toll from those with high incomes, as well as in wage distribution. The disparity in wages among occupational groups is slight (Selbyg, 1987). As they do in the United States, however, capitalists earning money from investments have available to them the usual loopholes that effectively preserve their control of the nation's wealth. The elimination of poverty does not always carry with it the elimination of great wealth. Every system is full of contradictions.

Trust in the Social System

Security is provided by the social system. Economic security is available to all, even to malingerers. Extended sick leave provides 100 percent of their pay to people suffering from such intangible conditions as back pain and nervousness from stress. Money is provided by the employer for the first two weeks, then by the government thereafter.

Social workers have a great deal of authority within the social system, especially in regard to child welfare and public welfare. (For a critical analysis, see van Wormer, 1990.) Professionally trained practitioners work with families in need; they arrange for people in economic difficulty to receive allotments from the state. Because the stigma attached to receiving aid is absent or very slight, no stigma attaches to working at the "social office."

Trust in the system that is for the most part not corrupt and that provides help when needed is logical. A latent effect of the tendency to turn to the state for help is reflected in the small minority of elderly people who live with their families or in nursing homes. Most often they live in easily accessible apartment buildings, where they receive extensive home help and health care. The emphasis on independence, however, is often at the price of loneliness. The very system that takes care of sick and elderly people appears to reduce the responsibility of the family proportionately.

Kindness toward the Weak and Vulnerable

Even the dogs do not bite in Norway; they rarely even bark. Owners of disobedient dogs speak quietly to them. These remarkable animals ride the trains with their owners and often accompany them to work. This illustrates one aspect of Norwegian life that is consistent with other aspects—kindness and nonaggression.

The kindness toward children in Norway is evidenced in law and social custom. Laws forbid corporal punishment against children by teachers and by parents. These laws are widely accepted and vigorously enforced. Norwegian visitors to the Anglo-American countries often remark on the shocking display of violence against children they encountered there. Americans, in contrast, often remark that children in Norway are babied and pampered. Indeed they are! Very large babies are pushed around in baby carriages and continue to take the bottle as long as they wish. They do not start school before age seven and are not taught to read before then.

Norway is not a punitive society. By international standards, criminals receive remarkably light sentences. The treatment of children, poor people, and even criminals is all of a pattern, and this pattern is characterized by individual and systematic kindness to people of all sorts.

IMPLICATIONS FOR U.S. SOCIAL POLICY

To grasp the meaning of poverty or its absence is to grasp the sense of cultural style. The poverty that exists so ubiquitously in

America, North or South, and the poverty that is prevented in a country like Norway mirrors the larger system. To understand a living system, it is necessary to look at a constellation of factors, not in and of themselves, but in their relationships and in their contexts (Bateson, 1984). To know one living system in its uniqueness is to learn of another in terms of the contrast.

Change will come in the United States when the values begin to change and emulate those in Norway. Generally, the laws in a society are consistent with traditional or current values. Hoefer (1988) used the example of Sweden's shift in politics and social welfare policies to illustrate the theory of changes in personal values (postmaterialism) as related to structural change.

To change the social system with reference to poverty in the United States, the country will need to change its values. For instance, both the collective good and individual protections will have to be emphasized above individual growth. Leaders in both the public and private sectors will have to articulate this consciousness. Coverage in the mass media will help. Once a collective sense of urgency is established (such as a demand for national health care), the mobilization of forces to carry out the prerequisite tasks will follow. I emphasize the word "urgency" because a passive belief system will not suffice. The equivalent of wartime fervor, however, would breed rapid mobilization and concomitant change.

Recently, U.S. national leaders talked of a "kinder, gentler society." Also, some action has been taken to shift from counterproductive defense spending to a reform of public welfare spending. Social workers, individually and as a profession, are speaking out for a reprioritizing of interests (Day, 1989). The consensus of social workers seems to be that they must work toward policy change (Hartman, 1989). They must also work toward achieving value change. But whether these diverse "voices in the wilderness" will lead to institutionalization of the efforts will depend on the national sense of urgency and the belief that something can be done.

Meanwhile, Norway is an example of the possible. The solution is simple and described by Selbyg (1987) as follows: "Norway is a welfare state, a country where extensive systems of social care and social insurance make most residents who find themselves in a difficult economic situation legally entitled to aid from the government" (p. 72). Instead of the work ethic, a helping ethic prevails. This ethic is not an individualistic, Band-Aid approach but rather a universal, preventive one, a policy consistent with a value system based on care and absolute security. Norway has found another way and, in my opinion, a far better way.

REFERENCES

Bateson, M. C. (1984). *With a daughter's eye: A memoir of Margaret Mead and Gregory Bateson.* New York: William Morrow.

Blau, J. (1988). On the uses of homelessness: A literature review. *Catalyst, 6*(2), 5–27.

Day, P. (1989). The new poor in America: Isolationism in an international political community. *Social Work, 34,* 227–232.

Ekstrom, J. (1988, July–August). *Cross cultural adaptation of drug and alcohol educational program.* Paper presented to the 35th International Congress on Alcoholism and Drug Dependency, Oslo, Norway.

Hartman, A. (1989). Homelessness: Public issue and private trouble [Editorial]. *Social Work, 34,* 483–484.

Henriksen, J. F. (1988). On being retired in Norway: Is the welfare state living up to expectations? *Norseman, 6,* 8–10.

Hoefer, R. (1988). Postmaterialism at work in social welfare policy: The Swedish case. *Social Service Review, 62,* 383–395.

Kohlert, N. (1989). Welfare reform: A historic consensus. *Social Work, 34,* 303–306.

Milgram, S. (1977). Nationality and conformity. In S. Milgram et al. (Eds.), *The individual in a social world: Essays and experiments* (pp. 159–173). Reading, MA: Addison-Wesley Press.

Norge laerer USA on helsetjeneste for barn. [Norway teaches USA about health services for children.] (1990, March 28). *Aftenposten,* p. 11.

Selbyg, A. (1987). *Norway today.* Oslo: Norwegian University Press.

Stevens, R. (1989). Cultural values and Norwegian health services: Dominant themes and recurring dilemmas. *Scandinavian Studies, 61*(2–3), 199–212.

van Wormer, K. (1990). The hidden juvenile justice system in Norway: A journey back in time. *Federal Probation, 54*(1), 57–61.

Zimbalist, S. (1988). Winning the war on poverty: The Swedish strategy. *Social Work, 33,* 46–49.

This chapter was originally published in the May 1994 issue of Social Work, *vol. 39, pp. 324–327.*

Single Mothers in Sweden: Work and Welfare in the Welfare State

Marguerite G. Rosenthal

Welfare reform is once again on the U.S. agenda. Calls to "end welfare as we know it" echo from the White House and many statehouses as well. Like earlier attempts, new efforts are aimed at moving single mothers to self-sufficiency through job training, incentives for employment, and temporary help with medical coverage and child care for welfare recipients entering the work force. Increasingly, however, the calls for change include punitive measures: compelling mothers who cannot find work to participate in workfare programs, curtailing benefits to families when recipient mothers have additional children, and setting time limits for the receipt of public assistance. As before, current reform measures are based on the following interpretation of welfare dependency: Recipients do not work because they have insufficient preparation or skills for work, lack adequate social skills, have inappropriate attitudes to acquire a job, or are simply too used to receiving public assistance and prefer receiving it to working.

The most recent federal attempt at moving recipients into the work force, the Family Support Act of 1988, was ironically formulated on the eve of a massive economic recession. The act, which governs the states' implementation of the Aid to Families with Dependent Children (AFDC) program, placed the burden for recipients' unemployment on personal deficiencies rather than on structural ones. Through provisions for mandatory education and training, the legislation aimed to reduce the welfare rolls and poverty by putting welfare mothers to work (Hagen, 1992; Hagen & Lurie, 1992; Nichols-Casebolt & McClure, 1989). The Clinton administration's attention to welfare reform takes place even as it acknowledges chronic unemployment flowing from profound structural changes in the economy. Yet, as evidenced in the president's 1994 State of the Union address, the connection between economic dislocation and welfare dependency—in contrast to dependency on unemployment insurance—is absent. In public rhetoric, at least, the problem is seen to be the chronic dependency and deficiency of the welfare recipient.

When the focus of reform is, instead, on the question of eliminating poverty rather than reforming welfare recipients, another issue arises: whether the problems of the very poor are better addressed by targeting social expenditures on the most needy versus instituting universal programs as more appropriate and more politically viable (Skocpol, 1990).

The American approach to single motherhood, work, and welfare stands in stark contrast to that of most other industrialized countries. A growing body of literature points to the economic vulnerability of single-parent families because of the limited income a single earner can produce, the low wages that many working women earn, and the adequacy or inadequacy of income transfer programs. In making comparisons the literature also finds that American single-parent families have remarkably higher and more persistent poverty rates than do those in other industrialized countries, largely because the benefit structure for single mothers in the United States is very low (Goldberg & Kremen, 1990; McFate, 1991; Smeeding, Torrey, & Rein, 1988; Zopf, 1989).

This article examines the situation of single mothers and their families in Sweden, the country acknowledged to be the most advanced welfare state. Through this examination, the author hopes to contribute to the American discussion of how best to meet the needs of such families and to illuminate the complexities of welfare reform.

SWEDEN'S APPROACH TO SOCIAL WELFARE

Among the industrialized countries, Sweden consistently stands out as the country where poverty appears to have been most successfully reduced (Duncan et al., 1991; Goldberg & Kremen, 1990; Kahn & Kamerman, 1983; Kamerman & Kahn, 1988; McFate, 1991; Sidel, 1986; Smeeding et al., 1988). Sweden has often been examined by comparative social policy analysts as the society where commitments to the general welfare of the population have been kept. Destitution, homelessness, substandard housing, hunger, malnutrition, and untreated health problems, all problems of poverty, have been virtually eliminated in Sweden.

A caveat is needed: In the September 1991 national elections, the Social Democrats, the long-term political office holders and architects of the renowned Swedish welfare state, were defeated in what was seen as a potential turning point in the nation's 50-year effort to articulate its advanced welfare state. There is a vigorous debate about which aspects of the Swedish welfare state are likely to be altered as the country moves to join the European Economic Community and privatization increases. These changes, it is posited, will undercut some of Sweden's social benefits—particularly those associated with high wages, full employment, and a large public sector—to make Sweden's industrial products competitive on the European market (Larsson, 1991). Conservatives argue that high labor costs, including associated high labor-related social welfare benefits, increase the price of products to competitive disadvantage.

The new conservative government has moved to increase economic expansion by lowering taxes on higher-income groups, thus reducing, at least temporarily, the amount of money available for public services (Schmidt, 1992; Swedish Institute, 1991b). Persson (1992) predicted the loss of 50,000 to 60,000 public-sector jobs, most of them held by women. A less-dire interpretation of the future, however, is that Sweden's basic welfare structure will remain intact and that, at worst, Sweden will become more like Germany, whose welfare system, though less elaborate than Sweden's, is nonetheless far more extensive than our own (Barkan, 1992). A Swedish political scientist, taking an even more sanguine position, noted that most members of the new incumbent bourgeois parties actually support the principles of the universal welfare state but advocate for increased choice for consumers and promote public competition and limited private options as well (Rothstein, 1992). Whether they survive or not, Sweden's welfare state provisions at their recent height demonstrate how a modern industrial society, one devoted to social equality and security, can provide well for its population.

Single-Parent Households in Sweden

Sweden is not immune to the economic and social stresses posed by growing numbers of single-parent households. Such families account for about 20 percent of families with children, although the path to single parenthood in Sweden differs from that in the United States. For instance, teenage parents are almost unknown in Sweden, and the mean age for first-time mothers is about 27 (Hoem & Hoem, 1987). However, the common pattern of having children in arrangements of cohabitation—seen as a less-stable family arrangement than formal marriage—as well as a high divorce rate result in many single-parent families; analysts have predicted that they will be a continuing and even growing phenomenon in Sweden (Popenoe, 1986).

Reducing Poverty

Several recent studies have examined Sweden's approaches to dealing with economic stress, particularly that experienced by families with children. For example, Zimbalist (1988) reported that Sweden has reduced poverty to a bare minimum, probably the lowest in the world. Kamerman and Kahn (1988) cited the Swedish system of social welfare benefits as very effective in meeting the economic needs of families with children. Most recently, a comparative study of eight countries—Australia, Canada, West Germany, Norway, Switzerland, the United Kingdom, the United States, and Sweden—found that the United States had the highest percentage of children below the U.S. poverty line, whereas Sweden had the lowest (Smeeding et al., 1988). Likewise, Kamerman and Kahn (1988) and Rosenthal (1990) reported that although Swedish single mothers and their children are economically disadvantaged, they are not impoverished, and in fact most have disposable incomes that approach those of families with two parents. Sweden's very low rate of poverty among children, about 5 percent compared to about 20 percent in the United States using the U.S. poverty line as the measure, is tied to the generosity of its income transfer programs, including its means-tested social assistance (Smeeding et al., 1988).

American social welfare analysts interested in examining the differences between the U.S. and Swedish responses to economic need have paid particular attention to the various universal welfare programs of the Swedish welfare state. For instance, Zimbalist (1988), in comparing U.S. and Swedish strategies for combating poverty in the post–World War II period, stated, "In Sweden, public social benefits . . . [are] made available on an increasingly universal—that is, not means-tested—basis, whereas in the United States more and more emphasis . . . [is] placed on rigorous means-testing of welfare programs" (p. 48).

In addition to universal health care and pension rights, Sweden's key universal non-means-tested welfare benefits for families with children are child allowances and state-supported child support payments. These benefits play an important part in increasing disposable income for families with children (Kahn & Kamerman, 1983; Kamerman & Kahn, 1988).

Child allowances, which were about $78 (or 485 Swedish crowns) per month per child in 1989, are provided by the state to all families with children younger than 19. They are adjusted yearly to equal about 5 percent of the average wage and are not taxed (Eriksson, 1987; Kamerman & Kahn, 1988; Ministry of Finance, 1989).

Advance maintenance allowances are child support payments made to the custodial parent by the state in cases of separation or divorce when the noncustodial parent fails to provide regular support. The state then seeks reimbursement from the noncustodial parent. In 1989 the monthly advance maintenance allowance was about $145 (or 930 Swedish crowns), an amount almost double the basic child allowance and also nearly twice the average amount collected from absent fathers (Eriksson, 1987; Kamerman & Kahn, 1988; Ministry of Finance, 1989). In 1988, 16 percent of all children up to age 17 were receiving maintenance advances (National Social Insurance Board, 1989).

The advance maintenance allowance, like many other social welfare benefits in Sweden, is calculated as a percentage of the minimum income needed to provide for an individual's fundamental needs. This base amount is recomputed annually to adjust to consumer price variations and is set by the National Pensions Board. The maintenance advance is computed at 40 percent of the base.

Because the number of children being supported by the advance maintenance payments has been steadily rising, the costs to the state, as well as the presumed disincentives to marriage, are currently under discussion in Sweden (National Social Insurance Board, 1989). In 1990 a special commission appointed to study these matters issued a first report. Several reforms were proposed, the general trend of which was to make these benefits means-tested rather than automatic (Socialdepartementet, 1990).

Combining the child allowance and the advance maintenance allowance, then, a mother with two children can expect to receive about $445 per month in publicly supported children's benefits, regardless of her other income. This amount represents about 60 percent of the base amount and about 30 percent of average earned income. These universal benefits exceeded the median U.S. grant of $360 for a family of three in 1988 (Levitan, 1990).

WOMEN WORKERS IN SWEDEN

As important as social welfare benefits are to providing a steady and basic support for single-parent families, they must not obscure the importance that earned income plays in the Swedish household. The Swedish concept of full employment, a basic tenet of the long-prevailing but now out-of-office Social Democratic party, includes not only the right to a job for everyone who wants one but also the expectation that all adults, including parents of young children, will participate in the labor force.

Sweden's proactive full-employment policies, as well as many of its other social policies, are frequently ascribed to the strong ties organized labor has had with the Social Democratic governments (Esping-Andersen, 1990). In Sweden 90 percent of earners are employees, and 90 percent of these are unionized. This situation contrasts sharply with the United States, where current estimates are that only about 16 percent of workers are unionized (Heckscher, 1988).

Through considerable government planning and intervention, the Swedish unemployment rate has remained around 2 percent for nearly 20 years (Esping-Andersen, 1990; Ginsburg, 1983; Swedish Institute, 1991b). The low unemployment rate is tied directly to labor market policies that involve the government in active and comprehensive job referral programs; training and retraining for workers with obsolete skills; government loans to stimulate new job creation in private industry; and, very importantly, job creation in the public sector in times of economic slowdown.

Women workers have shared in the benefits won for working people in Sweden. Indeed, in the arena of work force participation for women, Sweden offers important lessons—and warnings—for policymakers. Women began entering the paid labor force in considerable numbers following the post–World War II industrial boom. Beginning in the 1960s, married women, including those with young children, joined the labor force as permanent employees in increasing numbers (Scott, 1982). By 1985, 80 percent of all Swedish women were working outside of the home; those not working were almost exclusively older than 50 (Gustafsson, 1987), and women constituted 48 percent of the work force in 1990 (Swedish Institute, 1991b).

Economic and Social Policies to Assist Women Workers

The increased participation of women in the paid labor force did not come about by accident. Labor shortages in the 1960s led to the immigration of substantial numbers of foreign workers (mostly from Finland and Southern Europe) who, the powerful unions feared, threatened to lower wage rates.

Consciously devised economic policies induced many married women to go to work. The most important were tax changes that eliminated income taxes based on a family's income in favor of separate taxation of all earners. This policy ended deductions for dependents; a man supporting a wife and two children was taxed at the same rate as a single man, and each working adult's income was taxed separately; families were not penalized by having a larger combined income.

Another important policy generated the "solidaristic" wage agreements, which were labor contracts supported by Sweden's powerful labor confederations that minimized wage differentials between high- and low-wage earners. The contracts were negotiated centrally by three labor confederations and an employers' confederation, and they set wages nationally. Women's wages, typically at the low end of the scale, were raised as a result of this policy, and consequently paid work became more profitable for women (Scott, 1982). (Among other recent changes in Sweden, the established pattern of centralized bargaining is being increasingly replaced by decentralized negotiations [Martin, 1991; Swedish Institute, 1991a]. This new collective bargaining pattern threatens job stability and earnings for women, because it is associated with part-time and temporary work arrangements [Acker & Hallock, 1992].)

Several other important pieces of social legislation, designed to facilitate women's work force participation, were either created or elaborated on during the 1960s and 1970s. Parental leave, enacted in 1974, is an earned benefit that since July 1991 entitles either parent of a newborn or adopted child to 18 months of full-time leave compensated at 90 percent of full-time earnings, and the employee's job is held while he or she is on parental leave. Parents of children younger than eight also have the statutory right to work a maximum of six hours a day (with a corresponding reduction in income), and either parent may stay at home to care for a sick child for up to 60 days per year for each child (Swedish Institute, 1991a).

Government-supported child care was also greatly expanded in the late 1960s and 1970s to accommodate the needs of working mothers. Despite its comparative availability, however, universal child care is not yet a reality; in 1989 although nearly all mothers of young children were working, only 49 percent of their children were cared for in publicly provided settings, and the shortage of spaces for very young children was described as acute (Swedish Institute, 1990).

The strength of Sweden's educational and vocational training systems is a component of the success that Sweden has had in achieving full employment. All educational facilities in Sweden, from primary education through university and skills training, are public and free. Moreover, university students and adults in skills training receive stipends during training. School is compulsory for children through age 16. Most students continue their educations in an upper-secondary-school program geared either toward university preparation or a specific vocational field. A majority of students pursue vocational subjects. (Only about 15 percent of working-class children prepare for entrance to a university.) Retraining is available for older workers who need to develop further skills to obtain regular employment (Swedish Institute, 1984).

There is general agreement in the literature that this complex of economic, social, and skills development policies has been successful in integrating women into the work force. Parental leaves and child care policies have especially assisted women in balancing the demands of the workplace and the home (Kamerman & Kahn, 1988; Ruggie, 1984). Efforts and policies to equalize women's and men's work choices, salaries, and responsibilities in home and child care, however, have been less successful (Liljeström, Mellstrom, & Svensson, 1978; Rosenthal, 1990; Ruggie, 1984; Scott, 1982). Women take parental leave, work reduced hours, do housework, and manage the home and children. These differences in tasks are related to inequalities in the labor force that clearly affect women's earning capacities.

Women's Jobs and Earnings

Pronounced sex segregation and part-time work for women, two outstanding features of the Swedish labor market, have profound consequences for single mothers. In 1986, 43 percent of working women were employed part-time, working an average of 26 hours per week (Sundström, 1987). At the same time, women's job options were quite restricted, and most worked in same-sex–dominated occupations such as secretarial work, nursing, shop assistants, cleaners, child caretakers, home helpers, teachers, and kitchen staff (National Labour Market Board, 1987). Although these occupations pay less than most men's jobs, because of the solidaristic wage policy, women do better than American female wage earners. Women who worked full-time earned 78 percent of men's wages in 1985 (Acker, 1988). However, because so many worked part-time, women earned only 37 percent of the total yearly wages (Ericsson & Jacobsson, 1985).

Economic incentives, social welfare supports, and normative expectations of work result in a very high labor force participation by single mothers. In 1980, 87 percent of single mothers worked, only 2 percent were counted as full-time homemakers, another 2 percent were listed as unemployed, 7 percent were studying, and the remainder were not accounted for. In contrast, 76 percent of married mothers worked, 18 percent were at home, 3 percent were students, and no data existed for the remainder (Gustafsson, 1990).

NEED FOR SOCIAL ASSISTANCE

Despite the extent of social welfare benefits and the high labor force participation of single mothers, the most recent data demonstrate that the need for means-tested social assistance—the Swedish equivalent of public assistance—has not been eliminated. In 1985, 40 percent of families headed by single mothers received social assistance during some of the year (Nordic Council of Ministers, 1988).

Use of social assistance has been found to be particularly associated with increases in unemployment, because some workers have not been employed long enough to qualify for unemployment benefits. The financial crises precipitated by divorce are also associated with receipt of social assistance. Temporary and part-time work reduce earned income, and there is an increasing use of women workers for this contingency work force (Acker & Hallock, 1992). All of these factors disproportionately affect single mothers, who then turn to social assistance to supplement earnings and other benefits. The numbers of single-parent families using social assistance grew by 50 percent between 1980 and 1984 (Gustafsson, 1988a). A Swedish poverty researcher found that single-parent families and immigrants are disproportionately represented among those families who receive social assistance (Gustafsson, 1988a). Assistance is also used by single adults with marginal attachment to the work force and non-Swedish residents (Marklund, 1992).

No precise information about persistent dependence on social assistance is available. There are data that show that the average length of time single-parent families receive assistance is only 4½ months (Nordic Council of Ministers, 1988), although a Swedish researcher concluded that there is a strong likelihood that a significant percentage of families rely on assistance for a lengthy period of time (Gustafsson, 1988a).

Unlike the situation in the United States, where public assistance is frequently the only source of income for recipients, social assistance in Sweden supplements other income sources, including wages and other transfer benefits. It is used during transitional periods when other sources of earned income are lost or interrupted, and it is probably used to supplement earned income for large families. Social assistance remains an important source of income for appreciable numbers of single-parent families in Sweden despite other generous welfare entitlements.

Assistance is required by national law to provide a "reasonable level of living" for recipients. Assistance is administered by municipalities, and actual grant levels vary from municipality to municipality, but nearly all jurisdictions come close to providing at least the minimum amount suggested by the national welfare administration. Other sources of income, such as child allowances and maintenance allowances (child support), are deducted from the social assistance grant. In August 1988 the monthly assistance grant was computed at $808 (5,050 Swedish crowns) for a single mother with two children younger than seven (personal communication with B. Åkerlind, Socialistyrelsen, August 1988). This generous level of assistance ensures that recipients do not live in abject poverty, in contrast to American public welfare recipients, who uniformly live below the meager poverty line.

The housing subsidy is another means-tested welfare benefit that is paid according to income and family size. It is an additional benefit for families receiving social assistance and on average covers about 40 percent of housing costs. Again, single-parent families are more likely to receive this benefit than are two-parent families; in 1979, 80 percent of single parents received the subsidy, but only 26 percent of two-parent families did so. Single parents also received priority for publicly supported child care slots and paid lower fees (Gustafsson, 1990).

POVERTY IN SWEDEN

Sweden has not established an official poverty line, but the assistance grant level, 58 percent of the median income in 1985, is beginning to be used as a measure of poverty. Clearly, Sweden's poverty threshold is conceptualized at a very generous level, a fact that may partially explain why researchers have only recently begun to examine who should be considered poor in their country.

Approximately 12 percent of all families—presumably families who did not receive social assistance for one reason or another—had incomes below 58 percent of the median income in 1985 (Gustafsson, 1988b). Single-parent families were overrepresented among families experiencing economic difficulty, particularly those with several children. Other large families also experienced poverty disproportionately (Gustafsson, 1990). Research also shows that without transfer payments, 42 percent of all families would have been in poverty (Gustafsson, 1988b).

CONCLUSION

As U.S. welfare experts, politicians, and journalists continue to debate the merits of work requirements for public assistance recipients, the Swedish experience offers some important lessons. Far from undermining a work ethic, the Swedish social welfare system has supported it through a relatively cohesive set of programs that include the education system, labor market intervention, a tax system that encourages all adults to work, and social welfare provisions that assist working mothers. As a consequence, nearly all single mothers in Sweden work, and they are more likely to work full-time than are their married peers. However, there is an established and growing pattern of part-time work for women. As a consequence, Swedish women cannot rely exclusively on wages or even wages and universal transfer programs to protect them and their children from poverty. Means-tested social assistance, provided at a comparatively generous level, is an important, if often intermittent, support system for a large percentage of single-parent families.

Using a standard measure of poverty set at 50 percent of median income, Smeeding and Rainwater found that 5.5 percent of Swedish single-parent families lived in poverty in 1987, compared to an astounding 53.3 percent of U.S. single-parent families (cited in McFate, 1991).

Other recent comparative research (Duncan et al., 1991) has shown that single-parent families with two children in Sweden who rely exclusively on transfer benefits—social assistance, child allowances, maintenance payments, and housing allowances—receive 64 percent of the median family income for the country. With half-time work at minimum wage, the income of this family rises to 67 percent of the median. In the United States, similar families with no earned income receive only 27 percent of the median; with half-time work at minimum wage, single-parent families are still poor, receiving only 39 percent of the median. At least for Sweden, apparently maintaining a high level of transfer support has not served as a disincentive to work. Most single mothers work even though working makes only a marginal economic difference. At the same time, transfer payments are needed to keep single working mothers and their children out of poverty.

Of course the Swedish model will not transfer itself easily to the United States, where the emphasis on individualism and the Poor Law tradition keep alive the principles of self-sufficiency and less eligibility. Sweden industrialized late, and industrialization was accompanied by a strong and lasting trade union movement. This movement, combined with simultaneous organizing among the small farmers, are factors that provide part of the explanation for Sweden's development of its "third way":

advancing capitalism while also developing a comprehensive welfare state (Esping-Andersen, 1990).

In a context of weakened unions, fragmentation of the working and nonworking poor populations, deregulation, and a collapsing tax structure, U.S. social policymakers must pragmatically have less-comprehensive goals than aspiring to achieve a Swedish-like welfare state. This country must, of course, work to overcome these difficulties by supporting unionization, by urging greater regulation, and by advocating for a fair and comprehensive tax structure geared to domestic rather than military needs.

In the more limited debate about work and welfare, however, the United States can also make use of information from other countries. Among the lessons to be learned from Sweden are these: Substituting work for public assistance will not remove most single-parent families from poverty, and universal benefits, such as child allowances, are unlikely to meet the needs of the poorest of the poor, including those who work. If our goal is to eliminate or at least minimize poverty, we can, like the Swedes, champion an approach that combines work with welfare at levels that provide a minimum but decent standard of living.

REFERENCES

Acker, J. (1988, August). *A contradictory reality: Swedish women at work in the 1980s.* Paper presented at the annual meeting of the Society for the Advancement of Scandinavian Studies, Eugene, OR.

Acker, J., & Hallock, M. (1992, March). *Economic restructuring and women's wages: Equity issues in the U.S. and Sweden.* Paper presented at the Women, Power and Strategies for Change Seminar sponsored by the Swedish Information Service and held at New York University, New York.

Barkan, J. (1992). Sweden remodels: Have the Swedes tossed out social democracy? *Democratic Left, 20*(1), 6–8.

Duncan, G., Gustafsson, B., Hauser, R., Hausman, P., Jenkins, S., Messinger, H., Muffels, R., Nolan, B., Ray, J.-C., & Voges, W. (1991). *Poverty, inequality and the crisis of social policy.* Washington, DC: Joint Center for Political and Economic Studies.

Ericsson, Y., & Jacobsson, R. (1985). *Side by side: A report on equality between women and men in Sweden, 1985.* Stockholm: Gotab.

Eriksson, I. (1987). *Some facts on single parents in Sweden.* Stockholm: Ministry of Health and Social Affairs.

Esping-Andersen, G. (1990). *The three worlds of welfare capitalism.* Princeton, NJ: Princeton University Press.

Family Support Act of 1988, P.L. 100-485, 102 Stat. 2343.

Ginsburg, H. (1983). *Full employment and public policy: The United States and Sweden.* Lexington, MA: Lexington Books.

Goldberg, G. S., & Kremen, E. (Eds.). (1990). *The feminization of poverty: Only in America?* Westport, CT: Greenwood Press.

Gustafsson, B. (1988a, November). *The income safety net—Who falls into it and why?* Paper presented at the Welfare Trends in the Nordic Countries Conference, Oslo, Norway.

Gustafsson, B. (1988b, November). *Poverty in Sweden, 1975–1985.* Paper presented at the Welfare Trends in the Nordic Countries Conference, Oslo, Norway.

Gustafsson, S. (1987). *The labor force participation and earnings of lone parents: A review of Swedish politicies and institutions with some comparisons to West Germany.* Stockholm: Arbetslivscentrum.

Gustafsson, S. (1990). Labour force participation and earnings of lone parents: A Swedish case study including comparisons with Germany. In *Lone-parent families: The economic challenge* (OECD Social Policy Studies No. 8). Paris: Organisation for Economic Co-operation and Development.

Hagen, J. L. (1992). Women, work, and welfare: Is there a role for social work? *Social Work, 37,* 15–20.

Hagen, J. L., & Lurie, I. (1992). *Implementing JOBS: Initial state choices* (summary report). Albany: State University of New York, Nelson A. Rockefeller Institute of Government.

Heckscher, C. C. (1988). *The new unionism: Employee involvement in the changing corporation.* New York: Basic Books.

Hoem, B., & Hoem, J. M. (1987). *The Swedish family: Aspects of contemporary developments.* Stockholm: University of Stockholm, Section of Demography.

Kahn, A., & Kamerman, S. B. (1983). *Income transfers for families with children: An eight-country study.* Philadelphia: Temple University Press.

Kamerman, S. B., & Kahn, A. (1988). *Mothers alone: Strategies for a time of change.* Dover, MA: Auburn House.

Larsson, G. (1991, November). *The end of Swedish social democracy? The 1991 Swedish election and its implications.* Paper presented at the Minda de Gunzberg Center for European Studies, Harvard University, Cambridge, MA.

Levitan, S. A. (1990). *Programs in aid of the poor.* Baltimore: Johns Hopkins University Press.

Liljeström, R., Mellstrom, G. F., & Svensson, G. L. (1978). *Roles in transition.* Stockholm: Schmidts Boktryckeri A. B.

Marklund, S. (1992). The decomposition of social policy in Sweden. *Scandanavian Journal of Social Welfare 1,* 2–11.

Martin, A. (1991). *Wage bargaining and Swedish politics: The political implications of the end of central negotiations.* Cambridge, MA: Harvard University, Minda de Gunzburg Center for European Studies.

McFate, K. (1991). *Poverty, inequality and the crisis of social policy: Summary of findings.* Washington, DC: Joint Center for Political and Economic Studies.

Ministry of Finance. (1989). *The Swedish budget, 1989/90.* Stockholm: Author.

National Labour Market Board. (1987). *Statistics: Equality in the labour market.* Stockholm: Author.

National Social Insurance Board. (1989). *Social insurance statistics: Facts 1989.* Stockholm: Author.

Nichols-Casebolt, A. M., & McClure, J. (1989). Social work support for welfare reform: The latest surrender in the War on Poverty. *Social Work, 34,* 77–80.

Nordic Council of Ministers. (1988). *Kvinnor uch main i Norden: Fakta om jamstalldheten 1988* [Women and men in the Nordic countries: Facts on equal opportunities 1988]. Copenhagen: Author.

Persson, K. (1992, March). *Women and power: Why have we not made more headway in Sweden?* Paper presented at the Women, Power and Strategies for Change Seminar sponsored by the Swedish Information Service and held at New York University, New York.

Popenoe, D. (1986). What is happening to the family in Sweden? *Social Change, 36,* 1–7.

Rosenthal, M. G. (1990). Sweden: Promise and paradox. In G. S. Goldberg & E. Kremen (Eds.), *The feminization of poverty: Only in America?* (pp. 129–155). Westport, CT: Greenwood Press.

Rothstein, B. (1992, April). *The crisis of the Swedish Social Democrats and the future of the universal welfare state.* Paper presented at the Minda de Gunzberg Center for European Studies, Harvard University, Cambridge, MA.

Ruggie, M. (1984). *The state and working women: A comparative study of Britain and Sweden.* Princeton, NJ: Princeton University Press.

Schmidt, W. E. (1992, February 23). In a post–cold war era, Scandinavia rethinks itself. *New York Times,* p. E-3.

Scott, H. (1982). *Sweden's "right to be human"; Sex-role equality: The goal and the reality.* Armonk, NY: M. E. Sharpe.

Sidel, R. (1986). *Women and children last: The plight of poor women in affluent America.* New York: Penguin Books.

Skocpol, T. (1990, Summer). Sustainable social policy: Fighting poverty without poverty programs. *American Prospect, 2,* 58–70.

Smeeding, T., Torrey, B. B., & Rein, M. (1988). Patterns of income and poverty: The economic status of children and the elderly in eight countries. In J. L. Palmer, T. Smeeding, & B. B. Torrey (Eds.), *The vulnerable* (pp. 89–119). Washington, DC: Urban Institute.

Socialdepartementet. (1990). *Samhällsstöd till underhållsbidragsberättigade barn: Idéskisser och bakgrundsmaterial* [Advance maintenance allowances for custodial parents: Ideas and background material]. Stockholm: Regeringskansliets Offsetcentral.

Sundström, M. (1987). *A study in the growth of part-time work in Sweden.* Stockholm: Arbetslivcentrum.

Swedish Institute. (1984). *Fact sheet on Sweden: Facts and figures about youths in Sweden.* Stockholm: Author.

Swedish Institute. (1990). *Fact sheets on Sweden: Child care in Sweden.* Stockholm: Author.

Swedish Institute. (1991a). *Fact sheets on Sweden: Social insurance in Sweden*. Stockholm: Author.

Swedish Institute. (1991b). *Fact sheets on Sweden: The Swedish economy*. Stockholm: Author.

Zimbalist, S. E. (1988). Winning the war on poverty: The Swedish strategy. *Social Work, 33*, 46–49.

Zopf, P. E. (1989). *American women in poverty*. Westport, CT: Greenwood Press.

This chapter was originally published in the May 1994 issue of Social Work, *vol. 39, pp. 270–278.*

Part III

POPULATIONS

Effective Coping Strategies of African Americans

Alfrieda Daly, Jeanette Jennings, Joyce O. Beckett, and Bogart R. Leashore

W hat are the coping strategies that have enabled African Americans not only to survive but also to achieve against all odds? Are they shaped, at least in part, by cultural patterns and characteristics that have survived from life on the African continent to the present? If so, what does this suggest for social work practice and social welfare policies and services? This article discerns successful coping styles among African Americans that reflect the transmission of African belief systems and cultural values.

This article identifies several studies that explored the Africentric orientation to coping and resolving problems. These coping mechanisms are reviewed across system levels: individual, family, community, and organization. Implications for social work practice with African Americans are discussed and future research efforts are suggested.

TRADITIONAL AFRICAN CULTURAL PATTERNS

Despite their unique experience during and after slavery, African Americans have been viewed and judged by most social scientists with the same worldview applied to the dominant culture. Differences from established dominant norms have been interpreted negatively or, at best, neutralized. Herskovits (1935) was among the few American scholars in the first half of the 20th century who described the highly developed political and legal systems, literature and art, and arrangements of interpersonal and family relations on the West African coast, the major area from which slaves were brought to America. Possibly among the first American theorists to discuss distinct worldviews and values of African Americans were Kluckhorn and Strodtbeck (1961) and Parsons and Shils (1967).

More recently, Houston (1990) pointed to the structure, content, and practice of religion in African American churches as evidence that African culture survived the African diaspora. He described the large number of African priests who were among slaves brought to America as providing some of the means through which this cultural adaptation took place. These priests provided a degree of stability, affective experience, and group cohesiveness through which some of the coping strategies, based on their cultural past, could emerge. Houston stated, "Because of the many covert, subliminal, nonverbal, and otherwise seemingly innocuous means of culturally transmitting and conditioning personality from parent to offspring, it is possible that personality represents the most profound and intense of all African survivals" (p. 119).

Nobles (1972, 1980), Ak'bar (1984), Baldwin (1985), and Asante (1988) are among contemporary scholars who have identified an Africentric approach to philosophy and human behavior and contributed to the development of what has come to be known as the Africentric paradigm. This paradigm proposes that in African culture humanity is viewed as a collective rather than as individuals and that this collective view is expressed as shared concern and responsibility for the well-being of others (Ak'bar, 1984; Ho, 1987; Houston, 1990; Schiele, 1990). In fact, most African languages did not have words for "alone" and "ownership" at the time of initial contact with Europeans.

The Africentric paradigm acknowledges feelings and emotions as well as rational and logical ways of thinking equally. Materialism and competition are supplanted by spiritual awareness and by cooperation with others (Ak'bar, 1984; Baldwin, 1985; Ho, 1987; Turner, 1991). A belief system that recognizes and appreciates the rich heritage and experiences of African Americans, including the devastating impact of oppression as manifested by racism and discrimination, emerges from this perspective (Everett, Chipungu, & Leashore, 1991). Scholarship using this perspective identifies positive aspects of African American life richly embedded in spirituality and a worldview that incorporates African traits and commitment to common causes (Grier & Cobb, 1968; Hill, 1971; Houston, 1990; Nobles, 1972, 1980; Miller, 1993). In understanding African cultural survival and the African American personality, social and behavioral science and research have moved from viewing African American behavior as deviant to appreciating its unique cultural heritage.

Friendship, compassion, sharing, honesty, courage, and self-control are among the virtues upheld in African communities, whereas selfishness, theft, cheating, and greed are vices that are quickly addressed and corrected (Houston, 1990; Khoapa, 1980; Mbiti, 1969; Menkiti, 1984; Turner, 1991). In African society, social structures and organizations include every member in mutual sharing and responsibility for others. Emphasis on the interpersonal and on sharing kinship beyond blood ties evolved into a political structure that resembles socialism (Houston, 1990). However, Khoapa (1980) differentiated African socialism from European or Marxist socialism: African socialism focuses on universal charity and codes of conduct that give dignity to people regardless of their station in life, in contrast to Marxist societies where citizens are viewed as belonging to the state, which centralizes planning with little input from lower level workers. It is the positives of this Africentric perspective that are the basis of this article.

AFRICAN CULTURAL SURVIVAL AND COPING STRATEGIES AT THE INDIVIDUAL LEVEL

Numerous scholarly works detail the life patterns of descendants of African slaves in contemporary times (Billingsley, 1992; Clark, 1965; Frazier, 1964; Grier & Cobb, 1968; Hacker, 1992). African Americans experience pressures that can be explained by the stigmas of race or racial origin and that are unlike those encountered by other groups that have immigrated to America (Hacker, 1992). The health and well-being of African American males are examples of the efficacy of indigenous coping skills. Racism and discrimination have historically blocked the door to opportunity for many African Americans. Yet many African American males have been successful (Gary & Leashore, 1982; Hacker, 1992). Much of their success can be attributed to individual and family resilience, the ability to "bounce back" after defeat or near defeat, and the mobilization of limited resources while simultaneously protecting the ego against a constant array of social and economic assaults. To varying degrees, success results from a strong value system that includes belief in self, industrious efforts, desire and motivation to achieve, religious beliefs, self-respect and respect for others, responsibility toward one's family and community, and cooperation.

Traditionally and conventionally, social and behavioral science research has largely ignored African American males who actively assumed the role of provider for their families. However, there is an emerging body of literature that focuses on African American males from within rather than from without the context of family life. Their relationships and socialization with their children and family and spousal satisfactions are also of interest (Allen, 1981; Braithwaite, 1981; Cazenave, 1979; Gary & Leashore, 1982; Madhubuti, 1990; McAdoo, 1981; Staples, 1977). Two analyses of data from the *National Survey of Black Americans 1979–1980* (Jackson & Gurin, 1987) illustrate the research that is emerging. In the first analysis, Taylor, Leashore, and Tolliver (1988) examined the provider role as perceived by 771 African American males. Over half (54 percent) perceived themselves as providing very well for their families. Generally, younger men were the least likely to perceive themselves as good providers, whereas those 65 and older were the most likely to report that they performed very well in the provider role. A second analysis (Stewart, 1990) examined family life satisfaction among married African American males and found that home ownership, family closeness, and general life satisfaction were positively related to family life satisfaction.

The findings of these analyses suggest that African American men perceive greater success and satisfaction as they mature. The African American community collectively may provide a major structure that enables the development of self-esteem and general life satisfaction for African American males over time. This structure includes the tradition of giving honor and recognition to those in the African American community who have faithfully fulfilled their responsibilities to their families and communities. These men are not dependent on individual achievements such as the amount of earnings to feel good about themselves. Instead, they celebrate fulfilling their role as providers within parameters defined by their community. This perspective is in contrast to the dominant culture, which rewards individualism, competitiveness, and material achievements. Thus, the propensity toward collective in contrast to individualistic identity continues to provide a coping mechanism that enables these African American men to be successful and, indeed, to resist the onslaught of negative images that the dominant culture attributes to them.

AFRICAN CULTURAL SURVIVAL AND COPING STRATEGIES AT THE FAMILY LEVEL

Public awareness of spouse abuse as a social problem has increased since the 1970s; shelters and other services for battered women and their children have been established. Much attention has been given to this problem in the popular, scholarly, and professional literature. Although domestic violence exists among all socioeconomic, racial, ethnic, and gender groups, little attention has been given to its dynamics among African Americans. For example, only four citations on African American battered women emerged from a search of psychological, sociological, and social work literature for the years 1967 to 1987 (Coley & Beckett, 1988).

Despite the limited studies, evidence indicates that African American women coping with domestic violence, in contrast to white women, were particularly sensitive to the influence of family and social support systems. Social supports such as an extended family, the presence of nonnuclear family members in the home, or long-time residence in a neighborhood led to a substantial decrease in spouse assaults among African Americans, whereas the same factors led to a substantial increase in assaults among white people (Coley & Beckett, 1988). Although African American and white women used the same range of services, African American women were more hesitant than white women to use some services. For example, African American women seldom used shelter services. Whereas African American women were more likely to turn to medical services, this was the resource least likely to be sought by white women. In contrast, mental health services were the preferred resource sought by white women, but African American women were unlikely to seek counseling services. The literature suggests that African Americans frequently perceive these services as contrary to their cultural experiences and insufficient to meet their needs (Bingham & Guinyard, 1982).

The domestic violence literature suggests that some African American women may view and interpret their battering experiences differently than white women (Beckett & Coley, 1987; Richie, 1981; Vontress, 1973). African American women are more likely to view their physical abuse from the perspective of racial oppression or racial and sexual oppression, and white women use the perspective of sexual oppression. African American women are unlikely to see the violence solely in individual, family, or power terms. Thus, African American women are likely to view battering as the African American male's displaced anger and aggression in response to racism and his constant struggle to assume or maintain economic and other social roles typically expected of males in America. Finally, white men who are reported to the criminal justice system for spouse abuse are more likely to be referred to the mental health system, and African American men are more likely to remain in the criminal justice system without a referral (Beckett & Coley, 1987; Hacker, 1992).

The interaction of race with other social support variables supports the argument that African cultural survival in the African American community provides a supportive structure for women and families in which family violence is a problem. Although the specific processes of this support are not well elaborated in the literature, it is clear that family, neighbors, and the community provide advice, counseling, and shelter and that this assistance has provided a palliative effect. Such assistance is also consistent with the African value of the extended family and caring for the well-being of others. This collective aid to the family can be viewed as support of African survival in the resolution of domestic violence.

AFRICAN CULTURAL SURVIVAL AND COPING STRATEGIES AT THE COMMUNITY LEVEL

Although the social work literature has recognized the existence and importance of the extended family and community in the resolution of familial problems of African Americans, the mechanisms that have shaped this phenomenon have not received much attention. Extended kin and kinship networks have historically managed to buttress psychological isolation and poverty and have been recognized as an alternative means of service provision (Ross, 1978; Stacks, 1974). If services are not available or accessible, the importance of the family and community networks becomes even more salient. Elderly parents with adult dependent children provide an excellent example of the Africentric perspective of community support. These adult children are unable to fulfill the normal role of moving toward independence and mastery of self-help skills (Stanfield, 1973). Thus, parents become perpetual parents providing economic, social, and emotional support (Jennings, 1987).

Continuing care as one ages requires an extended network of family and friends who are willing to supplement each other's care (Bass, 1990; Taylor & Chatters, 1986). This care may be for the aging parent as well as the adult dependent child. To appreciate the situation of these families, it is imperative to recall that these elderly African American parents lived and raised their children in a segregated society. The segregated society offered few services and opportunities for African American families (Ross, 1978). Consequently, survival depended on their ability to adapt to the various programs and policies of the several states that seemed determined to isolate, alienate, segregate, subordinate, or otherwise diminish their civic and social stature in the body politic (Ross, 1978).

The residuals of segregation affect this population of elderly parents and their children today. For example, African American parents whose children had congenital and developmental disabilities generally kept their children at home, where they were often integrated into the community. There were few, if any, residential facilities available for African American families. Further, few rehabilitation, supportive, or community-based services were available for African American families whose children had handicapping conditions.

More recently, research on why parents choose to keep their children at home identify social class and social and psychological stressors as important determinants. Stressors range from those that are directly related to the child (that is, the severity and nature of the disability) to those that affect the family (that is, lack of financial resources). Individuals vary in how they respond to the same event. What one person perceives as aversion stimuli may be perceived as neutral or even benign by another. Thus, for some lower socioeconomic and African American families, a disability may be perceived by the caregiving members of the family as having less effect than other stressors that present a threat to survival (for example, eviction, hunger, unemployment, or severe illness). The relative weight of the stressor is thus contextually determined.

The higher one's social class, the greater one's financial resources are and the more skills one has in negotiating with the service delivery system. Middle-class families with a mentally retarded child are more likely to use the available services than are lower-class and nonwhite families. On the other hand, families without financial resources or access to formal service systems must rely heavily on informal support networks. Communities offer individuals a level of care that institutions cannot provide. Like other people, "the quality of life for . . . disabled people is at its best when they can live in their home" (Gartner, 1990, p. 1). Home care provides a normalizing environment, allows contact with neighbors and friends with whom the individual may have grown up, and diminishes isolation. Many practices from the African American community have been adopted by mainstream society, including the mainstreaming of individuals with disabilities into the community. The mode of care has shifted the focus of care to the community. Again, it appears that the African value of caring for others within the family structure and the community provided a source from which successful coping strategies emerged.

AFRICAN CULTURAL SURVIVAL AND COPING STRATEGIES AT THE ORGANIZATIONAL LEVEL

Societal changes concomitant with the expansion of civil rights and affirmative action have resulted in increased numbers of African Americans in management. Organizational literature on African Americans in the workplace is largely limited to identifying problems (Bush, 1977; Herbert, 1974; Jones, 1973, 1986) and differential experiences between members of ethnic groups and the dominant culture (Cox & Knono, 1986; McNeely, 1989; Mueller, Parcel, & Tanaka, 1989). The black church has been the focus of a few studies (Billingsley, 1992; Frazier, 1964). In general, however, little attention has been focused on identifying variations in managerial approaches of African Americans.

Schiele (1990) suggested an Africentric organizational model in which he identified three points of divergence with mainstream organizational theory. He stated that mainstream theories (1) focus on productivity and efficiency, (2) use materialistic achievements as the major criterion for measuring success, and (3) view human beings individualistically with communal and familial relations most likely perceived as potential interference in corporate matters. In contrast, Schiele stated that an organization shaped by the Africentric paradigm is characterized by how the group preserves itself rather than its productivity. This does not diminish the importance of goals, but goal attainment is defined in the context of survival. Thus, resource procurement and use replace efficiency and productivity as standards. The communal view of human identity may lead to the sharing of similar work tasks in the workplace rather than an extensive division of labor. Group consensus in decision making is preferred over a strict hierarchical structure. Finally, the organization is open to its environment because it is concerned with its preservation. Boundaries between the organization and the community are less marked; the survival of the community and the organization are related.

A study comparing the African American and white managers of an urban county department of social services provides an opportunity to examine empirical data for evidence of African American survival in the workplace (Daly, 1993). The effects of environmental organizational texture on management of these offices were also examined; half the offices were located in the inner city, and the remaining offices were located in suburban areas. Two distinctive management styles emerged as the environment became more intense and turbulent.

African American managers increased their support of staff in response to increased environmental turbulence and also encouraged and facilitated increased problem-solving communication. This is consistent with a management style that encourages mutual involvement in resolving problems as African culture does. White managers responded to an increase in turbulence of environments by increasing support to workers, but they did not change communication patterns. Staff in offices managed by white people perceived their managers as more supportive than staff in offices managed by African Americans, whereas staff in offices with African American managers perceived their work group as more supportive. It appeared that these work groups formed strong, horizontal bonds in their work relationships rather than seeking encouragement from their managers when facing turbulent conditions. Staff in offices managed by African Americans in turbulent environments also scored higher on job satisfaction than staff in offices with African American managers in nonturbulent environments and staff in offices managed by white people in both turbulent and nonturbulent offices.

The evidence suggests that the work group plays a much stronger role in offices in which African Americans are managers in turbulent environments. This finding appears to support the presence of African survival mechanisms in management styles and resulting work patterns. The implication is that individualistic, goal-focused motivational programs may have less satisfactory results with an African American work group than with a work group from the dominant culture, particularly when programs and policies are imposed from outside the work group (that is, from management or policymakers).

IMPLICATIONS FOR PRACTICE, POLICY, AND RESEARCH

Group identity plays a significant role in the attainment of ego strength and self-esteem among African Americans through affirmation from their group. This group-derived ego strength can then mediate against assaults on the self from the wider society. Family frequently serves as a buffer. Family is conceptualized beyond the nuclear family and may encompass distant relatives and "fictive kin," or members who are not blood relatives. Family values among African Americans include a strong sense of responsibility for each other, respect for elders, sharing material needs, and caring for each other (Billingsley, 1992; Ho, 1987; Stacks, 1974). It appears that these African survival mechanisms that have shaped the ethics of caring and sharing in relation to one's group are learned in the family and community. Surviving cultural values have provided an indigenous structure and means for addressing social issues such as pushing for rights, defending against external threats, and coping with domestic violence. These values have provided the community with the resilience to make effective responses against the violence and oppression of slavery and legalized segregation. Thus, the family cannot be underestimated as a mechanism of survival in the African American community.

The assessment of African American circumstances in social work practice should emphasize the identification of coping skills and capacities for developing them to enhance individual, family, and community functioning. Social workers require knowledge and understanding of traditional values and beliefs held by African Americans. The practitioner who works with African American clients should be comfortable in working across systems levels and should fully appreciate factors in each that may affect their clients' well-being, so that appropriate interventions can be planned. One example of an appropriate intervention at the individual level is the development of ego-oriented casework techniques that enable the client system to develop resilience as awareness of community support systems, such as the church, are identified and used.

Organizations can be developed and used to refine social services delivery systems so that they better serve African Americans. Inadequate attention has been given to race and its effect on sociocultural variables in addressing issues such as child welfare, domestic violence, and health care in the African American community. Planners need to develop greater sensitivity to systemic variables that engender negative images and assessments of African Americans and all people of color. The European and Western perspectives in which social workers are trained affects the interpretation of behavior as well as the questions asked in planning policy initiatives (Airhihenbuwa, DiClemente, Wingood, & Lowe, 1992). Thus, differences observed may be assessed in negative terms rather than as coping styles with origins from another culture.

Policy and service initiatives frequently fail to address and at times exacerbate the very problem they are intended to resolve because they run counter to African American cultural styles; one example is the education policy that takes children out of their community, effectively preventing them from maintaining bonds with their caretakers. Policy and service initiatives that involve community participation in planning can be empowering for the residents, and residents who invest in the development of such initiatives may become vested in successful outcomes.

Policy and program planners need to be conscious of the presence of African American males in the lives of African American women and children. Too often, interventions are based on the assumption that if a male is physically absent from the family, he has no involvement with the family. The emotional presence of these males may be obvious in many ways. Social workers may be more comfortable in working with females and unwittingly miss the importance of the men in their clients' lives. Not only does this eventually lead to further marginalization of these men, but it is counter to building the healthy relationships needed to develop indigenous coping strategies for assaults on African American family life. The professional literature about African American men has largely focused either on the most dysfunctional or on those with the most serious needs and problems. Attention to working- and middle-class African American men in the literature is relatively rare. Issues and problems of daily living that confront African Americans should be a part of social work curriculum and training programs. These daily stresses should be explicated in training and staff development and addressed in research. Because socioeconomic status and other demographic factors may shape the nature and source of these problems, they should be addressed in designing intervention strategies. More attention to people of color in policy, research, and practice and in the literature should result in an improved framework in which to bring attention to these groups in social work education and practice.

Finally, research related to identifying and understanding African American cultural traits is needed. There is a need for more research from a nondeficit model in which the dominant culture does not set the behavioral standard. The use of the Africentric perspective based on an African worldview and values is one way this may be accomplished. Research on differences between nonwhite ethnic groups and the dominant culture should be sensitive to cultural barriers that lean toward a negative interpretation of differences rather than recognition of how difference in worldview may explain these variations. In identifying the successful coping strategies that enabled African Americans to survive slavery, poverty, and segregation, more effective intervention strategies can be offered.

REFERENCES

Airhihenbuwa, C. O., DiClemente, R. J., Wingood, G. M., & Lowe, A. (1992). HIV/AIDS education and prevention among African Americans: A focus on culture. *AIDS Education and Prevention, 4,* 267–276.

Ak'bar, N. (1984). Afrocentric social services for human liberation. *Journal of Black Studies, 14,* 395–413.

Allen, W. R. (1981). Moms, dads and boys: Race and sex differences in the socialization of male children. In L. E. Gary (Ed.), *Black men* (pp. 99–114). Beverly Hills, CA: Sage Publications.

Asante, K. A. (1988). *Afrocentricity.* Trenton, NJ: Africa World.

Baldwin, S. (1985). *The costs of caring: Families with disabled children.* London: Routledge & Kegan Paul.

Bass, D. (1990). *Caring families: Supports and interventions.* Silver Spring, MD: NASW Press.

Beckett, J. O., & Coley, S. (1987). Ecological intervention: A case example with a black family. *Journal of Counseling and Human Service Professionals, 2,* 1–18.

Billingsley, A. (1992). *Climbing Jacob's ladder: The enduring legacy of African American families.* New York: Simon & Schuster.

Bingham, R., & Guinyard, J. (1982, August). *Counseling black women: Recognizing societal scripts.* Paper presented at the 90th Meeting of the American Psychological Association, Honolulu.

Braithwaite, R. L. (1981). Interpersonal relations between black males and black females. In L. E. Gary (Ed.), *Black men* (pp. 83–97). Beverly Hills, CA: Sage Publications.

Bush, J. A. (1977). The minority administrator: Implications for social work education. *Journal of Education for Social Work, 13*(1), 15–21.

Cazenave, N. A. (1979). Middle-income black fathers: An analysis of the provider role. *Family Coordinator, 28,* 583–593.

Clark, K. (1965). *Dark ghetto.* New York: Harper & Row.

Coley, S. M., & Beckett, J. O. (1988). Black battered women: Practice issues. *Social Casework, 69,* 483–490.

Cox, T., & Knono, N. (1986). Differential performance appraisal criteria: A field study of black and white managers. *Group and Organization Studies, 11*(1–2), 101–119.

Daly, A. (1993). African American and white management styles: A comparison in one agency. *Journal of Community Practice, 1*(1), 57–79.

Everett, J. E., Chipungu, S. S., & Leashore, B. R. (1991). *Child welfare: An Africentric perspective.* New Brunswick, NJ: Rutgers University Press.

Frazier, E. F. (1964). *The Negro church in America.* New York: Schocken.

Gartner, A. (1990). *Supporting families with a child with a disability: An international outlook.* Baltimore: Paul H. Brookes.

Gary, L. E., & Leashore, B. R. (1982). High risk status of black men. *Social Work, 27,* 54–58.

Grier, W. H., & Cobb, P. M. (1968). *Black rage.* New York: Basic Books.

Hacker, A. (1992). *Two nations: Black and white, separate, hostile, unequal.* New York: Charles Scribner's Sons.

Herbert, A. W. (1974). The minority administrator: Problems, prospects and challenges. *Public Administration Review, 42,* 556–563.

Herskovits, M. J. (1935). Social history of the Negro. In C. Murchison (Ed.), *A handbook of social psychology* (pp. 207–267). Worcester, MA: Clark University Press.

Hill, R. (1971). *Strengths of the black family.* New York: National Urban League.

Ho, M. K. (1987). *Family therapy with ethnic minorities.* Newbury Park, CA: Sage Publications.

Houston, L. N. (1990). *Psychological principles and the black experience*. New York: University Press of America.

Jackson, J., & Gurin, G. (1987). *National survey of black Americans, 1979–1980* (ICPSR 8512). Ann Arbor, MI: University of Michigan.

Jennings, J. (1987). Elderly parents as caregivers for their adult dependent children. *Social Work, 32*, 430–433.

Jones, E. W. (1973). What it's like to be a black manager. *Harvard Business Review, 51*, 108–116.

Jones, E. W. (1986). Black managers: The dream deferred. *Harvard Business Review, 64*, 84–93.

Khoapa, W. A. (1980). *The African personality*. Tokyo: United Nations University.

Kluckhorn, F., & Strodtbeck, F. (1961). *Variations in value orientations*. Westport, CT: Greenwood Press.

Madhubuti, H. R. (1990). *Black men: Obsolete, single, dangerous*. Chicago: Third World Press.

Mann, P. (1984). *Children in care revisited*. London: Batsford Academic and Education.

Mbiti, J. S. (1969). *African religions and philosophy*. New York: Praeger.

McAdoo, H. P. (Ed.). (1981). *Black families*. Beverly Hills, CA: Sage Publications.

McNeely, R. L. (1989). Race and job satisfaction in human service employment. *Administration in Social Work, 13*(2), 77–96.

Menkiti, I. A. (1984). Person and community in African traditional thought. In R. A. Wright (Ed.), *African philosophy* (pp. 171–181). New York: University Press of America.

Miller, A. T. (1993). Social science, social policy and the heritage of African American families. In M. B. Katz (Ed.), *The underclass debate* (pp. 254–289). Princeton, NJ: Princeton University Press.

Mueller, C. W., Parcel, T. L., & Tanaka, K. (1989). Particularism in authority outcomes of black and white supervisors. *Social Science Research, 18*, 1–20.

Nobles, W. W. (1972). African philosophy: Foundations for black psychology. In R. L. Jones (Ed.), *Black psychology* (pp. 18–32). New York: Harper & Row.

Nobles, W. W. (1980). African American family life: An instrument of culture. In H. P. McAdoo (Ed.), *Black families* (pp. 77–86). Beverly Hills, CA: Sage Publications.

Parsons, T., & Shils, E. (1967). *Toward a general theory of action*. Cambridge, MA: Harvard University Press.

Richie, B. (1981). Black battered women: A challenge for the black community. In I. N. Toure (Ed.), *An overview of third world women and violence*. Washington, DC: Rape Crisis Center.

Ross, E. (1978). *Black heritage in social welfare, 1860–1930*. Metuchen, NJ: Scarecrow Press.

Schiele, J. H. (1990). Organizational theory from an Afrocentric perspective. *Journal of Black Studies, 21*, 145–161.

Stacks, C. (1974). *All our kin: Strategies for survival in a black community*. New York: Harper & Row.

Stanfield, J. (1973). Graduation: What happens to the retarded child when he grows up? *Exceptional Child, 39,* 548–552.

Staples, R. (1977). *Black masculinity.* San Francisco: Black Press.

Stewart, R. (1990). *Familial satisfaction among African American married men.* Unpublished doctoral dissertation, Howard University, Washington, DC.

Taylor, R. J., & Chatters, L. (1986). Patterns of informal support to elderly blacks: Family, friends, and church members. *Social Work, 29,* 432–438.

Taylor, R. J., Leashore, B. R., & Tolliver, S. (1988). An assessment of the provider role as perceived by black males. *Family Relations, 37,* 426–431.

Turner, R. J. (1991). Affirming consciousness: The Africentric perspective. In J. E. Everett, S. S. Chipungu, & B. R. Leashore (Eds.), *Child welfare: An Africentric perspective* (pp. 36–57). New Brunswick, NJ: Rutgers University Press.

Vontress, C. (1973). Racial differences: Impediments to rapport. In J. Goodman (Ed.), *Dynamics of racism in social work practice* (pp. 80–89). Washington, DC: National Association of Social Workers.

This chapter was originally published in the March 1995 issue of Social Work, *vol. 40, pp. 240–248.*

16 The Endangerment of African American Men: An Appeal for Social Work Action

Paula Allen-Meares and Sondra Burman

W e live in a nation strained by racism, hostility, and hatred. Our communities and neighborhoods are overcome by violence, fear, and apathy. Our homes, which were once considered safe havens, have now become the sites of increasing acting out of frustration and anger. Due to inequities, oppressive conditions, and uncontrollable stresses, individuals are turning against themselves, their loved ones, and others to vent their feelings of helplessness and hopelessness. Many African American men are especially caught up in this cycle of violent behaviors and victimization and consequently are becoming an endangered species (Gibbs, 1984, 1988; Staples, 1987). The adverse consequences of this cycle—including major injury and death—will affect the future of African American men, their families, and generations to come. Society's level of concern says much about us as a nation.

Many studies have reported on the extent of violence in the African American community, citing alarming statistics and predictions. Relatively high victimization rates of violent crimes have been reported for individuals who are African American, male, poor, young, or single. According to the Bureau of Justice Statistics (1985), African American men have an unusually high likelihood of being murdered; African Americans are more than five times as likely to be the victims of homicide as white people (Hawkins, 1986). Homicide is the leading cause of death of African American men between ages 15 and 34, and since 1960, the suicide rate for African American men between ages 15 and 24 has tripled (Gibbs, 1988). In 1992, of the 23,760 homicide victims reported, 50 percent were African American and 48 percent were white, a disproportionate amount considering that African Americans are only 11 percent of the population.

Eighty-four percent of violent crimes perpetrated against African Americans were by African Americans (Bureau of Justice Statistics, 1990). Ninety percent of those arrested for homicide were men; 55 percent (10,728) were African American, and 43 percent (8,466) were white (U.S. Department of Justice, 1993). In 1990, African Americans were 35.7 percent of the prison population, compared with 50 percent for white people (Criminal Justice Institute, 1991). These figures are startling but do not examine the structural forces that engender crime: inadequate education and job training, unemployment and underemployment, and the inequitable distribution of wealth and power (Seidman & Rappaport, 1986).

Because the justice system places a higher value on white men than on African American men, the latter have had disproportionately higher incarceration and death penalty rates (Poussaint, 1983). Investigations of crimes against African Americans are given low priority. Crimes against white people are more stringently punished. Excessive force, police brutality, harassment, and false arrests against African Americans are widespread (Feagin, 1986). As Radelet and Vandiver (1986) pointed out, "Equality for blacks has not yet been achieved in American society, least of all in the criminal justice system. The idea that all of us are born with an equal chance of eventually dying in the electric chair remains a myth" (p. 189).

Despite the risks of school failure, family estrangement, homicidal violence, and stress-related illnesses that beset African American men from the vulnerable underclass, there is a growing number of middle-class African Americans who excel in family, community, and national leadership roles (Bowman, 1989). Since 1970, the number of African Americans earning over $35,000 a year has risen by almost one-third. Yet there was also a general decline in middle-class incomes between 1970 and 1984, resulting in an increase in lower-income families (Malveaux, 1988). Thus, the gap between economically disadvantaged and middle-class African Americans is growing. A vast majority of African Americans are excluded from the economic and political participation that would improve their standard of living. This loss of human resources and talents to the economy is the high cost of racism (Tidwell, 1991).

Despite the growth in the African American middle class, there continues to be a marked differential in the incomes and poverty levels of African Americans and white people in this country. According to the U.S. Department of Commerce (1992), African American families had a median income of $21,550, whereas the median income of white families was $37,780. Thirty-three percent of African Americans were living in poverty, compared with 11 percent of white people; and African Americans were more than twice as likely as white people to be among the working poor.

Why should the profession of social work be concerned by these staggering data? Is there cause for alarm and justification for taking action to alleviate the conditions and circumstances that contribute to the high-risk status and demise of people in our midst? This article attempts to answer these questions by presenting a history of events that led to the current crisis for African American men who have underachieved and lack the opportunities, skills, and power to rise above their places in society.

INSTITUTIONAL RACISM

Despite equal opportunity laws and affirmative action policies, many African Americans are struggling on a day-to-day basis. Unemployment in the African American community continues to rise, female-headed families on public welfare live at bare subsistence levels, and children are being victimized as the poorest of the poor, with little hope of surmounting their essentially predetermined destinies. These conditions arose from years of deprivation, oppression, and bias, exacerbated by institutional racism that goes unrecognized by the dominant forces at large; contemporary racism is much more subtle than the blatant exclusionary practices of the past (Tidwell, 1991).

Institutional racism is a product of the societal arrangements and structures that exclude African Americans and other people of color from necessary resources and power that would establish the determination to change their oppressed conditions (Pinderhughes, 1989). Public schools fail to provide them with satisfactory educations and marketable skills (Staples, 1987). The discrimination that exists in jobs, housing, and the availability of health and social services undermines the ability to gain control of self and community (Morales, 1981). Inequality and economic stagnation, inflamed by an enduring history of oppression and institutional racism, have fueled a sense of outrage at a system that promises, but does not deliver, opportunity for all.

According to Feagin (1986), "The end of slavery as a legal condition did not end the subordination of black Americans" (p. 180). Although almost 130 years have passed since the 13th Amendment to the Constitution abolished slavery, discriminatory practices and oppressive conditions have continued to relegate a vast majority of African Americans to a form of imposed submission through extreme poverty, exclusion from job opportunities that would provide security and stability, and the denigration of pride in self and the African American culture. African Americans are still attempting to obtain basic human and civil rights that were legally but immorally confiscated with the infamous Dred Scott decision of 1857. These elements have contributed to the devaluation of African American lives both outside of and within the African American community.

Scholars have argued that the devaluation of African Americans and their culture has resulted in psychological scarring, violence, and victimization. In reporting on black-on-black homicide, Poussaint (1983) remarked, "Institutional racist practices place a positive value on whiteness and a negative one on Blackness. . . . Many of the problems in the Black community are related to institutional racism, which fosters a chronic lack of Black self-respect, predisposing many poor Blacks to behave self-destructively and with uncontrollable rage" (pp. 163, 166). Despair, low self-esteem, and rage become forces of destruction, homicide, and suicide. An adolescent who lives in poverty and sees his father unemployed and the family suffer, and who is surrounded by destitution, disparagement, murder, and crime, is vulnerable to striking out against others and himself. Survival and optimistic life chances are not part of his destiny without major endemic and societal changes. And these are not in his foreseeable future.

A devalued status, racial stereotypes, and high crime rates have led to the societal perception of violence as "normal" in African American communities and families (Hawkins, 1987). Yet this image belies the historical facts of close-knit and protective kin that have survived despite forced separations and intolerable circumstances.

THE AFRICAN AMERICAN FAMILY

Franklin (1988) poignantly stated, "The family is one of the strongest and most important traditions in the black community" (p. 23). This family strength was continually demonstrated by the mutual support provided by early slaves to rise above excessive abuses and cruelties. Freed slaves searched frantically for their divided loved ones. Although migration to the urban North temporarily separated families, many were reunited to maintain the strong bonds of nuclear and extended kinships. Even through the Great Depression of the 1930s, the typical family was cared for by two parents (Gutman, 1976). As late as the 1960s, 75 percent of African American families were headed by a husband and wife.

But through the years, the forces of racial practices, policies, and attitudes weakened the family fabric (Franklin, 1988). By the 1980s, there were more than 1.5 million African American female-headed families in the United States, resulting in poverty for these families (Baker, 1988). Nevertheless, there has been an ongoing debate about the causative factors of the problems and disintegration of these families. Thirty years ago, Moynihan (1965) perceived a matriarchal structure that was destructive; however, Bell, Bland, Houston, and Jones (1983) argued against the position that female-dominated families led to inadequate, irresponsible, and absent fathers. Actually, most African American families were egalitarian, and spouses shared in decision making, negating the myth of the black matriarchal family system (Staples, 1982).

POLICY ISSUES

In a caustic report on the social welfare system, Murray (1984) blamed the deteriorating conditions of African Americans and poor people on expanded federal policies of the 1960s. His solution was to scrap existing assistance programs such as Aid to Families with Dependent Children, Medicaid, food stamps, unemployment insurance, worker's compensation, subsidized housing, and disability insurance. His solution was to put working-age people to work. The supposition was that without these subsidies, people would become more responsible and motivated to seek employment. Yet several researchers challenged these concepts and reform measures. Sampson (1987) reported that family disruption was created by exceedingly high African American poverty levels and male joblessness rather than liberal welfare policies. Stoesz and Karger (1990) commented, "If workers are unable to earn enough to be economically self-sufficient, how can welfare recipients be expected to become economically independent of public assistance?" (p. 147).

Murray's (1984) assumptions do not fit the reality of many African American experiences. He stated,

> Our schools know how to educate students who want to be educated. Our industries know how to find productive people and reward them. Our police know how to protect people who are ready to cooperate in their own protection. Our system of justice knows how to protect the rights of individuals who know what their rights are. . . . In short, American society is very good at reinforcing the investment of an individual in himself. (p. 234)

For those who realize the poor quality of many urban public schools, the severe lack of jobs, and the discriminatory practices of many police officers, it is difficult to comprehend that ours is a system of justice protecting the rights of all citizens. Unless equitable and fair practices materialize, and sufficient training and employment are readily available, federal welfare policies should not be made the scapegoat for the harsh conditions and corresponding behaviors experienced by the disenfranchised. Pessimism and feelings of powerlessness and hopelessness are the consequences of generational deprivation and bias that culminate in the destruction of the individual, families, and society at large. These factors have been especially devastating for African American men.

THE DILEMMA OF THE AFRICAN AMERICAN MAN

What happens to an individual who perceives the larger society as hostile, intolerant, and uncaring; opportunities for survival and advancement as limited; and little hope of rising above the status quo? There can be little doubt that depression, frustration, anger, and pessimism can result. Self-esteem and self-worth are violated, and feelings of powerlessness and helplessness to combat a society where one does not "fit in" can play havoc on thought processes and emotional states. The consequences of deleterious and demeaning experiences can create a climate for alienation, unrestrained rage, physical assaults, homicides, and suicides. Lives that could have been productive are lost.

According to Sampson (1987), "[Historically] there is nothing inherent in black culture that is conducive to crime" (p. 348). It is the feelings of powerlessness to alter the economic deprivation and isolation that create the negative behaviors evidenced in many African American men. Unemployment and the lack of marketable skills and adequate incomes can lead to crime and imprisonment; alcohol and drugs are a means of escape from the awareness of "their superfluous existence in a country that de-values and fears them" (Staples, 1987, p. 10). Williams (1984) summed up the results most succinctly: "poverty, in addition to racial inequality, provides 'fertile soil' for criminal violence" (p. 289).

The ultimate tragedy is that African Americans who experi-ence these conditions feel trapped in an unalterable life situation (Hendin, 1978). As Harvey (1986) expressed,"There is a definite relationship between the inability of young Black men to find employment; the increasing number of female-headed house-holds in the Black community; the economic and psychological trauma endured by the Black poor; and the high rates of homi-cidal activity among young, impoverished Black males" (p. 164). The results are the endangerment of a people, a culture, and the constructive search for a better quality of life. Actions that con-vey racism and discrimination create apprehensions in the Afri-can American community. Parents fear that their sons will not be respected, will be feared because of the color of their skin, and will be "beaten down" (Boyd-Franklin, 1992). Their children of-ten fail in schools and drop out, reacting to a sense of failure with disruptive, violent, and self-destructive behaviors (Allen-Meares, 1990; Comer, 1985). These stark realities sow the seeds of disillu-sionment and projections of hostility and animosity toward an unrelenting society that restricts upward mobility and success. Certainly, the availability of guns and other lethal weapons and media coverage of violence in various forms can cause emula-tion of aggressive behaviors that counteract frustration and anger.

Social workers, policymakers, and other professionals must heed the warnings of the disruptiveness engendered by years of subjugation, prejudice, and inequities. Already these factors have produced an alarming rate of destruction to individuals, families, communities, and the society at large.

SOCIAL WORK'S ROLE

Social work interventions have focused on problems in living based on a person-in-environment paradigm. Our historical mission has been to care and advocate for the disadvantaged, disenfranchised, and oppressed—those who are left behind and face an alien world and daily struggle. Our goals have been to enhance functioning and coping, to provide services and resources, and to act as a bridge between the individual and organizational systems. It behooves us to take action to right unfairness and injustice and to seek to improve the quality of life of those in need.

Yet when viewing the inequities and social conditions that afflict many African American men and their families, there appears to be a discomforting silence from the social work profession. Interventions focus on individual pathology and antisocial activities, rather than the unfair and intolerable practices of larger systems and institutions that create dissension and corresponding malfunctioning. It is for this reason that social workers are thought to be agents of social control instead of advocates for social change.

In acknowledging the high-risk status and problems of African American men, social work must address stresses in the environment. Discriminatory practices and economic disparity reveal the plight of many families who are victims of their consequences. Inequities based on race and socioeconomic status, which limit economic, social, and political power, resources, and opportunities, spawn division and despair, ultimately creating a society of chaos and decline. If we look the other way, this trend will persist.

Implications for Practice

The profession needs to develop program strategies that strengthen social support networks and resources in the community. The church, which has been a mainstay in the lives of

African Americans, should be included in an integral role of support and assistance (Gary & Leashore, 1982). The church has taken on responsibility for helping teenage parents, fighting alcohol and drug abuse, and providing aid to indigent and ill people (Lincoln, 1989).

Outreach services that assist with financial and legal aid, housing, health care, job training, and employment possibilities will alleviate intolerable pressures and concerns. And policies ensuring gainful educational and employment opportunities, satisfactory wage scales, adequate benefits, and the elimination of discrimination and harassment are mandatory to deter pent-up aggression and restrictive and deteriorating lifestyles.

Society's discriminatory practices and negative valuations that reflect inferiority and inadequacy often yield a pervasive powerlessness in taking charge and directing one's own life (Solomon, 1976). To rectify this, emphasis must be placed on empowerment and personal control and the recognition of innate and cultural strengths. Thomas (1987) reported how many African Americans have found solutions to their enforced conditions that can be instructive to practitioners who seek to alter perspectives, attitudes, and motivation toward self-help and community interventions. Elements of these solutions include

- Believing that one is a worthy, useful human being with a place of dignity in society.
- Developing a sense of Afrocentric solidarity . . . strong bonds to deal with stress and a variety of environmental events.
- Eliminating pervasive helplessness, racial inferiority, and other victimizing social liabilities . . . a shift in social focus to what blacks can do for themselves. (pp. 159–160)

To provide impetus for change, factors that affect self-esteem, self-image, and self-worth must be addressed. Pride in self and heritage is necessary for healthy functioning. Active supports from role models, caregivers, and policymakers can make a difference for young and adult males and their families who are trying to persevere under extreme duress.

Proposed Model for Activism

The authors' proposed model for activism derives many of its concepts and strategies from the work of other social work scholars, researchers, and practitioners. It is basically a model that is attuned to the history, culture, and values of African Americans and particularly to the current state of social and economic affairs.

Morales (1981) described a form of activist practice that takes into consideration an awareness of racial, ethnic, and political factors in providing services to assist with social problems in Third World communities. This type of practice entails the active recruitment of bicultural and bilingual students and faculty in schools of social work and practitioners in social services agencies and the development of proactive intervention strategies such as advocacy, empowerment, and class action social work. The latter requires close, interdisciplinary collaboration (for example, between schools and the legal and health professions) on behalf of client welfare.

Trader (1977) reminded us that we must not ignore the realities of external environments of oppressed groups. Historical and current societal conditions must be taken into account when deriving theoretical frameworks and models to guide practice. Rather than concentrating on pathology and internal, psychic change, it is necessary to seek changes in the outer society. The goals of treatment are to learn the skills of independent and productive control of self through obtaining essential resources and eliminating external constraints. Therefore, the practitioner acts as the mediator between systems to promote individual and environmental change.

Devore and Schlesinger (1991) remarked, "The interface between private troubles and public issues is an intrinsic aspect of most approaches to social work practice" (p. 175). Their model of ethnically sensitive practice calls for attention to both micro and macro issues and their consequences, including the results of racism, discrimination, and poverty. Knowledge of the community—its power structure, available resources, services, and networks—and an understanding of the culture and responses to traumas, conflicts, and tensions from an "insider" perspective are important to setting the stage for both micro and macro interventions.

Professional activism initially requires a firm foundation in schools of social work that can enlighten the future practitioner about its relevance and importance. Courses in ethnic diversity that focus on the historical and current context of cultures, problems, and concerns should be a part of both policy and intervention studies. A greater emphasis on the need for activism on behalf of oppressed and disadvantaged people should be incorporated into the curriculum. This information will provide basic knowledge and understanding of conditions alien to most students. Educational systems do have the power and influence to shape ideas, activities, and practice directions.

Social workers should seek strategies to address policies and practices that promote advocacy, social justice, social change, and knowledge and education for empowerment while activating change at macro and micro levels. The profession must raise awareness at the national and local (community) levels of the severity of the problems that African American men and their families face. Active leadership is needed to correct economic and social inequities and deprivations. When employment is so critical to survival and a sense of usefulness, more efforts must be made for equitable hiring practices in multiethnic communities. Local high schools, trade schools, and community colleges need more outreach in communities to help residents recognize what is available to improve education and job skills. Social workers must have greater participation in illuminating discrimination and harassment in the workplace and all institutions and agencies that serve people. Community organizing to fight crime and vulnerability to alcohol and drug abuse is necessary. Helping people obtain adequate health care, including providing transportation and reducing the waiting and red tape involved, will save and improve lives.

A primary function of the activist role will be working closely with the African American community as a team member to gain an in-depth understanding of indigenous support networks and strengths, actions that must be taken to resolve specific problems, and the approachable target systems that will be the focus of change. The numerous roles will include facilitating, mediating, and instructing at all levels to tie together the goals of the community and the individuals who are an integral part of its stability. In many cases, community programs will need to be developed and those in place will need to be expanded to provide additional resources and services. Programs such as Head Start and aid to the elderly population and ill people should reach more individuals. Key mediating institutions, such as the church and voluntary associations, that have had positive influences on African Americans should be provided more supportive, collaborative interventions from the social work profession. But at all levels, active participation of community members will be commensurate with achieving empowerment and ownership of the ventures.

The aim of the activist is to provide hope for constructive change so that optimism can replace despair and concrete solutions can alleviate daily struggles. Change will provide the motivation for individual striving and accomplishment and will reduce what Gary and Leashore (1982) called "the high-risk status of African-American males in this society" (p. 57) that endangers them and their families in the present and future. Activism at the community, state, and national levels is the key to successful functioning and the promise of equality for all. And we, as social workers, can make a difference through a vision, a dedication, and a commitment.

REFERENCES

Allen-Meares, P. (1990). Educating black youths: The unfulfilled promise of equality. *Social Work, 35,* 283–286.

Baker, F. M. (1988). Afro-Americans. In L. Comas-Diaz & E. H. Griffith (Eds.), *Clinical guidelines in cross-cultural mental health* (pp. 151–181). New York: John Wiley & Sons.

Bell, C. C., Bland, I. J., Houston, E., & Jones, B. E. (1983). Enhancement of knowledge and skills for the psychiatric treatment of black populations. In J. C. Chunn, P. J. Dunston, & F. Ross-Sheriff (Eds.), *Mental health and people of color: Curriculum development and change* (pp. 205–237). Washington, DC: Howard University Press.

Bowman, P. J. (1989). Research perspectives on black men: Role strain and adaptation across the life cycle. In R. L. Jones (Ed.), *Black adult development and aging* (pp. 117–150). Berkeley, CA: Cobb & Henry.

Boyd-Franklin, N. (1992, July). *African-American families in therapy.* Paper presented at a workshop sponsored by the National Association of Social Workers, Springfield, IL.

Bureau of Justice Statistics. (1985). *Risk of violent crime* (U.S. Department of Justice Special Report). Washington, DC: U.S. Government Printing Office.

Bureau of Justice Statistics. (1990). *Criminal victimization in the United States, 1990* (U.S. Department of Justice Special Report). Washington, DC: U.S. Government Printing Office.

Comer, J. P. (1985). Black violence and public policy. In L. A. Curtis (Ed.), *American violence and public policy* (pp. 63–86). New Haven, CT: Yale University Press.

Criminal Justice Institute. (1991). *The correctional yearbook, 1990.* Washington, DC: U.S. Government Printing Office.

Devore, W., & Schlesinger, E. G. (1991). *Ethnic-sensitive social work practice* (3rd ed.). New York: Macmillan.

Feagin, J. (1986). Slavery unwilling to die: The background of black oppression in the 1980s. *Journal of Black Studies, 17,* 173–200.

Franklin, J. H. (1988). A historical note on black families. In H. P. McAdoo (Ed.), *Black families* (2nd ed., pp. 23–26). Newbury Park, CA: Sage Publications.

Gary, L. E., & Leashore, B. R. (1982). High-risk status of black men. *Social Work, 27,* 54–58.

Gibbs, J. T. (1984). Black adolescents and youth: An endangered species. *American Journal of Orthopsychiatry, 54,* 6–21.

Gibbs, J. T. (1988). *Young, black, and male in America: An endangered species.* Dover, MA: Auburn House.

Gutman, H. (1976). *The black family in slavery and freedom.* New York: Pantheon.

Harvey, W. B. (1986). Homicide among young black adults: Life in the subculture of exasperation. In D. F. Hawkins (Ed.), *Homicide among black Americans* (pp. 153–171). Lanham, MD: University Press of America.

Hawkins, D. F. (Ed.). (1986). *Homicide among black Americans.* Lanham, MD: University Press of America.

Hawkins, D. F. (1987). Devalued lives and racial stereotypes: Ideological barriers to the prevention of family violence among blacks. In R. L. Hampton (Ed.), *Violence in the black family* (pp. 189–205). Lexington, MA: Lexington Books/D.C. Heath.

Hendin, H. (1978). Suicide: The psychosocial dimension. *Suicide and Life-Threatening Behavior, 8,* 99–117.

Lincoln, C. E. (1989). Knowing the black church: What it is and why. In J. Dewart (Ed.), *State of black America 1989* (pp. 137–149). New York: National Urban League.

Malveaux, J. (1988). The economic statuses of black families. In H. P. McAdoo (Ed.), *Black families* (2nd ed., pp. 133–147). Newbury Park, CA: Sage Publications.

Morales, A. (1981). Social work with third-world people. *Social Work, 26,* 45–51.

Moynihan, D. (1965). *The Negro family: The case for national action.* Washington, DC: U.S. Department of Labor.

Murray, C. (1984). *Losing ground.* New York: Basic Books.

Pinderhughes, E. (1989). *Understanding race, ethnicity, and power.* New York: Free Press.

Poussaint, A. F. (1983). Black-on-black homicide: A psychological–political perspective. *Victimology, 8,* 161–169.

Radelet, M. L., & Vandiver, M. (1986). Race and capital punishment: An overview of the issues. In D. F. Hawkins (Ed.), *Homicide among black Americans.* Lanham, MD: University Press of America.

Sampson, R. J. (1987). Urban black violence: The effect of male joblessness and family disruption. *American Journal of Sociology, 93,* 348–382.

Seidman, E., & Rappaport, J. (Eds.). (1986). *Redefining social problems.* New York: Plenum Press.

Solomon, B. B. (1976). *Black empowerment: Social work in oppressed communities.* New York: Columbia University Press.

Staples, R. (1982). *Black masculinity: The black male's role in American society.* San Francisco: Black Scholar Press.

Staples, R. (1987). Black male genocide: A final solution to the race problem in America. *Black Scholar, 18*(3), 2–11.

Stoesz, D., & Karger, H. J. (1990). Welfare reform: From illusion to reality. *Social Work, 35,* 141–147.

Thomas, C. W. (1987). Pride and purpose as antidotes to black homicidal violence. *Journal of the National Medical Association, 79,* 155–160.

Tidwell, B. J. (1991). More than a moral issue: The costs of American racism in the 1990s. *Urban League Review, 14*(2), 9–28.

Trader, H. P. (1977). Survival strategies for oppressed minorities. *Social Work, 22,* 10–13.

U.S. Department of Commerce. (1992). *The black population in the United States.* Washington, DC: Economics and Statistics Administration.

U.S. Department of Justice. (1993). *Crime in the U.S. 1992.* Washington, DC: Federal Bureau of Investigation.

Williams, K. R. (1984). Economic sources of homicide: Reestimating the effects of poverty and inequality. *American Sociological Review, 49,* 283–289.

This chapter was originally published in the March 1995 issue of Social Work, *vol. 40, pp. 268–274.*

African American Men's Perceptions of Racial Discrimination: A Sociocultural Analysis

Lawrence E. Gary

Although the United States is a nation where multiethnicity and cultural diversity are integral attributes of its character, recent data and racial incidents show that people of color, especially African American men, continue to experience racial discrimination in many sectors of society (Ezorsky, 1991; Hacker, 1992; Jaynes & Williams, 1989). Institutional causes, manifestations, and consequences of racial exploitation have existed historically since 17th-century colonial America. It has been argued that the entire edifice of the social, cultural, judicial–legal, and economic structures of U.S. society was built on the key reality of racial discrimination (Bell, 1980; Cose, 1992; Higginbotham, 1978).

In recent years, considerable attention has been given to the high-risk status of African American men (Gary, 1981; Gibbs, 1988; Monroe & Goldman, 1988; Staples, 1982). Government statistics on income, health, education, employment, and criminal justice suggest that, compared with white men, African American men are not coping very well in this society. For example, African American men have higher morbidity and mortality rates, experience greater unemployment and underemployment, earn less, are more likely to become victims of homicide, spend more time outside of marriage and family life, and have higher rates of incarceration and criminal victimization than white men (Akbar, 1991; Gary, 1981; Hutchison, 1994).

The disturbing plight of African American men has deteriorated to the point that they are now called an "endangered species" (Gibbs, 1988; Monroe & Goldman, 1988; Staples, 1987). Some social indicators suggest that despite racial oppression, African Americans, including men, have made social progress in a number of areas (Farley & Allen, 1987; Jaynes & Williams, 1989; Pinkney, 1984). But black people and white people have different perceptions of the significance of racism in American society. From an institutional perspective, there is considerable evidence that racial discrimination is a most significant factor in the degraded status of African American men (Feagin & Feagin, 1978; Goldberg, 1990; Hacker, 1992; Sigelman & Welch, 1991).

There is a need to gain better information about how African American men perceive racial discrimination in U.S. society. It is within this context that the investigation discussed in this article was undertaken. This article explores how demographic factors, stressors, and sociocultural patterns predict perceptions of racial discrimination among African American men. The research questions were

- Do demographic variables such as age, education, income, or marital status predict perceptions of racial discrimination among African American men?
- Is there a relationship between sociocultural patterns and perceptions of racial discrimination among African American men?
- Do life stress factors explain perceptions of racial discrimination among African American men?
- What is the relative importance of demographic, sociocultural, and stressor variables in influencing perceptions of racial discrimination among this group?

EARLIER RESEARCH

Although a number of works have examined the impact of racial discrimination on U.S. society, only a few have specifically targeted African American men's perceptions of racial discrimination (Cose, 1992; Hacker, 1992; Jaynes & Williams, 1989; Sigelman & Welch, 1991; Taylor, 1992). It is important to make a distinction between racial prejudice and racial discrimination. *Racial prejudice* describes an individual's attitude about a particular ethnic group. *Racial discrimination* is a behavior in which an individual or group treats people of a particular ethnic group unfairly on the basis of their race (Dovidio & Gaertner, 1986; Sigelman & Welch, 1991).

The perceptions of discrimination held by African Americans involve both the extent and the character of the individual awareness of being perceived and treated differently because of race alone. This holds true for individuals as well as the collective and remains distinct from actual discrimination. The consequences of accurately identifying incidents of racial prejudice or discrimination range from the barely significant to the life-threatening. From the perspective of the African American individual, many life situations occur that require the individual to discern whether he or she failed in a specific endeavor or, alternately, was a victim of racial discrimination. Thus, the manner in which African Americans perceive racism has an inevitable effect on their sense of well-being and how they cognitively structure their social reality.

Indeed, the danger of misinterpreting prejudice, particularly underestimating racism, is embedded in the very folklore of African Americans. Sigelman and Welch (1991) found that African Americans perceived the prevalence of racial discrimination as being considerably greater than white Americans perceived it. In addition, their research suggested that African Americans and white Americans have contrasting explanations of the origins and causes of racial inequality.

In analyzing African Americans' perceptions of racial discrimination, one approach has conceptualized racial discrimination as occurring in discrete domains. Some of the possible domains of racial discrimination examined in the national surveys—such as those by Louis Harris and Associates (1989) and the ABC News/*Washington Post* polls (cited in Sigelman & Welch, 1991)—include education, housing, employment, and wages. In summarizing these surveys, Sigelman and Welch observed that African Americans were more likely to perceive racial discrimination in employment (getting a job, wage discrimination) than they were in education (getting a quality education) or housing (getting decent housing). Sigelman and Welch concluded that

> Blacks are moving ahead in education, but their employment situation has worsened relative to that of whites. Even though those blacks who are employed are gaining on whites in salary and occupational status, in the real world that blacks are perceiving, black males pay at least a 12 percent salary penalty for being black. (pp. 54–55)

Other studies have examined African Americans' perceptions of racial inequality in other domains. For example, Hagan and Albonetti (1982) found that in their survey of 1,078 respondents, African Americans perceived considerable racism in the criminal justice system. Davis (1971) found that perceptions of racism are key to stated explanations of crime offered by African Americans. Another study (Farrell, Dawkins, & Oliver, 1983) found a widespread apprehension about the role played by family planning clinics in African American communities. The fear of genocide was documented by several questionnaire items. Respondents perceived that family planning and birth control had the racially discriminatory objective of decreasing the number of African Americans. Gender was a significant factor in the response; African American men expressed greater fears of genocide than African American women. In addition, older respondents and less educated respondents were much more likely to fear genocide.

Braddock and McPartland (1987), in their discussion of the significance of their finding that perceptions of de facto racial segregation were perpetuated throughout the life cycle, concluded that an individual's background of integration versus segregation was an important determinant of the individual's perception of discrimination. Another study (Hecht & Ribeau, 1987) indicated that racial identity had an effect on the perception of racial discrimination or racism. Hecht and Ribeau found that 61 African Americans differed in their social interactions with white people based on their use of the racial identity labels of "Afro-American," "black," or "black American." Aspects of communication such as emotional expressiveness, understanding, and acceptance were found to be more dissatisfying to African Americans who identified themselves as black American and Afro-American than among those who identified themselves as black.

A study of the effect of the racial composition of an area on African American perceptions found that the degree to which an area was populated by African Americans did not have an effect on how the group perceived its own strength (Evans & Giles, 1986). It is possible that African Americans' perceptions of racial discrimination are influenced by miscommunication because of culturally based differences between white people and African Americans (Kochman, 1981).

In their analyses of national surveys, Sigelman and Welch (1991) indicated that African Americans are more likely to perceive widespread discrimination against them as a group than against themselves as individuals. They downplay their personal experiences with discrimination compared with the experience of racial discrimination by the African American population as a whole. Sigelman and Welch concluded that "blacks perceive discrimination against blacks as a group as being most problematic in getting good jobs and getting appropriate pay for their jobs, the very same areas in which they are most likely to report having personally experienced discrimination" (p. 58).

What are the social and economic sources of the various perceptions of racial discrimination? Using probit analysis, Sigelman and Welch (1991) discovered that perceptions of racial discrimination were significantly related to gender and age. They showed that African American men were more likely to perceive themselves as victims of racial discrimination than African American women and that younger people were less likely to be targets of discriminatory treatment than older people. The analysis revealed contradictory results for the socioeconomic status measures. However, they did find that when all other variables were held constant, education had a significant positive effect on perceived discrimination: Better-educated African Americans were more likely to perceive greater discrimination than less-educated African Americans.

In their studies of racial discrimination as viewed by African Americans, researchers have tended to examine only a limited range of variables such as gender, age, and socioeconomic status in predicting African Americans' perceptions of discrimination against themselves. More consideration needs to be given to sociocultural variables such as racial consciousness, sex-role identity, religiosity, family and social networks, and social stressors. Studies show that the extent of perceived racial discrimination appears to be widespread. However, the measures of perceived racial discrimination continue to be rather crude. According to Sigelman and Welch (1991), racial discrimination would be shown to be even more widespread if measures were more refined. Some observers view the accuracy, or lack of accuracy, with which African Americans perceive racial discrimination as key to the development of pathological or functional ways of relating to major societal institutions (Ogbu, 1983).

SOCIOCULTURAL APPROACH

The research described in this article was guided by an ecological theoretical framework concerned with the interrelationships among individuals and between individuals and their environments. It focuses on the adaptive aspects of human beings in continuous transactions with the physical and social environments. It is concerned with the growth, development, and potentiality of human beings and with the characteristics of their environments that support or fail to support the expression of human potential (Germain, 1991).

Social perceptions are important aspects of adults' environments. Needs, beliefs, emotions, and expectations are components of the perceptual world of individuals as they interact with other individuals. For example, data suggest that previous life experiences lead one to expect the world to be a certain way (Clatterbaugh, 1990; Dovidio & Gaertner, 1986; Kochman, 1981; Majors & Billson, 1991).

Also, what a person holds to be true about the world can affect the interpretation of sensory signals or perceptions. A number of scholars have used an ecological framework for examining and organizing research on African American men (Akbar, 1991; Hutchison, 1994; Majors & Billson, 1991; Ogbu, 1983). Commenting on the usefulness of this conceptual framework, McAdoo (1993) stated, "Ecological theory allows one to evaluate the relationship between external social systems and internal family functioning. It also helps one to describe, explain, and predict the effects of racial discrimination in education and employment as well as experiences related to social isolation on the roles of African American men in their families" (p. 28).

The sociocultural variables examined in this article measure concepts that represent products of the interactions among and between individuals and their environments. These variables are consistent with the key concepts outlined by Germain (1991).

METHOD

Respondents

Respondents for this research came from a major mid-Atlantic East Coast city in which African Americans constituted 35 percent of the population. A multicluster sampling procedure was used to select a sample representative of noninstitutionalized African American community residents. This stratified random sampling strategy resulted in 1,018 respondents, 537 of whom were men. Because African American men have often been a difficult population to secure in field surveys, they were oversampled for this study. The male respondents from two samples were combined after conducting tests of independence using chi-square statistics. There were no statistically significant differences between the two samples of male respondents on demographic variables such as age, marital status, education, employment, and household size. The completion and response rates were 99 percent and 81 percent, respectively. Data were collected through face-to-face interviews administered by trained interviewers. More detailed discussion of the study design and methods of data collection may be found elsewhere (Gary, Brown, Milburn, Ahmed, & Booth, 1989; Milburn, Gary, Booth, & Brown, 1991).

Census data collected for the city confirmed that this sample represented a cross-section of African American men living in the community with respect to age, education, income, and marital and employment status. As shown in Table 17-1, most respondents (57.9 percent) were between the ages of 18 and 44 years. Forty-one percent had less than a high school education. Almost half (45.3 percent) of the respondents were married. Slightly more than one-fourth (28.1 percent) had household incomes of $25,000 or more per year. Nearly 70 percent of the respondents were employed.

Measurement

The perception of discrimination, the dependent variable, was measured by asking the respondents whether they had experienced racial discrimination within the past year in a number of social interaction situations: at work, from the police, at the bank, from waiters or waitresses, or from government agencies. Three categories of independent variables were obtained: demographic, sociocultural, and stressor.

Demographic Variables. The demographic independent variables included in the analysis were age (date of birth), marital status (married, divorced or separated, widowed, and never married), education (highest grade completed), household

TABLE 17-1
Demographic Characteristics of Respondents

Variable	No.	%
Age (in years)		
18–30	187	34.8
31–44	124	23.1
45–64	133	24.8
65 and over	93	17.3
Total	537	100.0
Marital status		
Married	240	45.3
Divorced or separated	98	18.5
Widowed	25	4.7
Never married	167	31.5
Total	530	100.0
Education		
8 years or less	105	19.6
9–11 years	114	21.3
12 years	153	28.6
Some college	163	30.5
Total	535	100.0
Annual household income ($)		
Less than 6,000	48	10.2
6,000–9,999	50	10.6
10,000–14,999	90	19.0
15,000–24,999	152	32.1
25,000 or more	133	28.1
Total	473	100.0
Employment		
Employed	364	69.9
Unemployed	157	30.1
Total	521	100.0

NOTE: Totals vary because of missing data.

income (all sources of income for all members of the household), and employment status (employed or unemployed).

Sociocultural Variables. The sociocultural independent variables were based on the following measures: family closeness, satisfaction with helping networks, friends' closeness, religiosity, racial consciousness, and sex-role identity. Family closeness was measured in terms of how close respondents believed their family members felt to one another. Responses on a Likert-type scale ranged from 1 = not too close to 3 = very close. Friends' closeness was measured by asking the respondents to indicate the extent to which they believed their friends were close to each other. Responses ranged from 1 = very close to 3 = not too close. For the measure of satisfaction with helping networks, respondents were asked to indicate their degree of satisfaction with the responses of others to their problems. Responses ranged from 1 = very dissatisfied or dissatisfied to 4 = very satisfied.

Religiosity, defined as involvement in institutionalized and personal religious activities such as praying, attending religious crusades, and listening to religious services on radio or television, was based on the Socio-cultural Religiosity Scale, developed by Kenney, Cromwell, and Vaughan (1977). For this analysis, a modified version of the scale was used consisting of 10 items to which respondents indicated on a five-point Likert-type scale from 1 = never to 5 = very often how often they were involved in religious activities. Total scores ranged from 10 to 50, with scores of 27 or less representing low levels of religiosity, 28 to 44 medium religiosity, and 45 or greater high religiosity. The Cronbach's alpha reliability coefficient for this scale was .89.

For the measure of sex-role identity, the short Bem Sex Role Inventory (BSRI) (Bem, 1974, 1977) was used. The BSRI contains 30 personality traits including 10 characteristics of the feminine sex-role stereotype, which sum to a femininity score (femininity scale); 10 characteristics of the masculine sex-role stereotype, which sum to a masculinity score (masculinity scale); and 10 not associated with either stereotype (androgynous). For example, traits from the masculinity scale include "ambitious," "dominant," and "self-reliant." Sample traits from the femininity scale include "affectionate," "gentle," and "understanding." During the interview, respondents were asked to specify on a scale from 1 = never or almost never true to 7 = always or almost always true how each BSRI characteristic described themselves.

Subsequently, the respondents were classified as conforming if their BSRI scores on the masculine scale were above the median and their scores on the feminine scale were below the median; they were classified as conflicting if their BSRI scores on the feminine scale were above the median and their scores on the masculine scale were below the median. In addition, if both scores were above the median (high masculine and high feminine), they were classified as androgynous. If both scores were below the median (low masculine and low feminine), the respondents were classified as undifferentiated. The Cronbach's alpha was .77 for the masculinity scale and .84 for the femininity scale.

The final sociocultural measure was *racial consciousness*, defined as the extent to which respondents identified with black people and were aware of racial oppression or discrimination. Measurement of racial consciousness was based on the respondents' responses to a five-point Likert-type scale ranging from 1 = strongly disagree to 5 = strongly agree. Twenty-two vignettes were used in this assessment (for example, vignettes included the following: Vernon thinks blacks get poor deals; Mary's mother tells her not to trust white men; Alex rarely talks to white people about serious matters because afterward he feels depressed). The maximum score was 110, indicating positive racial pride and awareness of racial oppression; the lowest possible score was 22. Scores of less than 45 indicated low levels of racial consciousness, 46 to 60 indicated medium racial consciousness, and 61 or greater indicated high levels of racial consciousness. The Cronbach's alpha reliability coefficient for this measure was .68.

Stressor Variables. The stressor (or stress-related) independent variables included stressful life events, daily hassles, and perceived health status. The presence of stressful life events in the lives of the respondents was assessed by a modified version of the Social Readjustment Rating Scale (Holmes & Rahe, 1967). Respondents were asked if a series of stressors such as illness or injury, trouble at work, the death of a spouse, a change in marital status, and so forth had happened to them within the past year. The number of such events was counted and scored as follows: no stress if there were no events, some stress if there were one to five events, and high stress if there were six or more events.

Perceived health status was measured by asking respondents to rate their physical health on a four-point scale ranging from 0 = poor to 3 = excellent. Although this single item does not capture the variability of multiple health conditions, studies using self-ratings of health suggest that subjective perceptions of health are significantly related to physicians' ratings and are a reasonably good measure of health status (LaRue, Bank, Jarvik, & Hetland, 1979; Maddox & Douglas, 1973; Mossey & Shapiro, 1982). It is assumed that being in poor health is stressful.

The final stress-related variable was "daily hassles." To assess this, a modified version of the Daily Hassles Scale (Kanner, Coyne, Schafer, & Lazarus, 1981) was used. Participants were asked to indicate whether they had experienced any hassles with parents, children, relatives, friends, employers, and so forth and to rate such a hassle on a four-point scale ranging from 0 = no hassle to 3 = a great deal of hassle. For purposes of analysis, raw scores, ranging from 0 to 56, were grouped into three categories, with a score of 0 indicating no hassles (low level), a score of 1 to 10 a medium level of daily hassles, and a score of 11 or greater a high level of daily hassles. The Cronbach's alpha coefficient for this scale was .94.

Analysis

Analysis examined the relationship between mean percentages on the racial discrimination variable and the three sets of independent variables. To determine which variables best predicted perceptions of racial discrimination, multiple regression analysis, both step-wise and forced entry, was used. The continuous forms of age, education, and household income were used in the multiple regression models. Dummy coding was used for marital status (married = 1, not married = 0) and employment status (employed = 1, not employed = 0). All analyses were conducted using SPSS-2 (Nie, Hull, Jenkins, Steinbrenner, & Bent, 1975).

RESULTS

Perceptions of Racial Discrimination

The frequency of racially discriminatory experiences was measured by a question asking respondents how many incidents of racial discrimination they had experienced within the past year. The gross number of incidents reported by each respondent was recorded as a numerical response based on these self-reports. Almost one-third (28.8 percent) of the respondents reported one racially discriminatory experience over the past year, and 10.9 percent reported two or more such experiences. So about 40 percent of the respondents reported that they had personally experienced some form of racial discrimination within the past year. When asked about the social context in which these racially discriminatory experiences had occurred, nine different social settings were provided. The workplace was the setting most often cited by those who said they had experienced racial discrimination (18.4 percent). The second most frequently identified social setting was government agencies (6.7 percent); 6.3 percent of the respondents experienced racial discrimination by the police.

Table 17-2 presents the distribution of perceptions of racial discrimination by demographic variables. Statistically significant relations exist between the respondents' perceptions of racial discrimination and age $[F(3, 474) = 18.18, p < .001]$, marital status $[F(3, 476) = 6.56, p < .001]$, education $[F(3, 480) = 6.56, p < .001]$, and employment status $[F(3, 456) = 9.73, p < .01]$. African American men who were young, unmarried, highly educated (some college or college graduation), and employed were more likely to perceive racial discrimination than old, married or widowed, poorly educated, and unemployed African Americans. Household income was not significantly related to perceptions of racial discrimination. One might surmise from this observation that perceived discrimination affects people regardless of their economic achievements.

As shown in Table 17-3, four of the six sociocultural variables were significantly related to the incidence of perceived racial discrimination. Family and friends' closeness did not have an effect on the dependent variable. However, satisfaction with helping networks did, although the direction of the relationship was not linear. Men who were satisfied with their helping networks were more likely to perceive racial incidents than were those who were neutral or dissatisfied with their helping system $[F(3, 470) = 6.38, p < .01]$.

Statistically significant relationships existed between respondents' perceptions of racial discrimination and religiosity $[F(2, 483) = 3.72, p < .05]$ and racial consciousness $[F(2, 470) = 3.33, p < .05]$. Religious men perceived less racial discrimination than nonreligious men. Men who were very conscious of their racial identity perceived more racial discrimination than men who were not racially conscious.

Sex-role identity had a statistically significant effect on perceptions of racial discrimination. Men who were masculine in their sex-role identity perceived more racially motivated incidents than men who expressed alternative sex-role identities. It is interesting to note that feminine-oriented respondents reported the

TABLE 17-2

Relationship between Incidence of Perceived Racial Discrimination and Demographic Variables

Variable	n	M
Age (years)		
18–30	175	.794
31–44	118	.720
45–64	110	.118
65 and over	75	.040
Total	478	.502
$F(3, 474) = 18.183, p = .000$		
Marital status		
Married	218	.321
Divorced or separated	82	.537
Widowed	24	.292
Never married	156	.763
Total	480	.500
$F(3, 476) = 6.555, p = .000$		
Education		
8 years or less	88	.068
9–11 years	101	.545
12 years	140	.607
Some college	155	.613
Total	484	.498
$F(3, 480) = 6.555, p = .000$		
Annual household income ($)		
Less than 6,000	44	.500
6,000–9,999	44	.432
10,000–14,999	85	.459
15,000–24,999	137	.562
25,000 or more	124	.581
Total	434	.528
$F(4, 429) = .298, p = .879$		
Employment		
Employed	345	.594
Unemployed	134	.269
Total	479	.503
$F(3, 456) = 9.729, p = .004$		

NOTE: Totals vary because of missing data.

least number of racially discriminatory incidents when compared with the masculine- or androgynous-oriented men.

Table 17-4 presents the distribution of racial incidents by stress-related variables. Self-report of health status was not related to

TABLE 17-3

Relationship between Incidence of Perceived Racial Discrimination and Sociocultural Variables

Variable	n	M
Family closeness		
Very close	271	.476
Fairly close	163	.528
Not too close	41	.610
Total	475	.505
$F(2, 472) = .352, p = .703$		
Satisfaction with helping networks		
Very dissatisfied or dissatisfied	54	.352
Neutral	30	.267
Satisfied	222	.437
Very satisfied	168	.482
Total	474	.496
$F(3, 470) = 6.382, p = .006$		
Friends' closeness		
Very close	149	.423
Fairly close	256	.484
Not too close	69	.652
Total	474	.489
$F(2, 471) = 1.219, p = .296$		
Religiosity		
Low	96	.458
Medium	329	.565
High	61	.180
Total	486	.496
$F(2, 483) = 3.724, p = .025$		
Racial consciousness		
Low	46	.174
Medium	357	.507
High	70	.671
Total	473	.490
$F(2, 470) = 3.331, p = .037$		
Sex-role identity		
Undifferentiated	109	.358
Feminine	66	.273
Masculine	122	.762
Androgynous	163	.472
Total	460	.493
$F(3, 456) = 4.479, p = .004$		

NOTE: Totals vary because of missing data.

TABLE 17-4

Relationship between Incidence of Perceived Racial Discrimination and Stressor Variables

Variable	n	M
Hassles score		
Equal to 0	35	.000
Between 1 and 10	143	.182
Higher than 10	264	.750
Total	442	.507
$F(2, 439) = 19.684, p = .000$		
Stressful event		
One	19	.210
Two	131	.107
Three or more	336	.664
Total	486	.496
$F(2, 483) = 15.427, p = .000$		
Health rating		
Excellent	182	.576
Good	195	.461
Fair	72	.569
Poor	37	.135
Total	486	.495
$F(3, 482) = 2.106, p = .099$		

NOTE: Totals vary because of missing data.

perceived racial discrimination. Statistically significant relationships existed between perceptions of racial discrimination and daily hassles [$F(2, 439) = 19.68, p < .001$] and stressful life events [$F(2, 483) = 15.43, p < .001$]. Men who had high levels of both chronic and acute stressors were more likely to report racial discrimination than were men who experienced lower levels of stressors.

Multivariate Analysis

Multiple regressions, both stepwise and forced entry methods, were used to examine the independent effects of the various demographic stressors and sociocultural variables on perceptions of racial discrimination. Table 17-5 presents the results of multiple regression analyses using the stepwise method. Of all the variables, six (daily hassles, stressful life events, marital status, racial consciousness, age, and sex-role identity) had independent effects on perceived racial discrimination [$F(6, 530) = 23.15$,

TABLE 17-5

Stepwise Multiple Regression of Perceived Racial Discrimination and Selected Variables

Variable[a]	Multiple R	R^2 Change	Simple r	Beta[b]
Hassles	.393	.155	.393	.297***
Stressful events	.418	.020	.277	.131**
Marital status	.430	.010	−.150	−.090*
Racial consciousness	.439	.008	.056	.106**
Age	.449	.008	−.286	−.104*
Sex-role identity	.456	.006	.068	.080*
Total R^2 = .207				
Adjusted R^2 = .199				
$F(6, 530) = 23.15, p = .000$				

[a]A dummy code was used for marital status (married = 1, not married = 0) and employment status (employed = 1, unemployed = 0).
[b]Beta = standardized coefficients.
*$p < .05$. **$p < .01$. ***$p < .001$.

$p < .001$] and together explained 20 percent of variance in the dependent variable. The forced entry method of multiple regression produced almost the same results (Table 17-6). Five of the six independent variables continued to be the best predictors of perceived racial discrimination. The exception was sex-role identity, although it almost approached statistical significance ($p = .073$). These data indicate that respondents who had perceived racial discrimination were young, single (never married, divorced, or separated), racially conscious, masculine in their sex-role identity, and exposed to a great deal of daily hassles and stressful life events.

DISCUSSION

When perception of racial discrimination was used as the dependent variable, several demographic, sociocultural, and stress-related factors were significantly related to this variable. Racial discrimination was most frequently perceived in the workplace, from government agencies, and from the police. These findings are consistent with Sigelman and Welch's (1991) analyses of national surveys that showed that African Americans reported experiencing more discrimination in employment than in housing

TABLE 17-6

Forced Entry Multiple Regression of Perceived Racial Discrimination and Selected Variables

Variable[a]	Beta[b]	t value	R
Friends' closeness	.035	.856	.062
Racial consciousness	.103*	2.551	.056
Marital status	−.102*	−2.463	−.150
Help satisfaction	−.044	−1.099	−.003
Sex-role identity	.073	1.804	.068
Stressful events	.138**	3.187	.277
Health rating	.010	.222	.072
Family closeness	−.068	−1.683	.036
Religiosity	−.035	.845	−.052
Income	.064	1.441	.039
Hassles	.324***	6.979	.393
Employment status	−.043	−.865	.133
Education	−.028	−.565	.154
Age	−.128*	−2.256	−.286

Multiple $R = .468$
$R^2 = .219$
Adjusted $R^2 = .198$
$F(14, 522) = 10.48, p = .000$.

[a]A dummy code was used for marital status (married = 1, not married =0) and employment status (employed = 1, unemployed = 0).
[b]Beta = standardized coefficients.
*$p < .05$. **$p < .01$. ***$p < .001$.

or education. Racial discrimination involving the police was not included in these surveys.

African American men's reports of racial discrimination from government agencies and the police should be a major concern to policymakers, who often supervise these public units. These findings imply that despite efforts to create equal employment opportunities, perceived disparities still exist. Similarly, the findings also indicate the inadequacies of legislative action and public policy mandates in addressing problems of racial acceptance in the daily lives and interpersonal behaviors of the population of the United States. Particularly disturbing is the knowledge that society's most concerted efforts to mandate fairness have occurred in the social settings cited in the survey—workplaces, public agencies, and police forces. These observations suggest the need for more innovative strategies to address discriminatory practices in the public as well as the private domains.

Factors closely associated with perceptions of discrimination included age, marital status, racial consciousness, social stressors, and sex-role identity. High levels of reported discrimination among those with high measures of racial consciousness can probably be best described in terms of the respondents' awareness and sensitivity. It is logical to assume that respondents with high levels of awareness with regard to racial and ethnic differences would be more inclined to identify discrimination or interpret behaviors as bias laden. This observation leads to the question of whether heightened awareness elicits higher levels of discrimination or merely greater sensitivity to the existence of discriminatory behavior. Experimental designs focusing on observable behavioral biases are needed to resolve this question. There is evidence that people of color are more attuned perceptually to detecting racial bias in specific social situations. A study of 175 undergraduates, including 106 African Americans, found that African American students perceived more unfairness than white students in responses to a hypothetical survey item that portrayed a white person being promoted over a black person (Sherman, Smith, & Sherman, 1983).

This research contradicts the findings of Sigelman and Welch (1991) with respect to age. The findings demonstrated that young African American men were more likely to perceive racial discrimination than older African American men. Sigelman and Welch found the reverse.

Moreover, married men, regardless of their age, reported less discrimination than did unmarried men. Both social support and role theories may be used to explain this finding. From the perspectives of these theories, being married in this society is a highly valued social role. Cultural mechanisms have been developed to support and protect a person, especially a man, in such a role. Reports dating back to the middle of the 19th century have shown that married people tend to have better health than unmarried people (Maykovich, 1980). Married men are likely to receive social support from their mates, other family members, and society in general. Brown, Gary, Greene, & Milburn (1992); Gary (1985); and Dressler and Badger (1985) showed that patterns of social affiliation were associated with a decreased risk for depression in the African American community. Thus, married African American men would be less likely to perceive racial discrimination because they are buffered by supportive cultural mechanisms from the effect of negative interactions in society.

On the other hand, there may be a cultural bias against single adult African American men. If this is the case, African American men, regardless of their age, would be subjected to more negative social interactions in various institutional settings and less social support within the context of the African American community and society in general.

Stressors both chronic and acute were significantly associated with perceptions of racial inequality. African American men who experienced high levels of stress—especially daily hassles (chronic types of stress)—were more likely to report racial discrimination than men with low levels of stress. These findings are consistent with those of Sigelman and Welch (1991) with respect to the effect of socioeconomic variables on African Americans' perceptions of racial inequality. For example, they found that African Americans who rented their living quarters and had trouble paying their bills and, thus, were under economic pressures were more likely to perceive racial discrimination than those who were homeowners and those who were not under economic pressure. To some extent, both of these variables as defined by Sigelman and Welch are stressors, and both can be classified as daily hassles or chronic stressors.

To reduce the incidence of perceived racial discrimination by African Americans, it is important to develop social policies and to design social programs that help reduce high levels of stress in the lives of African American men. Further research is needed to explore fully the relationship between racial discrimination as a stressor and its relevance to physical and mental health outcomes among this population. Stress theory might be an appropriate framework for understanding these relationships (Maykovich, 1980).

Perceptions of racial discrimination were significantly related to sex-role identity after controlling for other variables. Based on this observation and other findings, one can draw a hypothesis postulating that aggressive or assertive behavior (that is, the traditionally male role characteristic) among young African American men promotes reactive discrimination in the larger society.

Recent literature has emphasized the effects of changing gender expectations on masculine role identity (Clatterbaugh, 1990;

Franklin, 1984; Kimmel, 1987; Stearns, 1990). Traditionally, these discussions have taken place in the context of a male–female dichotomy without fully accounting for ethnic and cultural differences in gender orientation. Clatterbaugh maintained that contemporary attitudes and beliefs about masculinity should be understood from a variety of sociopolitical perspectives. One of these basic orientations is the "group-specific" perspective, in which the male sex role is defined in accordance with the needs and historical concerns of specific cultural, racial, and social groups. In this model, the combined group experience within the larger social setting influences and shapes gender definitions. Clatterbaugh's conceptualization is consistent with arguments relating to African American masculinity developed by Franklin (1984), Majors and Billson (1991), and others. Wilson (1990) specifically emphasized the negative influences of white racism in the development of maladaptive perceptions of masculinity among certain African American men.

CONCLUSION

The findings of this study about masculine role identity are important to social work practitioners, social scientists, policymakers, and educators because they document perceptions of heightened racial discrimination among traditionally masculine young African American men. It is important that social work practitioners and educators remain aware of the possibility that strategies designed to alleviate gender discrimination may be misconstrued by African American men as veiled attempts to devalue their experiences as victims of racism. Simultaneously, demands that African American men suppress their expressions of masculinity can be misinterpreted as attempts to further constrain their goal orientations, opportunities, and avenues to success. Progressive social policies must begin to address the inherent conflict in assisting different disadvantaged groups in society. Finally, the findings emphasize the need for the continued support of research and policy development centering around issues pertaining to social justice and equality.

REFERENCES

Akbar, N. (1991). *Visions for black men.* Nashville, TN: Winston-Derek.
Bell, D. A. (1980). *Race, racism and American law* (2nd ed.). Boston: Little, Brown.

Bem, S. L. (1974). The measurement of psychological androgyny. *Journal of Consulting and Clinical Psychology, 42,* 155–162.

Bem, S. L. (1977). On the utility of an alternate procedure for assessing psychological androgyny. *Journal of Consulting and Clinical Psychology, 45,* 196–205.

Braddock, J. H., & McPartland, J. M. (1987). How minorities continue to be excluded from equal opportunities: Research on labor markets and industrial barriers. *Journal of Social Issues, 43*(1), 5–39.

Brown, D. R., Gary, L. E., Greene, A. D., & Milburn, N. G. (1992). Patterns of social affiliation as predictors of depressive symptoms among urban blacks. *Journal of Health and Social Behavior, 33,* 242–253.

Clatterbaugh, K. C. (1990). *Contemporary perspectives on masculinity.* Boulder, CO: Westview Press.

Cose, E. (1992). *A nation of strangers: Prejudice, politics and the populating of America.* New York: William Morrow.

Davis, J. A. (1971). Justification for no obligation: Views of black males toward crime and the criminal law. *Issues in Criminology, 9*(2), 69–87.

Dovidio, J. F., & Gaertner, S. L. (Eds.). (1986). *Prejudice, discrimination and racism.* New York: Academic Press.

Dressler, W. W., & Badger, L. W. (1985). Depressive symptoms in black communities. *Journal of Nervous and Mental Disease, 173,* 212–219.

Evans, A. S., & Giles, M. W. (1986). Effects of percent black on blacks' perceptions of relative power and social distance. *Journal of Black Studies, 17*(1), 3–14.

Ezorsky, G. (1991). *Racism and justice: The case for affirmative action.* Ithaca, NY: Cornell University Press.

Farley, R., & Allen, W. R. (1987). *The color line and quality of life in America.* New York: Russell Sage Foundation.

Farrell, W. C., Dawkins, M. P., & Oliver, J. (1983). Genocide fears in a rural black community: An empirical examination. *Journal of Black Studies, 14*(1), 49–67.

Feagin, J. R., & Feagin, C. B. (1978). *Discrimination American style: Institutional racism and sexism.* Englewood Cliffs, NJ: Prentice Hall.

Franklin, C. (1984). *The changing definitions of masculinity.* New York: Plenum Press.

Gary, L. E. (Ed.). (1981). *Black men.* Beverly Hills, CA: Sage Publications.

Gary, L. E. (1985). Correlates of depressive symptoms among a select population of black men. *American Journal of Public Health, 75,* 1220–1222.

Gary, L. E., Brown, D. R., Milburn, N. G., Ahmed, F., & Booth, J. A. (1989). *Depression in black American adults: Findings from the Norfolk area health study: Final report.* Washington, DC: Howard University, Institute for Urban Affairs and Research.

Germain, C. B. (1991). *Human behavior in the social environment: An ecological view.* New York: Columbia University Press.

Gibbs, J. T. (Ed.). (1988). *Young, black and male in America: An endangered species.* Dover, MA: Auburn House.

Goldberg, D. T. (Ed.). (1990). *Anatomy of racism.* Minneapolis: University of Minnesota Press.

Hacker, A. (1992). *Two nations: Black and white, separate, hostile, unequal.* New York: Charles Scribner's Sons.

Hagan, J., & Albonetti, C. (1982). Race, class, and the perception of criminal injustice in America. *American Journal of Sociology, 88,* 329–355.

Harris, L., & Associates, Inc. (1989). *The unfinished agenda on race in America* (Study No. 883006/9, Vol. 1). New York: National Association for the Advancement of Colored People, Legal Defense and Educational Fund.

Hecht, M. L., & Ribeau, S. (1987). Afro-American identity labels and communication effectiveness. *Journal of Language and Social Psychology, 6*(3–4), 319–326.

Higginbotham, A. L. (1978). *In the matter of color: Race and American legal process—The colonial period.* New York: Oxford University Press.

Holmes, T. H., & Rahe, R. H. (1967). The social readjustment rating scale. *Journal of Psychosomatic Research, 11,* 213–218.

Hutchison, E. O. (1994). *The assassination of the black male image.* Los Angeles: Middle Passage Press.

Jaynes, G. D., & Williams, R. M. (Eds.). (1989). *A common destiny: Blacks and American society.* Washington, DC: National Academy Press.

Kanner, A. D., Coyne, J. C., Schafer, C., & Lazarus, R. (1981). Comparison of two modes of stress measurement: Daily hassles and uplift versus major life events. *Journal of Behavioral Medicine, 4,* 1–39.

Kenney, B., Cromwell, R., & Vaughan, C. E. (1977). Identifying the sociocultural forms of religiosity among urban ethnic minority group members. *Journal of the Scientific Study of Religion, 16,* 237–244.

Kimmel, M. S. (Ed.). (1987). *Changing men.* Newbury Park, CA: Sage Publications.

Kochman, T. (1981). *Black and white styles in conflict.* Chicago: University of Chicago Press.

LaRue, A. L., Bank, L., Jarvik, L., & Hetland, M. (1979). Health in old age: How do physicians' rating and self-rating compare? *Journal of Gerontology, 34,* 687–691.

Maddox, G. L., & Douglas, E. B. (1973). Self-assessment of health: A longitudinal study of elderly subjects. *Journal of Health and Social Behavior, 14*(1), 87–93.

Majors, R., & Billson, J. M. (1991). *Cool pose.* Lexington, MA: Macmillan.

Maykovich, M. K. (1980). *Medical sociology.* Sherman Oaks, CA: Alfred.

McAdoo, J. L. (1993). The roles of African American fathers: An ecological perspective. *Families in Society, 74,* 28–35.

Milburn, N. G., Gary, L. E., Booth, J. A., & Brown, D. R. (1991). Conducting epidemiologic research in a minority community: Methodological considerations. *Journal of Community Psychology, 19,* 3–12.

Monroe, S., & Goldman, P. (1988). *Brothers: Black and poor—A true story of courage and survival.* New York: William Morrow.

Mossey, J., & Shapiro, E. (1982). Self-rated health: Predictors of mortality among the elderly. *American Journal of Public Health, 72,* 800–808.

Nie, N. H., Hull, C. H, Jenkins, J. G., Steinbrenner, K., & Bent, D. H. (1975). *Statistical package for the social sciences* (2nd ed.). New York: McGraw-Hill.

Ogbu, J. U. (1983). Schooling the inner city. *Society, 117*(1), 75–79.

Pinkney, A. (1984). *The myth of black progress.* New York: Cambridge University Press.

Sherman, M. F., Smith, R. J., & Sherman, N. C. (1983). Racial and gender differences in perceptions of fairness: When race is involved in a job promotion. *Perceptual and Motor Skills, 57,* 719–728.

Sigelman, L., & Welch, S. (1991). *Black Americans' views of racial inequality: The dream deferred.* New York: Cambridge University Press.

Staples, R. (1982). *Black masculinity: The black male's role in American society.* San Francisco: Black Scholar Press.

Staples, R. (1987). Black male genocide: A final solution to the race problem of America. *Black Scholar, 18,* 2–11.

Stearns, P. N. (1990). *Be a man! Men in society.* New York: Holmes & Meier.

Taylor, J. (1992). *Paved with good intentions: The failure of race relations in contemporary America.* New York: Carroll & Graf.

Wilson, A. N. (1990). *Black-on-black violence: The psychodynamics of black self-annihilation in service of white domination.* New York: Afrikan World Infosystems.

This chapter was originally published in the December 1995 issue of Social Work Research, *vol. 19, pp. 207–217.*

Deconstructing Politically Correct Practice Literature: The American Indian Case

Emma R. Gross

S ocial work theory on practice with people of color contains unevaluated assumptions that render it problematic for these ideas to genuinely account for the life experiences of people of color in ways that can be meaningfully applied to the development of practice skills. The literature on social work practice with American Indians is an example (Blanchard & Barsch, 1980; Brown, 1978; Cross, 1986; Devore & Schlesinger, 1989; Edwards & Edwards, 1980; Farris, 1976; Goodtracks, 1973; Green, 1982; Kumabe, Nishida, & Hepworth, 1985; Lewis & Deer, 1980; Lewis & Ho, 1975; Lockyear, 1972; Lum, 1986; Morales & Sheafor, 1980; Morey & Gilliam, 1974; RedHorse, 1980; RedHorse, Lewis, Feit, & Decker, 1978; Unger, 1977). The literature constructs generalizations about American Indian cultures and worldviews that create the impression of one unified American Indian reality (Berkhofer, 1978; Houts & Bahr, 1972) by stating or implying that cultural values are similarly regarded across Indian tribes, communities, and cultures; by designating the authors who are American Indians themselves as credible and authoritative simply by virtue of their ethnicity; and by promulgating the view that American Indian values as defined are not only immutable but also essential for any true affiliation with a state of "Indianness." Thus, "real" American Indians are those whose attitudes and behaviors are closest to traditionalist (premodern) cultural orientations.

The result of this "politically correct" practice literature has been to foster the impression that American Indian realities are only one and monolithic. (In this article, *political correctness* is defined as standpoints that unconditionally value descriptions of American Indian life that romanticize or glamorize traditional belief systems and practices.) This impression hinders the development of reform strategies and interventions that take into account the realities rather than the mythologized views of Indianness (Berkhofer, 1978; Svensson, 1973).

In this article I argue that although there were valid reasons for using a political approach to writing the practice literature, the need now is for a fairer representation of the diversity that characterizes American Indian communities. In this way, more accurate helping strategies can be used with American Indians.

BACKGROUND

My interest in American Indian representation in the social work practice literature stems from more than 20 years of involvement with American Indian community development, educational research, and teaching projects. My perceptions about how the literature has helped construct politically correct, and therefore acceptable, images of American Indian life derive from personal experience as well as a close reading of the subliterature about American Indian values, perhaps the most discussed of all American Indian topics in the social work literature.

Red Power Movement and Political Correctness

Those who wrote during or immediately after the "Red Power" events of the late 1960s and early 1970s were impelled as much by the need to present American Indians in a favorable light as by the requirement to be scholarly in reporting. Scholars' mission was to change then-prevailing views of American Indians as helpless, hopeless, and doomed to inevitable destinies of drunkenness and poverty. Along these lines, both the Red Power and countercultural movements drew heavily on romanticized conceptions of American Indian imagery, many of them already deeply ingrained in American popular culture. Resurrecting the idea of American Indians as noble (if "savage") and perfectly in tune with nature seemed very much in keeping with the social activist ideal of empowering American Indians and tribes (Berkhofer, 1978; Cross, Bazron, Dennis, & Isaacs, 1989; Svensson, 1973). For example, not only did "hippies" adorn themselves with American Indian paraphernalia, but young members of Indian and non-Indian alternative cultures also adopted American

Indian myths, rituals, dances, art, and spiritual practices. (Today, American Indian cosmologies and spiritual practices have become the commonplace staples of many New Age, countercultural, and alternative projects.)

Moreover, one did not need to identify with radical or threatening political alternatives to credibly advocate for social change. One did not need to believe in sovereignty for American Indian tribes or in their self-determination as a separatist alternative to write about their oppression. One could be "for" American Indians without seriously challenging the sociostructural roots of Indian misery.

Thus, advocates of increased opportunities for American Indians chose a liberal ideology that focused on showing how they were worthy of positive regard by non-Indian populations and institutions. The strategy succeeded largely because it put forth images of American Indians as "like" non-Indians, only somewhat lacking in equal access and a fair chance at the American Dream. In the process, however, traditionalist, progressive, and even assimilationist differences were obscured. For example, with respect to political goals and social development aspirations, social activists and mainstream politicians behaved as if "Indian" always meant the same thing (Gross, 1989).

At the same time, the social work practice literature encouraged non-Indian social workers to believe that effective practice in Indian communities was "learnable." Social workers were as eager as the politicians to find a positive construction of "Indian," especially one that fit European American assimilationist biases. The achievement of the politically correct approach was to relegitimize American Indians as "worthy" of increased social spending and concern. In addition, this newly acquired positive regard for Indianness helped give privilege to American Indian political views and interests in ways previously unknown, thus favoring the pursuit of American Indian policy interests.

The total domination of the politically correct perspective also made it difficult, if not impossible, to derive views of Indianness that were congruent with the diversity of American Indian life and views. In addition, increased political regard for American Indian tribes, communities, and organizations has not led to better daily lives for the tens of thousands of American Indians experiencing acute poverty. Indeed, the politically correct injunction "hands off unless one is an American Indian" undermines both Indian and non-Indian efforts to do something about the unconscionable degree of poverty and neglect present in American Indian communities. Also, politically correct stances inhibited developing approaches to dealing with American Indian alcoholism that emphasized the role of personal responsibility and choice in getting sober. Instead, practitioners surmised that traditional cultural practices would provide superior solutions to any American Indian problem.

Political Correctness Backlash

The current backlash against political correctness, however, has not restored balance to practitioner perspectives on American Indian life. Unfortunately, the backlash is spearheaded by reactionary forces who would prefer to see American Indians lose their political and moral privilege altogether (Gross, 1989). For example, conservative voices are leading the battles against American Indian self-determination, antidiscrimination, and affirmative action initiatives aimed at empowerment.

DECONSTRUCTING POLITICAL BIAS

One way to reinvigorate the social work practice literature on American Indians is to examine how the discussion of values and the requirements of authorship have obscured the diversity of Indian life. In this article I use the deconstructivist methodology to re-examine the unarticulated assumptions that underlie the development of a written body of work that eventually becomes the established authority (canon) on a subject. In the American Indian canon, for example, the notion of traditional as more desirable signifies the unspoken conviction that Indianness is best exemplified by one whose attitudes, beliefs, behaviors, and appearance most closely approximate a romanticized ideal.

Using this methodology I also identify in what ways the literature overgeneralizes so that degrees of Indian "likeness" are misrepresented. The exegetic, nonempirical basis of the generalizations about values, as well as the assimilationist and reverential biases, prevent alternative views from being heard. American Indians who are alcoholics, gay, or for progressive rather than traditionalist solutions are typically denied expression in the canon, because there is no "permission" to take a critical perspective on what is being said about Indians.

Along the same lines, "official" constructions of Indianness elicit positive regard from non-Indians enamored of romantic imagery and also exacerbate American Indians' awareness of themselves as helpless and incompetent, yet heroic. Conundrums that stem from perceived and observed differences in the Indian experience are common and unresolved. For example, there is as yet no language for expressing the oscillations that exist between views of "Indian" as noble and drunken and between views of "white" as conscientious and deceitful. The point of deconstructivist analysis, then, is to untangle the meaning behind such contradictory messages to suggest new meanings that are more respectful of differences.

Finally, it is not my intention to detract from the necessary and significant political gains that fictionalizing and mythologizing Indian realities has accomplished. American Indians were and still are entitled to whatever rectification and compensation they can obtain from European American societies. The purpose of this critique is not to advance a neoconservative alternative to the nonnegotiable rights of American Indian populations. The purpose is to reopen the canon on American Indian practice (and that of other people of color as well) to writings that will focus attention on issues such as poverty, alcoholism, and unemployment in ways that will make it possible for both Indians and non-Indians to deal more effectively with the complex and partial (rather than universal) realities they are encountering.

Central to this endeavor is talking about American Indian problems without perpetuating conventional assumptions about white people as better off and white ways as superior. Unfortunately, this is much easier said than done. Eurocentric social work biases are not only prevalent, they have been profoundly internalized by many of the writers of the American Indian practice canon as well (Brown, 1978; DeAnda, 1984; De Hoyos, De Hoyos, & Anderson, 1986). To properly rewrite conventional–assimilationist perspectives in this literature, therefore, will require viewing American Indian realities in and of themselves as legitimate and diverse. Ultimately, deconstructivism legitimates practitioner enterprise that is sensitive to context and regional differences rather than the application of models that may be static and unresponsive to particularized differences (Hartman, 1992; Nuccio & Sands, 1992; Sands & Nuccio, 1992).

VALUES IN THE PRACTICE LITERATURE

The discussion of American Indian values in the practice literature helps illustrate why it is politically incorrect to challenge the established view of Indianness. The partial list of values in Table 18-1 is drawn from this literature and summarizes two ways in which the practice canon perpetuates the notion that true Indianness is traditional and fixed. First, although lip service is paid to the notion that it is not correct to generalize across cultures, authors have proceeded to do just that (Cross et al., 1989; Edwards & Edwards, 1980; Goodtracks, 1973; Lewis & Ho, 1975; RedHorse, 1980). Second, values are typically set forth as oppositional and dichotomous, in which case the best resolution of any dilemma is to want to acquire the American Indian stance (presumed traditionalist outlooks and behaviors) and, therefore, to ignore the complexities associated with modern and postmodern approaches to social problems in American Indian communities.

With respect to generalizations about American Indians, reference to the often-cited value of noninterference is an example of the contradictory messages found in the literature on values. For example, Goodtracks (1973) stated, "the author's experience indicates that the statements made in this article apply to the Navajo and the tribes of Northern and Southern Plains," and then later in the same sentence, he contradicts himself with, "much that is said here might also be true of the Pueblo and other tribes" (p. 34). The value of noninterference, he says, means that "in native Indian society . . . no interference or meddling of any kind is allowed or tolerated, even when it is to keep the other person from doing something foolish or dangerous" (p. 30). Such is the political correctness of this stance that no one came forward to point out that it is precisely social work's imperative to interfere in instances when someone is perceived to be doing themselves or others harm.

Obviously, Goodtracks's (1973) stance reflects the contradictory tension that has always existed between the idea of social work in American Indian settings and the fact that social work's functions of social control symbolize oppression as much as liberation. There are subtextual messages, too, about the viability

Table 18-1

Generalizations about Indian versus Non-Indian Value Orientations: Artificial Dichotomies in the Canon

Value Opposition	Established View of Indianness
Noninterference versus interference or intervention	Interference is like "meddling," the opposite of "self-determination"; individual autonomy and self-expression are more important than asserting control over others. An often-cited example of this value is "permissiveness" in Indian child-rearing practices (children are not allowed to interrupt adults, for example, but they may run rampant); discipline, however, can be harsh (Morey & Gilliam, 1974). In any case, no interference of any kind is allowed (Goodtracks, 1973).
Nonlinearity versus rationality or linearity	The preference is for intuition, mysticism, and spirituality: for experiencing life as cyclical rather than as a series of cause-and-effect relationships and as organic rather than inanimate. An Indian sense of time is often cited as an example; lateness among Indians is viewed as okay because time is a "natural" phenomenon, and Indians are respectful of natural rhythms by acting in accordance with their own sense of when it is right to act rather than in keeping with "clock time." On a more philosophical level, rejection of scientism (scientific method) is implied.
Extended family versus nuclear family	Community, tribe, or clan is more important than the individual. Elders, grandparents especially, are said to be more revered than anyone else. All family members are expected to act according to traditional, rigorously prescribed roles. Extended families can be relied on to meet all individual needs; help from outside this system is not wanted or tolerated.
Harmony with nature versus mastery over nature	Preference is for "at-one-ness" with the universe—with "fourleggeds" (animals), nature, and other human beings. All things are or ought to be in balance or equilibrium; disturbances (conflict, confrontation, dissonance) should be avoided.
Emotional control and stoicism versus emotionality	Value is placed on pride, on not being embarrassed publicly, and on dominating (rather than expressing) feelings.
Sharing versus ownership	Value is placed on giving and generosity, as in giveaways and potlatches, even if going without is the consequence.
Respect versus self-definition and self-fulfillment	Value is placed on knowing and adhering to one's "place" in life; the family-related themes are reverence for elders, nonnegotiable expectations about the roles and status of women, and the proper behavior of children. Value is placed on preservation (the status quo) rather than change.
Humor versus seriousness and intensity	Humor is a value frequently contrasted with the white tendency to take oneself and one's enterprise seriously (grimly). The preference is for seeing the irony ("cosmic joke") rather than pathos in misfortune and for accepting what comes one's way ("fate").

of "helping" and "being helped" and about the impossibilities of achieving either.

The notion that American Indians are unsuited for survival in the modern era is certainly fostered by plentiful illustrations of Indian decadence and decay (Shkilnyk, 1985). Lockyear (1972), for example, voiced another of the politically correct views: "With rare exceptions, the only achievements that Indian people . . . can point to with pride occurred long ago . . . in earlier centuries. . . . The Indian life-style provided a sense of heroism and adventure and brought them satisfaction and tranquility. . . . As a people they have been able to make little or no contribution to the present" (p. 72). But any desire to "help" has to run the gauntlet of political correctness, an effort that has seemingly proved too daunting for most, given the absence of any literature challenging established notions about who American Indians are and what they want. Thus, ideas about "helping," which are plentiful in the literature, must conform to the expectation that they also not appear to be critical about Indianness, presumably in reference to the assumption about universal values.

In lieu, therefore, of open-ended dialogues about how one ought to practice, social work practitioners are much more likely to encounter the platitudes found in textbooks. For example,

> Each tribe's culture is unique . . . and no social worker can be familiar with the cultures of some 200 tribes. . . . Some customs are generally characteristic of all Native Americans, and the authors suggest that social workers become familiar with these. The concepts of sharing, time, acceptance of suffering, and optimism, to name a few cultural traits common to most tribes, differ significantly from Anglo-Saxon traits. Social workers must realize these differences and proceed accordingly. (Morales & Sheafor, 1980, p. 265)

The advice given here also illustrates the extent to which empirically unfounded generalizations about American Indian attitudes and behaviors are common in the literature. Even attempts to implement practice wisdom are based on the unquestioned conviction that certain generalities should be taken as proved and universal (Green, 1982).

Furthermore, the discussion associated with values illustrates how these presumed traditionalist values have also become reified in opposition to Eurocentric value orientations. Thus, it is held that any "true" resolution of Indian identity must move toward the traditionalist position to become credible. American Indians who choose to assimilate or to in some other way depart from traditionalist values are left with no Indian identity references against which they might then positively regard themselves or be positively regarded by others. For example, American Indians who advocate for mineral resources development may be defined as "bad" Indians (meaning not in harmony with nature). Similarly, American Indians who are gay or lesbian may find themselves the targets of derision and rejection, much as the author of *Hanto Yo* (Hill, 1979) was for suggesting that American Indians can be homosexual.

AUTHORSHIP OF AMERICAN INDIAN LITERATURE

For the most part, writers of the practice literature on American Indians have had to be Indian themselves, or if not, at least related by marriage or adoption (Blanchard & Barsh, 1980; Carpenter, 1980; Goodtracks, 1973). One effect of this unwritten policy has been to ensure control over content as well as over the status and the rewards that have accompanied becoming the sole or "token" American Indian on social work faculties. Another effect has been to inhibit the development of a contemporary discourse on the subject of Indianness. Importantly, talking about American Indian topics has required possessing proper credentials, namely, being Indian oneself. Being legitimated as "Indian," then, has enabled one to get the attention of publishers and academic colleagues, especially those who were responsible for teaching content about people of color in social work courses. One's legitimate status as Indian, then, not only ensured access to non-Indian audiences and the prestige that went along with being an "authority" or "expert" on the subject, but also forever enabled exclusion from the ranks of anyone without this credential, which was very difficult to obtain indeed. "Perfect acceptance comes only with the loss of the worker's alien status, which cannot be achieved except through adoption by Indian people. To become one of the people is, of course, most unlikely, but not impossible" (Goodtracks, 1973, p. 34). The effect of this message has been to keep everyone out of Indian affairs who is not culturally or racially Indian. Nontraditional Indians, as well as non-Indians, were effectively silenced by this requirement.

The debate between influential American Indian writer Evelyn Blanchard (Blanchard & Barsh, 1980) and Ronald Fischler (1980), a non-Indian, also illustrates how perilous it is to write about American Indians when one is not Indian oneself. Their debate was on the merits of the Indian Child Welfare Act of 1978: "Fischler's call for an analytical view of folklore and mythology raises serious ethical questions. . . . One would have to question the validity of such observations and analyses by persons out-side the American Indian culture" (Blanchard & Barsh, 1980, p. 352). From this standpoint, which is not unique to Blanchard and Barsh, Fischler's opinions are not merely invalidated, they do not exist. They cannot exist, because Fischler is not an American Indian. Fischler is silenced.

As part of the politically correct stance, Fischler's views must be nullified before they are heard, in part because genuine dis-agreements exist about Indian child-rearing practices. But more importantly, the debate itself must be squelched before it results in a closer, sustained examination of child-rearing practices and beliefs in general. Being politically correct in this instance means being aware that too much power will be relinquished if Ameri-can Indians cannot be portrayed as well equipped by tradition to raise their own children.

DISCUSSION

Deconstructivist challenges to the existing wisdom enable one to find ways to open the literature to other perspectives, findings, and conclusions without remarginalizing the writers. The ques-tion is especially poignant in view of the fact that any attempt to rewrite the literature should avoid rejecting out of hand the au-thority and authenticity implied by insights that are grounded in personal experience. Academicians and practitioners can main-tain visibility and centrality for the writers and at the same time demythologize and critically re-evaluate the literature by becom-ing self-conscious about the act of writing and practicing. This task can be accomplished in at least two ways. First, reference to the literature on standpoint theory and its particular aptness for researching questions of relations between people of color and white people will be helpful (Collins, 1990). Second, there are guidelines that one can apply to one's own research or learning about practice with people of color. For example, Who is doing the analyzing and observing? What are their and my interests in pursuing the subject? Who will benefit from these writings and practices? How will the population at stake benefit? To what extent is my motivation tied to wanting to be politically correct? To what extent is my motivation tied to finding an easy answer (a model)? How is the literature or speaker generalizing in ways that perpetuate stereotypes? How willing am I to challenge the prevailing wisdom? What provisions are made for others to be heard? How willing am I to acknowledge differences of perspective as well as opinion on the question of Indianness?

Becoming self-conscious and critical about the writing of one's experiences is a meaningful way in which to highlight the positive subjectivities of social work practice. It is also a way to restore balance to the client–social worker relationship in that both are learning as they go along. The notion that social work is or ought to be "scientific" practice is especially prejudicial to establishing egalitarianism in that the stance implies knowing something "permanent," "true," "universal," and "essential" about the other, when none of this is true. The client and social worker have each others' perceptions and resources to work with and nothing more. The value of entering into one another's subjectivities in this case is especially effective practice precisely because it permits using one's self to "do" something in cases where otherwise no help may be forthcoming. Developing such a stance permits practitioners to know what they want to have happen with respect to intervening on behalf of others. A scientific–positivist stance, then, simply makes it harder to act because one is dependent on "knowing truth" beforehand.

Thus, a working hypothesis might be that interventions and relating may be perceived as helpful to the extent that the helper is clear headed and focused with respect to his or her own belief systems and not those presumed to belong to the consumer (Finn, 1991; Gross, 1987; Kleinfeld, 1973). In fact, clear-headedness about one's own beliefs is probably why religious missionaries (among others) have been effective in American Indian communities. Although missionaries' purpose is to dilute cultures by imposing their own, their clarity of purpose has been successful where liberal social work approaches have not. The reason for this is that liberal rapprochement is much more likely to seek to emulate American Indian ways, thus obfuscating any contrasts and leading to even more confusion about who is supposed to be offering what to whom.

CONCLUSION

Social work writers and practitioners, both Indian and non-Indian, will need to continue to approach differentness respectfully and helpfully. They will also need to identify and critically reevaluate those hidden assumptions and biases that typically, and unknowingly, affect their helping postures in ways that are counterproductive for the interests of populations currently at risk—and even, it would seem, for positive social growth and development in general.

REFERENCES

Berkhofer, R. F., Jr. (1978). *The white man's Indian: Images of the American Indian from Columbus to the present.* New York: Vintage Books.

Blanchard, E. L., & Barsh, R. L. (1980). What is best for tribal children? A response to Fischler. *Social Work, 25,* 350–357.

Brown, E. F. (1978). American Indians in modern society: Implications for social policy and services. In D. G. Horton (Ed.), *The dual perspective: Inclusion of ethnic minority content in the social work curriculum* (pp. 68–76). New York: Council on Social Work Education.

Carpenter, E. M. (1980). Social services, policies, and issues. *Social Casework, 61,* 455–461.

Collins, P. H. (1990). *Black feminist thought: Knowledge, consciousness, and the politics of empowerment.* New York: Routledge & Kegan Paul.

Cross, T. L. (1986). Drawing on cultural tradition in Indian child welfare practice. *Social Casework, 67,* 283–289.

Cross, T. L., Bazron, B. J., Dennis, K. W., & Isaacs, M. R. (1989). *Towards a culturally competent system of care: A monograph on effective services for minority children who are severely emotionally disturbed.* Washington, DC: CASSP Technical Assistance Center, Georgetown University Child Development Center.

DeAnda, D. (1984). Bicultural socialization: Factors affecting the minority experience. *Social Work, 29,* 101–107.

De Hoyos, G., De Hoyos, A., & Anderson, C. B. (1986). Sociocultural dislocation: Beyond *The Dual Perspective. Social Work, 31,* 61–67.

Devore, W., & Schlesinger, E. G. (1989). *Ethnic-sensitive social work practice* (2nd ed.). Columbus, OH: Charles E. Merrill.

Edwards, E. D., & Edwards, M. E. (1980). American Indians: Working with individuals and groups. *Social Casework, 16,* 498–506.

Farris, C. E. (1976). American Indian social worker advocates. *Social Casework, 57,* 494–503.

Finn, J. (1991). *Native American women, public policy and the self-identity: Historic interplay of the personal and the political* (Working Paper Series, No. 1990-91-01). Ann Arbor: University of Michigan, School of Social Work.

Fischler, R. S. (1980). Protecting American Indian children. *Social Work, 25,* 341–349.

Goodtracks, J. G. (1973). Native American non-interference. *Social Work, 18*(6), 30–34.

Green, J. W. (1982). *Cultural awareness in the human services.* Englewood Cliffs, NJ: Prentice Hall.

Gross, E. R. (1987). *Curanderismo, espiritismo, shamanism, and social work practice* (Working Paper Series, No. 87-88-3). Ann Arbor: University of Michigan, School of Social Work.

Gross, E. R. (1989). *Contemporary federal policy toward American Indians.* Westport, CT: Greenwood Press.

Hartman, A. (1992). In search of subjugated knowledge [Editorial]. *Social Work, 37,* 483–484.

Hill, R. B. (1979). *Hanta Yo.* New York: Doubleday.

Houts, K. C., & Bahr, R. S. (1972). Stereotyping of Indians and blacks in magazine cartoons. In H. Bahr, B. A. Chadwick, & R. C. Day (Eds.), *Native Americans today: Sociological perspectives* (pp. 100–114). New York: Harper & Row.

Kleinfeld, J. S. (1973, March). *Effective teachers of Indian and Eskimo high school students.* Unpublished paper, University of Alaska, Institute of Social, Economic, and Government Research, College.

Kumabe, K. T., Nishida, C., & Hepworth, D. H. (1985). *Bridging ethnocultural diversities in social work and health.* Honolulu: University of Hawaii, School of Social Work.

Lewis, R. G., & Deer, A. (Eds.). (1980). The Phoenix from the flame: The American Indian today [Special issue]. *Social Casework, 61*(8).

Lewis, R. G., & Ho, M. K. (1975). Social work with Native Americans. *Social Work, 20,* 379–382.

Lockyear, H. (1972). American Indian myths. *Social Work, 17*(3), 72–80.

Lum, D. (1986). *Social work practice and people of color: A process–stage approach.* Monterey, CA: Brooks/Cole.

Morales, A., & Sheafor, B. W. (1980). *Social work: A profession of many faces* (2nd ed.). New York: Allyn & Bacon.

Morey, S. M., & Gilliam, O. L. (1974). *Respect for life: The traditional upbringing of American Indian children.* Garden City, NY: Waldorf Press.

Nuccio, K. E., & Sands, R. G. (1992). Using postmodern feminist theory to deconstruct "phallacies" of poverty. *Affilia, 7*(4), 26–48.

RedHorse, J. G. (1980). American Indian elders: Unifiers of Indian families. *Social Casework, 61,* 490–493.

RedHorse, J. G., Lewis, R., Feit, M., & Decker, J. (1978). Family behavior of urban American Indians. *Social Casework, 59,* 67–72.

Sands, R. G., & Nuccio, K. (1992). Postmodern feminist theory and social work. *Social Work, 37,* 489–494.

Shkilnyk, A. M. (1985). *A poison stronger than love: The destruction of an Ojibwa community.* New Haven, CT: Yale University Press.

Svensson, F. (1973). *The ethnics in American politics: American Indians.* Minneapolis: Burgess.

Unger, S. (Ed.). (1977). *The destruction of American Indian families.* New York: Association on American Indian Affairs.

This chapter was originally published in the March 1995 issue of Social Work, *vol. 40, pp. 206–213.*

19

Self-Determination from a Pacific Perspective

Patricia L. Ewalt and Noreen Mokuau

Self-determination is viewed as a fundamental principle of social work. Indeed, Levy (1983) observed a "reflection in the social work literature of a preoccupation, if not an obsession, with the concept and ramifications of client self-determination" (p. 904). An examination of such a fundamental principle provides an opportunity to assess its relevance and applicability for multicultural populations.

It has been proposed that the principle of self-determination is universal. However, in its current use, the term "self-determination" is overly reliant on Northern European–American individualistic values; therefore, the practice implications for social work are substantial. Practice that urges individuals toward self-realization without consideration of group-oriented values is discordant with non-Western orientations (Budman, Lipson, & Meleis, 1992; Inclan & Hernandez, 1992; Pedersen, Fukuyama, & Heath, 1989; Tung, 1991) and may be inappropriate for many Western people as well (Papajohn & Spiegel, 1975).

This article examines prevailing interpretations of self-determination as suggested in the literature and also presents the high valuation on group preferences among Pacific peoples using case examples. The article suggests how social work practice can be improved through a reinterpretation of the meaning of self-determination.

INTERPRETATIONS OF SELF–DETERMINATION

Separation from the Group

Weick and Pope (1988) summarized *self-determination* as "clients' right to make their own decisions, their right to actively participate in the helping process, and their right to lead a life of their own choosing" (p. 10). Freedberg (1989) provided a similar definition: "self-determination, that condition in which personal behavior emanates from a person's own wishes, choices, and decisions" (p. 33). In composing this definition, Freedberg relied on an essay by Berlin (1975), "Two Concepts of Liberty," in which the author discussed the freedom or liberty to do or be what one wants to do or be without interference by other people and the idea that humans are capable of rationally determining their own actions.

Thus, self-determination is clearly linked with the literature from which the prevailing middle-class American ethic of individualism is drawn:

> The feeling of being in control is especially important to people whose parents and grandparents lived lives so dominated by insecurity that control—and self-reliance—became the prerequisites for nearly everything else. Greater control spells more security, and with sufficient security people can start to loosen unwanted social ties and to make more of their own choices about their lives. (Gans, 1988, p. 2)

Rooted in individualism, self-determination is discussed in terms of freedom of the individual to exercise self-direction and choice (Hollis, 1966) and of full development of the personality and an inner capacity for knowing what is best (Weick & Pope, 1988). Indeed, as Gans (1988) delineated, freedom from group expectations is regarded as self-reliance, a sign of strength. Separation from the group, as contrasted with belonging to the group, is viewed as providing the security that people desire (Schwartz, 1989).

Equivalence to Maturity

Separation from external influences on one's decision making is so highly valued in the United States that autonomy is considered to be a benchmark of one's maturity. Personal control is viewed as fundamental to one's self-development (Gans, 1988), and the assumption exists that the more a person feels and acts autonomous of the group, the more healthy and mature the person.

In the individualistic view, external forces are enemies of self-determination. External forces of society are seen as constant threats to the individual's freedom to choose (Lemmon, 1983;

Levy, 1983). Rarely is contributing to the group's well-being considered integral to self-determination, and rarely is placing the group's well-being first seen as signifying maturity.

GROUP WELL-BEING AS A COMPONENT OF SELF-DETERMINATION

A more complex understanding of self-determination, extending beyond identity solely with individualism, is provided by cultures other than those descended from Northern Europe. Inherent in many cultures are values that emphasize the collective over the individual as a perspective on self-determination. In addition, populations of color have experienced histories of oppression that have further affected their ideas of autonomy and maturity.

Oppression and Self-Determination

Dana (1981) emphasized the contrast between the views of middle-class, white Americans and people of color about self-determination:

> The core belief of middle-class, white America in autonomy, or immanent self-sufficiency, has never been a major component of the heritage of minority groups [American Indians, African Americans, Hispanic Americans, and Asian Americans].
>
> All four of these minority groups differ from most white, middle-class people in their world view. They typically experience less personal power, feel less control over their own lives, and they may also feel that they should not be directly responsible for themselves or experience greater control over their own lives. Such world view differences suggest that many current mental health and rehabilitation practices requiring responsibility, initiative, and personal involvement for their success simply will not make sense to many minority persons. (p. 354)

Pinderhughes (1983) provided insight into the relative meaninglessness of self-determination when people, their families, and their social groups are powerless: "The existence or non-existence of power on one level of human functioning . . . affects and is affected by its existence or nonexistence on other levels of functioning—for example, intrapsychic, familial, community–ethnic–cultural, and societal" (p. 332). Gutierrez (1990) explicated "the effect that [group] powerlessness has on reducing the ability to exercise personal control" (p. 149). Whereas white, middle-class people may desire self-reliance, people of color may "go it alone" out of despair. When the stresses become extreme and families are totally overwhelmed, they learn to function in an autonomous fashion and to value going it alone. This comes not from a goal of self-actualization and realization but from feeling a sense of being alone and without any help (Pinderhughes, 1983).

Yet this very separation from the group causes the family to become vulnerable through isolation. Enhancement of connection to and strengthening of the group is indicated as contrasting with strengthening of autonomy (Pinderhughes, 1983). Through considering the condition of oppression, one can appreciate that discerning appraisal is required to comprehend how the concept of self-determination may apply to each person. Self-expression is an insufficient criterion. Individual achievement, attained competitively and through deciding what is best for one's self or immediate family, may in fact be devalued both by the person and the group. As paradoxical as it may seem from an individualistic perspective, self-directedness may require a strengthening rather than a dissolution of the person's connection with and commitment to the group.

A PACIFIC PERSPECTIVE

Self-determination for the cultures of the Pacific region is defined by values of collective affiliation rather than by individualism. Pacific cultures are scattered across 64 million square miles of Pacific Ocean (Quigg, 1987) in the geographic areas of Melanesia, Micronesia, and Polynesia. There is a rich diversity among Pacific island cultures in historical origins, languages, social organization, levels of political integration, and lifestyle practices (Linnekin & Poyer, 1990; Oliver, 1988). Diversity also exists in acculturation and the degree to which Pacific peoples adopt the worldviews and values of American culture. However, within this diversity, there is a common emphasis on group affiliation that is the basis for a unique perspective on self-determination.

An essential element of Pacific island cultures is the affiliative nature of relationships: "The person is not an individual in our Western sense of the term. The person is instead a locus of shared biographies: personal histories of people's relationships with other people and with other things. The relationship defines the person, not vice-versa" (Lieber, 1990, p. 72). An individual is characterized by social relationships and a shared identity that comes from "sharing food, water, land, spirits, knowledge, work and social activities" (Linnekin & Poyer, 1990, p. 8). Illustrations of the importance of Pacific Islander group identity and cohesiveness are plentiful. For example, Micronesians such as the Trukese have traditionally relied on the matrilineage as a source of identity (Hezel, 1989). Polynesians such as the Maoris talk about "group rhythm" (Kanahele, 1986) and the importance of the gathering and uniting of people (Stirling & Salmond, 1985). The Chamorros of Guam in Polynesia emphasize traditional values of role interdependence and reciprocity (Untalan, 1991) in identity formation. The identities of the Solomon Islanders in Melanesia originate in strong attachments to the land and the interrelationships of the family system (Gegeo & Watson-Gegeo, 1985).

The pronounced value of group identity and cohesiveness among the diverse cultures of the Pacific region undergirds other major values and permeates lifestyle practices. The following sections examine the dominant position of values and practices of group affiliation among the two largest Pacific Islander populations in the United States—Hawaiian and Samoan.

Hawaiian Culture

In Hawaiian culture, the individual is viewed in the context of relationships. A person is defined by others and defines himself or herself by the quality of his or her relationships with family members, the community, the land, and the spiritual world (Ito, 1987; Mokuau & Tauili'ili, 1992). According to Handy and Pukui (1977), the Hawaiian concept of the individual is most clearly depicted in the matrix of the 'ohana (family). The family, which consists of relatives by blood, marriage, and adoption, extends on a genealogical continuum binding people from the past, present, and future. Emphasis is consistently placed on the needs of the family unit rather than on the needs of any individual member.

Three values that reflect the strong emphasis on relationships in the Hawaiian family and group are *laulima* (cooperation), *kokua* (helpfulness), and *lokahi* (unity). Kanahele (1986) described the integral nature of these values in Hawaiian culture:

> The term laulima means many hands, and it expresses perfectly the Hawaiian sense of all persons in the family

> working together for a common purpose. Once established
> in the behavior of the basic 'ohana unit, cooperation was eas-
> ily transferred to working with other 'ohana in a communal
> setting. . . . Inseparably linked with cooperation is the value
> of kokua. . . a willingness of individuals to work voluntarily
> with each other. (p. 347)

Each member of a family or group has a defined assignment, and members "collaborate in unity (lokahi), subordinating personal glory to reaching the goals of the whole group" (pp. 347–348). Contributions to unity and harmony are more valued in Hawaiian culture than are competitive success or self-satisfaction (Howard, 1974).

Lifestyle practices that support the value of group affiliation are numerous and include honoring commitments to family and friends, providing aid to people in need, and engaging in situations of cooperative fellowship, even when these situations incur material deprivation for oneself (Howard, 1974).

Vignette 1. Leialoha, a Hawaiian man, is a skilled automobile mechanic who is consistently called on by family and friends to repair their personal cars. He is not known for turning people down and has willingly serviced relatives' and friends' cars at the end of his work day and often on weekends. He refuses monetary compensation, even though he still struggles with his own financial worries, and is most appreciative of the companionship and food that are shared with him once cars are repaired. Sometimes his generosity has extended to giving away special and costly automobile tools that family members or friends have admired. The frequent requests by family and friends are testimony to people's confidence in Leialoha's skills and their recognition of his inclination to help others.

Vignette 2. Debra, a Hawaiian woman, was interested in practicing medicine in the community in which she had recently completed her medical education. Here she was offered a physician's position with a reputable family clinic and a good salary. Combined with her comfortable living quarters and her network of friends, remaining in this community was an attractive option for Debra. However, her family, and in particular her parents, wished for Debra to establish her practice in the community in which she was raised. To do so would require her to move from the city back to her native community. Although there were a few moments of hesitation, Debra quickly adjusted and aligned her values with those of her family. She reasoned that by returning to her native community she would be reunited with her family and be available to provide medical care to members of her family and a community with severe health problems.

Samoan Culture

Samoan culture places a strong emphasis on relationships. "Dominant values . . . in Samoan culture focus on the family, communal relationships and the church" (Mokuau & Chang, 1991, p. 159). The family is viewed as the most important agency of human interactions (Territory of American Samoa, Office of the Governor, 1990).

Life is organized around the *aiga* (family) or the *aiga potopoto* (extended family), which are hierarchal systems with clearly defined roles. The highly structured organization of the family defines an individual's roles and responsibilities and guides the individual in interactions with others. In Samoan culture, older people have status over young people, titled people such as *matais* (chiefs) have status over untitled people, men have status over women, and men and women have status over children (Brigham Young University, Language and Intercultural Research Center, 1977).

One Samoan proverb captures the importance of the family: *"Sei fono le pa'a ma ona vae"* (Let the crab meet with his legs). According to Fuhrel (1980), the crab is the family and the legs are the different members of the family. The proverb means that when there is a gathering of families and a decision is not made, a chief may indicate that he has to consult with his family before he can decide his answer.

Each family member works for the well-being of the entire extended family, which sometimes may be as large as an entire village (Mokuau & Tauili'ili, 1992). The church assumes a pivotal role in reinforcing the closely structured social order and harmonious functioning of the family. In turn, families support the activities and practices of the church through attending regularly and donating financial contributions and volunteer time. The values that support this group orientation include reciprocity (the mutual exchange of services, goods, and privileges), interdependence, and cooperation (Mokuau & Tauili'ili, 1992).

Several lifestyle practices reflect and reinforce the importance of relationships in Samoan culture. One of the best known ritualized practices of Samoan culture is sometimes referred to as "trouble" (*fa'alavelave*) (Calkins, 1962), the practice of mutual support during lifecycle events such as weddings, christenings, and funerals. It is referred to as "trouble" because of the constant depletion of resources to support the collective.

Sharing is also an inherent part of Samoan culture. Attached to sharing, however, is a cultural expectation that the person who receives a gift will reciprocate the act at some later time: "Families share with their neighbors and friends. . . . We give or share something with someone and they give something in return" (Tusa, 1982, p. 17).

Vignette 1. Pita, a Samoan man, moved to the western United States about six years ago with his wife and two children. When members of his extended family travel to the United States, they often stay with Pita and rely on his household for shelter, food, and other assistance. Last year, Pita's household of four expanded to include one uncle, two cousins, and four nieces and nephews. In addition to assisting and caring for extended family members when they visit, Pita also sends money back to his family in American Samoa for special events. Several *fa'alavelave* occurred last year, including the birth of a first son to his sister, the marriage of another sister, and the death of an elder, and each time Pita sent money home.

Vignette 2. Susan brings to her new home in the United States a sense of sharing and relationship that draws from her Samoan heritage. Examples relate to her generosity with Samoan products such as *tapa* (cloth), coconut soap, and fine mat that she has brought from Samoa to her new home. When a non-Samoan friend visited Susan's home and admired a *tapa* wall hanging that covered a large portion of the hallway wall, Susan went into her bedroom and came back with another large *tapa* product and offered it to her friend. The friend, very surprised and a little embarrassed, finally accepted the gift and desired to reciprocate Susan's gracious gesture.

CONTEXT OF OPPRESSION

As populations of color, Hawaiian, Samoan, and other Pacific Islander groups have historically experienced oppression from colonizing nations that have undermined the efforts of Pacific nations at self-government (Trask, 1989). The sovereign nation movement of Hawaiians in the 1990s is an example of a people collectively asserting their rights for self-governance (Mokuau, in press). Hawaiians are recognizing that political, economic, educational, and health benefits and privileges cannot occur as long as the entire population is disenfranchised. Self-determination for Hawaiians and other Pacific Islanders has greater meaning in the sense of the entire population's empowerment. As social work pioneer Bertha Capen Reynolds suggested, the self-directing potential of individuals cannot be increased without considering economic and political realities (cited in Freedberg, 1989).

IMPLICATIONS FOR SOCIAL WORK

Definition of Self-Determination

Self-determination has two definitions. One is concerned with self-direction—that "only the individual knows or can come to know what he or she needs in order to live and to grow fully" (Weick & Pope, 1988, p. 13). In this connotation, the client's self-direction for what to do and be is held preeminent over decisions that the professional authority might prefer. The burden of proof for a departure from this rule rests with the professional person.

The second definition is that one should be free to do or be what one wants without group restraints (Berlin, 1975; Freedberg, 1989; Gans, 1988). However, reference to one's own wishes separate from one's social ties is not necessarily appropriate. Decision making is more complex than separating into exclusive categories what is in other people's interest and what is in one's own interest. It is necessary to appreciate how contributions to group interest may ultimately strengthen the person as well.

In addition to non-Western peoples, reference to group rather than individual interests may be a dominant feature with Western people of lower socioeconomic class and women. For example, according to Schneider and Smith (1987), "whereas the middle class lays strong emphasis upon the self-sufficiency and solidarity of the nuclear family against all other kinship ties and groupings, [in] the lower class . . . the emphasis is upon keeping open the options—upon maximizing the number of relationships which involve diffuse solidarity" (p. 221). Similarly, women are more inclined toward a more collectivist orientation than are men (Benhabib, 1987; Gilligan, 1987; Kaplan, 1984; Leventhal-Belfer, Cowan, & Cowan, 1992). In this respect, there may be a convergence of feminine values with non-European values (Harding, 1987). The situation, however, is not so clear-cut as to support the notion that women necessarily desire to be collectivist in orientation. Indeed, in some definitions of feminism, it is deemed that "women should become more competitive, assertive, individualistic, and self-directed" (Nes & Iadicola, 1989). Costin (1992) attributed a decline in interest in the problem of cruelty to children to a diminishing connection between women's and children's issues within feminism, seemingly indicating an increase in individualism and a lessening of relational qualities within at least some forms of feminism. Variations related to gender nevertheless re-emphasize the importance of careful identification of the pathway each person desires to take toward self-determination. For some this may be a renewal, not a shunning, of obligations to others.

Assessment, Goal Setting, and Intervention

The principle of self-determination, in the sense of freedom from imposition of the social worker's goals, continues to apply from the earliest moments of contact with individuals, families, and groups. As Pinderhughes (1989) commented, traditional approaches have tended to emphasize diagnosis and cure as "fixed entities not dependent on the individual's perception of what is wrong and what needs fixing" (pp. 13–14). Hence, the assessment may tend to be based on what the professional thinks clients ought to view, rather than what clients do view, as wrong.

Self-determination, however, may include fulfilling group obligations, not necessarily ridding oneself of them. Part of the assessment entails assessing the extent of clients' identity with their cultural group of origin and whether they wish to strengthen this identity (Pinderhughes, 1989). Goal setting may include strengthening ties with extended family and community as ends in themselves and also as a support for achieving other desired goals.

Methods of choice in working with clients toward their goals are also an aspect of self-determination. As described by Dana

(1981), actions in conjunction with and under the influence of the extended family may be most desired. Therefore, observance of self-determination should be enhanced in all aspects of practice. The principle should, however, be separated from any inherent connection with self-directedness apart from group relationships.

Practice Theory

It appears that the fundamentally valid principle of self-determination has acquired, through use in a particular context, a culturally biased interpretation. Independence was prized over interdependence, individual status over group achievement. Instead, the values of interdependence should be given equal weight with independence as people define their problems and goals. Independence from group goals is not necessarily a measure of health or maturity.

Furthermore, each fundamental principle of social work should be subjected to scrutiny to assess cultural bias. Gould (1988) suggested a "recognition of ideological value imperatives and prescriptions underlying practice models" (p. 145). A systematic reanalysis is required of universal practice principles to determine if they are fundamentally flawed or culturally biased.

REFERENCES

Benhabib, S. (1987). The generalized and the concrete other: The Kohlberg–Gilligan controversy and moral theory. In E. F. Kittay & D. T. Meyers (Eds.), *Women and moral theory* (pp. 154–177). Totowa, NJ: Rowman & Littlefield.

Berlin, S. I. (1975). Two concepts of liberty. In F. E. McDermott (Ed.), *Self-determination in social work* (pp. 141–153). Boston: Routledge & Kegan Paul.

Brigham Young University, Language and Intercultural Research Center. (1977). *People of Samoa.* Provo, UT: Author.

Budman, C. L., Lipson, J. G., & Meleis, A. I. (1992). The cultural consultant in mental health care: The case of an Arab adolescent. *American Journal of Orthopsychiatry, 62,* 359–370.

Calkins, F. (1962). *My Samoan chief.* Honolulu: University of Hawaii Press.

Costin, L. B. (1992). Cruelty to children: A dormant issue and its rediscovery, 1920–1960. *Social Service Review, 66,* 183–184.

Dana, R. H. (1981). Epilogue. In R. H. Dana (Ed.), *Human services for cultural minorities* (pp. 353–355). Baltimore: University Park Press.

Freedberg, S. (1989). Self-determination: Historical perspectives and effects on current practice. *Social Work, 34,* 33–38.

Fuhrel, F. (1980). Proverbs: Let the crab meet with his legs. In M. Luaiufi, E. Fa'afeu, & F. Fuhrel (Eds.), *Fa'a Samoa Pea* (p. 65–68). Pago Pago: American Samoa Community College.

Gans, H. J. (1988). *Middle American individualism*. New York: Free Press.

Gegeo, D., & Watson-Gegeo, K. A. (1985). Patterns of suicide in West Kwara'ae, Malaita, Solomon Islands. In F. X. Hezel, D. H. Rubinstein, & G. M. White (Eds.), *Culture, youth and suicide in the Pacific: Papers from an East–West Center Conference* (pp. 182–197). Honolulu: University of Hawaii, Pacific Islands Studies Program.

Gilligan, C. (1987). Moral orientation and moral development. In E. F. Kittay & D. T. Meyers (Eds.), *Women and moral theory* (pp. 19–33). Totowa, NJ: Rowman & Littlefield.

Gould, K. H. (1988). Asian and Pacific Islanders: Myth and reality. *Social Work, 33*, 142–147.

Gutierrez, L. M. (1990). Working with women of color: An empowerment perspective. *Social Work, 35*, 149–153.

Handy, E.S.C., & Pukui, M. K. (1977). *The Polynesian family system in Kau, Hawaii*. Rutland, VT: Charles E. Tuttle.

Harding, S. (1987). The curious coincidence of feminine and African moralities: Challenge for feminist theory. In E. F. Kittay & D. T. Meyers (Eds.), *Women and moral theory* (pp. 296–315). Totowa, NJ: Rowman & Littlefield.

Hezel, F. X. (1989). Suicide and the Micronesian family. *Contemporary Pacific, 1*(1 & 2), 43–74.

Hollis, F. (1966). *Casework: A psychosocial therapy*. New York: Random House.

Howard, A. (1974). *Ain't no big thing: Coping strategies in a Hawaiian-American community*. Honolulu: University Press of Hawaii, East–West Center Books.

Inclan, J., & Hernandez, M. (1992). Cross-cultural perspectives and codependence: The case of poor Hispanics. *American Journal of Orthopsychiatry, 62*, 245–247.

Ito, K. L. (1987). Emotions, proper behavior (hana pono), and Hawaiian concepts of self, person, and individual. In A. B. Robillard & A. J. Marsella (Eds.), *Contemporary issues in mental health research in the Pacific Islands* (pp. 45–71). Honolulu: University of Hawaii, Social Science Research Institute.

Kanahele, G.H.S. (1986). *Ku kanaka, stand tall*. Honolulu: University of Hawaii Press and Waiaha Foundation.

Kaplan, A. G. (1984). *The "self-in-relation": Implications for depression in women*. (Work in Progress, Working Paper No. 14.) Wellesley, MA: Wellesley College, Stone Center for Developmental Services and Studies.

Lemmon, J. A. (1983). Values, ethics, and legal issues. In A. Rosenblatt & D. Waldfogel (Eds.), *Handbook of clinical social work* (pp. 845–852). San Francisco: Jossey-Bass.

Leventhal-Belfer, L., Cowan, P. A., & Cowan, C. P. (1992). Satisfaction with child care arrangements: Effects on adaptation to parenthood. *American Journal of Orthopsychiatry, 62*, 165–177.

Levy, C. S. (1983). Client self-determination. In A. Rosenblatt & D. Waldfogel (Eds.), *Handbook of clinical social work* (pp. 904–919). San Francisco: Jossey-Bass.

Lieber, M. D. (1990). Lamarckian definitions of identity on Kapingamarangi and Pohnpei. In J. Linnekin & L. Poyer (Eds.), *Cultural identity and ethnicity in the Pacific* (pp. 71–101). Honolulu: University of Hawaii Press.

Linnekin, J., & Poyer, L. (1990). Introduction. In J. Linnekin & L. Poyer (Eds.), *Cultural identity and ethnicity in the Pacific* (pp. 1–15). Honolulu: University of Hawaii Press.

Mokuau, N., & Chang, N. (1991). Samoans. In N. Mokuau (Ed.), *Handbook of social services for Asian and Pacific Islanders* (pp. 155–169). Westport, CT: Greenwood Press.

Mokuau, N., & Matsuoka, J. (in press). Turbulence among a native people: Social work practice with Hawaiians. *Social Work.*

Mokuau, N., & Tauili'ili, P. (1992). Families with Native Hawaiian and Pacific Island roots. In E. W. Lynch & M. J. Hanson (Eds.), *Developing cross-cultural competence* (pp. 301–318). Baltimore: Paul H. Brookes.

Nes, J. A., & Iadicola, P. (1989). Toward a definition of feminist social work: A comparison of liberal, radical, and socialist models. *Social Work, 34,* 12–21.

Oliver, D. L. (1988). *The Pacific Islands.* Honolulu: University of Hawaii Press.

Papajohn, J., & Spiegel, J. (1975). *Transactions in families.* San Francisco: Jossey-Bass.

Pedersen, P. P., Fukuyama, M., & Heath, A. (1989). Client, counselor, and contextual variables in multicultural counseling. In P. P. Pedersen, J. G. Draguns, W. J. Lonner, & J. E. Trimble (Eds.), *Counseling across cultures* (3rd ed., pp. 23–52). Honolulu: University of Hawaii Press.

Pinderhughes, E. B. (1983). Empowerment for our clients and for ourselves. *Social Casework, 64,* 331–338.

Pinderhughes, E. B. (1989). *Understanding race, ethnicity, and power.* New York: Macmillan.

Quigg, A. (1987). *History of the Pacific Islands Studies Program at the University of Hawaii: 1950–1986.* Honolulu: University of Hawaii, Pacific Island Studies Program.

Schneider, D. M., & Smith, R. T. (1987). Class differences and sex roles in American kinship and family structure. In R. N. Bellah, R. Madsen, W. M. Sullivan, A. Swidler, & S. M. Tipton (Eds.), *Individualism and commitment in American life: Readings on the themes of habits of the heart* (pp. 211–223). New York: Harper & Row.

Schwartz, E. E. (1989). Social work and individualism: A comparative review. *Social Work, 34,* 167–170.

Stirling, E., & Salmond, A. (1985). *Eruera: The teachings of a Maori elder.* Auckland, New Zealand: Oxford University Press.

Territory of American Samoa, Office of the Governor. (1990). *Mental health plan 1989–1991.* Pago Pago: Author.

Trask, H.-K. (1989). Empowerment of Pacific people. In D. S. Sanders & J. K. Matsuoka (Eds.), *Peace and development: An interdisciplinary perspective* (pp. 133–139). Honolulu: University of Hawaii, School of Social Work.

Tung, M. (1991). Insight-oriented psychotherapy and the Chinese patient. *American Journal of Orthopsychiatry, 61,* 186–194.

Tusa, S. A. (1982). Proverbs: We give the lo and get the lo in return. In M. Tu'ufuli, S. A. Tusa, & T. Timoteo (Eds.), *Fa'a Samoa Pea* (pp. 16–23). Pago Pago: American Samoa Community College.

Untalan, F. F. (1991). Chamorros. In N. Mokuau (Ed.), *Handbook of social services for Asian and Pacific Islanders* (pp. 171–182). Westport, CT: Greenwood Press.

Weick, A., & Pope, L. (1988). Knowing what's best: A new look at self-determination. *Social Casework, 69,* 10–16.

This chapter was originally published in the March 1995 issue of Social Work, *vol. 40, pp. 168–175.*

20 Not Simply "Asian Americans": Periodical Literature Review on Asians and Pacific Islanders

Rowena Fong and Noreen Mokuau

One of every four persons in the United States is a person of color (U.S. Bureau of the Census, 1991). In the total resident population of 248.7 million, the 1990 census revealed that 75.6 percent are white; 12.1 percent are black; 9.0 percent are Hispanic; 2.9 percent are Asian and Pacific Islander; and 0.4 percent are Native American, Eskimo, and Aleut. These numbers reflect an increase in racial and ethnic diversity in the 1980–90 decade, with the black population increasing by 13.2 percent; the Native American, Eskimo, or Aleut population by 38 percent; the Hispanic population by 53 percent, and the Asian and Pacific Island population by 108 percent. This increase for Asians and Pacific Islanders includes such diverse American groups as Japanese, Chinese, Filipinos, Koreans, Vietnamese, Laotians, Cambodians (now Kampucheans), Asian Indians, native Hawaiians, Samoans, Tongans, Fijians, and Chamorros (Guamanians).

Although they are the fastest-growing people of color, Asians and Pacific Islanders have been plagued by myths and misconceptions. One is that they are a "model minority," without any need of government or social services. Some have claimed that Asians and Pacific Islanders no longer qualify as a disadvantaged or underrepresented group and have subsequently excluded them from the protections of affirmative action laws (Gould, 1988). For example, all agencies of the U.S. Public Health Service, a 300-organization consortium, participated in developing a national plan with 637 objectives to improve the health of the nation; yet, because of lack of data on Asians and Pacific Islanders, only eight objectives targeted their concerns (Asian American Health Forum, 1990).

Real problems of Asian and Pacific Island peoples have been ignored. Native Hawaiians, for example, have experienced severe health difficulties, including startlingly disproportionate rates of cancer, diseases of the heart, and diabetes mellitus, but have only recently been recognized in federal initiatives as a population in need of services (Mokuau, 1990b). The lack of responsiveness to the needs of Asians and Pacific Islanders may derive from a lack of commitment and interest, but more probably it originates in the insufficient amount of accurate descriptive and analytical information and knowledge about the diverse groups that make up this growing population.

Demographers forecast that by the turn of the century more than one-third of the entire population of the United States will be members of nonwhite minority groups (Harris, 1988–89). A significant portion of that population will include Asians and Pacific Islanders (Gould, 1988). Thus, it is imperative that social workers stay informed about people of color and their concerns. If responsiveness to the concerns of minority groups, and of Asian and Pacific Islanders in particular, is related to the availability of information and knowledge, then it is important to promote the development of that knowledge. Scholars must be encouraged to examine and discuss a range of issues such as institutional racism, historical paths of immigration, acculturation adjustment, and so on. It also is important to examine the information currently available to assess its content, to identify strengths and gaps in the knowledge base, and to chart directions for future research. This article assesses the status of social work knowledge on Asians and Pacific Islanders by reviewing the social work periodical literature and identifying areas for future research.

METHODOLOGY

The authors investigated articles that had total direct practice content on Asians and Pacific Islanders from 1980 to 1991 in four major social work journals: (1) *Social Work,* (2) *Social Casework* (later *Families in Society*), (3) *Social Service Review,* and (4) *Journal of Social Work Education.* These four journals are recognized as major social work publications with a generalist perspective; they circulate among 3,000 to over 140,000 readers (Mendelsohn, 1992), and they have been included in other reviews of social work periodical literature (Corcoran & Kirk, 1990; Jayaratne, 1979; Lum, 1986; Thyer & Bentley 1986). The *Social Science Citation Index* was also used to target journal articles using the terms Asian American, Asian immigrant, Asian refugee, and Pacific Islander.

The articles with Asian and Pacific Island content were analyzed for the ethnicity, age, and gender of the target population and the practice focus of the article (for example, individuals, families, groups, or communities). Articles that included direct practice information referring or applying to Asians and Pacific Islanders were included in the study. Articles that discussed these groups only incidentally in their examples to demonstrate points were deleted from the study.

FINDINGS

Of the 230 issues of these journals reviewed, only 22 issues (10 percent) carried articles with direct practice themes with Asian American and Pacific Island populations. Within these 22 issues, only 24 articles had content on Asians and Pacific Islanders. Sixteen (67 percent) of the articles were found in *Social Work,* five (21 percent) were found in *Social Casework* or *Families in Society,* two (8 percent) were found in *Social Service Review,* and one (4 percent) was found in the *Journal of Social Work Education.*

Ethnicity, Age, and Gender

The findings about ethnicity can be divided into three broad categories: (1) differences between Asian Americans and Pacific Islanders, (2) specific ethnic groups versus generic ethnic groups, and (3) immigrants and refugees versus U.S.-born Asians and Pacific Islanders.

Twenty-two of the 24 articles (92 percent) focused on Asians and Asian Americans, and only two (8 percent) mentioned or focused on Pacific Islanders. One of the latter referred to Pacific/ Asian Americans (Ishisaka & Takagi, 1981) in the context of improving social work curricula. The other article focused on native Hawaiians (Mokuau, 1990a) and the use of a family-centered approach in direct practice.

Eleven articles (46 percent) were specific to an ethnic group. Four discussed the Vietnamese population (Matsuoka, 1990; Montero & Dieppa, 1982; Mortland & Egan, 1987; Timberlake &

Cook, 1984); three discussed the Chinese population (Cheung, 1989; Lum, Cheung, Cho, Tang, & Yau, 1980; Ryan, 1981); and one each discussed the Vietnamese Chinese (Land, Nishimoto, & Chou, 1988); Cambodian (Bromley, 1987); Asian Indian (Segal, 1991); and native Hawaiian (Mokuau, 1990a) populations.

Thirteen articles (54 percent) discussed Asians and Pacific Islanders as a collective, nonspecific ethnic group, which reflects the tendency to see Asians and Pacific Islanders as a single people (Kitano & Daniels 1988; U.S. Bureau of Census, 1991). Typically an author presented examples from three to six ethnic populations in a single article. Asian Americans were mentioned but were clustered together with "all minority groups" or "Third World peoples." For example, in the content of an article that mentioned Third World peoples, blacks, Hispanics, Asian Americans, and Native Americans were all included in one group (Morales, 1981). In another article, "minority groups of color" consisted of blacks, Chicanos, Asians, Native Americans, and Puerto Ricans (Lum, 1982). "Indochinese" included Vietnamese, Cambodian, and Laotian refugees (Baker, 1981).

Twelve articles (50 percent) were written about the immigrant and refugee populations. Four articles raised concerns about immigrants: Two discussed the elderly Chinese population (Cheung, 1989; Lum et al., 1980), one discussed Asian Indian families (Segal, 1991), and one discussed empowerment for Asian immigrants (Hirayama & Cetingok, 1988). Eight articles addressed issues involving refugee resettlement, focusing on Indochinese refugees. Of these articles, six devoted total coverage to a single refugee group (four for the Vietnamese, one for the Vietnamese Chinese, and one for the Cambodian populations), and two articles had a generic focus on Southeast Asian refugees or Indochinese refugees (Baker, 1981; Weiss & Parish, 1989). Among the various concerns addressing the refugee population were the use of a crisis intervention approach (Bromley, 1987); the awareness of differential acculturation and coping mechanisms (Matsuoka, 1990); the issue of Vietnamese youth and foster care (Mortland & Egan, 1987); the understanding of cultural background and coping patterns (Timberlake & Cook, 1984); and the adaptation of culturally appropriate counseling, preventive, and interventive services (Freed, 1988; Mokuau, 1987; Land et al., 1988; Weiss & Parish, 1989).

The majority of articles that discussed age and gender did not refer to a specific age or gender. Eighteen articles (75 percent) did not refer to a specific age group but implied adults. Two (8 percent) focused on the elderly population (Cheung, 1989; Lum et al., 1980). Four articles (17 percent) made specific reference to children or adolescents, either singularly or with parents and family (Jenkins, 1980; Matsuoka, 1990; Mortland & Egan, 1987; Segal, 1991). Some of the issues concerning children were adjusting to foster care (Mortland & Egan, 1987), establishing identity (Matsuoka, 1990; Segal, 1991), and struggling with peer rejection (Matsuoka, 1990).

Twenty-one articles (88 percent) did not refer to a specific gender. Two articles (8 percent) had non-gender-specific titles or content but used men in the samples (Land et al., 1988, Mortland & Egan, 1987). Only one article (4 percent) specifically addressed women, focusing on empowerment concerns (Gutierrez, 1990).

Practice Focus

The practice focus included the four categories of individuals, families, groups, and communities. The articles were divided into either some combination of the four categories or one sole practice focus. The majority of articles, 13 (54 percent), focused on individuals in combination with either the family, the group, or the community. Six (25 percent) articles focused on direct practice with the individual alone. Two articles (8 percent) focused on direct practice with families (Mokuau, 1990a; Segal, 1991). Two (8 percent) focused on groups (Chau, 1989; Longres, 1982), and one (4 percent) focused on communities (Morales, 1981).

DISCUSSION

The availability of 24 articles with content on Asians and Pacific Islanders in the periodical literature shows some effort by the social work profession to develop knowledge regarding the unique concerns of these populations. Of paramount importance is the promotion of the "dual perspective" (Norton, 1978)—the comparison of the perspective of the larger societal system with the perspective of the client's immediate family and community. Several articles emphasized such a perspective by identifying and describing frameworks for minority practice (deAnda, 1984;

Ishisaka & Takagi, 1981; Jenkins, 1980; Longres, 1982; Lum, 1982), by using empowerment as a goal for ethnic minority groups (Gutierrez, 1990; Hirayama & Cetingok, 1988), and by using ethnic-sensitive, prevention-based models (Land et al., 1988).

The information in the 24 articles begins to provide a foundation of knowledge on Asian and Pacific Islanders. However, the foundation is inadequate because it fails to capture the diversity of the ethnicity of the population, especially in light of increasing population numbers. This study showed that the literature still needs to distinguish between Asian Americans and Pacific Islanders, to separate Asian Americans into different ethnic groups, to distinguish between immigrants and refugees, to consider lifespan developmental differences in age, to focus more on gender differences in the various ethnic groups, and to strengthen the practice focus on communities.

The study did show one strength: the literature acknowledges that Asian Americans and Pacific Islanders are more group oriented than self oriented. Many articles focused on using direct practice techniques that involve the individual in combination with the family, group, or community. However, more community-focused research is warranted because of the importance of community in Asian populations.

Ethnic Diversity among Asians and Pacific Islanders

The majority of the articles discussed the many groups that form the Asian and Pacific Island population as one entity and thus tended to perpetuate the conception that all the groups are alike. One consequence of ignoring the heterogeneity of the population is that prescriptions for social work practice are predicated on a generic perspective, and the unique background and needs of specific subgroups are neglected. There are dangers that border on racism in responding to health concerns of native Hawaiians as if they were the same for Japanese Americans or evaluating problems of second-generation Chinese Americans with the same procedures as those used for newly arrived Vietnamese Chinese refugees. These practices betray an underlying ignorance of social and cultural evironments that affect the Hawaiian, Japanese, Chinese, and Vietnamese cultures.

Not only are there differences between Asian American and Pacific Island groups, there are differences among the various subgroups considered Asian American, as well as among those considered Pacific Island. For example, Filipinos are different from Japanese in involvement with gangs, and native Hawaiians are different from Chamorros with respect to cancer and heart disease. Perhaps the ethnic differences were ignored and ethnic groups were lumped together in the 1970s and earlier because there were not enough people in any single group to demand separate attention. However, with increasing populations, research needs to be done on individual ethnic groups.

In this study the Vietnamese received the most attention as an individual ethnic group, perhaps because of the repercussions of the Vietnam War. Information was lacking regarding other Asian groups such as Filipinos, Koreans, and Japanese. However, because of increases in population these groups should not be ignored. It is important that future periodical literature on Asians and Pacific Islanders begin to make clear the distinctions among the various groups and subgroups to ensure that social work practice is based on accurate assessments and culturally responsive strategies rather than on stereotypy.

Refugee and Immigrant Diversity among Asians

Refugees constituted a large segment of the growing Asian population in the 1980s, and they were discussed in one-third of the articles. Yet the lack of ethnic group distinctions made among the general populace of Asians and Pacific Islanders also applied to Asian refugee groups. Bromley (1987) noted that there is a tendency to view refugees as a homogeneous group. The Southeast Asian refugee group covered most often was the Vietnamese. Other articles treated Southeast Asian refugees—Vietnamese, Cambodian, Laotian, Hmong, and others—as a barely differentiable mass.

The social work literature reviewed here tended to focus on Vietnamese refugees. The Hmong, Laotian, and Cambodian populations are not Vietnamese and warrant their own research. These populations are different in religion, culture, language, and history. For example, many Hmong were converted to Protestant Christianity, and religion has a very profound effect on their social, economic, and political life (Trueba, Jacobs, & Kirton, 1990). The Vietnamese were influenced by the French, who were Catholic, although most Vietnamese remain Buddhist.

Refugees enter the social system at different points, are concentrated in different parts of the country (although most are in California), and draw on the social services system in different ways. For example, Vietnamese refugees may have had the opportunity to attend school, whereas Hmong refugees, whose education is based on oral traditions, may arrive unexposed to any formal schooling (Trueba et al., 1990).

There are also differences between immigrants and refugees. Refugees are people who leave their homelands involuntarily under coercion and with no guarantee of ethnic or cultural survival (Timberlake & Cook, 1984; Trueba et al., 1990). Immigrants, on the other hand, leave their lands of origin with some choice and with hope of maintaining some aspects of their ethnic identity, language, religious beliefs, and customs (Cheung, 1989; Lum, 1982; Sung, 1987).

However, differentiations between refugees and immigrants were not made in the literature reviewed here. As the Vietnam War affected composition of the the refugee population in the United States in the mid-1970s, reflected in the literature from 1980 to 1990, so may the 1997 political takeover of Hong Kong by the People's Republic of China affect the composition of the immigrant population and be reflected in the literature of the next century. Many Chinese people who live in Hong Kong are emigrating to the United States (Fong, 1992). Reports indicate that Hong Kong immigrants are increasing in numbers and needs as they come to the United States (Fong, 1992; Takaki, 1989). In the mid-1990s and into the 2000s, social work practitioners may see an increase in immigrant concerns. By not having sufficient information specific to the needs of these immigrants, social workers may categorize them as refugees and make inaccurate generalizations.

Lifespan Development and Gender

Although lifespan development looks at all ages—old age, middle adulthood, and youth—the majority of the articles in the study did not refer to a specific age. Two articles dealt with the elderly population, and four focused on young people. The articles written on the ethnic groups were not age specific and did not discuss lifespan development. In the field of gerontology, elderly people are not lumped into one group, but are subdivided into groups of young–old (ages 65–74) and old–old (ages 75 years and older) (Zastrow & Kirst-Ashman, 1990).

The research on individual ethnic groups needs to reflect the differences in lifespan development. A middle-adulthood issue plaguing Southeast Asian men is sudden unexplained death syndrome (Petzold, 1991). Beginning research is describing adult male refugees whose mean age is 33 years and whose cause of death is undetermined, except that they die in their sleep. More research is needed on this phenomenon, which occurs almost exclusively among Hmong adult refugee men.

Two articles in the study specifically addressed youth issues: one on Vietnamese youths and foster care, the other on generation gaps for Asian Indian youths. Another group that ought to be addressed is Amerasian refugee youths, children of American fathers who fought in the Vietnam War and Vietnamese mothers who were left behind in Vietnam. This problem is beginning to surface as the youths emigrate to the United States and are dealing with issues of identity crisis, peer rejection, suicidal tendencies, and anorexia nervosa (Kope & Sack, 1987; Williams & Westermeyer, 1983). This group is considered high risk because they are "considered outcasts in Vietnam as reminders of the war and experience racism and discrimination in the United States" (Huang, 1990, p. 293). Social work knowledge relevant to children and youths in refugee populations and in Asian or Pacific Island populations needs to be developed to address these and other problems.

Women comprise 51 percent of the Asian and Pacific Island American population, yet only one article was devoted entirely to women. This low percentage does not adequately cover the concerns of Asian and Pacific Island women. The problems plaguing these women are complex and diverse and are complicated by the social environment from which they came. For example, recent refugee Hmong women continue to struggle with issues of self-esteem connected to the bride-price tradition (a custom where the groom gives a payment to the bride's family ranging from $1,000 to $5,000). Women feel the psychological effect of being "owned by the husband" (Trueba et al., 1990, p. 70) and express hopelessness in having no control over their lives.

There is a bride-price tradition in China, too, and some Chinese immigrant women may still be plagued by this burden to some degree, but third-generation Chinese American women may not even know what a bride price is. For them, there are problems of self-esteem, but they stem from identity crisis or identity formation. Third-generation Japanese American women also have struggles, but theirs may be with ethnic identity as they face a 60 percent outmarriage rate (Spickard, 1989). In the future, researchers and direct practitioners need to consider a woman's ethnic origin, how long she has lived in the United States, and a host of culturally bound issues to understand the complexity of gender, race, and acculturation as they affect Asian and Pacific Island women.

Family and Community Practice Focus

The articles examined focused on practice with the individual, the family, a group, or a community. The majority of the articles reviewed examined a combination of individuals with families, groups, or communities. Although the emphasis on the individual in context of the family, group, or community is congruent with a dominant cultural value of these populations, the individual or self is not and should not be the starting point or sole focus of practice. Instead, the focus should be the ethnic family and community or collective, on which Asian and Pacific Island cultures are based (Ho, 1987; Mokuau, 1990a; Untalon, 1991).

Mokuau (1991) noted the central role that the collective has in the values and lifestyle practices of Asian Americans and Pacific Islanders, in particular for Japanese Americans, Chinese Americans, Filipino Americans, Vietnamese, native Hawaiians, Samoans, and Chamorros. For example, in Western culture, the individual is placed at the center, with all other relationships arranged around the self. However, in Japanese culture, the family is placed at the center, and the self is a part of a web of interpersonal relationships in which the person learns to subordinate the self to the family social unit and to emphasize solidarity and unity (Fugita, Ito, Abe, & Takeuchi, 1991).

The priority to start with and to include the family and the ethnic community as a practice focus is particularly important as U.S. society becomes increasingly an immigrant- and refugee-occupied society. It is important to know where or in what ethnic community the Asian or Pacific Island client places his or her roots and present affiliations. Whether they are immigrants or members of the third generation, their ethnic communities are a vital part of their lives. Social work practitioners and researchers need to accept that fact rather than ignore it in trying to "Americanize" them. Thus, the finding in this literature review that only one article focused on communities and two focused on direct practice with families indicates the current literature is grossly inadequate.

Recent information on the importance of the multiservice centers for various populations, including Chamorros (Untalon, 1991), Chinese Americans (Huang, 1991), and Vietnamese (Matsuoka, 1991), appear to emphasize the need to incorporate ethnic community considerations in this type of community practice and social services intervention. This is an area to expand on in the future as it relates to community-based services for groups from within the Asian and Pacific Island populations.

REFERENCES

Asian American Health Forum. (1990). *Healthy people 2000 fact sheet*. San Francisco: Author.

Baker, N. (1981). Social work through an interpreter. *Social Work, 26*, 391–400.

Bromley, M. (1987). New beginnings for Cambodian refugees—or further disruptions? *Social Work, 32*, 236–239.

Chau, K. (1989). Sociocultural dissonance among ethnic minority populations. *Social Casework, 70*, 224–230.

Cheung, M. (1989). Elderly Chinese living in the United States: Assimilation or adjustment? *Social Work, 34*, 457–461.

Corcoran, K. J., & Kirk, S. A. (1990). We're all number one: Academic productivity among schools of social work. *Journal of Social Work Education, 26*, 310–321.

deAnda, D. (1984). Bicultural socialization: Factors affecting the minority experience. *Social Work, 29*, 101–107.

Fong, R. (1992). History of Asian Americans. In S. Furuto, R. Biswas, D. Chung, K. Murase, & F. Ross-Sheriff (Eds.), *Social work practice with Asian Americans* (pp. 3–26). Newbury Park, CA: Sage Publications.

Freed, A. (1988). Interviewing through an interpreter. *Social Work, 33*, 315–319.

Fugita, S., Ito, K. L., Abe, J., & Takeuchi, D. T. (1991). Japanese Americans. In N. Mokuau (Ed.), *Handbook of social services for Asian and Pacific Islanders* (pp. 61–77). Westport, CT: Greenwood Press.

Gould, K. (1988). Asian and Pacific Islanders: Myth and reality. *Social Work, 33*, 142–147.

Gutierrez, L. (1990). Working with women of color: An empowerment perspective. *Social Work, 35*, 149–154.

Harris, L. (1988–89). The world our students will enter. *College Board Review, 150*, 23.

Hirayama, H., & Cetingok, M. (1988). Empowerment: A social work approach for Asian immigrants. *Social Casework, 69,* 41–47.

Ho, M. K. (1987). *Family therapy with ethnic minorities.* Newbury Park, CA: Sage Publications.

Huang, K. (1991). Chinese Americans. In N. Mokuau (Ed.), *Handbook of social services for Asian and Pacific Islanders* (pp. 79–98). Westport, CT: Greenwood Press.

Huang, L. (1990). Southeast Asian refugee children and adolescents. In J. Gibbs, L. Huang, & Associates (Eds.), *Children of color: Psychological interventions with minority youth* (pp. 278–321). San Francisco: Jossey-Bass.

Ishisaka, A., & Takagi, C. (1981). Toward professional pluralism: The Pacific/Asian-American case. *Journal of Education for Social Work, 17*(1), 44–52.

Jayaratne, S. (1979). Analysis of selected social work journals and productivity ranks among schools of social work. *Journal of Education for Social Work, 15*(3), 72–80.

Jenkins, S. (1980). The ethnic agency defined. *Social Service Review, 54,* 249–261.

Kitano, H. L., & Daniels, R. (1988). *Asian Americans.* Englewood Cliffs, NJ: Prentice Hall.

Kope, T., & Sack, W. (1987). Anorexia-nervosa in southeast Asian refugees. *Journal of the American Academy of Child and Adolescent Psychiatry, 26*(5), 795–797.

Land, H., Nishimoto, R., & Chau, K. (1988). Interventive and preventive services for Vietnamese–Chinese refugees. *Social Service Review, 62,* 468–484.

Longres, J. (1982). Minority groups: An interest-group perspective. *Social Work, 27,* 7–14.

Lum, D. (1982). Towards a framework for social work practice with minorities. *Social Work, 27,* 244–249.

Lum, D. (1986). *Social work practice and people of color: A process-stage approach.* Monterey, CA: Brooks/Cole.

Lum, D., Cheung, L., Cho, E., Tang, T., & Yau, H. (1980). The psychosocial needs of the Chinese elderly. *Social Casework, 61,* 100–106.

Matsuoka, J. K. (1990). Differential acculturation among Vietnamese refugees. *Social Work, 35,* 341–345.

Matsuoka, J. K. (1991). Vietnamese Americans. In N. Mokuau (Ed.), *Handbook of social services for Asian and Pacific Islanders* (pp. 117–130). Westport, CT: Greenwood Press.

Mendelsohn, H. (1992). *An author's guide to social work journals* (3rd ed.). Washington, DC: NASW Press.

Mokuau, N. (1987). Social workers' perceptions of counseling effectiveness for Asian American clients. *Social Work, 32,* 331–335.

Mokuau, N. (1990a). A family-centered approach in native Hawaiian culture. *Families in Society, 71,* 607–613.

Mokuau, N. (1990b). The impoverishment of native Hawaiians and the social work challenge. *Health & Social Work, 15,* 235–242.

Mokuau, N. (Ed.). (1991). Handbook of social services for Asian and Pacific Islanders. Westport, CT: Greenwood Press.

Montero, D., & Dieppa, I. (1982). Resettling Vietnamese refugees: The service agency's role. *Social Work, 27,* 74–81.

Morales, A. (1981). Social work with third-world people. *Social Work, 26,* 45–61.

Mortland, C., & Egan, M. (1987). Vietnamese youth in foster care. *Social Work, 32,* 240–245.

Norton, D. (1978). *The dual perspective.* New York: Council on Social Work Education.

Petzold, J. (1991). Southeast Asian refugees and sudden unexplained death syndrome. *Social Work, 36,* 387.

Ryan, A. S. (1981). Training Chinese-American social workers. *Social Casework, 62,* 95–105.

Segal, U. (1991). Cultural variables in Asian Indian families. *Families in Society, 72,* 233–242.

Spickard, P. (1989). *Mixed blood: Intermarriage and ethnic identity in twentieth-century America.* Madison: University of Wisconsin Press.

Sung, B. (1987). *The adjustment experience of Chinese immigrant children in New York City.* New York: Center for Migration Studies.

Takaki, R. (1989). *Strangers from a different shore.* Boston: Little, Brown.

Thyer, B. A., & Bentley, K. J. (1986). Academic affiliations of social work authors: A citation analysis of six major journals. *Journal of Social Work Education, 22*(1), 67–73.

Timberlake, E., & Cook, K. (1984). Social work and the Vietnamese refugee. *Social Work, 29,* 108–114.

Trueba, H., Jacobs, L., & Kirton, E. (1990). *Cultural conflict and adaptation.* New York: Falmer Press.

Untalon, F. (1991). Chamorros. In N. Mokuau (Ed.), *Handbook of social services for Asian and Pacific Islanders* (pp. 171–184). Westport, CT: Greenwood Press.

U.S. Bureau of the Census. (1991). *Race and Hispanic origin, 1990 census profile.* Washington, DC: Author.

Weiss, B., & Parish, B. (1989). Culturally appropriate crisis counseling: Adapting an American method for use with Indochinese refugees. *Social Work, 34,* 252–254.

Williams, C., & Westermeyer, J. (1983). Psychiatric problems among adolescent Southeast Asian refugees: A descriptive study. *Journal of Nervous and Mental Disease, 171,* 79-85.

Zastrow, C., & Kirst-Ashman, K. (1990). *Understanding human behavior in the social environment* (2nd ed.). Chicago: Nelson-Hall.

This chapter was originally published in the May 1994 issue of Social Work, *vol. 39, pp. 298–305.*

Hard-of-Hearing or Deaf:
Issues of Ears, Language,
Culture, and Identity

Helen Sloss Luey, Laurel Glass, and
Holly Elliott

Hearing impairment is one of the most common of all chronic disabilities, and it affects people's lives in profound and all-encompassing ways. People with hearing loss are subject not only to the particular difficulties that their disability might create, but also to any social or psychological problems that might require social work intervention. It is important, then, that all social workers understand the differences among deaf and hearing-impaired people and have tools for assessing the meaning of hearing loss for a particular client.

About 8 percent of all people have a significant hearing loss, and many more have losses classified as mild or moderate. Both prevalence and severity of hearing loss increase dramatically with age (Glass, 1985; Ries, 1985); the incidence of self-reported trouble with hearing is 33 percent for people ages 65 to 74 and 62 percent for people older than age 85 (Havlik, 1986). In contrast to the high prevalence of hearing impairment, only 1 percent of the population is profoundly deaf, and of those, only 22 percent (.22 percent of the whole population) lost their hearing before age 19 (Schein & Delk, 1974). People who were born deaf, then, actually are a very small percentage of the hearing-impaired population.

PROJECT ON ADULT ONSET HEARING LOSS

The Project on Adult Onset Hearing Loss was established in 1989 at the University of California, San Francisco, to explore the psychosocial and vocational characteristics and needs of people who had lost their hearing during adult life. The project was supported in part by a grant from the National Institute on Disability and Rehabilitation Research.

After conducting focus groups with 70 adults with acquired hearing loss in the San Francisco Bay Area, the project recruited people willing to participate in a three-hour, comprehensive, semistructured interview. Recruitment was done through two national self-help organizations: Self Help for Hard of Hearing People and the Association of Late Deafened Adults. Members of those groups were asked to submit names of people they perceived as coping successfully with adult onset hearing loss. Respondents could nominate themselves as well as others. The project staff interviewed 130 people in all, 104 of whom had an adult onset hearing loss.

All subjects were English speaking. The median age was 51. Sixty-eight percent of the respondents were female. Sixty-two percent had worked in administrative or professional positions. Sixty-six percent had earned a college or graduate degree, and 19 percent had completed community college or a special training program. Sixty-one percent of the respondents described their income level as comfortable or affluent, 32 percent as adequate, and 7 percent as marginal.

SOME LIMITS OF LABELS

Statistics alone demonstrate that there are differences within the hearing-impaired population, most notably in degree of hearing loss and age at onset. But labels and categories cannot predict how individuals communicate or where they feel comfortable. By convention, "deaf" refers to an audiological condition or absence of hearing; "Deaf" means culturally deaf and implies membership in a community. These designations will be used throughout this article. Examples of how labels differ are shown in the following portraits:

> Andrew seems to hear nothing. He understands speech only if it is very slow and clearly directed to him. He does not startle when a door slams. But he will tell you that he is not deaf; he is hard-of-hearing.
>
> *   *   *
>
> Paula understands more speech than Andrew, but she prefers to use sign language. With her hearing aid on, she hears her doorbell. She bristles at the label hearing impaired. "I'm not 'impaired,'" she says. "I'm Deaf."
>
> *   *   *

> After losing her hearing suddenly from tumors, Lisa enrolled in a sign language class. One day she decided to try out her new skills at a club for Deaf people. Using the signs she knew, she explained repeatedly that she too was deaf. But people did not seem interested in talking with her. In words and behavior she was told throughout the evening that she probably was not Deaf and she certainly did not belong.

As these composite portraits illustrate, self-definition—as deaf, Deaf, deafened, hard-of-hearing, or hearing impaired—is a complex issue. Some of the factors involved, paradoxically, have little to do with hearing level. To understand, social workers must look at the complicated and interrelated dimensions of hearing, language, culture, and politics.

HEARING AND COMMUNICATION

Audiologically, hearing can be limited in any degree and in any combination of pitches (frequencies). Hearing loss can affect both the volume and clarity of sound. A loss of volume can often be corrected well with hearing aids. Hearing aids can sometimes offer limited help with problems of clarity, but most people with this problem report that they hear but do not fully understand. For some people, these challenges are compounded by tinnitus—noises from inside the ear that are unrelated to sounds in the environment.

The most damaging thing about hearing loss is that it interferes with communication. Some people with hearing loss are able to understand speech by discerning meaning from fragments of sound, supplemented by visual clues from people's lip movements and facial expressions. This skill, speechreading, is difficult and taxing. Some people seem to have a talent for it, and others do not. Facility with the language being spoken helps, as does knowledge of the subject matter, good vision, confidence, relationship skill, and reasonable freedom from stress (Luey, 1980). Even at best, however, speechreading is demanding, tiring, and only partially accurate.

Generally, the worse hearing becomes, the harder it is to speechread and the more likely it is for people to think of themselves as deaf rather than hard-of-hearing. The people in our study described the different meanings that change in self-definition might have:

> I was profoundly deaf, but my audiologist, bless her heart, never used the word with me. So I . . . learned to live my life as if I was just "hard-of-hearing." And then I found out that I was deaf.

*   *   *

> For me, it is better being deaf than it was being hard-of-hearing. I know who I am. I know what I can and cannot do, whereas when I was hard-of-hearing, I never knew from day to day or hour to hour what I could and couldn't hear, and I tried so hard. This is so much easier.

Many people who see themselves as deaf choose to use a visual communication system as a supplement to or even a substitute for speechreading. That choice requires willingness both to learn a new system and to make yet another shift in self-definition:

> I don't sign. I think to do that is [in] some way to acknowledge something I don't want to acknowledge yet.

LANGUAGE EXPERIENCE AND CHOICE

To understand how people communicate, it is essential to know not only what mode they use (speech or speechreading, sign, or writing), but also what language. Although speech and writing will almost always be in English or the person's native spoken language, manual communication has many forms. Some sign systems are visual representations of English. American Sign Language (ASL), on the other hand, is a distinct and complete language and the native language of Deaf Americans. Understanding how English and ASL differ requires some knowledge of the ways in which language first develops.

Children with normal hearing learn to communicate in the language of their families and communities. When hearing loss begins in infancy or early childhood, it interferes with the child's exposure to spoken language. How well a child compensates depends on many factors, including the nature and severity of the hearing loss; family involvement; motivation; talent; and access to information, services, and educational options.

Some children who are born deaf or who lose their hearing in infancy or early childhood do not use a formal language fluently and easily until they enter an environment in which ASL is the dominant language—usually a residential school for deaf children. In such environments, almost all children become fluent in

ASL. Many also become bilingual—readers, writers, and sometimes speakers of English—with varying levels of fluency. Despite the fact that Deaf children tend to learn ASL with relative ease, few people who become deaf as adults find ASL relevant to their lives at all. Of those who choose to study it, only a minority ever become truly fluent.

The vast majority of people with hearing loss consider English (or the language of their culture) their first language. Within this group are people who grew up hard-of-hearing or deaf and who continue to communicate primarily by speaking or speechreading (aided by the use of residual hearing). In addition, there is a larger group who acquired their hearing loss later in life, after language and communication methods were established. If the hearing loss is severe, members of either group sometimes supplement their speechreading with a manual communication system that follows the linguistic structure of English—signed English. Cued Speech is yet another system; it is phonetically based and uses handshapes to represent specific speech sounds. All of these approaches are designed to enable an individual to communicate in English.

CULTURE

People whose primary language is ASL tend to come together. Such groups have existed for many generations and have established a particular culture. Many people marry within the culture and affiliate with formal and informal organizations that are part of it. In addition to language, the culture includes particular behaviors, norms, and beliefs.

People who have been affiliated primarily with the speaking and hearing world are generally aliens in the Deaf culture; they do not speak its language or understand its ways:

> I went to Deaf family camp once and I was astounded. Everyone who was married had a spouse like them. . . . And here I was. . . . My hearing was not different than some of them, and yet I have a hearing husband and all my kids were hearing.

>   *   *   *

> I had realized that most of the congenitally deaf I really don't connect with. It's like I can learn sign, but I'm not as skilled as a congenitally deaf person. I don't have their culture.

Another significant difference between culturally Deaf people and those who have become deaf are their feelings about deafness itself. People in the Deaf community and culture tend to perceive deafness not as a disability, but as an alternate lifestyle and culture (Padden & Humphries, 1988). Those who become deaf, on the other hand, miss their earlier access to spoken communication, and they miss sound. For them, deafness is both a disability and a loss; it is something to be mourned:

> Many is the time that I have cried myself to sleep because of my hearing loss. Especially after sessions of lovemaking with my husband. I could not hear what he was saying to me. And I would want to talk to my children over the telephone, and "I can't hear you, I can't understand you." It was pretty bad. A couple of times I contemplated suicide.

*   *   *

> [My doctor] said to me, "Aren't you lucky that you had your education behind you." I hated that man for saying that. I'm going to be deaf and he says I'm lucky.

Although most people with acquired hearing loss strive to maintain their familiar social and cultural world, some choose a partial affiliation with the Deaf culture (Wax, 1989). None of the people in our study ever became fully integrated into the Deaf community, but a few developed some significant ties to it:

> Learning about Deaf people made being deaf not so frightening and being able to help people again was really helpful to me.

> Because of being deaf, I became aware of minority groups, and the feeling of oppression . . . of not being equal to other people. I never saw that before. . . . Then, I wanted to do something. . . . So that's when I started volunteer work to help get better rights, equal rights, better laws for deaf . . . or hearing-impaired people.

The people who had built such bridges tended to be those who had lost their hearing early in their adult life, before social identity and vocational choices had been firmly fashioned.

In recent years, people with adult onset hearing loss have formed groups and organizations to address their social, cultural, and political interests. Self Help for Hard of Hearing People (SHHH) largely comprises culturally hearing people with relatively severe hearing losses. SHHH members usually are not comfortable with the word "deaf" and generally communicate by speechreading aided by special amplifying devices. Few SHHH members use manual communication of any form; some are beginning to use speech-to-text technology. SHHH members are largely middle class and middle age or older.

Association of Late Deafened Adults (ALDA) members have become profoundly deaf as adults. ALDA members tend to be younger than SHHH members, are ready to define themselves as deaf, and are interested in visual systems of communication. A high percentage of ALDA members have learned at least some sign language, and computer-assisted captioning is used routinely (Howe & Graham, 1990).

In many communities, there are local support groups for people with different kinds of hearing loss and language preferences. Some are affiliated with service agencies, and some are informal networks.

POLITICS

> I started to feel that some Deaf people resented me and didn't think I was deaf. They said "She's deaf but she signs like a hearing person." I was always made to feel that I was a hearing person and that I shouldn't be taking on a leadership role.

In addition to a shared culture, the Deaf community has a political agenda. Many culturally Deaf people have suffered misunderstanding and overt discrimination from the hearing world. Group members tend to see themselves as fellow victims of oppression. Some Deaf organizations are active in efforts to promote acceptance of ASL and recognition of the rights and abilities of Deaf citizens.

People who are not fluent in ASL, not culturally at home in the Deaf world, and not conversant with its political issues are likely to be perceived by the Deaf community as "hearies," regardless of their actual ability to hear. To Deaf people, the hearies represent a world that is at the very least different and, at worst, oppressive.

Hard-of-hearing, deaf, and deafened people also experience discrimination and misunderstanding. Many of them also have a political agenda. In some ways, their agenda overlaps that of the Deaf community. Like the Deaf community, SHHH and ALDA strive to increase community understanding about the rights and needs of hearing-impaired people. For example, all groups are trying to make television coverage of emergencies accessible to deaf and hearing-impaired people, both through captions and sign language interpreting. But SHHH has a particular interest in making assistive listening devices available in public places, whereas ALDA emphasizes expansion of text-based systems, such as real-time captioning. In their different ways, SHHH and ALDA strive to make spoken English more accessible to their constituents. Because their agenda is unrelated to ASL, it is perceived by some members of the Deaf community as a threat to Deaf language and culture.

IMPLICATIONS FOR SOCIAL WORK

The first thing a social worker needs to do when meeting a deaf or hard-of-hearing client is establish a way to communicate. A primary question is what language the client knows and prefers. Because most hearing-impaired people are not culturally Deaf, most clients with hearing loss will have good speech ability and prefer English or the spoken language of their culture. If the client speechreads, the social worker can help by finding a quiet, well-lit place to talk. He or she should face the client; speak slowly and clearly; rephrase anything the client misunderstands; and offer to write key words, names, or specific information. Some clients with good speech and knowledge of English prefer to involve an interpreter for important interactions, and they are entitled to that accommodation. Professional interpreters for the deaf are able to use both signed English and ASL and to select the language suited to the individual and situation.

Deaf clients who prefer ASL to English may state their preference directly or may show it in other ways, perhaps by not understanding spoken or written English or by writing in a way that seems unclear, awkward, or not idiomatic. It is important to remember that writing is not an adequate accommodation when working with such a client. Effective communication will require the involvement of a fully qualified, professional interpreter and possibly consultation from a specialist in deafness. Using a family member as a volunteer interpreter is not appropriate; it can violate a client's right to privacy and introduce bias into the communication process.

ASL is, as its name suggests, American. Deaf people from other countries may use a different sign language and need a highly specialized interpreter. Some interpreters know sign systems other than ASL, and some are able, through gestures and mime, to communicate with those Deaf people who, for a variety of reasons, have not learned any formal language at all. Once communication has been established, the focus needs to move away from hearing and back to the issue that brought the client to the social worker in the first place. In the course of this work, it is important to remain mindful of the impact of hearing loss on the client's life and situation. Particularly if recently acquired, hearing loss is likely to be a major clinical issue, affecting the client's relationships, work life, inner feelings, and response to particular services or programs. For other clients, most often those who have lived with deafness or hearing loss for many years, hearing status may be simply a given, a part of the context of life, and something to be accommodated, not stressed.

Hearing impairment can be an isolating condition, and some clients might want to make connections with other people or groups who can offer companionship, support, and a sense of shared mission. Before making referrals, however, the social worker must be aware of pertinent social, cultural, and political characteristics both of the client and of the group being considered. The right connection can help immensely:

> I get a tremendous amount of support in empathy, in knowing that I'm not alone . . . that other people have problems in the same areas that I have . . . how much we have in common.

But the wrong connection can leave people feeling more isolated than ever:

> The rehabilitation counselors tell us to learn ASL when we have no use for ASL . . . It's aggravating. I get very angry with it.

CONCLUSION

Understanding a person with a hearing loss is a complex and specialized clinical challenge. To be of help, a social worker must join each deaf or hearing-impaired person in a full and multifaceted exploration of all pertinent dimensions of life—hearing, communication, language, culture, and politics. The process takes time and may at first seem remote from the problem at hand. But the exploration is essential for developing a positive relationship, for assessing needs accurately, and for delivering high-quality service.

REFERENCES

Glass, L. (1985). Psychosocial aspects of hearing loss in adulthood. In H. Orlans (Ed.), *Adjustment to adult hearing loss* (pp. 167–178). San Diego: College Hill Press.

Havlik, R. J. (1986). *Aging in the eighties, impaired senses for sound and light in persons age 65 years and over: Preliminary data from the supplement on aging to the national health interview survey: United States, January–June 1984* (Advance data from Vital and Health Statistics Number 125). Hyattsville, MD: National Center for Health Statistics.

Howe, M., & Graham, B. (1990). The importance of captioning for late-deafened adults. *International Journal of Technology & Aging, 3*(2), 121–131.

Luey, H. S. (1980). Between worlds: The problems of deafened adults. *Social Work in Health Care, 5,* 253–265.

Padden, C., & Humphries, T. (1988). *Deaf in America: Voices from a culture.* Cambridge, MA: Harvard University Press.

Ries, P. W. (1985). The demography of hearing loss. In H. Orlans (Ed.), *Adjustment to adult hearing loss* (pp. 3–21). San Diego: College Hill Press.

Schein, J., & Delk, M., Jr. (1974). *The deaf population of the United States.* Silver Spring, MD: National Association of the Deaf.

Wax, T. M. (1989). Assessment dilemmas of late-onset hearing loss. In H. S. Luey, H. H. Elliott, & L. E. Glass (Eds.), *Mental health assessment of deaf clients: Special conditions* (pp. 141–157). San Francisco: University of California, Center on Deafness.

This chapter was originally published in the March 1995 issue of Social Work, *vol. 40, pp. 177–182.*

Part IV

EDUCATION

22 Solution-Focused Social Work: Metamessages to Students in Higher Education Opportunity Programs

Mary Robinson Baker and Joseph R. Steiner

S tudents who enter higher education opportunity programs (HEOPs), like other disadvantaged groups, frequently feel as if they are viewed as different, of limited ability or motivation, untrustworthy, and perhaps unwanted. In the authors' experience as academic advisors and educational social workers, the perceived devaluation of their race or socioeconomic status has caused many students in HEOPs to identify themselves with academic and career failure. Such students generally feel blamed and disempowered and subjected to the "us versus them" attitudes of schools and communities. "Us versus them" orientations concretize the students into separate, unequal, and perhaps even adversarial categories and create dichotomies such as black versus white or rich versus poor. Traditional problem-focused social work frequently reinforces this negative grounding in spite of the good intentions of social workers.

This chapter demonstrates the usefulness of a solution-focused methodology, especially with those who feel demeaned, disempowered, and oppressed. Special attention is given to students in higher education opportunity programs, but this methodology can be successfully used with others who feel separated by "us versus them" orientations.

HIGHER EDUCATION OPPORTUNITY PROGRAMS

In this chapter, the phrase "higher education opportunity program" has a broader meaning than it does in New York State, where the phrase refers only to publicly funded educational opportunity programs in private colleges and universities. HEOP here refers to all educational opportunity programs in higher education whether in public or private educational institutions or whether publicly or privately funded. HEOPs emphasize the educational development of students and the expansion of educational opportunities for those from economically and educationally disadvantaged backgrounds. They go beyond the narrow criteria of remedial programs, subsidized tuition, or specific colleges or universities. HEOPs build on the ideal of equal access to higher education for all citizens by extending opportunities "to persons who have been academically and economically disadvantaged" (New York State Education Department, 1990, p. vi).

Students in HEOPs

HEOPs serve people traditionally underrepresented in higher education. For example, in New York State for the 1989–90 academic year, 93 percent of the students in HEOPs had gross family incomes under $18,000 a year, and 61 percent had annual incomes below $8,300. Forty-two percent of the HEOP students were black, 29 percent were Hispanic, 19 percent were white non-Hispanic, and 9 percent were Asian (New York State Education Department, 1990). The majority of students in HEOPs are students of color because of the economic and educational disadvantages confronting nonwhite populations. These disadvantages appear to be particularly devastating for males: "People talk about the fact that the black male has been disappearing from college campuses; so has the Hispanic male, in a precipitous drop in the last 10 or so years—about 20 percent in terms of participation rates" (Barry, 1991, p. 5).

Philosophical Assumptions of HEOPs

The philosophical assumptions that support higher education opportunity programs as opposed to remedial programs are similar in many ways to the assumptions that accompany solution-focused social work versus problem-focused social work. Individuals are perceived to have the inner resources they need to develop and succeed (Saleebey, 1992). They activate success by creating a vision of their future, by working in a supportive environment, and by connecting with specific individuals who help students identify strategies and deal with barriers as they move toward the future. Relatively little emphasis is placed on understanding the causes and sustaining forces of problems or on looking back and studying the past. Much emphasis is placed on here-and-now development in relation to where one is going. The empowerment that results from dealing positively with roadblocks helps students move from the present to the future with hope, self-esteem, and confidence. Remedial programs, like problem-focused social work, contribute to problem fatigue and to feelings of being stuck in an "us versus them" struggle, in spite of the good intentions that the professors or social workers in these programs bring to their work.

BARRIERS TO EDUCATION FOR BLACK AMERICANS

"Us versus them" thinking is accentuated by many things, but race is still a dominant one. Steele's (1992) research revealed that despite socioeconomic disadvantages, black students began school with test scores that were fairly close to the test scores of white students their age. The longer they stayed in school, however, the more they fell behind:

> By the sixth grade blacks in many school districts are two full grades behind whites in achievement. This pattern holds true in middle school . . . and the record does not improve in high school . . .
>
> Even for blacks who make it to college, the problem doesn't go away . . . 70 percent of black students who enroll in four-year colleges drop out at some point as compared with 45 percent of whites. (Steele, 1992, pp. 68–70)

In addition, black students in college got lower grades even when they were well off financially, had higher test scores coming into college, and were highly motivated (Steele, 1992). For many black students, this pattern of lower grades causes their college degree to be "terminal," because low undergraduate grades usually preclude graduate training.

Chestang (1976) used the term "black experience" to denote the deferred dreams and frustrated aspirations of a people oppressed by society. He wrote, "Three conditions, socially determined and institutionally supported, characterize the black experience: social injustice, social inconsistency, and personal impotence" (p. 61). He defined *social injustice* as the denial of legal rights and *social inconsistency* as the institutionalized discrepancy between word and deed:

> In person-to-person transactions, it is the individual expres-
> sion of group rejection, a personalized injustice that attacks
> the individual without his group supports and the individual
> takes it personally. Each act of this institutionalized behavior
> deprives the black person of the feelings of self-worth and
> esteem he has derived from his attempts to achieve accep-
> tance through adhering to the values, norms, and beliefs
> prescribed by society. Since it expresses the informal and un-
> official rejection of blacks, social inconsistency leaves the in-
> dividual without recourse to regulatory agencies and courts
> of law. (Chestang, 1976, p. 62)

The feelings of impotence that result from social injustice and
social inconsistency produce a sense of powerlessness to influence one's environment. This sense of powerlessness is reinforced
by school and neighborhood activities and even by social work
practices that accentuate "us versus them" thinking:

> Tragically, such devaluation can seem inescapable. Sooner
> or later, it forces on its victim two painful realizations. The
> first is that society is preconditioned to see the worst in them.
> Black students quickly learn that acceptance, if it is won at
> all, will be hard-won. The second is that even if the black
> student receives exoneration in one setting—with the teacher
> and fellow students in one classroom, or at one level of school-
> ing, for example, this approval will have to be rewon in the
> next classroom at the next level of schooling. (Steele, 1992,
> p. 74)

Part of the economic and educational disadvantage that many
people from oppressed groups have internalized is "problem fatigue"—the belief that problems of race and poverty cannot be
solved, that black and white people live in separate worlds and
are separate, distinct, and unequal people (Steele, 1992). And yet,
whatever other factors may depress black achievement, they are
substantially reduced in a school atmosphere that is inclusive,
that affirms, and that builds on strengths (Steele, 1992).

One major university found that none of its colleges or schools
graduated more than 40 percent of all disadvantaged students
admitted between 1972 and 1982 (personal communication with
R. Cavanagh, vice president, and R. Boney, assistant vice president, undergraduate studies, Syracuse University, Syracuse, New
York, Spring 1993). HEOPs for three categories of students significantly improved graduation rates of nonwhite students in each
of these schools and colleges as well as the university as a whole.

The first category comprised students considered "inadmissible." These were state-supported students with weak academic preparation and performance who generally would not have qualified for admission to this university. The second category was made up of federally supported students who met the standards for admission but entered with clear academic risks. The third category consisted of university-supported students who were superior in the sciences. Each student entered an intensive six-week summer college preparation program available to any first-time college student.

In addition, staff in the higher education opportunity program developed ongoing supportive relationships with each student. They clarified expectations, listened, and advised. HEOP staff sought feedback from professors and helped prepare students to negotiate with professors, but they did not directly intervene with professors. These staff also participated with students in social events, including special events with alumni of the HEOPs. HEOP students did not do remedial work, but they individualized their academic loads; some students took five or more years and others less than four years to graduate.

In short, this special opportunity program helped to create vision, instill hope, and provide direction. The result was a large payoff in graduation rates. Between 1985 and 1992, over 50 percent of the students originally considered inadmissible and over 60 percent of the admissible but at-risk students graduated, some in less than four years. Over 98 percent of the disadvantaged students who graduated from high school with superior academic records between 1985 and 1992 graduated or will graduate. This is a significantly higher rate than for other students with similar academic records or for disadvantaged students who do not participate in the higher education opportunity program.

Disadvantaged students who are instilled with a sense of opportunity, vision, and community will tend to succeed even though their prior academic performance may be unpromising: "Doing well in school requires a belief that school achievement can be a promising basis of self-esteem, and that belief needs constant reaffirmation even for advantaged students" (Steele, 1992, p. 72). Doing well in higher education requires students, professors, and other staff to identify with the university and feel like contributing members with good prospects.

METAMESSAGES AND SOCIAL WORK

Metamessages refer to relationship messages (Satir, 1967; Watzlawick, Beavin, & Jackson, 1967) that pass between people as they interact. Metamessages are transmitted and received verbally and nonverbally, consciously and unconsciously. For example, two people may be talking about family, school, friends, or even the weather, and concurrently they are transmitting metamessages about their respect for and attraction to each other. Metamessages may convey admiration, appreciation, joy, contempt, disgust, ridicule, or scorn. Walter and Peller (1992) described metamessages in their discussion of the presuppositions social workers communicate based on the theoretical framework they employ. For example, a metamessage in the psychoanalytic and psychiatric traditions is that the individual is the problem, in that something within them is undeveloped, defective, or diseased, and that the something should be developed, fixed, or treated by "us." In a family systems perspective, the metamessage is that the family is the problem. For example, in the complex extended family in which many black children are raised, the problem is sometimes identified as an enmeshment or blurring of boundaries (Minuchin, 1974). In the extreme, this can be seen as a fusion or lack of self-definition (Bowen, 1976). The differentiation issue is particularly difficult for black young adults who are going beyond their families in education and professional and socioeconomic status. The level of differentiation necessary for mobility is often frightening to these students and their families and can result in the development of symptoms of dysfunction in family members (Boyd-Franklin, 1989).

In the social advocacy and social planning traditions, problems that disadvantage people generally are seen as organizational or community problems, including racism, ethnocentrism, and classism. Yet recent social work literature has given little attention to working with disadvantaged populations to undertake "transformative action to remove the conditions that oppress people" (McMahon & Allen-Meares, 1992, p. 537).

What do existing theoretical perspectives and the actions of social workers using them communicate to students in HEOPs? What are the metamessages that accompany such actions? What do social workers transmit about a student's worth, ability to contribute, and future prospects?

Metamessages in Problem-Focused Social Work

Problem-focused social work gives much attention to problems, their causes, and the factors sustaining them and to their intensity, frequency, and duration. For a description of the historical roots and current misuse of problem-focused social work, see Weick (1992). Problem-focused social work is "an exquisitely rational" (Scott & Miller, 1971) approach in which it is incorrectly assumed that if one can clearly identify problems and their causes and sustaining forces, one can plan and carry out successful intervention strategies. Problem-focused approaches are used in clinical, organizational, and community contexts.

For students in HEOPs, such an approach assumes that they will do well academically and socially if their problems are identified, if they show proper motivation, and if rational intervention strategies are planned and carried out. In face-to-face situations, a social worker using a problem-focused approach raises a series of questions: What is the problem? What are its causes? What is maintaining the problem? The locus of the problem may be within a student, his or her family, the school, or society at large. Too often, social workers in educational settings focus primarily on problems within students and their families. Unfortunately, this feeling contributes to more problem fatigue and more "us versus them" maneuvering.

Many questions that drive problem-focused clinical work do not transmit affirming metamessages that students are cooperative, resourceful, creative, fun to be with, insightful, worthy of a challenge, and open to discovery and growth. Problem-focused messages typically do not reduce the gap between the social worker and students. Social workers perceive the failure of students to comply with problem-focused interventions as the result of low motivation, resistance, and lack of readiness for "treatment" and as indicative of the need for long-term work (see Gitterman, 1983). Seldom is this failure seen as a byproduct of the limitations of problem-focused clinical practice, a failure to communicate positive metamessages, or an inability to overcome an "us versus them" orientation between workers and students.

Much of the social work practice literature regarding diversity is written from a problem-focused perspective. McMahon and Allen-Meares (1992), in reviewing articles proposing social work intervention with disadvantaged populations, found that "All articles proposing individual intervention had the same basic intentions: either increase ethnic awareness for social workers or the cultural adaptation of social work practices for the designated population" (p. 535). Social work literature is written to help social workers become more aware, but the emphasis is too often on "them," "their problems," and conditions that disadvantage "them." Conflict continues regarding intervention choice. Should social work help "them" deal with their disadvantaging environments, or should it target schools, communities, or other social entities to reduce vestiges of racism, ethnocentrism, or classism for "them"?

Focusing exclusively on problems, including racism, ethnocentrism, or classism, makes the problems more important than the students. Focusing exclusively on problems minimizes the celebration of what is human in those we serve, especially the resourceful, creative, joyful power of the human spirit. This celebration is especially significant to students.

Metamessages in Solution-Focused Social Work

HEOP students, like many others, benefit from counseling services that are accessible and responsive and that are more user friendly than traditional, problem-focused change efforts (Saleebey, 1992). Each of the solution-focused techniques in the following discussion facilitates mutuality among social workers and students. Such methods are a pleasant surprise to students who are not expecting positive affirmation and empowerment from social workers.

If It Works, Do It More! This solution-focused method (de Shazer, 1988) is simple, direct, and profound, and it is too frequently overlooked. In operationalizing this approach, attention is given to discovering what has worked for a specific student and then linking these past successful efforts to current situations in which the student has not as yet succeeded: "Focusing on progress achieved leads very naturally to the question of how it should be explained. . . . Clients' own ideas about what has helped them can be used as a starting point to develop further plans" (Furman & Ahola, 1992, p. 111).

For example, when talking to James, a solution-focused social worker asked him to discuss at length what study styles had worked for him. The focus was clearly on James and the affirmation of his resourcefulness. For example, in previous courses where James did well, what were the patterns? Did he skim some readings and study others? Did he read the introduction and conclusion before reading the body of a paper or book? What worked? Did he spread out study time over the course of a day, week, or semester, or did he concentrate it at one time? What was the nature of James' underlining, note taking, and reviewing? How did it help him? Did he study in his own room, a library, or a public lounge? What were his eating, exercising, sleeping, and socializing patterns? How have these contributed to good grades in the past?

Additional questions about class attendance, seating, participation, and relationships with professors are also important in determining what has worked: How much did James attend class when he did his best academic work? Where did he sit? Did he make comments, ask questions, clarify conflicts in the class, support or disagree with others, including the teacher? When did others notice that he was doing well? What did he expect of a professor in class? What did he expect of a professor beyond class, and did he communicate this directly? How did he respond, behaviorally, to professors who liked him, to professors who appeared to ignore or even dislike him? What were things that worked in specific classes and with specific professors?

The authors' experience has confirmed that these questions and the metamessages that accompany them help promote skill in dealing with difficult situations, facilitative humor, and acceptance of a challenge by the disadvantaged students in HEOPs.

Search the Exceptions. This solution-focused approach (de Shazer, 1985) is in direct contrast to the identification of problems and their corresponding causes and maintenance patterns. The emphasis is on the times the problem did not occur and what the student was thinking and doing at those times. When did the person not feel depressed, not feel rejected? For example, Sabrina spoke of a writer's block. Whenever she sat down at her desk to write a paper, her mind went blank. Rather than focusing on the problem and its causes (and there were many), the social worker began by normalizing the fact that it is a pretty human thing to block at times in spite of the anxiety and fear this causes.

The social worker then searched for exceptions by asking Sabrina when her ideas flowed freely. Where was she, and how did she bring this flow about? Sabrina could not remember an academic paper she had ever written that was not a personal battle, a personal struggle to put ideas on paper. Additional questioning revealed that Sabrina did daydream creatively and at times even enjoyed putting her thoughts on paper when she did not have to worry about sentence structure and spelling.

Further discussion, including elements of "If it works, do more of it," enabled Sabrina to construct and refine a solution. She decided to brainstorm about an assigned paper well ahead of time as she exercised, then write notes to herself so she would not forget. After exercising, she would go to a comfortable place in a student lounge and sketch out an outline for her paper. Later she would write the paper, also in a somewhat noisy lounge where she felt comfortable. Spelling and sentence structure were de-emphasized at this point, and her awareness of where she felt comfortable was emphasized, as was her ability to write from a structure—a concrete sketch— rather than from scattered, fleeting ideas. Sabrina became more aware of her own resourcefulness and ability to control fear. In addition, her difficulty with spelling and sentence structure became one small, correctable part of a developing identity rather than a major, rather static, disabling part of her self-definition.

Another student, Tamara, was referred to the social worker because she reportedly daydreamed excessively about her family and was especially worried about her younger sister. She was also falling behind and losing interest in her studies. During the first interview, Tamara spoke rather freely about the many problems in her family, including the alcohol and drug abuse of her father, his meanness when intoxicated, and her mother's efforts to protect the children. Tamara said she would like to forget about her family while she was in college but that she thought about them too much, especially her sister, and this interfered with her studies.

The social worker listened closely, validating her feelings, and asked, "How have you done as well as you have?" which is a common solution-focused question. Tamara smiled for the first time but did not answer. The social worker then searched for exceptions. She asked, "When can you really focus on your studies, even if only for a short time, and not think of your family?" (This question is preferable to "When are you thinking of your family when you are trying to do school work?")

Further analysis revealed that phone calls to her family were very upsetting, so Tamara tried to limit contact with her family. But Tamara discovered that she was able to focus on her studies for two or three days following phone conversations with her mother. Tamara's schoolwork improved significantly when she began speaking to her mother by phone every three to four days. Tamara likewise displayed increased ability to concentrate and accept challenges as she felt the affirming metamessages that accompanied this aspect of solution-focused social work.

Use Presuppositional Questioning. Presuppositional questioning is a type of questioning that influences students' perceptions in the direction of solutions (O'Hanlon & Weiner-Davis, 1989). A basic rule of thumb in constructing presuppositional questions is to make them affirming and open-ended, avoiding questions where one or two word answers such as "yes" or "no" are possible. For example, rather than asking "Do you like college?" the social worker should ask "What do you like about college?" The latter presupposes that some things have gone well even if others have not and also that the student can make those distinctions. Rather than ask, "Have you been the victim of racism or classism?" ask "How have you been able to grow and to flourish in spite of an environment of racism or classism?" The latter again presupposes that the student has done well in some areas and that her or his resourcefulness helped ensure success.

The hidden metamessages that accompany good presuppositional questions are that the student is motivated, creative, able, and worthy in spite of any economic and academic disadvantages they may have faced or may still be facing. Students in HEOPs not infrequently have initial difficulty talking with social workers about their successes, things that make them laugh, and their aspirations. Talking about personal problems or discriminatory practices is frequently more familiar and perhaps initially more comfortable for many students and social workers in HEOPs. However, for students to feel safe, connected, and engaged, key individuals must discover and assertively experience a student's positive traits.

Ask the Miracle Question. The miracle question is actually a series of questions that elicit descriptions of concrete and specific behaviors that would probably occur after a solution is found. For example, "Suppose that one night while you were asleep, there was a miracle and the problem was solved. How would you know? What would be different?" (de Shazer, 1988, p. 5). Or, "If a miracle happened tonight and you woke up with the problem solved, or you were reasonably confident you were on the right track to solving it, what would you be doing differently?" (Walter & Peller, 1992, p. 78). Or, "Let us say you woke up tomorrow, and didn't know the miracle occurred, what would be different? What would your friends notice? What would your professors, your parents, notice?" Some people may respond better to questions about a magic wand: "If you had a magic wand and the problem went away, what would you be doing differently?" (Walter & Peller, 1992, p. 79).

Powerful changes take place as students clarify a future that has fewer problems. For example, Christal described herself as a recently divorced 34-year-old student who was having multiple problems with her 14-year-old son. In addition, Christal recently had learned that she had multiple sclerosis (MS) after feeling tired, physically weak, and emotionally burned out. After listening to her and acknowledging her difficult situation, the social worker changed the focus by asking the miracle question. Christal's initial response was that she would not have MS and that she would be doing well in school. The social worker acknowledged that not having MS would be a miracle and then said, "but even if you had MS, what would be different if a miracle occurred?" With encouragement, Christal went on to describe her performance in classes, her relationships with professors and friends, and things she would be doing with her son and former husband and with a support group for people with physical limitations.

The worker then encouraged Christal to do one or two things she identified in responses to the miracle question. Christal selected talking to her professors and becoming active in a support group. Christal then began doing other things she identified. Some joint laughter and tears of joy also contributed to her successes. In addition, Christal appeared to be empowered by the questions, "Why haven't things gotten worse?" and "How did you keep things going as well as you did?" The miracle question, like these other two solution-focused questions, communicated strong, affirming metamessages that led to strong, affirming actions. Christal resourcefully did well in college and moved toward solutions in spite of the many problems in her life.

Use Metaphors. Use of metaphors represents a powerful tool in building rapport and in facilitating change (O'Hanlon & Weiner-Davis, 1989). Malcolm was a HEOP student who approached the social worker informally because his father was pushing him to take engineering courses before he completed certain math courses. Malcolm's father was a construction worker who was very heavily invested in Malcolm's becoming an engineer, because the father had wanted to become an engineer but could not go to college. Malcolm's father may also have suspected that Malcolm was being ignored, or worse, being directed away from engineering classes because he was black.

Later, when Malcolm introduced the social worker to his father, again informally, the conflict over what courses to take was verbalized. The father was adamant that Malcolm was ready to take engineering courses and he wanted the social worker's support to convince Malcolm of this. The social worker listened and then asked the father about what he did and how buildings were constructed. Malcolm's father became more detailed as he spoke about the importance of his work as a builder helping to construct foundations. He also acknowledged that many people do not realize the importance of a good foundation. This became the metaphor the social worker used for Malcolm taking more math courses. Math courses became the foundation for building a career as an engineer. What started out as a somewhat tense "us versus them" confrontation ended with mutual respect. In the end, Malcolm's father was laughing frequently with the worker and Malcolm. He left happily, readily agreeing on the importance of a good foundation.

The metamessages that accompanied this conversation were that Malcolm and his father were resourceful, motivated, responsible individuals. These metamessages were in sharp contrast to those that accompanied rational arguments about what Malcolm needed to overcome his deficiencies and academic problems before he could succeed in an engineering program.

IMPLICATIONS FOR SOCIAL WORK

Many students in HEOPs are hesitant to request formal, scheduled sessions with social workers. Thus, it is important for social workers to reach out and to make themselves available for informal, user-friendly, two-way conversations in public places. The solution-focused techniques presented here can be used in any place that students select to talk: public lounges, empty classrooms, or private interviewing rooms. In addition, we have found that such conversations are accompanied by much more laughter than is problem-focused interviewing. Victor Borge seems to have been correct when he said, "Laughter is the shortest distance between two people" (Borge, 1991). Facilitative laughter is a universal language. It reduces the gulf between "us and them"; it enables students and social workers to feel acknowledged and connected. Such laughter may also be accompanied by tears of joy and healing.

CONCLUSION

Students in higher education, including those students identified as educationally and economically disadvantaged, need positive affirmations. The metamessages associated with solution-focused social work transmit positive affirmations more consistently than do the metamessages that accompany much problem-focused social work. Developing hope in students, including those in HEOPs, is no small task. Colleges and universities cannot become a repository of national hope and a source of national leadership unless they strive to practice what they teach (Giamatti, 1988). The same can be said of social work.

REFERENCES

Barry, P. (1991). A new voice for Hispanics in higher education: A conversation with Antonio Rigual [Interview]. *College Board Review, 160,* 2–7.

Borge, V. (1991, April 12). *The positive power of humor and creativity* [Keynote address]. Sixth annual conference on the positive power of humor and creativity, Saratoga Springs, NY.

Bowen, M. (1976). Theory and practice of psychotherapy. In P. J. Guerin (Ed.), *Family therapy: Theory and practice* (pp. 42–90). New York: Gardner Press.

Boyd-Franklin, N. (1989). *Black families in therapy: A multisystems approach.* New York: Guilford Press.

Chestang, L. (1976). Environmental influences on social functioning: The black experience. In R.S.J. Cafferty & L. Chestang (Eds.), *The diverse society: Implications for social policy* (pp. 59–74). Washington, DC: National Association of Social Workers.

de Shazer, S. (1985). *Keys to solution in brief therapy.* New York: W. W. Norton.

de Shazer, S. (1988). *Clues: Investigating solutions in brief therapy.* New York: W. W. Norton.

Furman, B., & Ahola, T. (1992). *Solution talk: Hosting therapeutic conversations.* New York: W. W. Norton.

Giamatti, A. B. (1988). *A free and ordered space: The real world of the university.* New York: W. W. Norton.

Gitterman, A. (1983). Uses of resistance: A transactional view. *Social Work, 28,* 127–131.

McMahon, A., & Allen-Meares, P. (1992). Is social work racist? A content analysis of recent literature. *Social Work, 37,* 533–539.

Minuchin, S. (1974). *Families and family therapy.* Cambridge, MA: Harvard University Press.

New York State Education Department. (1990, December). *HEOP works: Annual report 1989–90.* Albany: State University of New York.

O'Hanlon, W. H., & Weiner-Davis, M. (1989). *In search of solutions: A new direction in psychotherapy.* New York: W. W. Norton.

Saleebey, D. (Ed.). (1992). *The strengths perspective in social work practice.* New York: Longman.

Satir, V. (1967). *Conjoint family therapy* (2nd ed.). Palo Alto, CA: Science and Behavioral Books.

Scott, B., & Miller, H. (1971). *Problems and issues in social casework.* New York: Columbia University Press.

Steele, C. M. (1992, April). Race and the schooling of black Americans. *Atlantic Monthly,* pp. 68–78.

Walter, J. L., & Peller, J. E. (1992). *Becoming solution-focused in brief therapy.* New York: Brunner/Mazel.

Watzlawick, P., Beavin, J. H., & Jackson, D. D. (1967). *Pragmatics of human communication.* New York: W. W. Norton.

Weick, A. (1992). Building a strengths perspective in social work. In D. Saleebey (Ed.), *The strengths perspective in social work practice* (pp. 18–26). New York: Longman.

This chapter was originally published in the March 1995 issue of Social Work, *vol. 40, pp. 225–232.*

23 Problems of Inner-City Schoolchildren: Needs Assessment by Nominal Group Process

Karen E. Gerdes and Rose Ann Benson

The National Commission on Children's (1991) report *Beyond Rhetoric* declared that after a decade of educational reforms, "America remains a nation at risk" (p. xxv). Nowhere has this nation's educational system failed more dramatically than in inner-city schools serving predominantly poor African American populations. In many northeastern urban centers, the school dropout rate for African Americans living in poverty is approaching 40 percent (U.S. Bureau of the Census, 1993). Illiteracy among students of color is also as high as 40 percent in some cities (Perry, 1988).

The illiteracy of so many children of color may not reflect so much the incapacity of students to learn as much as the inability of schools to be flexible enough to accommodate the diverse abilities, interests, and complex individual needs of inner-city students. Problems such as poverty, poor student health, parental illiteracy, and community and family violence are common to many inner-city schools (Committee for Economic Development, 1987). However, each inner-city school, and each child in that school, has unique concerns and specialized needs. In addition, both the school and the student may have unique abilities and resources that are available to assist in solving these problems.

A site-based multidisciplinary management system has been recommended as a key educational reform to ensure that schools meet the needs of all students (National Commission on Children, 1991; Streeter & Franklin, 1993). A site-based management system allows the principal, school social worker, psychologist, nurse, teacher and parent representatives, and students to work together to design and implement creative programs that address the specialized and individual needs of students in the school.

The first step in developing and implementing a successful site-based management system, as well as effective and competent school social work interventions, is a needs assessment. Needs assessment information prevents sole reliance on outside "professional formulations of service needs" (Siegel, Attkisson, & Carson, 1987). This chapter describes the use of nominal group process to identify and rank the most critical problems faced by students in an inner-city school.

NOMINAL GROUP PROCESS

The greatest usefulness of the nominal group process compared with other needs assessment approaches, such as surveys or the Delphi technique, is as a planning tool for increasing collaboration. It allows individuals in small groups to participate equally in identifying and ranking problems (Siegel, Attkisson, & Cohn, 1974). The nominal group approach is "designed to maximize creativity and productivity and to minimize argumentative style of problem-solving and competitive discussion" by obtaining information from both service providers (that is, school administrators and teachers) and consumers of service (that is, students) (Siegel et al., 1987, p. 79).

To effectively address the problems of disadvantaged children, site-based management teams and school social workers need to view students, parents, and teachers as resources and partners in the problem-posing and action strategy process. The nominal group process allows for a partnership perspective because it is a systematic and effective technique for assessing different perspectives.

The goal of the nominal group process as a collaborative effort is empowerment. Pinderhughes (1983) defined *empowerment* as "the perception of oneself as having some power over the forces that control one's life" (p. 39). Once perceived problems and differing perceptions have been identified through the needs assessment, the school social worker can use his or her knowledge of power dynamics and systemic process to create a context for dialogue and the constructive use of "power" by both students and teachers (Pinderhughes, 1983). For example, students and teachers can gain a sense of control and purposefulness by using their unique abilities and resources to critically assess the social and historical roots of the identified problems and to develop their own problem-posing situations and action strategies (Freire, 1973; Wallerstein & Bernstein, 1988).

METHOD

Participants

The faculty and students who participated in this study were in a prekindergarten to grade 9 inner-city school. The entire student population of 910 was African American. Eighty-five percent of the students (n = 773) lived in single-parent families, and more than 50 percent (n = 455) of the student population lived in poverty. The entire faculty (82 people) were also African American.

Procedures

The nominal group process was used to identify the most serious problems students faced based on student and faculty perceptions. The recommendations of Gilmore (1989) were followed:

1. Group size was limited.
2. Focus was limited to one question.
3. Each participant was given the opportunity to respond.
4. Each group made a preliminary selection and ranking of responses.
5. Each group discussed the preliminary results and conducted a final vote.
6. A tally was made of the final vote of all the groups.

Student Groups

A stratified random sample of approximately 5 percent of the student population in grades 1 through 9 was identified. At least four students were selected from each grade level. Students were randomly assigned to one of two groups within their appropriate grade levels: primary (grades 1 to 3), middle (grades 4 to 6), and junior high (grades 7 to 9). There were no discernable differences between groups within the same grade level. Each group consisted of seven students or fewer. The total number of students participating was 40.

Ninth-grade students were trained as facilitators in half-day sessions by social workers experienced in the nominal group process. The ninth-grade facilitators first experienced the nominal group process themselves. Afterward, the trainers discussed with the students how to give instructions and monitor the process without introducing bias. The ninth graders then facilitated the student groups. Teachers and administrative personnel were not present during the group process; however, the trainers supervised the ninth graders' facilitation of the process.

The students were asked to list on paper the problems they faced. The group facilitator then used a round-robin format in which each student named one problem on his or her list not previously mentioned. The round-robin cycle was repeated until all of the problems students had listed were discussed and recorded by the facilitator. The facilitator also took notes on the discussion of each problem.

Next, each student was asked to identify the seven most serious problems on the master list recorded by the facilitator and rank them from 1 = most serious to 7 = least serious. The facilitator added the rankings of each student in the group and calculated a group ranking from 1 to 7. Grade-level rankings were calculated by averaging the two group rankings from each grade level.

Faculty Groups

The nominal group process was used to assess the teachers' and administrative staff members' perceptions of the problems that students face. Sixty-five teachers (17 faculty were not present at the in-service meeting) and five administrative personnel (resource director or vice principal) were divided into 10 groups, with seven teachers or administrative personnel or fewer in a group. Social workers experienced in the nominal group process explained the procedures to the participants. Each individual was given directions to list on paper his or her perceptions of problems students faced. After sharing their lists in a round-robin format, each group ranked the seven top problems using the same process used by the students.

FINDINGS

Students

All of the students in grades 1 to 6 identified fighting as the most serious problem (Table 23-1). One of the primary-grade groups

Table 23-1

Students' Ranking of Problems at School, by Grade Level (N = 40)

Rank	Problem	Students Listing (%)
Grades 1–3		
1	Fighting	100
2	Problems with teachers	100
3	Behavior	100
4	Boring classes	92
5	Not enough time for lunch or recess	85
6	Dirty bathrooms	75
7	Teachers who do not listen	75
Grades 4–6		
1	Fighting	100
2	Drugs	100
3	Pregnancy	100
4	Behavior	100
5	Weapons in school	90
6	Dropping out	90
7	Teachers who do not listen	90
Grades 7–9		
1	Pregnancy	100
2	Drugs and drug deals	100
3	Stress	100
4	Behavior	100
5	Teachers who do not listen	100
6	Academic problems	87
7	Lack of security	80

identified "killing," a consequence of fighting, as one of the things they feared most. The junior high students were unanimous in reporting pregnancy as the most serious problem confronting students in the school, whereas the middle-grade groups listed pregnancy as the third most serious problem. The junior high students stated that the pregnancy problem was due in part to a lack of sex education. They also believed there should be easy access to birth control at school. Even the primary-grade groups recognized pregnancy as a critical problem confronting them; however, it was not one of the top seven problems they identified.

The middle-grade groups and the junior high groups identified drugs as the second most serious problem confronting students. Although several of the primary-grade students identified drugs as a problem, neither of the primary-grade groups as a whole viewed it as one of the seven most serious problems facing students. One primary-grade student named drugs like PCP, heroin, and cocaine, but the majority of students stated only that "drugs" were a problem.

All of the groups identified student behavior as one of the most serious problems, with the middle and junior high students ranking it fourth and the primary-grade students ranking it third. Behavior problems were identified as using foul language, acting up in class, and being disrespectful to teachers. Although students acknowledged they were disrespectful to teachers, students reported that lack of respect by teachers for them caused many of the problems. Many students stated that teachers sometimes provoked students by "calling them names" or belittling them in front of classmates.

The primary- and middle-grade groups ranked "teachers not listening" and other problems with teachers seventh, and the junior high groups ranked it fifth. In addition, students reported that teachers often "jumped to conclusions" and did not really care about students. Students seemed most offended that teachers often did not respect them and gave the impression that they "thought they were better than the students." As a result, students reported feeling "powerless" in the classroom.

Additional problems identified were weapons in school, dropping out of school, boring classes, not enough time for recess, dirty bathrooms, stress (defined by them as both negative peer pressure and pressure from teachers to perform), poor academic performance, and a lack of security. Students were adamant that school security was not adequate. Several individuals suggested that the school use metal detectors because they had seen weapons in school. A student reported, "Anyone could walk into the school and say they were going to the office and be allowed to wander" unescorted. Students felt that they were not "safe" at school. Because of shooting incidents that had occurred at other schools in the area, a few students were fearful they could be "shot or hurt at school."

Faculty

The faculty groups were quite consistent in their perceptions of the most serious problems students faced. They listed the following as the seven most serious problems that students faced: (1) low parental support and parental problems, (2) lack of motivation and positive values, (3) low self-esteem, (4) oppression and community isolation, (5) behavior problems, (6) peer pressure, and (7) poor attendance and tardiness. Ten teacher and administrator groups identified very different problems from the student groups (Table 23-2).

Teachers and administrators identified students' lack of motivation as a major problem. Several teachers suggested that the high rate of absenteeism and tardiness were related to "lack of

Table 23-2

Students', Administrators', and Teachers' Average Ranking of Problems at School

Average Rank	Students' Problem List and Percentage Listing (N = 40)	Teachers' and Administrators' Problem List and Percentage Listing (N = 70)
1	Pregnancy (100)	Low parental support and parental problems: few parenting skills, young parents, drug abuse, child abuse (100)
2	Drugs and associated problems (100)	Students' lack of motivation; students' lack of value system, gold chains and clothes more important than education (100)
3	Behavior: fighting, using foul language, showing a lack of respect for teachers, playing around too much (100)	Students' low self-esteem (100)
4	Teachers who do not listen and do not care about students (88)	Macro-level problems: oppression, community isolation, poor housing and living environment, violence (95)
5	Difficulties with schoolwork: failing grades, dropping out (88)	Students' behavior: lack of self-control (95)
6	Security: not enough security, security not strictly enforced, weapons in school (83)	Peer pressure (90)
7	Stress: peer pressure and pressure from teachers to perform (65)	Students' poor attendance and tardiness (80)

motivation" as well as problems students experienced at home (for example, neglect). They reported that "students did not want to be in school," "did not perceive education as an advantage," and "did not understand personal responsibility and accountability." As a result, teachers reported feeling "powerless" to teach because they spent much of their time and energy just trying to control the classroom. Some reported that administration rules were not consistently enforced, perhaps giving mixed messages about responsibility. For example, students were not allowed to wear oversized shorts hanging from their hips; however, some students were sent home to change and others were not.

Teachers and administrators also identified negative peer pressure as a problem. They perceived anti-drug campaigns such as "Just Say No" as not fully addressing the issue of group pressure and the forceful persuasion that often caused students to use drugs.

Teachers and administrators mentioned drug use among students but not often enough to make the top seven list. They reported that the students' parents were more likely than the students to be abusing alcohol or other drugs.

DISCUSSION

Students were more likely to identify their problems as concrete student behaviors (fighting, pregnancy, taking drugs, conflict with teachers) and teacher behaviors (teachers who do not listen). Faculty were more likely to identify student problems as abstract constructs (values, motivation, and self-esteem). When teachers did identify concrete problems, the primary focus was on parental behaviors (drug abuse, child abuse, and so forth). Students did not include macro-level (that is, societal) problems; however, teachers listed several macro-level problems. Faculty viewed oppression, community isolation, lack of appropriate housing, poverty, and drug-related violence as problems that directly affected the performance of students and their ability to function in the classroom.

Faculty and students agreed that student behaviors (ranked third by students and fifth by teachers) were a serious problem. Teachers and administrators perceived the behavior problems of students as a "lack of personal discipline" or "self-control," whereas students claimed their behavior problems were precipitated by "teachers who did not listen and did not respect students." Consequently, students identified the teacher–student relationship as a significant problem. However, faculty did not perceive teacher–student relationships or a lack of communication as problems. In general, teachers did not perceive any communication gap with students. Only one teacher identified "teacher insensitivity" as a problem.

Common Feelings of Powerlessness

Teachers reported feeling "powerless" to teach. Perhaps their feelings of powerlessness can be explained by their focus on problems over which they had no control such as parent behaviors and poverty. By placing blame on students and other factors outside their control, teachers were not forced to examine their role in the student–teacher relationship, nor were they forced to re-examine their own behavior. However, research does support the strong emphasis that teachers placed on parental behavior, especially as it related to children's self-esteem (California Task Force, 1990).

Students also reported feeling "powerless" because of the way they were treated by teachers who were trying to maintain control in the classroom. Fighting was the behavioral problem most often cited by students. Studies have indicated that violence can arise out of a feeling of powerlessness or wanting to feel significant (California Task Force, 1990). Perhaps the students felt threatened by teacher attempts to maintain control and the students responded to this powerlessness, in part, by fighting with each other.

The students in this study, inner-city African American children living in poverty, were victims of discrimination and oppression. Society had failed to provide a safe environment in which these students could thrive. The result of society's failure was the "disorganized functioning" of the students' families, which in turn inhibited the development of the students' self-esteem and social skills (Pinderhughes, 1983).

Responses to Powerlessness

The students coped with their ensuing feelings of powerlessness by adapting values and roles that eased their frustration and gave them a false sense of power. For example, being "tough" and "oppositional" (that is, fighting) were roles students assumed in an attempt to feel powerful. Teachers and adminstrators interpreted these attempts to gain power as evidence that students lacked self-control and a positive value system.

The teachers manifested a sense of fatalism, demonstrated by a lack of introspection of their behaviors, and instead focused on outside factors. Their "controlling" behaviors in the classroom were also attempts to ease their frustration and regain power. The teachers' actions were interpreted by students as a "lack of respect" toward students.

The teachers and students were caught in a vicious cycle, colluding in their own powerlessness. For example, a student perceived that his or her teacher was not listening; the student began to disrupt the class; the teacher responded by reprimanding and belittling the student to regain control of the classroom; the student directed threatening statements toward the teacher; and the teacher sent the student to the principal's office. Therefore, the slightest gesture by either the teacher or the student could cause the cycle to run out of control—the teacher could not teach, and the student could not learn.

IMPLICATIONS FOR SCHOOL SOCIAL WORK INTERVENTION

The present study suggests that school social workers should focus on the student–teacher relationship, address the pervasive sense of powerlessness identified by both students and teachers, and be more inclusive of parents. Unfortunately, this study did not include the perspectives of parents. As a logical extension of the current needs assessment, the school social worker can facilitate a respectful discussion (where listening is paramount) between students, parents, and teachers and administrators about their differing perceptions as well as their mutual sense of powerlessness.

The social worker can create a context or framework for the discussion by providing the following information: a definition of empowerment (Freire, 1973, Pinderhughes, 1983); an explanation of power dynamics and systemic processes (Pinderhughes, 1983); an elucidation of how powerlessness may have been internalized by the students (or teachers) as "their fault," rather than as a response to systemwide discrimination (Wallerstein, 1992); an exposition of how students, parents, and teachers may be colluding in their own powerlessness (Pinderhughes, 1983); and a Freirian framework for developing a problem-posing discussion and an action strategy (Freire, 1973; Wallerstein & Bernstein, 1988). For example, Wallerstein and Bernstein's Freirian approach can facilitate critical thinking and problem-posing discussions among students, parents, and teachers that may lead to action strategies. Participants are asked to describe what they see and feel; as a group, to define the many levels of the identified problem; to share similar experiences from their lives; to question why this problem exists; and to develop action plans to address the problem.

It is important to inform participants that although problem-posing discussions are nurturing and will increase the social support network among students, parents, and teachers, change will evolve slowly. The school social worker must also be careful not to neglect efforts to bring about change in the larger environmental and societal contexts that were mentioned by the teachers. Interventions that focus only on increasing the participants' internal locus of control without changing oppressive conditions may actually increase the frustration and perceived powerlessness of all parties (Wallerstein, 1992).

The nominal group process allows site-based management teams to promote partnership among students, parents, and teachers. The process is inclusive and empowering because it generates opinions from a variety of perspectives, thereby laying the groundwork for interventions that can be designed to meet the specific needs of students in any given school.

REFERENCES

California Task Force to Promote Self-Esteem and Personal and Social Responsibility. (1990). *Toward a state of self-esteem.* Sacramento: California State Department of Education, Bureau of Publications.

Committee for Economic Development. (1987). *Children in need.* New York: Author.

Freire, P. (1973). *Education for critical consciousness.* New York: Seabury Press.

Gilmore, G. D. (1989). *Needs assessment strategies for health education and health promotion.* Indianapolis: Benchmark Press.

National Commission on Children. (1991). *Beyond rhetoric.* Washington, DC: Author.

Perry, N. (1988, November). Saving the schools: How business can help. *Fortune,* pp. 42–56.

Pinderhughes, E. B. (1983). Empowerment for our clients and ourselves. *Social Casework, 64*(6), 39–46.

Siegel, L. M., Attkisson, C. C., & Carson, L. G. (1987). Need identification and program planning in the community context. In F. M. Cox, J. L. Erlich, J. Rothman, & J. E. Tropman (Eds.), *Strategies of community organization* (4th ed., pp. 71–97). Itasca, IL: F. E. Peacock.

Siegel, L. M., Attkisson, C. C., & Cohn, A. H. (1974). *Mental health needs assessment: Strategies and techniques* (National Institute of Mental Health Report). Bethesda, MD: National Institute of Mental Health.

Streeter, C. L., & Franklin, C. (1993). Site-based management in public education: Opportunities and challenges for school social workers. *Social Work in Education, 15,* 71–81.

U. S. Bureau of the Census. (1993). *Statistical abstract of the United States: 1993* (113th ed.). Washington, DC: U.S. Department of Commerce.

Wallerstein, N. (1992). Powerlessness, empowerment, and health: Implications for health promotion. *American Journal of Health Promotion, 6,* 197–205.

Wallerstein, N., & Bernstein, E. (1988). Empowerment education: Freire's ideas adapted to health education. *Health Education, 15,* 379–394.

This chapter was originally published in the July 1995 issue of Social Work in Education, *vol. 17, pp. 139–147.*

Asian and Pacific Island Elders: Issues for Social Work Practice and Education

Colette Browne and Alice Broderick

The increasing numbers of aging people and the dramatic growth of America's ethnic and minority populations have resulted in greater demands for gerontological social workers sensitive to multicultural issues. This need is further accentuated by recent studies and reports that document the shortage of professionally trained social workers to serve older adults and their families (National Institute on Aging, 1987; Peterson, 1988) and data from the 1990 census that document the dramatic growth in the number of minority Americans (Bryant, 1991).

Ten percent of Americans 65 and older belonged to minority groups in 1980, and projections estimate that 20 percent of the nation's elderly population will be minorities by the year 2050 (U.S. Senate, 1989). Three factors predict a higher proportion of elder minorities in the next two decades: (1) the proportion of minorities in the total population is rising; (2) the elderly population is growing faster in minority groups than it is in the white population (Morrison, 1990); and (3) immigration is expected to contribute to increasing numbers of minority aged people (Torres-Gil, 1990). This chapter examines selected sociodemographic characteristics of the Asian and Pacific Island elderly population and discusses the implications for gerontological social work practice and education in ensuring quality of life for these elders and their families.

DEFINITION OF THE POPULATION

The Asian and Pacific Island population is an extremely diverse population composed of more than 30 cultures. Asians include but are not limited to Japanese, Chinese, Koreans, Filipinos,

Vietnamese, Asian Indians, Thais, Hmong, Indonesians, Pakistanis, Cambodians, and Lao. Pacific Islanders include Polynesians (Hawaiians, Samoans, Tongans), Micronesians (Chamorros [the indigenous people of Guam] and other groups), and Melanesians (Fijians) (U.S. Bureau of the Census, 1988). Each of these Asian and Pacific Island groups represents a culture unique in language, values, lifestyles, history, and patterns of movement and adaptation to America (Yip, 1990).

According to Ishisaka and Takagi (1982), "Asian and Pacific Islander" is an umbrella term that emerged during the civil rights movements and minority protests in the 1960s. Use of the term was a political stratagem to garner support in numbers and to build on loyalty and common concerns. As such, it has been successful, and yet it has also masked the many differences among the groups included in the category.

Data from the 1990 census indicate that the Asian and Pacific Island population, comprising 7,273,662 of the nation's nearly 250 million people, doubled in size between 1980 and 1990 (U.S. Bureau of the Census, 1991). The prior census also reported dramatic surges in Asian and Pacific Islanders, identifying a 120 percent growth rate between 1970 and 1980 (U.S. Department of Health and Human Services, 1985). Whereas the total U.S. population grew by nearly 10 percent from 1980 to 1990, the Asian and Pacific Island population grew by 108 percent, compared with 6 percent for whites, 13 percent for blacks, 38 percent for Native Americans/Eskimos/Aleuts, and 53 percent for Hispanics (Bryant, 1991). Data from the 1980 census identified 221,509 Asian and Pacific Islanders who were 65 and older (U.S. Bureau of the Census, 1990).

Ethnic Diversity

A key factor in describing Asian and Pacific Island older adults is understanding their ethnic diversity. The Asian and Pacific Island population is primarily Asian (93 percent), and the largest Asian groups are the Chinese, Filipinos, Japanese, Asian Indians, Indochinese, and Koreans (Liu & Yu, 1985). Of the remaining 7 percent who are Pacific Islander, Hawaiians are the most numerous (66 percent), followed by Samoans (15 percent), Chamorros (12 percent), and smaller numbers of other Pacific Islanders (Liu & Yu, 1985).

Geographic Location

The six states with the highest number of Asian and Pacific Islanders are California, Hawaii, New York, Texas, Illinois, and New Jersey (U.S. Bureau of the Census, 1991). Leung (1990) noted that the Asian American population is becoming more geographically dispersed, with the result that most communities will feel the presence of larger numbers of Asian and Pacific Islanders.

Gender Ratios

Of the 221,509 Asian and Pacific Islanders older than age 65 in 1980, 116,436, or 52.6 percent, were women. However, the ratio of females to males in the elderly population varied substantially by ethnic group. Among whites 65 and older, for example, there were 71.3 men for every 100 women in 1970. For elderly Japanese, the ratio was 76.7 per 100; for Chinese, 131.7 per 100; and for Filipinos, 431.4 per 100 (Markides & Mindel, 1987). These differences can be attributed primarily to the restrictive immigration policies of earlier years and are reflected in living arrangements and marital status. For example, a high proportion of Filipino males are single, and Chinese males are more apt to live alone than are elderly white males (Pacific/Asian Elderly Research Project, cited in Hooyman & Kiyak, 1991). Information on the lives of older Asian and Pacific Island women is virtually nonexistent.

Income and Poverty

Older Asian and Pacific Islanders, like other minority elders, have a lower economic status than white older Americans. According to the 1980 census, the median income of Asian and Pacific Island elders (those 65 years and older) was less than that of white older adults—$5,551 for men and $3,476 for women, compared with $7,408 for white men and $3,894 for white women (Yip, Stanford, & Schoenrock, 1989). Huge discrepancies exist in poverty rates among Asian and Pacific Island elders. The highest percentage of these elders with incomes reported below the poverty line were Vietnamese (36 percent), Hawaiian (26 percent), Samoan (23 percent), Asian Indian (20 percent), Chinese (16 percent), and Korean (16 percent) (Liu & Yu, 1985). Kim (1983) documented poverty levels as high as 40 percent among Asian and Pacific Island women older than 75.

Health Status

Information on the health status of Asian and Pacific Islanders is sketchy at best (U.S. Department of Health and Human Services, 1985). Theories have been proposed to explain the differential mortality of Asian and Pacific Islanders in the United States, including the impact of socioeconomic status, culture, and lifestyle (U.S. Department of Health and Human Services, 1985) and the devastating effect of oppression (Mokuau, 1990).

If longevity is a reliable indicator of good health, then certain members of the Asian and Pacific Island populations have the best health in the country. Chinese and Japanese Americans in particular have longer life expectancies than white Americans. However, Asian and Pacific Islanders in general have higher rates of tuberculosis, hepatitis, anemia, and hypertension than white Americans. Data also suggest that Japanese and Chinese American elders have a greater prevalence of multiinfarct dementia (Hasegawa, 1989) and are at greater risk of osteoporosis (Yano, Wasnich, Vogel, & Heilbrun, 1984) than the general population.

In general, Southeast Asians, many of whom are recent immigrants and refugees, and Pacific Islanders have poorer health than other Asians. Native Hawaiians, for example, experience proportionately more deaths from heart disease, cancer, diabetes, and accidents than all other ethnic groups residing in Hawaii (Mokuau, 1990). Furthermore, The Report of the Secretary's Task Force on Black and Minority Health (U.S. Department of Health and Human Services, 1985) noted that death rates among foreign-born Chinese, Japanese, and Filipinos are higher than among their American-born counterparts. Such statistics reveal wide differences among the ethnic subgroups that make up Asian and Pacific Island elders and suggest that aggregated data may be weighted toward the relatively healthy Asian subgroups rather than toward recent immigrants and Pacific Islanders (U.S. Department of Health and Human Services, 1985).

Service Use

Data suggest that minority elders do not receive health and social welfare benefits comparable to their needs (Cuellar & Weeks, 1980; Liu & Yu, 1987; Yip et al., 1989). A recent study on mental health service use reported that Asian and Pacific Islanders used fewer emergency room services and made fewer visits to office-based physicians than did white elders (Hu, Snowden, Jerrell, & Nguyen, 1991). Such data may suggest that Asian and Pacific Island elders delay seeking medical care until they are acutely ill. Delays such as this may be one reason why Asian and Pacific Island elders have a higher number of hospital days than white elders (Morioka-Douglas & Yeo, 1990).

Even though Asian American elders appear to have more mental health problems than their white counterparts (Kuo, 1984), mental health services use rates suggest low service use. Liu and Yu (1987) reported that the suicide rate for elderly Chinese women was 10 times that for white women. Liu and Yu also reported higher rates of suicide for the oldest (75 years and older) Chinese, Japanese, and Filipino men than for white men of similar ages (cited in Leung, 1990).

Researchers have listed a number of reasons for this apparent underuse of services. Among those identified are financial and language problems, a distrust of government programs, a belief that services based on a Western model of wellness are irrelevant, and the perception that staff are not culturally sensitive (Cox, 1991; Dhoomer, 1991; Sue & Sue, 1977). Gould (1988) suggested that professional views may also be to blame for low social services use rates, as Asians have been stereotypically identified as members of a model minority with no problems.

Cultural Values and Beliefs

Although there is diversity among Asian and Pacific Islanders and there are changes in values that result from assimilation, acculturation, and generational patterns, there appear to be certain values that are held in high esteem by all Asian and Pacific Islanders. These are the importance of the family and the great respect accorded to older adults. Family interdependence and conformity are significant, with elders viewed as family decision makers and the keepers of family and cultural wisdom. Confucian ideals and beliefs around filial piety and respect for the aged have strongly influenced the Chinese, Japanese, and Koreans. Among Japanese, *oyakoko* (filial piety) is expected of all children, and Korean families respect and honor older adults. The Filipino culture places great value on the practice of *utang na loob* (sense of obligation) among the younger family members toward their older ones. The Hawaiian word for family is *ohana,* and it is often the *kupuna* (elders) that are looked to for answers to family problems. The family is equally as important to Samoans, and the *aiga* (extended family) in Samoa is organized by its oldest family member.

Other values and beliefs have been described by a number of researchers. Kitano (1990) and others have listed a number of values common to Japanese Americans that may also be relevant to other Asian groups (Yee, 1990). Among these are family obligation and reciprocity, obedience to rules and roles, a sense of fatalism, filial piety, *enryo* (self-effacement), and use of indirect methods of communication. The avoidance of *hiya* (shame) and the respect for authority among Filipinos and the importance of *che myun* (face saving) among Koreans are strong cultural values, as is the importance of harmonious relationships with people and nature stressed among Hawaiians.

ISSUES FOR SOCIAL WORK PRACTICE

The proportion of minority clients seeking services from social welfare agencies is likely to increase substantially as the number of acculturated elders grows (Yip, 1990). The increasing numbers of ethnic and minority aged people suggest that identification of barriers to service use and the design and adoption of strategies for the delivery of culturally sensitive programs will be critical issues for social work practice in the future.

Identification of Barriers to Service Use

Whether ethnic and minority elders underuse social services is debatable (Rivas, 1990; Torres-Gil, 1990). However, studies have identified language problems, illiteracy, economics, and cultural values as often creating difficulties in minority groups' access to services (Cuellar & Weeks, 1980; Gelfand & Barresi, 1987; Kamikawa, 1987). A critical step in gaining access is knowing that the services or resources exist. Unfortunately, minorities are often at a disadvantage in this respect.

Widespread lack of literacy in any language makes it more difficult to publicize programs for minorities. Many older ethnic minority members, especially recent immigrants, are literate but do not speak or read English. Markides and Mindel (1987) noted the effectiveness of minority-oriented television and radio in increasing use of services. Providing program literature in languages other than English and supplying information through mass media that do not require the ability to read may thus increase minority access to services. Social services located in ethnic communities, free transportation, and program affordability can also increase program accessibility.

Design of Culturally Sensitive Programs and Services

Underuse also occurs when services are not, or are believed not to be, sensitive to cultural differences (Markides & Mindel, 1987). A variety of administrative and cultural barriers prevent use of services by minority groups. Yip (1990), for example, noted that the Administration on Aging's policy of requiring those who accompany an elder to a meal site program to pay the full fee for their meals may discourage participation in the nutrition program. For elders who care for their grandchildren, the cost of buying the youngsters' meals can be prohibitive. Clinical practice requires culturally sensitive approaches, bilingual staff, and staff knowledgeable about the cultural and historical background and values of the target population.

Concrete suggestions emerged from a study by Lee (1987) of agencies working with older adults through the Older Americans Act of 1965. Agencies that were successful in serving minority elders had the following characteristics: a location close to where minority elders live, the use of Asian and Pacific Islanders as staff and board members, active outreach programs, and opportunities for staff education to ensure sensitivity to values and variations within Asian and Pacific Island elderly populations. Programs like On Lok in San Francisco and Hale Pulama Mau and the Korean Care Home in Honolulu are just some of the programs that attempt to provide such culturally relevant services. Additionally, diversity among the Asian and Pacific Island elderly populations should be recognized and reflected in the design and delivery of social and health services. A Japanese elder residing in Hawaii has had very different experiences from a Japanese elder from California whose experience with government has been colored by his internment in a camp during World War II. The issue of trust in government services may be a much larger issue for the latter than the former, and use rates may reflect this.

Caring for Asian and Pacific Island elders often requires approaches that respect the role of the family and therefore include families in the planning of interventions. Practitioners and researchers have suggested a number of practice strategies including the use of problem-oriented rather than client-centered therapies (Dhoomer, 1991), behavioral approaches (Sue, 1981), and the use of indigenous social supports as valuable resources. Browne and Onzuka-Anderson (1988) described the situation in Hawaii:

> Hawaiian elders prefer to use the family as the vehicle for meeting needs. The process of *ho–oponopono*, whereby families get together to air out differences, is still used today. A Filipino elder, on the other hand, may rely on his province club (a social club made up of individuals who emigrated from the same province in the Philippines) in addition to his extended family. On the neighbor islands, Japanese elders benefit from the *ken*, or neighbor group, also tied to the prefecture of origin, that can provide support. (p. 110)

Other cultural traditions that have been used by various Asian and Pacific Island populations include the Filipino *Bayanihan*, or "working together" spirit; Japanese *Ku* organizations; and the Portuguese fraternal and religious organizations. Social workers should make efforts to include such indigenous supports and resources in evaluating needs and planning services while remaining aware of changes in ethnic communities (Kitano, 1990). Lee's (1987) study supports Kitano's statement, for those agencies with successful track records with minority elders recognized the value of enlisting indigenous people to serve on their boards and as staff.

ISSUES FOR SOCIAL WORK EDUCATION

Toward an Ethnogerontological Social Work Curriculum

Social work education will need to respond to these demographic trends and take the lead in developing and implementing an ethnogerontological curriculum for a changing America. Elements of a curriculum sensitive to older adults are described elsewhere (Schneider, 1984), as are curricula for Asian and Pacific Islanders (Pacific Asian Mental Health Research Center, 1978). However, few curricula appear to be responsive to these demographic trends (Kim, 1990; Sakauye, 1990). Given the dramatic growth of the Asian and Pacific Island population, it is timely for schools to implement such ideas now. Although providing information on specific cultures adds to a knowledge base and promotes culturally sensitive practice, educators know all too well the risk they run of reinforcing stereotypes by providing such information.

Curriculum Content in the Class and Field

One strategy for promoting effective practice with Asian and Pacific Island elders is to promote a greater awareness among students of the heterogeneity among Asian and Pacific Island elders. A curriculum that includes topics related to historical background, levels of acculturation and assimilation, nativity, and the role of ethnicity in aging can promote such knowledge.

Historical Background. Because Asian and Pacific Islanders share experiences of racism, discrimination, and isolation, familiarity with the historical background of political and social events preceding a move to a new country is critical in understanding the older adult's adjustment. Whether one immigrated by choice (Chinese), was forced to flee (Vietnamese), or was colonized (Native Hawaiians) influences how one uses services, the kinds of services one selects, and the presence or absence of trust placed in the American bureaucracy to solve problems. For example, the absence of trust could be one reason why Native Hawaiians, as a colonized race, have been found to underuse social welfare programs (Mokuau, 1990). Becoming knowledgeable about a group's history can assist social work students in understanding the call for parallel services by certain populations and the critical need to advocate for the legal and civil rights of clients.

Levels of Acculturation and Assimilation. Acculturation encompasses a wide continuum including assimilation, that is, the adjustment minorities make to become members of the mainstream culture without losing their own cultural traits. Those who have low levels of acculturation and assimilation may still embrace nontraditional or Asian health practices and may hesitate to use Western health facilities until acutely ill. For example, the Chinese interpretation of illness as an imbalance of the yin and yang is alien to Western diagnosis and treatments. Likewise, differing degrees and levels of acculturation and assimilation result in changing family caregiving responsibilities, as noted by Kitano and Daniels (1988), with implications for retirement planning and the delivery of home and community supports. It is also possible that lower levels of acculturation and assimilation can bring positive results. Another example is the *aiga*, or extended family of Samoa, which generally attempts to deal with mental health issues of family members, resulting in treatment that may be more culturally compatible with its members than Western mental health services.

Nativity. Nativity is defined as the place where an individual was born. Data suggest that those who are born outside of the United States have lower levels of income and poorer health, both associated with not speaking English (U.S. Department of Health and Human Services, 1985). Social workers should be able to identify those most at risk for poor health and other factors that impinge on well-being in later life and should apply primary, secondary, or tertiary interventions to counteract such factors.

Role of Ethnicity in Aging. Ethnicity has been seen as having both positive and negative influences on the aging process. On one hand, ethnicity has been generally viewed as a resource and strength, as seen in the provision of familial support and other informal resources (Browne & Onzuka-Anderson, 1988; Kitano, 1990). On the other hand, ethnic minority elders have lower incomes and poorer health than white elders, a result of racial discrimination, oppression, and cultural barriers. Social work students need to see both sides so that they neither romanticize the ethnic minority elderly population nor see them only as victims.

Knowledge of the role of ethnicity in aging would allow social workers to understand the ways in which problems are culturally defined; identify help-seeking behaviors that are culturally acceptable; distinguish the potential conflict between cultural beliefs of the dominant culture and the minority culture; and, in the end, adapt social work strategies for the most effective use with nonwhite populations. The importance of understanding values previously discussed is also essential. For example, interventions should acknowledge the preference among Filipinos for family care of the aged, but also the potential shame (hiya) if one is not able to do so and must instead rely on government services. Additionally, the network of indigenous supports should not be neglected in the design of treatment outcomes. Although such an agenda may appear overwhelming to social work educators and students, a curriculum that stresses family involvement, respect for the aged population, and patience and openness to a culture different from one's own will be a first step toward culturally sensitive practice.

Critical Need for Data

The education of multicultural social workers requires effective strategies that are empirically based. Good services are data dependent, and at this time there are no systematically gathered national data on the minority aging population other than those of the U.S. Bureau of the Census and the National Center for Health Statistics. The absence of solid descriptive and epidemiological studies on the minority aged population and on multicultural aging leaves many gaps in knowledge and needs to be corrected. Data are lacking that critically examine the influences of race, ethnicity, gender, age, and other variables. The absence of even simple descriptive data on Asian and Pacific Island elderly women is a serious problem (Gould, 1989). Specific values more common in Asian communities than in their white counterparts have been outlined earlier in this article, but studies have yet to examine what effect changes in such values, as noted by Kitano (1990), will have in the social policy and service delivery areas that rely on family responsibility.

CONCLUSION

Social workers face a number of challenges as they enter the 21st century. The number of Asian and Pacific Island elders, typically overlooked by policymakers and planners, will increase dramatically by the next century. The availability of culturally sensitive programs and services will be significantly affected by the knowledge and skills of social workers in the field, as well as by the direction of social work schools in the development and implementation of a multicultural curriculum. Without effective planning and the infusion of such a multicultural curriculum, future social workers will be hampered in their efforts to promote quality of life for all of America's aged people.

REFERENCES

Browne, C., & Onzuka-Anderson, R. (1988). Community support systems for the elderly in Hawaii. In D. Sanders & J. Fischer (Eds.), *Visions for the future: Social work and Pacific-Asian perspectives* (pp. 95–112). Honolulu: University of Hawaii, School of Social Work.

Bryant, B. E. (1991, March 22). *The 1990 Census and the implication of change.* Paper presented at a meeting of the Population Association of America, Washington, DC.

Cox, D. (1991). Social work education in the Asia Pacific region. *Asia Pacific Journal of Social Work, 1,* 6–14.

Cuellar, J. B., & Weeks, J. (1980). *Minority elderly Americans: The assessment of needs and equitable receipt of public benefits as a prototype in area agencies on aging* (Final Report). San Diego: Allied Home Health Association.

Dhoomer, S. S. (1991). Toward an effective response to the needs of Asian-Americans. *Journal of Multicultural Social Work, 1*(2), 65–82.

Gelfand, D., & Barresi, C. (Eds.). (1987). *Ethnic dimensions of aging.* New York: Springer.

Gould, K. (1988). Asian and Pacific Islanders: Myth and reality. *Social Work, 33,* 142–147.

Gould, K. (1989). A minority feminist perspective on women and aging. In J. D. Garner & S. O. Mercer (Eds.), *Women as they age* (pp. 195–216). Binghamton, NY: Haworth Press.

Hasegawa, K. (1989, October). *Research update on cross-cultural aspects of Alzheimers' disease in Japan.* Paper presented at the Asia Pacific Alzheimers' Disease Conference, Honolulu.

Hooyman, N., & Kiyak, H. A. (1991). *Social gerontology.* Needham Heights, MA: Allyn & Bacon.

Hu, T., Snowden, L., Jerrell, J., & Nguyen, T. (1991). Ethnic population in public mental health: Services choice and level of use. *American Journal of Public Health, 81,* 1429–1434.

Ishisaka, A., & Takagi, C. (1982). Social work with Asian- and Pacific Americans. In J. Green (Ed.), *Cultural awareness in the human services* (pp. 122–156). Englewood Cliffs, NJ: Prentice Hall.

Kamikawa, L. (1987). *Health care: The Pacific/Asian perspective.* Seattle: National Pacific/Asian Resource Center.

Kim, P. K. (1983). Demography of the Asian-Pacific elderly: Selected problems and implications. In R. L. McNeely & J. L. Cohen (Eds.), *Aging in minority groups* (pp. 29–41). Beverly Hills, CA: Sage Publications.

Kim, P. K. (1990). Asian American families and the elderly. In M. S. Harper (Ed.), *Minority aging: Essential curricula content for selected health and allied health professionals* (DHHS Publication No. HRS P-DV-90-4, pp. 349–363). Washington, DC: U.S. Government Printing Office.

Kitano, H. L. (1990). Values, beliefs, and practices of the Asian-American elderly: Implications for geriatric education. In M. S. Harper (Ed.), *Minority aging: Essential curricula content for selected health and allied health professionals* (DHHS Publication No. HRS P-DV-90-4, pp. 341–348). Washington, DC: U.S. Government Printing Office.

Kitano, H., & Daniels, R. (1988). *Asian Americans.* Englewood Cliffs, NJ: Prentice Hall.

Kuo, W. H. (1984). Prevalence of depression among Asian Americans. *Journal of Nervous and Mental Disorders, 172,* 449–457.

Lee, J. (1987). *Development, delivery, and utilization of services under the Older American's Act: A perspective of Asian American elderly.* Unpublished doctoral dissertation, University of Illinois, Urbana.

Leung, P. (1990). Asian Americans and psychology: Unresolved issues. *Journal of Training and Practice in Professional Psychology, 4*(1), 3–13.

Liu, W. T., & Yu, E. S. (1985). Asian/Pacific American elderly: Mortality differentials, health status, and use of health services. *Journal of Applied Gerontology, 4,* 35–64.

Liu, W. T., & Yu, E. S. (l987). Ethnicity and mental health. In *The Pacific/Asian Mental Health Center annual research review* (pp. 3–18). Chicago: University of Illinois.

Markides, K., & Mindel, C. (1987). *Aging and ethnicity.* Newbury Park, CA: Sage Publications.

Mokuau, N. (1990). The impoverishment of Native Hawaiians and the social work challenge. *Health & Social Work, 15,* 235–241.

Morioka-Douglas, N., & Yeo, G. (l990). *Aging and health: Asian/Pacific Island American elders* (SGEC Working Paper Series No. 3). Stanford, CA: Stanford Geriatric Education Center.

Morrison, M. (1990). Economic well-being and the aging of minority populations. In S. A. Schoenrock, J. L. Roberts, & J. Hyde (Eds.), *Diversity in an aging America: Challenges for the 1990s.* San Diego: National Resource Center on Minority Aging Populations.

National Institute on Aging, National Institutes of Health. (1987). *Personnel for health needs of the elderly through the year 2020* (DHHS-NIH Publication No. 87-2950). Washington, DC: U.S. Department of Health and Human Services.

Older Americans Act of 1965, P.L. 89-73, 79 Stat. 218.

Pacific Asian Mental Health Research Center. (1978). *Training mental health workers to serve Asian Americans.* Unpublished manuscript.

Peterson, D. A. (1988). *Personnel to serve the aging in the field of social work.* Washington, DC: Andrus Gerontology Center, University of Southern California, Los Angeles, and the Association for Gerontology in Higher Education.

Rivas, E. (1990, April/May). OAA 1991 reauthorization raises concerns about declines in minority participation. *Aging Connection,* pp. 8–9.

Sakauye, K. (1990). Differential diagnosis, medication, treatment and outcomes: Asian American elderly. In M. S. Harper (Ed.), *Minority aging: Essential curricula content for selected health and allied health professionals* (DHHS Publication No. HRS P-DV-90-4, pp. 331–339). Washington, DC: U.S. Government Printing Office.

Schneider, R. L. (1984). *Council on Social Work Education series in gerontology* (Vols. 1–4). Washington, DC: Council on Social Work Education.

Sue, D. (1981). *Counseling the culturally different.* New York: John Wiley & Sons.

Sue, D. W., & Sue, S. (1977). Barriers to effective cross-cultural counseling. *Journal of Counseling Psychology, 24,* 420–429.

Torres-Gil, F. (1990, April/May). The challenge of pluralism. *Aging Connection,* pp. 1–3.

U.S. Bureau of the Census. (1988). *Asian and Pacific Islander population in the United States, 1980.* Washington, DC: U.S. Government Printing Office.

U.S. Bureau of the Census. (1990). *Statistical abstract of the United States, 1980. The national data book.* Washington, DC: U.S. Government Printing Office.

U.S. Bureau of the Census. (1991, April). *Census and you* (Press Release CB91-100). Washington, DC: U.S. Government Printing Office.

U.S. Department of Health and Human Services. (1985). *The report of the Secretary's Task Force on Black and Minority Health: Vol. 1. Executive summary* (Publication No. 491-313/44706). Washington, DC: U.S. Government Printing Office.

U.S. Senate. (1989). *Aging America: Trends and projections* (Information paper to the Special Committee on Aging, U.S. Senate). Washington, DC: U.S. Government Printing Office.

Yano, K., Wasnich, R. D., Vogel, J. M., & Heilbrun, L. K. (1984). Bone mineral measurements among middle-aged and elderly Japanese residents in Hawaii. *American Journal of Epidemiology, 119,* 751–764.

Yee, B. (1990). *Variations in aging: Older minorities.* Galveston: Texas Consortium of Geriatric Education Centers.

Yip, B. (1990). Cultural changes. In S. A. Schoenrock, J. L. Roberts, & J. Hyde (Eds.), *Diversity in an aging America: Challenges for the 1990s.* San Diego: National Resource Center on Minority Aging Populations.

Yip, B., Stanford, E., & Schoenrock, S. (1989). *Enhancing services to minority elderly.* San Diego: National Research Center on Minority Aging Populations.

This chapter was originally published in the May 1994 issue of Social Work, *vol. 39, pp. 252–259.*

25 Building Strong Working Alliances with American Indian Families

Cass Dykeman, J. Ron Nelson, and Valerie Appleton

School social workers, counselors, and psychologists all work closely with students at risk for academic failure. One population at great risk is American Indian children. An element common to all tribal cultures is the salience parents and other elders have in the lives of these children. Thus, successful interventions with American Indian children can grow only out of a strong working alliance between school-based psychological and social welfare professionals and American Indian families. This chapter outlines the cultural knowledge on which such alliances can be built.

LITERATURE REVIEW

Professional literature in school social work, counseling, and psychology has thoroughly documented the at-risk status of American Indian children (Bert & Bert, 1992; Cahape & Howley, 1992; Coladarci, 1983; Dodd & Nelson, 1993; Dodd, Nelson, & Hofland, 1994; Gade, Hurlburt, & Fuqua, 1986; Gartrell, Jarvis, & Derksen, 1993; Herring, 1989; Hurlburt, Gade, & Fuqua, 1985). For instance, American Indian students have the highest dropout rate among all ethnic and racial groups (Reyhner, 1991). The professional literature has also reported that for American Indian children, self-esteem decreases as years of schooling increase (Luftig, 1983; Mitchum, 1989).

The literature unequivocally identifies the greatest potential source of help for these children—their parents and other adults (American Indian Science and Engineering Society, 1990; Herring, 1989; Martgan, 1979; Youngman & Sadongei, 1974). Yet stereotypical beliefs held by teachers and other educators alienate this most important resource (Burton, 1980).

American Indians value trust and understanding more than any other attributes in social workers, counselors, and psychologists (LaFromboise & Dixon, 1981; Lewis & Ho, 1979). These attributes form the basis of strong working alliances. Such alliances can combat school–home alienation and in turn can ameliorate at-risk status in children. For instance, Plas and Bellet (1983) pointed out that school psychologists can forge alliances through a greater understanding of the American Indians' unique cultures and value structures.

The best way to meet the needs of children is to support and build on the strengths of their families (National Information Center for Children and Youth with Disabilities, 1992). A wealth of techniques for getting parents involved exists in print (Fish, 1990; Hollifield, 1992; Inger, 1993, Jackson & Cooper, 1993; Palestis, 1993; Peterson & Warnsby, 1993; Schurr, 1993; Vandegrift & Greene, 1992). These techniques explain various ways to invite parental involvement in their child's schooling. However, school social workers, counselors, and psychologists must first understand the culture of any family to form an alliance and elicit parental involvement.

Families respond to invitations when the adult members have the confidence that they will be well received and respected. Thus, many cultural styles, values, and family structures in American society demand cultural awareness by school personnel. Moreover, this awareness is necessary to effectively carry out the techniques for getting parents involved.

KEY CULTURAL FACTORS

Cultural knowledge can help school social workers, counselors, and psychologists create effective working alliances with American Indian families. Cultural understanding can eliminate longstanding assumptions that American Indian children are deficient in their preparation for school and that their families have given them a poor start in life by fostering a more positive view of such children and their families. Also, cultural knowledge aids specialists in enhancing cultural sensitivity in the school (Murphy & Deblassie, 1984). Six cultural characteristics of American Indians influence the education of their children: geographical isolation, cultural heterogeneity, extended family, role of children, group primacy, and traumatic educational history.

Geographical Isolation

Although some American Indians live in urban areas, the majority live in rural settings (Bearcrane, Dodd, Nelson, & Ostwald, 1990). For instance, in Montana there are seven reservations, all of which are located in remote rural areas. Rural families frequently encounter concerns that urban families do not have to deal with. Hedge (1984) identified a variety of factors inhibiting interaction between families and school professionals in rural areas. In general, five of the identified factors pertain to American Indian families: (1) Rural communities' mores and values are different from those in urban areas; (2) rural families are reluctant to get involved with school authority figures; (3) vast distances, inclement weather, impassable roads, travel expenses, and time-consuming driving impede travel for the family and school staff; (4) adolescents frequently leave home at early ages; and (5) financial demands of services such as medical attention and baby sitting are often insurmountable.

Although geographical isolation significantly influenced the formation of American Indian cultures, the influence of cultural patterns transcends geography. Specifically, Red Horse et al. (1979, cited in Fenelon, Khoxayo, Kwiat, & Rodriguez, 1993) found that family values and communication patterns are not lost even if language and cultural orientation are reduced or even nonexistent.

Cultural Heterogeneity

The term "American Indian" serves as a sweeping label for 300 to 400 distinct ethnicities that speak at least 250 different languages (Churchill, 1985; Locke, Pfeiffer, Ridley, Simon, & Whiteman, 1977). As Gilliland (1992) pointed out, there are no "general" Indians. Therefore, no absolute universal cultural norms exist for American Indians. For example, a school social worker may elect to award an eagle feather to each member of an Adult Children of Alcoholics group during their final session. American Indians from many American Indian nations would view this as a culturally appropriate act on the part of the school social worker. However, Little Bear (1986, cited in Gilliland, 1992) stated that the granting of such an award to a female Cheyenne would be considered a spiritual taboo. Thus, in spite of positive intentions, the social worker's action could further distance the students and the students' families from the school.

In a counseling analogue study with American Indian students, LaFromboise (1992) found that American Indians gave a different meaning to interventions than the meanings the white counselors had intended. Accordingly, effective school social workers, counselors, or psychologists learn the cultural characteristics of the specific American Indian populations with whom they work (Dodd et al., 1994; Gilliland, 1992).

In addition to tribal cultural heterogeneity, considerable differences exist within each nation with respect to level of acculturation to the majority culture. Degree of acculturation ranges from total assimilation into the majority culture to retention of ancestral language, values, attitudes, and beliefs. Those who have retained their American Indian culture may be monocultural or bicultural (able to function in either culture). Tharp (1989) described bicultural status as accommodation without assimilation.

Some modern American Indians may feel completely displaced and uncomfortable in the majority culture and, at the same time, uncomfortable in traditional American Indian cultures (Glatt, 1965). Gilliland (1992) cautioned school personnel to not draw quick conclusions in this area:

> Don't make the mistake of thinking that the old tribal ways and values no longer have meaning for your students, or conversely, of expecting that most of your students are well grounded in their own tribal heritage. Every native child is somewhere in between the two cultures. He may be doing everything the way of the dominant culture and appear to have lost all native culture; still he may deep down feel the way he is doing things is wrong. His inner feelings may still be Indian. (p. 22)

Thus, school social workers, counselors, and psychologists must take the initiative not only to study the particular nation in their locality, but also to explore the personal aspect of each individual's cultural identity.

Extended Family

One of the greatest strengths common to American Indian cultures is the extended family. The importance given to family cannot be overstated. Children may view other members of their family such as aunts or grandparents as additional parents. It is common to find grandparents, aunts, uncles, cousins, or even friends of the family actively participating in the rearing of a child. These relationships may or may not be formalized by a tribal ceremony or court order. Thus, such arrangements are not necessarily indicative of a family's inability to care for a child; rather, they may reflect close family and friendship ties. Family welfare is considered more important than individual welfare. Child rearing is seen as the entire family's responsibility. For example, an extended-family member might be responsible for teasing children exhibiting inappropriate behavior.

Role of Children

American Indians respect children. Traditionally, American Indian people have been permissive and accepting of children. Although children are disciplined by adults, albeit with milder rebukes than the harsh verbal and physical expression of white counterparts, children are accorded the same degree of respect as adults (Hynd & Garcia, 1979). For example, young children are present and actively participate in events such as pow-wows. Furthermore, American Indian legends and stories have been passed down by older family members to both young children and adults.

Group Primacy

In American Indian cultures, people are judged by their contribution to the group rather than by individual achievement (Hynd & Garcia, 1979). Many young American Indian children perform better when involved in group activities. Even addressing children from across the classroom may be aversive to children who have been taught to value the group more than individual accomplishment. Thus, in contrast to the white family's emphasis on individual achievement and ownership, American Indian families place more emphasis on the group and community.

Traumatic Educational History

Although American Indians recognize schooling as a means to success and formal education as a necessity (Bearcrane et al., 1990), there is a legacy of fear and ambivalence. This legacy began when young American Indian children were taken forcibly from their family homes and placed in distant boarding schools where everything Indian, including language, was forbidden (Bearcrane et al., 1990). This practice dates from 1568 and ceased only in the middle half of this century (Eder & Reyhner, 1986; Laird, 1970). Such experiences evolved into stories used to frighten children: "If you are not good the missionaries or federal agents will take you to boarding school" (Bearcrane et al., 1990, p. 2). American Indians still pass on the frightening stories of harsh treatment in school. When American Indian children attend schools where the teacher is much more directly controlling than their parents and discipline more direct and harsh than they are accustomed to, the children may be frightened and withdraw. Nevertheless, American Indians generally hold a positive view of formal education, viewing it as a necessity to make vertical moves within the greater society.

IMPLICATIONS FOR PRACTICE

No school social worker, counselor, or psychologist can work effectively without attending to the specific cultural groups present at their work site. Without such an effort, human services professionals would cut off American Indian students from the key supports for their success—their family and people. School-based social workers, counselors, and psychologists do not have to create new work for themselves to serve as a catalyst for the formation of strong working alliances between American Indian families and schools. This alliance building best takes place through the common tasks of school-based psychological and social welfare professionals, such as prereferral activities, pedagogical consultation, and psychotherapeutic interventions. One note of caution—as noted above, generalities about American Indian culture have their limits. Any school social worker, counselor, or psychologist considering using the suggestions outlined in this section must take care to ensure these generalities fit the populations found at their work site.

Prereferral Activities

In comparison to the general student population, American Indian students are overrepresented in special education classes and underrepresented in gifted classes (Chinn & Hughes, 1987).

A number of researchers have suggested that the implementation of a prereferral intervention system would lead to more appropriate educational placements for American Indian students (Chinn & Hughes, 1987; Dodd & Nelson, 1993, in press; Dodd et al., 1994; Nelson, Smith, Taylor, Dodd, & Reavis, 1991). In any prereferral system, the establishment of a teacher assistance team is critical. The purpose of such a team is to make suggestions about educational procedures and practices that can be implemented by teachers in the regular classroom (Dodd & Nelson, in press). In reference to teacher assistance teams and ethnic diversity, Dodd and Nelson stated,

> Special education placement committees frequently interpret cultural and linguistic differences as deviant and the way to reduce the number of placements is to reduce the number of referrals. Therefore, teacher assistance teams could function to introduce appropriate procedures that are effective with youngsters who are linguistically and culturally different from the mainstream. To do this requires that at least one member of the team must be knowledgeable about the particular linguistic and cultural differences of the child being considered.

The accrediting bodies for social worker, counselor, and psychologist preparation programs all require coursework in multiculturalism. Thus, a school-based social worker, counselor, or psychologist could be assigned to serve as the team member who ensures that cultural issues are examined as Dodd and Nelson (1993) recommended. If a school social worker, counselor, or psychologist does not have a good working knowledge of a student's culture, this professional should work to ensure that an adult member of that culture is added to the team. This additional member could be a parent or other relative (Bromley & Olsen, 1994; Dodd & Nelson, in press; Sands, 1994).

Pedagogical Consultation

The classroom can be a very difficult and even hostile environment for American Indian students. Traditional Anglo American pedagogy often runs counter to American Indian learning styles and values (Swisher, 1990). School social workers, counselors, and psychologists can help teachers create more effective classrooms through direct consultation on American Indian cultures.

Two areas where a consult can lead to immediate instructional improvement are instructional speech patterns and instructional delivery.

Instructional Speech Patterns. There exist marked differences between Anglo American and American Indian speech in terms of cadence, tone, and quantity. American Indians tend to be less verbose and speak with a slower cadence and in lower tones than other Americans (Dodd et al., 1994; Gilliland, 1992; Honig, 1991; Taylor, 1991). As a result, Anglo American instructional speech can appear both rude and aggressive to American Indian children (Gilliland, 1992). Teachers who can modulate their speech patterns to better reflect American Indian cultural preferences will find their instruction to be more efficacious. For example, teachers can increase their wait time for a student response before moving to the next student for the answer. Increasing such wait time can enhance the quality of student responses (Dodd et al., 1994; Rowe, 1987).

Instructional Delivery. Traditional classroom instructional practices reflect the majority culture from which they emerge. In terms of this cultural influence, Gilliland (1992) stated,

> Whereas a large proportion of European-Americans learn easily through lecture, sequence, and the building of a concept from details, a greater percentage of Native Americans learn most easily when watching, imaging, and reflecting are emphasized. Many Native Americans learn most comfortably when we begin with a holistic view of a subject and are more concerned with feelings than with cold evidence. (p. 52)

In light of these differences, Gilliland suggested that teachers of American Indian students do the following in their classrooms: give students extended periods of observation before requesting the performance of a skill, create cooperative learning environments within the classroom, and allow students to respond with a demonstration rather than a verbal description. Swisher (1990) also cited the value of cooperative learning experiences for American Indian children. Besides the ideas presented above, Dodd and Nelson (in press) advised teachers to holistically explain or show a completed task before introducing the sequential steps required to accomplish that task.

Psychotherapeutic Interventions

To varying degrees, school social workers, counselors, and psychologists conduct psychotherapeutic interventions. The best predictor for the outcome of such interventions is the level of helping alliance between a therapist and client (Horvath & Greenberg, 1994; Horvath & Symonds, 1991; Luborsky, 1994). Such an alliance is based on a sense of collaboration on goals and tasks as well as a bond between therapist and client (Bordin, 1994). In psychotherapy, a client's failure to reveal the intimate details of his or her inner life or family dynamics after a brief period is often viewed as resistance by Anglo American therapists. However, the majority culture norm of quick self-disclosure does not extend to American Indians (Honig, 1991). Gilliland (1992) noted that American Indian students take a longer time than other students to reveal family or school problems to a counselor. Thus, school-based social workers, counselors, and psychologists should not read slow-developing self-revelatory behavior in their American Indian clients as a manifestation of resistance or as a therapeutic rupture. Professionals who engage in psychotherapeutic interventions with American Indian students must focus on rapport building for a longer period than is common with other students.

School social workers, counselors, and psychologists can enhance their work with American Indian students by integrating into their practice the key cultural factors outlined earlier in this article. For example, a school social worker planning a family therapy intervention can solicit from both a student and his or her parents information on which other family members should participate. This inclusion of extended family members taps a major strength of the American Indian family structure and thus increases the chances for a positive outcome. Also, extended family members can be invited to parent conferences concerning a student.

Because the strict adult–child social divisions in the majority culture are not present in American Indian culture, the inclusion of the student in such conferences will increase the relevance of these meetings for all participants. The addition of even elementary school students in parent–school professional conferences is becoming the suggested practice for all schools (Guyton &

Fielstein, 1989; Little & Allan, 1989). Finally, it is important to note that these inclusive practices can build stronger alliances between American Indian families and school social workers, counselors, and psychologists. Traditional Anglo American educational practices with American Indians have sought to reduce the influence of American Indian families. American Indian boarding schools are just the most pernicious example of these practices. By inviting family members to participate in the education of an American Indian student, the school social worker, counselor, or psychologist empowers American Indian families as agents of education and takes the first step toward healing a painful educational legacy of exclusion and isolation.

Besides familial cultural factors, school social workers, counselors, and psychologists who recognize the group primacy ethic among American Indian students can design even more effective psychotherapeutic interventions for these students. In other words, instead of relying on treatment modalities rooted in Anglo American culture (for example, individual talk therapy), a school social welfare or psychological professional can use techniques that better match the cultural preferences of American Indian students (Herring, 1989, 1990, 1992; LaFromboise & Dixon, 1981; Lofgren, 1981; Orlansky & Trapp, 1987; Trimble, 1981). One example of this matching would be the use of an art therapy group by a school social worker. Several researchers have noted the efficacy of art therapy with American Indian clients (Ashby, Gilchrist, & Miramontez, 1987; Burt Dtati, 1993; Dufrene, 1990; Ferrara, 1991; Lofgren, 1981). The use of art therapy in a group context capitalizes on the American Indian group primacy ethic and the preference for holistic communication styles. Thus, art therapy groups provide American Indian students with an opportunity for more culturally relevant expressions of their concerns about family, peers, and school. Moreover, these groups can provide a sense of safety within a historically threatening, Anglo American institution—the public school.

CONCLUSION

The professional associations for school social workers, counselors, and psychologists all demand that their membership both work to elicit parent involvement and demonstrate cultural sensitivity (American School Counselor Association, 1992; National

Association of School Psychologists, 1984; National Association of Social Workers, 1994). These demands are especially relevant to work with American Indian students. These students view their families as their greatest resource. Therefore, school social workers, counselors, and psychologists must strive to build strong working alliances with these resources.

The greatest stumbling block to the formation of such alliances is professional ignorance of a way of life that differs in ideas, habits, history, and language from the majority culture (Dodd & Vasi, 1970). School social workers, counselors, and psychologists can overcome this ignorance only through a firm understanding of the cultural characteristics outlined in this article. Moreover, such understanding is necessary if the cultural heritage and the identity of American Indians are to be preserved.

REFERENCES

American Indian Science and Engineering Society. (1990). *A parent's handbook.* Boulder, CO: Author. (ERIC Document Reproduction Service No. ED 343 742)

American School Counselor Association. (1992). *Ethical standards for school counselors.* Alexandria, VA: Author.

Ashby, M. R., Gilchrist, L. D., & Miramontez, A. (1987). Group treatment for sexually abused American Indian adolescents. *Social Work with Groups, 10,* 21–31.

Bearcrane, J., Dodd, J. M., Nelson, J. R. & Ostwald, S. W. (1990). Educational characteristics of Native Americans. *Rural Educator, 11,* 1–5.

Bert, C.R.G., & Bert, M. (1992). *Fetal alcohol syndrome in adolescents and adults.* Miami: Independent Native American Development Corporation of Florida. (ERIC Document Reproduction Service No. ED 351 167)

Bordin, E. S. (1994). Theory and research on the therapeutic working alliance: New directions. In A. O. Horvath & L. S. Greenberg (Eds.), *The working alliance* (pp. 13–37). New York: John Wiley & Sons.

Bromley, M. A., & Olsen, L. J. (1994). Early intervention services for Southeast Asian children. *Social Work in Education, 16,* 251–256.

Burt Dtati, H. (1993). Issues in art therapy with culturally displaced American Indian youth. *Arts in Psychotherapy, 20,* 143–151.

Burton, C. L. (1980, April). *Counseling Native American high school and college students.* Paper presented at the Eighth Annual Conference on Ethnic and Minority Studies, LaCrosse, WI. (ERIC Document Reproduction Service No. ED 190 330)

Cahape, P., & Howley, C. B. (1992). *Indian nations at risk: Listening to the people.* Washington, DC: U.S. Department of Education, Indian Nations at Risk Task Force. (ERIC Document Reproduction Service No. ED 339 588)

Chinn, P. C., & Hughes, S. (1987). Representation of minority students in special education classes. *Remedial and Special Education, 8,* 41–46.

Churchill, W. (1985). The situation of indigenous populations in the United States: A contemporary perspective. *Wicazo Sa Review, 1,* 30–35.

Coladarci, T. (1983). High school among Native Americans. *Journal of American Indian Education, 23,* 15–22.

Dodd, J. M., & Nelson, R. J. (1993). American Indian bilingual education: Making prereferral activities culturally relevant. *National Association of Bilingual Education News, 16,* 6–7, 25.

Dodd, J. M., & Nelson, R. J. (in press). Prereferral activities: One way to avoid biased testing procedures and possibly inappropriate special education placements for American Indian students. *Journal of Educational Issues of Linguistic Minority Students.*

Dodd, J. M., Nelson, R. J., & Hofland, B. H. (1994). Minority identity and self-concept: The American Indian experience. In T. M. Brinthaupt & R. P. Lipka (Eds.), *Changing the self: Philosophies, techniques and experiences* (pp. 307–336). Albany: State University of New York Press.

Dodd, J. M., & Vasi, J. J. (1970). Let's add inter-racial communication to the curriculum. *New York State Education Journal, 57,* 34–36.

Dufrene, P. (1990, April). *Exploring Native American symbols.* Workshop presented at the 30th National Art Education Association Conference, Kansas City, MO. (ERIC Document Reproduction Service No. ED 334 124)

Eder, J., & Reyhner, J. (1986). The historical background of Indian education. In J. Reyhner (Ed.), *Teaching the Indian child: A bilingual multicultural approach* (pp. 31–56). Billings: Eastern Montana College.

Fenelon, J., Khoxayo, P., Kwiat, J. A., & Rodriguez, B. M. (1993). Counseling culturally and linguistically diverse students. *Illinois Schools Journal, 72,* 15–32.

Ferrara, N. (1991). Luke's map of the journey: Art therapy with a Cree Indian boy. *Journal of Child and Youth Care, 6,* 73–78.

Fish, M. C. (1990). Best practices in family–school relationships. In A. Thomas & J. Grimes (Eds.), *Best practices in school psychology* (pp. 371–382). Washington, DC: National Association of School Psychologists.

Gade, E., Hurlburt, G., & Fuqua, D. (1986). Study habits and attitudes of American Indian students: Implications for counselors. *School Counselor, 34,* 135–139.

Gartrell, J. W., Jarvis, G. K., & Derksen, C. (1993). Suicidality among adolescent Albertan Indians. *Suicide and Life-Threatening Behavior, 23,* 366–373.

Gilliland, H. (1992). *Teaching the Native American.* Dubuque, IA: Kendall/Hunt.

Glatt, C. A. (1965). Who are the deprived children? *Elementary School Journal, 65,* 407–413.

Guyton, J. M., & Fielstein, L. L. (1989). Student-led parent conferences: A model for teaching responsibility. *Elementary School Guidance & Counseling, 24,* 169–172.

Hedge, D. (1984). Successful rural family–professional relationships. *Rural Special Education Quarterly, 5,* 4–5.

Herring, P. (1989). Counseling Native American children: Implications for elementary school counselors. *Elementary School Guidance & Counseling, 23,* 272–281.

Herring, P. (1990). Understanding Native American values: Process and content for counselors. *Counseling and Values, 34*, 134–137.

Herring, P. (1992). Seeking a new paradigm: Counseling Native Americans. *Journal of Multicultural Counseling and Development, 20*, 35–43.

Hollifield, J. (1992). *The league of schools reaching out: Getting parents going.* (Report No. 1, pp. 1–5). Baltimore: Center of Families, Communities, Schools, and Children's Learning.

Honig, B. (1991). *The American Indian: Yesterday, today, and tomorrow.* Sacramento: California Department of Education.

Horvath, A. O., & Greenberg, L. S. (1994). Introduction. In A. O. Horvath & L. S. Greenberg (Eds.), *The working alliance* (pp. 1–9). New York: John Wiley & Sons.

Horvath, A. O., & Symonds, B. D. (1991). Relation between working alliance and outcome in psychotherapy: A meta-analysis. *Journal of Counseling Psychology, 38*, 139–149.

Hurlburt, G., Gade, E., & Fuqua, D. (1985). *Study habits and attitudes of Indian students: Implications for counselor involvement.* Winnipeg, Manitoba, Canada: University of Manitoba. (ERIC Document Reproduction Service No. ED 272 349)

Hynd, G. W., & Garcia, W. I. (1979). Intellectual assessment of the Native American student. *School Psychology Digest, 8*, 446–454.

Inger, M. (1993). Getting parents involved. *Education Digest, 58*, 32–34.

Jackson, B. L., & Cooper, B. S. (1993). Involving parents in urban high schools. *Education Digest, 58*, 27–31.

LaFromboise, T. D. (1992). An interpersonal analysis of affinity, clarification, and helpful responses with American Indians. *Professional Psychology: Research and Practice, 23*, 281–286.

LaFromboise, T. D., & Dixon, D. N. (1981). American Indian perception of trustworthiness in a counseling interview. *Journal of Counseling Psychology, 28*, 135–139.

Laird, D. B. (1970). *De-Indianizing the American Indian: An essay on the education of the American Indian.* Ann Arbor: University of Michigan. (ERIC Document Reproduction Service No. ED 062 027)

Lewis, R. G., & Ho, M. K. (1979). Social work with Native Americans. In D. Atkinson, S. Morton, & D. Sue (Eds.), *Counseling American minorities* (pp. 51–58). Dubuque, IA: William C. Brown.

Little, A. W., & Allan, J. (1989). Student-led parent conferences. *Elementary School Guidance & Counseling, 23*, 210–218.

Little Bear, D. (1986). Teachers and parents: Working together. In J. Reyhner (Ed.), *Teaching the Indian child: A bilingual multicultural approach* (pp. 222–231). Billings: Eastern Montana College.

Locke, P. A., Pfeiffer, A. B., Ridley, J. B., Simon, S. M., & Whiteman, H. (1977). The American Indians. In M. J. Gold, C. A. Grant, & M. N. Rivlin (Eds.), *In praise of diversity: A resource book for multicultural education* (pp. 80–124). Washington, DC: Teacher Corps, Association of Teacher Educators.

Lofgren, D. E. (1981). Art therapy and cultural difference. *American Journal of Art Therapy, 21*, 25–30.

Luborsky, L. (1994). Therapeutic alliances as predictors of psychotherapy outcomes: Factor explaining the predictive success. In A. O. Horvath & L. S. Greenberg (Eds.), *The working alliance* (pp. 38–50). New York: John Wiley & Sons.

Luftig, R. L. (1983). Effects of schooling on the self-concept of native American students. *School Counselor, 30,* 251–260.

Martgan, R. H. (1979). *Elementary guidance program.* Window Rock, AZ: Bureau of Indian Affairs, Navajo Area. (ERIC Document Reproduction Service No. ED 186 161)

Mitchum, N. T. (1989). Increasing self-esteem in Native-American children. *Elementary School Guidance & Counseling, 23,* 266–271.

Murphy, S., & Deblassie, R. R. (1984). Substance abuse and the Native American student. *Journal of Drug Education, 14,* 315–321.

National Association of School Psychologists. (1984). *Principles for professional ethics.* Washington, DC: Author.

National Association of Social Workers. (1994). *NASW code of ethics.* Washington, DC: Author.

National Information Center for Children and Youth with Disabilities. (1992). *A parent's guide: Accession programs for infants, toddlers, and preschoolers with disabilities.* Washington, DC: Author.

Nelson, J. R., Smith, D. J., Taylor, L., Dodd, J. M., & Reavis, K. (1991). Prereferral intervention: A review of research. *Education and Treatment of Children, 14,* 243–253.

Orlansky, M. D., & Trapp, J. J. (1987). Working with Native American persons: Issues in facilitating communication and providing culturally relevant services. *Journal of Visual Impairment and Blindness, 81,* 151–155.

Palestis, E. (1993). Prize-winning parent involvement in New Jersey. *Education Digest, 58,* 14–17.

Peterson, C. I., & Warnsby, E. (1993). Reaching disengaged parents of at-risk elementary schoolers. *Education Digest, 58,* 22–26.

Plas, J. M., & Bellet, W. (1983). Assessment of the value attitude orientations of American Indian children. *Journal of School Psychology, 21,* 57–64.

Red Horse, J. G., Lewis, R., Feit, M., & Decker, J. (1979). Family behavior of the urban American Indians. In G. Henderson (Ed.), *Understanding and counseling ethnic minorities* (pp. 307–317). Springfield, IL: Charles C Thomas.

Reyhner, J. (1991). *Plans for dropout prevention and special school support services for American Indian and Alaska Native students.* Washington, DC: U.S. Department of Education, Indian Nations at Risk Task Force. (ERIC Document Reproduction Service No. ED 343 762)

Rowe, M. B. (1987). Wait time: Slowing down may be a way of speeding up. *American Educator, 11,* 38–43, 47.

Sands, R. G. (1994). A comparison of interprofessional and team–parent talk of an interdisciplinary team. *Social Work in Education, 16,* 207–219.

Schurr, S. (1993). Sixteen proven ways to involve parents. *Education Digest, 58,* 5–8.

Swisher, K. (1990). Cooperative learning and the education of American Indian/Alaskan Native students: A review of the literature and suggestions for implementation. *Journal of American Indian Education, 29*, 36–43.

Taylor, G. (1991). Time is round. *Journal of Navajo Education, 8*, 48–49.

Tharp, R. G. (1989). Psychocultural variables and constants: Effects on teaching and learning in schools. *American Psychologist, 44*, 349–359.

Trimble, J. E. (1981). Value differentials and their importance in counseling American Indians. In P. B. Pederson, J. E. Draguns, W. J. Lonner, & J. E. Trimble (Eds.), *Counseling across cultures* (pp. 203–226). Honolulu: University of Hawaii Press.

Vandegrift, G., & Greene., A. L. (1992). Involving parents of the at-risk: Rethinking definitions. *Educational Leadership, 50*, 57–59.

Youngman, G., & Sadongei, M. (1974). Counseling the American Indian child. *Elementary School Guidance & Counseling, 8*, 273–277.

This chapter was originally published in the July 1995 issue of Social Work in Education, *vol. 17, pp. 148–158.*

26 Culturally Relevant School Programs for American Indian Children and Families

Cynthia Franklin, John Waukechon, and
Peggy S. Larney

According to the 1990 census there are approximately 2 million American Indians in the United States, an increase of a half a million Indian people since 1980. These statistics are believed to underrepresent the actual numbers of American Indians living in urban areas, where Indians tend to blend with Euro-American culture.

American Indians are a diverse people from distinct cultures that represent over 500 nations and speak more than 200 different languages. Cherokees have the largest tribal affiliation, whereas the Navajo have the largest reservation and trust lands. Most states have substantial Indian populations, but the majority of American Indian children and families live in California, Oklahoma, New Mexico, Arizona, Alaska, North Carolina, and Washington. California, Oklahoma, Arizona, and New Mexico each have over 100,000 American Indians living in the state (Hodgkinson, Outtz, & Obarakpor, 1990; McQuiston & Brod, 1985; Reyhner, 1990; Thompson, Walker, & Silk-Walker, 1993).

Review of the research literature indicates that American Indian children and their families are an extremely vulnerable population and are at greater risk than other ethnic groups for developing serious psychosocial problems such as alcoholism, substance abuse, low self-concept, suicide, and other psychiatric disorders (Dana, 1993; Nel, 1994; Yates, 1987). Consequently, American Indian children are categorized as an "at-risk" population by many school districts. Thompson et al. (1993), however, cautioned practitioners to view this research with skepticism. Because of unrepresentative samples, these characterizations of

American Indians are stereotypes drawn from a select few individuals. Researchers emphasize that there are large intragroup differences among American Indians and intergroup differences among tribes.

Regardless of their individual vulnerabilities, most American Indian children and their families are poor. Hodgkinson et al. (1990) estimated that the poverty rate for American Indian families was considerably higher (24 percent) than the rate for the general population (10 percent). According to Reyhner (1990), living conditions on reservations are especially impoverished, with 45 percent of residents living below the poverty line. Twenty-one percent of families on reservations, for example, live without piped water, and 16 percent are without electricity. Approximately 100,000 American Indian children between the ages of five and 17 years live on reservations, but the majority live in low-income urban areas. The Los Angeles metropolitan area, for example, has the largest population of urban American Indians (McQuiston & Brod, 1985; Reyhner, 1990). Urban American Indians differ from those on reservations because they are usually one or two generations removed from their tribal heritage and its customs.

This chapter reviews current issues concerning American Indian families and the education of Indian children. Urbanization of American Indians and its implications for their relationships with the public schools are highlighted. The chapter discusses the need for culturally relevant school programs for American Indian children and their families and highlights several American Indian educational reform movements aimed at achieving this goal. The American Indian Education Act of 1972 (P.L. 92-318) programs are discussed and illustrated with two examples from Texas.

AMERICAN INDIAN CHILDREN AND PUBLIC EDUCATION SYSTEMS

Throughout their history public education systems have greatly affected American Indian children and their families. In the name of education many atrocities were committed against Indians; children were separated from their families and sent to residential boarding schools run by the federal government (Thompson et al., 1993). In 1990, only one-third of American Indian children who lived on reservations attended Bureau of Indian Affairs (BIA) schools. Approximately 90 percent of all American Indian children attended public schools instead of reservation or BIA schools (Reyhner, 1990). Conservative estimates indicate that in 1990 approximately 390,000 Indian children attended public elementary and secondary schools.

American Indian students have the largest dropout rate among ethnic groups. The National Center for Education Statistics (1988) reported that in 1987, 35.5 percent of Indian students dropped out of school in comparison to 27.7 percent of Latino students and 22.2 percent of African American students. Reports from American Indian tribal leaders and other sources indicate that the dropout rates for American Indian students may be higher than reported by many school districts. In a cohort dropout study, for example, Eberhard (1989) found that the dropout rate was substantially higher for American Indian students than the rate calculated by the school district. A report from the Center for Indian Education, derived from longitudinal studies conducted between 1969 and 1989 (Swisher, Hoisch, & Pavel, 1991), stated that the best estimate of the American Indian dropout rate was 24 percent to 48 percent.

American Indian students are also more likely to be referred for special education than other students. Nel (1994) noted that a report from the BIA stated that 11 percent of American Indian sophomores were in special education compared with 7 percent of Latino students and 9 percent of African Americans. Cummins (cited in Nel, 1994) attributed the failure of American Indians in school to relationships between teachers and students and school and ethnic communities' intergroup power structures.

Four factors, identified by Cummins (cited in Nel, 1994), may improve the relationships between schools and American Indian communities and empower Indian students: (1) including language and culture as a part of the school program; (2) encouraging partnership and participation from American Indian parents and communities; (3) actively promoting intrinsic reward for the use of their native language; and (4) advocating for students in the school assessment process. Nel (1994) also discussed the need to teach American Indian children about the dominant school culture. Several authors have also pointed to the benefits of positively orienting American Indian students to their own culture as well (Lake, 1990; McQuiston & Brod, 1985; Ogbu, 1987).

AMERICAN INDIAN EDUCATION REFORM MOVEMENT

There is an active American Indian education reform movement in the United States aimed at helping public schools be more culturally sensitive to American Indian students by incorporating the students' history, language, and culture into the school environment. As with any reform movement, many of the substantive changes are initiated from grassroots constituencies such as American Indian parents and tribal leaders. Professional groups such as the National Indian Education Association, Coalition for Indian Education, Coalition of Indian Controlled School Boards, and the American Indian Special Interest Group of the American Educational Research Association were established as a result of these reforms and advocate for their continuation.

The BIA has contributed to the American Indian education reform movement by using the Goodlad (1994) model to identify effective school correlates for providing culturally relevant and successful school programs for American Indians. Correlates identified for effective schools include

1. a clear school mission that incorporates respect for the Native American culture
2. assessment of comprehensive needs and monitoring of student progress, including individualized, social, and community assessments
3. appropriate curriculum and instruction that incorporates a culturally based curriculum
4. ample opportunity to learn and to spend time on tasks, meaning that schools must adopt a student-centered rather than a content-centered focus
5. high expectations that establish rewards consistent with American Indian cultures
6. safe and supportive environment, including counseling and increased safety from exposure to alcohol and other drugs around the school
7. good home, school, and community relationships that bridge alienation and involve American Indian parents and communities in the school
8. instructional leadership in the form of supportive services from the BIA and American Indian leaders (Gipp & Fox, 1991).

AMERICAN INDIAN EDUCATION ACT

Perhaps the most relevant educational policy reform that has contributed to improved education for American Indians is the American Indian Education Act of 1972 (P.L. 92-318). This act provided funding for special programs for Indian children in reservation schools and for the first time also provided funds for urban American Indian children attending public schools (Reyhner & Eder, 1990). In 1975 the act was amended to require that committees of American Indian parents be involved in the oversight and guidance of the special school programs. Amendment guidelines also encouraged community-run schools and culturally relevant reforms in curriculum, such as bilingual curriculum materials.

The American Indian Education Act was reauthorized in 1988 as Title V and in 1994 as Title IX (Indian, Native Hawaiian, and Alaskan Native Education) as a part of P.L. 103-382, the Improving America's Schools Act of 1994. Title IX is a federal formula-grant program available to any local education agency that has 10 or more American Indian students enrolled. Funding is based on the number of students enrolled in a project. For purposes of Title IX programs, students are considered "Native American" if they are members of a nation, band, or group of Indians or a terminated group or if they are Alaskan Native. In addition, any student who has one parent or grandparent who was a member of any of these groups is eligible for services.

Readers unfamiliar with definitions of "Native American" should know that the definition in the act differs from the definitions used by the federal government and by many nations in defining requirements for membership in American Indian nations. The federal government, for example, often defines American Indians as people who have documented that they are at least one-eighth American Indian. American Indian nations, on the other hand, set their own standards for accepting members and may require varying percentages of Native American blood or documentation of an ancestor's name.

There is wide variation in the types of programs established through Title IX. For example, some programs are very small and only have funds to provide limited cultural awareness activities in the school or special curricular assistance such as visual learning libraries. Other programs include more comprehensive assistance to American Indian students and their families such as case management, referral, counseling, and direct advocacy for students as well as cultural awareness promotion in the school and community. Regardless of the interventions provided, two components that are common to all Title IX programs are academic assistance and cultural education.

TITLE IX PROGRAMS IN TEXAS

Six Title IX programs were developed to serve American Indian children in Texas. The 1990 census indicated that there were approximately 65,000 American Indians in Texas, the majority of them living in nonreservation areas. Title IX programs were developed in Ysleta Independent School District (ISD) (serving Tigua Indians); Eagle Pass ISD (serving Kickapoo Indians); and Austin, Dallas, Fort Worth, and Grand Prairie ISDs, which serve a variety of urban Indians. In addition to these programs, other programs are in the planning stages (for example, Houston). The two Texas Title IX programs discussed in this article, the American Indian Education Projects of the Dallas and Austin ISDs, serve as examples of the range and types of Title IX programs that a school district can offer to American Indian students and their families.

Dallas ISD American Indian Education Project

The Dallas ISD American Indian Education Project started in 1975 and is the oldest American Indian education program in Texas. The Title IX project serves 674 American Indian students, prekindergarten to grade 12, and their families representing 59 different nations. Half of the families are low income and in need of income assistance. Two full-time staff work for the project, and many volunteers help operate the programs offered. The budget for 1994–95 was $89,933.

Historically, Dallas served as a relocation center for American Indian families, and starting a program in the school district seemed like a natural extension of this effort. American Indian parents and community leaders became active in the development of the program, and the program quickly evolved to provide supplemental services to meet the special educational and culturally related academic needs of the American Indian students.

Currently, the Dallas program provides intensive personal and academic intervention and support services as well as cultural education. Three large events are sponsored to involve parents and American Indian communities in the school: a basketball tournament, a tribal–nontribal higher education fair, and an awards ceremony.

For nine years the Dallas program has sponsored a basketball tournament involving American Indian students throughout the north Texas area. This event provides an opportunity for American Indian students to congregate and celebrate their tribal heritage. The tribal–nontribal higher education fair brings tribal higher education officers and recruiters from the BIA-sponsored colleges and other colleges with strong Indian student populations. These individuals serve as examples and show students that there are culturally relevant colleges that they can attend. The awards ceremony is designed to honor American Indian students for successfully completing another year of school. This event is held toward the end of the school year and allows American Indian families to gather to honor their children.

Cultural education is provided in the form of in-service training to teachers and student services professionals, and other training is provided for community groups. The program also provides a resource manual on American Indians. Much of the training and education centers on debunking stereotypes and myths about American Indians that have been passed down through several sources including the professional literature. Examples of myths include the following:

- All American Indian children are visual learners.
- American Indian children do not make eye contact with authority figures.
- American Indians loathe competition.

Although some of these stereotypes may have been true for a few tribal cultures (but not all), most American Indian children in urban areas are far removed from such traditions or learning styles.

The training also emphasizes ways to produce pride in American Indian heritage by educating groups on the uniqueness of tribes and their triumphant histories. For example, many people do not know that the Cherokees were a prosperous and well-educated people who had their own advanced educational systems. In fact, white settlers often intermarried with the Cherokees so they could improve their social and economic status. In addition, training focuses attention on raising teachers' cultural sensitivity in the classroom by helping them understand how Euro-American culture may affect American Indian students. For example, teachers are coached on avoiding phrases such as "sit Indian style" or "Indian giver."

The Dallas ISD's American Indian Education Project also provides intensive personal counseling and assistance to American Indian children and their families. Staff serve as home–school–community liaisons among American Indian children, families, community agencies, and the school. If an American Indian student is having a problem in the school, the liaison interviews the students and family and sets up a problem-solving meeting with student, family, and faculty. Home visits are conducted to assess crisis situations and to intervene in problem areas such as truancy and imminent dropout. Staff also serve as case managers, making referrals to school programs and community agencies; they follow up on the status of students once they are in contact with these programs. A considerable amount of advocacy work is completed in the course of making referrals, such as helping students obtain appropriate assessment and tutoring services for their academic needs or obtaining needed assistance from social services agencies.

Although the Dallas American Indian Education Project has been in operation for the past 20 years, no formal program evaluations or outcome studies have been conducted on the program. No funding is provided for outcome research by the American Indian Education Act, and the school district has not provided the funds for an evaluation. Because the program is a supplemental service, it does not fall under the auspices of the Texas Education Agency, which might be another source or facilitator of funding for research. In the absence of research, staff rely on anecdotal reports, case studies, and descriptive information about the programs' effectiveness in providing services to large numbers of American Indian students, many of whom have had positive outcomes in their achievement tests and graduation rates.

Case Example

Sue was one-fourth Osage Indian. She was a 17-year-old junior who attended a school with a predominantly African American student population. She was an average student. Sue lived with her mother and two younger siblings, Tory, age 7, and Chris, age 14. The mother was unemployed and receiving Aid to Families with Dependent Children. The American Indian Education Program became involved with this family when Sue attended a school support group to discuss her American Indian heritage.

Through a newsletter produced by the Dallas program, the mother also contacted the program and sought to reclaim her tribal identification. According to family reports the mother is one-half Osage. She studied the Osage traditions and identified herself as an American Indian. She also taught her children about their heritage. The mother, however, was adopted in childhood, and her adoption papers were not available. The liaison worked with the mother to help her obtain the appropriate documentation. Some family members, however, did not want to be associated with their American Indian heritage, and one generation in the family did not seek documentation, thus making it harder for the mother or Sue to ever "officially" prove their heritage.

For three years Sue often came by the program office to say hello and for encouragement. The American Indian Education Program frequently gave her school supplies for her and her siblings. One day Sue and her younger sister came by the office to ask for help. Her brother had been expelled for carrying a knife and remained out of school. Her brother was referred to the school truancy program and several youth agencies that could intervene with him.

Sue suddenly dropped out of school without seeking advice from anyone. The liaison made a home visit to assess the situation. There were problems at home because her mother was drinking and using drugs, and her brother was fighting with the mother. Because of the home situation Sue was missing school, causing her to be cited for absenteeism and low grades.

Sue asked for help in obtaining her general equivalency diploma (GED), and the liaison gave her information about the test. Using the information provided, Sue went to the library, checked out GED books, studied on her own, and completed the tests, passing on the first try with high marks. Sue was very proud of her achievement and came by the program office to show her certificate so it could be placed in her folder. The program reinforced her accomplishments with a letter of congratulations. Sue discussed future goals of wanting to be "emancipated" from her mother so that she could live independently. She also wanted to take care of her sister. Sue was interested in entering junior college and studying to be a nurse's aide or a therapist. The liaison referred her to counselors in the junior college system who could help her enroll. Sue was also very proud of her American Indian heritage and wanted to further pursue documentation. She was referred to the American Indian Legal Project for assistance.

Austin ISD American Indian Education Project

The Austin ISD American Indian Education Project is small but active. The project serves 85 of the district's approximately 70,000 students (0.1 percent). For 1994–95, the total budget for the project was less than $10,000. Therefore, there is only one part-time staff member (project facilitator) who works nine hours per week. Most of the program is operated through parent volunteers and other community members.

The Austin project was started by a group of concerned central Texas parents, most of them American Indian. In the $1\frac{1}{2}$ years since the project facilitator was hired, both informal and formal needs assessments have been conducted involving Austin ISD parents, students, teachers, principals, and American Indians in the central Texas area. These assessments have included written forms, conversations with parents and students, staff observations, and spoken and written comments about various project events.

These methods of gathering information have consistently revealed three important needs of Austin's Native American students: American Indian identity reinforcement, acquisition of knowledge of tribal and cultural heritage, and help in staying in school. Specific methods of addressing these issues were created by the project facilitator in close consultation with the parents' advisory group, the Native American Parents' Committee, that works with the project. The methods developed to meet these needs have all been designed for a project with limited funding and personnel.

To address the needs of American Indian students for reinforcement of their Indian identity, the Parents' Committee and its support group, First Americans of Central Texas (FACT), sponsor an annual Powwow and Heritage Festival. Such an event offers children who live a great distance from tribal headquarters or homelands a chance to participate in a cultural activity that American Indian students in many parts of the country attend regularly. An end-of-the-year awards ceremony is held and serves the same purpose as the one held in Dallas. Because the Austin project serves 37 campuses, some of the students in the project are the only American Indian on their campus and rarely see other American Indians during the school day. The interaction provided by the awards ceremony is rare for these students and therefore important.

The dropout problem is addressed through a mentoring program. This program is attached to the districtwide Project Mentor. Adults interested in the education of American Indian students, most of them American Indians themselves, are trained to serve as mentors. Mentors meet with the children once a week at school to help with homework, to talk, and to be a friend. After the mentors are trained, the facilitator takes requests for mentors from parents of children served by the project. The mentoring program has been in effect only one school year, so it is too early to tell what effect, if any, it has had on the dropout rate of Austin's American Indian students. In fact, no program evaluations or outcome studies have been conducted on the Austin project. Given the limited nature of the program budget, no studies have been planned. Staff, however, gauge their progress by attendance rates at the planned cultural events and anecdotal consumer satisfaction reports from the Austin Indian community.

The three programs described are primarily educational in nature. But the Austin project has been called on to address family and social needs as well. Because the nature of this project is cultural and educational, intervention in family and social difficulties is entirely ad hoc. Families in economic difficulties, for example, often request help with purchasing school supplies. Common problems brought to the project's attention include academic and social problems in school and the possibility of dropping out of school. These cases challenge the part-time staff and require a great amount of referral and coordination.

Ad hoc interventions are provided by project staff and concerned members of the Central Texas Indian community when
crisis situations develop. Given the few personnel available in
the project office, emphasis is placed on referring children and
their families to school social workers, counselors, or community agencies who can meet their needs. In this way, the Austin
Title IX project serves as a liaison to support services rather than
as a provider of such services.

Families that retain enough cultural identification to call themselves American Indian also face additional challenges. When
children claim to be members of a tribe or descendants of tribal
members, their claims are often challenged. Many of the students
and families face cultural isolation in their attempts to retain traditions others now ignore or have forgotten. Other families and
children have retained little knowledge of the traditions of their
tribes; these students know they are American Indian but may
not know what that means.

Educational programs have been created in the past two years
to help reinforce and support the cultural identity of all the students in the Austin project. Through the implementation of cultural education meetings and classes in the community taught
by other American Indians, students and families are supported
in identifying with and drawing strength from their cultural
heritage.

Case Example

Wanda was a 16-year-old high school junior who dropped out of
school for one semester but later entered a alternative school run
by Austin ISD to complete her education. She was half American
Indian (Seminole and Choctaw) and half Mexican American. Her
mother was a full-blooded Indian, half Seminole and half Choctaw,
and her father was Mexican American. Her parents were divorced.

Wanda first came to the project seeking help with her gym class.
She did not have enough money to buy the clothes required for
participation in the class and was being penalized for not "dressing out" in gym. She was very embarrassed about her situation.
The American Indian Education Project worked with the school
to help her obtain the appropriate clothing. After that she became very active with the program.

Wanda was very eager to learn more about her American Indian heritage and brought her mother to community meetings.

The staff knew her mother from other community activities, and she was very supportive of her daughter's education. She had recently joined the parents' advisory committee.

Both Wanda and her mother reported feeling cut off from their American Indian heritage and were very thankful for the project. The family lived in a low-income neighborhood that was primarily Latino, and Wanda felt that people did not understand her American Indian heritage. At one time she said that she felt pressure to disavow her American Indian heritage in favor of her Mexican American heritage because it seemed like the more popular thing to do. She said she did not do so because she knew it would hurt her mother deeply.

Wanda married a full-blooded Alabama–Coushatta Indian, who left for the Marines. She also became pregnant but wanted to return to school. The American Indian Project referred her to an alternative school to continue her education.

In general, Wanda was a good student, especially excelling in mathematics. She volunteered to work in the mentor program and served as a mentor to an eighth-grade Indian student who was having difficulty with algebra. She also asked for help from a mentor when she was having difficulty with her government class. She was very active in the awards ceremony. The staff interacted with Wanda at school support group meetings for over a year and were very surprised when she decided to leave school in the middle of the last semester. Staff continued to make contact with her periodically through cultural education meetings in the community. Recently, she came by the office to talk over her situation and decided to return to the alternative school.

IMPLICATIONS FOR SCHOOL SOCIAL WORKERS

Texas does not have mandated school social work, and social workers are only beginning to work in school districts in the state (Danis, Franklin, & Schwab, 1993). As a consequence, school social workers have not yet taken on a significant role in the American Indian Education Projects in Texas, although some social workers play adjunct roles through referrals. Roles of the personnel involved in the American Indian Education Projects, however, are very similar to the roles and job descriptions of school social workers. These programs are appropriate examples of the types of services school social workers may deliver to American Indian students.

The cultural components of the programs are most significant, and school social workers should be more aware of the issues facing American Indian students, especially urban American Indians. Many urban Indians are poor and need economic assistance and social support to help them be successful in school. There is a great amount of variation in urban Indians' familiarity with tribal customs and cultures. Many urban American Indians are cut off or unfamiliar with their tribal heritage. Students should be assessed on an individual basis for their degree of identification. Many students are eager to learn about their heritage. Providing cultural education may serve as a rapport-building mechanism for parents and Indian communities as well as a bonding agent between the student and the school.

Some students and families who have been cut off from their roots feel a need to reconnect with their tribal affiliation. Requests to learn how to identify with one's tribe should be taken seriously. Students should be given information and opportunities to pursue tribal certification if they meet the criteria.

The eradication of the culture of the American Indians is greatly misunderstood, and many children and families have been stripped of their American Indian identity. Sometimes students who are members of tribes experience a lack of support for following Indian customs. For example, American Indian students may be expelled from school for wearing their hair long and refusing to cut it, as was the case in two school districts in Texas (personal communication with P. S. Larney, specialist, American Indian Education Project, Dallas ISD, March 12, 1995).

A more subtle but pervasive dilemma is faced by urban American Indian students who are Indian by heritage but are not formal members of a nation. These students may encounter resistance from others when seeking to identify with their heritage or when seeking tribal membership. School social workers can provide support groups to help students who are facing these dilemmas.

Finally, stereotypes of Indians prevail. Some students may be embarrassed or confused when faced with these stereotypes. Social workers should help school professionals understand the cultural contexts of American Indian students, including those who are cut off from tribal affiliations and customs. All American Indian students should be encouraged to respect and identify with their proud heritage.

REFERENCES

American Indian Education Act of 1972, P.L. 92-318, Title IV, 86 Stat. 334–345.

Dana, R. H. (1993). *Multicultural assessment perspectives for professional psychology*. Boston: Allyn & Bacon.

Danis, F., Franklin, C., & Schwab, A. J. (1993). Texas awakens: New partnerships in school social work. *Social Work in Education, 15*, 55–62.

Eberhard, D. R. (1989). American Indian education: A study of dropouts, 1980–1987. *Journal of American Indian Education, 28*, 32–40.

Gipp, G. E., & Fox, S. J. (1991). Promoting cultural relevance in American Indian education. *Education Digest, 57*(9), 58–61.

Goodlad, J. I. (1994). The national network for educational renewal. *Phi Delta Kappan, 75*, 632–638.

Hodgkinson, H. L., Outtz, I., & Obarakpor, C. (1990). *The demographics of American Indians: One percent of the people; fifty percent of the diversity*. Washington, DC: Institute for Educational Leadership.

Improving America's Schools Act of 1994, P.L. 103-382, Title IX, 108 Stat. 3518.

Lake, R. (1990). Fighting prejudice in education: An Indian's father's plea. *Education Digest, 56*(3), 20–23.

McQuiston, J. M., & Brod, R. L. (1985). Structural and cultural conflict in American Indian education. *Education Digest, 50*(4), 28–31.

National Center for Education Statistics. (1988). *Dropout rates in the United States*. Washington, DC: U.S. Government Printing Office.

Nel, J. (1994). Preventing school failure: The Native American child. *Clearinghouse, 67*, 169–174.

Ogbu, J. U. (1987). Variability in minority school performance: A problem in search of an explanation. *Anthropology and Education Quarterly, 18*, 312–334.

Reyhner, J. (1990). American Indians today: Population and education statistics. In J. Reyhner (Ed.), *Teaching American Indian students* (pp. 265–268). Norman: University of Oklahoma Press.

Reyhner, J., & Eder, J. (1990). A history of Indian education. In J. Reyhner (Ed.), *Teaching American Indian students* (pp. 33–58). Norman: University of Oklahoma Press.

Swisher, K., Hoisch, M., & Pavel, M. D. (1991). *American Indian, Alaskan, national dropout study* (National Education Association Project on School Dropouts). Tempe: Arizona State University, Center for Indian Education.

Thompson, J. W., Walker, R. D., & Silk-Walker, P. (1993). Psychiatric care of American Indians and Alaska Natives. In A. C. Gaw (Ed.), *Culture, ethnicity, and mental illness* (pp. 189–241). Washington, DC: American Psychiatric Press.

Yates, A. (1987). Current status and future directions of research on the American Indian child. *American Journal of Psychiatry, 144*, 1135–1142.

This chapter was originally published in the July 1995 issue of Social Work in Education, *vol. 17, pp. 183–193.*

27 Engaging Effectively with Culturally Diverse Families and Children

Frances S. Caple, Ramon M. Salcido, and John di Cecco

Despite the creation of numerous programs to help children achieve success, the public school system has fallen short of meeting this goal for all children. Culturally sensitive supports and interventions are receiving increased attention as key factors in the formulation of effective strategies for achieving the National Educational Goals (Goals 2000: Educate America Act, P.L.103-227). As increasing numbers of culturally diverse children enter schools, they will encounter students and professionals who are not of their cultural background. This situation is especially evident in the Los Angeles Unified School District, where students and staff are identified in seven major racial or ethnic groups. The 633,000 students enrolled in 1994 included 66.6 percent Hispanics, 14.4 percent African Americans, 11.6 percent whites, 4.8 percent Asian Americans, 1.9 percent Filipinos, 0.4 percent Pacific Islanders, and 0.3 percent American Indians. Further stratification within each of these ethnic groups creates even greater diversity among cultural backgrounds, and these students were greeted with even more diversity as they received services from the 30,100 professional staff who were 57.6 percent white, 16.3 percent African American, 16.3 percent Hispanic, 7.6 percent Asian American, 1.3 percent Filipino, 0.7 percent American Indian, and 0.1 percent Pacific Islander (Los Angeles Unified School District, 1995). The needs of these children, the unique and rich perspectives they bring to schools, and the dynamic forces with which they interact will determine the mass educational and social outcomes of the 21st century. Many of these children will experience problems deriving from fragmented and destabilizing service delivery systems (Gardner, 1990), insensitive staff, and in some cases a school environment that is nonsympathetic and rejecting.

Brown (1981) argued that one reason school social workers should be involved with minority[1] children and their families is based on the experiences of such families in a racist society. The literature on social work intervention with minority clients identifies strategies to combat oppression (Devore & Schlesinger, 1987; Hopps, 1982), use indigenous practice methods (Humm-Delgado & Delgado, 1986; Mokuau, 1991), emphasize cultural sensitivity (Green, 1982), and provide a comprehensive plan for assessment and treatment (Ho, 1992). These models of practice tend to emphasize the importance of culture and cultural differences. Although these approaches are of great value in understanding cross-cultural intervention, they offer limited knowledge about effective interaction skills with diverse students, parents, and communities in a school context. School social workers need to develop cross-cultural knowledge and intervention skills to assist culturally diverse parents in pursuing educational and functional goals for their children.

This chapter describes a cross-cultural practice model for use in school settings, recognizing the important role the school community plays in successfully preparing children to assume adult roles and engage in advanced learning. In addition, the use of interpreters is examined as one example of how such cross-cultural practice can be conducted effectively. We define the client system as the pupil and parent unit, recognizing the extended familial and community context as important to this discussion

---

[1]The authors are aware of and acknowledge certain merit in the current debate concerning the use of the term "minority" when used particularly to describe people of color. The term, as used in this chapter, does not refer to relative size of the group with which a family is identified or how they are valued. Rather, as sociologists use the term, minority families are those that have historically been in a subordinate position with regard to social and economic power, privilege, and prestige as compared with the dominant majority (Longres, 1991). This subordination results most typically "as a consequence of their race, ancestry and/or other characteristics" the dominant groups hold in low esteem (Taylor, 1994, p. 1). The authors prefer the term "culturally diverse" for purposes of this chapter, given that a wide range of family and child issues can be conceptualized within such a term.

of engagement and assessment of students from diverse racial and ethnic groups.

PREPARING FOR PRACTICE COMPETENCE

Their education has systematically provided social workers with basic knowledge for effective engagement with clients. There is less assurance that social work education has systematically included knowledge for effective practice with culturally diverse families and children. For example, in a recent informal survey conducted by the authors, participants in a continuing education session revealed that people completing social work programs more than five years ago had virtually no course content that highlighted cultural issues and needs. Furthermore, Allen-Meares (1992) emphasized that school social workers need a cross-cultural perspective for practice, but she noted the lack of adequate attention to such a perspective in the educational preparation of social workers and other school personnel. Given that school social workers assume various roles such as direct service provider and collaborator–consultant to other school personnel, there is some urgency to the need to explore means of intervening with culturally diverse families and children.

One of the critical markers of the beginning phase of social work treatment is that it lays the foundation for all treatment that follows. Therefore, it is vital that the professional entering the engagement period be competent in receiving and processing all that the client brings to the situation. Along with the generic knowledge and skills needed for engaging with any client, the practitioner must formulate one or more perspectives for practice, using specific knowledge, skills, and beliefs about particular characteristics of clients, their problems, and the environments in which they are striving to exist. Perspective building thus assumes a major part of the worker's mental preparation before engaging with clients. For example, a worker may formulate a perspective for crisis intervention after receiving a referral in which the presenting problem is stated in relation to a client's recent personal loss. A different perspective would be taken if the loss occurred years before.

Similarly, then, whether consciously acknowledged or not, the practitioner typically formulates a perspective for working with culturally diverse clients. The contents of these perspectives are drawn not only from specialized knowledge and skills but also from the values and beliefs of the social worker. Although generally there is some balance among these elements, in the absence of adequate knowledge or a way of organizing acquired knowledge, the practitioner may resort to formulating unbalanced, value-based, or biased perspectives.

UNDERSTANDING CULTURE THROUGH PERSPECTIVE BUILDING

Social workers seeking competence in cross-cultural practice soon realize the impossibility of acquiring specific knowledge about every racially, ethnically, or otherwise culturally diverse client. We have identified four principles as essential for developing a generic perspective for culturally competent practice: (1) there is no single American culture, (2) members of each cultural group are diverse, (3) acculturation is a dynamic process, and (4) diversity is to be acknowledged and valued.

There Is No Single American Culture

Despite the myth that has persisted in this regard, in reality American society is composed of multicultural environments based on one or more of the following: race, ethnicity, socioeconomic class, national or regional origin, sexual orientation, age, physical and mental ability, and gender. Cultural referents based on racial and ethnic differences are the ones most frequently highlighted and subjected to heated debate; differences may be recognized and discussed with somewhat less emotion when comparing the customs, beliefs, and attitudes of, for example, Northerners and Southerners or urban and rural dwellers.

Members of Each Cultural Group Are Diverse

There is no single profile that fits all members of any specific cultural group. Over the past two decades, social workers and other mental health professionals have sought to learn quickly core cultural elements of particular racial or ethnic groups. As a result, some or all of several conference and classroom presentations and written publications have contained specific descriptions of "typical" realities of African Americans, Hispanic/Latino populations, Asian Americans, and occasionally American Indians (Green, 1982; Taylor, 1994). More recently, some authors have pointed out concerns about the tendency of social services providers to stereotype clients on the basis of a generalized picture of people from particular racial and ethnic groups and have included some useful discussion of diversity within various groups (Boyd-Franklin, 1989; Browne & Broderick, 1994; Castex, 1994; Fong & Mokuau, 1994).

Although general material is helpful in broadening one's knowledge of a cultural group, Solomon (1976) noted a limited use for such material in forming initial hypotheses about a client's situation. For example, a social worker who is helping a Latino family may hypothesize the following: "If in most Latino families the father is the dominant member and spokesperson, this may be true in the family with whom I am sitting right now." This hypothesis provides only a starting point and cannot be substituted for the practitioner's actual engagement activity, which must be direct exploration of this particular family's reality.

Given that in the social work treatment process there can be no reliance on the worker's acquired knowledge of how Americans behave or how members of a given ethnic group behave, the most direct and accurate source of data concerning cultural realities is the client. The social worker must be willing to assume the role of social worker–learner (Green, 1982). Specifically, the social worker must begin immediately to explore directly with the client, within the context of the client's cultural values and lifestyles, the meaning of life events and presenting problems, any history of past or current oppression, and the client's relative acculturation to the dominant culture.

Acculturation Is a Dynamic Process

Acculturation is a dynamic "process of adopting the cultural traits or social patterns of another group, esp. a dominant one" (*Random House Webster's College Dictionary*, 1992, p. 10). A common conceptualization of acculturation considers only the client's status in this regard. Actually, all members of a multicultural society, including social workers, are subject to some degree of acculturation as they commingle and interact with other members of the society. In the most general terms, this phenomenon is observable as native-born Americans eat foods indigenous to other countries and as immigrants from those countries seek out American cuisine or as hairstyles, clothing, music, dance, and selected rituals are adopted from one group by members of another. The understanding and appreciation of such cultural exchanges are vital for the promotion of professional competence in cross-cultural practice.

To some extent, all children engage in a process of acculturation throughout their school years. Although some family cultures are similar to that of the school, each child will make some adaptive shifts from one system to the other. Thus, it is not uncommon for families to report a different set of child behaviors at home than reported by school personnel. In addition, immigrant children may be at a different level of acculturation to dominant American culture than their parents, and this fact may require special attention in the engagement and ongoing treatment process.

Most schoolchildren will make such shifts between family and school cultures without much difficulty; the child perceives the norms of the school and behaves accordingly. The greater the incongruity between the personal culture of the individual and the culture of the system in which interaction occurs, the more dynamic the process of acculturation becomes. The potential for conflicts is particularly high when the cultural imperatives of one group are ignored or openly dismissed as irrelevant in person–environment transactions. The social worker should be prepared to recognize, assess, and negotiate resolution of such conflicts. One approach to conflict resolution would include the facilitation of an accurate perception of cultural differences and the open sharing of cultural beliefs and norms by all parties engaged in the social work process.

Diversity Is to Be Acknowledged and Valued

The distinct diversity of each client system, and of the various groups to which clients belong, is to be acknowledged and valued as providing real and potential sources of strength for the client's overall functioning and well-being. This principle is consistent with the core social work value and practice of assuming a nonjudgmental attitude toward clients. In the professional relationship the social worker assumes a nonjudgmental attitude by genuinely demonstrating acceptance, especially in the engagement phase but throughout the treatment process as well.

In every culture there exist some expectations and codes of behavior around areas of discipline, time, health, and religious beliefs. A worker's understanding of what these values are, where they fall on a value continuum of traditional to modern, and how they interface with behavioral expectations of the education system regarding children's learning are key elements of cross-cultural practice in school settings.

People from diverse racial and ethnic groups have experienced different forms of oppression and racism in their interactions with the majority culture. Placing these concerns into a cross-cultural perspective involves exploring the client's historical experiences with the majority culture and, if applicable, with migration and immigration. This history may include movement both within the United States and across foreign borders.

If the social worker has difficulty understanding the cultural reality described by the client, a cultural consultant may be helpful. This consultant would be an objective individual who is knowledgeable about the meaning of nuances of the client's specific cultural communication. Equally important is the worker's alertness to the likelihood that his or her own value systems and interpretations of life events may interfere with the effective engagement of the client.

Observations have been made that the greater the similarity between "the cognitive and affective characteristics of the client and the worker, the greater the chance for effective communication" (Green, 1982, p. 54). Likewise, the greater the similarity between the client's and the social worker's value systems, the greater the chance of effective service delivery (Longres, 1991). An early and ongoing task of the social worker is the assessment of the worker–client situation to identify cultural similarities and differences and provide clues for potential conflicts. Conflicts may arise because of positively or negatively biased behaviors or attitudes toward the client. Ongoing self-awareness checks with a professional consultant can be useful. A worker's ethnocentrism—the attitude that "my values and beliefs are more noble than those of the client and are worthy of emulation"—will not promote worker competence and effectiveness. The worker's personal work should focus on increasing openness and acceptance of the client's reality as potentially useful to the client's resolution of present problems.

A FRAMEWORK FOR CROSS–CULTURAL PRACTICE

Several models of social work practice and "the ethnic reality" have been reviewed and discussed by Devore and Schlesinger

(1987). We find that the ecosystems perspective, as currently used in social work practice, provides the overarching framework most compatible with Devore and Schlesinger's view of cultural practice in school settings. The ecosystems perspective recognizes that there are specific enduring and transient relationships between and among individuals, families, other groups, institutions, and society at large and that transactions between or among these systems have profound effects on human behavior and functioning. Because the nature of these transactions is reciprocal, practice in school settings should address the problems created by person–environment interactions by assessing the entire ecosystem and intervening at the most appropriate points in the system to effect desired change. To address person–environment problems, the practitioner can use culturally sensitive interactions based on the perspective developed as described earlier and by identifying and using appropriate problem-solving techniques (Germain, 1973, 1991; Meyer, 1983; Zastrow & Kirst-Ashman, 1994). The effectiveness of problem solving depends on the worker's understanding of and sensitivity to the client's cultural beliefs, lifestyle, and social support systems.

The worker who uses the ecosystems framework assumes various roles—enabler, facilitator, coordinator, mediator, and teacher—as she or he moves across system boundaries in dealing with the transactions between the client system and the school ecosystem. A primary emphasis of treatment is to empower the client system (pupils and their families) and intervene in other parts of the ecosystem that create barriers to empowerment. The social worker emphasizes activities based on the cultural strengths of the client system. The focus of treatment ultimately is to improve the goodness of fit between the client and others in the ecosystem, including the social worker. Therefore, interventions may be directed toward the family, specific members of the family, the teacher, or others in the ecosystem.

Basic Skills for Cross-Cultural Practice

Several authors have identified the importance of determining and applying specific skills in cross-cultural practice (for example, Gallegos, 1984; Green, 1982; Lum, 1986). The core skills proposed here for working with diverse clients are synthesized from cross-cultural models, social work skills, and practice wisdom.

Common Basic Skills. In the beginning stages of intervention it is recommended that social workers take basic steps to establish an initial positive relationship. A major problem in most public schools is the lack of positive, cooperative relationships among students, staff, parents, and administration (Curiel, 1991). In building positive interactions, basic etiquette should be observed to convey respect, including making proper introductions, asking how the client wants to be addressed, and using common courtesies. The practitioner should spend a few minutes getting acquainted with the clients in a relaxed manner. Ivey (1977) stressed the importance of establishing and maintaining eye contact at this stage. These initial interpersonal exchanges contribute to the client's perception of the practitioner as helper.

Interaction between practitioner and client may also be influenced by the parents' perceptions of the roles of the worker. In the countries of origin of some immigrant clients, the social work role is not known, and some of these clients may view the practitioner as a government agent. Therefore, the task of the practitioner is to explain his or her professional role and the function of the services he or she can provide. Sue and Sue (1990) emphasized the importance of credibility when working with Asian clients. To strengthen the client's confidence in the worker's abilities, workers should display all degrees and other items indicating professional competence on the walls of their offices and should present their professional title to the client.

Relationship-Building Skills. The building of the worker–client relationship is the next task after observing courtesy protocols. Our observation in working with parents is that minority parents often feel powerless to express their needs to professionals if they feel the practitioner will not "hear" them. Thus, an important part of establishing rapport is being an effective listener and demonstrating attention and interest in the client's communications. The practitioner's use of facilitation skills can demonstrate to clients a desire to truly listen. Chamberlain et al. (1985) defined *facilitation* as short utterances used by the practitioner to prompt the client to continue talking. Ivey and Authier (1978) suggested nodding the head, using phrases such as "mm hmm" and "tell me more," and repeating one or two words spoken by the client as approaches to promote a continuing conversation. These behaviors convey interest and acceptance.

Communication Skills. Effective cross-cultural practice requires effectiveness not only in listening and facilitation, but also in spoken communication. Ivey and Authier (1978) proposed that one way the effective practitioner can engage in culturally appropriate behavior is by generating an infinite array of selective communication skills including open- and closed-ended questions, paraphrasing, reflection of feelings, and summarization. Ivey's (1977) work on cross-cultural skill development (microcounseling) set the groundwork for developing universal cross-cultural communication skills. After using paraphrasing, reflection of feelings, and summarization, the practitioner then repeats the information he or she has gathered and specifically asks the client if the information is accurate. In our model, we conceptualize this validation step as a "cultural check."

Understanding the Client's Definition of the Problem. Definitions of problems are culture specific and complex. Sue and Zane (1987) argued that defining a problem is a culturally bound activity. Members of a particular cultural group may not agree with the definition of a problem provided by members of the dominant culture (Gold & Bogo, 1992). Green (1982) noted that it is critical to recognize how the client views the problem. Pedersen (1988) explained that each person perceives the world from his or her own cultural point of view, and one skill practitioners can use is to perceive the problem from the client's cultural point of view. The nature of the client's worldviews and values interacts with the behavioral norms that the client has adopted (Mokuau & Shimizu, 1991).

The problems or issues discussed need to be well identified and conceptualized by the client. The school social worker should ask parents or family units what the problem means to them, their family, and their culture. Various cultures have developed their own indigenous models of service, help-seeking behaviors, and belief systems. The school social worker must have or seek knowledge of the array of culturally specific imperatives and responses available in a particular school's ecosystem to understand the client's cultural definition of the problem. These cultural perceptions may then lead to a decision to work with the entire extended family, respected community leaders, and other natural helpers (Morales & Salcido, 1995).

Working with Interpreters

There are instances in cross-cultural practice when the social worker needs an interpreter to manage communication across language and cultural systems. Because language is the major mechanism for conveying cultural contents and meanings, special attention must always be given to the client's use of language. Even when English is the native language of both the worker and the client, there may be subtle or clear confusion due to regional origins, age, or racial differences. For example, teenagers' use of language may need some "interpretation" in the social work practice situation.

An interpreter is most necessary when the client speaks the worker's language either insufficiently or not at all. Agencies who used interpreters for non-English-speaking clients demonstrated success (Kline, Acosta, Austin, & Johnson, 1980), although in contrast to the clients' high satisfaction ratings, the workers reported feeling ineffective and concerned that they did not accurately convey an understanding of the clients and that the clients would not return for future services. These divergent worker and client perceptions suggest that the interpretation process must convey not only words, but also other types of information to establish relationships among worker, client, and interpreter. Communication of subtle affect and signals for key relationship guideposts such as respect, deference, or attention are subject to a wide range of cultural expression. Body language, despite the popular belief in its universality, may in fact convey quite different meanings in various cultures and is just one of many factors that may contribute to confusion in the interpretation process. Glasser (1983) and Owan et al. (1985) recommended that social workers be sensitive to issues of power and subordination when using interpreters and pointed out that the class and social status of the interpreter and the client may negatively interact in the interpretive process.

Interpretive Approaches. Baker (1981) identified two contrasting interpretive approaches he called the verbatim style and the independent intervention. With verbatim style, or instantaneous interpretation, words are translated as closely as possible, and the participation of the interpreter in the content of the interview is kept to a minimum. With independent intervention, on the other hand, the interpreter is a cultural bridge enabling the worker to understand the client's behavior, body language, and perceptions.

Allowing the interpreter to take a more active role in the interview process may be productive provided he or she understands the social work process and the purpose of the interview.

Interpretation is more cumbersome when cultural and linguistic differences are greatest. Interpretation of European languages with similar speech forms and worldviews is not as difficult as interpretation between English and Hmong, for example. Because language reflects cultural ideas and worldviews, it is unhelpful to translate verbatim the Hmong phrase "Our ancestors are rejoicing at the rising of the sun and the tea being poured by my mother's sister," which means "You have gained our trust and acceptance as you understand our world and the importance of our forefathers. It's great to see you and you are welcome as a member of our family." In addition, Owan et al. (1985) noted that confidentiality is an unfamiliar concept in many Southeast Asian cultures. In such cultures, talking publicly about taboo subjects might be considered deviant by both client and interpreter. It would be assumed that all public agencies would then know the client's personal business and family history, placing him or her in a dangerous and vulnerable position. Clearly, the interpreter needs considerable skill to convey meaning across both linguistic and cultural systems.

Preparing for the Interview. Planning for interpretation (Freed, 1988) is akin to developing a team approach; both social worker and interpreter must understand the purpose and focus of the social work interview and agree on the type of interpretation to be provided. The worker should conduct a briefing with the interpreter before the interview to assess attitudes and characteristics of the interpreter that may affect the interview process. Orienting the interpreter as to the interview's purpose and preparing him or her for content that may be sexual, graphic, or emotionally laden will help him or her function while the clinician directs difficult interviews. Marcos (1979) observed interpreters who compensated for disordered thought and inappropriate affect of clients in client mental status examinations to make their interpretation appear adequate and thereby please the clinicians. Because these interpreters lacked understanding of the purpose of the interview and the nature of the social work process, they were unable to focus on and convey critical information in the interpretation process.

After the Interview. After each interview, the social worker should debrief the interpreter to elicit subtle information about the client that may not have emerged during the interpretation process. For example, the interpreter should report if the client did not always make sense or spoke with a particular accent or articulation problem. The interpreter may reveal confusion regarding inappropriate affect, ambivalence, or blunted expression of mood or emotion. The interpreter's observations regarding aspects of the client's language such as baby talk, poor syntax, or difficulty with expression also assist the clinician in formulating a more developed assessment of the client. Using the interpreter as a cultural guide helps the social worker place the client's behaviors in a cultural context. The interpreter can help the social worker understand the norms, expectations, and values of the culture so that the worker can assess the client's functioning in his or her ethnic or cultural community.

Scarcity of Skilled Interpreters. Unfortunately, skilled interpreters with ideal characteristics are not always available. When a member of the client's social network, such as a child, neighbor, or relative, is asked to interpret, the social worker must think carefully about the effect on the social and familial functioning of the client. Interviews requiring a minimum of distortion, intense emotional material, or an investigative function are likely to fail if conducted with a family member or friend as the interpreter. Agencies should develop contacts with interpreters in ethnic communities as a development activity to serve targeted linguistic populations.

CONCLUSION

Cross-cultural social work is anchored in a definition of culture that acknowledges the many dimensions that affect the engagement process with children and families. There is no single American culture, nor is there a single profile that fits all members of any specific cultural group. Knowledge of cultural groups, however, is useful in both engaging with and assessing the unique cultural perspective of clients. To understand the client's worldview, the social worker must consider the client's immigration or migration history and his or her history of interaction with the dominant culture and other powerful groups. School social workers who apply this framework will then view person–environment transactions from a more culturally sensitive standpoint. Understanding of self, including cultural consultation for self-awareness checks, is a necessary adjunct to successful work across cultural systems. Competent practice with culturally diverse clients is an ongoing process of developing self-awareness; increasing one's generic and specific knowledge about cultural groups and their interactions; and sharpening practice skills that facilitate communication and understanding among client, school, and social worker.

REFERENCES

Allen-Meares, P. (1992). Prevention and cross-cultural perspective: Preparing school social workers for the 21st century. *Social Work in Education, 14*, 3–5.

Baker, N. G. (1981). Social work through an interpreter. *Social Work, 26*, 391–397.

Boyd-Franklin, N. (1989). *Black families in therapy: A multisystems approach.* New York: Guilford Press.

Brown, J. A. (1981). Parent education groups for Mexican-Americans. *Social Work in Education, 3*, 22–31.

Browne, C., & Broderick, A. (1994). Asian and Pacific Island elders: Issues for social work practice and education. *Social Work, 39*, 252–259.

Castex, G. (1994). Providing services to Hispanic/Latino populations: Profiles in diversity. *Social Work, 39*, 288–296.

Chamberlain, P., Davis, J. P., Forgatch, M. S., Frey, J., Patterson, G. R., Ray, J., Rothchild, A., & Trombley, J. (1985). *The therapy process code: A multidimensional system for observing therapist and client interactions.* Eugene: Oregon Social Learning Center.

Curiel, H. (1991). Strengthening family and school bonds in promoting Hispanic children's school performance. In M. Sotomayor (Ed.), *Empowering Hispanic families: A critical issue for the 90's* (pp. 75–95). Milwaukee: Family Service America.

Devore, W., & Schlesinger, E. (1987). *Ethnic-sensitive social work practice* (2nd ed.). Columbus, OH: Merrill.

Fong, R., & Mokuau, N. (1994). Not simply "Asian Americans": Periodical literature review on Asians and Pacific Islanders. *Social Work, 39*, 298–305.

Freed, A. O. (1988). Interviewing through an interpreter. *Social Work, 33*, 315–319.

Gallegos, J. (1984). The ethnic competence model for social work education. In B. W. White (Ed.), *Color in a white society* (pp. 1–9). Silver Spring, MD: National Association of Social Workers.

Gardner, S. (1990, Winter). Failure by fragmentation. *California Tomorrow*, pp. 3–9.

Germain, C. B. (1973). An ecological perspective in casework practice. *Social Casework, 54*, 323–333.

Germain, C. B. (1991). *Human behavior in the social environment: An ecological view.* New York: Columbia University Press.

Glasser, I. (1983). Guidelines for using an interpreter in social work. *Child Welfare, 62*, 468–470.

Goals 2000: Educate America Act, P.L. 103-227, 108 Stat. 125(1994).

Gold, N., & Bogo, M. (1992). Social work research in a multicultural society: Challenges and approaches. *Journal of Multicultural Social Work, 2*(4), 7–22.

Green, J. (1982). *Cultural awareness in the human services.* Englewood Cliffs, NJ: Prentice Hall.

Ho, M. K. (1992). *Minority children and adolescents in therapy.* Newbury Park, CA: Sage Publications.

Hopps, J. (1982). Oppression based on color [Special issue: Social work and people of color]. *Social Work, 27*, 3–5.

Humm-Delgado, D., & Delgado, M. (1986). Gaining community entree to assess service needs of Hispanics. *Social Casework, 67*(2), 80–89.

Ivey, A. (1977). Cultural expertise: Toward systematic outcome criteria in counseling and psychological education. *Personnel and Guidance Journal, 55*, 296–302.

Ivey, A., & Authier, J. (1978). *Micro counseling.* Springfield, IL: Charles C Thomas.

Kline, F., Acosta, F., Austin, W., & Johnson, R. (1980). The misunderstood Spanish-speaking patient. *American Journal of Psychiatry, 137*, 1530–1633.

Longres, J. (1991). Toward a status model of ethnic-sensitive practice. *Journal of Multicultural Social Work, 1*(1), 41–56.

Los Angeles Unified School District. (1995). *Fall ethnic survey report, Los Angeles Unified School District* (Publication No. 123). Los Angeles: Author.

Lum, D. (1986). *Social work practice and people of color: Process-stage approach.* Monterey, CA: Brooks/Cole.

Marcos, L. (1979). Effects of interpreters on the evaluation of psychopathology in non-English speaking patients. *American Journal of Psychiatry, 136*, 171–174.

Meyer, C. H. (Ed.). (1983). *Clinical social work in the eco-systems perspective.* New York: Columbia University Press.

Mokuau, N. (Ed.). (1991). *Handbook of social services for Asian and Pacific Islanders.* New York: Greenwood Press.

Mokuau, N., & Shimizu, D. (1991). Conceptual framework for social services for Asian and Pacific Islander Americans. In N. Mokuau (Ed.), *Handbook of social services for Asian and Pacific Islanders* (pp. 21–36). New York: Greenwood Press.

Morales, A. T., & Salcido, R. (1995). Social work practice with Mexican Americans. In A. T. Morales & B. W. Shaefor (Eds.), *Social work: A profession of many faces* (7th ed., pp. 527–552). Boston: Allyn & Bacon.

Owan, T. C., Bliatout, B., Lin, K.-M., Liu, W., Nguyen, T. D., & Wong, H. Z. (Eds.). (1985). *Southeast Asian mental health: Treatment, prevention, services, training, and research.* Washington, DC: U.S. Department of Health and Human Services.

Pedersen, R. (1988). *A handbook for developing multicultural awareness.* Alexandria, VA: American Association for Counseling and Development.

Random House Webster's college dictionary. (1992). New York: Random House.

Solomon, B. (1976). *Black empowerment: Social work in oppressed communities.* New York: Columbia University Press.

Sue, D., & Sue, D. (1990). *Counseling the culturally different.* New York: John Wiley & Sons.

Sue, S., & Zane, N. (1987). The role of culture and cultural techniques in psychotherapy. *American Psychologist, 42,* 37–45.

Taylor, R. (1994). Minority families in America: An introduction. In R. L. Taylor (Ed.), *Minority families in the United States: A multicultural perspective* (pp. 1–16). Englewood Cliffs, NJ: Prentice Hall.

Zastrow, C., & Kirst-Ashman, K. (1994). *Understanding human behavior and the social environment* (3rd ed.). Chicago: Nelson-Hall.

This chapter was originally published in the July 1995 issue of Social Work in Education, *vol. 17, pp. 159–170.*

A Developmental Framework for Cultural Competence Training with Children

Darlene Grant and Dennis Haynes

School social workers are challenged to assist teachers and the educational system in preparing students for an increasingly diverse world. Estimates suggest that by the year 2020 half of U.S. children of school age will be of color—a 25 percent to 40 percent change in composition in some school settings (Axelson, 1993; Leckrone, 1993; York, 1994). Nationally, enrollment in elementary and secondary schools was 46.2 million in 1990 and is expected to increase to 51.8 million by 1998 and 53 million by 2002 (U.S. Department of Education, 1991). It is projected that by 2000, African Americans will constitute the majority population in 53 major U.S. cities (York, 1994). By 2015, Hispanic Americans and Latinos will outnumber African Americans in the United States (York, 1994). And by 2050 there will be more people of color than white people in the United States (Axelson, 1993; York, 1994).

It is estimated that by 2020, the number of school-age children needing English instruction and other types of cross-cultural intervention to succeed in school will reach more than 4 million (York, 1994). Statistics from the Children's Defense Fund (1992) suggest that intercultural disparity continues in basic skills and achievement. The impact of change in the cultural and ethnic composition of schools is manifest in an increase in charged intergroup conflicts (York, 1994).

To improve cultural relations, students and teachers must become not only culturally sensitive but also competent in cross-cultural interaction. The task of training students to meet increasingly high educational and sociobehavioral standards is a large one. Social workers have a historical mission to work in partnership with schools to provide pupil services to achieve these standards. School social workers, prepared through professional education to provide services to poor and oppressed populations, to people who are discriminated against, and to people wanting or needing enrichment in various psychosocial areas of functioning (Council on Social Work Education, 1992), play an important role in developing strategies and methods to combat ethnocentrism, group hatred, prejudice, and violence. The knowledge, values, and skill base of the social work profession promote respect for the positive value of diversity and an understanding of the mechanisms that contribute to the propagation of all forms of discrimination so that social change and social justice are possible. Furthermore, the practice theories social workers use as frameworks for intervening in human development and behavior can be logically applied to cultural competence training (Lum, 1992). The challenges diversity presents for student relations and achievement, however, dictate that school social workers further develop their skills in multicultural practice.

Little recognition has been given to school social workers' potential to assist schools with multicultural education. Social work training and literature do little to prepare school social workers with specific skills to help school systems and students cope with diversity (Leckrone, 1993). This chapter summarizes a developmental framework for cultural competence training with children that school social workers may use to guide their practice. Formulated from psychosocial and ecological theories, the framework synchronizes cultural competence training with children's developmental levels and cultural learning readiness in cognitive, affective, and behavioral areas. To lay a foundation, the history of cross-cultural training and the role of public schools and multicultural issues concerning childhood development are presented.

HISTORICAL ROLE OF PUBLIC SCHOOLS IN CULTURAL TRAINING

For nearly two centuries public schools have played a significant role in determining the quantity and tenor of cross-cultural interactions for children and adults in the United States. Evidence that education played more than a limited role in people's lives did not appear until the late 19th and early 20th centuries, when education was used to assimilate immigrant children (Banks, 1993; La Belle & Ward, 1994). Public schools were instruments of acculturation, with the primary goal being to socialize children to the dominant group's language, values, and behavioral standards. Cross-cultural training in schools has traditionally occurred in an American society that has associated differences in intelligence and ability to learn with the race and economic status of the child's family, thus shortchanging the children of poor people and people of color. As such, cross-cultural training was first developed and implemented in the sterile vacuum of classroom settings as schools presented culturally biased information.

In the early 19th century, boarding schools were used to separate Native American children from their cultural and tribal bonds and practices (La Belle & Ward, 1994). Remnants of this practice remain in some areas in the 1990s. The educational needs of Mexican American and other Hispanic immigrants and migrant workers were effectively ignored by the dominant group during "three hundred years of Hispanic presence and influence in America" (La Belle & Ward, 1994, p. 9). The effects of this neglect remain in some areas as the debate rages over bilingual education in the United States.

World War I introduced suspicion and intolerance of cultural diversity. In this environment the goal of schools was a monocultural society. African Americans were relegated to separate and inferior schools, and schools accepted only complete assimilation of American values from all other students (La Belle & Ward, 1994). Racism, Naziism, anti-Semitism, and homophobia were rampant (Banks, 1993; La Belle & Ward, 1994; York, 1994).

Intercultural education with a focus on pride in one's cultural heritage and tolerance of differences became popular in the 1940s and early 1950s. Later and more current ideals regarding cultural pluralism have their roots in this period, which focused on changing the attitudes of the American people. Cross-cultural education followed the end of World War II. Training addressed the needs of a war-weary society concerned with international peace (Banks, 1993; York, 1994). Race riots in Detroit during the war had highlighted the need to concentrate on improving relations at home as well as abroad. The educational movement did not, however, "address structural racism, poverty, or the empowerment of subordinate groups" (La Belle & Ward, 1994, p. 17). The goals of training and education became political. Any emphasis on appreciation and value for cultural differences was absent;

training focused instead on the transfer of American technology, social norms, and values (York, 1994).

The civil rights movement called attention to the need to address education's role in spreading intolerance and its support of institutional racism. Up to this point, early attempts at cross-cultural training were founded on the expectation that children of color would change to become more like white children (York, 1994). Following orders for desegregation, "success was measured by how quickly and well minority children became invisible in white schools" (York, 1994, p. 64). At this time the cross-cultural training focus began to shift from training children to training teachers in an effort to prepare them to teach increasingly diverse students.

The current multicultural movement in the United States is the direct product of the civil rights movement of the 1960s and 1970s. Much of the insights, approaches, techniques, and research used today emanate from the intergroup education focus of that period. This historical retrospect highlights the developmental nature of the process through which the educational and broader societal systems have advanced to advocate the pluralistic stance of today. School districts and schools have not moved to this point in concert. As with human development, schools have progressed in their attention to the value of multicultural education and training at varying paces.

PRINCIPLES OF CULTURAL TRAINING

Approaches

Multicultural training goals include the expectation that participants will experience shifts in feelings, thoughts, and behaviors concerning themselves and others who are different from themselves. Cross-cultural training strategies are complex and vary depending on the characteristics of the school setting and learning readiness of the children. For example, a school social worker in an inner-city public school might present training differently from a school social worker in a rural setting. Similarly, students in either setting will gain different benefits from the training depending on issues that affect their learning readiness in this area. York (1994) identified five core characteristics of all cross-cultural training:

> (1) training occurs within a limited time, (2) goals and out-
> comes of training are tied to events people find distressing
> and confusing in a new culture, (3) training is trainee-centered,
> (4) the motivations that propel trainees into programs and
> their intentions for success vary greatly, and (5) the training
> may be addressed to all cultures (culture-general) or to one
> culture in particular (culture-specific). (pp. 66–67)

According to Banks (1993), current multicultural education approaches do one or more of the following: incorporate curriculum content about cultural heroes and holidays (contributions
approach); permit the addition of content and perspectives without changing the basic structure of the curriculum (cultural ad-
ditive approach); enable students to view issues from different
perspectives (transformation approach); empower students to
make reflective decisions and take personal, social, and civic action (decision-making and social action approach); offer strategies designed to increase academic achievement of students in
poverty and students of color (achievement approach); and extend opportunities for students to develop and apply more positive attributes toward other racial, gender, and cultural groups
(intergroup education approach). Public schools choose the approach that suits their needs best.

Strategies

Given the range of approaches, strategies used to develop culturally competent and skilled students are either knowledge-
oriented, awareness-oriented, or skill-oriented (Pedersen & Ivey,
1993) or affect-oriented (Chau, 1990).

Knowledge-oriented strategies focus on providing students
correct and sufficient information about their own and other cultures. Training methods include lectures, group discussions, and
written and visual materials. Training that emphasizes cognitive
understanding has dominated the field of intercultural training
(Bennett, 1986). It is content focused, fact focused, and culturally
specific. To effectively train students, school social workers must
be knowledge competent, which requires an understanding of
the socioeconomic role of racial and ethnic groups in the United
States, specific knowledge about the culture of their students, a
clear and explicit knowledge of the generalist practice literature,
and knowledge of institutional barriers that bar people of color
from access to services (Pedersen & Ivey, 1993).

Awareness-oriented strategies emphasize affective goals and experiential processes (Bennett, 1986). They focus on students' ability to see situations from their own and others' viewpoint with accuracy. These strategies include experiential cultural awareness through fieldwork and role play, cultural values clarification, or cultural immersion. In cultural immersion, the social worker or trainer provides a simulated environment for students to live and work in. In this environment students interact with role models from other cultures. Children are active in their learning and function as a group to bring into consciousness each student's own emotions and responses. Experience provides the basis for explicated opinions, attitudes, and assumptions of the students. School social workers providing multicultural training must be aware of their own cultural backgrounds, aware of those assumptions and value biases socialized by their cultural backgrounds, comfortable with cultural differences between practitioner and students, and sensitive to circumstances that might require referral of a student to a culturally similar practitioner (Pedersen & Ivey, 1993).

Skill-oriented strategies emphasize the ability to perform accurately in multicultural interactions by matching the appropriate strategy to the situation. These strategies include cognitive–behavioral modification; structured interaction; and micro skills training, which includes attending behaviors, influencing skills, and integrative skills. Skill-oriented training assumes that knowledge, awareness, and affective competencies of students have been previously addressed. School social workers providing this type of training must be able to do three things: "(1) generate a wide variety of verbal and nonverbal responses appropriate to a wide range of cultures, (2) both send and receive verbal and nonverbal messages accurately and appropriately to or from culturally different people," and (3) intervene at the system or institutional level on behalf of the student (Pedersen & Ivey, 1993, p. 22).

Affect-oriented strategies emphasize the emotions involved when dealing with value-laden diversity issues (Chau, 1990). These strategies focus on the evocation and processing of feelings and subsequently the students' ability to empathize with others. Strategies include role plays, audiovisual presentations, field experiences using resource people from the host culture

(Pedersen & Ivey, 1993), and cultural immersion. School social workers providing affect-oriented training must be able to

- provide a safe environment for the evocation, sharing, and processing of feelings
- provide clear boundaries and limits for affective skill development
- guide students through feelings
- monitor students' stress levels and change the focus of or discontinue an exercise when it becomes counterproductive
- supplement students' repertoire of feelings with ones that accommodate skills in cross-cultural interaction.

CHILD DEVELOPMENTAL LEVELS

The multicultural training literature has tended not to clarify the application of training to distinct groups, but the field of early childhood education is an exception. Writers have been specific in applying multicultural education concepts to the developmental levels of children (Ramsey, 1982; York, 1991).

Infancy and Toddlerhood

Developmental issues in infancy and toddlerhood lay a foundation for children's cultural learning readiness. Newborns have an innate preference for human faces over objects. At four months, infants can tell the difference between familiar people and strangers, and by six months they have begun to actively explore their surroundings. Infants learn to trust or mistrust based on their experiences with caregivers. In these early years, children's development of self-concept plays an important role in their learning to accept others. Children also learn which feelings are acceptable and which feelings to deny and hide.

Preschool Age: Three to Four Years

Children's awareness of similarities and differences develops as early as preschool age (three to four years), when children readily identify cultural differences in customs, language, and skin color and can make choices and show preferences based on external characteristics. They can match people and objects with categories. Preschoolers act out situations from home life and mimic caretaker biases. Aggression is usually expressed physically. Their thinking is limited and inconsistent. This age group is prone to overgeneralize and to oversimplistically jump to conclusions. They are susceptible to believing stereotypes because they base associations on how things look. Preschoolers also tend to focus only on one detail, often minor, at a time. Children's attitudes toward their own race and toward other racial groups start to form in the preschool years. European American children develop a positive association with the racial label of white and negative attitudes toward people who are different (York, 1991). At this age children from all racial and ethnic groups have learned more about human diversity (York, 1991).

Early School Age: Five to Seven Years

By early school age, children begin to understand the concept of group membership and to socialize with peers. Prosocial and antisocial behaviors develop. Children tend to choose friends of the same sex and race. Early school–age children enjoy exploring the cultural heritages of themselves and others. Children of color can identify their own ethnicity, but it is not until age seven that they develop negative attitudes toward other ethnic groups. Early school–age children can begin to identify the limitations of stereotypes as they struggle to discriminate between real and pretend concepts. By this age, children's thinking allows them to realize that things such as gender and skin color stay the same in individuals even though they may change from one person to the next. Children in this age group are developing moral judgment and understand the concept of fair and unfair. They may, however, be rigid and rule bound in their behavior. Insults tend to be used in the expression of aggression.

Middle School Age: Eight to 12 Years

By middle school age, children are more interested in and aware of the broader social and cultural environment. However, it is important to stress both similarities and differences, as children are more likely to incorporate new information when seen in relation to previous knowledge. They demonstrate an increased reliance on logic and are able to consider more than one attribute at a time. Middle school–age children need help to see the correspondence between their own lives and those of others. These children use the concept of group membership to distinguish themselves from others. Children of color demonstrate more attachment to their own ethnic group, and by ages 11 or 12 these children are fully aware of social classifications and their ethnic group's place in society. Some researchers indicate that racial attitudes of children of this age are set after age nine, unless they experience some major event or life change (York, 1991). Middle school–age children have increased cooperation skills and are better able to describe feelings and empathize. In addition, social responsibility to the community can be fostered. This age group is sensitive to social norms, expectations, and peer pressure and is preoccupied with self-evaluation.

Early Adolescence: 13 to 17 Years

Adolescents are able to think hypothetically, reason abstractly, and self-reflect. They are preoccupied with their own thoughts. This age group has the capacity to integrate the past, present, and future; to determine the consistency and inconsistency of statements; and to anticipate consequences. Adolescents develop the flexibility to realize that their beliefs are not shared by all others, and they begin to experience multiple role expectations. This age is often a period of heightened emotional sensitivity and conflicted relationships. Membership in a peer group is extremely important to provide adolescents with a sense of social belonging. If the adolescent does not have or fit in with a peer group, then he or she experiences a sense of isolation. The self-concept of the adolescent is susceptible to changes in status with peers. Adolescents of color are especially vulnerable to exclusion and rejection from majority culture peers and conflict with their own ethnic-group values.

DEVELOPMENTAL FRAMEWORK FOR CULTURAL COMPETENCE TRAINING

In the authors' framework, movement of students from cultural incompetence to cultural sensitivity to cultural competence is assumed to be developmental. Several authors have suggested that student development of cultural competence requires multiple training foci on knowledge, affect, and skill (Carney & Kahn, 1984; Orlandi, 1992; Stevenson, Cheung, & Leung, 1992; York, 1994).

The idea of a matrix depicting the multidimensional aspects of multicultural competence is not a new one. Orlandi (1992), in his efforts to define cultural competence, presented a table in which levels of competence for knowledge, affect, and skill are expressed on a continuum from low to high. The objective of training is to move students from the lowest or intermediate levels to the highest level of competence in all dimensions. We propose an alternative to the multidimensional approach: To maximize effectiveness, cultural competence training should focus on the one dimension—that is, knowledge, affect, or skill—most closely related to children's level of psychosocial development (Table 28-1).

Cultural Competencies

Knowledge Competence. The objective of knowledge competence is a cognitive understanding of cultural similarities and differences on the micro (student) level. Students with the least knowledge competence are unaware of similarities and differences; knowledge-competent students know both general and specific cultural content. In the developmental sequence of training, knowledge content of cultural similarities and differences is the first area of focus. Knowledge competence increases as students supplement awareness of their own culture with an understanding of similarities and differences with others' cultural traditions, family structures, roles, heroes, dress, foods, celebrations, and other cultural content.

Affective Competence. Affective competence builds on knowledge competence and ranges from apathetic to sympathetic to empathic. Affect-competent students have moved from a cognitive understanding of cultural similarities and differences to an affective response to the cultural differentness of others. Such students are able to perceive and communicate their own feelings and to respond accurately to others' perceptions and communications regarding cultural similarities and differences on the mezzo, or interpersonal, level.

Skill Competence. Skill competence builds on knowledge and affective competencies and constitutes the application phase of development. Skill-competent students have become socially proactive in confronting cultural bias and challenging ethnocentrism, group hatred, prejudice, and violence. Such students build on their knowledge and affective competencies (self-understanding and empathic attitudes toward others) to intervene with groups and institutions at the macro level.

Table 28-1

Developmental Framework for Cultural Competency Training with Children

Child Developmental Level	Training Objective	Cultural Learning Readiness Stage	Knowledge Competence	Affective Competence	Skill Competence (Application of Training Principles)	School Social Worker Training Focus
Early school age (5 to 7 years old)	Knowledge: Child self-awareness	Culturally incompetent (denies or minimizes cultural difference)	Unaware	Apathetic	Unskilled	Support
Middle school age (8 to 12 years old)	Affect: Other-awareness	Culturally sensitive (accepts differences and adapts responses)	Aware	Sympathetic	Minimally skilled	Interact
Early adolescence (13 to 17 years old)	Skill: Social action	Culturally competent (integrates experiences)	Knowledgeable	Empathic	Highly skilled	Challenge

Cultural Readiness Stages

Cultural readiness suggests that children are differentially ready, over and above their developmental capabilities, to receive new information, to be accepting of differences, and to move toward integration of characteristics related to cultural competence. Familial and community support and involvement in the development of cultural competence are important ingredients for a child's readiness.

Cultural readiness relates to the development of a positive self-concept not predicated on highlighting the positive attributes of self over the negative attributes of others who are different. Experience with extended caregivers and significant others from other cultures contributes to a capacity to be understanding, aware, receptive, and empathic. Cultural readiness emphasizes the importance of uniqueness and access to people who are role models for inclusivity. A child raised in a prejudiced and biased setting may not be as prepared to develop sensitivity to cultural difference as the child who has been exposed to different cultures. The culturally isolated child may lack family or systemic support for exposure to and integration of information that is counter to the stereotypes learned at home. Cultural readiness relates to having enough information and experience to discriminate between stereotypes and the richness of individuals who are different. It also relates to children's understanding of the idea of the interrelatedness of human beings beyond ethnic and social classifications. Students progress through three stages of cultural readiness: cultural incompetence, cultural sensitivity, and cultural competence.

Culturally Incompetent Students. Culturally incompetent students lack cultural knowledge, affective, and skill competencies and have limited experience with others who are culturally different. They are unaware of difference or deny its existence by overemphasizing similarity. They minimize the importance of cultural learning. To the extent that they acknowledge difference, they have blaming and stereotypic attitudes and tend to behave negatively toward and to influence others to insult those different from themselves.

Culturally Sensitive Students. Culturally sensitive students tend to be other focused, with increased cultural knowledge, affective, and skill competencies. They have moved from exhibiting a blaming external focus to imitating accepting behaviors to assuming more personal responsibility for their responses to others. They are able to accept differences and to adapt their own culturally learned responses to be more open to people different from themselves.

Culturally Competent Students. Culturally competent students are culturally knowledgeable, empathic, and highly skilled. They are able to integrate new experiences with old ones and are fluid in their view of differences. They not only appreciate, respect, and value cultural difference, but also are committed to and active in protecting cultural pluralism and in promoting social equality and change. They see and act beyond themselves and their peers in specific and concrete tasks to influence the broader community and societal context.

Developmentally Appropriate Training Objectives and Activities

What skill should the worker focus on developing with children at each developmental stage? What activities move the child toward cultural competence at each stage?

Early School Age. The training objective for early school–age children is to provide knowledge with the goal of creating self-awareness as a member of a group. The emphasis is on self-awareness and intrapersonal understanding within a micro context. Children gain self-awareness as they explore their own cultural heritage and the heritage of others with the support and encouragement of the trainer. Training emphasizes prosocial behaviors and develops the concepts of fairness and respect for others. These children are able to begin to move beyond stereotypic labels and categorizations.

When training early school–age children, the school social worker should concentrate on cultural knowledge competence. The worker should model support and encouragement of cultural diversity for the students and provide a highly structured and supportive learning environment that encourages exploration of diverse views. The student's cultural knowledge base can be expanded through information and facts, reading, role plays, media simulations, role models, guest speakers, and parent presentations.

Middle School Age. The training objective for middle school–age children is to develop attitudes of other-awareness as demonstrated through empathic responses. Children at this age are able to describe feelings, to cooperate, to empathize, and to be more socially responsive; however, these skills need to be fostered through interaction with peers. This other-awareness needs to be framed within the student's own context, because students are more likely to be able to incorporate new learning when viewed in relation to self-knowledge.

In multicultural training the school social worker should focus on cultural affective competence through peer interaction (the mezzo level). Affective competence builds on the knowledge competence of early school age. Students can be encouraged to examine their attitudes through structured value clarification exercises, personal journals, written critical incidents, video simulations, and role plays. This other-awareness enables them to develop empathy, cooperation, and social responsibility.

Early Adolescence. In early adolescence students are able to integrate experiences from past, present, and future perspectives. Their ability to self-reflect at this stage allows students to be critical in their thinking and to confront inconsistencies. The training objective for this developmental level is to get students to act on these inconsistencies (skill competence). Positive peer mentoring by older adolescents models the skills of inclusivity and flexibility. These students, motivated by challenge and experiential learning, are able to expand their commitment beyond self and peers to the arena of social activism (the macro level).

By building on students' knowledge and affective competencies enhanced in the earlier developmental stages, school social workers can develop early adolescents' cultural skill competence. The emphasis is on the interdependence of self, others, and society. The challenge to act is fostered by experience in cross-cultural encounter groups, direct involvement with diverse people and settings, and cultural immersion. Inconsistencies are best confronted by the students themselves and by older adolescent peer mentors. School social workers can guide students in devising and participating in problem-solving activities in the neighborhood and community through collaborative learning and macro-skill-building exercises.

IMPLICATIONS FOR SCHOOL SOCIAL WORKERS

Culture Brokering

The school social worker is "culture broker" (Lefley, 1986, p. 91) in the schools when interfacing with other agencies and when involved in the community. In this capacity, the school social worker bridges gaps in knowledge, affect, and skills and provides training within the school, for other agencies involved with children and families, and in the community. Brokerage also involves the development of links facilitating the exchange of information and clarification of boundaries and areas of necessary overlap among school social worker, teacher, parent, and community. The culture broker also advocates for strategies within the family, school, and community that reinforce and support what students learn in cultural competence training. The broker also functions as a consultant in areas of community outreach, network development, and programmatic research.

Program Evaluation

Evaluation is a critical program component that promotes the accountability of multicultural training programs to school social workers, school administration, teachers, students, parents, and community members. Program, staff, family, and student strengths and weaknesses, as well as program outcome, should be evaluated. The three main purposes of evaluation are to identify relationships between program involvement and changes in knowledge, affect, and skill in participants; to provide a framework for accountability, program change, and development; and to contribute to the practice knowledge base so that school social workers and other professionals and laypeople can read about what worked and what did not in which setting with which age-specific groups of children. Program outcome evaluation should take into consideration the different stages of child development and the different levels of objectives, learning skills, competence, and student response. Each measurement, whether qualitative or quantitative, should match the appropriate dimensions of interest, including valid or invalid objectives; strong or weak learning skills; high or low student response; and evident or not evident self-awareness, other-awareness, or social action involvement.

School social worker involvement may be evaluated during initial and continuing assessment of barriers to and support of desired outcomes in working with children using this developmental framework. Barriers might include lack of parental support for student participation, lack of funding, or after-school programming that excludes subgroups of students, such as those who ride school buses and have no other way of getting home. The evaluation protocol should also assess the theoretical soundness of the training design, operationalization, and student outcome and satisfaction. Evaluation should also facilitate continual monitoring and modification of measurement approaches, objectives, levels of competence, and training foci and micro, mezzo, and macro program impact.

CONCLUSION

The cultural competence training framework presented in this chapter is flexible enough to provide a base for developing programs on the community, district, and national levels for children from early school age to early adolescence. The framework meets students where they are on the cultural competence continuum, building on the abilities and capabilities that they bring to learning and cross-cultural experiences. Because the framework can be adapted to fit the setting, outcomes for students should generalize from one setting to another as students learn to adapt to increasing demands on their intrapersonal, interpersonal, and interdependent competence and skills.

This development-based framework enables school social workers to effectively provide multicultural training in a dynamic and ever-changing society. This framework is expected to remain viable across settings; responsive to the changing dynamics of society, schools, and communities; and current as perspectives on cultural competence change.

REFERENCES

Axelson, J. A. (1993). *Counseling and development in a multicultural society.* Pacific Grove, CA: Brooks/Cole.

Banks, J. A. (1993). Education and cultural diversity in the United States. In A. Fyfe & P. Figueroa (Eds.), *Education for cultural diversity: The challenge for a new era* (pp. 49–68). New York: Routledge.

Bennett, J. M. (1986). Modes of cross-cultural training: Conceptualizing cross-cultural training as education. *International Journal of Intercultural Relations, 10,* 117–134.

Carney, C. G., & Kahn, K. B. (1984). Building competencies for effective cross-cultural counseling: A developmental view. *Counseling Psychologist, 12*(1), 111–119.

Chau, K. L. (1990). A model for teaching cross-cultural practice in social work. *Journal of Social Work Education, 26*(2), 124–133.

Children's Defense Fund. (1992). *The state of America's children.* Washington, DC: Author.

Council on Social Work Education. (1992). *Curriculum policy statement for baccalaureate and master's degree programs in social work education.* New York: Author.

La Belle, T. J., & Ward, C. R. (1994). *Multiculturalism and education: Diversity and its impact on schools and society.* Albany: State University of New York Press.

Leckrone, M. J. (1993). Multicultural education. *School Social Work Journal, 17*(2), 1–10.

Lefley, H. P. (1986). The cross-cultural training institute for mental health professionals: Reeducating practitioners in cultural and community perspectives. In H. P. Lefley & P. B. Pedersen (Eds.), *Cross-cultural training for mental health professionals* (pp. 89–111). Springfield, IL: Charles C Thomas.

Lum, D. (1992). *Social work practice and people of color: A process-stage approach* (2nd ed.). Pacific Grove, CA: Brooks/Cole.

Orlandi, M. A. (1992). Defining cultural competence: An organizing framework. In M. A. Orlandi (Ed.), *Cultural competence for evaluators* (pp. 293–299). Rockville, MD: U.S. Department of Health and Human Services.

Pedersen, P. B., & Ivey, A. (1993). *Culture-centered counseling and interviewing skills: A practical guide.* Westport, CT: Praeger.

Ramsey, P. G. (1982). Multicultural education in early childhood. *Young Children, 37*(2), 13–24.

Stevenson, K. M., Cheung, K.F.M., & Leung, P. (1992). A new approach to training child protective service workers for ethnically sensitive practice. *Child Welfare League of America, 71*(40), 291–305.

U.S. Department of Education. (1991). *Projections of education statistics to 2002.* Washington, DC: National Center for Education Statistics.

York, D. E. (1994). *Cross-cultural training programs.* Westport, CT: Bergin & Garvey.

York, S. (1991). *Roots and wings: Affirming culture in early childhood programs.* St. Paul, MN: Redleaf Press.

This chapter was originally published in the July 1995 issue of Social Work in Education, *vol. 17, pp. 171–182.*

Part V

HEALTH CARE

29 Perceptions of Social Support and Psychological Adaptation to Sexually Acquired HIV among White and African American Men

Larry M. Gant and David G. Ostrow

I n recent studies of the psychosocial coping activities of HIV-infected individuals, the presence and use of social support has gained importance as an indispensable component of psychological care (Flynn, Smith, Bradbeer, & Watley, 1991; Lackner, Joseph, Ostrow, Kessler, & O'Brien, 1991; Ostrow, Fraser, et al., 1991; Reisbeck, Buchta, Hutner, Oliveri, & Schneider, 1991). In particular, much has been learned about the mental health and psychosocial impacts of the human immunodeficiency virus (HIV) epidemic among self-identified gay men, primarily those residing in epicenters of acquired immune deficiency syndrome (AIDS) such as San Francisco and New York.

However, more information is needed regarding groups commonly ignored by current research. Few studies exist, for example, on the mental health of men who have sex with men but do not self-identify as gay or bisexual, of men of color who experience an increase in psychosocial pressures without a corresponding increase in community-based resources, and on the much broader socioeconomic distribution of men at risk of infection through homosexual activities (Mays & Cochran, 1987). For instance, one study of HIV-infected gay white men found relationships among active–behavioral coping, lower mood disturbance, satisfaction with social support, and higher self-esteem (Namir, Wolcott, & Fawzy, 1987). In another study of 29 HIV-infected gay white men, however, active–behavioral coping was significantly related to greater mood disturbance and lower social support (Wolf et al.,

1991). Finally, Hays, Chauncey, and Tobey (1990) found friends and fellow persons with AIDS to be the greatest source of social support for a sample of 24 gay white men, with size of the social support network correlated with mental health measures.

The assumption that the relationships between social support and perceptions of psychosocial and mental health functioning in the presence of AIDS are similar for African American and white men is unwise, problematic, and difficult to substantiate for three reasons. First, ethnic distinctions in help-seeking for mental health problems and physical problems are well documented (for example, Broman, 1987; Dressler, 1985; Sussman, Robins, & Earls, 1987). Second, African Americans and white people differ in the relative use of formal and informal social support systems (Antonucci & Jackson, 1990; Broman, 1987; Neighbors & Jackson, 1987).

Third, African American men who have sex with men face issues that may be qualitatively different from those of their white counterparts, including differential expressions of homophobia in certain African American subpopulations (Friedman, Sotheran, & Abdul-Quader, 1987; Loiacano, 1989). Although this chapter will provide brief examples to develop this point, we refer the reader to Dalton's (1989) classic article for a fascinating and more extended discussion.

African American men who have sex with men have minimal interaction with existing social support networks within the gay white male community (Friedman et al., 1987). Research suggests that this population faces isolation and alienation stemming from real or perceived racism in traditional gay community organizations and depends more heavily on support systems oriented outside the white gay community, particularly family support systems (Icard, 1986; Mays & Cochran, 1987). However, many times family support for African American men is compromised; families may rally around when the physical illnesses of the person become manifest but criticize his sexual orientation and the route of transmission (Icard, Schilling, El-Bassel, & Young, 1992). The reliance of African American men with HIV on informal social support systems that hold negative or stigmatizing attitudes toward HIV infection, sexual orientation, and homosexual or bisexual behavior may negatively affect their psychosocial and mental health status (Dalton, 1989; Icard et al., 1992; Loiacano, 1989).

We emphasize that there is no evidence whatsoever that homophobia is greater in African American than non–African American communities; rather, homophobia may be expressed quite differently in African American communities than in other communities. In many African American communities, the issue of homosexuality has been handled in a complex, ambivalent manner characterized by "boisterous homophobic talk, tacit acceptance in practice, and a broad-based conspiracy of silence" (Dalton, 1989, p. 219).

In studying the differences between white and African American men's patterns of social support, socioeconomic status (SES) factors must be controlled for, especially when race is considered a critical determinant of health or help-seeking behavior (Wilkinson & King, 1987). Rodin and Salovey (1989) observed the following:

> Race and ethnic variables are confounded with socioeconomic factors that may influence health and disease. Low socioeconomic status usually results in a less stable physical environment, a less stable and supportive social environment, altered perceptions of oneself and one's group, and altered capacities to adapt psychologically and behaviorally. (p. 549)

However, Kessler and Cleary (1980) challenged the widely held belief that all racial differences in coping behavior and social support use are explainable by class or SES difference. It is therefore important that a study examining racial patterns of adaptation to stress and of social support separate SES effects and access to care from cultural factors independent of SES.

The study described in this article sought to examine the roles of social support in the mental health and behavioral adaptation of men with homosexually acquired HIV infection. The study also examined whether the sources, functions, or effects of social support differed among African American and white men with HIV. We hypothesized that social support from family would be strongly predictive of mental health outcomes among African American study participants but not white study participants and that social support from friends would be strongly predictive of mental health outcomes for white men but not for African American men.

The findings in this article are based on data collected for a biracial cohort study of social support among gay and bisexual white and African American men in southeastern Michigan. The findings also reflect the experience of social support among this population. Considerable caution should be used in generalizing these findings to other gay and bisexual male populations and to female populations.

METHOD

Subjects

All of the men were recruited from the HIV/AIDS program of the Henry Ford Hospital Medical Center of Detroit, Michigan. All had medical insurance coverage and volunteered for the study. A cohort of 40 men, 20 African American and 20 white, with HIV infection but not AIDS participated in this study. Of this group, one participant chose not to complete major portions of either the baseline or nine-month follow up assessment procedures; his results were deleted from the analysis. Nine months after baseline assessment, follow-up evaluations were performed on 33 of the remaining 39 eligible study participants (17 African American, 16 white). Of the six dropouts, three had moved out of state, two were too ill to participate, and one could not be located.

Measures

Each subject was given intensive psychiatric, face-to-face neuropsychological, behavioral, and psychosocial assessments at entry (1989 to mid-1990) and were re-examined an average of nine months later. After physical examinations, blood draws, and interviews, each man was given a take-home self-report questionnaire assessing social support, mental health, and other psychosocial factors. During the follow-up examinations, several alternative measures of coping behaviors and styles and social support were pilot tested. The measures of particular interest for this investigation—those of social support and mental health—were administered only during the follow-up examinations and interviews.

Social Support

A modified version of the O'Brien and Wortman (1993) social support questionnaire was evaluated and used in this study. The modifications were made after the results of pilot study observations in this cohort showed differences in the direction of correlations between social support and mental health outcome measures (Ostrow, Whitaker, Frasier, & Cohen, 1991).

Four subscales were derived: (1) social conflict (for example, "Do you feel misunderstood by the people in your personal life?"), (2) objective social integration (for example, "How active are you in the groups or clubs you belong to?"), (3) material social support from family (for example, "Is there a family member who would help take care of you if you were confined to bed for several weeks?"), and (4) material social support from friends (for example, "Is there a friend who would help take care of you if you were confined to bed for several weeks?"). Alphas for the overall social support questionnaire were .84 for the entire sample, .77 for the African American respondents, and .89 for the white respondents. Overall and race-specific alphas for each of the two material social support subscales were all greater than .80.

Mental Health

Three self-report measures that have been used extensively in studies of mental health and people with AIDS/HIV were used in this study: the Profile of Mood States (POMS) (Buros, 1978), the Beck Depression Inventory (Beck, 1979), and the UCLA Loneliness Inventory (Ostrow, Whitaker, et al., 1991). The Profile of Mood States is a 65-item self-report symptom scale measuring current mood or affect. It consists of six factor analytically derived subscales for anxiety, anger, depression, confusion, fatigue, and vigor that are summed to generate a total mood disturbance score. Total, affective, and cognitive scale scores from the Beck Depression Inventory were used. Finally, the UCLA Loneliness Inventory was used because of prior findings of its correlation with overall mental health and risk behaviors among HIV-infected men (Kelly, Dunne, Raphael, & Bickham, 1991; Pace, Brown, Rundell, & Paolucci, 1990; Rundell & Brown, 1990). All three measures of mental health were normed with racially mixed groups, including representative percentages of African American men and women (Beck, 1979; Ostrow, Whitaker, et al., 1991; Rundell & Brown, 1990).

Statistical Methods

For all subsequent analyses, Spearman correlations were first computed to identify social support measures that were most closely associated with the three general indexes of mental health. Z-transformed correlations were used to test whether correlations were significantly different between white and African American respondents.

RESULTS

The African American and white men did not differ in mean age (35.2) or years of education (15.1 years) (Table 29-1). There was, however, a substantial if nonsignificant difference in reported average yearly income (African American, $19,400; white, $29,800). Differences in residential location reflect the geographic segregation commonly found in urban (African American respondents) and suburban (white respondents) areas. There were no significant differences in CD-4 counts, major depression status (Table 29-2), or infection classifications under the Centers for Disease Control Classification System (O'Malley, 1989) (Table 29-3) between the two subsamples.

Correlations between Social Support and Mental Health Measures

All Participants. In an analysis of the grouped data (Table 29-4), all correlations between social support and general mental health variables were statistically significant except one (material social support from family and anger/hostility). Not surprisingly, social conflict correlated positively with increased tension/

Table 29-1

Demographic Characteristics and CD-4 (T-Helper Cell) Counts

Characteristic	African American Respondents ($n = 20$)		White Respondents ($n = 20$)		Total	
	M	*SD*	*M*	*SD*	*M*	*SD*
Age (years)	34.5	8.2	35.8	7.3	35.2	7.7
Years of education	14.5	2.0	15.8	2.1	15.1	2.1
Yearly income (thousands of $)	19.4	12.8	29.8	18.0	24.7	16.3
Residence	Urban		Suburban			
CD-4 count[a]	637	388	575	268	601	320

[a]The CD-4 count is the number of white cells (T4 lymphocytes) present per cubic millimeter of blood.

Table 29-2

Major Depression States of Cohort as Determined by Beck Depression Inventory Scale

Characteristic	Baseline				Follow-up			
	Total		African American	White	Total		African American	White
	n	%			*n*	%		
No depression	25	64	15	10	24	73	11	13
Depression within past 6 months	7	18	2	5	9	27	5	4
Depression more than 6 months ago	5	13	1	4	NA	NA	NA	NA
Depression unknown time ago	2	5	1	1	0	0	0	0
Total	39	100	19	20	33	100	16	17

NOTE: NA = not applicable.

Table 29-3

Participants' HIV Infection Classifications Using Centers for Disease Control (CDC) Classification System for HIV Infections

Characteristic	Baseline				Follow-up			
	All		African American	White	All		African American	White
	n	%			n	%		
II (asymptomatic infection)	15	39	7	8	3	9	2	1
III (persistent generalized lymphadenopathy)	7	18	2	5	11	34	4	7
IV A (constitutional disease)	0	0	0	0	0	0	0	0
IV B (neurological disease)	0	0	0	0	2	6	1	1
IV C1 (specified secondary infectious diseases listed in the CDC surveillance definition of AIDS)	0	0	0	0	2	6	2	0
IV C2 (other specified secondary infectious diseases)	17	43	10	7	14	42	9	5
IV D (secondary cancers)	0	0	0	0	1	3	0	1
IV E (other conditions)	0	0	0	0	0	3	0	0
Totals	39	100	12	20	33	100	18	15

Table 29-4

Correlations of Social Support with Mental Health Indicators for All Subjects (*N* = 32)

| | Type of Social Support | | | |
Mental Health Indicator	Social Conflict	Objective Social Integration	Material Social Support: Family	Material Social Support: Friends
Tension/anxiety[a]	0.546*	−0.399*	−0.326**	−0.491*
Depression[a]	0.587*	−0.525*	−0.472*	−0.602*
Anger/hostility[a]	0.679*	−0.339**	−0.256	−0.397*
Depression[b]	0.529*	−0.317**	−0.382*	−0.419*
Loneliness[c]	0.596*	−0.643*	−0.346*	−0.499*

[a]Measure used was the Profile of Mood States (Buros, 1978).
[b]Measure used was the Beck Depression Inventory (Beck, 1979).
[c]Measure used was the UCLA Loneliness Inventory (Ostrow, Whitaker, et al., 1991).
*$p < .05$. **$p < .10$.

anxiety, depression, anger/hostility, and loneliness. Increased objective social integration, material social support from family, and material social support from friends were associated with lower scores across all indexes of mental health.

White Participants. The pattern of correlations between social support and mental health measures for the white participants was very similar to that identified for all subjects (Table 29-5). With the exception of the correlations between material social support from family and tension/anxiety, depression, and anger/hostility, the direction and significance of the correlations are the same for white respondents as for all respondents. Social conflict is again correlated with high scores on all measures, and, with the exceptions noted above, objective social integration, material social support from family, and material social support from friends were significantly and negatively associated with all measures.

African American Respondents. The pattern of correlations between social support and mental health measures differed dramatically for the African American respondents (Table 29-6). Correlations between social conflict and the mental health indexes were in the same direction and statistically significant, if somewhat weaker, than the correlations noted in the total sample and

Table 29-5

Correlations of Social Support with Mental Health Indicators for White Males (N = 15)

| | Type of Social Support | | | |
Mental Health Indicator	Social Conflict	Objective Social Integration	Material Social Support: Family	Material Social Support: Friends
Tension/anxiety[a]	0.823*	−0.619*	−0.358	−0.852*
Depression[a]	0.792*	−0.683*	−0.415	−0.783*
Anger/hostility[a]	0.834*	−0.597*	−0.486**	−0.719*
Depression[b]	0.560*	−0.463**	−0.557*	−0.441*
Loneliness[c]	0.781*	−0.719*	−0.466*	−0.663*

[a]Measure used was the Profile of Mood States (Buros, 1978).
[b]Measure used was the Beck Depression Inventory (Beck, 1979).
[c]Measure used was the UCLA Loneliness Inventory (Ostrow, Whitaker, et al., 1991).
$*p < .05. **p < .10.$

white subsample. Although the correlations between the remainder of the social support measures and the mental health indexes were in the same direction as the other patterns, these correlations were extremely weak or nonsignificant. In fact, with two exceptions—objective social integration with loneliness and material social support from family with depression—there were no significant correlations between measures of social support and measures of general mental health in the African American sample. Especially surprising, in light of the literature citing the importance of family in the social support networks of African Americans, is the lack of significant associations between material social support from family and tension/anxiety, anger/hostility, depression, and loneliness. Only one association, between depression and material social support from family, was significant.

DISCUSSION

People infected with HIV are at high risk for developing serious psychological and neuropsychological dysfunction (Fan, Connor, & Villarreal, 1991). Such impairment can interfere with access to and use of resources critical to enhanced quality of life and increased longevity of the individual. In this study, social support

Table 29-6
___

Correlations of Social Support with Mental Health Indicators for African American Males (N = 17)

	Type of Social Support			
Mental Health Indicator	Social Conflict	Objective Social Integration	Material Social Support: Family	Material Social Support: Friends
Tension/anxiety[a]	0.417**	–0.193	–0.270	–0.149
Depression[a]	0.487*	–0.326	–0.473*	–0.335
Anger/hostility[a]	0.543*	–0.100	–0.132	–0.234
Depression[b]	0.473*	–0.261	–0.219	–0.156
Loneliness[c]	0.451**	–0.552*	–0.183	–0.289

[a]Measure used was the Profile of Mood States (Buros, 1978).
[b]Measure used was the Beck Depression Inventory (Beck, 1979).
[c]Measure used was the UCLA Loneliness Inventory (Ostrow, Whitaker, et al., 1991).
*$p < .05$. **$p < .10$.

was hypothesized to be a critical element of adaptive responses to HIV infection. Because social support can be obtained from informal self-help support groups, there is much potential for promoting such groups, either naturally as they occur in the individual's personal environment or purposefully as in specifically developed supportive interventions.

At the outset of the study, we expected that because of the isolation from traditional gay organizations and ambivalent support networks identified in the literature, the African American respondents would have less access to resources and thus greater risk of developing mental illness than the white respondents. Given the role that social support appears to play in facilitating adaptive mental health among men with HIV, and given the acknowledged importance of the family as a primary social support group among African American populations, we expected to find a strong inverse relationship between the indicators of mental health and reported social support from the family. We did not expect to find relationships between mental health indicators and social support from friends for the African American men in the sample. We expected to find exactly the reverse relationship for the white men in the sample. That is, we expected that social support and mental health outcomes would be found among friends and not family.

To some extent, our expectations for the white men in the sample were confirmed. The relationship between mental health indicators and material social support from friends was as anticipated; material social support was strongly associated with lower reported scores on all mental health indicators. The pattern, while evident, was weaker for material social support from families.

Our expectations for the African American men in the sample were only partially confirmed. We expected and found weak, nonsignificant relationships between the mental health indicators and material social support from friends. We also expected to find strong inverse relationships between social support from family and mental health indicators. We believed that absence of social support would lead to mental illness or would at least be correlated with mental illness. Of all the expected associations, we thought this would be the most obvious and hence the strongest relationship. Instead, we found a pattern of weak, nonsignificant relationships (with the previously mentioned exception of relationship between depression and material social support from the family). Why did this occur?

Unfortunately, methodological limitations of the current study do not allow us to answer this question. We provide an extended discussion of seven major methodological shortcomings in the hope that future investigations will address and resolve these limitations and conjectures.

First, it is possible that the measures of social support we used were not sensitive to the various dimensions of social support from either friends or family for African American men. Other models of social support reflect alternate dimensions of support (for example, emotional support or psychological support). Perhaps African American men with sexually acquired HIV do not seek material, resource-based forms of social support, but rather more emotional or psychological kinds of support, from their families. Investigation with an instrument that allows respondents to describe the type of social support they receive from their families may provide a better, clearer indicator of social support. The authors are currently field-testing such an instrument (Antonucci, 1986) with small groups of African American and white men with sexually acquired HIV.

Second, African American men may feel so conflicted by the compromised nature of social support (that is, support provided for the disease but not for the route of acquisition) that they prefer not to seek material social support from their families (or, apparently, their friends). We noted high associations between social conflict and the mental health measures and the lack of associations between material social support and mental health. It is possible that African American men may feel so conflicted that they perceive receiving social support as more painful than beneficial (Loiacano, 1989).

Third, the relationship between social support and mental health could be mediated by a third factor—the stage of disease. These men tested positive for HIV but were asymptomatic. The African American men may simply have decided that they were not sick enough to call on the material social support resources of their families. It is possible that the progression of the disease may be associated with the use of material social support. The more the disease overtly manifests itself in the symptomatic stages, the greater the perceived need for social support.

Fourth, the African American men with sexually acquired HIV may have feared the disclosure of the disease and the route of transmission—in this case acquired by having unprotected sex with HIV infected men—more than their white counterparts in the study. Several qualitative studies and anecdotal reports suggest that African American men who have sex with other men may consider or identify themselves as bisexual rather than gay. Alternately, African American men who have sex with other men may choose not to assign themselves with the value-laden and lifestyle-implicative terms "gay" or "bisexual," but rather use a simple description of the behavior (for example, having sex with men).

African American men who have sex with other men, then, may often reject the gay or bisexual indicator of sexual expression in favor of the behavioral description. However, although they themselves may be comfortable with this self-identification, they may feel that family and friends (at least female friends and male friends who do not have sex with men) would perceive them as gay or homosexual and therefore disapprove of them or even terminate the relationship. The fear of disclosure of this route of transmission may therefore prevent African American men from seeking either social support in general or material social support in particular from family or friends.

Fifth, it is possible that the significant associations between social conflict and general mental health outcomes reported by these African American men reflected more the general stresses and conflict of being African American in the United States rather than either specific stresses related to sexual expression ("outness") or HIV/AIDS-related stresses. Unfortunately, we did not ask questions about AIDS ethnocentrism (race-relevant beliefs that African American men may hold regarding their risk of HIV/AIDS) (Peterson et al., 1992). Participants responded to several items addressing HIV/AIDS-related stresses, but these items had very low interitem reliability and thus were not reported.

Sixth, it is possible that socioeconomic status determines access to social support. This possibility is raised given the previously cited comments of Rodin and Salovey (1989) and Kessler and Cleary (1980). Because of the careful selection of an economically and educationally matched sample, and given the lack of significant educational and economic differences between the white and African American gay and bisexual men, it seems that this conjecture has been adequately resolved and needs no further consideration for this study.

Finally, it is possible that the African American men may have lied about their mental health. Certainly, the issue of African Americans disclosing information to white interviewers is a serious methodological problem (Mays & Jackson, 1991). However, in this project the interviewer knew the respondents extremely well and had worked for several years in the clinic. It is hoped that the African American men did not perceive him as a stranger collecting information and therefore gave honest answers. Additionally, if one considers as valid the notion that the African American men lied about their mental health, one would wonder about the extent to which they lied in their other responses to the survey.

This study, although largely descriptive in nature, has several practice implications. Readers of past and current studies that indicate a relationship between social support and mental health status of men with HIV have developed both formal and informal social support groups. Without a better understanding of the types of social support, it is conceivable that support groups that are avowedly "supportive" may actually have negative consequences, especially if the social support is focused on the identification of social conflict issues (for example, "no one understands me," "I feel misunderstood by my friends," "I feel misunderstood by my family").

Support groups for HIV-positive African American and white men who have acquired HIV through unprotected sex with other men may be more heterogeneous than initially thought. The distinctly different perceptions of sexual expression held by African American and white men may lead to conflict over several topics. For instance, the issue of "coming out" may be much more problematic or irrelevant for African American men than white men, simply because the definition of sexual expression is not desired.

Social workers who work with African American men with sexually acquired HIV need to explore fully their client's notions of social support, and if a family of origin or choice is identified as a potential resource, the worker may wish to explore the kind of support desired by the client from his family. Material social support may not be desired at the current time.

Likewise, the social worker working with such clients may wish to pay more attention to the clients' stage of the disease. If the client declined the support of the family in earlier, asymptomatic stages of the disease, it is possible the client may reconsider seeking family social support as the disease moves to the symptomatic stages.

Finally, this study reflects the need to understand what social support is and what it means, both theoretically and practically. At the very least, the worker should endeavor to understand what social support means for African American and white men with sexually acquired HIV and to assume neither that all social support is good and positive social support nor that what is perceived as social support for some is equivalently perceived as social support for all.

REFERENCES

Antonucci, T. C. (1986). Measuring social support networks: Hierarchical mapping technique. *Generations, 10*, 10–12.

Antonucci, T. C., & Jackson, J. S. (1990). The role of reciprocity in social support. In B. R. Sarason, I. G. Sarason, & G. R. Pierce (Eds.), *Social support: An interactional view* (pp. 219–250). New York: John Wiley & Sons.

Beck, A. T. (1979). *Cognitive therapy of depression*. New York: Guilford Press.

Broman, C. L. (1987). Race differences in professional help seeking. *American Journal of Community Psychology, 15*, 473–489.

Buros, O. K. (Ed.). (1978). *The eighth mental measurements yearbook.* Highland Park, NJ: Gryphon Press.

Dalton, H. L. (1989). AIDS in blackface. *Daedalus, 118,* 205–227.

Dressler, W. W. (1985). The social and cultural context of coping: Action, gender, and symptoms in a southern black community. *Social Science and Medicine, 21,* 499–506.

Fan, H., Connor, R. F., & Villarreal, L. P. (1991). *The biology of AIDS.* Boston: Jones & Bartlett.

Flynn, R., Smith, A. P., Bradbeer, C., & Watley, J. (1991, August). *The role of social support in modifying the relationship between stress and self-reported physical symptoms, cognitive deficits and psychopathology in gay men with HIV infection: A pilot study.* Paper presented at the First International Conference, Biopsychosocial Aspects of HIV Infection, Amsterdam, The Netherlands.

Friedman, S. R., Sotheran, J. L., & Abdul-Quader, A. (1987). The AIDS epidemic among blacks and Hispanics. *Milbank Quarterly, 65,* 455–499.

Hays, R. B., Chauncey, S., & Tobey, L. A. (1990). The social networks of gay men with AIDS. *Journal of Community Psychology, 18,* 374–385.

Icard, L. (1986). Black gay men and conflicting social identities: Sexual orientation versus racial identity. *Journal of Social Work and Human Sexuality, 4,* 83–93.

Icard, L., Schilling, R. F., El-Bassel, N., & Young, D. (1992). Preventing AIDS among black gay men and black gay and heterosexual intravenous drug users. *Social Work, 37,* 440–445.

Kelly, B., Dunne, M., Raphael, B., & Bickham, C. (1991). Relationships between mental adjustment to HIV diagnosis, psychological morbidity and sexual behaviour. *British Journal of Clinical Psychology, 30,* 370–372.

Kessler, R. C., & Cleary, P. D. (1980). Social class and psychological distress. *American Sociological Review, 45,* 463–478.

Lackner, J. B., Joseph, J. G., Ostrow, D. G., Kessler, R. C., & O'Brien, K. (1991). *Predictors of psychological distress in a cohort of gay men: The role of social support and coping.* Paper presented at the First International Conference, Biopsychosocial Aspects of HIV Infection, Amsterdam, The Netherlands.

Loiacano, D. K. (1989). Gay identity issues among black Americans: Racism, homophobia and the need for validation. *Journal of Counseling and Development, 68,* 21–25.

Mays, V. M., & Cochran, S. D. (1987). Acquired immunodeficiency syndrome and black Americans: Special psychosocial issues. *Public Health Reports, 102,* 224–231.

Mays, V. M., & Jackson, J. S. (1991). AIDS survey methodology with black Americans. *Social Science and Medicine, 33,* 47–54.

Namir, S., Wolcott, D. L., & Fawzy, F. (1987). Coping with AIDS: Psychosocial and health implications. *Journal of Applied Social Psychology, 17,* 309–328.

Neighbors, H., & Jackson, J. S. (1987). Barriers to medical care among adult blacks: What happens to the uninsured? *Journal of the National Medical Association, 79,* 489–493.

O'Brien, K., & Wortman, C. B. (1993). Social relationships of men at risk for AIDS. *Social Science Medicine, 36,* 1161–1167.

O'Malley, P. (1989). *The AIDS epidemic: Private rights and the public interest.* Boston: Beacon Press.

Ostrow, D. G., Fraser, K., Nelson, C., Schork, T., Thomas, C., Whitaker, R., Gant, L., & Fisher, E. (1991). *Social support and mental health among a biracial cohort of HIV-infected homosexual/bisexual men.* Paper presented at the First International Conference, Biopsychosocial Aspects of HIV Infection, Amsterdam, The Netherlands.

Ostrow, D. G., Whitaker, R. E., Frasier, K., & Cohen, C. (1991). Racial differences in social support and mental health in men with HIV infection: A pilot study. *AIDS Care, 3,* 55–62.

Pace, J., Brown, G. R., Rundell, J. R., & Paolucci, S. (1990). Prevalence of psychiatric disorders in a mandatory screening program for infection with human immunodeficiency virus: A pilot study. *Military Medicine, 155*(2), 76–80.

Peterson, J. L., Coates, T. J., Catania, J. A., Middleton, L., Hilliard, B., & Hearst, N. (1992). High risk sexual behavior and condom use among gay and bisexual African-American men. *American Journal of Public Health, 82,* 1490–1494.

Reisbeck, G., Buchta, M., Hutner, G., Oliveri, G., & Schneider, M. M. (1991). *Coping, social support, and well-being of HIV-infected homosexuals, hemophiliacs and women: A qualitative–quantitative comparison.* Paper presented at the First International Conference, Biopsychosocial Aspects of HIV Infection, Amsterdam, The Netherlands.

Rodin, J., & Salovey, P. (1989). Health psychology. *Annual Review of Psychology, 40,* 533–579.

Rundell, J. R., & Brown, G. R. (1990). Persistence of psychiatric symptoms in HIV-seropositive persons. *American Journal of Psychiatry, 147,* 674–675.

Sussman, L. K., Robins, L. N., & Earls, F. (1987). Treatment-seeking for depression by black and white Americans. *Social Science and Medicine, 24,* 187–196.

Wilkinson, D. Y., & King, G. (1987). Conceptual and methodological issues in the use of race as a variable: Policy implications. *Milbank Quarterly, 65,* 56–71.

Wolf, T. M., Balson, P. M., Morse, E. V., Simon, P. M., Gaumer, R. H., Dralle, P. W., & Williams, M. H. (1991). Relationship of coping style to affective state and perceived social support in asymptomatic and symptomatic HIV-infected persons: Implications for clinical management. *Journal of Clinical Psychiatry, 52,* 171–173.

This chapter was originally published in the March 1995 issue of Social Work, *vol. 40, pp. 215–224.*

30 Estimating Rates of Psychosocial Problems in Urban and Poor Children with Sickle Cell Anemia

Oscar A. Barbarin, Charles F. Whitten, and Sandy M. Bonds

P roblems of adjustment occur among all children, irrespective of health status. However, chronically ill children and their siblings experience these problems at rates twice as high as those for healthy children. (See Barbarin, 1990, for a review of the research.) Children with sickle cell anemia (SCA) are no exception. The disease is also associated with increased risk of several adverse developmental outcomes. Available data on adjustment to SCA suggest that dysfunction may occur in several domains: psychological functioning (for example, anxiety, depression, fear, preoccupation with death, and diminished self-esteem), academic functioning (for example, poor grades, school failure, and school dropout), social functioning (for example, isolation and poor relations with peers), and family functioning (poor relations with parents and siblings) (Anderson, Werzman, & McMahon, 1986; Conyard, Krishnamurthy, & Dosik, 1980; Evans, Burlew, & Oler, 1988; Hurtig & White, 1986; Nadel & Portadin, 1977; Nevergold, 1987). For example, 24 adolescents with SCA were less successful in school and less satisfied with their bodies; they spent less time in social activities and exhibited depressive symptoms more often than disease-free adolescents matched for race, gender, age, and socioeconomic status (SES) (Morgan & Jackson, 1986). However, in light of inconsistencies in the findings of several studies, the extent of psychosocial impairment associated with SCA is not entirely clear.

Failure to account adequately for the potential effects of gender, age, income, and illness severity on psychosocial adjustment has contributed to the ambiguity of the existing body of research

(Barbarin & Soler, 1993). For example, boys experience significantly more adjustment problems than girls (Hurtig & White, 1986), and children from low SES families experience more adjustment problems than children from high SES families (Lemanek, Moore, Gresham, Williamson, & Kelley, 1986). *Illness severity*, defined as the frequency of serious pain episodes, has been related to high levels of depressive symptoms (Nadel & Portadin, 1977) and to problems of school adjustment (Hurtig, Koepke, & Park, 1989). Consequently, discrepancies among published conclusions about psychosocial risks may be explained in part by differences among the samples in gender, SES, or illness severity (Hurtig & Park, 1989).

Currently, no credible estimates exist of the prevalence of psychosocial difficulties in children with SCA. As a result, the most pressing needs of the children at greatest risk of adjustment problems have not been identified. This information could inform the development of social work services and channel more precisely resources to the children who need them most. The study in this chapter helps provide that information by concentrating on poor children in urban areas, an important subgroup of children with SCA. It examines adjustment in social, psychological, academic, and medical domains. It was expected that the risk of adjustment difficulties across these domains would be related to gender, family income, and frequency of serious pain episodes.

METHODS

Participants

The study sample consisted of 327 children four to 17 years old who were being treated for SCA at an urban midwestern children's hospital. Data were drawn from interviews with the children and their parents during an annual psychosocial assessment. Fifty-six percent ($n = 182$) of the children were male, and 44 percent ($n = 145$) were female. A total of 144 children (44 percent) were four to eight years old, 117 (36.8 percent) were eight to 13 years old, and 66 (20.0 percent) were 13 to 17 years old.

Procedure

As part of the preventive health care provided by the Comprehensive Sickle Cell Clinic at the hospital, an annual medical examination is conducted for all patients. A component of this examination is a psychosocial assessment of the patient and the family. Because the assessment is a regular part of the annual medical examination, information on more than 95 percent of children treated for SCA at the hospital clinic is available. The group on whom data are available is representative of poor and urban children treated for SCA, the largest group treated at the clinic.

The psychosocial assessment is a structured interview of parents or guardians and patients conducted in the outpatient clinic by clinical nurse practitioners or social workers. The interview, which was developed by medical and social work staff, covered demographics; problems currently experienced by the family; issues related to financial needs and resources; access to medical care; medical, social, academic, and work problems; mood ratings of patient and parent; parental concerns and expectations; family impact of the illness; and family functioning. The content of the interview was based on issues that surfaced over a number of years as concerns expressed by family members and clinic staff. The assessment interview uses both open-ended questions and numerical ratings to gather information. Use of standardized psychological tests was judged to be inappropriate and inadequate because of their bias toward psychopathology and because they do not provide coverage of the issues of greatest concern in the study of illness adjustment with urban African American children.

In the case of children younger than 16, parents or guardians were the primary sources of information. However, in separate interviews children older than eight answered some of the same questions posed to guardians regarding health status, self-perception, school performance, and psychological functioning. Questions in some domains related to school performance and social functioning (for example, going out with friends) were omitted because of their inappropriateness for very young children, particularly those not enrolled in school.

Because we were interested in the frequency of parental concerns and wished to express it in terms of percentage of children affected, all responses were converted to a yes–no format; the respondent indicated whether the child experienced the problem. This approach yielded information regarding the frequency of concerns but did not indicate the intensity or severity of the problem.

Domains and Problems

The problems covered in the psychosocial assessment are arranged by adjustment domains: illness, social, academic, psychological, and family.

Illness Adjustment. Problems of living with the illness measured whether the illness was viewed and experienced as a problem that disrupted day-to-day life. Teasing measured whether the ill child was known to have been teased about some aspects of his or her illness. Delayed growth indicated whether the child was below average in size. Diminutive stature and delayed onset of puberty are common sequelae to SCA. Barriers to medical care identified the experienced difficulty in obtaining medical care for the ill child because of one of the following impediments: lack of transportation or funds for transportation, inability to obtain time off from work, or lack of medical insurance or money to pay for care.

Social Adjustment. Characterization of the child as shy or lonely, having problems getting along with friends, or lacking a close friend indicated social adjustment problems.

Academic Adjustment. These items covered several issues indicative of how the children were functioning in school: failing grades, retention in grade, lack of motivation, conflict with teachers, transportation problems, or need for special education program. Questions related to this domain were asked of children who had begun elementary school by the time of the interview.

Psychological Adjustment. Problems in the emotional expression of the ill child, including anger, fear, moodiness, depression, shame, and hopelessness were rated.

Family Adjustment. Problems of family adjustment related to parent, child, and sibling fears were assessed. Parental fear indicated depth of the parents' fears about the child's SCA or its complications. Parental worry indicated the parents' concern about and protectiveness of the physical welfare of the ill child or anxiety about the child's future prospects. Sibling adjustment to the illness assessed problems siblings had in response to the illness including jealousy, avoidance of the ill child, acting out, fear, and overprotection.

RESULTS

Demographic Characteristics

Mothers were 96 percent of the 327 informants and fathers only 3 percent. An equal proportion (40 percent) of these mothers were married or divorced or widowed; 20 percent were never married. The mean years of education completed was 12.0 for mothers and 11.8 for fathers. Forty-seven percent of families had three or more children. Many families had more than one child with SCA. About 27 percent of children reported having a sibling with SCA. The sample represented in this study was urban and largely, although not exclusively, poor. The median family income for the sample was under $6,000 per year, whereas the 1980 median income for African American families in the same metropolitan area was $15,931. Most of the families received some form of public assistance: Aid to Families with Dependent Children (AFDC), Supplemental Security Income (SSI), or disability payments. Over a fourth (27 percent) of the families reported not having enough income for basic necessities. Only 32 percent had private health insurance, and 25 percent had difficulty paying out-of-pocket expenses related to outpatient doctor visits, transportation, and medicines.

Problems

Frequencies were tabulated for each problem in the psychosocial assessment, and percentages were computed to indicate the proportion of the total sample experiencing difficulty on that issue. Table 30-1 provides the percentages for problems reported most frequently in the total sample. It is as useful to note items from the psychosocial assessment that do not appear on Table 30-1 as it is to note those that were experienced more frequently by the sample. Items in the assessment interview related to family relations and functioning revealed very low rates of problems in the family. Very small percentages of families reported conflict or emotional alienation among family members.

Three illness adjustment problems affected many children and families: activity disruption (problem living with SCA), teasing, and delayed growth. About one of three children with SCA was teased because of the illness or some visible sequelae of the illness. In addition, 27 percent of parents reported delayed growth.

Table 30-1

Percentage of Children with Problems on Indexes of Psychosocial Adjustment to Sickle Cell Anemia by Pain, Age, and Gender

Adjustment Domain	Total (n = 327)	Pain Episodes[a]		Age (Years)			Gender	
		None (n = 91)	Some (n = 233)	Younger than 8 (n = 144)	8 to 13 (n = 117)	14 to 17 (n = 66)	Male (n = 182)	Female (n = 145)
Illness adjustment								
Activity disruption	23	10	24	15	28	27	18	31
Teasing	32	20	38	14	32	36	30	33
Delayed growth	27	25	27	21	31	25	28	25
Social adjustment								
Shyness	42	46	41	42	43	41	40	43
Loneliness	26	18	30	28	26	25	25	26
No close friendship	23	20	25	25	24	20	17	19
Too few friends	18	21	13	8	21	18	15	16
Academic adjustment								
Problems at school	34	33	34	25	38	31	35	31
Course failure	19	15	21	10	17	31	21	17
Retention in grade	23	29	21	5	36	38	27	17
Poor grades	19	20	19	4	31	30	19	19
Poor motivation	12	14	10	3	22	14	16	7
Psychological adjustment								
Anger	33	19	38	14	30	36	28	35
Fear	38	33	40	14	39	39	32	45
Moodiness	41	36	43	36	46	47	39	45
Hopelessness	26	23	36	29	26	25	26	26
Depression	26	19	21	24	31	25	24	27
Shame	26	19	31	29	24	31	25	29
Family adjustment								
Sibling jealousy	15	11	11	16	17	12	14	18
Sibling overprotection	29	21	21	39	30	12	26	33
Sibling acting out	9	6	10	11	8	5	8	9
Sibling fear	27	25	28	27	28	26	26	28
Poor sibling relations	9	9	14	9	11	7	9	9
Parental fear	56	45	60	64	51	46	55	57
Parental worry	38	62	77	84	66	67	72	76

[a]Data missing on three cases.

Social adjustment was problematic for many children. Shyness, loneliness, and lack of a close friend were reported most frequently. More than two of five children were characterized as shy, one in four had problems with loneliness, and more than one in five had no close friend. About one of every three children had problems at school. At the time of the interview almost one in five had failed a course; among those in high school, the number increased to almost one in three. The same pattern held for the number of children who were held back at least one grade level. With respect to the psychological domain, about one in three children was depicted as angry and fearful, and one in four exhibited depressive symptoms, including moodiness, hopelessness, depression, and shame. Data on sibling responses to the illness indicated that at least one of four siblings was fearful or overprotected the ill child. Parental fear was reported by over half of the respondents, and parental worry about the ill child was reported by 38 percent of families.

The study tested assertions made in previous research about the effects of income, age, gender, and disease adjustment (Lemanek et al., 1986). Because the data took the form of frequencies, we used log-linear analysis to assess the effects of demographic variables and pain on adjustment. We used the SPSS program to test a specific class of log-linear models called logit models. This analytical approach permitted us to assess the goodness of fit of a model that states that the observed frequency of a particular problem depends on a class of independent variables or the interactions among them.

In this study gender, age, and occurrence of pain were independent variables. The null hypothesis tested was that the observed frequency of a problem in a given group (for example, experiencing serious pain in adolescent females or children younger than eight) was not different from the frequency expected if the independent variable had no influence at all on the occurrence of a problem. Accordingly, the dependent variable in the analysis is the log of the probability that a problem might occur. It is the log of the ratio of the odds of a problem occurring to the odds that a problem does not occur in a given group or subgroup. If the null hypothesis is to be rejected, the residual for the effect tested must be significantly greater than 0. This analytical approach tests the main effects of and interactions among the independent variables on the frequencies of problems.

First, simple models were tested for the effect of income. Total annual family income was assessed by asking parents to indicate which of seven income clusters they fell into—from under $3,000 to over $21,000 in increments of $3,000. For analysis these were reduced to three groups: under $6,000, $6,000 to $12,000, and over $12,000. No significant effects were found on the adjustment problems for income, with the exception of impediments to care. Low-income families more frequently reported barriers to medical care than higher-income groups.

On average children in the sample experienced 4.3 episodes of pain serious enough to seek medical assistance at a hospital emergency room. However, there was considerable variability in the frequency of pain. Some children had no serious pain episodes during that year; others had as many as 20 episodes per year. About 28 percent of the sample ($n = 91$) experienced no serious pain episode, 21 percent ($n = 69$) experienced one episode, and 20 percent ($n = 66$) experienced two episodes. Ten percent ($n = 33$) experienced three episodes, 9 percent ($n = 29$) experienced four episodes, 3 percent ($n = 10$) had five, 3 percent ($n = 10$) had six, and 5 percent ($n = 16$) had seven to 20 episodes. In the logit analyses the dichotomous variable compared those who had serious pain episodes to those who had none that year. The sample was divided into three age groups: four to seven years, eight to 13 years, and 14 to 17 years.

Logit models were tested to assess the significance of main effects for and interactions among pain, gender, and age on the likelihood of adjustment problems. The .05 level was accepted as the standard of significance. Results of these analyses show significant main effects of gender on disease adjustment problems and retention in grade (Table 30-2). Girls were significantly more likely than boys to experience the illness as a problem on a day-to-day basis, but boys were more likely than girls to be held back a year in school. Significant main effects on age occurred with respect to failing a class and overprotection by a sibling. Adolescents more frequently failed a class than younger children, and younger children were overprotected more often by their siblings than older children and adolescents.

Pain has a significant effect on several different adjustment problems: Illness-related problems of activity disruption and teasing were more likely to be experienced by those with pain than

Table 30-2

Coefficients for Problem Areas Testing Effect of Gender, Pain, Age, and Their Interactions on Children with Sickle Cell Anemia

Adjustment Domain	Gender (G)	Pain (P)	Age(A)	G×P	G×A	P×A	G×P×A
Illness adjustment							
Activity disruption	.24*	.32*	-.15*	.02	.11	.15	-.17
Teasing	.06	.23*	.05	.01	.01	.02	.01
Delayed growth	.07	.03	.10	.04	-.08	-.09	.09
Social adjustment							
Shyness	.02	.12	.00	.10	.06	.06	.02
Loneliness	.16	.21	.27	.10	.08	.09	.13
No close friends	.05	.10	.12	.08	.03	.02	.03
Too few friends	.15	.19	.09	.08	.05	.06	.09
Academic adjustment							
Problems at school	-.21	.05	.24	.07	.07	.09	.11
Course failure	.08	.17	.26*	.00	.01	.15	.07
Retention in grade	.18*	.08	.04	.02	.14	.04	.02
Poor grades	.01	.16	.00	.06	.05	.10	.04
Poor motivation	.15	.18	.09	.13	.04	.10	.03
Psychological adjustment							
Anger	.14	.24*	.03	.09	.00	.19*	.17
Fear	.25*	.15	-.14	.04	.00	.09	.13
Moodiness	.03	.09	.10	.03	.09	.09	.03
Hopelessness	.05	.21*	.10	.07	.00	.22*	.01
Depression	.03	.31*	.12	.04	.07	.11	-.17
Shame	.08	.31*	.03	.03	.03	.03	.03
Family adjustment							
Sibling jealousy	.03	-.20	.08	.00	.03	.05	.12
Sibling overprotection	.06	.01	.31*	-.31*	.00	.06	.03
Sibling acting out	.06	.24	.08	.20	.07	.06	.01
Sibling fear	.09	.11	.16	.09	-.27*	.21	.06
Poor sibling relations	.00	.15	.00	.00	.00	.11	.00
Parental fear	.02	.20*	.07	.04	.00	.04	.08
Parental worry	.17	.22*	.16	.06	.13	.08	.20

*p < .05.

those without pain. Children with pain were more likely to be angry, hopeless, depressed, and ashamed than children who had not experienced serious pain episodes. Moreover, the parents of children with pain were also more likely to be fearful and to worry than parents of children without serious pain episodes. There were significant relationships between gender, pain, and sibling overprotection. Females who experienced pain were more likely to be overprotected than the other groups. Finally, there was a significant gender–age interaction for sibling fear; siblings of young females were more fearful than other groups.

DISCUSSION

If frequency of occurrence is used as a gauge of problem magnitude for the sample, problems related to social relations, isolation, and shyness constituted the most serious area of concern. The experience of day-to-day problems related to the illness may have interfered with the development of intimate social relations. In many ways this finding is surprising, given the scant attention paid to social adjustment in research on children's adjustment to chronic illness.

From the standpoint of validity, parents' reports did not stand alone. Teachers have also characterized seriously ill children as more socially isolated and less well adjusted in social interactions than their peers who are not ill (Noll, Bukowski, Rogosch, & Leroy, 1990). Perhaps illness and stigma associated with SCA attenuate initiation and reciprocation of social interaction both by the ill child and potential friends. Social isolation observed among ill children is particularly disconcerting because of what it augurs for social relations in adult life.

Rates of academic problems among children with SCA are also a serious concern. There was no significant relationship between academic functioning and the measure used to estimate illness effect. In the absence of a control group and a significant effect for pain, questions naturally arise about the ability to draw logical connections between academic problems observed in the sample and the disease itself. Fortunately, the academic functioning of African American children has been the subject of numerous empirical studies using large representative samples. For example, the Child Health Supplement of the National Health Interview Survey (U.S. Department of Health and Human Services, 1981) gathered data on a national representative sample of African American children. The children with SCA in the study had rates of school failure that were twice as high as those for the national sample of African American children matched for income.

Moreover, the possibility that frequency of less-severe pain, which could not be reliably measured in this study, might be related to deterioration of academic performance cannot be ruled out. The occurrence of subtle pain may be disruptive enough to decrease the motivation necessary to succeed academically. Daily pain diaries might be used to explore this possibility. It is also possible that parental concern about a premature death associated with SCA may lower parental expectations and maturity demands and may diminish incentives for children to sustain a level of effort needed to perform well. It is important to understand the processes affecting the academic performance of children with SCA because of their consequences for financial independence and emotional well-being in adulthood.

Gender, absolute income, and age have very limited roles in determining the risk of adjustment problems. The data revealed that these variables are less robust and significant mediators of psychosocial outcomes than reported in many previous studies on smaller samples of children and adolescents with SCA. Although the study did find several important differences between males and females, between young children and adolescents, and between low- and moderate-income families, the differences were not large. The failure to replicate previously observed relations between income and adjustment must be interpreted with caution. The sample used represents a very narrow income range of poor to very poor families. If a broader range of incomes were included, the data might be consistent with other studies.

With the exception of the disruptiveness of the illness on a day-to-day basis and its effect on being held back in school, males and females experienced roughly the same chances of having or not having adjustment difficulties. Males, however, seemed to be more vulnerable to dysfunction in the academic arena, but this circumstance is true even for children who are not ill (Pharr & Barbarin, 1981). Similarly, the effect of age is relatively minor. Adolescents are more likely to experience academic failure than younger children. That difference may simply be an artifact. Adolescents have been in school longer and consequently have had more opportunities to fail. A likely explanation of the higher rates of failure is that skill deficits accumulated during elementary school begin to surface in ways that cannot be avoided or easily managed at the junior and senior high school level. Transitions from elementary school to middle and senior high schools are demanding for all children, and they may be doubly difficult for ill children.

No matter what accounts for the age trend in academic problems, the existence of academic difficulties for a large number of children with SCA is indisputable. Clearly much has to be done in a preventive way to help children build a solid foundation of skills and motivation in elementary schools. In addition, academic support programs throughout the middle and high school years are needed as well.

The result of the log-linear analysis provided convincing evidence of effect related to the occurrence of serious pain episodes. It shows clearly that children who experience serious pain are significantly more likely to have symptoms such as depression than children who do not experience pain. Estimates of depressive symptoms fall most frequently in the range of 10 percent to 15 percent. Although these estimates are often flawed methodologically, a history of pain is an important mediator of adjustment. Merely being diagnosed with SCA may not be enough to predict problems of adjustment. Though pain is the most widely occurring physical effect associated with SCA, some children do not have serious pain episodes. This finding may partially explain why some studies that failed to control for pain episodes or severity did not find differences in adjustment between children with SCA and controls who were not ill.

Another important finding from the study is the high level of fear that family members have about the illness. At first glance this fear may appear to be an uncomfortable though unavoidable reaction that is inconsequential in the larger scheme. Such fears may flow from a pattern of beliefs and behaviors driven by the specter of the child's fragility and conviction that pain places the child at death's doorstep. When such beliefs color the family's appraisal of the situation, parents may unnecessarily circumscribe the child's range of activities. The use of family-focused psychoeducational intervention as part of comprehensive health care is an important first step in addressing this anxiety. Emphasis is also needed in the teaching and nurturing of social skills for children with problems in this domain. Recent work on peer relations offers much information that is useful in understanding and intervening in this domain. Finally, given the importance of pain to adjustment, teaching children to live fully and to cope in spite of pain is particularly important. The data suggest that the most judicious use of resources might be to invest in a combination of preventive early intervention followed up with services and resources targeted specifically to those groups having difficulty.

Although this chapter concentrates on problems reported with highest frequency, it is illuminating to note the problem areas included in the clinical assessment that were not frequently regarded as problems. The data related to family functioning suggest an especially favorable picture of family life for this group. Moreover, in light of prior research, the rates of some problems are surprisingly low. For example, problems related to apathy, low motivation, low self-concept, or conduct disorder were not often reported. Thus, maladjustment in these domains is far from absolute or inevitable.

In conclusion, the results of the study show clearly that the most significant and widespread problems for children with SCA arise in the social and academic arenas. Illness severity places children at greater risk of teasing and of psychological symptoms. Moreover, males and adolescents are particularly vulnerable to problems in academic settings. The increased risk faced by males, adolescents, and those with frequent pain make these groups suitable targets for preventive psychosocial interventions by medical social workers.

REFERENCES

Anderson, J., Werzman, M., & McMahon, L. (1986). Psychosocial adjustment, family functioning and sickle cell disease. *American Journal of Diseases of Children, 140,* 297.

Barbarin, O. (1990). Adjustment to serious illness. In B. Lahey & A. Kazdin (Eds.), *Advances in clinical child psychology* (Vol. 13., pp. 377–403). New York: Plenum Press.

Barbarin, O., & Soler, R. (1993). Behavioral, emotional, and academic adjustment in a national probability sample of African American children: Effects of age, gender, and family structure. *Journal of Black Psychology, 19*(4), 423–446.

Conyard, S., Krishnamurthy, M., & Dosik, H. (1980). Psychosocial aspects of sickle-cell anemia in adolescents. *Health & Social Work, 5,* 20–26.

Evans, R. C., Burlew, A. K., & Oler, C. H. (1988). Children with sickle cell anemia: Parental relations, parent–child relation and child behavior. *Social Work, 33,* 127–130.

Hurtig, A., Koepke, D., & Park, K. (1989). Relation between severity of chronic illness and adjustment in children and adolescents with sickle cell disease. *Journal of Pediatric Psychology, 14,* 117–132.

Hurtig, A., & Park, K. (1989). Adjustment and coping in adolescents with sickle cell disease. *Annals of the New York Academy of Sciences, 565,* 172–182.

Hurtig, A. L., & White, L. S. (1986). Children and adolescents: The unexpected terrain of emotional development. In L. Hurley & T. Viera (Eds.), *Sickle cell disease: Psychological and psychosocial issues* (pp. 24–40). Urbana: University of Illinois Press.

Lemanek, K., Moore, S., Gresham, F., Williamson, D., & Kelley, M. (1986). Psychological adjustment of children with sickle cell anemia. *Journal of Pediatric Psychology, 11,* 397–410.

Morgan, S., & Jackson, J. (1986). Psychological and social concomitants of sickle cell anemia in adolescents. *Journal of Pediatric Psychology, 11,* 429–440.

Nadel, C., & Portadin, G. (1977). Sickle cell crises: Psychological factors associated with onset. *New York State Journal of Medicine, 77,* 1075–1078.

Nevergold, B. S. (1987). Sickle cell disease and its effects on parental relations, family environment and self-perception of black adolescents. *Dissertation Abstracts International, 47*(9-A), 3315.

Noll, R. B., Bukowski, W. M., Rogosch, F. A., & Leroy, S. (1990). Social interactions between children with cancer and their peers: Teacher ratings. *Journal of Pediatric Psychology, 15,* 43–56.

Pharr, O., & Barbarin, O. (1981). Social suspension: A problem of person–environment fit. In O. Barbarin, P. Good, O. Pharr, & J. Siskind (Eds.), *Institutional racism and community competence* (DHHS-ADM 81, pp. 76–90). Washington, DC: U.S. Government Printing Office.

U.S. Department of Health and Human Services. (1981). *National Health Interview Survey, child health supplement.* Washington, DC: National Institute of Child Health and Human Development.

This chapter was originally published in the May 1994 issue of Health & Social Work, *vol. 19, pp. 112–119.*

31 Psychiatric Social Work and Socialism: Problems and Potential in China

Veronica Pearson and Michael Phillips

The People's Republic of China is no different from any other country in having a significant number of mentally ill citizens. The most extensive epidemiological study done in China found that the prevalence of schizophrenia is 6.06 per 1,000 in urban China and 3.42 per 1,000 in rural China (Research Coordinating Group, 1986), a total of approximately 4,500,000 people. Only about 2 percent of these individuals are hospitalized at any one time; over 90 percent of them are cared for by their families (Phillips, 1993). In contrast, only an estimated 40 percent of people with schizophrenia in the United States are cared for by their families (Torrey, 1988), and in the United Kingdom, 60 percent of those suffering their first episode of schizophrenia are cared for by their families (Perring, Twigg, & Atkin, 1990).

China has few community-based services to provide for the needs of mentally ill individuals and their families. Over the past decade some services such as work therapy stations (Xia, Yan, & Wang, 1987), factory liaison projects (Jiang, 1988), mobile psychiatric care units (Xia et al., 1987), and home programs (Leung, 1978; Shen, 1983, 1985) have evolved in the major urban centers, but these services reach only a tiny proportion of mentally ill people (Pearson, 1992). Moreover, the network of voluntary nongovernment agencies that provide ancillary services for mentally ill clients in Western countries does not exist in China.

The preponderance of family-based care and the lack of community facilities indicate that psychiatric social workers could provide needed services to mentally ill patients and their families in China. It would, however, be inadvisable to assume that because social work has demonstrated usefulness in Western cultures it will automatically be useful in a very different culture. This chapter discusses the practical and ideological problems of introducing this Western profession into the Chinese setting. We hope to show that there is a potential role for psychiatric social work but that such practice would inevitably assume Chinese characteristics.

HISTORY OF SOCIAL WORK IN CHINA

According to Fu (1983), who wholeheartedly supported the development of social work in psychiatric settings in China, several Chinese universities and medical schools had set up social work departments before the 1949 Revolution. Yanjing University in Beijing was the first to introduce social work in 1925, although not of a specifically psychiatric nature (Nann, He, & Leung, 1990). Some people were sent abroad to train as social workers. However, after 1949 psychiatric practice came under the influence of the Russian school of psychiatry, which was biologically oriented. Social sciences and sociology in particular fell into disrepute and social work with them. As Fu said, "It was considered that under the supreme socialist system social problems did not exist" (p. 333). The Cultural Revolution (1966 to 1976) took this view to even more extreme lengths.

It has taken four decades for this position to be seriously reviewed and for the authorities in the People's Republic to reach a more realistic appraisal of the human condition and the problems inherent in living. At the meeting of the Asia and Pacific Association of Social Work Education (APSWE) held in Beijing in December 1988, it was announced that the State Education Commission had decided to approve general social work studies in four universities (APSWE and Department of Sociology, Beijing University, 1988). Zhongshan University in Guangzhou, in conjunction with Hong Kong University's Department of Social Work and Social Administration, offered courses in social work in its Sociology Department in the 1986–87 school year (Nann et al., 1990).

In 1992, 35 delegates from China attended the first international conference on social work in Chinese communities held in Hong Kong. Also in 1992, the Chinese Ministry of Civil Affairs produced the first government "white paper" on social welfare in China. In the spring of 1994, the Association of Social Work Education was founded.

For social workers and those who believe that the profession has something to offer that transcends cultural boundaries, this was encouraging news. Yet the fact remains that social work as a formalized activity has been seen as a Western invention and has frequently been interpreted as a means to make the unacceptable face of capitalism more palatable. What place, then, can it have in the world's largest socialist country? Will social work with Chinese characteristics be recognizable as related to its foreign cousin?

A TENTATIVE FRAMEWORK

At first sight, there would seem to be many reasons why personal social work, which has long been associated with principles like self-determination, individuation, personal disclosure, and essentially nondirective techniques, would find it hard to take root in Chinese soil. In relation to training counselors for Asian Americans, Root, Ho, and Sue (1986) made a number of points that tend to be accepted as commonplace when dealing with Asian people: They are not comfortable expressing feelings, they expect the authority figure to dispense advice, and they are concerned about bringing shame to the family. Thus, the theory goes, they do not respond well to Western counseling techniques based on personal revelation and exploration. Our personal experience of interviewing and counseling patients and their families in China has led us to the conclusion that this view, although common, is too stereotyped. Family members expressed a great deal of emotion in interviews and spontaneously raised issues of a delicate and sensitive nature.

Clearly, a theoretical structure is needed for social work that can accommodate cultural diversity. Howe (1987) developed a framework that attempts to incorporate and connect several paradigms, typifying the ability to absorb and use diversity that has contributed to the usefulness and adaptability of social work theory. While suggesting strongly that social work practice always be informed by a coherent philosophy and theoretical foundation, Howe also acknowledged that individuals viewing the same phenomenon may bring different paradigms to explain it and, therefore, react differently to it.

The logic of this argument suggests that although the biological abnormality resulting in serious mental disorders (the "disease") may be the same the world over, the problems experienced by the patients and families (the "illness") and the methods of resolving these problems will vary widely depending on the sociocultural environment. What is needed is a framework that incorporates this diversity into one coherent whole, without demanding a convergence of differences.

Citing the work of Burrell and Morgan, Howe (1987) put forward a framework that takes into account the two themes he considered defining and universal in the generation of theories for social work. The first theme is the tension between order and stability on the one hand and conflict and change on the other, and the second is the subjective stance (that of a participant) versus the objective stance (that of an observer) (Figure 31-1). This framework generated four paradigms: (1) functionalists, whom Howe called "the fixers"; (2) interpretivists, or "the seekers after meaning"; (3) radical humanists, or "the raisers of consciousness";

Figure 31-1

Framework for Analyzing Social Theory

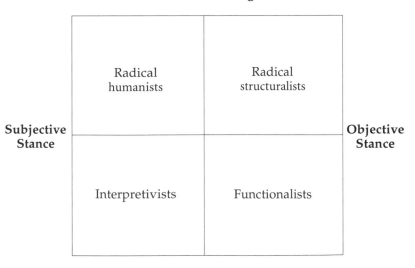

SOURCE: Adapted from Howe, D. (1987). *An introduction to social work theory* (p. 47). Aldershot, England: Wildwood House.

and (4) radical structuralists, or "the revolutionaries" (p. 49). Burrell and Morgan wrote that "The four paradigms define fundamentally different perspectives for the analysis of social phenomena. They approach this endeavor from contrasting standpoints and generate quite different concepts and analytical tools" (cited in Howe, 1987, p. 48).

The West, with its culture of democratic pluralism, accepts all four paradigms as legitimate aspects of professional social work. This acceptance is unlikely in the People's Republic. Which paradigm has greater cultural congruity with the Chinese setting? Despite, or perhaps because of, being a state created by revolution after a period of chaos, the People's Republic of China is a profoundly conservative country. Given China's long history of devastating social upheavals, the maintenance of order and stability is the government's highest priority, as it was in imperial times when the Confucian value of social harmony was paramount. The boundaries of the social work profession, like those of other professions in China, would be delineated by the state, and social workers would be expected to contribute to the overall goals of socialism. Thus, as Leung (1990) said, "The functions of [social] welfare in China are mingled with and subjugated to the political objectives of the government in maintaining social order" (p. 38).

Although the Chinese government is not prepared to accept social work's role as a provoker of societal change, it is prepared to accept its usefulness in the amelioration of personal problems. Thus, seekers after meaning, raisers of consciousness, and revolutionaries will not be accepted, but fixers may be welcomed. Can social work survive as a professional discipline if only functionalist social work is allowed to flourish?

The position in China is not, perhaps, as far from our own as we would like to imagine. In its desire to maintain order, China is like most other countries and certainly like those where social work thrives. The difference is that the others are prepared to tolerate variable and dissenting views and possibly even welcome them as a sign of their democratic spirit as long as they do not seriously threaten the established order. Thus, social work in most Western countries is part of the establishment and part of the informal mechanisms maintaining social control (Davies, 1985), and social workers practice honorably within this tradition.

Whether the system is capitalist or socialist, social problems are endemic, generated either by the social structure or through personal misfortune, from which no political system can protect its citizens. Private troubles and social issues have always been intertwined.

COMMUNITY AND FAMILY CARE IN CHINA

Informal versus Formal Care

A common but nonetheless accurate observation is that China is a family-centered country where caring for vulnerable citizens is mostly a family matter. Contrasts are frequently made between Western and developing countries over the question of attitudes toward families shown by mental health professionals. Pedersen and LeFley (1986) claimed that families are welcomed in developing countries as participants in patient care. This contrasts with the adversarial attitude often taken toward families of mentally ill people by Western mental health professionals and the concentration of writing and research, until recently, on pathogenesis in families rather than on coping (Falloon, Pedersen, & Al-Khayyal, 1986; Hatfield & LeFley, 1987).

LeFley (1987) developed this argument further. She claimed that in developing countries a social ambience that externalizes causation of mental illness, subscribes to a disease model (thus viewing the afflicted individual as sick rather than as a participant in his or her disability), and gears productivity to realistic expectancy levels results in more benign family relationships and lower rates of hospitalization. LeFley also contended that societies that show mutual interdependence rather than "independent functioning in the community," the catchphrase of our aftercare movement, appear to provide a more tolerant atmosphere for the severely psychiatrically disabled individual. She suggested that patients do better in societies in which mental health professionals emphasize family involvement, not because there is a lower level of disturbed family psychodynamics, but because it would be culturally incongruent not to involve the family in information and decisions regarding the patient. A large extended family, she observed, can provide a supportive network where the burden of caring for a mentally ill member may be spread around and thus diluted. Such family networks may also be able to fill a productive social role in a protected environment that maintains the self-esteem. Research showing reduced psychiatric chronicity in developing countries attributed it to less stress and fewer social demands on the patient (Jablensky, 1988).

Although LeFley's (1987) arguments may contain some general truths, many of the specifics as they relate to China do not hold true. To begin with, there is little community tolerance for mentally ill people, and such patients and their families are heavily stigmatized. Just as in the West, mental health professionals assume that families will care and cope, as they frequently do. However, in no way can it be said that they are seen as partners in care.

From the observations of the first author in psychiatric hospitals in Shashi City and in Beijing, doctors treating patients tend to dismiss the relatives' ability to comprehend what is going on and tend to be unwilling to share information. Even when a patient is admitted to a hospital, the relative, who may be staying with the patient in the hospital, is usually clueless as to the diagnosis of the patient's illness and what the implications and prognosis are. What little information relatives have is picked up from other relatives in similar positions, combining clues and trying to form a composite picture. Patients are told even less.

It is true that on a theoretical level the traditions of Chinese medicine include an awareness of the social contributions to illness. In practice the theory seems to make little difference, and doctors working in psychiatric settings adopt a preeminently biological model for at least two reasons. First, most psychiatric treatment is based on Western psychotropic medication rather than on traditional Chinese medicine. Second, attributing mental illness to environmental factors can be interpreted as blaming the political system for "causing" psychological disturbance. Psychiatrists (along with many other groups of people) were persecuted during the Cultural Revolution. They may feel that biological explanations are a safer option. Such explanations, of course, preclude any consideration of how social relationships may contribute to the onset, course, treatment, and outcome of the disorder.

Families are identified as a cheap caring resource in China as much as they are anywhere else. But the concomitant policy decision of seeking ways of strengthening their coping capacity has not been considered. Family care is the Chinese way, and families are expected to cope. There are times when the burden on individual relatives of family care can be very heavy indeed.

The whole concept of informal rather than formal care is predicated on the notion that not only the family but also other people involved with the patient are willing and able to help in whatever way they can. Chinese people are intensely private about family matters while being just as intensely curious about other people's affairs. Mental illness is considered to be a matter of great shame and stigma. It particularly affects the life chances of young unmarried people. Families go to great lengths to hide the fact of any illness. Consequently, mobilizing informal networks of care presents real difficulties because this level of intrusion into their private affairs would be intolerable for many people. This is not an uncommon reaction in other countries as well (Bulmer, 1987; Pinker, 1985).

Frequently, however, mentally ill people and their families must turn to outside sources of help. What little help there is outside hospital care is often organized on a neighborhood basis; for instance, psychiatric care units use retired people from the area. Work stations are administered at a neighborhood level. Health insurance, for the minority who have any, is organized through the work unit, so keeping hospitalization a secret from workmates is almost impossible. Most streets have wardens who keep an eye on general comings and goings and who report anything strange. As a result, it is hard to avoid official interest if the individual publicly manifests unusual behavior.

Professional versus Nonprofessional Intervention

Many tasks that are identified with professional social work are provided by informal networks of family, by volunteers in the form of retired workers, or by nonprofessional government functionaries. It is impossible for social workers to meet every social need that psychiatric clients have, and there will always be a major role for care provided by untrained people. But it is possible to identify needs that are not being met or are being met inadequately and require trained intervention. It could be argued that in the Chinese context, a number of these tasks should be taken up by psychiatrists, but psychiatrists' view of their own role tends to be very restricted. Most have no training in counseling techniques of any sort, most are unwilling to leave the confines of the hospital, and most are not attuned to the contribution of family and other relationships to psychic distress. These psychiatrists are not good at linking up with organizations and networks or seeing the broad rather than the narrow view of the patient's life.

By suggesting that there is a role for social workers in psychiatric settings in China, are we simply trying to extend a professional hegemony, and a Western one at that, or are there specific skills that social workers have that are necessary in the Chinese context? In our view, the context may be different, but the needs of psychiatrically ill people and their family members, whether in Western countries or China, are very similar. There are several major areas where the skills and approaches traditionally found in social work could be usefully imported.

Education. There is a need to develop and disseminate information to patients and relatives in a way that is easily understood and accessible to them. Other than being told to ensure that the patient takes the medicine, relatives receive very little other specific advice or guidance on useful strategies for managing the patient at home or for understanding the illness.

Training. To maximize the potential usefulness of retired workers and cadre support at the local level, training and support programs need to be implemented. Effective use of scarce social work time would be maximized by helping people involved at grassroots levels perform their tasks with more assurance, competence, and effectiveness.

Liaison. The traditional role of social workers as a bridge between the hospital and other organizations is very relevant for China. At the moment, discharged patients are not usually referred to local health centers, and no information is sent to these centers. Systems need to be devised that would ensure that the patient has access to care in his or her own locality. This access is most important to the majority of patients who live many hours away from a hospital.

A major liaison task is to coordinate with work units about ways to appropriately reintegrate a discharged worker into the work force with minimum embarrassment and damage to self-esteem. In areas where one or two major enterprises employ most people, developing a close link with the enterprises' health and personnel workers would probably be of great benefit.

Family Support. Many families are greatly strengthened in their capacity to cope with a mentally ill person if they know that there is someone to whom they can turn when crises arise or with whom they can simply let off steam. This resource does not always need to be a social worker. The potential for mutual aid among families with mentally ill members is largely untapped in China. Because the rural population is dispersed, mutual aid would be difficult to organize in the countryside, but it would be possible in cities. The stigma of mental illness makes the lot of relatives a lonely and isolated one. Although the idea of mutual aid organizations would be very new, there is certainly a discernible need for them. It is often claimed that Chinese people are rarely willing to discuss personal difficulties in front of strangers, but our experience in Hong Kong and China suggests that when the problem is both severe and stigmatizing, mutual sufferers benefit from sharing experiences and problems (Pearson, 1991). Mutual aid is also an appropriate concept to apply to patients, particularly in the development of social clubs or groups to provide an element of social life outside the home.

Counseling. Many consider counseling to be the core task of social work. The Chinese government banned interventions of this sort for many years, but mentally ill patients and their relatives have continued to experience personal distress. The majority of Chinese people share very restricted living space with family members; many families occupy just one room. Physical conditions are uncomfortable. Such an environment can become an emotional pressure cooker from which there is no escape. Children cannot go into their bedrooms and shut the doors. Parents cannot confine quarrels to their bedrooms. There are few places to go in the evening, so people stay at home. All emotions are on display for everyone to see and hear. Rather than being encouraged to pursue the goal of independent living, as might be the case in the West, Chinese psychiatric patients need help in coping with complex and difficult emotional environments, as do their relatives.

PROBLEMS AND PROSPECTS FOR SOCIAL WORK IN CHINA

Although it is possible to demonstrate a case for introducing psychiatric social work to China, the difficulties are obvious. Despite moves by the Chinese government to introduce social work into a selected few university curricula, there has been no sustained effort to define a social work role or to promote it across the country. As far as is known, these courses do not offer any specialist training in psychiatric social work. Anding psychiatric hospital, which the first author visited for eight days in December 1990, had two newly graduated social work practitioners from Beijing University. They majored in sociology but took the new social work courses, the precise content of which is not known. They had had no practical training or teachers who were social workers. Not surprisingly, they felt confused about their role. More importantly, other people did not understand their job title or did not have a clear idea of the work they were expected to do.

In a country where hierarchy is a prime organizational principle, these social work practitioners were at a disadvantage because nobody knew where to put them. Were they equivalent to the second-level psychiatrists with three years of training in medical college, as opposed to the first-level doctors with six-year university training? The social workers found this unacceptable because Beijing University is the most prestigious school in China, taking the cream of the school graduates, and is certainly much harder to get into than a medical college. If social work is to take off in China, then the various ministries involved, and there are many, need to coordinate their efforts at the national level, put resources into training, and define a job and a status in the structure for this newly created worker.

A second, related issue is that university students tend to see social work as a low class of activity unsuitable for graduates. Although they can imagine themselves as administrators and managers, they believe that direct contact with clients is best left to retired workers and low-level cadres (Leung, 1986; Nann et al., 1990).

As with everything else in China, the organization of social work in psychiatric settings is greatly complicated by the rural–urban divide. Nearly 80 percent of the population lives in rural areas. Because existing services are mainly located in hospitals and because patients and families think of hospitals as the source of services, it makes sense to locate social workers primarily in these settings. Ideally, social workers would also be responsible for outreach to the rural areas (preferably as part of a multidisciplinary team) to offer support, education, and training to psychiatric patients, relatives, and health workers. Staff based in hospitals in urban areas have shown little fondness for work in the rural areas, even on a part-time or rotational basis, so an outreach program would probably be very difficult to implement.

CONCLUSION

China has a clear need for psychiatric social work in areas that are not currently being covered by grassroots assistance or retired workers. Whether such practice will ever develop is open to debate. If it does develop, the shape it takes will undoubtedly be stamped by the Chinese culture. From our extensive practice and teaching experience in China, it is obvious that those interested in social work are attracted by the technology rather than the philosophy. Even in conservative practice settings in the West, social work is imbued with a certain feisty character that is prepared to take on officialdom if it is thought to be in the best interests of a client or class of clients. It is very difficult to imagine that spirit surviving in social work in China. Nonetheless, there is a job to be done, and social workers may be the most qualified to do it.

REFERENCES

Asia and Pacific Association of Social Work Education (APSWE) and Department of Sociology, Beijing University. (1988). *Seminar on social work education in the Asia and Pacific region.* Beijing: Authors.

Bulmer, M. (1987). *The social basis of community care.* London: Allen & Unwin.

Davies, M. (1985). *The essential social worker: A guide to positive practice* (2nd ed.). Aldershot, England: Wildwood House.

Falloon, R., Pederson, J., & Al-Khagyal, M. (1986). Family support versus family pathology. *Journal of Family Therapy, 8,* 351–369.

Fu, L. (1983). Re-evaluation of the role of social workers in clinical psychiatry. *Chinese Journal of Neurology and Psychiatry, 16*(6), 333–334.

Hatfield, A., & LeFley, H. (1987). *Families of the mentally ill: Coping and adaptation.* New York: Guilford Press.

Howe, D. (1987). *An introduction to social work theory.* Aldershot, England: Wildwood House.

Jablensky, A. (1988). Epidemiology of schizophrenia. In P. Bebbington & P. McGuffin (Eds.), *Schizophrenia: The major issues* (pp. 19–35). Oxford, England: Heinemann.

Jiang, Z. (1988). Community psychiatry in China: Organization and characteristics. *International Journal of Mental Health, 16*(3), 30–42.

LeFley, H. (1987). Culture and mental illness: The family role. In A. Hatfield & H. LeFley (Eds.), *Families of the mentally ill: Coping and adaptation* (pp. 30–59). New York: Guilford Press.

Leung, J.C.B. (1986). Some impressions of teaching a social work course in Guangzhou, China. *Hong Kong Journal of Social Work, 20*(2), 30–34.

Leung, J.C.B. (1990, September 3–5). *Social welfare with Chinese characteristics.* Paper presented at China and Hong Kong at a Crossroads, a conference organized by the Hong Kong Baptist College, Hong Kong.

Leung, S. (1978). Chinese approach to mental health service. *Canadian Psychiatric Association Journal, 23,* 354–359.

Nann, R. C., He, Z., & Leung, J.C.B. (1990). *Introducing social work and social work education in the People's Republic of China.* Hong Kong: Hong Kong University, Department of Social Work and Social Administration.

Pearson, V. (1991). Western theory, Eastern practice: Social groupwork in Hong Kong. *Social Work with Groups, 14,* 45–58.

Pearson, V. (1992). Community and culture: A Chinese model of community care for the mentally ill. *International Journal of Social Psychiatry, 38*(3), 163–178.

Pedersen, P., & LeFley, H. (1986). Introduction to cross-cultural training. In P. Pedersen & H. LeFley (Eds.), *Cross-cultural training for mental health professionals* (pp. 5–10). Springfield, IL: Charles C Thomas.

Perring, C., Twigg, J., & Atkin, K. (1990). *Families caring for people diagnosed as mentally ill: The literature re-examined.* London: Her Majesty's Stationery Office.

Phillips, M. R. (1993). Strategies used by Chinese families in coping with schizophrenia. In D. Davis & S. Hawell (Eds.), *Chinese families in the 1980's.* Berkeley: University of California Press.

Pinker, R. (1985). Social policy and social care: Divisions of social responsibility. In J. A. Yoder, J.M.L. Jonker, & R.A.B. Leaper (Eds.), *Support networks in a caring community.* Dordrecht, The Netherlands: Martinus Nijhoff.

Research Coordinating Group. (1986). An epidemiological investigation of mental disorders in twelve regions of China: Methodology and data analysis. *Chinese Journal of Neurology and Psychiatry, 19*(2), 65–69.

Root, M., Ho, C., & Sue, S. (1986). Issues in training counselors for Asian Americans. In P. Pedersen & H. LeFley (Eds.), *Cross-cultural training for mental health professionals* (pp. 199–209). Springfield, IL: Charles C Thomas.

Shen, Y. (1983). Community mental health care within primary care in the People's Republic of China: The home care program in the Beijing countryside. *International Journal of Mental Health, 12*(3), 123–131.

Shen, Y. (1985). Community mental health home care program, Haidian district in the suburbs of Beijing. In P. Pichot (Ed.), *Psychiatry, the state of the art: Epidemiology and community psychiatry* (Vol. 7, pp. 423–428). New York: Plenum Press.

Torrey, E. F. (1988). *Surviving schizophrenia: A family manual.* New York: Harper & Row.

Xia, Z., Yan, H., & Wang, C. (1987). Mental health care in Shanghai. *International Journal of Mental Health, 16*(3), 81–85.

This chapter was originally published in the May 1994 issue of Social Work, *vol. 39, pp. 280–287.*

32 NAFTA, American Health, and Mexican Health: They Tie Together

Dennis L. Poole

A t first glance, the North Atlantic Free Trade Agreement (NAFTA) seems to have little to do with health social work in America. The treaty was widely publicized as a pact that opens the economies of industrialized nations (United States and Canada) to a major Third World country (Mexico). It is a type of Marshall Plan in reverse. By liberalizing the movement of goods, services, and capital, NAFTA would help Mexico pay back its debt to these nations.

But closer scrutiny of the treaty unveils another scenario. Two years after the implementation of NAFTA, it is clear that the treaty will have major health and social consequences for people living in this hemisphere. Indeed, history may judge NAFTA as one of the most important social policy decisions of the United States this century.

Although NAFTA brings many risks, the treaty also offers great opportunities for international healing and partnerships. Both are long overdue, especially between citizens of the United States and citizens of Mexico. Many American social workers in health care and other fields have begun the healing process already by forming coalitions and networks with Mexican colleagues and organizations. They know firsthand that American health and Mexican health are inextricably tied. This was evident at the Third International Conference of Social Work, sponsored last summer by the National School of Social Work in Mexico. Appropriately titled "Civil Society: Catharsis or Mobilization?" the conference was strikingly different from most recent social work conferences. The major issues were not managed care, budget cutbacks, and block grants, but democracy, social justice, and civil society.

CIVIL SOCIETY AND HEALTH

Although civil society seldom gets mentioned in American social work literature, the quest for it has much to do with recent
changes in health and social services. In the United States, the
term "civil society" was established most effectively by Berger
and Neuhaus (1977) in the classic *To Empower People*, which entered "mediating structures" into the vernacular of policymakers and professionals. *Mediating structures* are institutions such
as families, churches, synagogues, voluntary associations, and
neighborhoods that come between individuals and the state.
Berger and Neuhaus argued that these structures are essential
for a vital democratic society and that public policy should foster and protect these institutions to achieve social goals. A generation of policymakers was later influenced by this view. They
believe that mediating structures can, and should, play a pivotal
role in social welfare. Hence, decentralization, localism, and
nongovernment interventions rivet their policy-making agendas,
which have achieved some success in recent years. Indeed, the
movement of many health social workers from institution-based
to community-based services stems, in part, from the quest of
these policymakers to strengthen civil society in America. They
want government to do less and mediating structures to do more
in the delivery of services to individuals and families.

But the quest for civil society holds special significance for
Mexican health social workers. Because the Mexican constitution
explicitly recognizes the civic right to health protection, the national health system is largely governmental. Only 4 percent of
the country's population of 90 million people purchase health
care through the private sector; everyone else gets care at government hospitals and public clinics (Frenk et al., 1994). As a result, virtually all Mexican health social workers are public
employees.

Being employed by the government can put health social workers in a tough position. The Mexican political system cannot be
considered democratic. It operates largely as a centralized, one-
party state with an extremely powerful presidency and subordinate legislative and judicial branches. The party in power, the
Institutional Revolutionary Party (PRI), has run the national government since 1928 and is often charged with vote-rigging and

civil rights violations (Heredia, 1994). Hence, political advocacy and social reform efforts carry much risk for health social workers in Mexico who earn their living from the government.

NAFTA has helped to change this situation in ways that were not expected or intended. In the early 1990s, when the Mexican government formed the NAFTA Advisory Council, only PRI-affiliated groups were represented. The Business Organizations for Foreign Trade was assigned public responsibility for coordinating the NAFTA effort. Government officials maintained that NAFTA was an economic issue; the treaty would create jobs and foster economic opportunities in Mexico. Workers, poor people, small farmers, and nongovernmental organizations were generally excluded from the NAFTA agenda-building process because they were not PRI-affiliated or were unlikely to reap benefits from the treaty for a long time (Heredia, 1994). In fact, small farmers and the rural poor population were not expected to fare well under the treaty initially. Early drafts of the trade pact called for a complete overhaul of the land tenure system in Mexico, including cutting agricultural subsidies to traditional farming communities and removing the constitutional guarantee of land grants to indigenous farmers. Revising this system would encourage foreign investors and corporate farmers to purchase land, which provides 70 percent of the nation's rural poor population with sustenance (Cavise, 1994).

The realization that the treaty would have dire consequences for the nation's rural poor population unleashed a supranational, nongovernment movement that has made true democratic reform in Mexico imperative. The movement—which social workers in cross-national coalitions joined—forced changes in the NAFTA pact to reflect a shared commitment to democratic practices and a respect for civil rights. These changes have put Mexico under greater international scrutiny, and they have increased the influence of nongovernment groups in domestic policy-making.

In this respect, NAFTA provided the political groundwork for the Third International Conference of Social Work, which allowed participants to address substantive issues related to democracy, social justice, and civil society in Mexico. The conference, in turn, directed attention to NAFTA-related challenges and opportunities, including health concerns at the U.S.–Mexico border.

BORDER HEALTH

Indeed, NAFTA has unleashed events that will dramatically affect health in Mexico and the United States, especially in border communities. One event is the sudden rush of U.S. health care companies to Mexico. Over the past two years, medical equipment suppliers, home health care providers, health maintenance organizations, health insurance firms, and American hospital companies have been pouring across the border to get a foothold on Mexico's private insurance market, estimated at about 4.5 million people. Investors are banking that NAFTA will improve the Mexican economy and will fuel the growth of Mexico's middle and upper classes (Mitchell, 1994; Skolnick, 1995).

But there are risks for investors. Mexico recently plunged into a deep economic recession. A free fall in the peso scared off billions of dollars in investments, pushed up inflation and interest rates, and forced people out of work. As a result, many middle-class families have been driven into poverty and forced to receive subsidized care at now overcrowded and underfunded government hospitals and clinics. Inflation and peso devaluation have also eroded the nation's public health budget, reducing government demand for the importation of some health goods (Fineman, 1995).

NAFTA brings other risks for Mexicans as well. In their rush for profits in Mexico, American health care companies could perform unnecessary procedures, discriminate against certain patient groups, or skimp on service quality. Disincentives for them to do otherwise are few. In Mexico, public policy is more lax, and the country lags behind the United States considerably in accreditation of health care facilities and certification of practitioners (Frenk et al., 1994).

In addition, NAFTA will significantly expand the *maquiladora* industry, which consists of "offshore" assembly plants owned mostly by U.S. firms. This industry lures hundreds of thousands of Mexicans from the interior of the country to the border. Although some experts (for example, Guendelman & Silberg, 1993) have reported otherwise, evidence is mounting that work in *maquiladora* industries can be hazardous to one's health. Denman (1990) found that the birthweights of infants of female *maquiladora* workers are significantly below internationally accepted standards. The findings were attributed to harsh working conditions, including exposure to toxins, long working days, and physically demanding work. Kopinak (1995) concluded that foreign capital exploits women at *maquiladora* industries by offering the least desirable jobs to them using the term *personal femenino* ("female personnel") in advertising for unskilled production personnel. Shields (1995) observed that *maquiladoras* avoid payment of health benefits. To avoid providing maternity leave, some companies apparently force pregnant women to quit their jobs by assigning them more difficult tasks to perform. Press and Rose (1995) reported that General Electric and Honeywell recently dismissed 100 workers for trying to establish a labor union at their plants. Thus, complaining about conditions at *maquiladora* plants can jeopardize one's job.

The long-term effects of NAFTA on health in border communities will probably be substantial. In 1990 there were an estimated 7 million people living along the nearly 2,000-mile U.S.–Mexico border. By the year 2000, El Paso, Texas, and its sister city in Mexico, Juárez, will have more than 2.3 million people living in the largest international metropolis in the world (Skolnick, 1995). Many migrants live in *colonias,* or unincorporated settlements on both sides of the border, which usually lack septic tanks, sewers, or running water (Frenk et al., 1994). Other community health problems associated with border life include high fertility rates, disparities in infant mortality, transfer of communicable diseases, pollution, and improper waste management (Shields, 1995; Warner, 1991). Poverty is a severe problem as well. Families often have to "bunch up" in one household to subsist on low-wage jobs in border communities (Kopinak, 1995; Young & Christopherson, 1986).

TIES BETWEEN MEXICAN HEALTH AND AMERICAN HEALTH

NAFTA countries must recognize that investments in economic partnerships will also require substantial investments in health and social services. As one public health official in El Paso observed, citizens on both sides of the border "share the same water, the same air, the same pollution, and the same diseases—none of which have any respect for that line drawn on the map that does little to separate our population" (Skolnick, 1995, p. 1647). The reality is that Mexican health and American health are inextricably and permanently tied together.

One determining factor is economics. U.S.–Mexico trade crossing by land was estimated at $55.4 billion in 1993, and NAFTA partners contributed 50 percent of U.S. export growth in the first quarter and accounted for nearly one-third of U.S. import growth. In the first quarter of 1994, Mexico's imports to the United States expanded by 22 percent, and U.S. exports to Mexico were expected to approach $50 billion by the end of the year, compared with $41.7 billion in 1993. If current trends continue, Mexico will soon surpass Japan as the second largest U.S. foreign market (Bureau of National Affairs, 1994). In addition, the U.S. economy demands Mexican workers. The number of Mexicans who cross the border each day to work is enormous. In New Mexico alone, 60 percent to 70 percent of the state's migrant workers live in Mexico and commute daily to work in New Mexican fields (Skolnick, 1995).

Another determining factor that links Mexican health and American health is immigration. The U.S. Bureau of the Census predicts that the United States will double its number of Hispanic families to almost 46 million in 2015, triple its size to over 68 million by 2035, and expand to almost four times its 1990 size by 2050. Two-thirds of these families will originate in Mexico (Day, 1993). Although it is easy to overestimate the amount of additional immigration that NAFTA will cause, it is clear at this point that the Mexican government has lost control of the single most potent inducement for migration to the United States—inflation (Cornelius & Martin, 1993).

Border states will not be the only states affected by NAFTA and Mexican immigration. Although the additional business brought about by NAFTA will be concentrated in the border states, other states with cities that have a large Mexican American population, like Chicago, will be affected by NAFTA-associated trade, despite the distance to Mexico (Santos, 1994). They, too, will attract emigrants from Mexico to their communities.

CHALLENGES AND OPPORTUNITIES

It is hoped that side agreements during NAFTA's dispute resolution process will allow individuals and nongovernmental organizations to bring health, labor, and quality-of-life issues into the dispute resolution process (Garvey, 1995). Meanwhile, severe challenges are emerging from the growing interaction between Mexico and the United States.

Health social workers can be helpful in at least five ways. First, at the policy level, they can join cross-national coalitions, such as the Tri-National Social Work Task Force and the Coalition for Justice in the Maquiladoras, to monitor the progress of NAFTA and to promote development of service infrastructure to accommodate economic growth. They can also push for changes in the trade pact to protect workers' rights; enforce fair labor standards; and promote environmental, occupational, and personal health. Furthermore, health social workers can support the development of financial mechanisms to pay for health services received on either side of the border as well as the establishment of Mexican medical care facilities for Mexican citizens living in the United States as seasonal workers (Frenk et al., 1994).

Second, health social workers can develop innovative solutions to border health problems. Formal channels of communication, referral, and follow-up between health providers on both sides of the border are urgently needed. El Paso's recent success in increasing its prenatal care and childhood immunization rates by working with leaders on both sides of the border sets a good example (Skolnick, 1995). Working with mediating structures such as families, neighborhood groups, and voluntary associations can be very effective as well. For example, volunteer community health aides can remove barriers to primary and preventive care by developing and implementing culturally appropriate health education and outreach services in border communities (Patton, 1995). The De Madres a Madres Program, started in a Houston inner-city Hispanic community, is a good example. Based on the concept of empowerment, this program uses indigenous volunteer mothers to form coalitions with civic groups and agencies to address health needs of Mexican Americans and other Hispanic immigrants (McFarlane & Fehir, 1994).

Third, NAFTA expands opportunities for international consortia and joint projects in health social work training. Although the treaty provides minimal references to personal health services, Annex 1210 permits "relevant bodies" to negotiate mutually acceptable professional standards and criteria for licensure and certification of professional service providers and to provide recommendations on mutual recognition (Frenk et al., 1994). The Task Force for International Social Work of the Council for Social Work Education has taken the lead in this area by urging faculty exchanges and joint research efforts and by working toward the development of a national accreditation body in Mexico. Several schools of social work have provided leadership as well, including the ones at University of Texas at Pan American, Tulane University, University of Calgary, and New Mexico State University, to name a few.

Fourth, health social work scholars can help by devoting more research to health and service utilization patterns of Mexican immigrants. Numerous studies (Applewhite, 1995; Chavez, 1986; De la Rosa, 1989; Giachello, 1988; Ginzberg, 1991; Lopez-Aqueres, Kemp, Staples, & Brummel-Smith, 1984; Nichols, Labrec, Homedes, & Geller, 1994; Trevino, Moyer, Valdez, & Stroup-Benham, 1991; Zambrana, Ell, Dorrington, Wachsman, & Hodge, 1994) have reported that families of Mexican origin tend to underuse services in the United States. Most of these studies have been conducted in border cities, where challenges associated with immigration are more obvious and pressing. But little is known about the health and social services utilization patterns of Mexican immigrants in other areas of the country, especially in metropolitan communities of nonborder states. This is unfortunate. The long-term viability of these communities will rest in part on their ability to address the needs of this rapidly expanding population.

Fifth, health social workers can help strengthen interactions between Mexicans and Americans by confronting "moral panic." Hostility surfacing in the form of expressed fears that Mexican immigration will boost welfare rolls, drive up health care costs, or turn the United States into a Third World country must be challenged. Regrettably, much of the debate over NAFTA and immigration has rested on unfounded fears.

In this regard, a few relevant facts can help promote international healing. One is that immigration from Mexico can strengthen American communities. Mexicans traditionally hold family and community values in high regard (Vega, 1990; Vega, Kolody, Valle, & Weir, 1991). Immigration can also improve community health. Mexicans have lower levels of low-birthweight babies, and they are less likely than Anglos to die from many chronic diseases, including cancer, heart disease, and pulmonary diseases (Frenk et al., 1994; Stolberg, 1993). Another relevant fact is that additional patrols at the U.S.–Mexico border cannot stop immigration. Increased apprehension of illegal entrants has never changed the basic pattern of Mexican migration, except perhaps to increase the flow of women and children seeking to be reunited with newly legalized family heads in the United States (Cornelius, 1992; Donato, 1993). Finally, Americans can be gently reminded that Mexican immigrants seek the same thing that attracted their own ancestors to the United States—hope.

REFERENCES

Applewhite, S. L. (1995). *Curanderismo:* Demystifying the health beliefs and practices of elderly Mexican Americans. *Health & Social Work, 20,* 247–253.

Berger, P., & Neuhaus, R. (1977). *To empower people.* Washington, DC: American Enterprise Institute Press.

Bureau of National Affairs. (1994, June 1). NAFTA: U.S., Mexican governors address. *BNA International Environment Daily.*

Cavise, L. (1994). NAFTA rebellion: How the small village of Chiapas is fighting for its life. *Human Rights, 21,* 36–42.

Chavez, L. R. (1986). Mexican immigration and health care: A political economy perspective. *Human Organization, 45,* 344–352.

Cornelius, W. A. (1992). From sojourners to settlers: The changing profile of Mexican migration to the United States. In J. A. Bustamante, C. W. Reynolds, & R. Hinojosa-Ojeda (Eds.), *U.S.–Mexico relations: Labor market interdependence* (pp. 155–195). Stanford, CA: Stanford University Press.

Cornelius, W. A., & Martin, P. L. (1993). The uncertain connection: Free trade and rural Mexican migration to the United States. *International Migration Review, 27,* 484–512.

Day, J. C. (1993). *Population projections of the United States, by age, sex, race, and Hispanic origin: 1993 to 2050.* Suitland, MD: U.S. Bureau of the Census.

De la Rosa, M. (1989). Health care needs of Hispanic Americans and the responsiveness of the health care system. *Health & Social Work, 14,* 104–113.

Denman, C. (1990). La salud de las obreras de la maquila: El caso de Nogales [The health of female assembly plant workers: The case of Nogales]. In G. de la Pena et al. (Eds.), *Crisis, conflicto, y sobrevivencia* [Crisis, conflict, and survival]. Guadalajara, Mexico: Universidad de Guadalajara Press.

Donato, K. M. (1993). Current trends and patterns of female migration: Evidence from Mexico. *International Migration Review, 27,* 748–771.

Fineman, M. (1995, October 1). Economic ills infect Mexicans. *Los Angeles Times,* p. A-1.

Frenk, J., Gomez-Dantes, O., Cruz, C., Chacon, F., Hernandez, P., & Freeman, P. (1994). Consequences of the North Atlantic Free Trade Agreement for health services: A perspective from Mexico. *American Journal of Public Health, 84,* 1591–1597.

Garvey, J. I. (1995). Trade law and quality of life—Dispute resolution under the NAFTA side accords on labor and the environment. *American Journal of International Law, 89,* 439–453.

Giachello, A. L. (1988). Hispanics and health care. In P. S. Cafferty, S. J. Pastora, & W. C. McCready (Eds.), *Hispanics in the United States: A new social agenda* (pp. 159–194). New Brunswick, NJ: Transaction Books.

Ginzberg, E. (1991). Access to health care for Hispanics. *Journal of the American Medical Association, 265,* 238–242.

Guendelman, S., & Silberg, M. J. (1993). The health consequences of maquiladora work: Women on the U.S.–Mexican border. *American Journal of Public Health, 83,* 37–44.

Heredia, C. (1994). NAFTA and democratization in Mexico. *Journal of International Affairs, 48,* 13–38.

Kopinak, K. (1995). Gender as a vehicle for the subordination of women. *Latin American Perspectives, 22,* 30–48.

Lopez-Aqueres, W., Kemp, B., Staples, F., & Brummel-Smith, K. (1984). Use of health care services by older Hispanics. *Journal of the American Geriatric Society, 32,* 435–440.

McFarlane, J., & Fehir, J. (1994). De Madres a Madres: A community partner-ship for health. *Health Education Quarterly, 21,* 381–394.

Mitchell, L. A. (1994, April 21). Health care revolution in Mexico opens door. *Arizona Business Gazette,* p. 1.

Nichols, A. W., Labrec, P. A., Homedes, N., & Geller, S. E. (1994). The utiliza-tion of Arizona medical services by residents of Mexico. *Salud Publica Mex, 36,* 129–139.

Patton, S. (1995). Empowering women: Improving a community's health. *Nursing Management, 26,* 36–41.

Press, E., & Rose, G. (1995). NAFTAmath. *Nation, 260,* 4–5.

Santos, F. (1994). NAFTA in the windy city. *Hispanic Business, 16,* 62–63.

Shields, J. (1995). Border health hazards. *Multinational Monitor, 16,* 22–23.

Skolnick, A. (1995). Crossing the "line on the map" in search of hope. *Journal of the American Medical Association, 273,* 1646–1648.

Stolberg, S. (1993, November 24). Health study ranks Latinos above Anglos. *Los Angeles Times,* p. A-1.

Trevino, F. M., Moyer, M. E., Valdez, R. B., & Stroup-Benham, C. A. (1991). Health insurance coverage and utilization of health services by Mexican, mainland Puerto-Rican and Cuban-Americans. *Journal of the American Medical Association, 265,* 233–237.

Vega, W. (1990). Hispanic families in the 1980's: A decade of research. *Journal of Marriage and the Family, 52,* 1015–1024.

Vega, W., Kolody, B., Valle, R., & Weir, J. (1991). Social support networks, social support and their relationship to depression among immigrant Mexican women. *Human Organization, 50,* 154–162.

Warner, D. (1991). Health issues at the U.S.–Mexican border. *Journal of the American Medical Association, 265,* 242–247.

Young, G., & Christopherson, S. (1986). Household structure and activity in Ciudad Juárez. In G. Young (Ed.), *The social and economic development of Ciudad Juárez* (pp. 229–258). Boulder, CO: Westview Press.

Zambrana, R., Ell, K., Dorrington, C., Wachsman, L., & Hodge, D. (1994). The relationship between psychosocial status of immigrant Latino mothers and use of emergency pediatric services. *Health & Social Work, 19,* 93–102.

This chapter was originally published in the February 1996 issue of Health & Social Work, *vol. 21, pp. 3–7.*

33 Curanderismo: Demystifying the Health Beliefs and Practices of Elderly Mexican Americans

Steven Lozano Applewhite

E ffective health care intervention with various ethnic groups requires special attention to cultural differences. This is especially true for elderly Mexican Americans, many of whom retain a strong attachment to indigenous values, including those about health care. Culturally specific beliefs and attitudes about folk healing play an essential role in elderly Mexican Americans' approach to their own health and use of health care resources. Despite this fact, little knowledge is available about the role of folk healing in the lives of this population.

MEXICAN FOLK HEALING

Mexican folk healing evolved from early Aztec and pre-Columbian civilizations. In Mexican American communities today, folk healing is referred to as *curanderismo*. In this article, *folk healing* is defined broadly as a set of health beliefs and practices derived from ethnic and historical traditions that have as their goal the amelioration or cure of psychological, spiritual, and physical problems. These health beliefs are based on notions that healing is an art that includes culturally appropriate methods of treatment delivered by recognized healers in the community who capitalize on a patient's faith and belief systems in the treatment process (Trotter & Chavira, 1981). It involves beliefs in "natural" and "supernatural" illnesses, a metaphysical connection to the spiritual world, and a view of God's divine will and centrality in all aspects of life. Healing is administered by individuals who have a divine gift *(don)* for healing and who intervene through natural or supernatural means of treatment.

Folk healing can be practiced informally with families and neighbors by individuals not recognized by the community as folk healers (Woyames, 1981) using home remedies such as herbs, candles, and other healing paraphernalia (Mayers, 1992), or it may be practiced by specialized practitioners known as *curanderos* (Trotter & Chavira, 1981). There are other well-known and respected folk medicine practitioners such as herbalists *(yerberos)*, bone and muscle therapists *(hueseros* and *sobadores)*, and midwives *(parteras)* (De La Cancela & Martinez, 1983). Because there is considerable overlap in practices and beliefs among practitioners and patients, labels have limited value in identifying discrete categories and functions of natural healers (Vega, 1980).

The best-known folk healer, the *curandero,* is recognized by the community to treat individuals with physical, spiritual, and psychosomatic illnesses as well as traditional folk illnesses (Mayers, 1992). A *curandero* may intervene at various levels, including the spiritual, mental, and material level (Trotter & Chavira, 1981). Traditionally, Mexican American communities have included a great number of *curanderos;* however, because their existence is a closely guarded secret to outsiders and even to many residents of the community, it is often impossible to estimate the number of *curanderos.*

Within any community, the extent of folk healing use varies depending on the strength of the traditional belief system and the availability of folk specialists. In communities such as border towns, folk healing is prevalent and a part of a dual health care system of conventional and traditional medicine (Trotter, 1982). The size of the community does not affect the use of folk healers as much as satisfaction with conventional medical care, language, self-perceived health status, and income (Higginbotham, Trevino, & Ray, 1990).

HEALTH CARE SERVICES UTILIZATION

A number of researchers have studied the determinants of and barriers to health care services utilization by Mexican Americans and other Latinos (Anderson, 1968; Anderson, Lewis, Giachello, Aday, & Chiu, 1981; Anderson & Newman, 1973; Veeder, 1983). Although these studies discussed the use of modern services, they generally failed to recognize folk healing. Other studies have emphasized ethnographic description of folk methods, beliefs, and remedies in the Mexican American population in general, but relatively few have examined the effects of ethnic group influences and cultural beliefs on the health care practices of elderly Hispanic people (Eve & Friedsam, 1979; Lopez-Aqueres, Kemp, Staples, & Brummel-Smith, 1984; Woyames, 1981).

Young (1980) developed an ethnomedical health belief decision-making model to describe health care service utilization in rural Mexico, identifying four factors that significantly influence the choice-making process: (1) gravity or perceived seriousness of the illness; (2) knowledge of home remedies; (3) faith in or perceived benefits of a folk remedy; and (4) accessibility of health care, including cost and availability (Young & Garro, 1982). In addition, Kay (1979) considered the remedies patients sought for particular illnesses such as home remedies, doctor's prescriptions, or over-the-counter medications and the type of professional services preferred such as folk providers or physicians.

The current study was developed from Young's (1980) model and explores cultural knowledge, belief and faith systems, and health care preferences and practices of elderly Mexican Americans. Five questions guided the study: (1) What do elderly Mexican Americans know about *curanderismo?* (2) How did they acquire their folk knowledge? (3) To what extent do they use folk knowledge to treat their health problems? (4) How do cultural beliefs and spiritual faith affect their health care behaviors? and (5) To whom do they turn for help during an illness?

METHOD

Study Design

Valle and Mendoza's (1978) *plática* methodology is considered culturally relevant and sensitive to data collection. The *plática* methodology, which is similar to Spradley's (1979) ethnographic interview, is like a friendly, informal conversation. This approach is well suited to elderly Mexican Americans, because it enables researchers to first establish a sense of confidence *(confianza),* trust *(respeto),* and mutual holistic sharing *(personalismo)*—critical concepts in the culture—before moving toward task-oriented activities. It further enables researchers to gain an insider's perspective about *curanderismo* based on life experiences, folk and spiritual beliefs, language preferences, and culturally specific behaviors.

Unlike the traditional anthropological approach that requires immersion in a cultural group for an extended period, this study, done in 1991, relied on ethnographies in selective areas using in-depth, semistructured, interactive interviews (Morse, 1991). These interviews, which averaged one to two hours, were conducted by a bilingual and bicultural investigator and research assistant who were proficient in Spanish and the Mexican culture. Participants chose whether to tape-record interviews and whether to speak Spanish or English. The interviews provided structure, consistency, and flexibility, allowing the interviewer to make adjustments in the interview schedule and ask additional questions in selected areas.

A set of questions for each category provided the context for moving from general to specific areas. Data were collected for each category and coded as key words, significant events, recurring patterns, and dominant group perspectives. Participants' perspectives were compared to find individual and group themes and interpret stated meanings. Data were recorded as verbatim statements (thick descriptions). To add greater clarity, quantitative data were used sparingly to emphasize general response patterns of open-ended questions. The author did not intend to quantify qualitative data in every category explored.

Participants

Elderly Mexican Americans were selected from two senior citizen centers in a major metropolitan area in Arizona. One center was in a densely populated, ethnically mixed urban area, and the other was in a small township of about 5,000 Hispanic residents between several predominantly Anglo communities. Participation was voluntary. Managers at the senior citizen centers were asked to identify elderly Mexican Americans who were willing to participate in the study, considered themselves knowledgeable about folk healing, had some prior experience with the topic, or were interested in participating regardless of their level of expertise. Twenty-five people agreed to participate in the study.

Participants received a detailed explanation of the purpose of the study, were assured of confidentiality, and were asked to select a time and place most convenient for an interview. All but one respondent preferred to be interviewed at the senior citizen centers on days they normally attended.

Study Limitations

One limitation of this study was that it did not allow the assessment of the impact of the participants' level of acculturation on their knowledge, beliefs, and practices. Another limitation is that the findings cannot be generalized to large populations because of the small sample size and the nature of qualitative, ethnographic research, which emphasizes individual perspectives of cultural phenomena.

FINDINGS

Demographic Profile

The mean age of the 25 participants was 76.6 years, and most (60 percent) were women. Their mean annual income was $5,623, and they had an average of 4.7 years of formal education. Fifteen participants (60 percent) were born in Mexico, and 14 (56 percent) had lived in their current residence for 15 years or longer. Most (90 percent) had lived the majority of their lives in the southwestern United States and had moved freely from the United States to Mexico and back.

The participants were either traditionalist (more comfortable with the Mexican culture than the Anglo culture) or bicultural (comfortable in both cultures) (Lum, 1992). Nearly one-third (32 percent of the 25 participants) were bilingual; nearly two-thirds (64 percent) preferred to be interviewed in Spanish. More than three-fifths (64 percent) were widowed; 13 (52 percent) lived alone, and 10 (40 percent) lived with relatives.

Cultural Knowledge

Although all 25 participants had difficulty precisely defining folk healing, they showed various levels of knowledge and beliefs about its nature, purpose, and types, which were largely influenced by their roles as observers, patients, and practitioners. Most (88 percent) had an understanding ranging from a faint familiarity to a working knowledge of methods and support systems.

Among the approaches used or heard about by participants were the use of home remedies and herbs, bone and muscle manipulation, midwifery, faith healing, spiritualism, tarot card reading, witchcraft, praying, and the use of religious icons and paraphernalia for spiritual and other related purposes. Spiritualism and witchcraft, considered by the participants to be malevolent forms of practice and deemed outside the mainstream of traditional folk healing, were still thought of as part of traditional beliefs and practices.

Participants first learned about folk medicine in early childhood, adolescence, and early adulthood. During these periods most (84 percent) indicated they had received folk treatments from family members, neighbors, or local *curanderos*, and later in life sought folk healers to treat their children for common conditions such as colic *(cólico)*, locked bowels *(empacho)*, fright *(susto)*, evil eye *(mal de ojo)*, and fallen fontanel *(caída de la mollera)*. A few (12 percent) recalled healing rituals involving candle lighting, praying, laying of hands, and spiritual cleansing *(barridas* or *limpias)*. One participant recalled witnessing an exorcism by a *curandero*.

As their health problems became more serious and chronic and their children grew older, participants shifted attention from their children to themselves. Skepticism about the efficacy of folk healing, along with strong religious beliefs, appeared in late adulthood. The participants turned less to healers and more to conventional health care providers, self-medications, home remedies, or God's divine will.

A few participants (12 percent) offered their perceptions about *curanderismo* based on myths, folk tales, and general hearsay. However, most (92 percent) believed that folk healing involved either malevolent or benevolent practices, with spiritualism and witchcraft having little relevance to treating health problems. Although most (92 percent) did not deny the existence of supernatural forces—good and evil spirits that can be summoned by spiritualists *(espiritualistas)*, witches *(brujas)*, and warlocks *(brujos)*—the issue was one of practical usefulness. Supernatural forces or conditions (illnesses caused by supernatural means requiring supernatural treatment) did not worry the participants; chronic debilitating conditions were their greatest concerns.

> Herbalism is fine [in old age], but not [spiritual] *curanderos*.
>
> *   *   *
>
> *Yerberos* know about herbs, but [spiritual] *curanderos* practice witchcraft, which is not the best kind of healing there is. Now that I am old I need doctors more than I need *curanderos* to cure me.
>
> *   *   *

> I'm not afraid of them [spiritual *curanderos*]. I believe there
> are bad ones and good ones depending on what you need.
> But I don't really use them. I usually just go to the doctor if I
> can. If not I just live with the pain and suffering.

Discussions about witchcraft elicited lowered voices, loss of eye contact, or fading interest. Despite the interviewers' careful attention to this sensitive topic, most participants (96 percent) were uneasy, indifferent, uninformed, unwilling, or skeptical in discussing it.

As expected, the participants were knowledgeable about herbalism (64 percent) and made clear distinctions between home remedies *(remedios caseros)* and self-medication with over-the-counter drugs *(remedios de la bótica)*. Many expressed a preference for home remedies instead of over-the-counter drugs for cultural reasons and their proved effectiveness. Cost was always seen as a drain on their fixed incomes and a barrier to obtaining prescription or even over-the-counter medication. Despite differences in regional backgrounds, participants used similar terms to describe home remedies.

Belief and Faith Systems

Young (1980) noted that faith in home remedies is a powerful dimension in health care choice making. This faith has been widely reported across several generations of research on Mexican Americans (Farge, 1977; Trotter, 1982).

More than three-fourths (76 percent) of the 25 participants believed that herbs were effective in treating mild illnesses *(enfermedades simples)* ranging from headaches to insomnia to more serious problems such as hypertension *(alta presión)* and nervous tension *(los nervios)*. However, herbs were not the first choice of treatment for more serious health problems. For these, some participants (12 percent) did not consult *yerberos* extensively and chose instead to treat themselves with their own herbs and teas, ointments, and home remedies or to seek modern medical treatment. Those who turned to *yerberos* visited herbal shops for advice on home remedies and to purchase herbs. One participant stated,

> I don't go see anyone when I have a health problem. Perhaps
> because there hasn't been an occasion to see a doctor. First of
> all I cure myself with herbs, teas, or other home remedies.

> When I do see a doctor, I inform him of the herbs I am taking,
> and he tells me to keep on taking them because he says I am
> healthier than even he.

Participants also held strong beliefs about divine intervention in health problems, which was common among elderly people in this study. With few exceptions elderly Mexican Americans placed their faith in God's will (*la fé en Dios; lo que Dios mande; la voluntad de Dios*) to deal with physical, social, and emotional problems accompanying old age:

> I don't use [folk healers]; I rely on the power of God. I don't
> go to anyone, not even the doctor. I don't have any faith in
> them. They do not do anything for me. They just charge me
> money. I have faith in God, for there is no problem that God
> cannot heal. God is merciful (*Dios es misericordioso*) and will
> always be with me.

A hint of fatalism (*así es la vida*, or "such is life") also accompanied the 25 participants' spiritual faith. Still, many (68 percent) discussed optimal health care as a combination of modern medicine, folk healing, and faith in the power of God to intervene in their lives. One woman captured the prevailing sentiment:

> Everything depends on one's faith because that has all to do
> with it. *Curanderos* may have a gift and doctors have the edu-
> cation, but it is through God's divine will (*la voluntad de Dios*)
> that they [healers or physicians] will be able to cure.

Preferences and Practices

Most of the 25 participants (80 percent) moved freely from traditional healing to modern health care depending on the type and seriousness of illness they had, whether it could be treated with home remedies, and whether they had faith in and the economic means to visit a physician. Both negative and positive views of modern health care and Mexican folk healing emerged. (Because participants offered positive and negative views about both types of health care approaches, percentages do not add to 100 in each category.) Forty-eight percent of the participants viewed some aspects of modern medicine negatively, and 84 percent viewed some aspects of it positively. In comparison, 36 percent viewed folk healing negatively, and 64 percent viewed it positively.

The 25 participants noted that even modern medicine could not eliminate chronic problems and declining health in old age.

Other negative views were the impersonal and disrespectful treatment by health care providers, communication problems, unfavorable health outcomes, fears that physicians actually do more harm than good, fears about surgery and possible death, and a general distrust of physicians and other health care professionals. Economic hardship was the most important factor influencing their views about modern health care, because most (85 percent) indicated that they did not have the money or health insurance to see a doctor regularly, even when they had a serious health problem. The participants harshly denounced modern health care services and their prohibitive fee-for-service costs. As expected, most (92 percent) had very limited knowledge of available services and even less information about patient rights and benefits.

Despite the fact that the 25 participants expressed skepticism about different aspects of modern medicine, the majority (85 percent) indicated that a physician was still their first choice of treatment. Participants believed that some major health problems and diseases in old age cannot and should not be treated by folk healers. Only 16 percent indicated they had consulted anyone other than a physician for a serious health condition, adding that lack of faith in modern medicine and lack of money influenced their decision to seek help from folk healers.

Still, almost half of the 25 participants (48 percent) indicated that they would consider consulting a *curandero* if their physician could no longer help them with an illness. Two participants reported going without modern health care or folk healing, believing that neither was a viable alternative for them at the time. Instead, they chose to treat themselves through self-medication and home remedies.

Thirty-two percent also expressed negative views of folk healing, including a personal fear of the supernatural; concerns about charlatanism and overcharging among *curanderos;* and the beliefs that they were too old and set in their ways to believe in *curanderos,* that old-age illnesses require modern medical treatment, and that faith in God is greater than any faith in healers. Participants stated,

> I would not turn to a *curandero* because my illnesses are more related to my old age, such as cataracts or falling down [broken bones]. These are major problems that need the attention of the doctor.

*   *   *

If doctors can't help, *curanderos* can do even less.

Favorable comments about folk healing included statements that *curanderos* prescribe good remedies and are effective; that folk healing is worth trying when all else fails; and that elderly people should place their confidence in *curanderos,* particularly older ones who may share similar health problems and cultural orientation. One participant stated,

> They [*curanderos*] may help with aches and pains when the doctors can't get rid of [the pain or condition]. They can give you ointments and massages for your circulation. Maybe they will not cure you completely, but they will give you some relief. Anything is worth a try.

Finally, when asked if they knew of folk healers in the community, fewer than one-third (32 percent) of the 25 participants indicated they personally knew a spiritual *curandero;* two-thirds (66 percent) knew of a *sobador* or *yerbero;* fewer than one-sixth (12 percent) used the services of a *curandero,* massage therapist, herbalist, or other folk healer; and slightly more than three-fourths (76 percent) chose to treat themselves with a common folk treatment, self-medication, or herbal remedy.

DISCUSSION

In this study the elderly Mexican American participants did not reject folk healing or modern medical treatment; rather, they chose the method that seemed most accessible and appropriate to the problem at hand. Few saw any conflict in using both approaches, for example, relying on modern health care for major medical problems and herbal remedies for minor ailments. This finding is supported by other studies (Higginbotham et al., 1990; Martin, Martinez, Leon, Richardson, & Acosta, 1985; Trotter & Chavira, 1980) that also reported that although Mexican Americans believe in folk healing, they generally underuse folk healers and prefer to consult physicians or resort to herbs and home remedies or self-medication (Anderson et al., 1981; Trotter, 1982).

The degree to which elderly Mexican Americans use folk healing may depend in part on their ties to traditional ethnic culture, health problems, and access to and satisfaction with modern health care (Mayers, 1992). Although elderly Mexican Americans are tied to their culture, because of their residence in the United States they are also influenced by Anglo culture and the medical advances in technology and health care generally available to them. Thus, it is not uncommon for members of a community, especially elderly Mexican American women (Martinez, 1981, cited in Mayers, 1992), who are influenced by traditional and modern cultures to adopt practices of both cultures and use both health care systems simultaneously to meet their needs (Anthony-Tkach, 1981; Chavez, 1984; Chesney, Thompson, Guevara, Vela, & Schottstaedt, 1980; Martin et al., 1985; Trotter, 1982). However, more comprehensive studies of elderly Mexican Americans should study the effects of acculturation on health care choices, the effects of religious beliefs on the use of folk medicine, the level of satisfaction with folk healers and physicians, income, and cohort behaviors.

RECOMMENDATIONS

Social workers and other health care professionals who serve elderly Mexican Americans need to assess a patient's cultural orientation toward folk healing before making recommendations for health care. Professionals can often predict a patient's preference for treatment based on the nature of the medical problem. Patients may believe that serious health problems and injuries require modern medical intervention and that less serious complaints can be effectively treated by folk healing. For those who have strong cultural and religious beliefs and access to traditional medicine, folk healing may be as effective as some forms of modern health care. For seriously ill patients who prefer folk healing, professionals must also consider the health and socio-psychological consequences of delaying necessary modern health care.

Furthermore, adequate health care for elderly Mexican Americans will not exist until accessible and affordable modern medical care is available to them. Some patients turn to folk healing because they cannot gain access to or afford modern health care. It is unknown to what extent this may cause a delay in seeking modern intervention and increase morbidity and mortality. Patients may avoid needed modern health care because existing health care systems, with their emphasis on efficiency and impersonality, conflict with their cultural values, particularly *personalismo.* Folk practices, which depend on personal relationships and community norms, may provide lessons for the reform of modern medical practice and health care service delivery.

Moreover, it would be useful for social workers and other health care professionals to evaluate the effectiveness of traditional herbal medication as compared to modern pharmacological equivalents. Health care professionals should also know how simultaneous use of folk and modern treatments may help or hinder health. Drug-taking behaviors must be explored to identify potential risk factors affecting older members of ethnic groups (Raffoul & Haney, 1989). For example, some home remedies and herbal medicines may interact adversely with prescription medications or may mask symptoms that should be diagnosed (Espino, 1988). Professionals may also want to study natural support systems such as treatment centers that offer a blend of folk or holistic treatment and modern treatment. Information about herbal shops *(yerberías)* and centers for alternative therapy *(centros de terapias alternativas)* or holistic massages *(masajes holísticos)* may reveal effective health care models.

Finally, effective health care depends on social workers and other health care professionals being knowledgeable about and respectful of the indigenous culture of patients. Indigenous beliefs and folk practices, which vary among elderly Mexican Americans, are not barriers to health care. Indeed, the use of folk medicine by elderly Mexican Americans may be overstated in some situations and overlooked in others, which further confounds the issue of whether this population over- or underutilizes health care services. Ultimately, traditional folk healing represents a time-honored alternative to conventional medicine that helps maintain healthful lifestyles for people who are tied to their ancestral cultures. Viewed in this way, social workers and other health care professionals can separate myths from realities to serve elderly Mexican Americans more effectively.

REFERENCES

Anderson, R. (1968). *A behavioral model of families' use of health services* (Research Series No. 25). Chicago: Center for Health Administration Studies, University of Chicago.

Anderson, R., Lewis, S., Giachello, A. L., Aday, L. U., & Chiu, G. (1981). Access to medical care among the Hispanic population of the southwestern United States. *Journal of Health and Social Behavior, 22,* 78–89.

Anderson, R., & Newman, J. (1973). Societal and individual determinants of medical care utilization in the United States. *Milbank Memorial Fund Quarterly, 51,* 95–124.

Anthony-Tkach, C. (1981). Care of the Mexican-American patient. *Nursing and Health Care, 2,* 424–432.

Chavez, L. R. (1984). Doctors, curanderos, and brujas: Healthcare delivery and Mexican immigrants in San Diego. *Medical Anthropology Quarterly, 15,* 31–37.

Chesney, A. P., Thompson, B. L., Guevara, A., Vela, A., & Schottstaedt, M. F. (1980). Mexican-American folk medicine: Implications for the family physicians. *Journal of Family Practice, 11,* 567–574.

De La Cancela, V., & Martinez, I. Z. (1983). An analysis of culturalism in Latino mental health: Folk medicine as a case in point. *Hispanic Journal of Behavioral Sciences, 5,* 251–274.

Espino, D. V. (1988, March). Medication usage in elderly Hispanics: What we know and what we need to know. In *Conference proceedings: Improving drug use among Hispanic elderly* (pp. 7–10). Washington, DC: National Hispanic Council on Aging.

Eve, S. B., & Friedsam, H. J. (1979). Ethnic differences in the use of health care services among older Texans. *Journal of Minority Aging, 4,* 62–75.

Farge, E. J. (1977). A review of findings of "three generations" of Chicano health-care behavior. *Social Science Quarterly, 57,* 407–411.

Higginbotham, J. C., Trevino, F. M., & Ray, L. A. (1990). Utilization of curanderos by Mexican Americans: Prevalence and predictors from H-HANES 1982–1984. *American Journal of Public Health, 80,* 32–35.

Kay, M. A. (1979). Health and illness in a Mexican American barrio. In E. H. Spicer (Ed.), *Ethnic medicine in the Southwest* (pp. 99–166). Tucson: University of Arizona Press.

Lopez-Aqueres, W., Kemp, B., Staples, F., & Brummel-Smith, K. (1984). Use of health care services by older Hispanics. *Journal of the American Geriatric Society, 32,* 435–440.

Lum, D. (1992). *Social work practice and people of color: A process-stage approach.* Pacific Grove, CA: Brooks/Cole.

Martin, H. W., Martinez, C., Leon, R. L., Richardson, C., & Acosta, V. (1985). Folk illnesses reported to physicians in the lower Rio Grande Valley: A binational comparison. *Ethnology, 24,* 229–236.

Mayers, R. S. (1992). Use of folk medicine by elderly Mexican-American women. In B. L. Kail (Ed.), *Special problems on noncompliance among elderly women of color* (pp. 121–133). Lewiston, NY: Edwin Mellen Press.

Morse, J. M. (1991). *Qualitative nursing research.* Newbury Park, CA: Sage Publications.

Raffoul, P. R., & Haney, C. A. (1989). Interdisciplinary treatment of drug misuse among older people of color: Ethnic considerations for social work practice. *Journal of Drug Issues, 19,* 297–313.

Spradley, J. P. (1979). *The ethnographic interview.* Chicago: Holt, Rinehart & Winston.

Trotter, R. T. (1982). Contrasting models of the healer's role: South Texas case examples. *Hispanic Journal of Behavioral Sciences, 4,* 315–327.

Trotter, R. T., II, & Chavira, J. A. (1980). *Remedios caseros:* Mexican American home remedies and community health problems. *Social Science and Medicine, 15,* 107–114.

Trotter, R. T., II, & Chavira, J. A. (1981). *Mexican American folk healing system.* Athens: University of Georgia Press.

Valle, R., & Mendoza, L. (1978). *The elder Latino.* San Diego: Campanile Press.

Veeder, N. W. (1983). Health services utilization models for human services planning. In R. M. Kramer & H. Specht (Eds.), *Readings in community organization practice* (pp. 304–314). Englewood Cliffs, NJ: Prentice Hall.

Vega, W. (1980). The Hispanic natural healer—A case study: Implications for prevention. In R. Valle & W. Vega (Eds.), *Hispanic natural support systems: Mental health promotion perspectives* (pp. 65–74). Sacramento: California Department of Mental Health.

Woyames, G. M. (1981). *Perceptions of curanderismo among elderly Mexican-Americans.* Unpublished master's thesis, University of Texas at Arlington.

Young, J. (1980). *Medical choice in a culture context: Treatment decision making in a Mexican town.* New Brunswick, NJ: Rutgers University Press.

Young, J. C., & Garro, L. Y. (1982). Variations in the choice of treatment of two Mexican communities. *Social Science and Medicine, 16,* 1453–1465.

This chapter was originally published in the November 1995 issue of Health & Social Work, *vol. 20, pp. 247–253.*

34 The Relationship between Psychosocial Status of Immigrant Latino Mothers and Use of Emergency Pediatric Services

Ruth E. Zambrana, Kathleen Ell,
Claudia Dorrington, Laura Wachsman,
and Dee Hodge

Young Hispanic families are of growing concern nationally and in Los Angeles. Although families of Mexican origin represent the largest sector of the Spanish-speaking population in California, there are significant numbers of families from El Salvador and Guatemala. In Los Angeles, currently 40 percent of the population is Hispanic, and the public school population is about 60 percent Hispanic (Valdivieso & Davis, 1988), a significant proportion being recent Mexican immigrants. Furthermore, public county facilities for prenatal and child health services are used predominantly by Hispanic women and children. These women tend to be younger (mean age of 23) and have higher fertility rates and lower income and educational levels than the general population (Valdivieso & Davis, 1988).

There has been an increasing recognition of the need to collect data on the fastest growing segment of the U.S. population. A major social problem is the welfare of young children, especially the plight of poor and minority children. In 1988 among all families in Los Angeles, 36.2 percent of Hispanic children lived in poverty, compared with 16 percent of white children. Furthermore, 71 percent of Hispanic children in single-parent households lived in poverty (Ong, 1989). Consistent empirical evidence has demonstrated that Hispanics, especially those of Mexican origin, tend to underutilize health care services in general and are least likely to have a usual source of care (Becerra & Greenblatt, 1983; Cornelius, 1993a, 1993b; Schur, Berstein, & Berk, 1987). These studies attribute low use of services to specific features of the population, namely, low level of education and income, lack of knowledge of available resources, and cultural and linguistic barriers (Council on Scientific Affairs, 1991; De la Rosa, 1989). Lack of health insurance was found to be directly related to lack of regular (or usual) source of care (Marin, Marin, Padilla, & De la Rocha, 1983; Marin, Marin, Padilla, De la Rocha, & Fay, 1981). Institutional barriers, such as high cost of medical care, lack of bilingual or bicultural personnel, discrimination, and immigration laws, have also contributed to low use or inappropriate use of health services (Becerra & Greenblatt, 1983; Giachello, 1988; Guendelman, 1983).

The purposes of the study described in this chapter were to identify and describe the sociodemographic and psychosocial characteristics of Latino immigrant mothers who use emergency pediatric services; to assess the association of maternal characteristics with perceived barriers to care; and to examine key predictors of utilization behavior, as measured by total number of pediatric visits in the past year and usual source of care, among immigrant Latino mothers.

FACTORS THAT INFLUENCE USE OF PEDIATRIC HEALTH SERVICES

Few studies have examined the utilization patterns of Latinos in the United States, and relatively little comparative research exists on the health of Latino children (Angel & Worobey, 1991). However, Marin et al. (1983), in a study of utilization patterns among Hispanics, found that 57 percent of the sample had never seen a private physician, and more than half (55 percent) of the respondents had used emergency rooms as their main access point to health care delivery systems. In a recent analysis of Latino mothers, the authors found that 50 percent of the women in single-parent households reported barriers to health care, one-third had no insurance, 20 percent had never had a routine medical exam, and 25 percent reported no physical exam for five years or more (Trevino, Trevino, Stroup, & Ray, 1988). A review of 500 pediatric medical charts for Latino children showed that 69 percent of the cases had only one reported visit in the past year. Physical exams, immunizations, and tuberculosis tests were the principal reasons for the visits, and nearly 20 percent of these visits were made in September for school-related purposes (Marin et al., 1981).

Additional investigations have sought to identify the factors that influence the mother's decision to seek pediatric services. In one study, 90 mothers were interviewed in a pediatrician's office. The results indicated that visits were most likely to occur when the child exhibited multiple symptoms and the mother was employed. Delayed visits were correlated with perceived cost of care. Overall, only 39 percent of the visits were judged to be appropriate (necessary and on time) by pediatricians (Kaftarian & Safer, 1987–88). In another study, Schwarz-Lockinland, McKeever, and Saputa (1989) examined factors that enhanced appropriate use of pediatric care. Their study of compliance with an antibiotic regimen for acute otitis media among Hispanic mothers found that when mother and child couples were seen individually by the same health care provider on separate clinic visits, and when verbal instructions were provided and a skill was acquired (such as drawing up medication into an oral syringe), compliance was high. The authors suggested that the acquisition of a new skill may have increased a mother's self-esteem and feelings of control, which enhanced both compliance and appropriate health-seeking behavior.

PSYCHOSOCIAL FACTORS AND HEALTH-SEEKING BEHAVIORS

A limited number of studies have examined the role that social and psychological factors play in influencing a mother's evaluation of her child's health and the decision to seek pediatric services. Several studies raised questions about the role of maternal stress and depression in childhood illness (Orr & James, 1984; Orr, James, Burns, & Thompson, 1989). Contemporary conceptualizations have proposed that a set of interrelated factors, namely, social class, culture, and psychosocial factors, influence a mother's assessment of the severity of symptoms and constrain her decisions concerning appropriate behavior. Acculturation and English language proficiency have also been found to have strong independent effects on a mother's report of poor health for her child, and these may reflect her own level of distress (Angel & Worobey, 1988). For example, in an analysis of

Mexican American mothers, the data showed that the least acculturated mothers reported their children to be in poorer health than the more acculturated mothers and that single mothers reported poorer health for their children than did married mothers. Furthermore, the authors found that Mexican American mothers who spoke only Spanish reported much higher rates of fair and poor health than either black or white two-parent and female-headed households. These data support the hypothesis that a mother's report of her child's health reflects her own perceptions and is likely to be influenced by her psychosocial status (Angel & Worobey, 1988).

A complex set of social and psychological factors influence a mother's decision to seek pediatric services, including work status of the mother, multiple symptoms in the child, marital status, culture, and emotional status. In addition, organizational or structural characteristics of the current health care delivery system present barriers to appropriate use of services for Latino women and children. Several studies have concluded that racism and discrimination are endemic in the delivery, administration, and planning of health care services. These factors seriously impede access to and use of these services by Hispanic families and their children (De la Rosa, 1989; Giachello, 1988; Ginzberg, 1991).

Currently, major urban areas such as Los Angeles are experiencing organizational strain on their health care systems, in part because of the dramatic increase of low-income and poor families, including immigrants. Mothers and children represent a significant portion of users of health care services. Mothers are the primary caretakers of the family and the primary health decision makers (Combs-Orme, 1990; Ell & Northen, 1990). For immigrant Latino mothers, there is still limited understanding of the constellation of factors that influence use of pediatric services.

METHODS

Sample

A purposive, sequential sampling procedure was used. The sample consisted of 80 Latino mothers. The women selected were between ages 18 and 40; born in Mexico, El Salvador, or Guatemala; had a child between infancy and age five; and had visited a large urban pediatric emergency room in Los Angeles County in 1990. All women who met these criteria were identified through medical charts by intake staff at the hospital and referred to the interviewer over a three-month period. The nature of the study was explained to potential respondents, and their participation was requested by bilingual and bicultural interviewers. When the participants agreed, they signed an informed consent agreement. The study site was selected because about 98 percent of the users of pediatric services were Hispanic children.

Instrument and Procedures

The instrument was designed to obtain information on the sociodemographic characteristics of the mother and information about the child's health care including reason for current visit, number of days of illness before current visit, the child's usual source of care, and the mother's perception of the child's overall health and the seriousness of the current illness. In addition, data were collected on the mother's perception of barriers to health care and on her own psychosocial functioning and health status.

A series of closed-ended items obtained information on the mother's age, place of birth, marital status, number of years in the United States, level of education, employment status, and health insurance coverage for the child (specifically Medi-Cal). A five-point Likert scale was used to measure the mother's assessment of her child's overall health (1 = excellent, 5 = poor), and a four-point scale measured the mother's perception of seriousness of current symptoms (1 = extremely serious, 4 = not serious).

Perceived barriers to health care services were measured on a 14-item scale adapted from the Hispanic Health and Nutrition Examination Survey (H-HANES). The respondent indicated yes or no to a series of questions asking whether she had been unable to get medical care for her child during the past year for reasons such as prohibitive cost, lack of child care, or lack of transportation. The sum of the affirmative responses constituted the total score with a range of 0 to 14. The Cronbach alpha for this scale yielded a coefficient of .84.

Five multi-item scales were used to assess the psychosocial functioning and health status of the mothers. The Subjective Self-Rating Health Scale (SSRH) was used to obtain their perceptions of their overall health status on a five-point scale (1 = excellent, 5 = poor). Two items were derived from the Functional Limitations

Battery, Dayton Medical History Questionnaire (Stewart, Ware, Brook, & Davies-Avery, 1978). The respondents were asked whether their health had limited their ability to carry out normal daily activities or had prevented them from carrying out their normal activities altogether during the past year. These items were rated on a three-point scale (1 = three months or more, 2 = three months or less, and 3 = no).

Five items were derived from the Form A Mental Health Battery, Dayton Medical History Questionnaire (Ware, Johnston, Davies-Avery, & Brook, 1979). The respondents' mental health status for the past month was rated on a six-item scale, with responses rated from 5 = all the time to 1 = never. For example, respondents were asked how much time they had been nervous or depressed during the past month. The sum of the responses to all items resulted in a total score ranging from six to 30. Higher scores indicated a higher level of mental distress over the past month. Reliability analysis of this scale yielded a Cronbach alpha coefficient of .68.

A life problems measure was derived from the Los Angeles County Epidemiological Catchment Area Study (Golding, 1985), which includes 13 life problem areas and asks respondents to indicate on a four-point scale how serious each problem has been in their lives during the past three months (1 = not a problem, 4 = a serious problem). Examples of problems are lack of money, family health problems, or employment difficulties. Scores ranged from 13 to 52, the higher score indicating a higher number of serious problems during the past three months. The reliability analysis yielded an alpha coefficient of .73.

Procidano and Heller's (1983) Perceived Social Support Scale was used to examine the mother's perception of her relationships with family members and friends. The family scale includes 10 items addressing relations with family members—for example, "My family is sensitive to my personal needs." The friend support scale includes 10 items such as "My friends give me moral support when I need it." Each item is measured on a three-point scale (3 = yes, 2 = don't know, and 1 = no). Scores ranged from 10 to 30 for each of the scales. The higher scores indicate a perception of greater social support from family or friends. Reliability analysis yielded an alpha of .67 for the family support scale and .75 for the friend support scale.

The Perceived Stress Scale (Cohen, Kamarck, & Mermelstein, 1983) was used to measure the respondents' perceptions regarding their ability to cope with their lives and their problems and the extent to which they felt in control during the past month. The instrument consists of eight items measured on a five-point scale (1 = never, 5 = always). Total scores ranged from eight to 40, the higher scores indicating that the respondents felt more in control of their lives and were better able to cope with problems. Reliability analysis yielded an alpha of .57, which raised concerns about the cross-cultural equivalency of this scale.

All measures were modified to incorporate central study concerns and to ensure linguistic and cultural sensitivity to respondents. Interviewers were of Hispanic origin, and all respondents were interviewed in Spanish. Interviews were conducted while the respondents were waiting to see the physician and, on average, took 40 minutes.

Analyses

Univariate descriptive statistics and bivariate analyses, including chi-square, t tests, and correlational analysis, were performed depending on the level of measurement of the variables concerned. Respondents from Mexico and Central America were compared to determine any significant differences between the two groups. Multivariate analysis was conducted to assess the independent effects of various factors associated with the major dependent variable, the number of pediatric health care visits during the past year for the total sample.

RESULTS

Sociodemographic Characteristics of Mothers

The sample consisted of 80 Hispanic immigrant mothers, of whom 59 were Mexican immigrants and 21 Central American (Salvadoran and Guatemalan) immigrants. Table 34-1 presents the characteristics of respondents by place of origin. The mean age of the respondents was 25.61 years (SD = 5.08). The mean educational level of respondents was 7.56 years (SD = 3.73). About two-fifths (43.8 percent) of all respondents were married, and 29.6 percent of all respondents reported working full-time. The mean number of household members was 5.70 (SD = 2.08). The average

Table 34-1

Sociodemographic Characteristics of Immigrant Latino Mothers

Sociodemographic Characteristic	Total (n = 80)		Mexican (n = 59)		Central American (n = 21)	
	M	SD	M	SD	M	SD
Age	25.61	5.08	25.20	5.12	26.76	4.90
Education	7.56	3.73	7.53	3.85	7.67	3.44
No. of years in the United States	6.90	5.11	6.82	5.44	7.10	4.17
Household size	5.70	2.08	5.85	2.26	5.29	1.42
	%		%		%	
Marital status						
Married	43.8		45.8		38.1	
Not married	56.2		54.2		61.9	
Employed						
Full-time	29.6		29.7		29.4	
Part-time	9.3		8.1		11.8	
Does not work	61.2		62.2		58.8	
Speaks English						
Yes	34.2		29.3		47.6	
No	65.8		70.7		52.4	
Medi-Cal coverage						
Yes	39.2		42.4		30.0	
No	60.8		57.6		70.0	

NOTE: Totals may not add to 100 due to rounding.

length of time in the United States for all respondents was 6.90 years (*SD* = 5.11). More than half (51.25 percent, *n* = 41) of the respondents had been in the Los Angeles area less than five years. Almost half (47.6 percent) of the Central American immigrants reported ability to speak English, compared with 29.3 percent of the Mexican immigrants. Medi-Cal coverage was reported by 42.4 percent of the Mexican immigrants but by only 30.0 percent of the Central Americans. There were no significant differences by immigrant group on the major sociodemographic factors including age of mother and child, level of education, marital status, employment, and number of persons per household. Thus, all further analyses were conducted on the total sample, but differences by place of origin are noted.

As expected, the respondents' ages were significantly associated with length of time in the United States ($r = .34, p < .01$), and the mothers' ability to speak English was positively associated with their level of education ($r = .37, p < .01$) and length of time in the United States ($r = .52, p < .01$). Mothers who spoke English had an average of 9.52 years of education and had been in the country for an average of $10^{1}/_{2}$ years. In contrast, non-English-speaking respondents had an average of 6.67 years of education ($F = 12.17, p < .01$) and had lived in the United States for an average of five years ($F = 27.87, p < .01$).

Health-Related Characteristics of Child

The mean age of the children was 18.52 months ($SD = 19.74$) (Table 34-2). All children were born in the United States. Overall, 62.5 percent of respondents reported that their children's health was good or very good, and 5.0 percent reported that their children's health was poor. The principal reasons given for the physician visit were ear, nose, and throat problems; flu-related symptoms

Table 34-2

Health-Related Characteristics of Latino Children

Health-Related Characteristic	Total (n = 80)		Mexican (n = 59)		Central American (n = 21)	
	M	SD	M	SD	M	SD
Child's age, months	18.52	19.74	17.07	18.69	22.60	22.44
No. of days sick before current visit	9.73	18.98	8.76	17.87	12.74	22.34
	%		%		%	
Mother's evaluation of—						
Child's current symptoms						
Not serious	29.5		32.8		20.0	
Serious	35.9		36.2		35.0	
Extremely or very serious	34.6		31.0		45.0	
Child's overall health						
Poor	5.0		5.1		4.8	
Fair	32.5		35.6		23.8	
Good	40.0		35.6		52.4	
Very good	22.5		23.7		19.0	

such as stuffy nose, coughing, or fever; intestinal-related problems such as diarrhea or vomiting; and accidents. The mothers
reported that their children had been sick for an average of 9.73
days (SD = 18.98) before the current visit.

Respondents evaluated the seriousness of the symptoms for
the current visit. One-third (34.6 percent) rated the symptoms as
extremely or very serious. An almost equal percentage rated the
children's symptoms as serious, and 29.5 percent (35.9 percent)
rated the symptoms as not serious. The mean for seriousness of
symptom evaluation was 2.24 (SD = 1.08). Correlation analyses
showed no significant relationships between total number of visits
during the past year and child-related variables—that is, age of
child, number of days sick before current visit, mothers' perception of children's health overall, or existence of children's usual
source of care.

Health Care Utilization Patterns and Barriers

Four items, with forced-choice response options, asked the respondents to indicate if they had a usual source of care for their
children. Two items asked where they usually took their children for routine checkups and immunizations and where they
usually took their children when they were sick. One item asked
for the number of pediatric visits in the past year. Respondents
reported an average of 6.29 (SD = 12.33) child health care visits
during the past year (Table 34-3). Sixty-five percent (n = 52) of
the sample reported a usual source of care. Central Americans
were equally as likely to report a usual source of care as Mexican
immigrants. The data revealed two major sources of regular health
care for children: 36.2 percent (n = 29) identified the pediatric
emergency room, and 42.5 percent (n = 34) reported other public
health facilities. Only 7.5 percent (n = 6) reported a private physician, and 13.7 percent (n = 11) reported other sources. Mexican
immigrants were $1\frac{1}{2}$ times more likely than Central American
immigrants to report use of the emergency room as a regular
source of care. Almost half (47.5 percent, n = 38) reported the
emergency room as usual health care source for a sick child,
whereas 36.2 percent (n = 29) reported other public health facilities. Trends were similar for both groups.

On average the respondents identified four barriers (M = 4.14,
SD = 3.51) to obtaining health care for their children during the

Table 34-3

Pediatric Health Care Utilization Characteristics

Characteristic	Total (n = 80)		Mexican (n = 59)		Central American (n = 21)	
	M	SD	M	SD	M	SD
No. of health care visits	6.29	12.33	6.96	14.22	4.42	3.27
No. of barriers to health care use	4.14	3.51	3.64	3.52	5.52*	3.16
	%		%		%	
Usual source of care						
Yes	65.0		62.7		71.4	
No	35.0		37.3		28.6	
Pediatric source of care						
Regular consultation						
Emergency room	36.2		40.7		23.8	
Private doctor	7.5		5.1		14.3	
Other public facility	42.5		39.0		52.4	
Other source	13.7		15.3		9.5	
When child is unwell						
Emergency room	47.5		49.2		42.9	
Private doctor	7.5		5.1		14.3	
Other public facility	36.2		37.3		33.4	
Other source	8.7		8.5		9.5	

NOTE: Totals may not add to 100 due to rounding.
*$p < .05$.

past year. Central American mothers reported a significantly higher number of barriers ($M = 5.52$, $SD = 3.16$) than Mexican immigrant mothers ($M = 3.64$, $SD = 3.52$, $p < .05$). The most frequently reported barriers were too long a wait in the clinic (56.2 percent, $n = 45$); too long to wait for an appointment (50.0 percent, $n = 40$); the cost of care (40.0 percent, $n = 32$); the staff not speaking Spanish (35.0 percent, $n = 28$); the lack of Latino staff (31.2 percent, $n = 25$); and lack of confidence in health care staff (31.2 percent, $n = 25$).

Psychosocial Profile of Mothers

More than half (56.2 percent, $n = 45$) of the women reported that their own physical health was only fair or poor, 27.5 percent ($n =$

22) reported generally good health, and 16.2 percent ($n = 13$) reported very good or excellent health. Almost 14 percent ($n = 11$)
indicated that their health had affected their ability to carry out
their usual daily activities, either at work or at home, for more
than three months during the past year, and 11.2 percent ($n = 9$)
were unable to go to work at all for more than three months.
Another 11.2 percent ($n = 9$) had been affected by health-related
problems for three months or less.

The average score on the life problems scale for all respondents was 24.0 ($SD = 6.36$). The women identified an average of
5.67 problems that had caused them some difficulty during the
preceding three months, ranging from minor to serious. The difficulties most frequently reported as a major or serious problem
included lack of English skills (60.0 percent, $n = 48$), lack of money
(58.7 percent, $n = 47$), difficulty finding or keeping a job (41.2
percent, $n = 33$), difficulty finding an affordable place to live
(38.7 percent, $n = 31$), and difficulty finding a safe place to live
(36.2 percent, $n = 29$). Major or serious problems with family
health or discrimination against family members were reported
by 18.7 percent ($n = 15$) of the respondents.

In addition, the respondents reported high levels of mental
distress during the past month, specifically feelings of nervousness and depression ($M = 14.34$, $SD = 5.00$). Almost one-third
(32.5 percent, $n = 26$) reported being nervous, and 25.0 percent ($n = 20$) reported feeling sad or depressed most or all of the time
during the past month. Central American women tended to re-
port a higher degree of mental distress ($M = 16.19$, $SD = 4.97$)
than Mexican immigrant women ($M = 13.68$, $SD = 4.89$, $p = .053$).
The scores on the Perceived Stress Scale ($M = 26.64$, $SD = 4.71$)
indicated that generally the respondents felt that they had been
"able to manage or be in control of their lives" and their problems only some of the time during the past month. Moreover,
21.2 percent ($n = 17$) reported that they "never or hardly ever felt
that they could manage," and only 15 percent ($n = 12$) reported
that they "felt they could cope with their lives and their problems most of the time." On the other hand, the respondents re-
ported relatively high levels of support from both family ($M = 21.98$, $SD = 5.24$) and friends ($M = 19.43$, $SD = 5.23$).

Correlation analyses were conducted to assess the associations
between maternal characteristics and perceived barriers to care.

A significant positive relationship existed between the scores on the life problems scale and the measure of mental health status (r = .43, $p < .01$) and perceived barriers to health care ($r = .49$, $p <$ .01). Alternatively, significant negative associations existed between the scores on the Perceived Stress Scale and mental health status ($r = -.32$, $p < .01$), life problems ($r = -.23$, $p < .05$), and perceived barriers to health care ($r = -.25$, $p < .05$). The relationship between the variables showed that those with a greater sense of control over their lives reported fewer difficulties; those reporting fewer difficulties over the past three months or who felt in greater control of their lives experienced lower levels of mental distress and also perceived fewer barriers to health care.

Multivariate Analyses

Five independent variables were included in a multiple regression model to assess the influence of these factors on the total number of pediatric visits during the past year. Two dummy variables were created: Medi-Cal coverage (1 = yes, 0 = no) and usual source of health care. Three continuous variables were included: age of child, number of years in the United States, and perceived barriers to health care.

As shown in Table 34-4, the multivariate model was significant, accounting for 19 percent of the variation in pediatric health care visits during the past year (model R^2 = .19, standard error of

Table 34-4

Multivariate Analysis: Number of Health Care Visits during the Past Year

Independent Variables	r	SE	Significant t	Correlation with Formal Visits
Intercept	2.443	.969		
Age of child	−.003	.005	.6030	−.004
Medi-Cal coverage[a]	1.991	.813	.0172	.376**
Usual source of care[a]	.812	.804	.3176	.155
No. of years in United States	.130	.076	.0925	.283*
Perceived barriers to health care	−.070	.120	.5635	−.156

NOTE: Model R^2 = .19, standard error of estimate = 2.95, $F < .01$.
[a] 0 = no, 1 = yes.
*$p \leq .05$. **$p \leq .01$.

estimate = 2.95, F < .01). However, when using the backward method of selection, only one variable, Medi-Cal coverage, was found to be a significant predictor of the total number of pediatric health care visits (model R^2 = .14, standard error of estimate = 2.99, F < .01). Additional multivariate analyses were conducted that included mother's education level instead of length of time in the United States (model R^2 = .16, standard error of estimate = 3.07, F = .058). A second set of analyses were conducted using the mother's psychosocial variables (life problems scale, mental health status, Perceived Stress Scale, and family and friend support scales) as independent predictors. These models were not significant.

DISCUSSION

The unprecedented growth of Latino immigrant groups in the Los Angeles area is contributing to a crisis for both the health care system and Latino families. The use of health care services by Latino families has been consistently documented as inadequate, especially in poor families (De la Rosa, 1989). Differential utilization patterns within Hispanic groups have also consistently demonstrated that Mexican-origin populations are the least likely to have public or private health insurance and show the lowest use of health care services (Cornelius, 1993a, 1993b; Trevino, Moyer, Valdez, & Stroup-Benham, 1991).

In comparing the social characteristics of our study sample to Mexican American respondents (Spanish interview) from the national H-HANES, our respondents were less likely to be in two-parent families (43.8 percent of our study sample versus 78.7 percent of the H-HANES study sample), although the data show similar household size (5.7 versus 5.5). In comparing parental assessment of child's health, 5.0 percent of the study respondents rated their children's health as poor compared with 1.2 percent of national sample; 32.5 percent of study sample compared with 22.9 percent of the national sample rated their children's health as fair; 40 percent of both samples rated their children's health as good. Only 22.5 percent of the study sample rated their children's health as very good to excellent compared with 34.1 percent of the national sample.

These data show that the study sample is more likely to be in female-headed households, and nearly 40 percent reported their children's health as poor to fair, confirming the relationships among acculturation, socioeconomic status, and single parenthood (Angel & Worobey, 1988, 1991). Clearly, the small sample size and the urban context in which this study was conducted represent limitations with respect to representativeness of the study participants. Thus, caution needs to be exercised in the interpretation and generalization of these findings to all Latino subgroups in different geographic regions.

Overall, this group of immigrant women demonstrated a fairly high incidence of mental distress, specifically feeling nervous or depressed. The women had to cope with a relatively high number of life problems, the most serious ones relating to their socioeconomic conditions. The psychosocial profiles show that as a group, the respondents felt overwhelmed and unable to cope with everyday life and experienced limited physical and mental health functioning. Not surprisingly, the data confirmed the reported high levels of anxiety and depression found among Mexican and Central American immigrants due to barriers to care such as lack of English language proficiency, lack of adequate employment, undocumented status, and perceived societal discrimination (Cervantes, Salgado de Snyder, & Padilla, 1988; Leslie & Leitch, 1989; Padilla, Cervantes, Maldonado, & Garcia, 1987; Padilla, Ruiz, & Alvarez, 1975). Social support from both family and friends was generally perceived by respondents as being available. However, other studies have found that Mexican immigrant mothers have a greater number of life problems and fewer family and social support resources than Mexican American mothers, a fact that may also contribute to their mental distress (Vega, 1990; Zambrana, Silva-Palacios, & Powell, 1992).

The physical and mental health status of the mothers was positively correlated with reported significant barriers to access to health care services for their children. For example, although 65 percent of the respondents reported a usual source of care, 36 percent also reported the emergency room as the site for usual care; these data suggest that respondents may perceive the emergency room as a primary and preventive health care site or that they find it to be most available and accessible site for routine pediatric care. Alternatively, the mothers' psychosocial health status may influence the delayed use of pediatric services. The delay may be related to the respondents' inability to manage everyday tasks due to mental distress.

Several studies have documented that lack of health insurance is a major barrier to timely and appropriate use of health care services (Behrman & Larson, 1991; Council on Scientific Affairs, 1991; Trevino et al., 1991). In this study, Medi-Cal health insurance coverage was the most significant predictor of the total number of pediatric care visits. Yet immigrants whose children are eligible for Medi-Cal by virtue of their birth in the United States tend not to use these benefits. Medi-Cal was not a sufficient variable in and of itself to influence timely and appropriate use of pediatric health care services. In fact, it appears that perceived barriers, which are highly associated with reported psychosocial stressors, contribute to delayed use of pediatric care.

These preliminary findings reveal a pattern of delayed care for children, use of emergency room services for primary care needs, that is, acute health problems, and respondents who are experiencing serious psychosocial difficulties in their everyday lives. The reported barriers to use of pediatric services show limited accessibility to nonemergency room preventive and primary care services in the Latino community.

CONCLUSION

The sociodemographic characteristics and psychosocial attributes of the Latino immigrant mothers in this study placed this group at high risk of delaying pediatric health care for their children. In fact, these data point to the need to systematically explore the interactive effect of sociodemographic characteristics, perception of seriousness of child's illness, mother's psychosocial status, and perceived barriers to care on Latino immigrant women's use of emergency pediatric health services. Several questions for future research emerged from this study. Is the evidence of overall poor health in Latino children related to this delayed care? What effect does delayed care have on the long-range health status of Latino children? What effect does the mother's mental and physical status have on children's mental and developmental status? What types of psychosocial interventions would be most appropriate for these mothers to decrease the delay in care? These questions can serve to guide future research in this area, research that needs to be formulated within a family context (Combs-Orme, 1990; Ell & Northen, 1990).

Latino mothers, by and large, have been marginal participants in the mainstream pediatric health care system; therefore, they have had little access to biomedical knowledge. For this reason, social workers (and other health care practitioners) can have a significant influence on the health of Latino mothers and children by taking their educational role seriously. Specifically, there are three steps that can be taken: (1) inform (through an interpreter, if necessary) Latino mothers in health care settings about the need for preventive and prompt care, diagnostic tests, and prodromal symptoms of major treatable diseases; (2) initiate and facilitate family support programs (Hutchins & Walch, 1989; Powell, Zambrana, & Silva-Palacios, 1990); and (3) promote community education on acute pediatric illnesses and preventive measures (for example, by providing a list of nonemergency pediatric resources in the residential community of the mother). Social workers practicing in pediatric programs should pay particular attention to the psychosocial needs of poor Latino mothers. A need for methods to routinely screen these women with respect to general psychosocial needs and psychological distress is strongly indicated. A variety of methods including the use of brief questionnaires might be instituted (Orr, James, & Charney, 1989). Efforts on the part of social workers to assist these mothers will not influence environmental conditions that can be addressed only at a social policy level. However, such efforts can reduce the negative subjective experiences of the mothers (Halpern, 1990) and ultimately influence the children's lives and health.

Closely related is the need for social workers to encourage the development of and training in cross-cultural education and awareness within the medical services arena and for an increase in the number of bicultural, bilingual staff among social services providers in urban facilities. In this way, the goal of providing culturally and linguistically sensitive delivery of pediatric health care services to Latinos can be attained. Social workers can also help Latinos by directing them to classes in English as a second language in community-sponsored programs so they can develop new language proficiency skills to improve communication with mainstream pediatric health care providers. Last, health care providers can initiate, support, and encourage legislative proposals to fund and increase the number of community-based health care

centers in Latino communities, thus improving accessibility to
primary and preventive health care services for this population.

REFERENCES

Angel, R. J., & Worobey, J. L. (1988). Single motherhood and children's health.
  Journal of Health and Social Behavior, 29, 38–52.
Angel, R. J., & Worobey, J. L. (1991). Intragroup differences in the health of
  Hispanic children. *Social Science Quarterly, 72*(2), 361–377.
Becerra, R., & Greenblatt, M. (1983). *Hispanics seek health care. A study of 1,000
  veterans of three war eras.* Lanham, MD: University Press of America.
Behrman, R. E., & Larson, C. S. (1991). Health care for pregnant women and
  young children. *American Journal of Diseases of Children, 145,* 572–574.
Cervantes, R. C., Salgado de Snyder, V. N., & Padilla, A. M. (1988). *Post-
  traumatic stress disorder among immigrants from Central America and Mexico*
  (Occasional Paper No. 24). Los Angeles: University of California, Los
  Angeles, Spanish-Speaking Mental Health Research Center.
Cohen, S., Kamarck, T., & Mermelstein, R. (1983). A global measure of
  perceived stress. *Journal of Health and Social Behavior, 24,* 385–396.
Combs-Orme, T. (1990). *Social work practice in maternal and child health.* New
  York: Springer.
Cornelius, L. (1993a). Barriers to medical care for white, black, and Hispanic
  children. *Journal of the National Medical Association, 85*(4), 281–288.
Cornelius, L. (1993b). Ethnic minorities and access to medical care: Where do
  we stand? *Journal of the Association for Academic Minority Physicians, 4*(1),
  16–25.
Council on Scientific Affairs. (1991). Hispanic health in the United States.
  Journal of the American Medical Association, 265, 248–253.
De la Rosa, M. (1989). Health care needs of Hispanic Americans and the
  responsiveness of the health care system. *Health & Social Work, 14,* 104–113.
Ell, K., & Northen, H. (1990). *Families and health care: Psychosocial practice.* New
  York: Aldine de Gruyter.
Giachello, A. L. (1988). Hispanics and health care. In P. S. Cafferty, S. J.
  Pastora, & W. C. McCready (Eds.), *Hispanics in the United States: A new
  social agenda* (pp. 159–194). New Brunswick, NJ: Transaction Books.
Ginzberg, E. (1991). Access to health care for Hispanics. *Journal of the American
  Medical Association, 265,* 238–242.
Golding, J. M. (1985). *An integrated role restriction and stress approach to gender
  differences in depression.* Unpublished doctoral dissertation, University of
  California, Los Angeles.
Guendelman, S. (1983). Developing responsiveness to the health needs of
  Hispanic children and families. *Social Work in Health Care, 8*(4), 1–15.
Halpern, R. (1990). Poverty and early childhood parenting: Toward a
  framework for intervention. *American Journal of Orthopsychiatry, 60,* 6–18.
Hutchins, V., & Walch, C. (1989). Meeting minority health needs through
  special MCH projects. *Public Health Reports, 104,* 621–626.

Kaftarian, S., & Safer, M. (1987–88). Determinants of seeking timely and necessary pediatric care. *Current Psychological Research and Reviews, 6*(4), 289–300.

Leslie, L. A., & Leitch, M. L. (1989). A demographic profile of recent Central American immigrants: Clinical and service implications. *Hispanic Journal of Behavioral Sciences, 11*(40), 315–329.

Marin, B. V., Marin, G., Padilla, A., & De la Rocha, C. (1983). Utilization of traditional and non-traditional sources of health care among Hispanics. *Hispanic Journal of Behavioral Sciences, 5*(1), 65–80.

Marin, B. V., Marin, G., Padilla, A. M., De la Rocha, C., & Fay, J. (1981). *Health care utilization by low-income clients of a community clinic: An archival study* (Occasional Paper No. 12). Los Angeles: University of California, Los Angeles, Spanish-Speaking Mental Health Research Center.

Ong, P. (1989). *The widening divide: Income, inequality and poverty in Los Angeles.* Los Angeles: University of California, Los Angeles Research Group on the Los Angeles Economy.

Orr, S. T., & James, S. A. (1984). Maternal depression in a urban pediatric practice: Implications for health care delivery. *American Journal of Public Health, 74,* 363–365.

Orr, S. T., James, S. A., Burns, B. J., & Thompson, B. (1989). Chronic stressors and maternal depression: Implications for prevention. *American Journal of Public Health, 79,* 1295–1296.

Orr, S. T., James, S. A., & Charney, E. (1989). A social environment inventory for the pediatric office. *Journal of Developmental and Behavioral Pediatrics, 10*(6), 287–291.

Padilla, A. M., Cervantes, R. C., Maldonado, M., & Garcia, R. E. (1987). *Coping responses to psychosocial stressors among Mexican and Central American immigrants* (Occasional Paper No. 23). Los Angeles: University of California, Los Angeles, Spanish-Speaking Mental Health Research Center.

Padilla, A. M., Ruiz, R. E., & Alvarez, R. (1975). Community mental health services for the Spanish-speaking surnamed population. *American Psychologist, 30,* 892–905.

Powell, D., Zambrana, R. E., & Silva-Palacios, V. (1990). Designing culturally responsive parent programs: A comparison of low-income Mexican and Mexican-American mothers' preferences. *Family Relations, 39,* 298–304.

Procidano, M. E., & Heller, K. (1983). Measures of perceived social support from friends and family: Three validation studies. *American Journal of Community Psychology, 2*(1), 1–24.

Schur, C. L., Berstein, A. B., & Berk, M. L. (1987). The importance of distinguishing Hispanic sub-populations in the use of medical care. *Medical Care, 25,* 627–641.

Schwarz-Lockinland, S., McKeever, L. C., & Saputa, M. (1989). Compliance with antibiotic regimens in Hispanic mothers. *Patient Education and Counseling, 13,* 171–182.

Stewart, W., Ware, J. E., Brook, R. H., & Davies-Avery, A. (1978). *Conceptualization and measurement of health for adults in the health insurance study: Vol. II. Physical health in terms of functioning.* Santa Monica, CA: Rand Corporation.

Trevino, F. M., Moyer, M. E., Valdez, R. B., & Stroup-Benham, C. A. (1991). Health insurance coverage and utilization of health services by Mexican, mainland Puerto-Rican and Cuban-Americans. *Journal of the American Medical Association, 265,* 233–237.

Trevino, F. M., Trevino, D. B., Stroup C. A., & Ray L. (1988). *The feminization of poverty among Hispanic households.* San Antonio, TX: Tomas Rivera Center, National Institute of Policy Studies.

Valdivieso R., & Davis, C. (1988). *U.S. Hispanics: Challenging issues for the 1990s.* Washington, DC: Population Reference Bureau.

Vega, W. (1990). Hispanic families in the 1980's: A decade of research. *Journal of Marriage and the Family, 52,* 1015–1024.

Ware, J. E., Johnston, S. A., Davies-Avery, A., & Brook, R. H. (1979). Conceptualization and measurement of health for adults in the health insurance study. *Mental Health, 3,* 115.

This chapter was originally published in the May 1994 issue of Health & Social Work, *vol. 19, pp. 93–102.*

Part VI

SERVICE DELIVERY

35 The Effect of Mental Health Practitioners' Racial Sensitivity on African Americans' Perceptions of Service

Sharron M. Singleton-Bowie

The prevalence of mental illness among African American adults is rapidly increasing and has serious ramifications for both society in general and the African American community. In spite of continuous efforts by the psychiatric community to refine the definition of and diagnostic criteria for chronic mental illness, large numbers of African Americans are diagnosed with the most severe disorders and are considered to have poor prognoses for recovery.

Although African American adults make up approximately 12 percent of the U.S. population (U.S. Bureau of the Census, 1991), their representation in the mentally ill population is disproportionately higher. African American men are hospitalized for psychiatric reasons at a rate 2.8 times greater than white men and African American women at a rate 2.5 times greater than white women (National Institute of Mental Health [NIMH], 1987). African American inpatients are diagnosed with schizophrenia at almost twice the rate of white inpatients—56 percent compared with 32 percent (NIMH, 1987). Keith, Regier, and Rae (1991) found that the lifetime rate of schizophrenic disorders for African American adults (2.1 percent) was significantly higher than that for both white (1.4 percent) and Hispanic (0.08 percent) groups. This disproportionate representation was also found to exist when comparisons were made by age and sex. Research conducted by several noted authors (Bulhan, 1975; Jones & Gray, 1986; Lawson, 1986; Solomon, 1988; Sue, 1977) indicated that African Americans are disproportionately diagnosed as schizophrenic or psychotic and make up a large percentage of people receiving services from public mental health facilities.

One aspect of human existence especially important to the African American population is the experience of racism. Some authors view racism as a factor contributing to mental illness among African Americans (Jones & Gray, 1986; Wilcox, 1973; Williams, 1986). African Americans who experience mental illness must face the symptoms of their illness as well as the racism found in the mental health profession. This racism reflects a society historically hostile to the very existence of African Americans (Carter, 1986; Jones & Gray, 1986; Solomon, 1988; Wilcox, 1973). Several studies have provided evidence of prejudice and bias in the mental health treatment of African Americans. The biased acts include misdiagnosis (Bell & Mehta, 1981; Jones & Gray, 1986; Loring & Powell, 1988; Mollica, Blum, & Redlich, 1980; Mukherjee, Shuckla, Woodle, Rosen, & Olarte, 1983; Poussaint, 1983; Solomon, 1988), abuse and neglect in mental health institutions (Collins, Rickman, & Risher, 1984), and excessive use of medication (Lawson, Yesavage, & Werner, 1984). Although much literature has been produced about African American culture and its relevance for treatment, very little attention has been given to racism and its possible effect on such treatment issues as resource provision, relationship development, and quality of life for people who are mentally ill.

Quality of life is a critical outcome variable for evaluating services for chronically mentally ill people (Baker & Intagliata, 1982; Franklin, Simmons, Solovitz, Clemons, & Miller, 1986; Lehman, 1983; Lehman, Ward, & Linn, 1982; Turner & Tenhoor, 1978). Although there have been numerous debates about the ability of mentally ill people to reliably report on the conditions of their lives, it has become evident that quality of life goes beyond access to material supports. Bigelow, Brodsky, Stewart, and Olson (1982) viewed quality of life as an abstraction that integrated and summarized all features of human existence found to be more or less desirable and satisfying. Scholars advocated that the areas to be assessed in the study of quality of life for chronically mentally ill individuals should include those most likely to be influenced by the care, treatment, and services provided them (Alexander & Willems, 1981; Baker & Intagliata, 1982; Franklin et al., 1986; Malm, May, & Dencker, 1981).

The research discussed in this chapter examines the level of awareness of racial oppression on the part of practitioners in a mental health delivery system and explores the relationship of this sensitivity to clients' perceptions of service delivery and the quality of their lives.

METHOD

The research explored three questions: (1) How sensitive were case managers to the existence of racially oppressive attitudes, beliefs, and behaviors in the mental health services system? (2) What effect did level of sensitivity to racial oppression have on the delivery of services to African American clients? (3) How did case managers' level of sensitivity to racial oppression affect client perception of the quality of life?

Answers to these questions were sought using data collected in the public mental health system of Washington, DC, where approximately 7,500 adult clients (5,300 of whom were outpatients) received a variety of services from the District of Columbia's Commission on Mental Health Services (CMHS, 1990) from September 1989 through October 1990. The study used a cross-sectional research design and multistage probability sampling procedures. In the first stage of sampling, selection was made from the population of African American adults diagnosed with schizophrenia who were listed on the rolls of the CMHS's community mental health system and who had been outpatients for a minimum of two years. In the second stage, individuals on the list were randomly ordered and their primary case managers identified. Where duplication of primary case managers occurred, second and subsequent matches were removed. This process resulted in 135 nonduplicated client–case manager pairs that were randomly ordered to produce a list.

Participants

Clients were contacted, one at a time, through the identified case manager and asked to participate in the study. Seventy-five clients agreed to participate. Clients who agreed to participate were interviewed using a quality-of-life questionnaire; case managers answered a written survey designed by the author. The requirements of a diagnosis of schizophrenia and the two-year outpatient status were used to control for the effects of the symptomatology of the disease and the outpatient experience.

Analysis of Data

Three statistical strategies were used in analyzing the data. Bivariate relationships were determined among primary variables using cross-classification procedures with chi-square statistics. The strength and direction of some relationships were measured using correlation coefficients. To further clarify relationship, ordinary least-squares multiple regression procedures were conducted.

Instruments

The Quality of Life Interview Schedule (Lehman, 1988) was used and involved a 45-minute face-to-face interview with the client. The measure examined quality of life objectively and subjectively in the domains of living situation, family relationships, social relationships, leisure, work, finances, safety, and health. Lehman (1983, 1988) confirmed construct validity for the objective, multi-item scales with principal-component factor analyses. Internal consistency reliabilities (Cronbach's alpha) ranged from .51 to .87, which he found to be acceptable. Internal consistency reliabilities on scales for subjective quality-of-life measures ranged from .67 to .87, and factor analysis confirmed their construct validities. Test–retest reliability correlations revealed significant levels of stability for most of the interview items and scales. Lehman's tests showed the instrument to be a valid and reliable measure of quality of life specific to chronically mentally ill patients.

Following an exhaustive but futile search for a standardized measure, the author created a questionnaire, the Sensitivity to Racial Oppression Scale, designed to ascertain worker sensitivity to the effect of racial oppression on the treatment process for mentally ill African Americans. Items on the questionnaire were generated from literature about racial oppression in psychiatry and related fields. Case managers were asked to agree or disagree with statements reflecting the following: personal views of African American clients, recognition of racial biases in the diagnostic and treatment process, and recognition of racially oppressive behaviors or attitudes exhibited by colleagues. Figure 35-1 presents selected statements from the questionnaire.

FIGURE 35-1

Selected Items from the Racial Oppression Sensitivity Scale

For the following statements please check the comment that **best** represents your thoughts or opinions regarding your African American clients.

1. African Americans are more likely than white people to be diagnosed schizophrenic.
   ____ strongly disagree
   ____ not sure but probably disagree
   ____ not sure but probably agree
   ____ strongly agree

2. Most non–African American mental health professionals tend to discount or ignore the importance of the African American experience with racism when working with African American clients.
   ____ strongly disagree
   ____ not sure but probably disagree
   ____ not sure but probably agree
   ____ strongly agree

3. I don't expect my African American clients to function as well as my non–African American clients.
   ____ strongly disagree
   ____ not sure but probably disagree
   ____ not sure but probably agree
   ____ strongly agree

Response options to the statements on a four-point Likert-type scale ranging from 1 = strongly disagree to 4 = strongly agree measured the worker's level of racial oppression sensitivity. Use of the scale allowed the worker flexibility in responding to each statement. For statistical purposes, the data were recoded to reflect simple agreement or disagreement with the statement. The minimum score was 23, and the maximum was 46. A score of 34 or less indicated agreement with fewer than 50 percent of the statements and indicated a low level of sensitivity to racial oppression. A score of 35 to 40 represented agreement with 51 percent to 70 percent of the statements and indicated a moderate level of sensitivity to racial oppression. A score greater than 40 represented agreement with at least 80 percent of the statements and indicated a high level of sensitivity to racial oppression.

An internal consistency reliability coefficient (Cronbach's alpha) was computed for the overall scale. An alpha of .89 indicated that the items in the scale were positively correlated with each other and that the overall scale was quite reliable. Factor analysis with varimax rotation allowed the author to test the content validity of the overall scale to determine if a central factor represented relationships among the statements.

The 23 items clustered around six underlying factors: Anglo-European-based racism, institutional racism's influence on agency policy and behavior, institutional racism's influence on treatment, racism's influence on the mental health of African Americans, racism's influence on the assessment process, and the perceptions of professionals of color about their African American clients. Sensitivity to racial oppression was treated as a multidimensional concept. The six factors around which the questions clustered are supported by literature demonstrating that these factors exist and affect mental health and service delivery (Bell & Mehta, 1981; Bulhan, 1975; Jones & Gray, 1986; Lawson, 1986; Loring & Powell, 1988; Poussaint, 1983; Solomon, 1988; Sue, 1977; Wilcox, 1973; Williams, 1986).

Demographic Characteristics of the Participants

Case Managers. Case managers were mostly female (69 percent, $n = 52$) and people of color (67 percent, $n = 50$), with a mean age of 40 years. Forty-one percent ($n = 31$) of the case managers had acquired a master's degree–level of education, but only 35 percent ($n = 26$) had either a bachelor's or master's degree in social work. Forty-four percent ($n = 33$) had more than five years of experience working with African American clients, and their current caseloads were overwhelmingly African American (86 percent of the total combined caseload count).

Clients. All 75 of the client participants were African American outpatients with a psychiatric diagnosis of schizophrenia. They were mostly single (62 percent) and male (81 percent), with a mean age of 40 years. Forty-nine percent had less than a 12th-grade education. Only 15 had experienced psychiatric rehospitalization during the previous calendar year. Generally, the client respondents reported being satisfied with the various aspects of their lives. Many (73 percent), however, reported problems in life areas relative to employment, finances, living situations, social relationships, and use of leisure time.

Limitations and Strengths

The small sample size, although sufficient for purposes of this research, limits the generalizability of the results. The selection process for the client population, although randomized, may have resulted in the selection of higher functioning clients, further limiting the generalizability of the data. Client self-report as the only source of the dependent variable poses other shortcomings for the study. Although Lehman's (1983) instrument has been shown to be both valid and reliable, there is the possibility of client responses being influenced by the interviewer's presence or the client's need to give socially desirable responses.

Strengths of the study include use of a valid and reliable quality-of-life instrument that has both objective and subjective measures and the use of a measure for racial oppression sensitivity that has high levels of validity and reliability and that allowed case managers to demonstrate racial oppression sensitivity regardless of race. In addition, data were generated that can be used to support arguments about causal factors because they demonstrated relationships.

RESULTS

Case Managers

Scores for the case managers on the Racial Oppression Sensitivity Scale ranged from 23 to 44, with a mean of 36 (moderate level of sensitivity). Almost half (48 percent, $n = 36$) showed low levels of racial oppression sensitivity. Three case manager characteristics demonstrated significant relationships with level of sensitivity: being a person of color [$c^2(2, N = 75) = 9.09, p < .01$], type of degree [$c^2(2, N = 75) = 6.07, p < .05$], and gender [$c^2(2, N = 75) = 6.01, p < .05$]. Nineteen (76 percent) of the 25 white case managers had low scores in racial oppression sensitivity compared with 19 (38 percent) of their colleagues of color. Thirty-six percent ($n = 9$) of case managers with social work degrees scored in the high range of sensitivity compared with 15 percent ($n = 7$) who had some other type of degree. Female case managers had higher levels of racial oppression sensitivity than their male counterparts. When these three variables were entered into a regression analysis, it was determined they were useful predictors for level of racial sensitivity. However, only ethnic status maintained its bi-variate statistical significance ($r = .355, p < .01$) (Table 35-1).

Clients

To address the two remaining research questions, clients' responses from the Quality of Life Interview Schedule were analyzed. Data about the delivery of services were amassed from the objective subscale Services and Continuity of Care and the subjective subscale Feelings about the Care Received (selected items from the Quality of Life Interview Schedule are given in Figure 35-2). Racial Oppression Sensitivity Scale scores were statistically associated with clients' feelings about the care they received ($r = .23$, $p < .05$) and whether they experienced difficulties in receiving services they felt they needed ($r = .24, p < .05$). These results indicated that clients whose case managers scored high on the Racial Oppression Sensitivity Scale felt better about the services they received and had less difficulty in receiving services.

To control for the possible effects of case manager demographic characteristics, especially the race of the case manager, on client perception of service delivery, a regression analysis was run using case manager's race (identified as minority status), gender, degree type, and racial oppression sensitivity as independent variables. The inclusion of minority-racial status in the regression allowed the estimation of the direct effects of case manager

TABLE 35-1

Standardized Coefficients for the Regression of Racial Oppression Sensitivity Scale Scores on Case Manager Degree Type, Racial Status, and Gender

Variable	Beta	SE
Degree type[a]: social work	.153	1.378
Racial status[b]: minority	.355*	1.419
Gender[c]: male	−.218	1.426
Adjusted $R^2 = .09$, $SE = 5.19$, $F = 4.39, p = .01$		

[a]Degree type was treated as a dummy variable; the reference category was "not social work."

[b]Racial status was treated as a dummy variable; the reference category was "nonminority."

[c]Gender was treated as a dummy variable; the reference category was "female."

*$p < .05$.

FIGURE 35-2

Selected Items from the Quality of Life Interview Schedule

Services and Continuity of Care Scale

I would like to ask you about services that you might have received during the past year. For each service I'd like to know:

   a. Did you need the service?

   b. Did you receive the service?

   c. Did you have any problem getting the service?

     1 = yes, 0 = no, 9 = not applicable/don't know

1. Assessment of your needs for service

2. Help getting food, clothing, shelter, assistance in applying for benefits

3. Medical care for physical problem(s)

Subjective Scale

How do you feel about:

   ___ The care available to you if you need it?

   ___ Your life as a whole?

   1 = terrible

   2 = unhappy

   3 = mostly dissatisfied

   4 = mixed

   5 = mostly satisfied

   6 = pleased

   7 = delighted

SOURCE: Reprinted with permission from Lehman, A. (1983). The well-being of chronic mental patients: Assessing their quality of life. *Archives of General Psychiatry, 40*, 369–373.

race on client perception of service. In addition, an interaction term that represented the effects of racial oppression sensitivity on perception of service for each type of minority-racial status was added to the regression. The interaction term represents the indirect combined effects of minority-racial status and sensitivity on perception of service. The regression equations were found to be nonsignificant (Table 35-2); therefore, the partial correlations were also not significant. Case manager demographic characteristics had no direct or indirect bearing on client perception of service delivery. More important, client perception of service was not affected by the race of the case manager.

Quality of life was measured through client responses to the question, "How do you feel about your life as a whole?" posed at the beginning and conclusion of the interview. No association

TABLE 35-2

Standardized Coefficients for the Regression of Client Perceptions of Service Delivery on Case Manager Degree Type, Racial Status, Gender, and Racial Oppression Sensitivity

Variable	Beta	SE
Degree type[a]: social work	−.309	0.884
Racial status[b]: minority	.281	6.426
Gender[c]: male	−.415	0.935
Racial oppression sensitivity	−.047	0.129
Combined effects of case manager racial status and racial oppression sensitivity	.013	0.170
Adjusted R^2 = −.08, SE = 2.87, F = .24, p = .94		

[a]Degree type was treated as a dummy variable; the reference category was "not social work."
[b]Racial status was treated as a dummy variable; the reference category was "nonminority."
[c]Gender was treated was a dummy variable; the reference category was "female."

was found between the case managers' level of racial oppression sensitivity and clients' perceptions of their quality of life.

DISCUSSION

Overall, the case managers in the study had a moderate level of sensitivity to racial oppression. Race, gender, and degree type influenced racial oppression sensitivity at both the bivariate and multivariate levels. People of color, females, and those with social work degrees were more sensitive to the issues of racism and oppression present in the mental health arena. This finding may be due to the fact that people of color and women generally have encountered life experiences that make them more sensitive to the presence of oppression at various social levels. It is also possible that the Council on Social Work Education's mandate to include content on the oppression of various groups in the curricula of schools of social work produces individuals with higher levels of sensitivity to racial oppression. The overall low sensitivity of the total group of case managers, however, contrasts with the high percentage of case managers of color in the group. Perhaps this dichotomy indicates a tendency of workers to incorporate the values and behavior of the larger society in direct opposition to their own life experiences and personal views.

These results have serious implications for those in the mental health arena. The literature shows that insensitivity to racial oppression has resulted in a high rate of psychiatric institutionalization among African Americans (Bulhan, 1975; Jones & Gray, 1986; Keith et al., 1991; Lawson, 1986; Solomon, 1988; Sue, 1977). Even more important, it has been demonstrated that this insensitivity can lead to misdiagnosis and maltreatment of a most vulnerable population (Bell & Mehta, 1981; Collins et al., 1984; Jones & Gray, 1986; Lawson et al., 1984; Loring & Powell, 1988; Mollica et al., 1980; Mukherjee et al., 1983; Poussaint, 1983; Solomon, 1988). The most effective means of overcoming such attitudinal and behavioral barriers is to deal directly with issues of racial oppression. In this way, mental health professionals become aware of the existence of racial oppression in psychiatry and are sensitized to the contribution they each may make to the process.

It is clear from the findings that moderately and highly sensitive case managers are, perhaps, more attentive to the emotional and material needs of their African American clients. Case managers who are sensitive to the dilemma faced by African Americans in general, and especially those who are mentally ill, are perhaps more likely to create an empathic and supportive relationship with their African American clients while at the same time removing barriers to services and resources. To the extent that previous research has established the existence of racial oppression insensitivity in the mental health arena, it becomes important to be attentive to its effect on the functioning of the practitioner as well as the client. Agencies charged with the responsibility of providing care and support services to mentally ill African Americans must be sensitive to covert attitudes and behaviors that are counterproductive to the helping process. Agencies can institute policies, procedures, and training to help workers, regardless of ethnicity, be more sensitive to racial oppression.

CONCLUSION

This research has implications for practitioners and agencies involved in providing services to mentally ill African Americans. Although there was no statistical connection between case managers' levels of sensitivity to racial oppression and client perception of quality of life, there were relationships established between racial oppression sensitivity and other objective and subjective measures. The connection between level of worker sensitivity and client's perception of difficulty in service delivery and satisfaction with services is a significant finding even though the strength of the relationship was modest. This information points to the need for mental health practitioners to increase their awareness of their own attitudes and behavior toward mentally ill African American clients. An increase in the racial oppression sensitivity of the practitioner alone could contribute to an increase in client quality of life.

The Racial Oppression Sensitivity Scale provides a means for agencies and practitioners to test their own levels of racial sensitivity and to determine if training specific to working with mentally ill African Americans is needed. The scale poses questions specific to the many dimensions of racial oppression in the mental health arena and provides information that can be used to shape training as well as generate additional research.

The social work profession has long been a leader in providing insight and innovative means of working with oppressed populations, in part because of the emphasis placed on content about oppression in the social work education curriculum. Practitioners need to recognize oppression at both the individual and agency levels. They must be equipped with the knowledge and skills to counter oppression. To this end, a consideration of racial oppression content specific to mental health in social work curricula is warranted.

REFERENCES

Alexander, J., & Willems, E. (1981). Quality of life: Some measurements requirements. *Archives of Physical Medicine and Rehabilitation, 62*, 261–265.

Baker, F., & Intagliata, J. (1982). Quality of life in the evaluation of community support systems. *Evaluation and Program Planning, 5*, 69–79.

Bell, C. C., & Mehta, H. (1981). Misdiagnosis of black patients with manic–depressive illness. *Journal of the National Medical Association, 72*, 141–145.

Bigelow, D., Brodsky, G., Stewart, L., & Olson, M. (1982). The concept and measurement of quality of life as a dependent variable in evaluation of mental health services. In G. Stahler & W. Tash (Eds.), *Innovative approaches to mental health evaluation* (pp. 345–356). New York: Academic Press.

Bulhan, H. (1975). Black Americans and psychopathology: An overview of research and theory. *Psychotherapy, 22*, 370–378.

Carter, J. (1986). Deinstitutionalization of black patients: An apocalypse now. *Hospital and Community Psychiatry, 37*, 78–79.

Collins, J., Rickman, L., & Risher, D. (1984). Training psychiatric staff to treat a multicultural patient population. *Journal of the National Medical Association, 75,* 851–856.

Commission on Mental Health Services. (1990). [Patients on the rolls of the CMHS as of October 1990]. Unpublished raw data.

Franklin, J., Simmons, J., Solovitz, B., Clemons, J., & Miller, G. (1986). Assessing quality of life of the mentally ill: A three-dimensional model. *Evaluation and the Mental Health Professions, 9,* 376–388.

Jones, B., & Gray, G. (1986). Problems in diagnosing schizophrenia and affective disorders among blacks. *Hospital and Community Psychiatry, 37,* 61–65.

Keith, S. J., Regier, D. A., & Rae, D. (1991). Schizophrenic disorders. In L. N. Robins & D. A. Regier (Eds.), *Psychiatric disorders in America* (pp. 33–52). New York: Free Press.

Lawson, B. (1986). Racial and ethnic factors in psychiatric research. *Hospital and Community Psychiatry, 37,* 50–53.

Lawson, W., Yesavage, J., & Werner, P. (1984). Race, violence, and psychopathology. *Journal of Clinical Psychiatry, 45,* 294–297.

Lehman, A. (1983). The well-being of chronic mental patients: Assessing their quality of life. *Archives of General Psychiatry, 40,* 369–373.

Lehman, A. (1988). A quality of life interview for the chronically mentally ill. *Evaluation and Program Planning, 11*(1), 51–62.

Lehman, A., Ward, N., & Linn, L. (1982). Chronic mental patients: The quality of life issue. *American Journal of Psychiatry, 139,* 1271–1276.

Loring, M., & Powell, B. (1988). Gender, race, and DSM-III: A study of the objectivity of psychiatric behavior. *Journal of Health and Social Behavior, 29*(1), 1–22.

Malm, U., May, P., & Dencker, S. (1981). Evaluation of the quality of life of the schizophrenic outpatient: A check list. *Schizophrenia Bulletin, 7,* 34–42.

Mollica, R., Blum, J., & Redlich, F. (1980). Equity and the psychiatric care of the black patient, 1950 to 1975. *Journal of Nervous and Mental Disease, 168,* 279–286.

Mukherjee, S., Shuckla, S., Woodle, J., Rosen, A., & Olarte, S. (1983). Misdiagnosis of schizophrenia in bipolar patients: A multiethnic comparison. *American Journal of Psychiatry, 140,* 1571–1574.

National Institute of Mental Health. (1987). *Mental health, United States, 1987.* Washington, DC: U.S. Department of Health and Human Services.

Poussaint, A. (1983). The mental health status of blacks—1983. In J. D. Williams (Ed.), *The state of black America—1983* (pp. 187–239). New York: National Urban League.

Solomon, P. (1988). Racial factors in mental health service utilization. *Psychosocial Rehabilitation Journal, 11*(3), 4–12.

Sue, S. (1977). Community mental health services to minority groups. *American Psychologist, 32,* 616–624.

Turner, J., & Tenhoor, W. (1978). The NIMH community support program: Pilot approach to a needed social reform. *Schizophrenia Bulletin, 4,* 319–344.

U.S. Bureau of the Census. (1991). *Census of the United States, 1990.* Washington, DC: U.S. Government Printing Office.

Wilcox, D. (1973). Positive mental health in the black community: The black liberation movement. In C. Willis, B. Kramer, & B. Brown (Eds.), *Racism and mental health* (pp. 463–524). Pittsburgh: University of Pittsburgh Press.

Williams, D. (1986). Epidemiology of mental illness in Afro-Americans. *Hospital and Community Psychiatry, 37,* 42–49.

This chapter was originally published in the December 1995 issue of Social Work Research, *vol. 19, pp. 238–244.*

In-Home and Community-Based Service Utilization by Three Groups of Elderly Hispanics: A National Perspective

Denise Burnette and Ada C. Mui

bout 5 percent of all people in the United States ages 65 and older are Hispanic (U.S. Bureau of the Census, 1990). However, whereas the older white population is expected to grow by 92 percent between 1990 and 2030, the older Hispanic population is expected to grow by 395 percent (U.S. Senate Special Committee on Aging, American Association of Retired Persons, Federal Council on the Aging, and U.S. Administration on Aging, 1991). The complex needs and considerable diversity within this burgeoning population present challenges for social work practice and public policy that are now just beginning to be appreciated.

This study uses data from the 1988 National Survey of Hispanic Elderly People (Davis, 1990) to examine the status and needs of Mexican American, Cuban American, and Puerto Rican elderly people and the determinants of in-home and community-based health care and social services utilization for these groups. Implications for social work practice and public policies to improve access to services are discussed.

LITERATURE REVIEW

Recent analyses of data from the U.S. Bureau of the Census and several national data sets (including the National Study to Assess the Service Needs of Hispanic Elderly [Lacayo, 1980], the Hispanic Health and Nutrition Examination Survey [Trevino, 1990], and the National Survey of Hispanic Elderly People [Davis,

1990]) have begun to document the serious financial, health, and social problems that Hispanic elderly people face in the United States (Andrews, Lyons, & Rowland, 1992; Angel & Angel, 1992; Bastida, 1984; Krause & Goldenhaur, 1992; Maldonado, 1989; Moscicki, Rae, Regier, & Locke, 1987; Narrow, Rae, Moscicki, Locke, & Regier, 1990). Hispanic elderly people experience both the absolute and relative disadvantages suffered by most older ethnic and racial groups. For example, in comparing a national random sample of all older Americans (Commonwealth Fund, 1986) with Hispanic elderly people in a companion data set (Westat, 1989), Andrews et al. (1992) found that Hispanic elderly people fared worse on almost all major dimensions of health and well-being, particularly in income, health status, facility with English, educational attainment, and functional status. People with low incomes or in poor health were especially vulnerable.

Despite their needs, Hispanic elderly people tend not to use long-term care services (Eribes & Bradley-Rawls, 1978; Greene & Monahan, 1984; Starrett, Wright, Mindel, & Tran, 1989). This pattern is consistent with that of other elderly people of color, who tend to underuse all types of formal services (Hu, Snowden, Jerrell, & Nguyen, 1991; Kart, 1991; Mui & Burnette, 1994), including those designated for poor and marginally poor people. These elderly people are much poorer than same-age white people, yet they constitute less than 3 percent of participants in all poverty programs for elderly people (Kamikawa, 1991).

Empirical data on formal service utilization by elderly people of color are limited, and patterns and reasons for persistent underuse are complex and poorly understood (Kulys, 1990). Starrett, Wright, et al. (1989) pointed out that research on formal service utilization by Hispanic elderly people has been stymied by inadequate funding and various methodological problems, including the fact that most studies have been purely descriptive (see also Becerra & Zambrana, 1985; Estrada, 1985). Furthermore, most researchers have ignored the diverse cultural, historical, demographic, and ecological conditions of Hispanic subnational groups in the United States (Aguirre & Bigelow, 1983), merging Mexican Americans, Cuban Americans, and Puerto Ricans into one "Hispanic" category.

Studies that used inferential statistical models to examine among- and within-group differences in large national samples of Hispanic elderly people revealed substantial group variations that exert both direct and indirect effects on socioeconomic status (Biafora & Longino, 1990; Guarnaccia, Good, & Kleinman, 1990; Lacayo & Crawford, 1980) and on physical, social, and psychological well-being (Angel & Angel, 1992; Bean & Tienda, 1987; Krause & Goldenhaur, 1992). Group variations also created differential patterns of need and service utilization (Starrett, Todd, & De Leon, 1989; Starrett, Wright, et al., 1989).

THEORETICAL FRAMEWORK

In a widely used behavioral model of health-related service utilization, Andersen and Newman (1973) posited that utilization is a result of the interaction of predisposing, enabling, and needs-for-care factors. *Predisposing factors* are sociodemographic characteristics and health-related attitudes that existed before an illness episode. *Enabling factors* are social and economic resources that facilitate or impede service utilization. *Needs-for-care factors* are illness- or impairment-related conditions for which services are sought.

The Andersen–Newman model has been extended to predict health care and social services utilization by elderly people (Wan, 1989; Wolinsky, 1990). For example, Ward (1977) suggested that age, gender, race, education, health beliefs, and service utilization patterns established earlier in life may predispose an elderly person to becoming an effective service user. Family income, social supports, and other resources also contribute to service utilization (Bass & Noelker, 1987; Coulton & Frost, 1982; McAuley & Arling, 1984; Nelson, 1993).

Using the Andersen–Newman model, Starrett and his colleagues confirmed the importance of needs for care and income variables and identified other predictors of service utilization for Hispanic elderly people. Overall social services utilization is low (Starrett, Wright, et al., 1989); environmental awareness is the strongest direct predictor of utilization (Starrett & Decker, 1984), followed by needs for care, family income, and ethnicity (Starrett, Bresler, Decker, Walters, & Rogers, 1990); and predictors of utilization differ among Mexican Americans, Cuban Americans, and Puerto Ricans (Starrett, Todd, & De Leon, 1989; Starrett, Wright, et al., 1989).

METHOD

Data Sources and Sample

Data are from the 1988 National Survey of Hispanic Elderly People (Davis, 1990). The study, a part of the Commonwealth Fund's (1986) project on elderly people living alone, used a telephone survey to obtain a profile of the health, economic, and social circumstances of people of Hispanic origin ages 65 and older. Between August and October 1988, trained bilingual interviewers gathered information on living arrangements, years since migration to the United States, economic resources, health and functional status, social networks, family support, and psychological well-being.

The survey provided a nationally representative sample of Hispanic people ages 65 and older living within telephone exchanges with at least 30 percent concentrations of Hispanic residents in three subuniverses in the continental United States. Using random digit dialing, 48,183 households were contacted, resulting in completed interviews of 2,299 Hispanic elderly people. The overall response rate was 80 percent. Details of sample selection and survey procedures are described elsewhere (Westat, 1989). The analyses in the study reported here are based on a subsample of Mexican Americans (n = 773), Cuban Americans (n = 714), and Puerto Ricans (n = 368). Other Hispanic groups were not included because their numbers were limited.

Several caveats should be made about the sampling and procedures. First, people unable to participate in telephone interviews because of severe physical or cognitive impairments are underrepresented. Second, low-income individuals who are less likely to have a telephone in the home are underrepresented; however, the U.S. Bureau of the Census indicated that about 92 percent of Hispanic elderly people live in households with telephones (Westat, 1989). Finally, all data are self-reported, and survey constraints prohibited independent verification of responses.

Measurement of Variables

Independent Variables. Independent variables, including predisposing, enabling, and needs-for-care factors, and their measures are presented in Table 36-1. Missing data on income were excessive, so education was used to measure social class standing (Krause & Goldenhaur, 1992). Receipt of public assistance provided a rough measure of income but was unreliable because

TABLE 36-1

Measures of Predisposing, Enabling, and Needs-for-Care Factors

Variable	Measure
Predisposing factor	
Age	Younger than 80 = 0, 80 and older = 1
Gender	Female = 0, male = 1
Length of stay in the United States	Number of years
Puerto Rican, Mexican American, or Cuban American	Binary variable: Cuban American is reference group
Enabling factor	
Education	Categorical, with higher score denoting more education or training
Living arrangement	Lives alone = 1, lives with others = 0
English language ability	Able to speak English = 1, able to read English = 1, able to write English = 1
Number of children	Number
Frequency of contact with children	Number of times each week
Recipient of public assistance	Recipient of food stamps, SSI, or Medicaid
Needs-for-care factor	
ADL impairments (a = .86)	Number of impairments
IADL impairments (a = .82)	Number of impairments
Self-rated health	1 = excellent to 4 = poor
Doctor visits	Number of visits during the past 12 months
Hospital utilization	Have been in hospital overnight during the past 12 months: yes = 1, no = 0
Psychological distress (a = .71)	Number of symptoms in past few weeks
Unmet service needs (a = .86)	Total number of in-home and community-based services needed
Service utilization	
In-home services	Number of services
Community-based services	Number of services

NOTES: SSI = Supplemental Security Income; ADL = activities of daily living; IADL = instrumental activities of daily living.

the proportion of eligible people who received these services was unknown. Two dummy variables, Mexican American and Puerto Rican, were created to examine subgroup differences, with Cuban Americans serving as the reference group.

Psychological distress was assessed by self-reported experience in the past few weeks of feeling restless, lonely, bored, depressed, or upset (each coded dichotomously). A principal components analysis with varimax rotation was performed, and the five items were summed to create a composite score of psychological distress.

Utilization of a service type not being specifically examined was included as an independent variable in each regression model to control for the role of other contacts with the service delivery system. Thus, the number of community-based services used appears in the model for assessing the likelihood of in-home services utilization and vice versa.

Outcome Variables. Utilization of in-home services (Meals on Wheels, home health aides, visiting nurses) and community-based services (senior citizen centers, congregate meals, transportation, church programs, telephone assurance programs) was examined. As dependent variables, service utilization was coded 1 for users of at least one of the services in the category and 0 for nonusers.

Data Analysis

Descriptive statistics were used to generate a profile of service utilization by the three groups of Hispanic elderly people. Twenty-one variables were entered into a hierarchical regression model; the predisposing factors were entered first, followed by the enabling and needs-for-care factors and finally the national origin group variables (Bass, Looman, & Ehrlich, 1992). This strategy provided a rigorous analytic procedure for examining prediction equations with dichotomous outcomes (Cox, 1978; Hosmer & Lemeshow, 1989).

Logistic coefficients indicated the direction and magnitude of an independent variable's association with an outcome measure. Coefficients were interpreted as in ordinary least-squares regression, with parameter estimates indicating the change in log odds of being in a category with a unit change in the independent variable, with the effects of all other variables in the model controlled.

These estimates were then converted to odds ratios and tested for statistical significance (Hosmer & Lemeshow, 1989).

The relative impact of each independent variable on each type of service utilization was determined by comparing corresponding Wald c^2 statistics (Selvin, 1991). The probability of a respondent using each type of service was thus estimated by calculating the odds ratio through the antilogs of the parameter estimate of each independent variable. For example, an odds ratio of 1.58 for in-home service utilization means that a respondent is 58 percent more likely to use the service than not, whereas an odds ratio of .30 would indicate a 70 percent less likelihood. Zero-order correlations of the 21 variables in the model ranged from .07 to .42, and there was no evidence of problems with multicollinearity.

RESULTS

About one-fifth of the Mexican Americans (20.7 percent) and Cuban Americans (21.1 percent) were ages 80 or older, making them somewhat older than the Puerto Ricans (16.3 percent) (Table 36-2). Nearly two-thirds (65.8 percent) of the Puerto Ricans were unmarried, and they more often lived alone (36.7 percent) than the Mexican Americans (22.1 percent) and the Cuban Americans (21.0 percent). The Mexican Americans least often used Medicaid and food stamps, whereas fewer Puerto Ricans had private insurance. The Cuban Americans had the least facility with English language skills.

The Cuban Americans were in better physical and functional health than the Mexican Americans and the Puerto Ricans (Table 36-3). A larger percentage of the Cuban Americans reported being in either excellent or good health and were the least impaired on nearly every activity of daily living (ADL) and instrumental activity of daily living (IADL).

The Puerto Ricans reported much higher use of homemaker services and visiting nurses than the other two groups, and they also used more transportation services and services at senior citizen centers during the past year (Table 36-4). The Mexican Americans, on the other hand, reported greater use of Meals on Wheels and church programs. This group also reported having more living children and more frequent contact with children each week.

TABLE 36-2
Sociodemographic Characteristics of the Elderly Hispanic Sample

	Percentage of		
Characteristic	Mexican American (N = 773)	Cuban American (N = 714)	Puerto Ricans (N = 368)
Age (years)****			
65–69	37.7	32.3	39.9
70–74	23.0	23.9	24.2
75–79	18.6	22.7	19.6
80–84	13.7	12.8	9.5
85 and older	7.0	8.3	6.8
Gender			
Women	62.5	62.5	66.6
Marital status****			
Married	51.1	53.1	34.2
Not married	48.9	46.9	65.8
Education****			
No education	25.6	4.0	11.6
Grade school	34.8	23.8	40.3
High school	21.4	39.6	22.8
College	10.6	20.3	18.4
Postcollege	7.6	12.3	6.9
Living arrangement****			
Alone	22.1	21.0	36.7
With others	77.9	79.0	63.3
Public assistance			
Medicaid****	34.4	46.1	53.3
Food stamps****	15.4	40.2	36.1
SSI	12.2	13.2	16.5
Private insurance****	27.9	31.8	16.3
Self-assessed English skills			
Able to speak****	46.3	36.7	51.4
Able to read****	56.3	43.4	51.9
Able to write****	44.9	34.5	41.0

NOTE: SSI = Supplemental Security Income.
****$p < .0001$.

Significant predictors of in-home service utilization included being age 80 and older, living alone, having fewer living children, more often using public assistance and community-based services, having higher levels of ADL and IADL impairment, and having more hospitalizations (Table 36-5). A comparison of Wald c^2 statistics shows that hospital utilization was the strongest pre-

TABLE 36-3

Physical and Psychological Well-Being of the Elderly Hispanic Sample

	Percentage of		
Characteristic	Mexican American (*N* = 773)	Cuban American (*N* = 714)	Puerto Ricans (*N* = 368)
Perceived health status****			
Excellent	12.4	16.6	10.4
Good	30.3	37.4	24.3
Fair	44.8	37.1	51.1
Poor	12.5	8.9	14.2
Psychological distress			
Feeling restless****	23.7	22.3	36.9
Feeling lonely***	25.2	22.6	33.2
Feeling bored****	26.8	23.9	37.5
Feeling depressed*	29.1	27.7	35.9
Feeling upset*	11.8	8.1	11.7
ADL impairment			
Bathing*	16.2	11.9	17.9
Dressing*	11.3	10.4	16.3
Eating	4.9	4.6	7.3
Getting in and out of bed****	22.8	15.6	28.0
Walking****	30.3	18.1	35.6
Going outside****	20.3	15.6	25.8
Using the toilet	8.4	5.7	8.4
IADL impairment			
Preparing meals**	17.9	11.9	19.8
Managing money****	13.8	7.3	14.7
Using the phone****	16.3	7.4	10.6
Shopping for groceries*	22.1	17.4	22.8
Doing heavy work****	39.3	31.8	44.8
Doing light work**	15.0	13.0	20.7

NOTES: ADL = activities of daily living; IADL = instrumental activities of daily living.

*$p < .05$. **$p < .01$. ***$p < .001$. ****$p < .0001$.

dictor, followed by community-based services utilization and then age. Respondents ages 80 and older were 96 percent more likely and those living alone were 74 percent more likely to have used at least one in-home service during the past 12 months. Respondents using public assistance and community-based services were 28 percent and 43 percent more likely, respectively, to have used an in-home service, whereas those with more living children were

TABLE 36-4

Social Support of the Elderly Hispanic Sample

	Percentage of		
Characteristic	Mexican American (N = 773)	Cuban American (N = 714)	Puerto Ricans (N = 368)
In-home services[a]			
Homemaker services****	6.7	4.8	16.0
Visiting nurse****	8.9	9.5	17.9
Home health aide	4.1	5.7	6.8
Meals on Wheels****	8.5	3.4	3.5
Community-based services[a]			
Transportation****	8.9	18.1	22.6
Senior citizen centers****	12.0	9.4	19.8
Congregate meals**	14.9	10.2	15.8
Telephone assurance programs	4.7	3.5	4.1
Church programs****	8.4	2.7	5.4
Informal support network[b]			
Mean number of children*	4.6	2.0	3.8
Mean number of visits with children per week*	2.5	1.6	1.3

[a]c^2 statistic was used.
[b]Analysis of variance was used to test the differences between means.
*$p < .05$. **$p < .01$. ****$p < .0001$.

38 percent less likely to do so. Hispanic subgroup membership had no effect, controlling for other variables in the model.

Significant predictors of community-based service utilization included being age 80 and older, living alone, using public assistance and in-home services, having lower levels of IADL impairment, and being Puerto Rican (Table 36-6). A comparison of Wald c^2 statistics shows that in-home services utilization was the strongest predictor, followed by living alone and using public assistance. Respondents ages 80 and older and those living alone were 55 percent and 76 percent more likely, respectively, to use community-based services. Respondents using public assistance and in-home services were 25 percent and 58 percent more likely, respectively, to use community-based services. Those with higher levels of IADL impairment were 17 percent less likely to use community-based services. Puerto Ricans were 43 percent more likely than Cuban Americans to use community-based services, controlling for other variables in the model.

TABLE 36-5

Logistic Regression Analysis of In-Home Service Utilization by the Elderly Hispanic Sample

Variable	Unstandardized Logit Coefficients	SE	Odds Ratio[a]	Wald c^2
Predisposing factors				
Age (80 and older = 1)	.67	.21	1.96**	10.33
Gender (male = 1)	−.14	.19		
Length of stay in the United States	−.01	.01		
Enabling factors				
Education	−.03	.02		
Living alone	.56	.21	1.74**	7.14
Able to speak English	.03	.23		
Able to read English	−.14	.30		
Able to write English	.13	.31		
Number of children	−.48	.24	.62*	3.81
Number of visits with children per week	.07	.06		
On public assistance[b]	.25	.10	1.28*	6.47
Community-based services utilization	.36	.09	1.43****	15.66
Needs-for-care factors				
ADL impairment	.18	.07	1.20***	8.00
IADL impairment	.16	.08	1.20*	4.54
Self-rated health	.02	.12		
Doctor visits	.01	.01		
Hospital utilization	1.19	.18	3.30****	40.83
Psychological distress	−.04	.07		
Unmet service needs	.04	.04		
Hispanic subgroups				
Mexican American	−.14	.29		
Puerto Rican	−.10	.24		
Intercept	−2.51****			
Model c^2	249.74****			

NOTES: ADL = activities of daily living; IADL = instrumental activities of daily living.

[a]Odds ratios were calculated for the significant coefficients.

[b]Recipients of either food stamps, Supplemental Security Income, or Medicaid.

*$p < .05$. **$p < .01$. ***$p < .001$. ****$p < .0001$.

DISCUSSION

The data reported in this study support and extend the findings of previous studies that have used the Andersen–Newman model

TABLE 36-6

Logistic Regression Analysis of Community-Based Service Utilization of the Elderly Hispanic Sample

Variable	Unstandardized Logit Coefficients	SE	Odds Ratio[a]	Wald c^2
Predisposing factors				
Age (80 and older = 1)	.44	.18	1.55*	6.24
Gender (male = 1)	.05	.14		
Length of stay in the United States	.00	.00		
Enabling factors				
Education	−.01	.02		
Living alone	.57	.16	1.76***	13.14
Able to speak English	.08	.17		
Able to read English	.35	.22		
Able to write English	−.12	.22		
Number of children	.08	.20		
Number of visits with children per week	.02	.04		
On public assistance[b]	.22	.07	1.25**	9.26
In-home services utilization	.46	.11	1.58****	17.62
Needs-for-care factors				
ADL impairment	.12	.06		
IADL impairment	−.18	.07	.83**	7.13
Self-rated health	−.01	.09		
Doctor visits	.01	.01		
Hospital utilization	−.14	.16		
Psychological distress	.03	.05		
Unmet service needs	−.05	.03		
Hispanic subgroups				
Mexican American	.10	.20		
Puerto Rican	.35	.18	1.43*	3.84
Intercept	−1.69****			
Model c^2	9.22****			

[a]Odds ratios were calculated for the significant coefficients.
[b]Recipients of either food stamps, Supplemental Security Income, or Medicaid.
*$p < .05$. **$p < .01$. ***$p < .001$. ****$p < .0001$.

to evaluate service utilization by Hispanic elderly people. Needs-for-care factors were the strongest predictors of in-home services utilization, followed by enabling and then predisposing factors. On the other hand, enabling factors made the greatest contribution to community-based services utilization.

The elderly Puerto Ricans in this study were somewhat younger than the Mexican Americans and Cuban Americans, and the proportion of the Puerto Ricans who were unmarried and living alone was more similar to the overall elderly population than to the other Hispanic groups (U.S. Senate Special Committee on Aging et al., 1991). Older people who live alone are less likely to have reliable informal support systems and may be at increased risk of need for services to assist with daily tasks and to increase socialization (Soldo, 1986). Hispanic elderly people who live alone may be particularly vulnerable because of high levels of poverty, especially among women (Maldonado, 1989).

The Mexican Americans and Puerto Ricans had less formal education than the Cuban Americans, suggesting that these groups may experience greater financial strain (Andrews et al., 1992). This finding is consistent with literature reviewed by Krause and Goldenhaur (1992). However, fewer Mexican Americans reported receiving Medicaid and food stamps, perhaps because of differential awareness and availability of services. Knowledge of services is a powerful determinant of service utilization (Chapleski, 1989; Snider, 1980; Starrett et al., 1990). High concentrations of ethnic groups may facilitate the dissemination of knowledge and availability and accessibility of services (Holmes, Holmes, Steinbach, Hausner, & Rocheleau, 1979). The dispersion of Mexican Americans in rural areas may contribute to a lack of awareness of and hence lower participation in services.

Return migration also affects Hispanic groups differently. Unlike Mexican Americans and Puerto Ricans, Cuban Americans generally do not return to Cuba because of adverse political conditions. This may be one reason why elderly Cuban Americans constitute a higher proportion of Hispanics than Puerto Ricans or Mexican Americans (Aguirre & Bigelow, 1983). The stability of this migration pattern may also help explain why Cuban Americans benefit from close-knit ethnic enclaves that help preserve their original culture and native language (Angel & Angel, 1992; Boswell & Curtis, 1984; Perez, 1986).

The greater likelihood that older elderly people will use both types of services is perhaps due to increased frailty. Previous studies using the Andersen–Newman model to explain service utilization by older adults consistently reported that illness or disability explained most of the variance in service utilization (Coulton & Frost, 1982; Wan, 1982; Wolinsky & Johnson, 1991).

That the use of public assistance and in-home services predicted the utilization of community-based services and vice versa is likely attributable to the benefits of already being in the service delivery system. Having fewer children predicted in-home services utilization only perhaps because elderly people of color often depend on family for this more intensive, hands-on care. Predictors of in-home service utilization were ADL and IADL impairment and hospital use. The Mexican Americans and Puerto Ricans were neither more nor less likely than the Cuban Americans to use in-home services, which is an important finding given that the Cuban Americans had uniformly higher levels of economic, physical, and psychological well-being.

IADL impairment, which indicated the ability to perform housekeeping and out-of-home activities such as shopping and money management, was the only needs-for-care predictor of community-based service utilization. The Puerto Ricans were 43 percent more likely than the Cuban Americans to use community-based services, but the Mexican Americans were neither more nor less likely to use this type of service.

CONCLUSION

Social workers can make the current service delivery system more responsive to an increasingly racially and ethnically diverse population of older Americans. Focusing outreach efforts on those with the greatest needs and at the same time increasing the general level of knowledge about services can compensate for some of the common structural barriers to services (Starrett & Decker, 1984).

Social workers can improve access to services by decreasing barriers such as inadequate income and insurance and by promoting individual and programmatic sensitivity to cultural norms, customs, and beliefs (De La Rosa, 1989; Para & Espino, 1992; Rivera, 1990). They can also seek to maximize the powerful influence of "lay referral structures" that can impede or promote use of professional services by elderly people of color (Birkel & Reppucci, 1983; House, Landis, & Umberson, 1988).

Finally, empowerment, or the process of self- and mutual help to gain mastery, is a cultural tool traditionally used by Hispanics to ameliorate stress from socioeconomic and political conditions (Sotomayor, 1989). Community human services networks can be used effectively to assess community resources, encourage intra-agency cooperation, and target appropriate services to their most vulnerable constituents.

REFERENCES

Aguirre, B. E., & Bigelow, A. (1983). The aged in Hispanic groups: A review. *International Journal of Aging and Human Development, 17,* 177–201.

Andersen, R. M., & Newman, J. F. (1973). Societal and individual determinants of medical care utilization in the U.S. *Milbank Memorial Fund Quarterly, 51,* 95–124.

Andrews, J. W., Lyons, B., & Rowland, D. (1992). Life satisfaction and peace of mind: A comparative analysis of elderly Hispanic and other elderly Americans. *Clinical Gerontologist, 11*(3–4), 21–42.

Angel, J., & Angel, R. J. (1992). Age at immigration, social connections, and well-being among elderly Hispanics. *Journal of Aging and Health, 4,* 480–499.

Bass, D. M., Looman, W. J., & Ehrlich, P. (1992). Predicting the volume of health and social services: Integrating cognitive impairment into the modified Andersen framework. *Gerontologist, 32,* 33–43.

Bass, D. M., & Noelker, L. S. (1987). The influence of family caregivers on elders' use of in-home services: An expanded conceptual framework. *Journal of Health and Social Behavior, 28,* 184–196.

Bastida, E. (1984). The elderly of Hispanic origin: Population characteristics for 1980. *Mid-American Review of Sociology, 9*(1), 41–47.

Bean, F. D., & Tienda, M. (1987). *The Hispanic population of the United States.* New York: Academic Press.

Becerra, R. M., & Zambrana, R. E. (1985). Methodological approaches to research on Hispanics. *Social Work Research & Abstracts, 21*(2), 42–49.

Biafora, F. A., & Longino, C. F. (1990). Elderly Hispanic migration in the United States. *Journal of Gerontology, 45,* S212–S219.

Birkel, R. C., & Reppucci, N. D. (1983). Social networks, information-seeking, and the utilization of services. *American Journal of Community Psychology, 11,* 185–205.

Boswell, T. D., & Curtis, J. R. (1984). *The Cuban-American experience: Culture, images, and perspectives.* Totowa, NJ: Rowman & Allanheld.

Chapleski, E. E. (1989). Determinants of knowledge of services to the elderly: Are strong ties enabling or inhibiting? *Gerontologist, 29,* 539–545.

Commonwealth Fund. (1986). *Problems facing elderly Americans living alone: A national survey* (Report of the Commonwealth Commission on Elderly People Living Alone). Baltimore: Author.

Coulton, C., & Frost, A. K. (1982). Use of social and health services by the elderly. *Journal of Health and Social Behavior, 23,* 330–339.

Cox, D. (1978). *Analysis of binary data.* London: Chapman & Hall.

Davis, K. (1990). *National Survey of Hispanic Elderly People, 1988*. Ann Arbor, MI: Inter-University Consortium for Political and Social Research.

De La Rosa, M. (1989). Health care needs of Hispanic Americans and the responsiveness of the health care system. *Health & Social Work, 14*, 104–113.

Eribes, R. A., & Bradley-Rawls, M. (1978). The underutilization of nursing home facilities by Mexican-American elderly in the Southwest. *Gerontologist, 18*, 363–371.

Estrada, L. F. (1985). The dynamics of Hispanic populations: A description and comparison. *Social Thought, 11*, 23–39.

Greene, V. L., & Monahan, D. J. (1984). Comparative utilization of community-based long-term care services by Hispanic and Anglo elderly in a case management system. *Journal of Gerontology, 39*, 730–735.

Guarnaccia, P. J., Good, B. J., & Kleinman, A. (1990). A critical review of epidemiological studies of Puerto Rican mental health. *American Journal of Psychiatry, 147*, 1449–1456.

Holmes, D., Holmes, M., Steinbach, L., Hausner, T., & Rocheleau, B. (1979). The use of community-based services in long-term care of older minority persons. *Gerontologist, 19*, 389–397.

Hosmer, D. W., & Lemeshow, S. (1989). *Applied logistic regression*. New York: John Wiley & Sons.

House, J. S., Landis, K. R., & Umberson, D. (1988, June 28). Social relationships and health. *Science*, pp. 540–545.

Hu, T., Snowden, L. R., Jerrell, J. M., & Nguyen, T. D. (1991). Ethnic populations in public mental health: Service choices and level of use. *American Journal of Public Health, 81*, 1429–1434.

Kamikawa, L. (1991, Fall/Winter). Public entitlements: Exclusionary beneficence. *Generations*, pp. 21–24.

Kart, C. S. (1991). Variation in long-term care service use by aged blacks. *Journal of Aging and Health, 3*, 511–526.

Krause, N., & Goldenhaur, L. M. (1992). Acculturation and psychological distress in three groups of elderly Hispanics. *Journal of Gerontology, 47*, S279–S288.

Kulys, R. (1990). The ethnic factor in the delivery of social services. In A. Monk (Ed.), *Handbook of gerontological services* (2nd ed., pp. 629–661). New York: Columbia University Press.

Lacayo, C. G. (1980). *A national study to assess the service needs of the Hispanic elderly*. Washington, DC: Library of Congress.

Lacayo, C. G., & Crawford, J. K. (1980). *A national study to assess the service needs of the Hispanic elderly*. Los Angeles: Asociacion Nacional Pro Personas Mayores.

Maldonado, D. (1989). The Latino elderly living alone: The invisible poor. *California Sociologist, 12*(1), 8–21.

McAuley, W. J., & Arling, G. (1984). Use of in-home care by very old people. *Journal of Health and Social Behavior, 25*, 54–64.

Moscicki, E. K., Rae, D. S., Regier, D. A., & Locke, B. Z. (1987). The Hispanic Health and Nutrition Survey: Depression among Mexican Americans, Cuban Americans, and Puerto Ricans. In M. Gaviria & J. D. Arana (Eds.),

Health and behavior: Research agenda for Hispanics (Simon Bolivar Research Monograph Series No. 1, pp. 145–159). Chicago: University of Illinois Press.

Mui, A. C., & Burnette, D. (1994). Long-term care service use by frail elders: Is ethnicity a factor? *Gerontologist, 34,* 190–198.

Narrow, W. E., Rae, D. S., Moscicki, E. K., Locke, B. Z., & Regier, D. A. (1990). Depression among Cuban Americans: The Hispanic Health and Nutrition Examination Survey. *Social Psychiatry and Psychiatric Epidemiology, 25,* 260–268.

Nelson, M. A. (1993). Race, gender, and the effect of social supports on the use of health services by elderly individuals. *International Journal of Aging and Human Development, 37,* 227–246.

Para, E. O., & Espino, D. V. (1992). Barriers to health care access faced by elderly Mexican Americans. *Clinical Gerontologist, 11*(3–4), 171–177.

Perez, L. (1986). Cubans in the United States. *Annals of the American Academy of Political and Social Science, 487,* 126–137.

Rivera, R. (1990). *The effects of social class on health care utilization of Puerto Ricans in the United States.* Unpublished doctoral dissertation, Brandeis University, Waltham, MA.

Selvin, S. (1991). *Statistical analysis of epidemiologic data.* New York: Oxford University Press.

Snider, E. (1980). Factors influencing health services knowledge among the elderly. *Journal of Health and Social Behavior, 21,* 371–377.

Soldo, B. J. (1986). Household types, housing needs, and disability. In R. J. Newcomer, M. P. Lawton, & T. O. Byerts (Eds.), *Housing an aging society: Issues, alternatives, and policy* (pp. 10–20). New York: Van Nostrand Reinhold.

Sotomayor, M. (1989). Empowerment and the Latino elderly. *California Sociologist, 12,* 65–83.

Starrett, R. A., Bresler, C., Decker, J. T., Walters, G. T., & Rogers, D. (1990). The role of environmental awareness and support networks in Hispanic elderly persons' use of formal social services. *Journal of Community Psychology, 18,* 218–227.

Starrett, R. A., & Decker, J. T. (1984). The utilization of discretionary services by the Hispanic elderly: A causal analysis. *California Sociologist, 7,* 159–180.

Starrett, R. A., Todd, A. M., & De Leon, L. (1989). A comparison of social service utilization behavior of the Cuban and Puerto Rican elderly. *Hispanic Journal of Behavioral Sciences, 11,* 341–353.

Starrett, R. A., Wright, R., Mindel, C. H., & Tran, T. V. (1989). The use of social services by Hispanic elderly: A comparison of Mexican American, Puerto Rican, and Cuban elderly. *Journal of Social Service Research, 13,* 1–25.

Trevino, F. M. (Ed.). (1990). Hispanic Health and Nutrition Examination Survey, 1982–1984: Findings on health status and health care need. *American Journal of Public Health, 80*(Suppl.), 6–70.

U.S. Bureau of the Census. (1990). *U.S. population estimates by age, sex, race and Hispanic origin: 1989* (Current Population Reports, Series P-25, No. 1057). Washington, DC: U.S. Government Printing Office.

U.S. Senate Special Committee on Aging, American Association of Retired
   Persons, Federal Council on the Aging, & U.S. Administration on Aging.
   (1991). *Aging America: Trends and projections, 1991 edition* (DHHS Pub. No.
   FCoA 91-28001). Washington, DC: Authors.
Wan, T.T.H. (1982). Use of health services by the elderly in low-income
   communities. *Milbank Memorial Fund Quarterly, 60,* 82–107.
Wan, T.T.H. (1989). The behavioral model of health care utilization and older
   people. In M. Ory & K. Bond (Eds.), *Aging and health care* (pp. 52–77). New
   York: Routledge.
Ward, R. A. (1977). Services for older people: An integrated framework for
   research. *Journal of Health and Social Behavior, 18,* 61–78.
Westat. (1989). *A survey of elderly Hispanics* (Report of the Commonwealth
   Fund Commission on Elderly People Living Alone). Rockville, MD:
   Author. (Available from Westat, Inc., 1650 Research Boulevard, Rockville,
   MD 20850)
Wolinsky, F. D. (1990). *Health and health behavior among elderly Americans: An
   age-stratification perspective.* New York: Springer.
Wolinsky, F. D., & Johnson, R. J. (1991). The use of health services by older
   adults. *Journal of Gerontology, 46,* S345–S357.

This chapter was originally published in the December 1995 issue of
Social Work Research, *vol. 19, pp. 197–206.*

37 Providing Services to Hispanic/Latino Populations: Profiles in Diversity

Graciela M. Castex

Social workers in many settings find themselves providing services to clients characterized as Hispanics or Latinos, a group with which they may have had little experience. Although the literature makes frequent reference to Hispanics as a very diverse group, there has been little discussion of the socially important differences and similarities among Hispanics and how these differences and similarities may affect the provision of services. Instead, discussions about the provision of social services to Hispanic people often quickly focus on cultural attributes taken as common among subgroups, primarily Mexican Americans (or Chicanos), Puerto Ricans, and Cubans. Questions that may arise in the mind of the practitioner are, What is the Hispanic population? If subgroups are diverse, in what ways are they diverse, and in what ways are they similar? What does it mean for culturally and racially diverse peoples to be perceived as members of a single ethnic group, and what are the implications of a client's ascription to this diverse group for practice?

Hispanic clients pose increasing challenges for social workers. This already large group is growing rapidly, and indicators such as age distribution and low median income levels indicate a rapidly increasing need for social services. The high numbers of recent immigrants, who often have limited English (Moore & Pachon, 1985) and experience a host of cultural factors that differentiate them from others in the population, add to the complexity of the challenge.

This chapter profiles the Hispanic/Latino population in the United States. It very briefly places the interactions of this group in the context of contemporary theories of ethnicity and discusses

the diversity and similarities among members of the Hispanic/
Latino group by examining key social features. The common experience of ascription to an ethnic minority in the United States
has served as a primary unifying force that gave impetus—in a
bidirectional process with state institutions—to the creation and
maintenance of the Hispanic/Latino group.

HISPANICS: A STATISTICAL PROFILE

In April 1990, according to the U.S. Bureau of the Census, there
were approximately 22 million people of Hispanic origin (referred
to as Hispanics in the census literature) living in the United States
out of a total population of 248.7 million. Hispanics, with 9.0 percent of the population, constituted the second largest minority
group in the country after black Americans, with 12.1 percent.
Because some census respondents identified themselves as both
black and Hispanic, however, non-Hispanic blacks are only 11.8
percent of the nation's population. Furthermore, although census estimates are not available, the general assumption is that
Hispanics are more likely to be undercounted than non-Hispanics
(U.S. Bureau of the Census, 1991b, 1991c, 1991d).

The social needs of Hispanics are underlined by their standing in four social indexes:

1. poverty: In 1992, 26.2 percent of Hispanic families had incomes below the poverty level, compared with 10.3 percent
   of non-Hispanic families. Twelve percent of the children in
   the United States were Hispanic in 1992, but 21 percent of
   the children living in poverty were Hispanic; of all Hispanic
   children, 39.9 percent lived in poverty in 1992 (U.S. Bureau
   of the Census, 1993a).
2. income: The 1992 median income of non-Hispanic white
   households ($33,388) was 46.1 percent higher than that of
   Hispanic households ($22,848) (U.S. Bureau of the Cen-
   sus,1993b).
3. family composition: Hispanics had a higher ratio of single-
   parent families (30 percent) than non-Hispanics (20 percent),
   and the ratio rose to 43 percent for the Puerto Rican–origin
   Hispanic subgroup (U.S. Bureau of the Census, 1991a).
4. demographics: The Hispanic population is young compared
   with non-Hispanics, with median ages in 1990 of 26.0 and

33.5 years, respectively; 30 percent of Hispanics and 21 percent of non-Hispanics are less than 15 years of age. Although accurate long-range demographic forecasts are difficult (one census projection predicts a Hispanic population of 128.3 million by 2050), short-range phenomena such as a high proportion of group members at or near childbearing age, a relatively high fertility rate, and high documented and undocumented net immigration rates guarantee a continued rapid growth of the Hispanic population during the next generation (U.S. Bureau of the Census, 1993c, 1993d).

ETHNIC GROUP CONCEPT

The Hispanic/Latino group, created by a federal order in the late 1970s, constitutes a valid social category that can be called an ethnic group and is increasingly regarded as such by those so ascribed. However, this usage may be counterintuitive for those trained to equate a list of cultural traits—a "culture"—with the ascription of ethnic status. But the U.S. government defined and formally created the Hispanic ethnic group on May 4, 1978. According to the Office of Management and Budget (1978), a Hispanic is "a person of Mexican, Puerto Rican, Cuban, Central or South American or other Spanish culture or origin, regardless of race" (p. 19269).

This definition largely focuses on the countries of origin and assumes that people in those countries have a common "Spanish culture," which is also shared by some people living in the United States. Although "Hispanic" was chosen by the federal government as the name of the group, many people so ascribed preferred to call themselves by another name, such as Latino or Latina. The formation of the Hispanic group should not be seen as unique; Native Americans and African Americans are two other examples, and similar phenomena are common in other countries.

The creation of an ethnic group in a dialectic with the state is a common social process. For the Hispanics in the United States, the process was bidirectional, involving state institutions and those so ascribed, to identify, control, and provide needed services to members of the new group (Castex, 1990; Enloe, 1981; Hayes-Bautista & Chapa, 1987; Nelson & Tienda, 1985).

If ethnic groups are regarded primarily as bearers of cultural traits, the bulk of which are passed from generation to generation, practitioners might assume that the federal government characterized Hispanics as belonging to a single group because they shared many significant cultural traits. Because this population is culturally diverse, from this culture-based perspective (which current anthropological and sociological ethnicity theory largely rejects) the designation "Hispanic" might be regarded as confusing at best.

The standard perspective among social theorists regarding the nature and functioning of ethnic groups—which began to be rigorously established in the late 1960s and early 1970s by Barth (1969), Cohen (1974), and Vincent (1974), among others—considers ethnicity to arise from groups interacting with other groups and social structures. In this perspective no ethnic group can exist without other groups to interact with: An ethnic group cannot exist in isolation. Ethnic identity is always expressed in dynamic processes of interaction with others. Barth (1969) pointed out that although particular cultural traits (for example, language or religion) may be important in the formation of a group and in the maintenance of group boundaries, no one can predict which traits will prove important in advance or which will continue to be ethnically significant in the future. Others have expanded Barth's arguments, elucidating the ways in which the state and other social structures affect ethnic group mobilization, maintenance, demobilization, and the joining together or splitting apart of groups to form new groups (Enloe, 1981; Horowitz, 1985; Wolf, 1982).

This perspective has directly or indirectly begun influencing discussions of ethnicity and cultural awareness in social work (Green, 1982; Pinderhughes, 1988, 1989). An understanding of Hispanic, or any other, ethnicity is impossible in the older paradigm; members of ethnic groups were presumed to "carry" a whole list of cultural traits, which sound suspiciously like stereotypes. The alternative viewpoint, however, emphasizes the need not only to value but also to expect diversity in a group. This view conditions exceptions and encourages development of strategies that avoid stereotypes when addressing the needs of the client.

HISPANIC ETHNICITY IN PRACTICE

Social workers need to keep in mind many features and issues deriving from the Hispanic client's ethnic status, in addition to the client's individual needs. Practitioners should prepare intellectually, emotionally, and clinically in anticipation of serving the Hispanic client. Prime features often regarded as ethnically significant and certainly important when interacting with clients include (but are not limited to) national origin, language, family names, religion, racial ascription, and immigration or citizenship status.

National Origin

Hispanics come from 26 nations according to the federal definition. There are significant differences among these nationalities; the languages, economic resources, educational systems, status structures, and customs vary dramatically from country to country. In addition, individual countries are often very ethnically diverse. The countries included by the Census Bureau are in North America (United States, Mexico), Central America (Guatemala, Honduras, El Salvador, Belize, Nicaragua, Costa Rica, Panama), the Caribbean (Cuba, Puerto Rico, Dominican Republic), South America (Venezuela, Colombia, Ecuador, Peru, Bolivia, Chile, Paraguay, Argentina, Uruguay, Brazil, French Guiana, Suriname, and Guyana; the last three, lacking Spanish origin, are sometimes referred to as non-Hispanic South America, and the state language of Brazil is Portuguese), and Europe (Spain).

A social worker probably encounters clients coming from fewer countries, however. Persons describing themselves as of Mexican origin on the 1990 census constituted 60.4 percent of the Hispanic total, Puerto Ricans were 12.2 percent, and Cubans were 4.7 percent of the total. The catchall "other Hispanic" category covered 22.8 percent of Hispanics and included persons from all the other defined countries as well as some very old Hispanic communities in the United States (U.S. Bureau of the Census, 1991b).

The historical experiences of each country with the United States and the European colonialists are very different and can affect the ethnic self-identification of clients. Immigrants' attitudes toward the United States especially may be conditioned by these histories; long-time Dominican residents in New York, for example, sometimes express reluctance to become U.S. citizens; they still associate the United States with the suppression of the popular revolt in the Dominican Republic in 1965 and the subsequent

military occupation by U.S. forces (personal communication with
A. Goris, Hunter College instructor, Department of Puerto Rican
Studies, March 17, 1992). Similarly complex feelings may be described by Mexicans, Nicaraguans, Salvadorans, Chileans, and
Cubans. The feelings may not always be negative, but the actions of the state may evoke reactions dating from before the
client's emigration or may even have contributed to the emigration. National background also affects the ease of obtaining legal
residence status or, at times, refugee status. Practitioners working with Hispanic clients need to do the following:

- Ask where the client is from. What is the client's nationality?
- Ask if the client is a member of an ethnic group within that
  nationality.
- Become familiar with the group history and the history of
  the group's migration.
- Identify formal or informal providers of services directed
  toward members of this national group, such as religious
  and civic organizations, sports clubs, political organizations,
  and political officeholders.

Language

Many non-Hispanics assume that most Hispanics speak the same
language—Spanish—or that their near forebears spoke it. This
assumption follows the 19th-century tendency to equate language, nationality, and ethnic status, even though the relationship of language and ethnicity has always been complex in the
United States (Smith, 1989; Worsley, 1984). In fact, the home language of 3.05 million of the 14.61 million Hispanics counted in
the 1980 census was not Spanish (Moore & Pachon, 1985).

Hispanics in the United States and residents of the 25 other
countries of origin speak five major European languages (Spanish, Portuguese, French, Dutch, and English). They also speak
such major Native American languages (each with millions of
speakers) as Quechua, Mayan (a family of languages), Aymara,
and Guarani, as well as many other Native American languages
and creole dialects. Such language diversity is not a trivial point:
Spanish may be a second language for many Spanish-speaking
Hispanic immigrants. Immigrants from highland Guatemala

(Mayan), highland Peru and Bolivia (Quechua and Aymara), and coastal Honduras (Garifuna, a creole language; Castex, in press) are common in the United States.

The assumption that Hispanics are normally fluent and literate in Spanish sometimes has damaging practical consequences for individual Hispanics, particularly in work-related situations. For example, a monolingual Spanish caseload should not be assigned to students or workers whose facility with the language is limited to discussions of the weather.

Similarly, not all Hispanic clients are fluent in Spanish. The situation may be even more complex, however. An agency sensitive to the needs of its clients, for example, may have materials and forms printed in Spanish, and the social worker may presume that all clients can read them. But some clients may not be literate in Spanish. Or some may speak both English and Spanish but may only be able to read English, making discussions of forms and legal documents very complex.

In addition, Hispanic clients speak a number of regional Spanish dialects. Speech in any language can serve as a social marker, however. The social worker should be sensitive, therefore, to situations in which the speech of the interviewer may indicate a status that differs from the client's. The interviewer's social status as indicated by Spanish usage may be higher or lower than that indicated by his or her English usage (Green, 1982; Kadushin, 1983).

The social worker attempting to communicate with Hispanic clients will find it helpful to

- find out what language the client communicates best in
- be sensitive to the possibility that people who are in crisis or who are experiencing powerful emotions may have additional difficulties communicating in a second or third language
- use trained people as interpreters or translators if such action seems appropriate and review literature on interviewing techniques when using interpreters.

Family Names

Many Hispanics have surnames that differ from those traditionally regarded as Spanish. While "Juan Garcia" is used colloquially as the Spanish equivalent of "John Smith," some Hispanics really are named Smith. And some Garcias in the United States are not Hispanic. The founding father of Chile was named O'Higgins, and the names of the current presidents of Peru, Argentina, and Chile—Fujimori, Menem, and Aylwin—are Japanese, Syrian, and Welsh in origin, respectively. Especially since 1800 there have been waves of migration to Latin America and the Caribbean from all over the world, particularly from Italy, France, Germany, and the Middle East but also from East Asia, Eastern Europe, and sub-Saharan Africa.

Regarding a surname as an indicator of ethnic status reached the height of absurdity when the Census Bureau tried to develop statistics on Hispanics on the basis of Spanish surnames. In preparing for the 1970 census, Spanish surnames were defined as any surname listed more than 25 times in the 1962 Havana, Cuba, telephone directory, thus excluding Cubans named Johnson or Lipshitz. The Havana list supplemented a 1950 list derived from the Mexico City and San Juan, Puerto Rico, directories. Had Eamon de Valera's mother not returned to Ireland from Brooklyn when he was a child, the first president of the Irish Republic would have been counted as Hispanic because his name began with "de." The "Martin" problem signaled the surname system's collapse, as thousands of people of British ancestry became "hispanized" because their last name appeared more than 25 times in a telephone directory (U.S. Bureau of the Census, 1975).

An additional source of confusion for practitioners may result from the Spanish language naming system, which differs from traditional English practice. Patrilineal descent is traced in naming through the second to the last name. The mother's maiden name (her father's) becomes a child's last name. In other words, Juan Garcia Jones's father's name is Garcia and his mother's name is Jones. Juan will pass on the Garcia name to his children as their second to last name, and so on.

Under Spanish common law, women do not acquire their husband's name on marriage. Garcia's mother, Señora Jones, is legally a Jones, not a Garcia. Forms including a husband's name—Señora Jones de Garcia—rarely have other than honorific status. Passports, airline tickets, and such are often issued in maiden names, which some countries require women to use when signing official documents. Therefore, social workers can make no assumptions about marital status or feminist attitudes because a couple uses different surnames.

Social workers will find it useful to

- make no firm assumptions about language use, ethnic status, or recent heritage based on a name
- ask a client how to pronounce or spell a name
- remember that persons in the same household may have different surnames (married names may have no legal standing, and the extended family may include aunts, uncles, cousins, grandparents, grandchildren, even godchildren and godparents, living together)
- keep in mind that some people may not use their legal names because they fear attention from immigration authorities.

Racial Ascription

Racial ascription is generally regarded as cultural rather than biological among social theorists. The particular biological traits that significantly determine racial ascription vary from society to society. Skin color, hair texture, class status, and other traits may all interact differentially to determine racial ascription; therefore, ascription is primarily a cultural phenomenon. A white Dominican, for example, may be *trigueño* (mixed, literally "wheat-colored") in Puerto Rico and black in Georgia (Harris, 1964; Mintz, 1971; Stephens, 1989).

Hispanics are racially diverse by any system of definition. Individual Hispanics might be characterized in the United States as white or European American, Native American, African American, East Asian, South Asian, and perhaps other racial types. In many countries, discrimination based on ascription as an *indio* (Native American) may be the most socially significant racial designation. But even then, to live like a *blanco* (white or European) is often to become one (Comitas, 1967; Harris, 1964).

The U.S. census of 1990 identifies Hispanics as a category separate from race. When asked to identify race in a separate question, Hispanic respondents identified themselves as follows: white, 11.5 million; black, 770,000; American Indian, 165,000; Asian, 305,000; other race, 9.5 million. These figures communicate a significant message: Whereas 51.7 percent of the Hispanic population identified itself as white, 42.7 percent of the Hispanics self-identified as another race. Hispanics constitute 97.5 percent of the other race category for the nation as a whole. Most of these self-identified racially as Hispanic, Latino, Chicano, La Raza, mestizo, or some other term that referred to Hispanic origin (U.S. Bureau of the Census, 1991d).

Clients who may have become classified as African American only after their arrival in the United States may be experiencing serious racial discrimination for the first time. As a result, the practitioner must keep in mind the need to consult with the client regarding his or her racial status and to be sensitive to the possibility that he or she may have experienced a dramatic change in social status because of the U.S. system of racial ascription. Such a change can affect self-esteem, relations with others, and real opportunities.

Religion

Perhaps the majority of Hispanics are Roman Catholics, but there are very large (and growing) Protestant Hispanic populations both in the United States and in the countries of origin, as well as significant populations of other faiths. In addition, the beliefs and practices of many Hispanics have been influenced by or derive directly from African and Native American belief systems that may be syncretized with Christian or Catholic beliefs in forms such as santeria. For example, the botanicas (stores that sell herbal medicines and religious images) are communal centers in the expression of the spiritist beliefs that inform santeria (Borello & Mathias, 1977).

The cultural component and practices of Hispanic believers may differ quite extensively from the practices of non-Hispanic coreligionists in the United States (McCready, 1985). Hispanics and the once largely Irish hierarchy of the Catholic Church in the United States, for example, have had a long and complex struggle to achieve mutual understanding (to put the matter politely). Although differences between Hispanic Methodists and non-Hispanic Methodists may exist, most Protestant denominations are relatively less hierarchical and therefore in practice more open to different styles of observance (Weyr, 1988).

The Catholic Church and other denominations have developed many programs to address the social needs of Hispanics. These vary locally and run the gamut from soup kitchens to legal assistance for immigrants. Umbrella organizations encompassing other faiths have also been active, especially in working with immigrants and refugees. When making referrals, religious institutions may be important resources. It is important to keep in mind that

- religious institutions involving a variety of faiths may provide organizational support for and leadership to Hispanic communities.
- if it appears relevant, social workers should determine clients' religious affiliations, if any.
- social workers should make no assumptions about clients' experiences in their native country. For example, some Hispanics have experienced severe religious discrimination in their country of origin.

Ascription by Self or Others

Most Hispanics, when asked to describe their cultural heritage or ethnic identity, will first respond with a reference to their nationality (such as Mexican, Puerto Rican, Peruvian), even in the second or third immigrant generation. If one were to ask them about any broader self-identification, the term Hispanic would until recently rarely be heard; Latino or Latina is more common (Hayes-Bautista & Chapa, 1987).

When determining ethnic status, however, it is useful to look at the social context in which it is expressed. A single person can have many ethnicities, including a national ethnicity and a supraethnicity, when dealing with large-scale social institutions such as national or international systems or encompassing state structures. (Changes in state structures almost invariably radically affect ethnic expression. Contemporary Yugoslavia and the former Soviet Union, British India in 1947, and Austria–Hungary in 1918 are striking examples.)

Hispanics are a composite group with enough feelings of similarity to aid coalition forming when confronting large-scale structures, which in turn may find it convenient to regard Hispanics as a single group (Greeley, 1977; Royce, 1982). In other situations this large-scale sense of selfhood need not be called into play—in a neighborhood of Hispanics nationality might be the identifying factor; in a neighborhood of Mexican Americans, other local or ancestral criteria might come into play.

The state and the larger society, the "others," have named the Hispanic. In many respects, naming is the result of and a response to oppression and exploitation: One might speak of "greaser" or "wetback" ethnicity. By a purification of terms, such terms have come to refer to the more acceptable Hispanic or Latino ethnicity.

There are problems with the term "Hispanic." It reminds many persons so ascribed of the colonial exploitation of the Spanish state; many Hispanics have no ancestors from the Iberian Peninsula. The term "Latino," however, also excludes the Native American, African, Asian, or non-Latin European backgrounds of many Hispanics. But ethnicity may transcend terminology in the search for symbolic effectiveness. In situations in which ethnic identification may be important, the social worker might find it helpful to let people identify themselves, to remember that ascriptions may vary by social context, and to remember that individuals may not see themselves as members of the group they have been placed in.

Immigration or Citizenship Status

One great division in the Hispanic community is between those who have the legal right to both live and remain in the United States ("documented") and those who do not ("undocumented"). In addition, there are numerous classifications of documented status (such as refugee status) that affect access to public services. Legal status affects mobility, employment availability, the ability to assert rights, and even the ability to plan for the future on more than a day-to-day basis.

The date of entry into the United States is a key piece of information for those providing services to almost any immigrant. A verifiable entry date may render the undocumented client eligible for a regularization of status under various laws that offer protection and amnesties. For all immigrants, date of entrance communicates information about the opportunities in the United States at the time of migration and conditions in the country of origin at that time.

All noncitizens, even undocumented noncitizens, have rights, however. These include a child's right to schooling, the right to basic medical care, and the right to due process. Immigrants' rights group are sources of materials setting forth the rights of noncitizens and the policies of local governments and agencies in defense of those rights (National Center for Immigrant Students, 1991; New York Department of City Planning, 1990).

No matter how the client looks, sounds (even if there is no trace of a Spanish accent), or behaves, a social worker should consider whether or not documentation status is affecting the issues a client brings to the relationship. Social workers will find it useful to

- become acquainted with the services available to aid documented and undocumented people with various statuses.
- be sensitive to the possibility that clients who appear evasive or resistant to suggestions may be frightened about revealing undocumented status. Social workers can emphasize the degree of confidentiality that they can offer clients and include some legal advice about agency, local, and federal policies.
- keep abreast of current immigration regulations.

CONCLUSION

During the 19th century and early in the 20th century, Hispanics were legally discriminated against in the United States; they have always suffered from oppression, violence, and disrespect (Moore & Pachon, 1985). This suppression of group members, sanctioned by the state at various levels as well as by other social institutions and combined with the mounting rate of post–World War II immigration, led to the creation of the population we now call Hispanic or Latino. The population began to form a group as part of multidirectional interactions among component groups as well as interactions among the new group, federal and state authorities, and other institutions that were attempting to address perceived needs and pressures in an administratively convenient manner (Enloe, 1981; Moore & Pachon, 1985; Weyr, 1988). This process has led to an increasing group consciousness both organizationally and symbolically, as indicated by the ethnic self-identification in the 1990 census.

Yankauer (1987), reviewing a series of articles on terminology, commented that "whatever cohesion exists within the diverse groups covered by the term 'Hispanic,' it is the product of prejudice and discrimination directed against them" (p. 15). When confronted with the special needs and challenges of a large and growing population, the government began labeling, and the component groups tended to band together to more effectively confront the state and other discriminatory groups or institutions. Individuals tend to identify themselves as Hispanic or not depending on the level of interactions with other systems. Large systems tend to elicit responses of the amalgamated group; interactions at the neighborhood and more personal levels are likely to elicit more restricted identifications. Peeling the onion of Hispanic ethnicity may well lead to additional ethnicities, depending on the group or institution with which it is interacting.

REFERENCES

Barth, F. (1969). Introduction. In F. Barth (Ed.), *Ethnic groups and boundaries* (pp. 3–38). Boston: Little, Brown.

Borello, M. A., & Mathias, E. (1977, August–September). Botanicas: Puerto Rican folk pharmacies. *Natural History*, pp. 65–73.

Castex, G. M. (1990). An analysis and synthesis of current theories of ethnicity and ethnic group processes using the creation of the Hispanic group as a case example. *Dissertation Abstracts International, 51,* 07A (University Microfilms No. 90-33820).

Castex, G. M. (in press). Hondurans. In K. T. Jackson (Ed.), *Encyclopedia of New York City.* New Haven, CT: New York Historical Society and Yale University.

Cohen, A. (1974). Introduction: The lesson of ethnicity. In A. Cohen (Ed.), *Urban ethnicity* (pp. ix–xxiv). London: Tavistock.

Comitas, L. (1967). Education and social stratification in Bolivia. *Transactions of the New York Academy of Sciences, 9*(7, Series 2), 935–948.

Enloe, C. H. (1981). The growth of the state and ethnic mobilization: The American experience. *Ethnic and Racial Studies, 4,* 123–136.

Greeley, A. (1977). Minorities: White ethnics. In J. B. Turner (Ed.-in-Chief), *Encyclopedia of social work* (17th ed., Vol. 2, pp. 979–984). Washington, DC: National Association of Social Workers.

Green, J. W. (1982). *Cultural awareness in the human services.* Englewood Cliffs, NJ: Prentice Hall.

Harris, M. (1964). *Patterns of race in the Americas.* New York: W. W. Norton.

Hayes-Bautista, D. E., & Chapa, J. (1987). Latino terminology: Conceptual bases for standardized terminology. *American Journal of Public Health, 77,* 61–68.

Horowitz, D. L. (1985). *Ethnic groups in conflict.* Los Angeles: University of California Press.

Kadushin, A. (1983). *The social work interview.* New York: Columbia University Press.

McCready, W. C. (1985). Culture and religion. In P.S.J. Cafferty & W. C. McCready (Eds.), *Hispanics in the United States: A new social agenda* (pp. 49–61). New Brunswick, NJ: Transaction Books.

Mintz, S. (1971). Groups, group boundaries and the perception of race. *Comparative Studies in Society and History, 13,* 437–450.

Moore, J., & Pachon, H. (1985). *Hispanics in the United States.* Englewood Cliffs, NJ: Prentice Hall.

National Center for Immigrant Students. (1991). Immigrant students' right of access. *New Voices, 1*(1), 4.

Nelson, C., & Tienda, M. (1985). The structuring of Hispanic ethnicity: Historical and contemporary perspectives. *Ethnic and Racial Studies, 8,* 49–74.

New York Department of City Planning, Office of Immigrant Affairs. (1990). *Immigrant entitlements made (relatively) simple* (DCP No. 90-14). New York: Author.

Office of Management and Budget. (1978, May 4). Directive 15: Race and ethnic standards for federal statistics and administrative reporting. *Federal Register, 43,* 19269.

Pinderhughes, E. (1988). Significance of culture and power in the human behavior curriculum. In C. Jacobs & D. D. Bowles (Eds.), *Ethnicity & race: Critical concepts in social work* (pp. 152–166). Silver Spring, MD: National Association of Social Workers.

Pinderhughes, E. (1989). *Understanding race, ethnicity, and power.* New York: Free Press.

Royce, A. P. (1982). *Ethnic identity.* Bloomington: Indiana University Press.

Smith, A. (1989). The origins of nations. *Ethnic and Racial Studies, 12,* 340–367.

Stephens, T. M. (1989). The language of ethnicity and self-identity in American Spanish and Brazilian Portuguese. *Ethnic and Racial Studies, 12,* 138–145.

U.S. Bureau of the Census. (1975). *Comparison of persons of Spanish surname and persons of Spanish origin in the United States* (Technical Paper 38). Washington, DC: U.S. Government Printing Office.

U.S. Bureau of the Census. (1991a). *The Hispanic population in the United States: March 1990* (Current Population Reports, Series P-20, No. 449). Washington, DC: U.S. Government Printing Office.

U.S. Bureau of the Census. (1991b). *Resident population distribution for the United States, regions, and states, by race and Hispanic origin: 1990* (Press Release CB91-100). Washington, DC: Author.

U.S. Bureau of the Census. (1991c). *Census Bureau releases counts on specific racial groups* (Press Release CB91-215). Washington, DC: Author.

U.S. Bureau of the Census. (1991d). *Census Bureau releases 1990 Census counts on Hispanic population groups* (Press Release CB91-216). Washington, DC: Author.

U.S. Bureau of the Census. (1993a). *Poverty in the United States: 1992* (Current Population Reports, Series P-60, No. 185). Washington, DC: U.S. Government Printing Office.

U.S. Bureau of the Census. (1993b). *Money income of households, families, and persons in the United States: 1992* (Current Population Reports, Series P-60, No. 184). Washington, DC: U.S. Government Printing Office.

U.S. Bureau of the Census. (1993c). *Population projections of the United States, by age, sex, race, and Hispanic origin* (Current Population Reports, Series PS-25, No. 1104). Washington, DC: U.S. Government Printing Office.

U.S. Bureau of the Census. (1993d). *Hispanic Americans today* (Current Population Reports, Population Characteristics, Series P-23, No. 183). Washington, DC: U.S. Government Printing Office.

Vincent, J. (1974). The structuring of ethnicity. *Human Organization, 33,* 375–378.

Weyr, T. (1988). *Hispanic U.S.A.: Breaking the melting pot.* New York: Harper & Row.

Wolf, E. (1982). *Europe and the people without history.* Berkeley: University of California Press.

Worsley, P. (1984). *The three worlds: Culture and world development.* Chicago: University of Chicago Press.

Yankauer, A. (1987). Hispanic/Latino—What's in a name? *American Journal of Public Health, 77,* 15–17.

This chapter was originally published in the May 1994 issue of Social Work, *vol. 39, pp. 288–296.*

Predictors of Economic Status of Southeast Asian Refugees: Implications for Service Improvement

Miriam Potocky and Thomas P. McDonald

Immigrants are a growing segment of the ethnic population of the United States, and practice with immigrants has been identified as an important substantive area for the social work profession (NASW, 1990; Ryan, 1992). Immigrants cope with a number of challenges, including language differences, cultural differences, and ethnic discrimination. One special class of immigrants—refugees—faces a particularly difficult adjustment process. *Refugees* are people who do not leave their native countries voluntarily but rather are forced out as a result of human rights violations. Since 1980 almost 1.5 million refugees have resettled in the United States, the largest group of which are Southeast Asians (U.S. Committee for Refugees, 1993). This population will continue to constitute a large proportion of newly arriving refugees in the future as a result of the continuing Communist domination of Southeast Asia.

One area of Southeast Asian refugee adaptation that has been of greatest concern to policymakers, social services providers, and the general public is economic integration. This concern is driven by a high rate of public assistance use by these refugees. Approximately 40 percent of Southeast Asian refugees who have been in the United States up to two years receive public assistance of some type (Office of Refugee Resettlement, 1991). As a result of this concern, recent theory development and empirical investigation have focused on identifying the factors that influence refugees' economic integration.

Kuhlman (1991) developed a comprehensive model of economic integration of refugees. The model postulates six categories of factors that influence economic integration: (1) character-istics of refugees, such as demographic and ethnocultural vari-ables; (2) flight-related factors, such as cause of flight and type of migration; (3) host-related factors, such as economic and cultural variables in the host society; (4) policies, including international, national, regional, and local; (5) residence factors in the host coun-try, including length of residence and secondary migration (move-ment within the host country); and (6) noneconomic aspects of adaptation, such as acculturation.

Kuhlman (1991) proposed that "this model can serve as a frame-work for assessing and analyzing the economic integration of refugees" (p. 17). With respect to applying the model in research, he noted that "a partial analysis is usually more feasible than a comprehensive one and can be most useful, provided the overall picture is kept in mind" (p. 19). A number of studies have under-taken such a partial analysis (Bach & Carroll-Seguin, 1986; Caplan, Whitmore, & Bui, 1985; Tran, 1991; Uba & Chung, 1991; Westermeyer, Callies, & Neider, 1990). These investigations have found that specific predictors of refugee economic adaptation include English proficiency, household composition, length of time in the United States, type of sponsorship, education, gen-der, age, history of trauma, and health and mental health status.

The present study, which was part of a larger investigation (Potocky, 1993, in press), was developed to add to these lines of inquiry. The study was designed to extend existing research in three ways. First, existing studies have been limited to investiga-tions of short-term economic integration. This cross-sectional study investigated the adjustment of refugees who had been in the United States up to 15 years. Second, most prior studies have examined only a single indicator of economic status, such as pub-lic assistance use, employment, or household income. This study examined all three of these to obtain a broader assessment of Southeast Asian refugees' economic status. Finally, this study addressed several variables in economic integration that have thus far received only limited attention, such as citizenship.

METHOD

This study focused on Southeast Asian refugees in California, which has the largest proportion of Southeast Asian refugees in the United States (Office of Refugee Resettlement, 1991). The study used data from the 1990 Census of Population and Housing Public Use Microdata Sample for California, which is a 1 percent stratified random sample of the state's residents (U.S. Bureau of the Census, 1993). Respondents completed a questionnaire addressing over 125 items such as place of birth, income, and employment, in addition to basic demographic information. Instruction guides for completing the questionnaire were available in 33 languages.

Sample

For the present study, Southeast Asian refugees were operationally defined by selecting all persons in the census sample who were born in Vietnam, Laos, or Cambodia and who had arrived in the United States since 1975. Only people living in households and over age 15 were selected. Thus, in some cases the sample includes multiple individuals over age 15 living in the same household.

The Public Use Microdata Sample includes a weighting factor (derived from the stratified sampling procedure) for each household and person, which is designed to increase the accuracy of estimates of the characteristics of the total population (U.S. Bureau of the Census, 1993). This weighting factor was applied in all the analyses in this study. Consequently, a weighted sample size was used that represents the total population of Southeast Asian refugees over age 15 in California households (number of persons = 325,403; number of households = 102,180). The characteristics of this population are provided in Table 38-1.

Independent and Dependent Variables

The dependent construct, economic integration, was represented by three separate variables: employment status, public assistance use, and household income. The selection of independent variables was guided by Kuhlman's (1991) theory of refugee economic adaptation and by prior empirical literature (for example, Bach & Carroll-Seguin, 1986; Caplan et al., 1985; Tran, 1991). All variables in the census data set that were related to economic integration theoretically or empirically were selected for analysis, resulting in 18 independent variables (see Table 38-1). These 18 variables represent three of the theoretical factors: characteristics of refugees (for example, gender and age), residence in host coun-

TABLE 38-1

Characteristics of Southeast Asian Refugees in California Households

Characteristic	M	%	SE
Percentage employed		44.5	1.0
Percentage receiving public			
assistance		24.5	1.0
Sex			
Male		51.2	1.0
Female		48.8	.0
Age (years)	34.6		.0
Place of birth			
Vietnam		69.2	1.8
Laos		17.1	1.4
Cambodia		13.7	1.3
Ethnicity			
Vietnamese		53.5	1.0
Chinese–Vietnamese		17.7	.8
Cambodian		11.5	.7
Laotian		8.8	.6
Hmong		6.4	.5
All other		2.1	.3
Education (years)	11.2		.0
Length of residence in United			
States (years)			
0–3		13.5	.9
4–5		11.4	.8
6–8		15.1	.9
9–10		29.4	1.2
11–15		30.6	1.2
Percentage who made secondary			
migration to California		9.3	1.1
English-speaking ability			
Very well		23.9	1.3
Well		34.7	1.4
Not well		30.4	1.4
Not at all		11.0	.9
U.S. citizens		34.1	1.5
Percentage who have a disability			
that limits or prevents work		10.6	.6
Household income ($)	33,214		96
No. of persons in household	5.1		.0
Households headed by			
married couple		71.2	1.8
Households with nonrelatives		20.2	1.6
Households with children		77.0	1.6
Households with people			
age 65 and over		18.1	1.4
Households with subfamilies		15.9	1.4
Households speaking language			
other than English at home		98.2	.7
Households with U.S. natives		3.2	1.2

try (for example, length of residence), and noneconomic aspects of adaptation (for example, English-speaking ability and U.S. citizenship). No variables were available in the census data to represent the remaining three factors; therefore, like prior empirical investigations, the present study constituted a partial analysis of the comprehensive theoretical model.

Variable Definitions and Coding

All dichotomous variables were coded 0 to indicate the absence of the characteristic and 1 to indicate its presence. Place of birth, consisting of three categories (Vietnam, Cambodia, and Laos), and ethnicity, consisting of six categories (Vietnamese, Chinese–Vietnamese [people of Chinese ethnicity who had lived in Vietnam], Cambodian, Laotian, Hmong, and "all other"), were each dummy coded with Vietnam and Vietnamese, respectively, as the reference (omitted) categories. Years of education was coded on a 17-point scale ranging from 1 = none to 17 = doctorate degree. Length of residence in the United States was coded into five categories of approximately three years each. Secondary migration (interstate movement within the United States after arrival) was derived from a variable that indicated the respondent's place of residence five years before the census. All people who lived in another state in 1985 were coded as secondary migrants; all others were coded as not secondary migrants. This latter category included both people who moved directly to California from Southeast Asia and those who moved to California more than five years before the census after having initially settled in another state.

English-speaking ability was coded on a scale ranging from 1 = very well to 4 = not at all. A separate variable, use of a language other than English at home, denoted whether household members spoke a language besides or in addition to English in the home. Finally, U.S. natives were defined as people born in the United States who were not of Southeast Asian ethnicity. This variable therefore reflects the presence of people in the household who are neither Southeast Asian refugees nor their U.S.-born descendants.

Analysis Strategy

For each of the three dependent variables, a separate regression equation consisting of the 18 independent variables was computed. In all three regressions, all of the independent variables were entered simultaneously. For the dichotomous dependent variables of employment status and public assistance use, logistic regressions were conducted. The unit of analysis was the individual person. For these analyses, the sample was randomly split into approximately equal halves. The logistic regression equations were computed on the first half of the sample and then verified on the second half.

For the continuous dependent variable of household income, a multiple regression was conducted. The unit of analysis was the household. For this analysis, person variables were aggregated to the household level. The categorical variables of gender, citizenship, secondary migration, and disability were aggregated by summing. Thus, the new variables represent the total number of females, total number of citizens, total number of people who made a secondary migration, and total number of disabled people—all over age 15—in the household. The continuous variables of age, length of residence in the United States, and years of education were aggregated by taking their means. Thus, the new variables represent the average age, average length of residence, and average years of education of all people over age 15 in the household. With regard to ethnicity and place of birth, the characteristics of the householder (the person in whose name the home was owned or rented) were used in the analysis. Finally, the aggregated measure of English-speaking ability was linguistic isolation (whether a household had any members over age 15 who spoke English very well).

RESULTS

Because the analyses were based on weighted estimates of total population characteristics rather than on a sample from which population characteristics were inferred, statistical significance was not meaningful because the large population size made all effects statistically significant. Therefore, significance statistics are not included in this presentation of the results. However, this does not affect the interpretation of the overall usefulness of the equations in explaining variance or the practical significance of the effect of each independent variable.

Overall Regression Results

Table 38-2 shows the overall regression results for each equation. With respect to household income, the multiple regression equation accounted for approximately 37 percent of the variance in the dependent variable. With respect to employment status, the logistic regression equation correctly classified 75.3 percent of the cases in the computation sample. In logistic regression, the classification rates are evaluated in the context of prior probabilities (that is, the observed frequency distributions). The distribution

TABLE 38-2

Overall Regression Results

Multiple Regression Results for	R	R²	Adjusted R²	SE
Household income	0.61083	0.37311	0.37297	24,384.36073

Logistic Regression Classification Table for	Predicted		% Correct
	No	Yes	
Employment status			
Computation sample			
Observed			
No	73,242	20,267	78.3
Yes	21,359	53,300	71.4
Overall			75.3
Verification sample			
Observed			
No	67,145	19,838	77.2
Yes	19,513	50,739	72.2
Overall			75.0
Public assistance use			
Computation sample			
Observed			
No	117,000	9,165	92.7
Yes	22,321	19,682	46.9
Overall			81.3
Verification sample			
Observed			
No	110,838	8,671	92.7
Yes	20,462	17,264	45.8
Overall			81.5

of employment was approximately 55 percent unemployed and 45 percent employed (Table 38-1). Thus, based on this knowledge alone, if the researcher predicted that every member of the sample was unemployed, this would result in a 55 percent accuracy rate. Therefore, the additional information provided by the regression model increased the accuracy of prediction by approximately 20 percent. With respect to public assistance use, the equation correctly classified 81.3 percent of the cases in the computation sample. The frequency distribution of public assistance use was approximately 75 percent not receiving public assistance versus 25 percent receiving it; therefore, the regression model increased predictive accuracy by approximately 6 percent. For both employment status and public assistance use, the classification results for the verification sample were nearly identical to those of the computation sample, indicating that the equations performed equally well at classifying cases that were not used as the basis for the computation of the logistic coefficients.

Variable Effects

To assess the degree of multicollinearity among the independent variables, the tolerances of the variables were examined. The tolerance is a value ranging from 0 to 1. Low tolerances indicate the presence of high multicollinearity, which poses a threat to the interpretation of the regression coefficients (Pedhazur, 1982). In the present data set, none of the tolerances were less than .50, indicating that the independent variables were sufficiently uncorrelated so that each regression coefficient could be interpreted as reflecting the unique effect of the variable with which it is associated.

Table 38-3 shows the effect of each independent variable on the indicators of economic status. In logistic regression, the value of e^b "is the factor by which the odds change when the . . . independent variable increases by one unit" (Norusis, 1990, p. B-43). If e^b is greater than one, the odds of the event occurring are increased; if e^b is less than one, the odds are decreased; and if e^b is equal to one, the odds are not changed. The value of R in logistic regression is analogous to ß in multiple regression and is useful for comparing the relative effects of the independent variables.

The results indicate that having a household headed by a married couple; having nonrelatives or subfamilies (that is, married

TABLE 38-3

Effects of Person and Household Characteristics on Economic Status

	Economic Status					
	Employment[a]		Public Assistance Use[a]		Household Income ($)	
Characteristic	e^b	R	e^b	R	b	b
Sex (0 = male; 1 = female)	.524	-.110[b]	.804	-.035	-1,058	-.034
Age (years)	1.004	.016	1.044	.169[b]	163	.049
Place of birth (reference = Vietnam)						
Cambodia	.902	-.004	1.283	.011	2,960	.034
Laos	1.078	.000	.655	-.016	-6,319	-.080
Ethnicity (reference = Vietnamese)						
Chinese–Vietnamese	2.171	.092[b]	.804	-.022	-1,125	-.013
Hmong	.446	-.024	1.950	.023	-4,564	-.038
Laotian	.568	-.018	3.154	.041	-1,525	-.015
Cambodian	.847	-.007	1.909	.028	-10,092	-.106[b]
Other	.207	-.044	4.491	.059	-49	.000
Education (1 unit = approximately 1 year)	1.183	.174[b]	.879	-.144[b]	2,308	.253[b]
Length of residence in United States (1 unit = approximately 3 years)	1.146	.056	.920	-.035	598	.023
Secondary migration[a]	.759	-.026	2.143	.076	152	.004
English-speaking ability (1 = very well to 4 = not at all)	.810	-.050	1.383	.078[b]	-2,764	-.044
U.S. citizenship[a]	2.210	.114[b]	.469	-.088[b]	6,926	.287[b]
Disability	.311	-.092[b]	1.503	.044	-1,622	-.034
Number of persons	.939	-.042	.901	-.064	2,933	.235[b]
Household headed by married couple[a]	1.146	.018	.707	-.044	3,715	.056
Presence of nonrelatives[a]	1.348	.038	.583	-.062	9,596	.113[b]
Presence of children[a]	.576	-.067	3.966	.131[b]	-6,847	-.094
Presence of people age 65 and over[a]	.751	-.036	1.043	.004	-1,798	-.020
Presence of subfamilies[a]	1.356	.034	.689	-.039	10,069	.099
Language other than English spoken at home[a]	2.897	.045	1.253	.007	-1,210	-.003
Presence of U.S. natives[a]	.534	-.036	1.663	.028	2,184	.011

[a]0 = no, 1 = yes.
[b]Five most important predictors for each economic status indicator.

couples, nuclear families, or single-parent families that are related to but do not include the householder or the householder's spouse) in the household; and having greater education, greater length of residence, greater English-speaking ability, and U.S. citizenship all had enhancing effects on all three indicators of economic integration. In other words, these characteristics increased the odds of employment, decreased the odds of public assistance use, and increased household income. Being of an ethnicity other than Vietnamese and Chinese–Vietnamese, having children or people aged 65 and older in the household, and being disabled all had impeding effects on all three economic status indicators. The remaining variables (for example, language spoken at home) had differing effects on each of the indicators of economic integration: In some cases the effect of the variable was enhancing, whereas in other cases it was impeding.

Education and citizenship repeatedly emerged among the five most important predictors for all three economic status indicators, and ethnicity was among the most important for two of the indicators. Each additional year of education increased the odds of employment by 1.18 and decreased the odds of public assistance use by 0.88. Each additional year of mean education of household members increased household income by about $2,300. Southeast Asian refugees who had become citizens, compared with those who had not, had more than twice the odds of being employed and less than half the odds of receiving public assistance. Each additional citizen in the household (controlling for total number of people) increased income by almost $7,000. Economic status varied widely by ethnicity. For example, refugees of Chinese–Vietnamese ethnicity were more than twice as likely to be employed and had 0.80 the odds of receiving public assistance compared with Vietnamese refugees. On the other hand, Vietnamese refugees had over $10,000 more in annual household income than Cambodians.

DISCUSSION

The overall regression results of this study (the classification rates for employment and public assistance use and the percentage of variance explained for household income) indicate that the 18-variable regression model has good usefulness in predicting the economic status of this population of Southeast Asian refugees.

(It should be noted that the apparently low improvement in prediction of public assistance use is a function of the high prior probability.) Furthermore, the interpretation of predictors of refugees' economic status may be perceived as complex due to the intercorrelations among many of the variables (for example, length of residence, English-speaking ability, education, and citizenship are all correlated). However, this study has demonstrated that the multiple correlations among these variables are not large enough to pose a threat to interpretation. Thus, the findings of this study are particularly useful for identifying the unique, independent risk factors for poor economic adjustment of Southeast Asian refugees. The major risk factors identified by this study have implications for improvement of refugee resettlement policies, programs, and practices.

Education

Education emerged as one of the five most important predictors of all three measures of economic status. This finding is particularly important in light of the fact that the members of this refugee population on average had not completed high school (Table 38-1). It has been noted that "by the year 2000, there will be a significant decline in jobs requiring only a high school degree and an increase in jobs requiring at least one year of college education" (Belcher & Rejent, 1993, p. 298). Thus, refugee adults without a high school education must be urged and helped to obtain a general equivalency diploma, and college education should also be strongly advocated.

Furthermore, the equivalency of educational programs in the Southeast Asian countries and the United States requires further investigation. For example, it is likely that six years of education in Vietnam is not equivalent to the same years of schooling in the United States or in other Southeast Asian countries. Also, the limitations of the census data precluded an analysis of whether the respondent's educational level was attained in the country of origin or in the United States after arrival.

Citizenship

Citizenship was also among the five most important predictors of all three measures of economic status. The attainment of citizenship encompasses a number of issues, including length of residence, English-speaking ability, and acculturation to American norms. Because the first two of these variables were accounted for in this study, it appears that acculturation may be a unique underlying trait that enhances economic integration. This finding suggests that resettlement policies, programs, and practices should promote *bicultural competence,* which refers to the ability to practice American norms without giving up the traditional norms and values of one's native culture. However, for many refugees, applying for citizenship constitutes a major change in self-identity and frequently represents an admission of final defeat with regard to hopes of returning to the homeland. These feelings are strong inhibitors to seeking citizenship. Further investigation is needed with regard to this issue and its effect on refugee economic adjustment.

Ethnicity

Ethnicity also emerged as an important variable in identifying Southeast Asian refugees at risk for poor economic status. In general, people of Chinese–Vietnamese and Vietnamese ethnicity fared better on all the economic status indicators than people of Laotian, Hmong, and Cambodian ethnicity. The Vietnamese and the Chinese–Vietnamese probably fared better because they came from a more Westernized, urbanized society than did the other ethnic groups (Canda, 1988). In addition, it is possible that the Chinese–Vietnamese newcomers received support for economic integration from the already established Chinese American community in California. Similarly, the more recent Vietnamese arrivals would have had the benefit of a social support infrastructure from ethnic enclaves—for example, "Little Saigons"—formed by the earlier arrivals. No such existing communities were in place for the newcomers of the other ethnic groups.

These findings indicate that resettlement policies, programs, and practices cannot treat Southeast Asian refugees as one homogeneous population. Although they all come from roughly the same part of the world, the ethnic groups within this population vary greatly with regard to history, language, culture, and other characteristics. Thus, services must be tailored to the unique needs of each specific ethnic group. The exact nature of these needs and the types of services that are most effective for each group remain to be determined.

English-Speaking Ability

Like prior research (for example, Bach & Carroll-Seguin, 1986; Office of Refugee Resettlement, 1991; Tran, 1991), this study showed that better English-speaking ability was associated with better economic status. Compared with a refugee who spoke English very well, one who did not speak English at all had about half the odds of being employed and over 2½ times the odds of being on welfare. Linguistically isolated households had over $8,000 less in household income than nonlinguistically isolated households. English as a second language (ESL) training is a key component of current refugee resettlement policies and programs. The findings of this study support the inclusion of this element. However, the present results showed that 41.4 percent of the Southeast Asian refugee population did not speak English well, even though 86.5 percent of the population had been in the United States more than three years (Table 38-1). This finding suggests that ESL classes are not adequately reaching the population or are not helping their clients achieve an adequate level of competence. These apparent shortcomings require further investigation.

Length of Residence

The results of this study suggest that length of residence is of considerably less importance in economic improvement than has been indicated by previous research (for example, Bach & Carroll-Seguin, 1986; Caplan et al., 1985; Tran, 1991). Each approximately three additional years of residence increased the odds of employment by only 1.15, decreased the odds of welfare use by only .92, and increased household income by less than $600. Thus, compared with a newly arrived Southeast Asian refugee, one who has been in the United States 10 years is 1½ times as likely to be employed, has three-fourths the odds of being on welfare, and has $1,800 more in annual household income. These changes over a 10-year period cannot be considered substantively significant. In addition, 86.5 percent of the refugees in this study had been in the United States more than three years, yet 55.5 percent were not employed and 24.5 percent were receiving public assistance (Table 38-1). These data indicate that the upward mobility of Southeast Asian refugees once they arrive in the United States is limited; much of their later economic status appears to be determined by their status early after arrival. This finding is supported by a recent study in California that showed that "if a refugee is not working within 12 months in this country, the chance of that refugee being at work after 5 years here is only five percent" (U.S. Committee for Refugees, 1992, p. 6).

Household Composition

The findings of this study with respect to the presence of nonrelatives and subfamilies replicate the findings of prior research (for example, Bach, 1988; Caplan et al., 1985). A substantial proportion of Southeast Asian refugees live in large extended-family households. Refugees in these households have better economic status than those in smaller, nuclear family-type households, indicating that these families use a strategy of pooling resources to achieve economic integration.

Additional family composition variables that were found to be important were the presence of children and the presence of people aged 65 and over. Southeast Asian refugee households with children fared much worse on all three indicators of economic status than households without children. This finding is important in light of the fact that an extremely large proportion of Southeast Asian refugee households have children (77 percent in this study; see Table 38-1) (Office of Refugee Resettlement, 1991). In addition, the presence of people aged 65 and over in the household was associated with lower economic status on all three indicators. As is true for members of American society as a whole, the necessity of caring for children and elderly household members affects labor force participation, earnings potential, and welfare use. Thus, Southeast Asian refugees would benefit from overall welfare reform and workplace legislation aimed at providing affordable and accessible child care and elder care for all American families.

Secondary Migration

The results of this study showed that Southeast Asian refugees who made a secondary migration to California within the previous five years had three-fourths the odds of being employed and more than twice the odds of receiving welfare compared with refugees who either came directly to California or who made a secondary migration more than five years previously. This finding appears to bear out prior assertions that Southeast Asian refugees in other states move to California specifically to take advantage of its liberal public assistance programs (H.R. Rep. No. 99–132, 1985). Bach (1988) found that Southeast Asian refugees outside California were much more likely to be poor than refugees in California because California's welfare eligibility rules allow people to combine earned income with public assistance. Thus, a move to California may be a necessary survival strategy. This problem must be addressed at the national policy level. A restructuring of the refugee resettlement program as suggested by this study would enhance all Southeast Asian refugees' opportunities for improvement in their economic status, thereby decreasing the necessity of secondary migration to California.

Generalizability of the Study

Two types of generalizability are relevant to this study: generalizability to Southeast Asian refugees in states other than California and generalizability to non–Southeast Asian refugees in California and in other states. Both types of generalization require caution because of large differences in state policies and programs and among different refugee groups. Thus, the present study should be replicated in other states and with other refugee groups to determine the extent to which the findings generalize.

SUGGESTIONS FOR FUTURE RESEARCH

A number of areas for future research have been identified, including evaluating the effectiveness of ESL classes, further exploring the issue of citizenship and its relationship to economic adjustment, and determining the most effective service approaches for each refugee ethnic group. Because of the vast differences between the ethnic groups, it would be useful to conduct a multiple comparison to determine whether the predictor variables have a similar effect on the economic integration of each group. A similar comparison could be conducted with respect to time of arrival. Among all refugee populations, the upper socioeconomic classes flee their country first, followed by those less fortunate. Thus, the predictors of economic integration for each of these arrival groups would be expected to differ.

In addition, further investigation is needed into the idiosyncratic effects of some of the variables, that is, their varying

enhancing and impeding effects on the three measures of economic integration. These fluctuations may be due to statistical or
measurement error. A more rigorous analytical technique such
as structural equation modeling might address this issue.

Finally, because of the nature of the available census data, this
study was limited to a focus on the characteristics of the refugees
as opposed to characteristics of their environment. As noted, this
study examined three factors within Kuhlman's (1991) comprehensive theoretical model: characteristics of refugees, length of
residence, and noneconomic aspects of adaptation. Future studies should address the other three theoretical factors: flight-
related factors, host-related factors, and policies, all of which are
concerned with environmental effects. Relevant flight-related
factors include the cause of the flight (for example, type of persecution suffered in the country of origin) and the type of migration (for example, airplane flight directly to the United States
versus escape by boat and lengthy stay in a refugee camp). Relevant host-related factors include the economic strength of the
local community, the influence of existing ethnic enclaves, and
the attitudes of native-born citizens toward the refugees. Finally,
the effects of policies regarding asylum, work permits, and public assistance eligibility need to be addressed.

REFERENCES

Bach, R. L. (1988). State intervention in Southeast Asian refugee resettlement
    in the United States. *Journal of Refugee Studies, 1,* 38–56.
Bach, R. L., & Carroll-Seguin, R. (1986). Labor force participation, household
    composition, and sponsorship among Southeast Asian refugees. *Interna-
    tional Migration Review, 20,* 381–404.
Belcher, J. R., & Rejent, D. (1993). Using company-owned housing and
    workfare to fill the need for low-wage workers: A solution or step
    backward? *Social Work, 38,* 297–304.
Canda, E. R. (1988). *Southeast Asian refugees in Iowa: Cultural background, needs,
    and services.* Iowa City: University of Iowa School of Social Work, Refugee
    Training and Family Service Project.
Caplan, N., Whitmore, J. K., & Bui, Q. L. (1985). Economic self-sufficiency
    among recently arrived refugees from Southeast Asia. *Economic Outlook
    USA, 12,* 60–63.
H.R. Rep. No. 99-132, 99th Cong., 1st Sess. 7 (1985).
Kuhlman, T. (1991). The economic integration of refugees in developing
    countries: A research model. *Journal of Refugee Studies, 4,* 1–20.

National Association of Social Workers. (1990). *Facts on refugees.* Silver Spring, MD: NASW, Child and Family Well-Being Development Education Program.

Norusis, M. J. (1990). *SPSS/PC+ advanced statistics 4.0.* Chicago: SPSS.

Office of Refugee Resettlement. (1991). *Refugee Resettlement Program: Annual report to Congress, FY 1990.* Washington, DC: U.S. Government Printing Office.

Pedhazur, E. J. (1982). *Multiple regression in behavioral research.* Fort Worth, TX: Holt, Rinehart & Winston.

Potocky, M. (1993). *The economic integration of Southeast Asian Refugees in California.* Unpublished doctoral dissertation, University of Kansas School of Social Welfare.

Potocky, M. (in press). Toward a new definition of refugee economic integration. *International Social Work.*

Ryan, A. S. (Ed.). (1992). *Social work with immigrants and refugees.* New York: Haworth Press.

Tran, T. V. (1991). Sponsorship and employment status among Indochinese refugees in the United States. *International Migration Review, 25,* 536–550.

Uba, L., & Chung, R. C. (1991). The relationship between trauma and financial and physical well-being among Cambodians in the United States. *Journal of General Psychology, 118,* 215–225.

U.S. Bureau of the Census. (1993). *Census of population and housing, 1990: Public use microdata samples technical documentation.* Washington, DC: U.S. Government Printing Office.

U.S. Committee for Refugees. (1992). *Refugee Reports* interview with ORR director Chris Gersten. *Refugee Reports, 13*(10), 6–10.

U.S. Committee for Refugees. (1993). Refugees admitted to the United States by nationality, FY 80–93. *Refugee Reports, 14*(3), 10–11.

Westermeyer, J., Callies, A., & Neider, J. (1990). Welfare status and psychosocial adjustment among 100 Hmong refugees. *Journal of Nervous and Mental Disease, 178,* 300–306.

This chapter was originally published in the December 1995 issue of Social Work Research, *vol. 19, pp. 219–227.*

Index

The Editors

Patricia L. Ewalt, PhD, is dean and professor, School of Social Work, University of Hawaii, Honolulu. She has a master's degree in social work from Simmons College School of Social Work and a PhD in health care policy, research, and administration from the Florence Heller School for Advanced Studies in Social Welfare, Brandeis University, Waltham, Massachusetts. She is the editor of Social Work.

Edith M. Freeman, PhD, is professor, University of Kansas School of Social Welfare, Lawrence. She has an MSW from the University of Kansas School of Social Welfare and a PhD from the Departments of Psychology and Human Development and Family Life. She is the editor of Social Work in Education.

Stuart A. Kirk, DSW, is Ralph and Marjorie Crump Professor of Social Welfare, School of Public Policy and Social Research, University of California, Los Angeles. He has an MSW from the University of Illinois at Urbana and a DSW from the University of California, Berkeley. He is the editor of Social Work Research.

Dennis L. Poole, PhD, is professor, University of Central Florida, Orlando. He has an MSW from West Virginia University and a PhD from the Florence Heller School for Advanced Studies in Social Welfare, Brandeis University, Waltham, Massachusetts. He is the editor of Health & Social Work.

The Contributors

Paula Allen-Meares, PhD, *is dean and professor, School of Social Work, University of Michigan.*

Valerie Appleton, EdD, *is assistant professor, Department of Applied Psychology, Eastern Washington University.*

Steven Lozano Applewhite, PhD, *is associate professor, Graduate School of Social Work, University of Houston.*

Mary Robinson Baker, MSW, CSW, *is social worker, Ithaca City School District, Ithaca, NY.*

Oscar A. Barbarin, PhD, *is professor, Psychology and Social Work, and director, University Center for the Child and Family, School of Social Work, University of Michigan.*

Arnold Barnes, PhD, *is assistant professor, Indiana University School of Social Work.*

Joyce O. Beckett, PhD, *is professor, School of Social Work, Virginia Commonwealth University.*

Rose Ann Benson, PhD, *is head swimming coach, San Jose State University.*

Sandy M. Bonds, BS, PNP, *is pediatric nurse practitioner, Sickle Cell Center, Children's Hospital, Detroit.*

Alice Broderick, MSW, MPH, *is director of Options for Elders, Honolulu.*

Colette Browne, MSW, DrPH, *is associate professor and chair of the gerontology concentration at the School of Social Work, University of Hawaii.*

Sondra Burman, PhD, *is assistant professor, Rutgers, The State University of New Jersey.*

Denise Burnette, PhD, ACSW, *is associate professor, Columbia University School of Social Work.*

Frances S. Caple, PhD, *is associate dean, School of Social Work, University of Southern California.*

Graciela M. Castex, EdD, ACSW, *is assistant professor of social work, Department of Sociology and Social Work, Lehman College, City University of New York.*

Alfrieda Daly, PhD, *is assistant professor, School of Social Work, Rutgers, The State University of New Jersey.*

Larry E. Davis, PhD, *is associate professor of social work and psychology, George Warren Brown School of Social Work, Washington University.*

Kate DeLois, PhD, *is assistant professor, University of New England.*

John di Cecco, MSW, *is restructuring planned coordinator, Division of Student Health and Human Services, Los Angeles Unified School District.*

Claudia Dorrington, PhD, *is lecturer, Department of Sociology and Social Work, Azusa Pacific University.*

Diane Drachman, PhD, *is associate professor, School of Social Work, University of Connecticut.*

Cass Dykeman, PhD, *is assistant professor, Department of Applied Psychology, Eastern Washington University.*

Kathleen Ell, DSW, *is professor, School of Social Work, University of Southern California.*

Holly Elliott, MS, *is coprincipal investigator, Project on Adult Onset Hearing Loss, Langley Porter Psychiatric Institute, University of California at San Francisco.*

Paul H. Ephross, PhD, *is professor, School of Social Work, University of Maryland at Baltimore.*

Rowena Fong, MSW, EdD, is associate professor, School of Social Work, University of Hawaii.

Cynthia Franklin, PhD, is associate professor, School of Social Work, University of Texas at Austin.

Petra Galindo, LCSW, PPSC, is social worker, School Mental Health Unit, Los Angeles Unified School District.

Maeda J. Galinsky, PhD, is Kenan professor, School of Social Work, University of North Carolina at Chapel Hill.

Larry M. Gant, MSW, PhD, is associate professor, School of Social Work, University of Michigan.

Lawrence E. Gary, PhD, is professor, School of Social Work, Howard University.

Karen E. Gerdes, PhD, is assistant professor and BSW Program director, Arizona State University.

Laurel Glass, MD, PhD, is professor emeritus of anatomy and psychology, University of California Medical School, San Francisco.

Linnea GlenMaye, PhD(c), is instructor, Antioch University.

Ketayun H. Gould, PhD, is professor emerita, School of Social Work, University of Illinois, Urbana–Champaign, and partner, Independent Scholars Associated.

Darlene Grant, PhD, is assistant professor, School of Social Work, University of Texas at Austin.

Emma R. Gross, PhD, MSW, is associate professor, Graduate School of Social Work, University of Utah.

Lorraine M. Gutiérrez, PhD, is associate professor, School of Social Work, University of Michigan.

Dennis Haynes, PhD, is assistant professor, School of Social Work, University of Texas at Austin.

Dee Hodge, MD, *is physician, Department of Pediatrics, University of Southern California.*

André G. Jacob, PhD, *is dean, Department of Social Work, Université du Québec.*

Jeanette Jennings, PhD, *is associate professor, College of Social Work, University of Tennessee at Knoxville.*

Peggy S. Larney, BBA, *is specialist, American Indian Education Project, Dallas Independent School District.*

Bogart R. Leashore, PhD, *is dean, Hunter College School of Social Work.*

Helen Sloss Luey, MS, LCSW, *is director of social services, Hearing Society for the Bay Area, San Francisco.*

Thomas P. McDonald, PhD, *is associate professor, School of Social Welfare, University of Kansas.*

Maureen K. McEntee, MA, CCC, IC/TC, *is founder and director, Stand Fast, Warwick, RI.*

Noreen Mokuau, DSW, *is professor, School of Social Work, University of Hawaii.*

Ada C. Mui, PhD, ACSW, *is associate professor, Columbia University School of Social Work.*

J. Ron Nelson, PhD, *is associate professor, Department of Applied Psychology, Eastern Washington University.*

Jack Nowicki, LMSW-ACP, *is family counselor, Youth Options, Austin, TX.*

David G. Ostrow, MD, PhD, *is professor, Center for AIDS Intervention Research, University of Wisconsin–Milwaukee.*

Veronica Pearson, BSc Economics, MSc, CQSW, D Phil, is associate professor, Department of Social Work and Social Administration, University of Hong Kong.

Michael Phillips, MD, is director, Research Center of Psychological Medicine, Shashi Psychiatric Hospital, Shashi, Hubei Province, People's Republic of China.

Miriam Potocky, PhD, is assistant professor, School of Social Work, College of Urban and Public Affairs, Florida International University.

Enola K. Proctor, PhD, is Frank J. Bruno professor of social work and director, Center for Mental Health Services Research, Washington University.

Marguerite G. Rosenthal, PhD, is associate professor, School of Social Work, Salem State College.

Ramon M. Salcido, DSW, is associate professor, School of Social Work, University of Southern California.

Janice H. Schopler, PhD, ACSW, is associate dean and professor, School of Social Work, University of North Carolina at Chapel Hill.

Sharron M. Singleton-Bowie, DSW, ACSW, LICSW, is associate professor, School of Social Work, Barry University.

Paul R. Spickard, PhD, is associate dean for the social sciences, Brigham Young University–Hawaii, and research director, Institute for Polynesian Studies, Laie.

Joseph R. Steiner, PhD, ACSW, QCSW, is professor, School of Social Work, Syracuse University.

Katherine van Wormer, PhD, is associate professor, University of Northern Iowa, Department of Social Work.

Laura Wachsman, MD, is physician, Department of Pediatrics, Los Angeles County Plus, USC Medical Center, University of Southern California.

John Waukechon, MA, is facilitator, American Indian Education Project, Austin Independent School District, Austin, TX.

Charles F. Whitten, MD, is distinguished professor emeritus of pediatrics and associate dean for special programs, Wayne State University School of Medicine.

Michael Yellow Bird, PhD, is assistant professor, School of Social Welfare, University of Kansas.

Ruth E. Zambrana, PhD, is professor and Enoch chair, College of Nursing and Health Sciences, and director, Center for Child Welfare, George Mason University.

Cover design by The Watermark Design Office

Interior design by Bill Cathey

Typeset in Lucida Sans and Palatino by Bill Cathey

Printed by Boyd Printing Company on 60# Windsor